To Chuck,

In the hope That we
see a Turn Toward democracy.

with all best wishes,

Ted Morgan

12 / '10

What Really Happened to the 1960s

What Really Happened to the 1960s

How Mass Media Culture Failed American Democracy

Edward P. Morgan

University Press of Kansas

Published by the University Press of Kansas (Lawrence,
Kansas 66045), which was organized by the Kansas Board
of Regents and is operated and funded by Emporia State
University, Fort Hays State University, Kansas State
University, Pittsburg State University, the University of
Kansas, and Wichita State University

Library of Congress Cataloging-in-Publication Data

Morgan, Edward P., 1945–
   What really happened to the 1960s : how mass media
culture failed American democracy / Edward P. Morgan.
        p.   cm.
   Includes bibliographical references and index.
   ISBN 978-0-7006-1756-2 (cloth : alk. paper)
1. United States—Social conditions—1960–1980. 2. Social
movements—United States—History—20th century.
3. Counterculture—United States—History—20th century.
4. Democracy—United States—History—20th century.
5. Politics and culture—United States—History—20th
century. 6. Mass media—Political aspects—United States.
7. Social movements—United States—Public opinion.
8. Counterculture—United States—Public opinion.
9. Hippies—United States—Public opinion. 10. Public
opinion—United States. I. Title.
   HN59.M65 2010
   306'.1—dc22   2010027342

British Library Cataloguing-in-Publication Data is available.

Printed in the United States of America
10 9 8 7 6 5 4 3 2 1

The paper used in this publication is recycled and contains
30 percent postconsumer waste. It is acid free and meets the
minimum requirements of the American National Standard
for Permanence of Paper for Printed Library Materials
Z39.48–1992.

To Mary Lou

Contents

(A photograph section follows page 170)

Preface

As this book goes to press, fifty years have passed since the student sit-ins of 1960 reenergized the civil rights movement, and forty years since authorities shot and killed students at Kent State and Mississippi State Universities. Yet the mass media's fixation with "the Sixties" seemingly never ends.

I begin the book with a discussion of how the unending "battles of the 1960s," as candidate Barack Obama put it, were a significant and at times poignant backdrop to the 2008 presidential campaign. Such is the nature of political discourse in the American mass media culture. Something called "the Sixties" is alluded to again and again at regular intervals: presidential campaigns, repeated acts of war by the United States, outbursts of mass protest, episodes of racial unrest, abortion battles, charges of "political correctness," to say nothing of media-saturated anniversaries of iconic sixties events, from Martin Luther King's "I Have a Dream" speech to Woodstock.

I maintain that the mass media's "Sixties" discourse is chiefly one of ghosts, accusations, and smoke and mirrors that has long played on audience emotions and diverted public attention to what is essentially a symbolic form of spectator politics. In a commentary that represents perhaps the archetypal media culture representation, commentator Andrew Sullivan referred to these as the "debilitating, self-perpetuating family quarrel of the Baby Boom generation that has long engulfed all of us."[1] Sullivan is right in one sense; this media discourse is debilitating if we aspire to a democratic way of life. It provides the public with an endless stream of imagery, distorted claims, and personalities they can loathe, embrace, or emulate—and not much else. Indeed, this political culture is both hyper-political and depoliticized; hyper-political because it is dominated by blame-them rhetoric heightened by imagistic media, yet depoliticized in two important ways: the nation's political institutions too often serve up essentially symbolic solutions that fail to resolve deep-seated problems that have over time become worse, and a correspondingly disillusioned and disempowered public is drawn into a culture of consumption and entertainment that provides them with a compensatory but ultimately erosive sense of empowerment.

On the other hand, the archetypal media argument is also wrong in two respects. These "battles of the 1960s" were not, and are not, a generational quarrel. Notwithstanding media representations, sixties battles were about racism, poverty, war, meaningful education, the rat race, sexism, and ecological destruction. But, second, these political concerns are not even battles of the sixties.

Lo and behold, while minorities and women have made great gains within the social mainstream, contemporary American life is marked by wars the people oppose yet cannot stop; poverty and a racially identifiable underclass that lives without hope; an educational system increasingly driven by the bottom line that leaves young people more trapped in a rat race than were their sixties forebears; ongoing violence toward women in a society that continues to bombard us with images of pumped-up militarism; and an ecosphere that is showing far more fundamental signs of deterioration than it did in the earlier era of Earth Day environmentalism.

Yet during the actual battles of the 1960s, a lot did happen that has left us with both imagistic memories and emotional scars, and these are largely what the media discourse is referring to, directly or indirectly, in speaking of "sixties battles" or "family quarrels." It is my contention that overcoming these residues can occur only if we as a nation engage in an open and honest discourse about our not-so-distant past—a kind of truth and reconciliation process that helps heal the wounds to which people still cling. We need a reckoning with this past that we can learn from, not a discourse that keeps a distorted past alive while simultaneously trying to bury it.

In these pages, I offer an interpretive reading that simultaneously seeks to explain what happened in the 1960s era and what happened to that history. More broadly, I offer a reading of how the United States evolved from the post–World War II era down to the present moment. As I proceed, it is important for the reader to bear in mind three points.

First, I place the mass media at the center of this story, yet I need to qualify what this means. I refer to the mass media in a structural sense—that is, I speak of characteristics of mass media that are grounded in the broader political economy and thus shape media outcomes systemically. As corporate institutions that seek mass markets in order to remain economically viable, the media are subject to dynamics that invariably shape what we the public get from them. These national *mass* media thus are the locus for our common political discourse, even as a wide range of smaller, independent media provide a richly vital discourse that is significantly different and, in today's Internet at least, wide open to any and all perspectives.

It is important, then, to recognize that I am referring to institutional characteristics of media within which a wide range of often very competent professional journalists work. I am not suggesting a form of collusion on the part of individual media actors, be they reporters, editors, or corporate executives. Also, in referring to the common ground of "legitimate" media discourse—as distinct from those perspectives that are excluded from that common ground—I am really writing about a set of ideological assumptions that informs, and limits, the nation's public discourse throughout its political institutions: courts, legislative arenas, and executive bodies. I concentrate on the mass media because I am primarily concerned with characteristics of these institutions that I argue have had a deleterious effect on the nation's public discourse. Thus when I speak of media "effects," I am referring to ways in which the institutional dynamics of the media interact with wider forces in society to produce a kind of logic that shapes political action—not that any specific media account "caused" a specific public response. The latter effort lies well beyond the range of this book, if not the capabilities of social science.

Actually studying the media in and about the sixties is a formidable task. Many others have examined pieces of the puzzle, and I draw on their work. Most of my own hands-on analysis of national mass media has concentrated on the weekly newsmagazines—*Time, Newsweek, U.S. News & World Report,* and, to a degree, *Life*—and the *New York Times,* all of which are readily available through various electronic archives. Television is more difficult, and much television before 1968 is not even available. For the most part, I have relied on a number of systematic efforts to examine television coverage of specific aspects of the sixties era. I have also examined alternative media accounts of sixties phenomena I study. While these media played an enormously important role in raising awareness, debating issues, and creating community within the social movements of the sixties, my thesis focuses primarily on the mass media "commons" that perform the crucial function of keeping many of the perspectives of alternative media outside the boundaries of legitimate discourse. The same is true today as a tremendously vital independent media discourse continues to provide a rich progressive critique of the American mainstream yet is marginalized by the mass media culture.

Second, in writing a critical interpretation of the institutional characteristics of mass media discourse, I am offering a reading of our past and the mass media that itself lies outside the boundaries of conventional media discourse. Most fundamentally, my argument revolves around contradictions between capitalism and democracy and the way these have played out in the United States since World War II. Along with an increasing number of voices around the world, this perspective sees these contradictions becoming increasingly problematic in the years ahead.

In most characterizations, this is a view from the Left, although I hasten to add not the "Left" as it is typically characterized in the mass media. My particular perspective is also grounded in a vision of a democratic way of life, and this has important implications for both the nation's discourse and the Left. I argue that the Left's historical exclusion from legitimate discourse in the United States is a fundamental, undemocratic flaw of our common discourse. Indeed, I argue with respect to the 1960s era that this exclusion had significant ramifications for both the trajectory of that era and the fragmentation of the Left. Coupled with a highly imagistic media culture, the responses to the sixties have produced a culture of ideological and identity enclaves across the population, in the process sharpening divisions and reducing—not enhancing—the likelihood of a democratic conversation among the citizenry. Yet that is precisely what I conclude we sorely need if we are to confront the growing problems we face—"we" meaning the American people and the people of the world, and "we" meaning the fragmented enclaves of the Left as well.

Finally, I am aware that my argument makes significant generalizations about activities in and since the sixties. Having lived through and been actively involved in the sixties, I am very mindful of the deep emotions and antagonisms that can trigger a wide range of responses to claims made about that era. Those emotions and antagonisms are, in fact, part of my subject. I make no claim to a definitive explanation of the sixties era, nor is it my intention to rehash and second-guess old struggles and strategies. To my knowledge, no one can claim immunity from shortcomings, mistakes, or excesses. I revisit this past because it can tell us a lot about where we are today and why we are there. It can also shed important light on the kinds of complex issues we face if we are to strengthen rather than lose our democratic way of life. And finally, the sixties era was permeated by a sense—not universally shared, it must be noted—that people can join together and act in ways that shape their world. Notwithstanding President Obama's "audacity of hope" rhetoric, we have largely lost our collective sense of hope that we, the people, can shape our future. We need to understand how and why this has happened.

This book is the culmination of many years of conversation, study, writing, and rewriting. Along the way, my thinking has benefited greatly from conversations with a wide range of colleagues and friends, particularly at conferences on the meaning and legacies of the 1960s and on the "Sixties-List," at one time a rich conversation among teachers, scholars, and activists organized by Kali Tal. There have obviously been too many to remember, but I know I benefited from conversations with John Andrew, Stanley Aronowitz, John Baky, Michael Bibby, Wini Breines, Nick Bromell, Bob Buzzanco, Peter Carroll, Alice Echols, Bill Ehrhart, Marc Flacks, Michael Foley, Bruce Franklin, Todd Gitlin, Van Gosse, Susan Jeffords, Richard King, Peter Ling, Don Luce, Staughton Lynd, Paul Lyons, Roz Payne, Charlotte Ryan, Barbara Tischler, Jeremy Varon, Ellen Willis, and the many folks who have kept alive the important memories at Kent State University, particularly Carol Barbato and Laura Davis, the primary organizers of the 2009 Democracy symposium.

I would especially like to thank the friends and colleagues who read portions of the manuscript and generously shared their reactions with me: Bill Ayers, Dan Berger, Barbara Epstein, Dave Dellinger, Dick Flacks, Alex Grosskurth, Bill Grover, Ron Jacobs, Ed Herman, George Katsiaficas, Kathleen Kelly, Doug Kellner, Jama Lazerow, Jack Lule, Rick Matthews, Bob McChesney, Carey McWilliams, Nancy McWilliams, Mark Crispin Miller, John Pettegrew, Gary Olson, Matthew

Rinaldi, Bill Riches, Bob Rosenwein, David Stiegerwald, and Cathy Wilkerson all provided valued readings of my evolving argument at different times over the last decade or so. Marilyn Young gave a particularly helpful read of several chapters in the early going, as well as a response to my article in the *Radical History Review*. Bill Gamson's insight on several chapters was especially useful, as were his suggestions and consultation as I pursued the publication of the book. In addition, he generously invited me to present my thesis to his workshop at the Media Research and Action Project. I would also like to express special thanks to two men who have been important sources of inspiration as well as support. Both Noam Chomsky and the late Howard Zinn have read and responded generously to several pieces of my work, while their own writing and speaking has been crucial to the vitality of a wider community of which I am part. Even though publication of this book provides a kind of closure, the conversation is ongoing and important to me.

Over the years, I have benefited from the help of a number of students who scouted and uncovered valuable media pieces and secondary studies. I thank Sarah Van Beurden, Elric Kline, Claudia Anewalt, Amanda Barnes, Hannah Behrmann, Lauren Brinker, David Stanley, and Noah Sunflower for their contributions. More generally, with their fresh engagement in the subject material of this book, my many students have continuously helped me to refine and rearticulate my thinking; I will always be grateful to them for the vitality they have brought to my life. Many thanks also to Judy Smullen, who gave a much bulkier manuscript two careful readings and was a great help in my effort to make it a more coherent and relatively concise whole. Thanks, too, to Roseann Bowerman, one of Lehigh University's very valuable librarians, for her help in tracking down a wide variety of resources. And, finally, thanks to the folks at the University Press of Kansas: my editor, Fred Woodward, for his patience, experience, and intelligence as I plodded through the revision process; and Susan Schott, Jennifer Dropkin, Sara Henderson White, and Eric Schramm for their skill and understanding in preparing the manuscript for publication.

I am extremely grateful to my whole family for their forbearance and support through what I'm sure seemed an endless span of time in which I wrestled with "the book." Most of all, I am grateful to Mary Lou, who has really had to live in intimate relationship not only with the author but, at times it must have seemed, the book itself. Her love and support, along with that of my family, helped me see it through. I dedicate the book to her with love and gratitude.

What Really Happened to the 1960s

1

The Past as Prologue: Distorted History —

Declining Democracy

History always constitutes the relation between a present and a past. Conse-
quently fear of the present leads to a mystification of the past. . . . If we "saw"
the . . . past, we would situate ourselves in history. When we are prevented from
seeing it, we are being deprived of the history which belongs to us.
   —John Berger, *Ways of Seeing*, 1977

With the destruction of history, contemporary events themselves retreat into
a remote and fabulous realm of unverifiable stories, uncheckable statistics,
unlikely explanations and untenable reasoning. For every imbecility presented
by the spectacle, there are only the media's professionals to give an answer.
   —Guy De Bord, *Comments on the Society of Spectacle*, 1988

The democratic ideal . . . is that the people are capable of and ought to be
making their own history. . . . The reason that democracy persists as an ideal
at all is that people at times have transcended their everyday lives in order to
make history.
   —Richard Flacks, *Making History*, 1988

Forty years after the tumultuous year of 1968 ushered in an era of political backlash and market liberalization, Americans turned out in record numbers and
elected Barack Obama as the first African American president. At the precise
moment the national networks could officially declare Obama the winner, NBC
anchor Brian Williams observed, "We have news. There will be young children
in the White House for the first time since the Kennedy generation. An African
American has broken the barrier as old as the republic; an astonishing candidate, an astonishing campaign. A seismic shift in American politics."[1] As Williams continued, viewers watched campaign supporters' jubilant celebration in,
of all places, Chicago's Grant Park, where forty years earlier a phalanx of Chicago policemen, with billy clubs flailing, charged into a crowd of antiwar protesters in one of the sixties era's pivotal events.

   While the multiracial and multigenerational Obama crowd celebrated, tears
streaming down the faces of young African American women, NBC asked for
the thoughts of Congressman John Lewis, a former civil rights activist. Lewis's
words were poignant: "Well, I must tell you, this is unreal, it's unbelievable. But
I tell you, the struggle, the suffering, the pain and everything that we tried to

do to create a more perfect union, it was worth it." Recalling that Martin Luther King Jr. "had tears coming down his face" when President Lyndon Johnson concluded his historic introduction of the Voting Rights Act of 1965 with the movement's credo, "We shall overcome," Lewis continued,

> I think about Robert Kennedy and the countless individuals that stood in those unmovable lines in Selma. I think about those three young civil rights workers in Mississippi, two whites from New York and an African American from Mississippi who was beaten, shot and killed. So some people gave their very life and some of us gave a little blood to make tonight possible. It is a night of gratitude. I tell you, I feel more than lucky, but I feel very blessed to live to see this day.[2]

Greeting his supporters a short while later, President-elect Obama used words that recalled King's final public address the night before he was killed in April 1968: "The road ahead will be long. Our climb will be steep. We may not get there in one year, or even in one term. But America, I have never been more hopeful than I am tonight that we will get there. I promise you, we as a people will get there."[3]

For millions of viewers it was powerful television that resonated with the struggles of the 1960s era, to say nothing of the nation's tragic racial history. Indeed, ever since Obama was considered a potential candidate, the mass media speculated about how resonances from the 1960s era might influence the 2008 race. From February 2007 to election day, 1,790 articles from LexisNexis's major U.S. and world news publications discussed Obama and the 1960s.

From the beginning, media commentary speculated about the historic nature of Obama's candidacy and whether or not the United States was ready to elect a black president, hearkening back to the 1960 candidacy of John Kennedy, the first Catholic to be elected president. Obama's eloquence and charismatic personality, his youthful appeal to younger voters, and his rhetoric calling for change from the jaded politics of the past all contributed to the Kennedy comparisons.

While candidate Obama may have welcomed this particular media fixation, his effort to speak in a "new voice" meant he had to distinguish his campaign from much of the political discourse that had dominated presidential elections in the decades since the brief Kennedy years.[4] For Obama, this meant, as he declared on September 15, 2007, "I come from a new generation of Americans. I don't want to fight the battles of the 1960s."[5] Even this declaration echoed John Kennedy's inaugural reference to the torch passing to "a new generation of Americans."

Why did candidate Obama feel compelled to make such a statement? What did he mean by it? Clearly, at a time when public opinion reflected alarm over the nation's economic nosedive and opposition to the nation's war in Iraq, it made sense to frame one's candidacy around the theme of change. But what have "the battles of the 1960s" come to represent in American political discourse? What do the media mean by "the sixties"? Further, what would a "seismic shift in American politics," as Brian Williams put it, look like? How much difference does a "new generation" make in American politics, anyway?

These are questions left unexamined in the media. Much of mass media discourse on the sixties is about ghosts, accusations, and smoke and mirrors, and much of it is meant to play on audience emotions and, where these are available, potent memories of long ago days. Aside from indisputably powerful imagery, rhetoric, and symbolism, it is hard to locate much political substance in this media discourse. The same could be said about mass media's political discourse in general. More often than not revolving around symbolic appeals to emotion, manipulation of images, attack and counterattack, and at times breathtaking distortion, the media spectacle largely distracts the public from the kind of public conversation through which democratic citizens gain an understanding of their common interests and concerns.

The media culture's "Sixties," however, played a crucial historical role in producing this contemporary media discourse. The mass media have been the major vehicle used by the Right and the corporate center in fanning the flames of ideological backlash against sixties-era social movements. They have also been the principal vehicle for the commercial exploitation of sixties-era impulses. In combination, I argue, these responses have produced conditions that simultaneously demand and discourage collective action on the part of the public.

"The Sixties" in Mass Media Discourse

Presidential campaigns have for more than forty years exploited symbols, images, and personalities from the 1960s era as a means of mobilizing political support for their candidates and political agendas. For the most part, these campaigns have come from the right side of the political spectrum. Over time, they have blamed "the Sixties" for just about everything they see as wrong with America. Beginning as far back as Barry Goldwater's 1964 presidential campaign, political forces on the Right have used sixties-era media images to tap into the fears and resentments that the spectacle has spawned and thus to buttress their political agendas aimed largely at what they like to call "Big Government." During the 1960s, these attacks began to pull significant populations — most notably the white South and portions of the Catholic working class — out of the Democratic Party's New Deal coalition into the Republican camp.

With the economy floundering in the early to mid-1970s, capitalism's elites sought to redress what they saw as the "excess of democracy" or "democratic distemper" of the sixties era in order to move public policy to the right.[6] Rightist and corporate agendas converged with the election of Ronald Reagan in 1980, a turning point that not only produced the neoliberal (or what is misleadingly called a "free market") regime that dominated American politics for at least the next twenty-eight years,[7] but succeeded in transforming American political discourse in the process. The Reagan agenda implemented earlier corporate calls for a sharp reduction in liberal government, a major shift toward privatization and free-market policies, and a new surge in military spending coupled with a more aggressive U.S. foreign policy—a reversal of the so-called "Vietnam syndrome."

Despite policies geared to the interests of corporations and the wealthy, neoliberalism enjoyed wide electoral success because it was ushered in by rhetoric that effectively played off public images of the sixties—threatening black militants, rebellious students, Viet Cong flag–waving antiwar protesters, self-indulgent and stoned hippies, and "man-hating" or "family-hating" women—that had alienated significant portions of the population. Via a process I call "visual thinking" or visual association, the conservative "Machiavellians," as Tom Hayden has accurately labeled them,[8] produced a populist spin for policies that favored economic elites by blaming the images on an "Eastern liberal elite." The folksy, avuncular Reagan persona became a kind of nostalgic commercial for traditional verities and "family values" that allegedly flourished in a visually mythologized past before the era of "riots, assassinations, and domestic strife over the Vietnam war," as Reagan described the 1960s.[9] All things "liberal"—permissive parenting, indulgent campus authorities, domestic government programs, and the media—were blamed for the generational unrest of the past.

Curiously, this longstanding campaign against the "bad sixties" succeeded with considerable help from the very "liberal media" the campaign persistently attacked. Like the ideological backlash, the commercialization of the sixties began during the sixties era as news media and advertisers began to zero in on images of what they saw as new and increasingly provocative behaviors of a large baby boom population. News media coverage of sixties-era protests began to frame public understanding of protest around the most common visual denominator, a seemingly "rebellious generation," around mid-decade—roughly the same time that protests began targeting national policies and institutions, *and* the same time that the national backlash began. Commercial interests responded by adopting the language of youthful alienation and a stance of "cool" skepticism as they began to transform the "youth culture" into a "hip" youth market.

Over the same time period, entertainment television and popular movies began to air themes popular with sixties youth. By 1971 CBS had introduced Norman Lear's sitcom *All in the Family*, which juxtaposed two sides of the popularized sixties divide—young liberals versus their working-class parents, presented in the familiar generational frame. Twelve years later, NBC's *Family Ties*, a sitcom that President Reagan claimed as his favorite TV show,[10] played off another generational clash, this one between the young Reaganite Alex P. Keaton and his liberal sixties-generation parents. With musical scores and themes that evoked baby boomer nostalgia, films like the Reagan era's *The Big Chill* (1983) and the 1994 blockbuster *Forrest Gump* provided audiences with representations of the sixties era that confirmed everything the Right claimed. Advertisers appealed to hip consumers by using rebellious sixties songs to sell everything from sneakers to raisins to accounting firms. More generally, as documented by Thomas Frank, advertisers and the business world widely appropriated the values of countercultural rebellion for their own commercial purposes.[11]

The interaction between ideological attack and commercial exploitation provides crucial insight into the deterioration of American political discourse during and since the 1960s. On the one hand, the commercially driven, highly imagistic stuff of mass media acts as a kind of advertisement for an increasingly expressive America "liberated" from past restraints. On the other hand, ideological rhetoric, much of it propaganda, plays on fears and resentments aroused by imagery to offer a return to the "good old days." Yet the neoliberal policies actually implemented by successive administrations further erode the public's ability to shape its common destiny, providing fuel for more of the same dynamic.

At the same time, the political polarization and social fragmentation that occurred during the sixties has been greatly exacerbated by the two media culture responses. The ideological backlash has unleashed a warlike political discourse in which political adversaries are treated as enemies worthy only of attack. The market response to our fragmentation is to play to our different tastes, from cable TV channels geared to target audiences to the Internet's personalized pitch to individual consumers. The market offers us what Lawrence Grossberg has called individual "affective empowerment"[12] instead of the real thing—thereby introducing what I call a "market dialectic" that erodes and supplants a more democratic dialectic.[13]

As the Obama election coverage suggests, the mass media not only provide profoundly evocative moments that resonate with historic 1960s events and personalities, they fill the airwaves and print media with snapshot reminders of sixties pop culture, iconic personalities, and banal references to the baby boom generation—the latter so tiresome that advertisers appeal to millions of younger, "hipper" Americans by ridiculing "Boomers" and the sixties.

The media culture's sixties fixation has evolved over time. The initial generational explanation, dominant during the Reagan–*Big Chill* years, meant the sixties ended when the baby boomer generation grew into their careerist and acquisitive adult years—a frame that was somewhat paralleled by the early "declensionist" histories of the sixties.[14] A second generational explanation evolved as media fixations with the sixties persisted despite the political entrenchment of neoliberalism and the maturation of baby boomers. Attention to right-wing baby boomers (e.g., George W. Bush) and allegedly "left-wing" baby boomers (e.g., Bill Clinton) in positions of power,[15] the spreading "culture wars" of the 1990s, and histories that reread the sixties as a civil war between Right and Left[16]—all helped to configure the sixties as a metaphor for a divided America.

In light of this persistent media attention, is it surprising that the mass media have also been obsessed with the question of whether we were "over" the sixties—as if the sixties were a stage in growing up—since, well, the late sixties themselves? Beyond their rhetorical flourish, the media are asking a political question: when will the political issues and social divides of the sixties era no longer be salient in American politics? But they are also obeying economic and political imperatives linked to the size of the baby boom population bulge. In the media's reflexive generational frame, the two considerations converge seamlessly: the social divides of the sixties dominate the culture because they are generational. Thus, for example, in December 2007, Andrew Sullivan argued that candidate Obama, "unlike any of the other candidates," was positioned to "take America—finally—past the debilitating, self-perpetuating family quarrel of the Baby Boom generation that has long engulfed all of us."[17] Representations like these illustrate shortcomings in popular discourse about the sixties today. Indeed, much of what passes for history in conventional thinking is actually the public memory preserved for us by the mass media.

I would suggest three fundamental problems with the typical media fare related to the sixties: (1) it fundamentally distorts history by, among other things, removing serious consideration of the conditions that generated hopeful, democratic activism and by reducing potent social movements involving millions of people to a few iconic leaders or images; (2) it is part of a general media discourse that undermines the possibility of democracy; and (3) it fails to address the 800-pound gorilla in the room that no one mentions—namely, systemic characteristics of capitalism that contribute in fundamental ways to the social ills with which Americans and the rest of the world struggle.

First, the sixties era has been so thoroughly reconstructed in mass media discourse that, despite being extensively documented in historical scholarship, one of its defining qualities has largely disappeared from public memory: namely, the surge in democratic empowerment in which large numbers of Americans of all ages organized themselves to confront and transform a range of injustices rooted in American institutions. Instead, the mass media frame the sixties as the product of an unusually restless and rebellious generation, a distortion that essentially makes this past politically irrelevant. In the first place, the implication that the change agents in the sixties were all young or that most of the baby boom generation was activist is simply wrong. Furthermore, this public memory largely denies us collective awareness of the contexts, experiences, and beliefs that were catalysts to the dramatic actions of the past, thereby obscuring important connections between this past and the troubles of today's world. Finally, and most profoundly, the broader meaning of citizen assertiveness in the sixties—that it represented the inspiring potential for a more vital, accountable, and humane democracy—has largely vanished from public discourse—except for symbolically suggestive, visceral moments like election night 2008.

Second, as noted above, this generational frame has long been part of a diversionary and counter-democratic public discourse that substitutes simplistic visual association for thought. However alienating or entertaining the political spectacle may be, it is fundamentally depoliticizing because it distances us from substantive politics that confront and deal with the problems of the day. At the same time, it has seemingly politicized everything through its manipulation of affect. It produces a fragmented polity characterized by what I call an enclave mentality and a warlike discourse.

This counter-democratic discourse has come to define the public side of politics to such a degree that it permeates the nation's legislative and policy-making arenas as well as the nation's elections. Television news audiences, in particular, are bombarded with abbreviated and self-contained political dramas and human interest stories that draw attention away from the ways that American institutions shape the world. Increasingly over time, the spectator public is left with less and less understanding but with more and more feeling-based judgments aroused for or against one or another side in the nation's political conflicts. Indeed, feelings have become the currency of not only advertising but of media politics, as well.

Like the media's "Sixties," this counter-democratic discourse has evolved over the decades. During the Reagan years, the president's rhetoric often appealed to conservatives' sense that the nation's culture was in decline, that the pursuit of individual self-indulgence was out of control, that society's traditions—and traditional values—were threatened. These were and are legitimate and important political concerns, yet they, too, have been turned into divisive and diversionary politics. Rightist rhetoric has juxtaposed behaviors and images from the sixties era against an idealized era before the sixties, suggesting by spurious association that various manifestations of liberalism were to blame for the excesses that fed many Americans' perceptions that they were in danger of losing a way of life they valued. The Right's political rhetoric has also continually railed about hot-button, emotionally arousing issues—prayer in schools, court-ordered school desegregation, the changing sexual mores of youth, flag burning, gun control, and, of course, abortion—that in various ways project back into the sixties era.

Along with the world of consumerism and entertainment, these efforts have, on the one hand, depoliticized the polity, diminishing the public's ability to influence government policy, much less make history. Activist courts—both the oft-targeted, liberal Supreme Court of the long sixties era and the contemporary conservative Court—supplant legislative arenas while imbuing presidential elections with potent partisan politics heavy with symbolic meaning.[18] And, with both Republicans and Democrats on board, the neoliberal regime has turned more and more of the political realm over to the marketplace—an ironic result since the market accelerates the very forces that cause "conservative" constituencies (of all political stripes) to feel that their world is increasingly beyond their control. Not only do neoliberal policies and the Right's attacks sustain unending frustration for American conservatives, they diminish the realm of democratic politics within which popular concerns of all kinds can be aired and acted upon.

On the other hand, the backlash that has generated neoliberalism continually feeds on the fears and resentments of people who are disturbed by the sixties they witnessed or remember with the help of media imagery. Propaganda attacks against sixties stereotypes have over the years greatly inflamed public discourse, feeding an angry sense of victimhood on the part of both the targets of these attacks and those whose resentments can never be resolved by this highly symbolic media discourse.

The third fundamental problem with this media discourse is what it leaves out, or what it diverts our attention from: namely, a serious discussion of capitalism and the ways that it aggravates the very conditions that generate a great deal of agitation all across the political spectrum. Particularly in the United States, but increasingly throughout the globally capitalist world, the mass media are capitalist institutions that not only produce our diversionary media culture but help to keep serious discussion of capitalism outside the common ground of mainstream discourse and therefore off the political agenda. In these respects, then, we live in what I call a "market democracy"—or a democracy that is compatible with what C. B. Macpherson called a "market society"—that is, narrowed in meaning to a "system of government rather than a kind of society" and one that is made safe for and pervasively infiltrated by the imperatives of capitalism.[19] Through the market dialectic they spread, capitalism's media have a profoundly corrosive effect on democratic culture and, thus far at least, have effectively restricted the range of public debate.

Yet the policies of the neoliberal regime have also produced a world that, I suggest, desperately needs both a democratic civic culture and a full range of public debate. Turning the world over to the market has produced an accelerating erosion of the ecosphere and an ever-widening gap of inequality in American and global society, to say nothing of the persistence of destructive and arguably counterproductive American wars as well as great potential for future resource wars. Understanding the fundamental ways that capitalism contradicts democracy is an important first step in finding a way out of the discourse that has captured our politics and, far too often, captivated us. It also provides, I submit, an important framework for understanding how we got here—what happened to the 1960s, where the "sixties divide" comes from, and the central role the media have played in the transformation from the regime of New Deal liberalism to our current neoliberalism.

This understanding can also help us think about how to regain a sense of popular empowerment, well beyond the highly symbolic promises of an Obama administration. In contrast to the classic media fare, the history of sixties social movements provides important insights in this regard. As Robert Putnam observed in the year 2000, "Never in our history had the future of civic life looked brighter than it did at the end of the 1960s."[20] Certainly the sixties era produced a wide array of legislative reforms, ranging from the historic Civil Rights and Voting Rights Acts of 1964 and 1965 to the highly symbolic War Powers Resolution of 1973. It also produced substantial social and cultural change, most notably the entry of women and racial minorities into the broad mainstream of American life. Perhaps nothing resonates more powerfully from the experiences of activists in the sixties era, particularly in the earlier years, than their sense that they were part of a social movement that was making history, bringing America to a full reckoning with its tragic racial past and forging a future more compatible with the nation's democratic ideals.[21]

Yet, at the same time that America's democratic promise was being heralded, the media culture of the time conveyed the clear impression that the nation was coming apart. The American public was deeply divided over the war in Vietnam, racial polarization was inflamed, and media consumers had been buffeted by a long sequence of violent shocks: political assassinations, racial insurrection, police brutality, a nightmarish war, militant protest, an alienated youthful counterculture, and a political discourse charged with the strident rhetoric of backlash. In contrast to social movements' sense of making history, a 1968 statement adopted by the Columbia University chapter of Students for a Democratic Society asserted, "We felt helpless in the history of our times"[22] — a feeling many Americans continue to experience. Despite the awakenings of important new social movements focusing on the liberation of women, gay and lesbian rights, ecology, and neighborhood preservation, the end of the decade stood in stark contrast to the idealistic and hopeful zeitgeist of the early sixties — or, at least, so it seemed in the political spectacle recorded by the mass media.

Between a sense of hopeful empowerment and a sense of feeling helpless in the history of the times, ideological backlash against and commercial exploitation of sixties' social movements were becoming more pronounced. The political structure was becoming increasingly resistant and repressive while capitalism's media culture offered what was increasingly a feeling of empowerment as at least a partial compensation for the real thing. In order to understand what has happened to the 1960s, we must understand what happened in the 1960s.

How Mass Media Derail Democracy: An Overview

I argue that the interaction between mass social movements, mass media, and the institutions of political authority during and since the 1960s reflect historically recurring tensions between, on the one hand, a market-based capitalist economy and the elite political domination it engenders and, on the other, the dynamics of a vital democratic polity. Contradictions within the prevailing system invariably produce forms of opposition and resistance, typically through some form of protest. Indeed, American history can be read as the history of groups with fundamental grievances militantly agitating for and ultimately achieving some level of reform.[23] As they play out through the media culture, then, the contradictions between capitalism and democracy help to explain both the evolving media spectacle of the 1960s and the subsequent turn toward neoliberalism and the privatization of political life in the years since.

The concept of hegemony is appropriate to this analysis since it refers to elite domination of the mass of people, not through coercion as in authoritarian or traditional totalitarian systems but through the people's consent.[24] Hegemony occurs via the penetration throughout the culture of an ideology, a belief system that "this is the way things are." To the degree that "the way things are" becomes the way things must (or should) be in the popular imagination, the relations of domination and power in society are legitimized. Hegemony is maintained through a never-ending process of "negotiation" in which elites anticipate and seek to incorporate the very forces that rise up to challenge them, or potentially might do so. Commercial interests in particular—including, of course, the media—are constantly attempting to anticipate shifts in the public's tastes so they can package their products in ways that sustain public demand, so it is hardly surprising that much of this negotiation occurs in the realm of culture, increasingly via the media. Electoral campaigns operate in much the same manner. Yet when popular political challenges become sufficiently potent, political elites either repress them by force or they respond in ways that accommodate grievances within prevailing institutional structures and ideologies—i.e., without altering the basic structure of hegemony.

From this vantage point, the sixties era can be seen as a pivotal period within the historical span from the Second World War to the present, a time in which the hegemony of the post–World War II culture was subjected to profound challenges, many of them efforts to push society in a more democratic direction responsive to a variety of new political voices and new demands for public accountability. During and after the sixties era, both political elites and commercial media responded to these challenges through a variety of "negotiations" (backed up by the coercive authority of the state), and hegemony was reestablished. Reflecting the ideological and commercial imperatives of corporate institutions, the mass media played—and continue to play—a major role in these negotiations between the challenges to and the restoration of hegemony.

Although I place the mass media at the center of the transformation of political discourse and culture, I hasten to add that the media culture obviously reflects the broader institutional context of commercial imperatives, political power, and ideology. Thus I speak of the mass media in the macro- or structural sense of an institution that plays a crucial role in shaping the polity's common discourse. It is the nation's common discourse that is my primary focus, rather than the measurable impact of a particular media presentation. As I note in the Preface, professional journalists work within constraints and influences imposed by the imperatives of these corporate institutions; practices that make unquestioned sense within this structure may become, in the larger context, part of the problem. Finally, I need to make clear that I am by no means suggesting that these media are all-powerful. Indeed, the way different audiences respond differently to what they encounter in the media is crucial to my analysis.

In brief, I argue that the mass media of the sixties era helped to invite and spread that era's protest activity, but they did so on terms reflecting broader structures of which they were part. As a result, they simultaneously helped to shape, marginalize, and ultimately contain protest movements. Along with the powerful ideological voices who enjoy significant, if not dominant, access to the media, they have been the major facilitators of our diversionary politics and warlike discourse ever since.

I suggest that two systemic characteristics of the emerging postwar media became crucial to the contestation and maintenance of hegemony. First, what the media, by their behavior, consider to be legitimate discourse for public consumption encompasses a range of viewpoints that embrace rather than challenge the system's foundational myths, ideological beliefs, and institutions. Second, as commercial enterprises, the mass media must aggressively seek and engage readers and audiences. The ideological commons of mass media discourse can be traced back to their origins as mass-market enterprises, while the imperative of attracting and engaging audiences took on new intensity with the postwar rise of television.

I argue that both characteristics contradict and undermine a democratic culture. Democratic discourse is inclusive. At great cost to our public discourse, the mass media exclude critical conversation about fundamental flaws in the nation's policies and institutions. Democratic discourse should also enlighten and inform the people so they achieve a level of understanding that enables them to act as citizens. The mass media's main function clearly should not be to distract the public from engaging in and learning about their society and its institutions. Furthermore, in combination, these forces produce dynamics that have telling implications for efforts to challenge and contest prevailing conditions—as they did in the sixties.

Reflecting their need to appeal to mass markets, these media typically strive for bipartisan balance as the first rule in their efforts to maintain their so-called objectivity. As a result, the political discourse available in mass media is restricted to conflicting interpretations among competing elites, which means it is bound by the common ideological beliefs promulgated by the powerful and inculcated through society's educational and cultural institutions.[25] Most fundamentally, these include the belief that the system and its institutions work, that they largely work for the good of all, and that American intentions abroad are noble. As Daniel Hallin observed in his study of media reporting on the Vietnam War, a "Sphere of Consensus" in the mass media encompasses those beliefs not regarded as controversial by journalists, political officials, and much of the public—including, for example, the United States' motives in the war. The norms of objective journalism do not apply to the sphere of consensus; in this realm, Hallin found, journalists did not act as disinterested observers, but as "patriots."[26]

Beyond this consensus, however, lies the "Sphere of Legitimate Controversy," the "region of electoral contests and legislative debates" whose "limits" are "defined primarily by the two-party system. . . . Within this region objectivity and balance reign as the supreme journalist virtues." Legitimate media discourse is contained within these two spheres. Beyond the sphere of legitimate controversy, as Hallin put it, "lies the Sphere of Deviance, the realm of those political actors and views which journalists and the political mainstream of society reject as *unworthy of being heard*."[27]

The boundaries of mass media discourse thereby constrict the range of ideas and arguments given the status of legitimacy in the polity, and thus these media act as crucial gatekeepers in maintaining foundational ideological beliefs. In Hallin's study, the media became a "boundary-maintaining mechanism" during the Vietnam War, playing the role of "exposing, condemning, or excluding from the public agenda those who violate or challenge the political consensus."[28] As Edward Herman and Noam Chomsky have widely documented in their work on mass media, "views that challenge fundamental premises or suggest that the observed modes of exercise of state power are based on systemic forces will be excluded."[29] Todd Gitlin defined the news media's "dominant hegemonic principles" as "*the legitimacy of private control of commodity production; the legitimacy of the national security state; the legitimacy of technocratic experts; the right and ability of authorized agencies to manage conflict and make the necessary reforms; the legitimacy of the social order secured and defined by the dominant elites; and the value of individualism as the measure of social existence*."[30]

Despite the vehemence of sixties protest movements—or more recent protests—the boundaries of mass media's ideological commons have remained to the current day.

By effectively excluding the critical perspectives and argumentation of outsiders, the media simultaneously delegitimize, marginalize, and disempower them. As William Gamson and Gadi Wolfsfeld have put it, outsiders find that the mass media speak "mainstreamese." As a result,

> movements are pushed to adopt this language to be heard since journalists
> are prone to misunderstand or never hear the alternate language and its
> underlying ideas. But it is a common experience of movement activists

to complain that something has been lost in translation. Movements that accept the dominant cultural codes and do not challenge what is normally taken for granted will have less of a problem, but for *many* movements this would involve surrendering fundamental aspects of their raison d'être.[31]

In a world in which criticism of society's foundational institutions and beliefs is excluded from legitimate discourse, outsiders often seek to compensate for their arguments' lack of resonance within the media by using visually potent symbols or more forceful and disruptive forms of communication. Visual potency, protest size, and movement militancy thereby become the crucial determinants of a protest's impact on the politically powerful. Each can inject new issues onto the public agenda and can influence the actions of officialdom. Yet relevant policy debates, where legitimate and supposedly credible political actors define the parameters of discussion, occur elsewhere: in the media's framed news analysis and in legislative and corporate arenas where outsider arguments are similarly excluded or effectively marginalized.

Driven by the imperatives of commercialism, the introduction of television in the years following World War II greatly accelerated media culture's emphasis on powerful imagery, colorful personalities, dramatic action, and even violent conflict. Indeed, the rise of television as a commercial medium was a crucial catalyst for the rise of the postwar "market democracy" and for generating the all-too-familiar contemporary media culture with its shrinking sound bites, its shock imagery, and its fixation with celebrity and scandal.

Over the course of the sixties era, the media were drawn to the more dramatic and imagistic features that made protest "newsworthy" at the same time that they largely excluded protest arguments that challenged consensual ideological beliefs. Typically, the protesters became the story, not the issues and arguments the protesters raised. In the visual media, the behaviors or appearances of protesters increasingly came to define their identity as outsiders, dwelling in Hallin's "Sphere of Deviance."[32] Appearances and behaviors that signified their outsider status often had opposing visceral effects on mainstream audiences versus those predisposed by past experiences to be sympathetic to protesters' critical arguments.

In combination, I would suggest that these fundamental characteristics of mass media and conventional discourse introduced a contradictory dynamic into the political realm that has profound implications for democracy. Reflecting Albert O. Hirschman's dichotomy of "exit" and "voice,"[33] exclusion from common discourse encouraged protesters to exit or withdraw in order to find their own convivial realms of discourse — as different groups repeatedly did in the sixties era. Yet the media tendency to be visually inclusive sent protesting outsiders the message that they should adapt themselves to media imperatives if they sought to express their voice to the wider society.[34] The contradictory dynamic of visual inclusion and substantive exclusion substituted being seen for being heard as a vehicle of empowerment, thereby substituting appearance and behavior for voice. Outside of the actual impact protest size and militancy may have, this dynamic threatens to introduce the market dialectic into political protest.

Protesters and the media thereby engaged in a kind of dance in which each provided something for the other. Yet the media were the dance partners who determined the tune, or the acceptable meanings, of the protest. The media often chose the most colorful or dramatic behaviors as visual representations of a protest at the same time that they clearly distinguished between the arguments of legitimate insiders and illegitimate outsiders. Typically the mass media offered legitimate insider explanations of the outsider behaviors they covered, thereby delegitimizing the protesters' cause unless that cause could be conveyed visually.

Protests that were able to convey their meanings in a way that was visually potent and fit within the boundaries of legitimate discourse were most likely to receive a favorable hearing within the arenas of government policy making. Indeed, probably the two most effective examples of this kind of communicative protest in the entire era were the civil rights protests in Birmingham and Selma in 1963 and 1965. Both communicated their potent meaning through the media's visual coverage as opposed to the media's texts. Given the fact that the protests' target, the Jim Crow South, deviated from national norms of equal rights recently legitimized by the Supreme Court, the rest of America could perceive the movements' meaning when the media's cameras recorded Alabama authorities violently attacking nonviolent protesters seeking those rights. Each protest, in turn, was a catalyst for one of the two historic civil rights laws passed during the sixties era—an enduring testament to the power of media-based direct action protest—and a hugely significant catalyst to the era's remaining protest movements. The other major "legitimate" protest of the era, the 1969 Moratorium against the war in Vietnam, was legitimate because by that date a majority of Americans and much of the elite were against the war, and because the protesters tended to be a peaceful cross section of the American public who appeared in sharp contrast to both earlier and later antiwar protests.

The dynamic was, and is, different for any form of protest argument that lay outside the boundaries of legitimate discourse. I am by no means suggesting that the outsider arguments made by protesters or polemicists were (or are) consistently cogent or even on target. However, each of the sixties era's movements included central arguments that fell outside the boundaries of legitimate discourse: namely, that poverty was endemic in the American economy and racism embedded in society's institutions, that a main function of the universities was to select and appropriately train society's managerial classes, that the war in Vietnam was an illegitimate and horrifying act of American aggression against a tiny nation that posed no threat to the United States, that society was hopelessly entangled in the pursuit of artificially scarce material goods to the detriment of deeper human connections, and that society's institutions reflected and per-petuated gender roles that not only subjugated women but repressed men as well, with profound implications for society as a whole. Even a public figure as distinguished and legitimate in his "I have a dream" oratory and commitment to nonviolence as Martin Luther King Jr. experienced widespread media denuncia-tion when he crossed the boundaries of legitimacy, most profoundly when he spoke out against the war in Vietnam.

The protests by these system-critical movements and their leaders helped to motivate liberals inside the boundaries of legitimate discourse to speak to the issues raised by the protests: to call for social welfare programs, to push for phased withdrawal from Vietnam, and to advocate equal rights for women. Yet the "something lost in translation," to borrow Gamson and Wolfsfeld's phrase, was acknowledgment that the systemic critiques of outsiders might have valid-ity. Along with formative experiences of police and government repression, the steady and horrifying escalation of the war, and the abusive scorn heaped on the women's movement, this exclusion fueled rising frustration and alienation within the era's social movements. It also helped to produce the growing, radi-cal sense that something called "the system" was the problem since the system's legitimate leaders seemed incapable of addressing issues the protesters raised.

With television growing in importance, politics generally became more symbol-driven, at least for audiences consuming the media spectacle. Protest politics followed suit. Visual symbols—peace signs, Viet Cong flags, raised fists, styles of dress, Ché Guevara icons, prowling panthers, burning American flags, even guns and bombings—became increasingly important vehicles for convey-ing movement meanings. They became, in effect, shortcuts for communicating the meaning of protest gatherings, and they simultaneously became important signifiers of social identity, especially among the young. As symbolic shortcuts, however, they were open to widely divergent subjective interpretation by sym-pathetic onlookers, skeptical if not hostile public audiences, and, importantly, the forces of backlash who emphasized the visual association between the im-ages and their favorite target of the time: liberal government.

As the era's social movements began mobilizing in significant numbers against national institutions and policies around 1964 and 1965, protest was almost by definition outside the boundaries of legitimate discourse. At that very time, the nation's media landed on a compelling explanation for the rising tumult against the impoverishment and racial isolation of the nation's cities, against the na-tion's universities, and against escalation of a foreign war. Unable or unwilling to comprehend critiques of the very norms and assumptions held by members of the media and the rest of the "establishment," the media speedily gravitated toward an explanatory frame for the era's activism that appeared disproportion-ately populated by young people. The notion of a "generation gap" and a "rebel-lious generation" began to catch on.

It was in this precise time frame that what critics on the Right view as the nightmare of "the Sixties" began. As columnist Jonathan Yardley put it in 1987, "The Sixties . . . actually began around 1965 and ended about a decade later."[35] Increasingly, as the system began to resist the growing tidal wave of protest, participation in the media spectacle would become a compensatory form of affective empowerment in which feeling empowered began to supplant being empowered—except for the degree to which militancy actually produced a desired political response. It is no coincidence that, as John Sanbonmatsu has argued, 1965 was the year in which "expressivism became the dominant 'spirit' of the movement."[36]

As is the case with advertising, the affective empowerment offered by news media attention was likely to be appealing to the degree that it compensated for a sense of powerlessness or alienation from the mainstream culture. As Jerry Rubin once put it, "Just being on TV makes [a boring demonstration] exciting. . . . Television creates myths bigger than reality. . . . [It] packs all the action into two minutes—a commercial for the revolution."[37] As a young black male remarked in the aftermath of the 1965 Watts riot, "We won, because we made the whole world pay attention to us."[38] In reality, while the riot may have produced a temporary rush that felt like winning, and while it may have provoked action in some governmental quarters, these same dramatic media images were useful to those who sought to close off the longer-term prospects for building a more democratic society. Furious protesters at the 1968 Democratic Convention chanted, "The whole world is watching," confident that television coverage of police brutality would turn viewers against the police. In fact, the majority of the American public responded by siding with the police.

With no legitimacy in mainstream discourse, outsiders' very separation from that discourse in turn became an important part of their social identity, particularly in the case of younger participants. The exclusion of their authentic, if formative, voices accentuated their need to seek compatible community among others so excluded. In important ways, the separation of black nationalists, experimental schools, countercultural communes, women's consciousness-raising groups, and cultural feminist communities provided these groups with what Sara Evans and Harry Boyte have called "free spaces," or "environments in which people are able to learn a new self-respect, a deeper and more assertive group identity, public skills, and values of cooperation and civic virtue."[39] The same dynamic produced the lively alternative media or "underground press" that flourished in the sixties era.[40] In different form, the independent media of the left have remained a vital arena for political exchange ever since the sixties era—though it, too, is effectively marginalized by if not invisible in the mainstream culture.

Yet outside of the impact of personal conversations with family members, friends, and personal acquaintances, outsiders' growing isolation from the rest of society had significant ramifications for late-sixties discourse. Age segregation seemed especially telling, particularly for younger Americans passing through formative stages of identity development. With their voices excluded from mainstream media, outsiders' communication with the wider culture was increasingly defined in media terms, that is, by their provocative actions and appearances. Their delegitimation, in turn, left them vulnerable to both the media spectacle's invitation and its confirmation of their identity among their peers in the world of outsiders. Sharpened by events, isolation, and the implications for identity, what had been important "free spaces" tended to become defended enclaves defined by group identities, harsh internal expectations of "correct" behavior and belief, and angry attack against incorrect others. Both structurally through outsiders' isolation and procedurally through their actions and interactions, discourse within movement groups in the latter sixties deviated sharply from the kind of "free interaction" among and within social groups productive of "recognition of mutual interests" that a democratic theorist like John Dewey once envisioned.[41]

For many, the convergence of events and their delegitimation by society was a devastatingly painful experience, often leaving them with a profound sense of betrayal by the society that had encouraged their beliefs and allegiance. The horror of the war they witnessed their nation waging in their name, the intense contradiction between the idealized world they grew up in and the events they witnessed or the state violence they experienced, and finally their radical separation from society—all cut deep and spawned profound levels of anger, even rage. Within this pain, anger, and isolation lay the fertile soil of "victimspeak." Though different people behaved in different ways, their anger and pain were authentic and valid.

It should not be surprising that protest became increasingly militant. Not only did successive administrations carry on the unceasing horror of the war in defiance of growing public antipathy, not only did the experience of police violence spawn violence, but the media encouraged militancy as the only way to express a radically critical "voice" within mass media discourse. The media not only excluded anything that sounded remotely like radical analysis, but routinely used the word "radical" to describe militant action regardless of whether that action was informed by radical or systemic analysis. In effect, the media advertised militancy as the vehicle for radical criticism. In a similar way, they advertised the counterculture to younger teenagers with alluring images of lifestyles that gave form to their inner drives and dissatisfactions. Both media representations offered forms of apparent "empowerment."

As spin-offs of the market dialectic, affective empowerment and the expression of public identities were ultimately compatible with the always adaptable forces of commercialization, and thus not only news media but advertisers, entertainment television, and movies all began to zero in on the provocative appearances and behaviors of a large baby boom population. Simultaneously, the forces of corporate and electoral backlash fed off these same images to mobilize public support on behalf of their interests. Both strains helped to restore capitalism's hegemony and usher in the era of neoliberalism.

Then and Now: What Are the Stakes?

Though the Obama election of 2008 certainly provided a moment of historic symbolism matched by the upbeat rhetoric of political change, it will take several years to determine the election's historical significance. In light of this book's focus on media, symbolism, and sixties-era social movements, I offer three reflections on the symbolism of the Obama election. The first, suggested earlier, is that the Obama election recalled the symbolism of John F. Kennedy's election: the youth, eloquence, and can-do charisma that helped give "unwitting charge" to large numbers of Americans—particularly younger ones, many of whom had been moved by the awakening civil rights struggle. Called into political engagement, many of those activists helped to ensure that political change was real, not just rhetorical. Eventually, they also challenged the war the Kennedy administration had a major hand in escalating.

President Obama was elected at a time when the entire world was struggling under the increasingly devastating grip of globalizing capitalism and Rightist-dominated, neoliberal politics, a partnership that continues to prevail. The composite picture—profound global and domestic inequality, dehumanizing poverty and a criminalized underclass, global warming and ecological deterioration, aggressive American wars in Iraq and Afghanistan, and potential for future wars over increasingly scarce energy and water resources—has suggested to many that the prevailing model does not work. Despite these crises, however, the nation's political discourse continues to be dominated by an improbable "debate" between a market-embracing, centrist Obama administration and another round of nativist, right-wing attacks, now aimed at an alleged "socialist" administration.

Yet the world is alive with grassroots struggle, much of it beneath the radar of mass media. Paul Hawken has written about what he termed a "blessed unrest" of global grassroots activism focusing on issues of social justice and environmental sustainability. Though largely unnoticed by the mass media, Hawken suggests this unrest may be the "largest social movement in all of human history." As he put it, "If you look at the science that describes what is happening on earth today and aren't pessimistic, you don't have the correct data. If you meet the people in this unnamed movement and aren't optimistic, you haven't got a heart."[42] In a world plagued by war, shattering poverty, and ecological erosion, the "blessed unrest" of global grassroots activism is a sign that millions of people the world over recognize the need for transformation.

It remains to be seen if the Obama election gives unwitting charge to these global struggles, though it certainly seems clear that the eyes of much of the world have looked to Obama for a change in the direction of American leadership. One lesson we can learn from the democratic impulses of the 1960s era is that the answer depends on us, not on the Obama administration—a lesson reinforced by that administration's performance in office.

A second important piece of the Obama election is its symbolic connection to the history of people in struggle, its hopeful reminder that "ordinary folk," as Toni Morrison once put it, are capable of making history.[43] There is far too much powerful evidence of "ordinary folk" making history in the long sixties era for us to settle for the distracting silliness we find in our media culture. We can learn how people in that era struggled with issues of war, inequality, identity, and environmental despoliation—where and how they succeeded and where and why they failed. And we can learn a great deal from their interaction with the mass media. Though the media of that time were significantly less commercialized than those of today, the two crucial features of their interaction with sixties social movements remain central to prospects for greater democracy in the future. Indeed, the mass media are a crucial manifestation of the forces that require transformation if a more aware, democratic culture is to emerge.

The final piece of symbolism from the Obama election is the way the candidates' campaign rhetoric suggested a new tone of reconciliation, an effort to reach across the social divides so people could begin to understand each other. Indeed, amid the rancor of everyday discourse, the occasional political leader pleads for greater civility in our politics. Yet the rancor continues. Indeed, Obama's election seems to have triggered astonishing new levels of vitriol. In an anything-goes media culture in which the truth increasingly is whatever you want it to be, some warn that we are veering dangerously close to a form of fascism.[44]

If conditions suggest that a fundamental shift toward a more fully democratic culture is imperative, the experiences of sixties social movements recounted in this book, as well as the rich American tradition of political and community organizing, suggest that it is possible. We can no longer afford to remain in our own self-serving enclaves. We need to attend to and restore the commons. While political organizing dilemmas will continue to arise, democratic empowerment requires both community building and expanding awareness of the systemic forces that erode democracy.

Ultimately, democracy is not something done to people, but a process and a way of life pursued with an expanding community of others. It is a learned art that, as Frances Moore Lappé and others have argued, draws on our fundamental human capacity for empathy and our quest for transcendent meaning.[45] In the end, democracy is not only a worthy pursuit, but is becoming an increasingly imperative one.

2

Roots of the Sixties: Contradictions between Capitalism and Democracy in Postwar America

Democracy is . . . more than a form of government . . . it's a way of life. . . . The cure for the ailments of democracy is more democracy.
—John Dewey, *The Public and Its Problems*, 1927

The twentieth century has been characterized by three developments of great political importance: the growth of democracy, the growth of corporate power, and the growth of corporate propaganda as a means of protecting corporate power against democracy.
—Alex Carey, *Taking the Risk out of Democracy*, 1997

Taken as a whole, the sixties era was a time of vehement democratic assertiveness sandwiched between two eras dominated by political elites and the imperatives of capitalism. I suggest that the pendulum swing from capitalist domination to democratic opposition and back—or from market dialectic to democratic dialectic and back—reflects deeper contradictions between capitalism and democracy, contradictions that became particularly significant in the United States after World War II and provided catalysts for the rise of sixties-era social movements.

Capitalism vs. Democracy

In large part because the modern forms of democracy—representative government, competitive elections, secret ballots, basic rights of privacy and free expression—evolved in nation-states where capitalism had taken root, democracy and capitalism are conventionally thought of as two sides of the same coin. Yet the two are derived from and justified by two quite different conceptions of human beings and their potential.

Capitalism and its companion political theory, liberalism, are grounded in a view of humans as essentially self-interested beings with a potentially self-aggrandizing nature that needs to be restrained by impersonal safeguards: laws and the checks and balances of government and the mechanism of the competitive marketplace. Born in opposition to the arbitrary or excessive domination of monarchs, both liberalism and capitalism gained legitimacy through their celebration of individual freedom from political control. In the liberal lexicon, society is an abstracted arena of self-interested, competing individuals. Thus a proponent of "free market" neoliberalism such as former British prime minister Margaret Thatcher can proclaim, "There is no such thing as society, only individual men and women and their families."[1]

By contrast, democracy is grounded on the notion of individuals in social interaction connected to a wider community. In contrast to Thatcher's pronouncement, democratic society reflects the connections among human beings, grounded in their common humanity. While restricted to a narrow citizenry, the ancient Athenian city-state emphasized democratic politics imbued with the values of equality, public spiritedness, and meaningful participation in the life in common. As political philosopher Hannah Arendt put it, "The *polis* was for the Greeks ... their guarantee against the futility of individual life, the space protected against this futility and reserved for the relative permanence, if not immortality, of mortals."[2]

In modern parlance, democracy has reflected the view that humans contain the potential to develop in either socially constructive or antisocial directions, so it advocates environments that are conducive to the development of our "better selves." As democratic theorist C. B. Macpherson contended, "Any adequate twentieth century theory of democratic society must assert an equal effective right of the members to use and develop their essential human capacities. ... Democracy maximizes men's ability to exercise those capacities."[3] In traditional liberal-democratic thought, participation in public life was crucial to this development. For John Stuart Mill, through such participation the individual learns to "weigh interests not his own; to be guided, in case of conflicting claims, by another rule than his private partialities."[4]

Democracy thus rests on a foundation different from the self-interested individualism of capitalism—not that individuals aren't entirely capable of being aggressively self-interested, but that human beings are much more than this. The common strand of democratic community over the ages revolves around human empathy.[5] In the 1940s, political scientist E. E. Schattschneider argued that democracy "begins with an act of imagination about people," that they are "equal in the one dimension that counts: each is a human being, infinitely precious because he is human."[6] In recent years, neurobiological research has documented the fact that human empathy is hard-wired into the human brain, that humans have innate needs for collaboration and meaning.[7]

Thus, as Frances Moore Lappé has argued, there is a fundamental contradiction between the social dynamics that grow out of institutions that assume and thereby encourage the pursuit of individual self-interest and those that encourage humans' empathic and collaborative capabilities.[8] As John Dewey maintained, democracy "is moral because [it is] based on faith in the ability of human nature to achieve freedom for individuals accompanied with respect and regard for other persons and with social stability built on cohesion instead of coercion."[9]

Capitalism, too, rests for considerable legitimacy on the metaphor of individuals freely engaging in transactions that are mutually empowering because they are freely entered into—most notably the transactions between employer and employee and between seller and buyer. Though one can readily imagine market exchanges in which both parties are "empowered," capitalism's foundational belief is an ideological abstraction because real people in real societies do not find themselves free from a variety of forces that constrain or influence their work and consumption choices. The extrinsic incentives of success in schooling and work, the threat of unemployment, the manipulation of latent needs and status anxieties by advertising—all shape and constrain human behaviors and limit people's perceptions of what is possible.

The contradiction within capitalism between its reliance on self-interested individuals and its legitimizing justifications ultimately generates contradictions between capitalism and democracy. Perhaps the most fundamental constraint produced by capitalism is the inequality that results from the accumulation of wealth in the hands of business owners and the class inequality that derives from it. Left to its own devices, capitalism has universally produced extreme inequality—from lavish wealth to extreme impoverishment and deprivation. Indeed, too much equality is dysfunctional in capitalism, depriving it of the material incentives and status anxieties that keep workers and consumers alike motivated when their work or their lives are less than intrinsically fulfilling. It has been one of the great ideological illusions of capitalism that poverty can be eliminated within a system that is grounded on the uneven accumulation of wealth.[10] The kind of base-line equality conducive to universal human development, to say nothing of decent lives for all human beings, is inconceivable in a system shaped by capitalism's imperatives.

The contradiction of inequality thereby produces demands for intervention by the state to provide democracy's base-line equality. Yet, by lending itself to the accumulation of great wealth in relatively few hands, capitalism produces "elite democracy" as its form of democratic political decision making. Legitimized by the argument that competitive elections and other safeguards like free expression make public policy ultimately accountable to popular priorities, elite democracy is, at best, minimal democracy. Indeed, what we commonly refer to as the American democracy rests on institutions and processes designed to restrict rather than express popular rule.[11] As political theorist Sheldon Wolin has put it, "The Founders hoped to combine the principle of rule by a republican elite with the principle of popular consent: real politics for the few, formal participation for the many."[12]

Tension around capitalism's inequality came to a head in the United States in the latter decades of the nineteenth century as industrial capitalism took off. The historic struggle for labor rights—like the slave revolts, abolitionist movement, and women's suffrage movement—was one of many recurring chapters in American history in which groups disempowered by capitalism and/or formally excluded from the polity demanded inclusion as empowered citizens. Whereas powerful elites initially used the state to crush labor organizing, the persistence of labor struggle, aided by its legitimation by democratic values as well as the potential for spreading unrest, generated the extension of significant rights to American workers.

Twentieth-Century Capitalism: The Expanding State and Mass Media

These tensions played out in the early twentieth century, at a time when the nation's media were themselves becoming profitable mass enterprises attempting to appeal to wider swaths of the general public, aided by technological innovations like the teletype and photograph. Seeking legitimacy in mass markets, the new mass media cast off much of their prior narrow partisanship and adopted the professional norms of journalism.[13] As documented by W. Lance Bennett and others, nonpartisan "neutrality," a standardized story format for reporting the news, and the use of "documentary reporting practices" provided the foundations of modern media routines. Furthermore, as market forces became increasingly imperative, journalistic norms created the "conditions that systematically favor the reporting of narrow, official perspectives" by pushing journalists toward a passive stance of reporting the interpretations of competing "credible" sources. In Bennett's phrasing, professional journalism thereby created the "paradox of objective journalism" whereby "news is biased not in spite of, but precisely because of, the professional journalism standards intended to prevent bias."[14] Since they must compete for mass audiences, the news media also seek to frame news stories in ways that "make sense" within the conventional wisdom of public opinion.

The quest for mass audiences produced a second fundamental shift in the news media that tied them even more tightly to the interests of capitalism: the reliance on significant advertising revenue to support the news enterprise. In Michael Schudson's words, the rise of mass-circulation newspapers meant that the "means of enlightenment became a marketplace of sensation," as newspapers themselves became responsive to the forces of consumerism.[15] As Neil Postman has argued, as news content veered toward a form of entertainment, it became increasingly irrelevant to a world that citizens could act upon.[16]

Finally, the rise of mass communications corresponded historically with the rise of mass propaganda, or what Garth Jowett and Victoria O'Donnell have defined as "the deliberate and systematic attempt to shape perceptions, manipulate cognitions, and direct behavior to achieve a response that furthers the desired intent of the propagandist."[17] As Jacques Ellul wrote in his classic treatise, modern mass propaganda manipulates emotion so as to "short-circuit" critical thought.[18] Indeed, one of the earliest successful uses of mass propaganda was the campaign engineered by the "father of public relations," Edward Bernays, and the Creel Commission to overcome public resistance to U.S. entry into World War I. Bernays made his embrace of elite democracy clear: "The conscious and intelligent manipulation of the organized habits and opinions of the masses is an important element in democratic society. . . . It is the intelligent minorities which need to make use of propaganda continuously and systematically."[19]

Mass communications thereby provided elites with an effective new vehicle for dealing with the threat of too much democracy. In conjunction with war-delayed wage demands, the growth of the organized labor movement produced the Great Steel Strike of 1919, and the suffragette movement produced the Nineteenth Amendment in 1920. As the eminent liberal journalist Walter Lippmann observed, between 1880 and 1920, the franchise was extended from 10 to 15 percent of the population to 40 to 50 percent.[20] Concerned that the mass media could be used by various polemicists to manufacture opinion, Lippmann's push for professional norms reflected his embrace of elite democracy. Echoing the reasoning of James Madison over a century earlier, Lippmann argued in 1921 that only the "responsible men" of the "political classes" could discern the nation's "common interests." These distinguished members of the elite should therefore use the new mass media to "manufacture" the "consent" of "ignorant and meddlesome outsiders" who were better suited to be "interested spectators of action."[21]

Political scientist Harold Lasswell echoed Lippman in the early 1930s, observing that the new "democratic assertiveness" abroad in the land "compelled the development of a whole new technique of control, largely through propaganda." Lasswell argued against "democratic dogmatisms," such as the belief that people are "the best judges of their own interests."[22] As the late social critic Alex Carey has documented, mass propaganda played a significant role when the contradictions between capitalism and democracy produced an aroused populace during three distinct political eras: the years following World War I and World War II and following the 1960s.[23]

Capitalism has therefore not only produced elite forms of democracy through the variety of ways that accumulated capital and the ideology of the "free market" dominate the activities of political institutions, but capitalism has greatly enhanced that domination through its own mass media—the primary means by which the public is informed about politics and policy. When competing elites within the polity and its media system converge in their commitment to the ideologies and institutions of capitalism, public discourse cuts off a range of considerations that may have vital consequences for the mass of people in and outside the polity. Ultimately, such a polity serves the hegemony of capitalism, even as capitalism adapts and adjusts to the kinds of tensions it produces. Democracy, on the other hand, agitates against those forms of inequality and domination—poverty and deprivation, status anxieties, or the consumer-driven distractions of mass media—that subvert the empowerment of each voice.

An additional tension between capitalism and democracy derives from the growth of the state in response to the imperatives and contradictions of capitalism. In the United States, these emerged with particular force during the first half of the twentieth century, laying the groundwork for the post–World War II world that spawned the sixties era.

Capitalism is legitimized by the ideological assertion that the aggregation of individual self-interest adds up to the common good—originally proclaimed via what Adam Smith referred to as the "invisible hand" of the marketplace.[24] In reality, this crucial legitimation of capitalism founders on a variety of contradictions between individual self-interest and the common good, including the common good of capitalism itself. Belief in the self-correcting virtue of the market is such a mainstay of so-called free-market ideology that former Federal Reserve chairman Alan Greenspan expressed his "shocked disbelief" at its breakdown in the economic crisis of 2008.[25] Yet the very existence of a "competitive" marketplace, crucial to capitalism's legitimation, produces the contradictory effect that self-interested enterprises strive to control, if not eliminate, that competitive market. In this sense, even the term "free market" is an ideological construction. Furthermore, in their quest to accumulate capital, competing individual enterprises are driven to maximize their production. In the aggregate, this imperative invariably generates production that outstrips demand. This overproduction, in turn, generates capitalism's familiar boom and bust cycles, including the devastating downward spiral of depression.

Finally, the pursuit of individual self-interest contradicts the common good in another way that has become increasingly significant over the past forty years. Within capitalism, decisions are based on individual units—individual consumers, individual automobile drivers, individual enterprises, individual local governments, or even nation-states competing for capital. In a "free" market, where capital is mobile, it is in each unit's interest to maximize its use of resources, even if this ultimately works against the common good—the core principle of Garrett Hardin's "tragedy of the commons."[26] Moreover, since private capital is the primary source of jobs and potential tax revenue, the ideology of "what's good for business is good for everyone" becomes politically persuasive.[27] As capitalism has globalized, these dynamics have spread beyond the range of existing state political authority, yet these "micro-motives," as Thomas Schelling has described them,[28] ultimately produce "macro-consequences" that have become impossible to ignore: environmental degradation, damage to the human immune system, and, ultimately, erosion of the global ecosphere.

All the contradictions contained within the self-interest foundation of capitalism have produced pressures for state intervention in the economy. As capitalism has grown, the state has grown. Early antitrust interventions were, in theory, designed to protect capitalism against the monopolies it produces under laissez-faire policies. Triggered by economic crises like the Great Depression and the recession of 2008–09, government has managed capitalism's boom and bust tendencies through fiscal and monetary policies and through government protections, subsidies, and bailouts for private sector enterprises. In brief, for capitalism to "work"—to say nothing of working relatively equitably and non-destructively—state intervention is required. As Immanuel Wallerstein has argued, despite the anti-state rhetoric of free-market ideology, the growth of state power has been "absolutely crucial for capital." Indeed, he contends, "states are needed most of all not by reformers and not by [egalitarian social] movements but by capitalists."[29] Yet within the pervasive free-market ideology of mainstream media discourse, state intervention is framed as a government constraint on capitalism—sometimes justified by other social goods, other times because of the exceptional cases of greedy firms or CEOs and careless or inefficient operators, rather than being systemically required by capitalism.

A final reason for the growth of the American state in the twentieth century was the increasing role played by the United States in the rest of the world, particularly as it evolved through the two world wars and their aftermaths. While conventionally framed in terms of "defending freedom," the emergence of the United States as an increasingly dominant world power is critically linked to maintaining the profitability of American capitalism. As was the case of U.S. domination of the Western hemisphere, historically claimed as the nation's special "sphere of interest," the growth of global U.S. hegemony in the post–World War II era has reflected the imperative of protecting American dominance of capitalism's system of global development.[30]

Along with the rise of industrial capitalism and the capitalist mass media, the growth of the state has had profound effects on democracy in the United States. For one, it has accentuated the role of government at a distance from the people. Through much of the American republic's first century, one could find references to a richly democratic social fabric in the participatory traditions of everyday American life. From Thomas Jefferson's vision of politics as an inherently social and ennobling arena of human action fundamental to human happiness to Alexis de Tocqueville's observations about the vitality of American "voluntary associations,"[31] one finds references to a "public sphere" where citizens freely discussed public concerns relevant to everyday life—without interference from government.[32] While democratic struggle has helped to expand the inclusiveness of the public sphere, its civic vitality has eroded as the role of the state and mass media have grown.

Political debate over the growth of the state has commonly divided along "liberal" and "conservative" lines depending on which interests were affected by government intervention and which government was doing the intervening. Historically, that debate has been framed within the ideology of liberalism, upholding the virtues of the capitalist economy. With rare historical exceptions, critics of capitalism could only be found outside the boundaries of legitimate political discourse. When their voices rose to a level that threatened to affect public discourse in the years after the First and Second World Wars, capitalist interests helped to mobilize "red scares" and widespread anticommunist propaganda that effectively suppressed and marginalized these critics.[33]

Postwar America: Market Democracy and the Pax Americana

The contradictions between capitalism's imperatives and fundamental democratic impulses came to a head in the post–World War II era, spawning, among other things, forces that would generate the social movements of the 1960s. The Great Depression had brought capitalism's contradictions to a critical breaking point. Along with elite and state responses to the Depression, the U.S. entry into the Second World War brought about a sea change in the American political economy.

First, the widespread poverty and unemployment of the Depression era helped to spawn an increasingly militant organized labor movement, producing, among other things, more potent collective bargaining rights through the Wagner Act of 1935. Fearing aggressive labor demands resulting from wartime wage freezes, corporate elites went on the offensive to contain the labor threat. As Elizabeth Fones-Wolf put it, even before 1945, "the business community faced the twin challenges of a struggle for control within the workplace and the defense of the free enterprise system from the growing intrusiveness of the federal government."[34] In contrast to the leftward turn toward social democracy in postwar Europe, a combination of forces moved the United States rightward toward a "market democracy" subservient to a resurgent market economy.

Attacking unions' "monopoly power," the National Association of Manufacturers (NAM) and its allies identified government regulation of the economy with communist subversion, thus helping to mobilize congressional support for passage of the Taft-Hartley Act in 1947, significantly weakening the newly recognized collective bargaining power of organized labor. Business propaganda by the NAM, the Chamber of Commerce, and the Advertising Council converged with that of groups like the American Legion in launching the Red Scare against alleged communist infiltration of labor and government—a campaign that helped to remove the more militant trade union voices from organized labor and produce the Truman administration's imposition of loyalty oaths and eventually McCarthyism.

The attack on organized labor was only one side of the corporate public relations blitz. Building on earlier anti–New Deal efforts, the corporate sector launched a massive campaign designed to win public opinion over to the side of business, the "free-enterprise" system and the Republican Party.[35] In political scientist V. O. Key's words, the "dissemination of political ideology" produced an "almost overwhelming propaganda of doctrine" and the "saturation of media with advertising calculated to sell ideas rather than merchandise."[36] The NAM launched a national campaign to immerse workers and their families in films and discussions designed to indoctrinate them with the "values and symbols associated with the American way of life, including patriotism, freedom, individualism, competition, and abundance through increased productivity."[37] In Alex Carey's account, the campaign identified the traditional American free-enterprise system with "social harmony, freedom, democracy, the family, the church, and patriotism."[38]

So effective was this campaign that, while making wage concessions to striking unions, the corporate sector succeeded in defeating labor's broader campaign for industrial democracy and blunting the militancy of labor—producing what was benignly labeled a management-labor "truce" that helped to absorb blue-collar workers into the American mainstream. By 1950, the nation's political agenda had shifted significantly to the right.[39] The ideologies of growth and anticommunism were politically hegemonic. Both revolved around free enterprise as the foundation of the American way, and both Republicans and Democrats embraced them. This ideological consensus was so pervasive in the 1950s that the era spawned the belief that the United States had realized the "end of ideology," a phrase that first appeared in a journal of the CIA-financed Congress for Cultural Freedom.[40]

The New Deal had solidified the role of the state in managing the economy. One postwar payoff of this heightened government role was that domestic public policy helped to bring to fruition some of the "American way of life" advertised in corporate public relations campaigns.[41] The G.I. Bill provided returning World War II veterans with financial support to pursue technical or university training, start-up loans for small businesses, and federally underwritten mortgages that would enable them to realize the American dream of home ownership. The resulting construction boom not only helped to fuel postwar prosperity but also the historic suburbanization of American society. Furthermore, automobile producers and oil and rubber interests lobbied intensively for passage of the

Interstate Highway Act of 1956, which resulted in 41,000 miles of super-highway construction connecting suburbs and cities as well as the nation's major metropolitan areas — thereby accelerating car ownership, geographic mobility, suburbanization, and the loosening of extended family ties. While producing lifestyle benefits for millions of Americans, these changes ultimately helped to create an American archetype of economic development that would later lead to urban decline, environmental degradation, hazards to public health, and sprawl.

Between 1945 and 1960, the American social landscape was transformed. As documented by historian William Chafe, a majority of Americans did not own their own homes during the war; most bought their food at neighborhood groceries; car ownership was not yet a reality for most Americans; "only 37 percent believed their children would have better opportunities in life than their own"; and radio and movies were the primary forms of entertainment while TV represented "an eccentric idea offered by a few esoteric inventors." By contrast, Chafe generalized,

> Fifteen years later, a new world had come into being. Ribbons of highways connected inner cities to suburban developments that sprouted everywhere. Sixty percent of all Americans now owned their own homes. TV antennae perched on nearly every roof, families sat down to eat frozen dinners purchased at the supermarket in a nearby suburban shopping mall, and they then argued over the correct cost of the latest consumer gadget on TV's quiz show, "The Price is Right." Jet planes had reduced coast-to-coast travel to five hours, the two-car family was as much the rule as the exception, and families of the middle class debated whether to take an out-of-state vacation or build a new addition on the house. Between 1947 and 1960 the average real income for American workers increased by as much as it had in the previous half-century.[42]

As a result, nearly 60 percent of the American people had achieved a "middle-class" standard of living by the mid-1950s, as compared to only 31 percent prior to the Depression.[43]

By itself, however, the New Deal did not put the U.S. economy on durable footing. That came from the enormous industrial stimulus resulting from the U.S. entry into World War II. The war greatly expanded the U.S. role in dominating the world's capitalist system, ushering in what was variously called the *Pax Americana* and the "American century," and what the Trilateral Commission later hailed as the successful "defense shift" in government priorities.[44] With the United States emerging from the war with a national economy and military prowess unmatched in the world, American foreign policy was buttressed by a widespread culture of patriotism and belief in the nation's special mission of defending freedom in the world.

With postwar public discourse caught up in the fervor of anticommunism and the economy grappling with recessionary pressures, government policy planners called for the doubling of military spending in the top-secret National Security Council report, NSC-68. In words that echo later references to the "Vietnam syndrome," General Motors president and later U.S. secretary of defense Charles E. Wilson warned that "the revulsion against war not too long hence will be an almost insuperable obstacle for us to overcome. For that reason, I am convinced that we must begin now to set the machinery in motion for a *permanent war economy.*"[45] In conjunction with the Korean War, U.S. defense spending increased fourfold between 1950 and 1953,[46] establishing defense spending or "military Keynesianism" as the primary pump for stimulating economic growth. At the same time, NSC-68 called for an aggressive U.S. position against alleged Soviet Union expansionism, a policy grounded in imperial underpinnings laid bare in an earlier secret memo by the State Department's George Kennan:

We have about 50% of the world's wealth but only 6.3% of its population. . . . We cannot fail to be the object of envy and resentment. Our real task in the coming period is to devise a pattern of relationships which will permit us to maintain this position of disparity without positive detriment to our national security. To do so, we will have to dispose of all sentimentality and day-dreaming; and our attention will have to be concentrated everywhere on our immediate national objectives. We need not deceive ourselves that we can afford today the luxury of altruism and world benefaction.[47]

Among other things, this policy would soon begin to collide in Indochina and elsewhere with another global legacy of the Second World War: anticolonialism.

In addition to fiscal and monetary policies and accelerated government demand in the form of defense contracts, long-term postwar economic growth was sustained by a massive influx of consumer demand. In essence, capitalism was to be sustained by the production of need.[48] Recognizing the centrality of this principle more than fifty years later, marketing professor Philip Kotler has observed, "If there are no more needs . . . then we have to invent new needs. . . . Capitalism is . . . a system where we've got to motivate people to want things so they'll work for those things. If there's no more things they want they won't work as hard: they'll want 35-hour weeks, 30-hour weeks and so on."[49] The promotion of consumerism had the additional functional advantage of helping to pacify the workforce.[50]

Building on prewar mass advertising and taking advantage of the new medium of television, consumerism converged with the promotion of a middle-class, suburban lifestyle to unleash the market dialectic and produce the market democracy of postwar America. Ideologically reinforced by the contrast between

American freedoms and the drab, authoritarian collectivism of Soviet communism, the emergent political culture advertised the empowerment of each individual American citizen. Yet it offered those citizens empowerment shaped by the imperatives of consumer capitalism rather than the kind of empowerment associated with a democratic civic culture. Compared to the public-spirited sense of national solidarity of the Second World War, the inward-turning culture of postwar America would prove lacking, ultimately eroding that civic culture.

Television and the Spread of the Market Dialectic

By 1960, almost 90 percent of American households owned at least one TV set.[51] In addition to quickly becoming the public's primary source of news, the rapid growth of television had two salient effects on the transmission of news, and thus on the spread of market democracy. First, unleashed by television's ability to produce a kind of one-to-one intimacy with viewers while conveying a visual recording of unfolding events, tele-journalism intensified the potential drama of news. Competition for viewers drives television to accentuate precisely those traits—conflict, violence, personal tragedy, and the like—that effectively grab and hold viewers' attention, thereby reinforcing the medium's emphasis on drama, personality, and ultimately diversionary entertainment.[52]

Second, by accentuating the visual side of news, television highlights the story as it is seen and experienced through the eye of the camera—whereas, as Neil Postman has maintained, print media intrinsically explore the meaning of events beyond what is seen.[53] In Susan Sontag's words, "Photographs furnish evidence. Something we hear about, but doubt, seems proven when we're shown a photograph of it." Televisual imagery provided viewers with, as Sontag put it, an "appearance of participation,"[54] which, in turn, invited viewers to respond with feelings toward what they saw, even to participate publicly by emulating or joining in what they saw.

It is commonly argued that television aids democracy by bringing politics closer to the people. I suggest that the growth of mass spectatorship actually reinforced capitalism's tendencies toward elite-dominated market democracy in a number of ways. Indeed, postwar intellectual thought legitimized these postwar trends by reasserting the imperative of elite democracy. Maintaining that "the electoral mass is incapable of action other than a stampede," economist Joseph Schumpeter argued that "democracy means only that the people have the opportunity of accepting or refusing the men who are to rule them." Schumpeter likened the polity to a controlled market where the "popular will" was "manufactured" in ways "exactly analogous to the ways of commercial advertising."[55] Prior to the 1960s' upheavals, the prevailing consensus of political scientists studying voting behavior was that apathy was good for democracy. As political scientist Bernard Berelson and his colleagues asked, "How could a mass democracy work if all the people were deeply involved in politics?"[56]

As if to fulfill the prophecy of elite theorists, postwar culture was dominated by an emphasis on consumption as the path to the good life for all Americans, an inward-turning suburbanized lifestyle, and an end-of-ideology two-party political consensus framed by anticommunism—the latter implying that politics was probably best left in the hands of experts. Television's development as a commercial medium greatly accelerated the spread of the self-contradictory market dialectic and the erosion of civic culture under market democracy. Indeed, it could be argued that a defining characteristic of market democracy is that in all its broad social manifestations—private consumption, advertised choice in the spectacle of electoral politics, commercially driven entertainment television, even TV news—it fosters illusions it cannot fulfill. In all these arenas, elites test for, anticipate, and manipulate deeper human emotions and drives that their offerings ultimately cannot satisfy.

As mass-market commercial enterprises, the media are driven by a dual imperative of maximizing the size of their audience or readership while simultaneously reaching or connecting with the individuals within that mass audience. On the one hand, this produces what might be described as a convergent or centripetal tendency, as the media and commercial marketers zero in on the most universally shared frames of reference. This imperative is one reason why appeal to emotion and to the widely shared myths and symbols of the nation's "imagined community"[57] have played such a central role in mass propaganda and mass advertising. During the 1950s, the American imagined community was remarkably monolithic, both socially and politically. Yet the very projection of that imagined community would fail to engage, and might even antagonize, those significant groups of Americans who in one way or another felt left out or resistant to the role the imagined community offered them. As significant tensions grew and the polity became more fragmented, commercial media had to adapt in order to connect with the varying subjective worlds of different populations.

The centrifugal force these tensions represented would become enormously important as sixties social movements emerged, and they have remained centrally important ever since. The tension between centripetal and centrifugal forces helps to explain why mass media discourse revolves around common, conventional meanings and emotionally gratifying human-interest stories even as the media cameras attend to an ever-wider range of behaviors, personalities, and identities. It also helps to explain why, once the monoculture of the 1950s broke apart, centrifugal forces intensified the quest for new media technologies—from cable TV to the Internet—that could effectively target increasingly fragmented audiences. The market instability produced by this fragmentation, in turn, helped to generate the turn toward media conglomeration. More and more media channels became owned and operated by fewer and fewer giant conglomerates.[58]

Through the medium of television, postwar mass marketers gained unprecedented entry into the homes and lives of American citizens. Because of its access to individual viewers in mass numbers and the potency of "living" visual advertising, television helped to usher in the "ferocious consumerism," in David Halberstam's phrase, of postwar America.[59] As ABC vice president Donald Coyle put it, television's "natural function" was to operate as "a giant pump fueling the machine of consumer demand, stepping up the flow of goods and services to keep living standards high and the economy expanding."[60]

As motivational researcher Ernest Dichter put it in 1956, "One of the basic problems of prosperity . . . is to demonstrate that the hedonistic approach to life is a moral, not an immoral one."[61] Private consumption was therefore framed by capitalism's ideological belief that, in the aggregate, individual consumption worked for the common good—producing what Lizabeth Cohen has called a "Consumer's Republic." For instance, a 1947 *Life* magazine photo essay included in Cohen's study portrayed one family's move from an old run-down house to a new, convenience-filled ranch-style suburban home. Citing a study financed by retailer Edward Filene, *Life*'s editors effused that the family's consumption pattern not only would "improve their own lives but also make possible a higher standard of living for all Americans."[62]

Early TV entertainment fare reinforced the desirability of this republic. In the late 1950s, television drew the viewing public into a world of happy suburban life: white, middle class, free of threatening conflict, blessed by comfort and household conveniences, held together by clearly defined gender roles and stereotypes, and ultimately reassured that the United States stood alone as the preeminent force for good in the world. In Sven Birkets's view: "Somewhere in the 1950s . . . television worked its way into the fabric of American life, [and] we grew accustomed to the idea of parallel realities—the one we lived in, the other that we stepped into whenever we wanted a break from our living. People born after the mid-1950s are the carriers of the new; they make up a force that will push us out of our already-fading rural/small town/urban understanding of social organization."[63] At best, undercurrents of criticism and larger issues of social justice and workplace alienation were brief blips on television's radar screen. Along with the real world of everyday life, the history of real people's struggles faded from public view. As Marty Jezer has put it, "The postwar years nailed the coffin shut on the American past."[64]

Legitimized by its contribution to the common good, consumerism introduced an ideology of individual self-improvement and self-entitlement that began to supplant the collectivist civic meaning Americans experienced during World War II. As psychologist Philip Cushman has put it, the cultural terrain of postwar consumerism was "oriented to purchasing and consuming rather than to moral striving; to individual transcendence rather than to community salvation; to isolated relationships rather than to community activism; to an individualistic mysticism rather than to political change." Whole industries from cosmetics and diet to pharmaceuticals and self-improvement grew up in the postwar world in order to "minister to the newly created needs."[65]

Translating latent human needs into commodities individuals could purchase, this culture aroused desires that, in several respects, it could not satisfy. As John Berger has written, the "purpose of publicity [advertising] is to make the spectator marginally dissatisfied with his present way of life. Not with the way of life of society, but with his own within it. It suggests that if he buys what it is offering, his life will become better. It offers him an improved alternative to what he is." Yet while advertising "begins by working on a natural appetite for pleasure," it "cannot offer the real object of pleasure."[66] A can opener as the "open sesame" to "freedom from tedium, space, work, and your own inexperience,"[67] the suggestive mastery offered by the Marlboro Man's rugged individualism, the short-term financial security provided by credit cards, or a burgeoning pharmaceutical industry promising nothing less than personal hygiene, popularity, and health—the examples from this era are profuse.

This pursuit of a "better self" meshed effectively with some of the more salient qualities of postwar life. Thus the accumulation of a house and the commodities to fill it offered "proof" that the material insecurities of the Depression had been left behind. Yet simultaneously, consumerism feeds an acute awareness of how one is being seen by others, as well as increasing privatism and isolation. As Berger put it, advertising offers the future buyer

> an image of himself made glamourous by the product or opportunity it is trying to sell. The image then makes him envious of himself as he might be. Yet what makes this self-which-he-might-be enviable? The envy of others. Publicity is about social relations, not objects. Its promise is not of pleasure, but of happiness: happiness as judged from the outside by others. The happiness of being envied is glamour.[68]

What Berger called "social envy" is relevant because it reflects the centrality of status anxiety for consumer-driven capitalism. Yet as Berger put it, "Being envied is a solitary form of reassurance. It depends precisely upon not sharing your experience with those who envy you."[69] The life of consumption offered self-isolating gratification. The "need" to "be envied" is closely linked to what David Riesman saw as the shift in the "social character" of middle-class Americans from "inner-directed" to "other-directed" orientations, the latter being the "tendency to be sensitized to the expectations and preferences of others." In 1961, he predicted that "the hegemony of other-direction lies not far off."[70]

As Cushman has argued, the "post–World War II self thus yearns to acquire and consume as an unconscious way of compensating for what has been lost."[71] As the sense of community, tradition, and shared meaning declined in postwar America, advertising increasingly revolved around nostalgia.[72] While channeling deep-seated human needs for companionship, love, and self-respect into consumption, consumerism simultaneously diverts people from the very experiences of place, community, and social interaction that might provide authentic gratification and a sense of being grounded. Being caught up in the dynamics of consumerism, the self is lost. Again, Cushman: "The self is empty, and it strives, desperately to be filled up."[73] The narcissism implicit in this world is perhaps most potently revealed in Berger's description of the forces at work on the human personality:

> The spectator-buyer is meant to envy herself as she will become if she buys the product. She is meant to imagine herself transformed by the product into an object of envy for others, an envy which will then justify her loving herself. One could put this another way: the publicity [advertising] image steals her love for herself as she is, and offers it back to her for the price of the product.[74]

Simultaneously by steering the populace toward individual lifestyle solutions rather than collective exchanges that lead to political outcomes, the world of consumerism erodes democracy. Market democracy, described by Berger as the society "which has moved towards democracy and then stopped half way," is the "ideal society" for generating "social envy," because the "pursuit of individual happiness has been acknowledged as a universal right. Yet the existing social conditions make the individual feel powerless. He lives in the contradiction between what he is and what he would like to be." Thus, advertising "turns consumption into a substitute for democracy."[75] In such a society, manipulated patriotism—in Chris Hedges's words, a "thinly veiled form of collective self-worship"—becomes an extension of the culture of narcissism.[76]

The market dialectic is grounded on the ideological construct that the market gives people what they want —a belief expressed by Roger King of King Brothers, syndicators of the television game shows *Wheel of Fortune* and *Jeopardy*: "The people are the boss. We listen to an audience, see what they want, and try to accommodate them."[77] The market dialectic is, however, fundamentally different from a democratic dialectic. First, individual market choices are always made within the boundaries of what is being offered, in a marketplace in which producers must reach the largest number possible. Second, the production of choices is a process generated from the top: marketing experts devise ways of measuring the public's "wants" in ways in which the experts' real objectives are obscured, and they then produce and package the "choices" for the public to consume. Third, the sole desired behavior of market audiences is consumption, not the expression of ideas, values, grievances, or imagined resolutions. Whether in commercial or political realms, the consumer dynamic provides no space for citizens to interact and derive their own collective values and priorities. Instead, it bypasses — indeed, draws us away from — the very realms within which we humans interact with each other to construct meaning. Finally, the imperative of market competition has driven commercialism to extend its reach further and further into the private, internal, and subconscious worlds people inhabit, and political advertising has been similarly invasive.[78]

Feeding upon the isolated and vulnerable individual, the media culture provides the language, aesthetic expression, historical "consciousness," exposition, and argumentation for us. In contrast to the active give-and-take of democracy, the people are not sovereign in the consumer dynamic. We don't "make our media," as James Twitchell put it;[79] we respond to our media, often unconsciously, and our responses become our "choices," our actions, our meaning-making. Commercialism is not our better judgment. Our better judgment comes from learning of our prejudices, insecurities, and narrow presuppositions through expressive interchange and reflection, through the educative interaction of democracy as a way of life. Commercialism is, instead, grounded in our *pre*-judgment.

Our freedom of choice among a seemingly ever-changing array of options enables us to feel empowered by the act of choosing; indeed, that act involves a kind of empowerment. The market society thereby achieves an ideological victory for capitalism by equating the marketplace with democracy and offering us feelings of empowerment at the same time that it erodes democratic civic life through its transformation of social space. In such a world, democracy becomes "merely a mechanism for choosing and authorizing governments," as Macpherson put it,[80] and legitimizing government actions — a far cry from the notion of democracy as a way of life.

Postwar Contradictions and the Rise of Democratic Assertiveness

Following an extraordinary period of national civic engagement in support of the U.S. war effort, the world produced by the dominant economic and political forces in the post–World War II era offered Americans two complementary meanings for public life. On the one hand, citizens were invited to participate in the noble experiment of postwar America, the pursuit of a privatized good life that would benefit society as a whole. On the other, their national loyalty was demanded in the face of a new and powerful totalitarian enemy, Soviet communism. With the nation's political agenda aimed at facilitating economic growth at home and Cold War initiatives abroad, it was left to individual Americans to optimize their place within the social order. However, the contradictions this world obscured unleashed forces that would produce a major transformation of the social landscape.

Essentially, this world contained two kinds of contradictions. One was an egalitarian contradiction that has always been present in U.S. history—namely the contradiction between the promise of equality and the variety of ways large groups of Americans have been denied full participation in society. The postwar political economy that seemingly promised a comfortable middle-class life to everyone—and, to a degree, delivered on this promise—contained two such egalitarian contradictions that were particularly significant in the sixties era. One was race and the other was gender, though agitation around these contradictions helped to crack open a variety of egalitarian social movements during and since the sixties.

The absorption of many working-class Americans into the middle classes helped to place the inequality experienced by African Americans in high relief. It also helped to trap millions of American women in a constructed social role as housewives. Whereas racial and gender inequality are theoretically incompatible with the performance-based ideology of capitalism, the historical reality of capitalism's inequality has disproportionately burdened women and racial minorities. These inequalities, in turn, are often exploited to exacerbate racial fears and gender stereotypes in ways that, among other things, deflect political consciousness grounded in common class interests. The tensions inherent in these conditions surfaced in the postwar years.

Perhaps the most important impetus for change came from the struggle by people of color throughout the Southern Hemisphere against Western colonialism. Within the United States, the contradiction between historical racial oppression and the experience of fighting against a particularly virulent form of Nazi racism helped ignite political agitation. Civil rights activism began to percolate during the 1950s—from the historic *Brown v. Board of Education* decision to the Montgomery bus boycott and beyond. With modest breakthroughs into public consciousness via mass media, early civil rights activity laid the groundwork for widespread agitation to take off in the 1960s. It helped to expose the contradiction of poverty amidst plenty, and it began to kindle in the hearts of black and sympathetic white Americans the radical hope that America's historic wrong could at last be righted. It beckoned the young, in particular, with a new civic charge: join us in making history.

In postwar society, the drive for equality and reconstruction of identity were compelling for women as well. The contradiction between the liberatory promise of postwar capitalism and the narrow, rigid social roles and identities reserved for women in that culture was the structural catalyst for the women's movement. A second crucial catalyst for much of the movement came from the fact that the same contradiction occurred in women's experiences within the other social movements of the time—movements that revolved around values of equality, empowerment, and democracy.

The other kind of contradiction alive in the postwar culture was more qualitative in nature and reflected the dynamics of market democracy described earlier. As was the case with the egalitarian contradictions, it wasn't a new phenomenon. Critics of capitalism and the market society had long dissected contradictions within capitalism, and a number of writers during the postwar era wrote widely disseminated critiques of postwar culture and society.[81] Many of these were important teachers of the young. However, the particular historical conditions spanning the era from the Depression to the 1950s meant that the qualitative contradictions of postwar culture would be more widely felt by younger Americans. At their core, however, the contradictions were and are systemic, not generational.

Consider the conditions of everyday life. The advertised good life of suburbia offered the lure of community, green space, ownership, and freedom to pursue happiness individual by individual, family by family. Yet, as with much of the good life advertised in the postwar years, the product undermined its ability to deliver on its promise. Rapid mass-production of housing, while aiding the postwar economic boom, also resulted in vast tracts of relatively cheaply made, lookalike "little boxes," as Malvina Reynolds's song put it.[82] At the same time, the interdependence of community life was stripped away by the segregation of the largely residential suburbs from urban centers of employment, culture, and politics. Aided by discriminatory real estate practices, most suburbs became virtually all white. Meanwhile, the out-migration of middle-class whites from American cities was matched by the in-migration of racial minorities at a time when entry-level, low-skill jobs were beginning to decline in urban areas of the North (and were often closed off by discriminatory unions).[83] Vital ethnic urban communities were subverted and racial isolation accelerated by urban planning and public policies like slum clearance, urban renewal, public housing projects, and highway construction. While middle-class Americans were being sold new opportunities for freedom and community—even as lawns, fences, and long commutes isolated them—the rich plurality of democracy's face-to-face political, social, and economic interdependence was shrinking in both urban and suburban settings.[84]

The contradictions contained in these life conditions were unlikely to be very obtrusive for many adult Americans who had survived the material insecurity of the Depression and experienced the monumental national effort against an expansionist totalitarian enemy. Indeed, they were prone to find the two meanings of postwar public life to be fundamentally persuasive, for the Depression and Second World War were important formative experiences in their own coming of age. Furthermore, they carried the high level of wartime patriotism and collective solidarity into forms of civic engagement that, in Robert Putnam's words, helped to generate "one of the most vital periods of community involvement in American history."[85]

By contrast, many of their children's experiences would be crucially different and would provide a catalyst for attitudes, responses to events, and behaviors that would later be popularly viewed as generational. On the one hand, lacking the formative experiences that gave meaning to their parents' quest for comfort and stability, they might feel—in keeping with Abraham Maslow's hierarchy of human needs[86]—that they had the freedom to look beyond material concerns for meaning in their lives. But they were simultaneously prone to feel the contradictions within the two dominant meanings for public life offered by postwar society, market democracy and the Cold War. The latter, played out with particular ferocity in Indochina, would reveal fundamental contradictions between the rhetoric that justified it and the reality of American foreign policy.

The age cohorts who came into consciousness during the postwar era might view their world with both heightened expectations of possibility and an undercurrent of potent disaffection. Their world offered them greatly expanded freedom while simultaneously appearing increasingly narrowed, depersonalized, and homogenized. Growing up in the aftermath of the war, many of the young were, in Paul Goodman's estimation, hungry for the romance of "patriotism," for a larger cause akin to what their parents had experienced, one that demanded personal engagement and sacrifice and "gave meaning to the affluent society."[87] Thus they were prone to respond to the invitation to action posed by postwar challenges to the prevailing order.

In 1964, political philosopher Herbert Marcuse was one of the writers critiquing the contradictions of "liberation" in postwar consumer culture. Marcuse argued that the "economic-technical coordination which operates through the manipulation of needs by vested interests" claims "the entire individual and thereby precludes the emergence of an effective opposition against the whole."[88] Given that he was writing just as "opposition against the whole" seemed to be erupting in society, one might argue that Marcuse's claim was at least premature, if not flat-out wrong. However, it bears noting that while the "opposition against the whole" that emerged in the sixties era was effective in many ways, it was not effective "against the whole." Indeed, postwar consumer culture may have had something to do with that.

3

An Awakening Democratic Dialectic: From Action to Empowerment in the 1960s

Ordinary people can be intimidated for a time, can be fooled for a time, but they have a down-deep common sense, and sooner or later they find a way to challenge the power that oppresses them.
—Howard Zinn, *You Can't Be Neutral on a Moving Train*, 2002

Action, in so far as it engages in founding and preserving political bodies, creates the conditions for remembrance, that is, for history.
—Hannah Arendt, *The Human Condition*, 1959

We are the ones we've been waiting for.
—Negro spiritual

As the 1960s began, the core ingredients of a democratic awakening were stirring and increasing numbers of Americans were becoming aware of the gap between democratic ideals and social realities. The civil rights movement that began to emerge in the 1950s helped to rekindle radical hopefulness while simultaneously modeling a praxis of individual and collective empowerment. Civil rights agitation was simultaneously a crucial catalyst for opening the door to counter-hegemonic consciousness, pointedly demonstrating that myths about the system working for everyone were false.

Despite their many differences, each of the era's social movements shared some aspects of the quest for democratic empowerment in liberal-capitalist America.[1] They embodied both expressive and instrumental aspects of empowerment; that is, they were simultaneously about expressing the values, perspectives, and identities of their participants and about seeking to change society's policies and institutions. These reflect aspects of democracy that range beyond the limited democratic meanings shaped by the imperatives of capitalism. In the actions that social movements took and in the words the actors spoke, we can discern a dynamic process of democratic empowerment that grew out of the world of the postwar United States.

What perhaps distinguished the sixties era most vividly was the rapid evolution of grassroots, collective empowerment struggles into mass mobilizations that captured the attention of the larger society and posed ideological challenges to the prevailing order. As the sixties era unfolded, tensions between the promises and realities of postwar America intensified enormously. All the sixties-era movements involved challenges to and departures from business as usual. Coming from outside the normal assumptions of everyday life, it became clear to participants and observers alike that the movements posed an ideological challenge to common assumptions about "the way things are."

While reflecting an expressive politics of personal liberation and identity formation, these mass mobilizations also began to effect significant changes in both political and cultural realms: new laws, public policies, and institutional reforms ranging from the historic Civil Rights Act and Voting Rights Acts to the War on Poverty and widespread educational reform, from affirmative action and abortion rights initiatives to environmental and consumer protection regulations. Mounting antiwar pressures placed restraints on war escalation and helped to bring the long war in Vietnam to an end. Cultural changes included major transformations in the public and private construction of racial, ethnic, gender, and sexual identity. All these changes were evidence of sixties movements' ability to change the world they encountered.

The Protest Imperative and Growing Importance of Media

Power concedes nothing without a demand.
   —Frederick Douglass, 1857

A strong case can be made that none of these transformations would have occurred in the absence of protest activism. Injustices affecting underrepresented groups in society often remain off the nation's political agenda for long spans of time. People resort to protest when their claims and grievances are not being addressed by the legitimate political authorities—when they are effectively voiceless within the polity. In other words, protest is, in itself, an action taken from outside the normal political processes of representative democracy. In this sense and from the vantage point of political officials and mainstream media, all protest is a form of outsider activity. Yet without it American history would be drastically different.

While most Americans are willing to acknowledge that the right to protest is legitimate if not important, the majority of Americans are typically predisposed to disapprove of specific protests. The civil rights movement has long enjoyed a hallowed reputation in American public memory, yet during the movement itself most protest activities were looked on with widespread skepticism, if not disapproval, by the American majority. During the 1961 Freedom Rides, for example, when nonviolent, mixed-race groups were violently attacked while riding together in interstate buses and sitting in the "wrong" waiting rooms, a

Gallup poll found that of the nearly two-thirds of Americans who were aware of them, 24 percent approved of Freedom Rides while 64 percent disapproved. A similar disparity showed up in public perceptions of the now-iconic 1963 March on Washington. By comparison, 66 percent approved of the Supreme Court ruling that ended segregation in buses, trains, and waiting rooms.[2]

Protest actions and protesters themselves span a wide range on two dimensions: the degree to which their views are radical or critical of society's foundational institutions and ideologies, and the degree to which they are militant or willing to take forceful or confrontational action to achieve their objectives. It follows that it is possible to advocate radical change by a whole range of strategies, militant or not. Alternatively, one may militantly pursue ends that range from adopting a desired public policy or ending a war to transforming the political and economic order. In sixties-era movements, activists were all over the map, ranging from those who sought change via electoral politics at one end of the spectrum to self-proclaimed street revolutionaries at the other end. Activists also varied widely in the degree to which they believed society's leaders or institutions could be influenced to fix specific problems or whether the institutions themselves—the "system" in the shorthand of the day—needed fixing. Both kinds of concern were incessantly debated within all sixties movements. As activism spread and encountered various form of resistance—evasion or dismissal by political leaders, state repression and police violence, and delegitimation of their discourse via exclusion from mass media—protests tended to become more expressively militant and increasing numbers of activists moved toward a more systemic or radical critique.

Underrepresented and relatively powerless groups have two main resources upon which they can call to muster instrumental power in American politics: their numbers and/or the moral persuasiveness of their argument. These resources, in turn, were organized into two primary types of protest action during the sixties era. Many involved what political scientist Frances Fox Piven and sociologist Richard Cloward have called "defiance," or the withdrawal of cooperation from institutions that required their participation in order to function properly or profitably—similar to the classic defiant action of the labor strike.[3] With varying degrees of success, examples ranged from the Montgomery bus boycott of 1955 to tenant strikes stimulated by the Community Action Program, and from the draft resistance, G.I. rebellion, and war tax resistance movements to the student strike of 1970. Needless to say, movements that withdraw participants needed for a system's operation are significantly empowered in the process; thus the bus boycott put a significant dent in bus company profits, which in turn increased pressures on local authorities to negotiate with movement leaders.

Activist Barbara Deming endorsed an aggressive version of nonviolent defiance when she argued, "This is how we stand up for ourselves nonviolently; we refuse the authorities our labor, we refuse them our money (our taxes), we refuse them our bodies, to fight in their wars. We strike. We go even beyond this and block and obstruct and disrupt the operation of that system in which we cannot feel like free men."[4] Later in the sixties era, many groups adopted militant tactics, particularly at the grassroots level, aimed at forcefully disrupting the operation of governmental institutions.

At the same time, even a brilliantly effective defiance action like the Montgomery boycott succeeded in part because it also involved a second resource: the intervention of an authoritative outside ally—in the Montgomery case, the federal courts. Again and again in the sixties era, outsiders typically engaged in protest actions aimed at effecting change by reaching and winning the sympathies of wider audiences and thus generating public pressure on officials. According to Michael Lipsky's seminal study of protest as a "political resource," such protest actions aim simultaneously at targets to be transformed and audiences to be won over. Protest effectiveness thus requires that protest audiences feel greater sympathy toward the protesters than toward the target of protests.[5] It also presumes that more favorable public opinion will at some point produce reform.

Depending on their specific objectives, of course, sixties protesters differed over which audiences were important: potential recruits, political allies, sympathetic publics, political elites, government or other authorities, or some combination of these. As Noam Chomsky observed, the antiwar movement had two principal targets: "the effect on decision-making and the effect on public opinion."[6] At the point that movements seek to grow from local grassroots activism to mass mobilizations, national organizing and the mass media become crucial to the effort to reach new participants and new locales. It is particularly at this point that the fundamental characteristics of mass media—their ideological predispositions, their commercial and organizational imperatives, and their journalistic routines—influence the way that protest groups reach wider audiences and ultimately help to define their meaning for media audiences, including many potential activists.[7] As William Gamson has observed, the "mass media are the most important forum for understanding cultural impact since they provide the major site in which contests over meaning must succeed politically" and they influence "broad cultural changes . . . in language use and political consciousness."[8]

In this manner, the media both recorded and influenced the actions of the era's protesters—and, over time, the trajectory of the sixties era. Direct action protest in the early years helped to launch the media spectacle of the later 1960s. As system resistance mounted and expressivism became increasingly prominent, the media spectacle began to encourage two forces: political backlash and what ultimately became affective rather than instrumental empowerment, thereby introducing the forces that would ultimately erode the democratic vitality alive in the sixties era. Nonetheless, while the spectacle influenced the forms of protest occurring later in the era, even those movements that emerged in the late sixties — women's liberation, gay rights, and environmental activism — contained the same empowerment dialectic that held great promise for a more democratic future.

Envisioning Democracy

In part because action was the most effective way to break through the barriers of common political discourse, much of the democratic vision expressed during the sixties era was embodied in the actions of the social movements of the time. As Murray Bookchin has put it, direct action embodied a "vision of citizenship and selfhood that assumes the free individual has the capacity to manage social affairs in a direct, ethical, and rational manner."[9] Still, a vision of a deeper, more participatory democracy repeatedly surfaced amid the activism of 1960s movements, most comprehensively in the Port Huron Statement published by Students for a Democratic Society (SDS) in 1962.[10]

SDS viewed genuine democratic participation as the antidote to one of the "defining features of social life today," the "decline of utopia and hope." Through participation, one could be brought "out of isolation and into community." Democratic politics were therefore a "necessary, though not sufficient, means of *finding meaning* in personal life,"[11] a means of breaking through the vacuous consumerism and rigid political and social norms of the 1950s. Though the "message of our society is that there is no viable alternative to the present," the young authors viewed their world with a sense of "urgency," observing that "the search for truly democratic alternatives to the present, and a commitment to social experimentation with them, is a worthy and fulfilling human enterprise, one which moves us and, we hope, others today."[12]

Reflecting the spreading scope of postwar market culture, SDS envisioned a participatory democracy grounded on meaningful conversation and engagement in decision-making in a variety of social settings: "As a *social system,* we seek the establishment of a democracy of individual participation, governed by two central aims: that the individual share in those social decisions determining the quality and direction of his life; that society be organized to encourage independence in men and provide the media for their common participation."[13] SDS also juxtaposed participatory democracy to the prevailing market system: "The economic experience is so personally decisive that the individual must share in its full determination; [and] . . . the economy itself is of such social importance that its major resources and means of production should be open to democratic participation and subject to democratic social regulations."[14]

The Port Huron Statement articulated a radically participatory vision of democracy that resounded again and again across the range of 1960s mobilizations.

On the eve of his assassination, Martin Luther King Jr. spoke of the civil rights movement "taking the whole nation back to those great wells of democracy."[15] At the Democratic National Convention in 1964, Mississippian Fannie Lou Hamer was asked if she sought equality with the white man. "No," she declared, "I want the true democracy that'll raise me and that white man up . . . raise America up."[16] As Charles Payne argued, the Student Nonviolent Coordinating Committee (SNCC) experience in the South was grounded in "participatory political forms" because, echoing theorists like John Dewey and John Stuart Mill, "people develop by participating, not being lectured to or told what to do."[17] And as Francesca Polletta has documented, one key point of the "endless meetings" of early SNCC and SDS activists was "to surmount differences in skills and educational background, not by denying them, but by reasoning and learning together on the basis of mutual respect."[18]

Sixties activists frequently testified to the power of the democratic deliberation they experienced within the movements of the day. As Carl Oglesby wrote of an SDS meeting in the fall of 1964, "That was an amazing meeting. I had never been around a bunch of people who were so smart and who were so sincere, in the sense that they listened to each other and they actually tried to meet one another's points. You could even see people have their minds changed because somebody showed them a reason or a fact that they hadn't known before."[19] The 1964 Berkeley Free Speech Movement included a huge, spontaneous rally at which, in Michael Rossman's recollection, "people are getting up there and talking, and people are listening. And people are voting on this, and people are voting on that. It's almost enough to make you believe that if it were given a chance, the democratic process might work. It just might work. People quoted books as if books were relevant. They talked about the Greeks, and they talked about theories of politics, as if it all *meant* something."[20]

Democracy is also closely associated with the principle of self-determination, the starting point for any society creating its own future. In announcing its 1965 antiwar march in Washington, SDS called for Vietnamese self-determination: "Only the Vietnamese have the right of nationhood to make their government democratic or not, free or not, neutral or not. It is not America's role to deny them the chance to be what they will make of themselves."[21] At the rally itself, Paul Potter characterized the war as the "cutting edge that has finally severed the last vestige of illusion that morality and democracy are the guiding principles of American foreign policy." Potter went on to link the march to a larger movement: "What is exciting about the participants in this march is that so many of us view ourselves consciously as participants as well in a movement to build a more decent society."[22] By contrast, government pursuit of the war demonstrated that the American people had "lost control of their government" and were excluded from any "role in the decisions which affect their lives," according to a 1965 flyer put out by the Berkeley Vietnam Day Committee.[23]

The War on Poverty's initial Community Action Program and a variety of community organizing efforts from Saul Alinsky's Woodlawn project to the SDS Economic Research and Action Project (ERAP) were grounded on the bottom-up, democratic empowerment of society's most profound outsiders, the poor. As Alinsky put it,

> To lose your 'identity' as a citizen of democracy is but a step from losing your identity as a person. People react to this frustration by not acting at all. The separation of the people from the routine daily functions of citizenship is heartbreak in a democracy. . . . In the end [the organizer] has one conviction—a belief that if people have the power to act, in the long run they will, most of the time, reach the right decisions.[24]

Paul Goodman's communitarian critique echoed this democratic dynamic: "The hope of community is in people deciding important matters for themselves."[25] Finally, reflecting its roots in the civil rights movement and the New Left, the women's movement sought democracy in personal relationships and movement practices. In Rosalyn Baxandall's recollection, "Both in New York Radical Women and Redstockings, we subscribed to *a new form of organization,* never articulated fully. It entailed no chairs and no hierarchy, innovations that came from the civil rights and antiwar movements."[26]

Personal action was the catalyst for empowerment because it liberated the actor from tacit complicity in an oppressive or unjust status quo. It also was the catalyst for experience, a potentially profound teacher. Movement experiences in the process of collective empowerment—activists' successes, their mistakes, and their failures—also enriched their understanding of democracy. The absence of a vibrant left tradition as an accessible part of legitimate American politics left many young people with the sense that they were "making it up as they went along." If the young people who flocked to sixties movements were prone to make mistakes, the elders who resisted the movements were prone to defend customs and institutions that suppressed human beings and violated the fundamental democratic imperative that democracy is grounded in the ability of people to learn from their mistakes. While highly imperfect in their expression, sixties social movements anticipated a fuller, richer democracy addressed to the world emergent in the postwar era.

Experiencing Democracy: The Democratic Dialectic in the 1960s

Like democracy itself, the democratic awakening of individual actors and social movements involved an interaction between the expression of participants' internal values, beliefs, and identities and their external, instrumental goals. The voices and experiences of sixties activists reveal a mutually reinforcing dialectic of awakened consciousness and efficacy, personal action and personal liberation, communal interaction and solidarity, radical hope, and collective empowerment. Although I identify discrete aspects of this empowerment process here, it is important to recognize that they do not occur in a step-by-step, linear manner, but are related and interactive parts of an evolving educative and empowering dialectic that is radically different from the market dialectic outlined in the previous chapter. Needless to say, movement activists not only interacted with others in the movement community, but also with authorities, the media, and via the media a variety of audiences among the wider public. These interactions ultimately helped shape the trajectory of the sixties era.

While my aim here is to distill common elements of a democratic dialectic, it is also important to bear in mind that the shifting historical context influenced the manner in which this dialectic played out. Many participants in the women's liberation movement, for example, experienced empowerment dynamics similar to those experienced by earlier civil rights activists, yet they did so in a late-sixties context strikingly different from the earliest days of the civil rights movement. Similarly, student cohorts entered and left college at different times, experiencing a campus (or post-campus) environment that was politicized in profoundly different ways. What came before influenced what came later, and the "master protest frame" visible in the media influenced the perceptions and actions of later groups, especially as new cohorts of young people came into political consciousness.[27] As the decade progressed, the context of prior activism, dramatic events, and media coverage provided a shifting field of self-definition for each wave of the newly politically conscious. In this sense, the trajectory of 1960s movements not only became an outcome of mass mobilizations and their interaction with the larger culture; it became a catalyst for subsequent movement experiences.

Furthermore, each of the egalitarian movements that sought liberation from exclusion and oppression—civil rights and black power, Chicano, Latino, American Indian, women's, gay/lesbian—went through a dynamic empowerment process that reflected the particular historical and cultural conditions of its oppression. Sixties-era movements also differed in the ideological hurdles they faced and the kind of internal "definitional processes," in Doug McAdam's phrase, that shifted the meaning that people attached to their condition.[28] For example, racial oppression in the South blatantly violated widely accepted norms in much of the country, while the women's movement went through a consciousness-raising experience that produced challenges to widely accepted norms. The task for the southern movement was, at great personal risk, to make visible to the rest of America a form of oppression that overtly violated consensual norms of human rights; the task for women's liberation was to convince the larger culture that conditions already familiar to and largely accepted by most people were, in fact, oppressive—arguably a more politically complex task, and one shared by other movements that challenged prevailing consensual norms.

Despite these significant variations, it is nonetheless possible to elicit from movement accounts a common dynamic of empowerment suggestive of a deep, strong, and radical democracy that is ultimately incompatible with the hegemony of capitalism. The dynamic of empowerment involves a dialectical interaction between awareness and action, subjective and objective, self and other, individual and collective, the "personal" and the "political." For the most part, this dynamic and the kind of democracy it suggests were, and are, invisible and largely incomprehensible in mass media discourse.

At the individual level, the dynamic of empowerment involves a personal awakening evoked by the interplay between an awareness of wrong and a sense of possibility that things could be otherwise, two factors that are crucial to any but the most impulsive decisions to act. As a spur to action, awareness involves consciousness that something in one's world is wrong and the corresponding sense that one has a right to address it.[29] In his study of political activism, Nathan Teske has identified "moral discovery" as a crucial catalyst to action. Teske's extensive interviews with diverse activists led him to conclude that "the experience of moral discovery among activists involves more than simply the discovery of new factual information. It also involves . . . [a] new paradigm for understanding how one ought to act and live one's life."[30] The shift Teske refers to may occur in relation to one's own oppression or that of others. Indeed, awakening internal consciousness is often conducive to empathy for others.[31]

Injustices are, of course, often internalized by the oppressed themselves, creating an internal obstacle to action. As a late-sixties Berkeley slogan put it, "Oppression means to think, 'What's wrong with me?'" when what might be "wrong with me" is that I have not asserted myself through action against forces that degrade and oppress me. Thus in Ralph Turner's words, new movements are "heralded by the redefinition of a condition heretofore viewed as misfortune, now newly viewed and deeply felt as an injustice."[32]

In many ways, the awakenings that occurred in the 1960s reflected the degree to which millions of Americans became aware of the normally obscure "dark side" of American political history. In effect, the veil of mythology was shredded by events. The prevailing ideology of a performance-based capitalist culture rationalizes the plight of victims of oppression as "their own fault." In elite democracy, this view is aided by the fact that the system's beneficiaries can point to the availability of the ballot box or public schooling, even by a correlation between standardized test scores and adult occupational rank, as "proof" of their claims. Moreover, in the dominant political discourse, if human suffering is openly acknowledged, it is often blamed on some reprehensible person. By contrast, for many movement participants, the ideology of a system that worked was pierced by the awareness that injustice was part of the fabric of everyday life in the United States. As Bernice Johnson Reagon put it, "The Civil Rights Movement exposed the basic structure of the country which, as it's set up, cannot sustain itself without oppressing someone."[33]

The sense that things could be different, that wrongs might be righted or a better way created through action — what Carol Mueller has called a "success expectation" — therefore becomes an important catalyst to action.[34] One's action, in turn, can accelerate this process, liberating one from one's fears and self-doubts and producing a surge in self-confidence that may in turn awaken an expanded sense of the possible. Action can produce new consciousness, a new sense of identity, launching one in an empowering new direction.

In many ways the civil rights movement that began to mobilize during the 1950s was the prototype for action and mobilization that occurred throughout the 1960s era, even as the master protest frame or zeitgeist of the decade was unfolding and changing. The centuries-old severity of Jim Crow and its slavery antecedent provided southern blacks with daily reminders that they were being wronged. Yet the longstanding intransigence of the system left them with little hope that things could be otherwise, leading some to internalize the belief that such was their fate.

In two different ways, the Second World War provided a historical catalyst to the postwar awakening. Black veterans' war experiences — not only their effective performance of all tasks that white soldiers performed (albeit in a segregated military), but their participation in an epic struggle against a racist regime — placed the illegitimacy of their second-class citizenship in unacceptably sharp relief. The horror of the Holocaust also generated intensified efforts to strike illegitimate forms of racism from the American system. Funding for renewed litigation by the National Association for the Advancement of Colored People (NAACP) ultimately led to the Supreme Court's *Brown v. Board of Education* decision in 1954. *Brown* not only legitimized the awakening postwar assertiveness of southern blacks; it gave them a sense they had an institutional ally in the national government.[35]

Individual experiences within this context also produced personal awareness that things could be different. Rosa Parks's decision on December 1, 1955, to disobey the Montgomery bus driver's demand that she vacate her seat in the "white" section of the bus proved to be historic, but it didn't occur in isolation. Along with several other early civil rights activists, Parks had participated in interracial empowerment workshops at the Highlander Folk School in Tennessee, she had been secretary of the Montgomery chapter of the NAACP, and on one earlier occasion she had refused to use the rear door of a Montgomery bus (resulting in her eviction). Circumstances had helped to shape her own consciousness — as well as that of others in the Montgomery black community — in ways that led to her 1955 refusal and the subsequent bus boycott. In her own words, the Highlander School experience was for Parks "the first time in my life I had lived in an atmosphere of complete equality with members of the other race. . . . *I felt it could be done* without the signs that said 'White' and 'Colored'—without any artificial barriers of racial segregation."[36]

The "fresh eyes" through which black veterans saw the injustice of Jim Crow were comparable to the experiences of "outsiders" who came into the South, even by those who saw southern injustice from a distance through photographs or television coverage. So it was for Diane Nash, one of the early SNCC leaders who traveled from Chicago to attend Fisk University in Nashville. As David Halberstam reports, when Nash encountered WHITE ONLY signs "for the first time in her life . . . it was as if someone had slapped her in the face."[37]

Similarly, young people who traveled south to participate in the Mississippi Freedom Summer in 1964 were stunned by the level of powerlessness and poverty they encountered and the degree to which it was enforced by racist brutality. As Doug McAdam's study revealed, the Freedom Summer volunteers were radicalized not only by the blatant racism, but also by the depth of the poverty they encountered and "what that said about the inherent goodness of America."[38] White reporters from other regions of the country who covered the civil rights movement in the South were often moved by the injustices they encountered, as well as the courageous assertiveness of movement activists.[39] Southern defenders of Jim Crow often blamed "outsiders" for the ferment of the movement; they were right in the sense that those challenging the hegemony of the southern system were seeing it from outside the ideological boundaries that sustained it.

Millions also came to moral opposition to the war in Vietnam through a similar journey outside the boundaries of ideology, discovering that their empathic connection to the war's victims could not be morally reconciled with the self-justifying pronouncements of successive national administrations. This awareness often built gradually through a succession of stories, photographs, and contextual information that challenged the conventional framing of the war. In a climate of contested meanings, a simple photograph could evoke an emotional response as powerful as that experienced by Diane Nash when she was first confronted with a WHITE ONLY sign. And clearly, this kind of awareness was fostered by many soldiers' direct experience "in country." At the same time, the growing antiwar protests provided a context for the awakening of moral consciousness and, for a time at least, a sense of possibility. As Doug Dowd recalled, in comparison to the quiescence of the Korean War period, the initial antiwar protests made it seem "obvious that something was happening that was absolutely brand-new. . . . And I began to feel very different about the possibilities of politics in the mid 1960s."[40]

In countless cases, the era's diverse range of individual decisions to act—decisions to attend a rally, to join a boycott or a sit-in, to risk arrest or refuse the draft, to start a free school or a women's health clinic, to confront or leave an abusive partner—unleashed a continuing spiral of growth, consciousness, and further action. As Douglas Lummis has argued, "What 'snaps' in the mind" when one acts "are the ideological bonds that prevent one from assuming that natural attitude of democratic common sense."[41] Internally, at least, action is liberating; it is a release from habitual accommodation to oppression or degrading conditions. Again and again, those who joined sit-ins in the South spoke of the "exhilaration" of acting, of doing what they knew was right. As John Lewis has recalled of the first day of the Nashville sit-in, the "fear fell away" despite the violent abuse he and others suffered at the hands of white toughs, despite his arrest and incarceration.[42]

The liberation of acting is, in turn, a step toward personal empowerment, toward constructing one's own identity freed from the strait-jacket imposed by society and its agents of socialization. At the personal level, this phenomenon is exactly what democratic empowerment means; it reflects one's unfolding "freedom to," a lifelong discovery of one's authentic self, one's mature voice, the discovery of which progressively frees one from manipulation by others and potentially from the disabling scripts of the unconscious. As Nathan Teske revealed in his study of political activism, action grounded on this kind of moral discovery often leads to a "lifelong commitment" that reflects "continuity of one's identity."[43]

Thus, as nonviolence trainer Jim Lawson put it, "ordinary people who acted on conscience and took terrible risks were no longer ordinary people. They were by their very actions transformed."[44] Activists' testimony bears Lawson out. After going to jail and joining in freedom songs, Bernice Johnson Reagon testified, "I had never been that me before. And once I became that me, I have never let that me go."[45] SNCC's Diane Nash referred to an "interior conversion" triggered by overcoming her debilitating fears through action.[46] Speaking of her personal transformation through participation in the Mississippi voter registration movement, Endesha Ida Mae Holland observed, "I became someone."[47] The liberation of acting, in turn, gave the actor a feeling of being empowered, especially when acting in concert with others. And expression of a new self opened doors of "new possibilities for aspiration," as Martha Nussbaum put it in reference to the women's liberation movement, or a "glimpse of a possibility," as Daniel Cohn-Bendit described the feeling running through the French student movement.[48] Imagining possibility helped to spur action, while action, in turn, helped to awaken imagination.

In contrast to the affective empowerment of market democracy, what turns the dialectic between action and awareness toward real democracy is the interaction between one's self and a larger community. One engages in collective interaction rather than merely feeling one's social identification with a larger social group visible in the wider media culture. This collective experience has two salient effects. One is that it reinforces the power of individual action; it amplifies the feeling of empowerment, the sense of liberation, the erasure of fear or internalized oppression, the exhilaration of acting, the sense of a new identity, even consciousness about the wrong that one acts against. As Doug McAdam has observed, the "tendency of people to explain their situation as a function of individual rather than situational factors" is "more likely to occur under conditions of personal isolation than under those of [social] integration."[49] To these reinforcing effects, of course, collective action adds the feeling of being in community. The other consequence of collective experience is that it offers the real possibility of instrumental political change, of having an effect on one's world. Rosa Parks's action, after all, became historic because it became the catalyst for the prolonged and successful collective bus boycott after local black activist E. D. Nixon proposed using her arrest as the basis for a federal court challenge against segregation.

Again and again in the 1960s, people who came together became aware of shared grievances produced by a combination of external oppression and their own inaction. In the early days of civil rights organizing at Fisk University in Nashville, students shared the hitherto secret wounds of humiliation they had experienced from Jim Crow racism. As they did so, in David Halberstam's account, "The words seemed to pour out. They were not alone. As far as the students were concerned, that was the first great lesson of these workshops. They had all felt the same pain and they all felt the same frustration. The more they talked the more they were bound to each other."[50] Similarly, in the early years of women's liberation, consciousness-raising groups became a crucial formative arena within which women broke through the barriers of private experience to share the diverse humiliations they encountered in relationships, school, and work environments. As Jo Freeman put it, "From this sharing comes the realization that what was thought to be individual is in fact common; that what was thought to be a personal problem has a social cause and a political solution."[51] Rosalyn Baxandall observed, "Suddenly I had new eyes to see with and a new way to look at the past and the future," while Ann Popkin remembered, "the fog before our eyes began to lift."[52] What Betty Friedan had labeled "the problem with no name" gained a name.[53]

The shared experience of collective action also counteracted the very fears that often prevent one from acting. In isolation, one is alone with one's fears, whether these be of ridicule, ostracism, bodily harm, or even death. Within the civil rights movement, fear was a long-established obstacle to action since the tripartite (social, economic, and political) oppression of southern blacks had for hundreds of years been reinforced by the very real presence of racist terror. In the early days of the civil rights awakening, the collective community meetings in black churches became a vehicle for reinforcing courage and producing, in the testimony of some, an almost ecstatic sense. Rev. Ralph Abernathy observed of the initial meeting that voted to extend the Montgomery bus boycott indefinitely, "The fear left that had shackled us across the years—all left suddenly when we were in that church together."[54] Bernice Reagon Johnson remarked of the movement's freedom songs, "a transformation took place inside of the people. The singing was just an echo of that. They could not stop our sound."[55] Abraham Wood recalled of the Birmingham protests in 1963, "When you are caught up in the emotion of the Movement and you commit yourself, you don't really worry about what's going to happen to you."[56] Sheyann Webb recalled of the 1965 Selma-to-Montgomery march, "When we crossed that bridge and started on down the road for Montgomery, the people just seemed like something had been lifted from their shoulders."[57]

In the late 1960s and early 1970s, women who confronted fellow New Left activists about their sexism often encountered humiliating ridicule. In a number of cases, they risked — as women continue to risk — violent abuse from male partners. Consciousness-raising groups provided an important foundation of support for these individual actions. Sometimes, they even led to collective actions — one example being the "truth squad," in which several women would "burst in unannounced on somebody's husband and confront him with a list of grievances."[58] Collective support also enhances one's sense of efficacy or "success expectation" — one reason activism invariably involves some kind of social network or support group. Throughout the egalitarian movements of the 1960s, people found support for their personal actions in movement communities and in the "master protest frames" accessible in the wider society.

Leadership, too, played a crucial role in reinforcing the sense of possibility through action. David Halberstam has described the way Jim Lawson inspired confidence among the Nashville students in 1959–60. Sensing the students' feelings of vulnerability, Lawson knew he had to "impress on them the viability of what he was talking about . . . that they could pull it off, young and uncertain though they were individually." Though their numbers were small, their "idea is not small," and thus their numbers would not remain small.[59] An important part of Martin Luther King's power as an orator was his ability to evoke in his audiences the confidence that they would prevail, that the tide of justice was on their side.

In addition to inspirational leadership, intrepid predecessors provided important role models for younger participants through their public actions. Courageous black women in the early civil rights movement had a particularly profound effect on a number of younger women, both black and white. Thus, for example, Black Panther Party activist Kathleen Cleaver noted, "While I was growing up . . . I saw Gloria Richardson standing face to face with National Guard soldiers, bayonets sticking from the guns they pointed at the demonstrators she led. . . . I saw Diane Nash speaking at Fisk University, leading black and white Freedom Riders onto Greyhound buses that got set on fire when they reached Alabama. . . . That's where I was determined to go."[60] The civil rights literature is full of such testimony.

Collective action took the sense of liberation to a more powerful level by reinforcing one's social identity as an activist. This collective confirmation produced some of the most intense communal bonding and vitality that activists had ever experienced. Howard Zinn noted of his participation in massive antiwar rallies that "for most of us, the movement was a life-giving force."[61] Ann Oakley described this vitality as an "extraordinary intimacy" in which one's "sensory world expands, becomes more intense."[62] Marilyn Milligan described the power of mass antiwar protests as "being with thousands of kindred spirits" and noted, "How often do we do that in life?"[63]

Finally, and critically, collective participation is what can produce real, instrumental power that effects change in external conditions. Jo Ann Robinson, who was highly involved in the Montgomery bus boycott of 1955, commented on the effect the boycott's outcome had on the participants:

> We felt that we were somebody. That somebody had listened to us, that we had forced the white man to give what we knew [was] our own citizenship. . . . And if you have never had the feeling that . . . you are [no longer] an alien, but that this is your country too, then you don't know what I'm talking about. It's a hilarious feeling that just goes all over you . . . that makes you feel that America is a great country and we're going to do more to make it greater.[64]

Robinson's description suggests some of the dizzying expectations unlocked when the oppressed engage in successful collective action. As Jackie Goldberg declared about her experiences in Berkeley's Free Speech Movement, "We realized that, my God, we could have an effect on history."[65] Rosalyn Fraad Baxandall captured similar feelings when she recalled of the women's movement, "What I'd like to convey . . . is the joy we felt. We were, we believed, poised on the trembling edge of a transformation." Not surprisingly, as Baxandall's comment suggests, collective action unlocked feelings of radical hopefulness, even illusions of imminent radical transformation.[66]

Feelings of collective empowerment rarely travel a direct route to objective empowerment in the larger political order. A crucial factor in the civil rights movement's success in removing Jim Crow practices was awakening the rest of the population to southern practices that on their face violated widely held norms of fairness. This meant that the rest of the nation had to see the violent forms of oppression that degraded and endangered the lives of southern blacks. This obviously required great personal courage and self-discipline in the movement, the brutal response of violent whites, and a sufficiently responsive national media that provided wider audiences with visible evidence. In addition to a host of local changes wrought by local actions, the transformative events in Birmingham and Selma, in particular, reached broad sectors of the national public via media coverage and ultimately influenced the White House and Congress to pass the two historic pieces of civil rights legislation: the Civil Rights Act of 1964 and the Voting Rights Act of 1965. These reforms put in motion a significant transformation of the South's Jim Crow culture. They also signified that historic reform was possible — in effect, putting the wider system on notice that it, too, would be subjected to grassroots agitation and mass mobilizations.

What happened, then, when movements had evolved to a level of significant personal transformation and collective feelings of empowerment, but encountered the sustained resistance of the broader political order, reinforced by a mass media closed off to the movements' meanings? Consider, for example, President Johnson's "War on Poverty." Within the broader liberal-reformism of the Poverty Program, the Community Action Program (CAP) briefly provided unprecedented direct funding for local poor communities to participate in shaping their own political agenda. The program's call for "maximum feasible participation" by the poor provided the inner-city poor with a crucial resource they obviously lacked: money that could be used to organize their communities. In Poverty Program director Sargent Shriver's words, "We inaugurated something called 'community action.' Therefore we expect action at the community level. And when you've got action, you've got arguments, you've got dissent, you've got differences of opinion. That's what we're financing. For the first time in the history of this country, poor people actually have a place and a way in which to express themselves. That's community action."[67]

Local community action agencies varied in the degree to which the voices of the poor community and local activists were empowered. Community action in Mayor Richard J. Daley's Chicago, for example, was known for its "minimum feasible participation."[68] Within Newark's community action program, the inner-city poor turned out in large numbers to air their various grievances and confront city decision makers, many participating in politics for the first time in their lives. Mary Smith, a Newark resident who had read the authorizing Economic Opportunity Act of 1964, "truly believed that it would solve our problems" and recalled that "there was such excitement in our community for the first time, hope, real hope." Funding for Newark's United Community Corporation (UCC) enabled resident Edna Thomas to attend six months of coursework and training at New York University. At first, she was "scared to death" at the prospect of attending a prestigious post-secondary institution but found that she "loved it. I didn't know I could do that much until I went to that school. . . . A lot of us came back prepared, and . . . looking at a new life."[69] James Walker, who moved from a factory job to become the personnel director of the fledgling UCC, remarked,

> Never in the history of this country had you ever seen the federal
> government saying to people in the community, "you can have as
> much participation in this as you want, and you can change your own

destiny." And people believed this. People who I had never seen out before—housewives dragging their kids off to meetings—because they really believed that they were participants in a structure that was going to better their lives.[70]

The "short, unhappy history" of the Community Action Program, to borrow David Stoloff's phrase, provides rich insights into the interaction between the democratic empowerment of the powerless and the "democracy" embraced by established elected officials.[71] In mainstream circles, democracy meant something quite different from what it meant to inner-city residents. For mayoral aide Donald Malafronte, the community action program "distorted democracy" by providing direct funding to "neighborhood participatory groups" rather than to elected city officials.[72] For Newark city councilor Lee Bernstein, community organizers from SDS "were going around trying to incite the black people to change things, to do things, to upset the city, and namely to upset me as the South ward councilman." As for the awakened hopes of the inner-city residents, as James Walker put it, "Unfortunately, it didn't work out that way. The more people became involved in the process, the more the power structure tried to take it away. And that brought about confrontation."[73]

In the heady atmosphere of personal liberation, feelings of empowerment, and radical hope, it is hardly surprising that emotions ran high, or that participants vented their anger at the nearest and most accessible targets. Often, in fact, the exhilarating feelings of liberation went hand in hand with a surge of anger at those who resisted the breakthrough in consciousness experienced by participants. Typically, this anger fed two kinds of behavior: an attack on those deemed responsible for the oppression or injustice, and/or a withdrawal into a safe haven or "free space" shared with like-minded others. In the case of the inner-city poor, long-simmering rage provided the fuel for the wave of what were widely called urban "riots"[74] that broke out in the "long, hot summers" of 1963–1968.[75]

From Collective Action to Democracy—or Not: Mass Media and the Sixties Trajectory

In a way, the Newark CAP experience is a kind of metaphor for the sixties trajectory as a whole, with the mass media playing two kinds of roles in that trajectory. Like the federal Community Action Program, the media provided a catalyst to empowerment for all protest groups. Simultaneously, like the official responses to the activism generated by Community Action, the media delegitimized and helped thwart the broad range of outsider activism. In assessing the media role in the pages that follow, we need to keep in mind several points about the democratic dialectic described above as well as what, briefly, one might expect from such a dialectic in a fully democratic culture.

First, as noted earlier, the democratic dialectic is radically different from the individualized dialectic that prevails in market democracy. Second, it is also invisible in the mass media,[76] meaning it is not conveyable to the wider society; it is private and isolated. Third, the dialectic of empowerment alive in the sixties era helped to produce a radical consciousness about the wider society. Fourth, the ideological boundaries that framed media attention to sixties activism thereby reinforced this radicalization as well as participants' feelings of isolation and alienation from the wider society. Like the prevailing ideology about victims of oppression, media coverage of protest was almost universally about the protesters, not the issues they raised nor the process that led to their protests.

By contrast, the continuity from community involvement and collective action to democracy requires, first, that a community's organized action gives the community a voice in the wider culture, a voice that has legitimacy because it is the community's authentic voice. The exercise of that voice, in turn, should ultimately produce the desired outcome or awareness that the desired outcome is legitimately outweighed by a larger collective good recognized as such—or some degree of compromise between these two. A democratic interchange produces mutual understanding. Clearly, the way in which the community expresses its voice matters, but it also needs to be recognized that in the case of a history of injustice and powerlessness there are deep-seated, pent-up emotions behind that voice. Leaders and organizers are important because they can help the community express its voice in ways that can be heard. But if the voices are delegitimized by the wider culture, militancy and violence become likely and "mainstream" leaders will become discredited in the eyes of their communities.

Outside of op-ed essays or letters to the editor, the commercially driven national mass media—whose range of legitimate discourse excludes serious consideration of arguments that challenge society's foundational beliefs and institutions—are structurally incapable of providing a democratic dialectic between an organized community and the wider sphere of society, including political authorities. Yet media coverage—particularly the media's visual coverage—provided a crucial and seductive vehicle for gaining the wider society's attention to issues that previously were off that society's political agenda. Therein lay a crucial paradox facing sixties-era movements, to say nothing of efforts by any outsider group to get its voice heard in society, especially when that society is permeated by the dialectic of consumerism and entertainment.

These media characteristics evolved through the sixties era as the era itself evolved. Coupled with the radicalizing impact of events, exclusion from media discourse had a particularly pronounced effect on young people at different times during the era as their democratic hope began to fade. On the one hand, their exclusion from the legitimate discourse had been a catalyst for the creation of democratic "free spaces" apart from the wider discourse. On the other, as events shattered their hope, their very isolation and "illegitimacy" produced decidedly undemocratic dynamics among young people caught up in the importance of their cause to their social identity — especially in a climate of repression-induced paranoia. Thus, for example, Charles Payne has written of the increasing "atmosphere of distrust and recriminations" in SNCC in the aftermath of the Mississippi Freedom Democratic Party debacle at the 1964 Democratic National Convention, leading SNCC's Mary King to observe, "This did not feel like SNCC to me. It was foreign — dissonant."[77] Later, in the early 1970s, as Heather Booth recalled, the women's movement evolved away from the "sisterhood of the earliest years to increasing sectarian battles over the meaning of 'true feminism,'" and Amy Kesselman remembered, "The cannibalistic debacle of the left in the late sixties shook me deeply. I began to question the wisdom of depending on the vicissitudes of a social movement for one's identity and source of satisfaction."[78] Similarly, the Black Panthers experienced a virulent schism between chapters loyal to Huey Newton or Eldridge Cleaver, and, as Cathy Wilkerson recalled of Weatherman, the leadership had "mastered the language of certainty and discovered the power of images," a "dazzling combination" that "set up much that followed," including the "most insidious assaults on other participants' ability to construct their own meaning of the ideas and realities we confronted."[79]

As a suggestive frame for understanding the evolution of the media spectacle, I would organize the long sixties era into three phases: an early phase from the first national manifestations of the civil rights awakening around 1954–1955 to the end of 1963, a middle or transition phase that lasted until 1968 (a turbulent transitional year in itself), and then a final phase from 1968 until around 1973. One can quibble about the years,[80] but my point is that there were distinguishable shifts in the media culture, in sixties movements, and the interactive dynamic between them — even, one may say, in the zeitgeist. Historical events were, of course, crucial to this evolution, but the mass media helped to spread the awakening sense of possibility, though they simultaneously helped to shape its presentation to others, in the process containing it — and, as visual images often do, stimulating but also constricting imagination.

From the mid-1950s on, readers of national newspapers like the *New York Times* and the *Washington Post* and weekly newsmagazines and photograph-intensive magazines like *Life* and *Look,* as well as the increasing numbers of television viewers, were able to see early evidence of an awakening insurgency in the South. The 1955 Mississippi murder of fourteen-year-old Emmett Till and the subsequent trial and acquittal of his killers jolted both white and black northern readers with its graphic display of southern injustice.[81] The 1957 desegregation of Little Rock's Central High School, particularly the images of armed National Guard troops escorting nine black students through a gauntlet of screaming, abusive whites, reverberated throughout the national media. In 1960, when four students sat down and demanded service at the Woolworth lunch counter in Greensboro, North Carolina, the images of their quiet persistence against a backdrop of abusive whites captured the imagination of more than a few northerners, calling them to join in the historic struggle.

Along with other forces—notably the election of the rhetorically gifted and televisually charismatic John Kennedy—the media helped foster a master protest frame that characterized the early phase of the sixties era, from the mid-1950s into the middle years of the 1960s. In important and varied ways, for many Americans these were years characterized by a kind of hopeful, democratic awakening, an effort largely geared to making American institutions work as many considered they were meant to. It was a time of possibility, a time that fed the awakening of imagination. In Morris Dickstein's phrase, these were the "green years" of the folk revival that captured interracial solidarity—as Bob Dylan's song put it, "The times they are a-changin'." Students began to challenge holdovers from the McCarthy era, like the House Un-American Activities Committee. Civil rights struggles pushed the Kennedy and Johnson administrations to introduce historic civil rights legislation and helped to heighten national awareness of poverty in America.

When President Kennedy was assassinated in 1963, television provided three days of saturation coverage of the event and its aftermath. In the process, the three national TV networks discovered that the powerful emotional appeal of dramatic public affairs could absorb a national audience. TV coverage also greatly legitimized the authority of television news and helped consolidate the role of TV journalists as cultural authorities.[82] Around the same time, protest activities began to shift to critique national conditions, institutions, and policies during the middle years of 1964–1965. These were the years in which the Johnson administration declared its War on Poverty with great fanfare, black rage first began to explode in the inner cities, and SDS got involved in community organizing in the urban ghettos of the North.

In one pivotal event in 1964, large numbers of mostly white students from the North, along with substantial national media attention, joined the Mississippi Freedom Summer project that produced the Mississippi Freedom Democratic Party's unsuccessful showdown with the national party at the Democratic National Convention in Atlantic City, sharpening the alienation of SNCC activists.[83] One veteran of Freedom Summer, Marshall Ganz, felt that the profound lesson of the convention experience was that party leaders and their allies "were afraid of young people, they were afraid of change, they were afraid of opening the doors to all the new ideas and fresh blood that wanted in. It was like they erected barriers and wanted to keep us out to their ultimate—not just to their shame but to their undoing."[84] Freedom Summer leader Robert Moses perceived the Mississippi experience as a telling turning point of the sixties era and beyond:

What happened in '64 symbolized the situation we're in now. That is, the national Democratic Party and political leadership of that time said, okay, there's room for these kinds of people, and it was professional people within our groups who were asked to become part—and actually did become part of—the Democratic Party. But on the other hand, they said there isn't room for these people: the grassroots people, the sharecroppers, the common workers, the day workers. There's room for them as recipients of largesse, poverty programs and the like. There isn't room for them as recipients in power sharing. A different scenario that could have worked its way out would have been for empowering the Freedom Democratic Party. There would have been struggle, and vicious struggle, but not armed struggle. Once it got into armed struggle and rioting and calling in the National Guard, it got into a polarization that we are not out of yet. It's one of the great tragedies of this country.[85]

Ignited in part by the Mississippi experience, these were the years that the Free Speech Movement erupted at Berkeley and a new wave of student activism spread on other college campuses. Disenchantment with the mainstream culture was also beginning to become visible as the media began to notice bohemian communities like New York's East Village and San Francisco's Haight-Ashbury. And finally, 1965 was the year in which the Johnson administration sharply escalated the war in Vietnam, triggering the first national protest of the antiwar movement.

The middle phase seems to have been characterized by a combination of a spreading democratic dialectic—activism and awareness spreading into new areas, new issues, accompanied by its growing sense of possibility—and a darkening of expectations about the system's ability to respond, a growing sense that the system was the problem. A range of events played an unmistakable role in this shift. For some activists, the assassination of President Kennedy was the first blow to their hope for a responsive national leadership. In spite of many criticisms of Kennedy, for SNCC's John Lewis, "when Kennedy died, I think something died within the movement itself. And I think something died within a lot of the young people." Lewis elaborated that he felt "there was a great deal of hope and a great deal of possibilities with Kennedy," that he was a "friend to the movement" and a "friend to young people in particular," because "he spoke their language."[86]

More fundamentally, however, as movements acted against national targets, these targets instinctively resisted activism, or at most translated activism meanings into reforms compatible with system maintenance. Growing awareness of the "sensory realities"[87] of the escalating war in Vietnam, along with a growing antiwar movement, made the war an increasingly pervasive source of contention. Representing a common sentiment in the mid-decade SNCC, Betty Garman testified to her "continual disappointment with the federal government . . . the white liberals . . . the Democratic party."[88] At his speech to the 1965 SDS antiwar rally in Washington, Carl Oglesby called for "disabusing" oneself of naïve political notions and recognizing that "we are dealing now with a colossus that does not want to be changed."[89]

As one would expect, media coverage of both protest and the war retained the structural characteristics that were present in the earlier period. The visual media emerged as a central stage for activists making claims against society, while the media's ideological boundaries became increasingly significant as movements mobilized against national institutions and the ideology that justified them. As the middle years evolved, discourse within the media sharpened even as the visual spectacle became more turbulent and colorful. In effect, as the "sphere of deviance" became more pronounced, the "sphere of legitimate controversy" expanded to incorporate new system-sustaining arguments between liberals and conservatives, doves and hawks.[90]

Early media skepticism and public antipathy toward protest of any kind continued, yet after Birmingham, the March on Washington, and Selma legitimized the civil rights cause, the media struggled to find a frame that would explain why protest was spreading to a variety of national arenas. Clearly something was happening beyond the usual local frame of a contest pitting two sides against each other. Spinning off northern student participation in Freedom Summer and aided by the fact that protest spread to campuses, the media discovered the frame they would use to explain the new turbulence awash in the land. It was the product of a new, postwar baby boom generation that, for a variety of reasons incessantly debated in the media by liberals and conservatives, was restless, questioning, and ultimately rebellious. The media began to examine shifting attitudes of college students and emergent forms of a "deviant" countercultural community.

The generational frame both flattered the young with media attention and diverted legitimate discourse away from the arguments the protest movements (and "outsider" leaders like Malcolm X) were making about poverty, racism in the nation at large, the immoral war, the vacuousness of market democracy and the rat-race, and the like. The dynamic of exit and voice fostered by exclusive discourse and inclusive visuals was in full sway, along with the expressive politics it encouraged. Indeed, many of the nation's youths seemed to embrace the generational frame, for in affective ways it seemed to corroborate their power. As Rennie Davis exulted to Milton Viorst, "Man, do you realize what we've got at our fingertips? This generation can actually command the media. We can shape public opinion."[91]

Yet, along with growing evidence of government repression and a backlash discourse, the ever-escalating war seemed to demand an increase in protest militancy. Sometime around 1968 — a year of staggering events that pummeled movement expectations that change was possible while simultaneously igniting a wave of youthful rebelliousness in much of the world—a shift began to occur. Many in the now-central antiwar movement were becoming increasingly dispirited as war continued in defiance of a public opinion majority who, for a variety of reasons, wanted it over. The backlash hardened with the election of Richard Nixon, and government repression escalated. At the same time, antiwar activism was spreading to younger activists shaped by the zeitgeist of the time and, as Mankoff and Flacks note, "socialized in conservative or conventional families."[92] More and more of the political media spectacle reflected the clash between the forces of "revolution" and reaction.[93]

Still, the democratic dialectic continued to push activism in new directions. Akin to the experience of black soldiers returning to the apartheid South after the war, the jarring experience of sexism within the grassroots democratic movements of the day was a catalyst to action for many women in these movements. Other movements containing a dynamic of identity reconstruction were emerging among Native Americans, Latinos, and gays and lesbians over the latter half of the sixties era. In the zeitgeist of the sixties era's final phase, the public face of these movements reflected the media spectacle of the time, yet they also began to represent a shifting plane to more personal and local actions, in part encouraged to move away from national action by the darkening zeitgeist. Other movements, most notably one that reflected emerging consciousness of environmental degradation, also had a public face that combined both media-capturing activism and liberal reformism—as well as a personal and local side revolving around both lifestyle change and direct action against local environmental hazards.

In brief, the final phase of the sixties era was one of endings and beginnings. Aided by the end of the Vietnam nightmare, what eventually ended was what the media culture likes to call "the Sixties." Yet the democratic dialectic continued within a society that was beginning to turn in a different direction. As that new direction became more dominant in the 1980s, the democratic dialectic persisted, although aside from sporadic mass mobilizations it has thus far largely done so in a more localistic frame, less noticed by the mass media. What the media have noticed has been framed as part of the continuing family quarrel within the baby boom generation, otherwise known as the "political battles of the 1960s."

4

Race, Class, and Gender: The Boundaries of Legitimate Media Discourse

*If you aren't careful, the newspapers will have you hating the people who are
oppressed and loving the people who are doing the oppressing.*
  —Malcolm X, speech at the Audubon Ballroom, Harlem, 1964

The southern civil rights movement has long been equated with the "good sixties" in the media culture's public memory. The prevailing civil rights story is
typically told on anniversaries of events like the March on Washington, during
Martin Luther King Day celebrations, in public school history books, or in occasional popular films or television documentaries on the status of race in the
United States. In the most prominent version of the story, the civil rights movement was led by the southern integrationist preacher Martin Luther King Jr., a
peace-loving man endowed with extraordinary vision and oratorical power. King
and his faithful followers challenged the racist practices of the South, provoked
a hostile response from racist rednecks, and pricked the conscience of a nation
that responded with historic legislation. The latter helped end Jim Crow and
take the United States at least partway toward the realization of King's "dream,"
probably the most commonly evoked symbol of the movement.

Other heroic-scale activists, most notably Rosa Parks, are recalled at appropriate times; indeed, Parks is popularly evoked as the woman who started the
movement with her singular action. What is most commonly left out of this story
is the awakening of a democratic dialectic in the spreading community of "ordinary folk" who became inspired to make their own history, and who, in the
process, reconstructed their social identity in the wider society. What is also left
out of this story is the connection between the civil rights struggle and broader
national challenges to dominant racial and gender constructions, to the combined burden of race and class in America's inner-cities, and to the student and
antiwar movements.

Media coverage during the 1960s contributed greatly to this public memory.
The narrowed texts of most national media accounts provided few glimpses of
the democratic dialectic, or even the historic nature, of the southern struggle.
As Charles Payne observed in connection with the voter registration drive, "The

press focused on big, dramatic events while neglecting the processes that led to them."[1] As for the historic meaning, it tended to come through to wider audiences via the imagery available in the media, though also through broad audience access to a few historic moments like King's 1963 "I Have a Dream" speech and Fannie Lou Hamer's "I Question America" speech at the 1964 Democratic National Convention. King's speech, of course, is part of the lore of the King holiday. While Hamer's speech was so powerfully moving when TV cameras first aired it that President Johnson preempted media attention with a hastily called press conference, its evocation of "ordinary folk" rising to challenge the nation's agenda has largely faded from popular memory.

Compared to other sixties-era movements, the southern civil rights movement enjoyed the most sympathetic mass media coverage and was correspondingly more successful than any other movement in communicating its meanings through the national media. When the struggle spread to the North, where racism and poverty were more deeply yet subtly embedded in national practices and institutions, media coverage was far less sympathetic. The angry voice of leaders like Malcolm X, the "black power" chants led by Stokely Carmichael, or the inflammatory rhetoric and threatening images of the Black Panther Party were largely interpreted to be forms of anti-white racism or black "supremacy," rather than efforts to reconstruct black Americans' identities in empowering ways. Thus all were summarily dismissed as "outsiders." The national media were also dismissive of Martin Luther King Jr.'s effort to bring the integrationist struggle to Chicago in 1966. The explosions of inner-city rage that began in 1964 became an increasingly significant part of the sixties spectacle and a catalyst to backlash, yet the experience of racially compounded class inequality was rarely comprehended as such within mass media discourse. Indeed, the era's distinctive official effort to understand the teeming rage of the inner cities was the presidential Kerner Commission, appointed by Lyndon Johnson in the aftermath of the Newark and Detroit riots of 1967. When the commission unveiled its report in 1968, concluding that the United States was fast becoming "two societies, separate and unequal," media attention was widely eclipsed by the fact that the political tide was turning, aided by White House efforts to minimize the document's visibility—ironic in light of the commission's finding that the "media have contributed to the schism" by largely ignoring the lives of black Americans.[2]

The women's liberation movement encountered similar media coverage. Though the media were for a while caustically dismissive toward "women's lib," they began fairly quickly to distinguish between the movement's legitimate liberal leaders and objectives—essentially reflecting the equal rights aims of civil rights—and manifestations of an outsider perspective that grew out of the movement's democratic dialectic and women's experiences in other sixties-era movements. Eventually, the liberal objectives of equal rights and opportunities for women were widely adopted throughout much of American culture while the images and rhetoric of the movements' more radical activists have been so widely attacked and linked to distortions of feminism that contemporary media culture has made much of the claim of many younger women: "I'm not a feminist, but of course I embrace the equal rights of women." Like the critique of Jim Crow, the claims of liberal feminism have been thoroughly legitimized—though still fought over—within mass media discourse. For the most part, the outsider voices of these movements have become the detritus of a widely disparaged and largely misunderstood past.

Racism and the Southern Exception

While reflecting much that had gone before, the student sit-ins of 1960 signaled the emergence of nonviolent direct action in the national consciousness. From the outset, media coverage of the sit-ins revealed three standard ways that mass media texts interpreted protest activity throughout the sixties era. One was the media's sense that protest itself was a kind of deviant act that lay outside the bounds of normal, legitimate political behavior. As Taylor Branch put it in reference to the civil rights movement, the media "stressed non-partisan calm as the essential pre-condition for racial progress—much like the clergymen who criticized King in Birmingham."[3] It should be noted, however, that in the absence of political agitation and direct action, the history of civil rights struggle made it abundantly clear that little if anything would change. As Ralph Abernathy of the Southern Christian Leadership Conference (SCLC) put it regarding the Kennedy administration,

> Both the president and the attorney general were eloquent in their commendation of civil rights. From time to time both endorsed our goals. . . . Unfortunately, it always took some significant initiative on our part for them to take positive steps, and we were certain that Congress would never move unless pushed to do so by President Kennedy.[4]

Second, as Todd Gitlin has noted, the archetypical media protest story followed the conventions of a crime story—meaning, among other things, that the story dealt with the event in question not only as an act of deviance, but in a very narrow frame of time, place, and causality. As Gitlin elaborated in his study of media coverage of SDS, "Journalism has traditionally equated insurgency and protest with deviance. . . . The style of the human interest story also deprecates collective motivations in favor of personal, idiosyncratic reasons. When reporters (and editors) ask demonstrators, 'Why are you here?' they are looking for singular reasons not political logic."[5] The very narrowness of the protest frame meant that mass audiences were left in the dark about the movements' meanings and significance, unless they were able to grasp these from the images that accompanied the often narrowly circumscribed texts—as occurred with the Birmingham and Selma protests.

Finally, from the outset, media coverage of sixties-era protests was preoccupied, one might even say obsessed, with violence and disorder. Indeed, the mass media's primary concern in assessing a civil rights struggle that remained remarkably nonviolent for years was whether the protests would unleash a massive wave of violence or racial warfare. No matter how nonviolent and disciplined a protest may have been, protest itself was persistently associated by media reports with violence or the threat of violence. Media accounts were sufficiently obscure in explaining events that they could be read as blaming nonviolent protesters for the violent reactions to protest—as, indeed, the forces of backlash were quick to do.

It should also be added that the mostly white, male, and middle-class media personnel were at least initially predisposed to report from a vantage point outside the protesters' own subjective realities—in this sense, reflecting the same racial, class, and gender blinders that pervaded most social institutions of the time. Reporters often grew more sensitive to the reasons for protest activity through their coverage, and pressure from racial and gender movements eventually helped integrate the journalism profession along with other occupational realms. Yet there has been virtually no change in the way the mass media attend to class differences. Class remains a lingering blinder in legitimate political discourse.

Media coverage of the southern civil rights movement did produce a particularly grating double standard in coverage: the deaths of "ordinary black folk" involved in the southern movement were largely passed over by the national media, whereas the deaths of white volunteers who joined the struggle became the focus of national media scrutiny. This media trait conforms to what Edward Herman and Noam Chomsky have documented as the mass media's tendency to divide the world into "worthy" and "unworthy victims"—the former being those given significant media attention and the latter largely ignored.[6] This differential treatment was itself an alienating confirmation for many black activists that they remained outsiders, a form of Other, in the eyes of mainstream media and the society it represented.

Nonviolent Sit-ins and the Threat of Violence

While media images of the 1960 student sit-ins were galvanizing young black and white Americans to join the history-making struggle, national news texts ranged from skeptical, if not hostile, to detached and narrowly circumscribed in explaining the issue to the rest of the American public. Among the newsmagazines, the most liberal, *Newsweek,* titled its first sit-in article "Squatter's Rights," reducing the "sit-down" to one in which "Negro college students" were protesting "the established Southern custom which permits them to be served at stand-up or take-out counters, but not on seats." In the absence of white violence, business proprietors were able to "shut off the protests" simply by "closing their counters or their stores." Overall, the article sketched a dispute between two groups of young people over who had "squatter's rights" to some lunch counter seats.[7]

A week later, as the sit-ins spread throughout the South, *Newsweek* inaccurately anointed King as the leader of "sit-down integration" and included a brief King interview, ominously titled "Full Scale Assault." The interview provided the opportunity for an important movement voice to be heard in the national media, even if it wasn't the voice of the student sit-in movement per se.[8] In the subsequent week's issue, the magazine balanced King's voice with an insert entitled "Terror?" that described Senator Richard Russell of Georgia declaring on the Senate floor that "professional New York agitators were fomenting Negro sitdown demonstrations in the South" in order to "start a race riot of terrible proportions."[9]

Reporting on the spreading "Turmoil in Dixie" in the same issue, *Newsweek* zeroed in on a confrontation between sit-in participants and an unruly crowd in Chattanooga, Tennessee. While a careful reading of the article reveals that the whites instigated the violence, *Newsweek*'s coverage ambiguously linked the nonviolent protest to violence. Under the heading "Violence erupted in the Deep South last week," *Newsweek*'s photograph showed a number of young black males facing the camera and confronting three visible white males seen from behind. The equally ambiguous caption read, "Face to Face: This tense moment in a Chattanooga lunchroom erupted seconds later." Indeed, the magazine seemed skeptical of the protesters' commitment to nonviolence. Introducing the "Negro high school students" as "neatly clad" and "at first soft-spoken," then noting their "orders" to remain nonviolent, *Newsweek* proceeded to describe how the tense confrontation with "hostile white students" "exploded into a bloody free-for-all," ambiguously referencing a "Negro brandishing a shovel," another activist who was arrested, and police "herd[ing] the rest of the Negroes . . . toward . . . their own district." *Newsweek* concluded its story ambiguously: "On the Tennessee-Georgia border, at least, it was clear that a 'peaceful' Negro protest was much easier planned than implemented." At the same time, the magazine pointedly distanced itself from "an ugly core of city toughs in leather jackets and with duck-tailed hair; and of hard-muscled, hard-faced country youths" who confronted the black protesters on the following day.[10] Violent white "toughs" were consistent media outsiders throughout the civil rights era; they have become iconic "bad-sixties" representatives for all resistance to desegregation in the media's retelling of the "good-sixties" civil rights story.[11]

By comparison, the *New York Times* headed its story on the sit-in confrontation "Sitdown Erupts into Racial Riot." The article contained far more detail about various objects "being thrown" during the first day's confrontation, including whites' claims that Negro activists had drawn "switch-blade" knives. The following day's front-page article, "Chattanooga Quells Racial Clash," included a photograph of a "fire hose being used" to "disperse a crowd of whites and Negroes." However, the photo was taken from behind the firemen and only showed a high, arching stream of water aimed in the general direction of a distant and racially indistinct group. With no evidence of the fire hose's impact, it conveyed little of the drama contained in later Birmingham photographs and television footage.[12]

Two weeks later, *Newsweek* seemed to find comfort in reporting from Tennessee that "calm and reasoning voices—from both Negroes and whites—finally were being raised." Against the well-positioned men of "caliber" who were "taking the lead" and giving "assurances that they wanted to be good neighbors," the magazine juxtaposed nonviolence trainer Rev. James Lawson, depicting him as the "Negro agitator behind Nashville's sit-down disorders." *Newsweek*'s preference for elite negotiations over the more potentially volatile direct action seemed clear. Noting that it "remained to be seen" how "these cities" would "solve the *sitdown problem*," the magazine suggested that "it seemed likely that Knoxville was pointing the way" and concluded the article with the legitimizing assurances of white industrialist George Dempster: "If we can't work this thing out peaceably and within the law here in Knoxville, where the Negro has been generally accepted and treated with dignity over the years, then in the name of God, where can it work?"[13]

The dramatic surge in sit-in activity clearly caught the attention of the national media. The *New York Times,* for example, published forty-six articles on the sit-ins during the month of February alone. In its March 28 issue, *Newsweek* led its "National Affairs" section with a three-page feature story titled "Next for the South?" beneath a map that revealed the location of the fifty-three communities in nine southern states that had witnessed sit-in demonstrations over the previous eight weeks. In classic binary fashion, the article asked, "What was this new wind sweeping the South? Was it, for integrationists, a heady wind of victory? Or was it, as many Southerners fear, an ominous wind, heavy with a threat of violence to come?" The magazine sought authoritative voices for its dichotomous balance, citing President Eisenhower's guarded support for "orderly" demonstrations, as opposed to former President Truman's declaration: "If anyone came to my store and sat down, I'd throw him out. . . . Private business has its own rights and can do what it wants."[14]

Black Deaths—White Deaths: The Double Standard

Dramatic and violent imagery became the watchword for media coverage and movement impact over the next two years. The Student Nonviolent Coordinating

Committee (SNCC) that grew out of the sit-in movement began a voter registration drive in rural Mississippi in 1961, focusing particularly on registering the poor sharecroppers of the Delta as a first step in their political empowerment. As Mary King of SNCC was later to observe, the campaign was

> dependent on the news media. . . . Public awareness was crucial to our strategy. Without national exposure and mobilized public opinion, there was no point to the struggle. The sacrifice would be lost in oblivion. The news media were therefore essential, for how else would the American people know about the machinery of injustice that tyrannized blacks in the South? . . . The civil rights movement could not succeed without significant coverage by the national news corps.[15]

SNCC workers engaged in a systematic effort to bring to national media attention the seemingly incessant attacks against the voter registration drive, particularly since media coverage was also viewed as a potential deterrent to violence at the hands of the "courthouse crowd" who "might beat our staff or provoke their beating with impunity—unless they believed that they were under some form of surveillance."[16]

Yet despite transmitting "news story after news story—about arrests, beatings, firebombings, night riders, church burnings"[17] to the national media, coverage was limited in several ways. AP and UPI wire service reports tended to carry stories written by local newspaper "stringers," and these reflected local biases against the activists. Typically, in Mary King's eyes, national stories had a "distant, flat" tone, although she noted that certain reporters who directly witnessed virulent attacks wrote with greater feeling of the momentous issues involved. Covering a mass meeting of activists, *New York Times* reporter Claude Sitton was threatened by several sheriff's deputies and "the air was let out of a tire of Claude's rented station wagon and sand was poured into the gas tank." As a result, King recollected, "Claude's coverage lost the distant, flat quality of most news reportage of the time and leaped to life. He had come to understand in a personal way the nature of the opposition to full black participation in the political and social life of the country, and his accounts were subsequently crackling with episode after episode that gave his readers a genuine sense of the high stakes involved."[18] Some animated reports filed by reporters who witnessed white intimidation were, however, transformed by editors in faraway places like New York City. As King observed, "One reporter showed me the story on Mississippi that he was filing with his editors at *Time*. It was well-researched and rousing copy with breadth and depth. When I saw later what the editors had run, it had an unrecognizable pall."[19]

At the same time, however, the independent progressive press carried article after article pulsating with the historic events in the South. Anticipating the underground press that was to flourish later in the 1960s, SNCC created their own newspaper, *The Student Voice,* and Tom Hayden of SDS sent reports from the voter registration front in Mississippi to the SDS mailing list, reports that were later collected in a pamphlet entitled *Revolution in Mississippi.* Anticipating things to come, a view of the civil rights movement from outside the boundaries of mainstream media discourse was beginning to bring the historic turbulence of civil rights activism to receptive audiences around the nation.

In 1961, Herbert Lee, a black farmer participating in the voter registration drive, was shot to death in full public view by a white state representative who was later acquitted. Lee's death was a momentary but powerful blow against the voter registration drive; it was also virtually invisible in the national newsmagazines. Outside of one perfunctory mention of Lee's death, the only *New York Times* report about Lee quoted the state representative's version of Lee's "ungovernable temper" and his account that "I must have pulled the trigger unconsciously," with no countervailing argument from any of the civil rights workers, including Robert Moses, who worked closely with Lee and was featured elsewhere in the story.[20] Civil rights activists involved in the voter registration drives were already learning painful lessons about the national media and national law enforcement. While the media were drawn to violence and visual drama, they were also prone to pass over the deaths of African Americans "unworthy" of notice. Over the next two years, violent harassment and assaults continued to batter the voter registration drive, largely ignored by the federal government and the national media.

Fully aware of the national double standard with respect to black deaths in the deep South, SNCC organizers deliberated at length before deciding to invite sympathetic, mostly white students from the North to join in their "Mississippi Freedom Summer" project of 1964. On the one hand, seeking the participation of highly educated, affluent northern white students contradicted SNCC's emphasis on the self-empowerment of Mississippi's rural poor. On the other, it virtually guaranteed close national attention to the Mississippi effort. SNCC and other civil rights organizations recognized that "political and social justice cannot be won [in Mississippi] without the massive aid of the country as a whole, backed by the power and authority of the federal government."[21] As Robert Moses observed, "These students bring the rest of the country with them. They're from good schools and their parents are influential. The interest of the country is awakened, and when that happens, the Government responds to that interest."[22] Moses later commented that Freedom Summer marked an attempt to "bring the law to the South by . . . bringing those the law covered to the South."[23]

SNCC's predictions were realized, in part because the group's communications office took pains to make sure that the northern volunteers' home newspapers received news reports. The *New York Times* intoned ominously, "South Girds for Crisis: Massive Assault on Racial Barriers Planned for This Summer

Creates Atmosphere of Tension."[24] In a feature story on June 25, the *Saturday Evening Post* subheading read, "At the Risk of Their Lives, Hundreds of Northern Students Are Challenging the Heart of the Deep South." As with other reports, this media attention concentrated on the white northern volunteers rather than Mississippi's black population or SNCC's field staff. As white SNCC worker Mendy Samstein observed,

> It was clear from the nature of the publicity derived from the [earlier] Freedom Vote campaign that the press would respond to the beating of a Yale student as it simply would not do to the beating of a local Negro. . . . During the Freedom Rally in Jackson which concluded the campaign, TV men from N.B.C. spent most of their time shooting film of the Yalies and seemed hardly aware of the local people and full-time SNCC workers.[25]

Beyond the boundaries of mass media discourse, the voices of the actual citizens striving for their own empowerment were largely unheard. While the deaths of Herbert Lee, Louis Allen (an eyewitness to Lee's murder), and other blacks involved in the voter drive were largely ignored by the national media, everything changed in 1964 when James Chaney, a twenty-one-year-old black Mississippian, Michael Schwerner, a twenty-four-year-old white social worker from New York, and Andrew Goodman, a twenty-one-year-old white student who had just arrived from New York, disappeared near Philadelphia, Mississippi. The contrast with the earlier lack of media coverage could not have been more dramatic, as the federal government searched for the three volunteers until their slain bodies were discovered six weeks later and then pursued their killers.[26] As Fred Powledge put it, "The murderers may have thought that their deed amounted to just a routine reaction to the 'invasion' of Mississippi by 'outsider agitators.' But the nation and world thought otherwise. This time, it was not just a case of another black man's being missing in Mississippi. Two whites—Northern whites—had disappeared. The FBI at first showed its usual reluctance to move past the note-taking stage, but President Lyndon Johnson changed all that."[27]

On July 3, *Life* ran a four-page spread about the murders, focusing explicitly on Andrew Goodman and his nonviolence training in Oxford, Ohio, prior to the journey to Mississippi.[28] On July 6, *Newsweek*'s four-page feature story led with photographs of Chaney, Schwerner, and Goodman and the recovered car they had been driving. The title read, "Mississippi—'Everybody's Scared,'" but the primary fear the magazine focused on was that of white Mississippians, for whom the "175 Northern students who arrived last week—and the 800 more still to come—seemed an invading army bent on destroying its way of life."[29] *Time* framed its coverage of the disappearances with the disdainful lead, "Despite its high purpose, the Negro revolution breeds violence and death," and provided details on the "indoctrination course" for northern college students.

As Doug McAdam has noted, the "combination of fear, history-making media attention, exposure to new life-styles, and sense of political mission that suffused the [Freedom Summer] project" produced for many of the northern volunteers, the "type of transcendent, larger-than-life experiences that would bind them to the movement for years to come."[30] Yet the profound discrepancy in northern news media coverage of black deaths and white deaths, the absence of real federal protection for the courageous SNCC field staffers, and the feelings generated by knowing that the white volunteers were needed if the movement wanted to attract attention in the North all helped to exacerbate racial tensions within the heretofore integrated movement in the South, particularly within SNCC. As Fred Powledge observed, "The contrast between the federal government's vigorous concern now, when Northern whites were involved, and its faltering actions in the past, when 'only' Negro lives were at stake, was amazing for some, saddening for others."[31] Robert Moses drew a broader conclusion:

> Before the summer project last year we watched five Negroes murdered in two counties in Mississippi with no reaction from the country. We couldn't get the news out. Then we saw that when three civil rights workers were killed, and two of them were white, the whole country reacted, went into motion. There's a deep problem behind that, and I think if you can begin to understand what that problem is . . . then maybe you can begin to understand this country in relation to Vietnam and the third world.[32]

In his later reflections on Freedom Summer, the project's Freedom Schools director Staughton Lynd has argued that "the Summer project was a tragedy because a strategy effective in winning the right to vote also disempowered blacks at the same time. Both sides in the Movement debate about whether to have a Summer Project proved correct. The casualties of the summer included not only the individuals who died, but the idea of an interracial movement for fundamental social change."[33] SNCC's Gwen Robinson (later Zaharah Simmons) suggested that the black power movement was at least in part a reaction to shifts in SNCC itself resulting from the increasing influence of moneyed northern whites over SNCC strategy.[34]

In effect, what the national media did was to cast the SNCC activists and their grassroots struggle as media outsiders, people whose experiences and voices were not taken seriously by the mainstream mass media, an experience largely repeated with the Mississippi Freedom Democratic Party's unsuccessful effort to be seated at the 1964 Democratic National Convention. SNCC's outsider status was reinforced by media labeling; the newsmagazines repeatedly dismissed SNCC activists as "hyper-militants." In 1965 *Newsweek* explored at length questions raised about communist connections within the civil rights movement, repeating a familiar refrain raised time and time again by opponents of civil rights. After reviewing and rejecting charges made against Martin Luther King Jr., *Newsweek* observed, "The anxiety about SNCC is less easy to dismiss." The balance of the article suggested that charges that "disciplined Communists have wormed their way into the group's operations" could not readily be refuted, and that SNCC's "far-out radicalism" was "at best irresponsible, and, at worst somewhat sinister."[35]

Martin Luther King Jr. as Insider and Outsider

Although the media anointed Martin Luther King Jr. as the undisputed voice of legitimate civil rights activism in the South, their treatment of him varied widely, depending on the degree to which King's words and actions transgressed the acceptable norms of legitimacy. When his was the reasonable, moderate voice of conscience about racial injustice in the South—typically in contrast to violent white racists or what the media liked to call the "militants" of SNCC—King clearly enjoyed a favorable spotlight from national media that eventually came to see much of his cause as just. But when his demands were viewed as too pushy or ill-timed, or when they reached beyond the cause of justice for southern blacks, the tone of media coverage changed significantly. The latter arose when King directed his voice of moral conscience at segregation in the urban North, the war in Vietnam, and the pervasiveness of poverty throughout the nation.

When King's SCLC brought its campaign into Birmingham in 1963, both *Time* and *Newsweek,* in Richard Lentz's words, "shared a distaste for a confrontation that they believed was forced by King," yet "where *Newsweek* entertained doubts, *Time,* as always, had certitude."[36] *Time*'s article, entitled "Poorly Timed Protest," noted, "To many Birmingham Negroes, King's drive inflamed tensions at a time when the city seems to be making some progress, however small, in race relations," and then went on to quote both black and white leaders who complained about King's campaign.[37] While also critical of King's timing, *Newsweek* waffled back and forth between criticizing King for bringing tensions to a head in Birmingham and responding sympathetically to the rising level of frustration among blacks in both North and South. *U.S. News* was typically more openly critical, characterizing King's campaign as a kind of invasion that was inciting racial hatred and was likely to do so elsewhere in the South as well. Despite King's growing national stature after the 1963 March on Washington speech and his 1964 Nobel Peace Prize, the newsmagazines repeated these themes when SCLC and SNCC combined forces to challenge segregation in Selma, Alabama. Both *Time* and *Newsweek* suggested King was beginning another unnecessary campaign, and both juxtaposed King against Sheriff Jim Clark, making clear their preference for the moderates in the middle (SNCC organizers in Selma were largely invisible). *Time* observed, "A new Selma city administration, with the cooperation of many businessmen, is trying hard to clear the town's dark racist reputation by steering a more moderate course."[38] In both cases, the dramatic photographs of police attacks on peaceful protesters abruptly changed the magazines' tone of detached skepticism. According to Lentz, *"Time* and *Newsweek* were forced to reinterpret King," placing him on the side of good against the savage attacks generated by Jim Clark and the Alabama state police, though both began to view King's insistence on carrying on the march to Montgomery with increasing skepticism.[39]

With passage of the 1964 Civil Rights Act and 1965 Voting Rights Act, the national media's attention shifted to the racial struggles outside the South, particularly in the aftermath of the 1965 Watts riot in Los Angeles. As he became increasingly prominent, King also shifted more of his attention to national concerns, leading to an erosion in what had been the national media's mostly favorable stance toward the heroic, if sometimes too willful, leader of the southern movement.

This erosion occurred on three particular occasions: in 1966, when King and the SCLC went into Chicago to campaign for legislation to ban housing segregation and address urban ills throughout the country; in 1967, when King spoke out forcefully against the war in Vietnam; and in 1968, when, prior to his death, he attempted to organize the Poor People's campaign in Washington, D.C. In these instances, media coverage blatantly reflected the conventional ideological assumptions about urban segregation, the U.S. role in Vietnam, and poverty and its link to economic inequality.

Early in 1966, the SCLC joined with the Chicago-based Coordinating Council of Community Organizations (CCCO) to address the myriad of inner-city ills that, in its thirteen-page proposal, it explicitly attributed to "economic exploitation," noting, "Every condition exists simply because someone profits by its existence. This economic exploitation is crystalized in the SLUM," which it labeled "a system of internal colonialism." The Chicago campaign, based in the city's sprawling southside slum, aimed to raise public consciousness about the appalling conditions of slum life, organize tenant groups to win concessions from absentee landlords, and eliminate segregated housing.

As with other campaigns, the national media greeted King's announcement with typical skepticism, but this time with a difference. In *Time*'s framing, the issue was narrowed essentially to urban segregation, which the magazine viewed as an outcome of a "free choice" real estate market. Thus there seemed little that a southern integrationist like King could offer the urban North. As occurred in Birmingham, black Chicagoans loyal to the political machine of Mayor Richard J. Daley criticized the SCLC campaign. Feeling that the campaign was floundering without significant media coverage—in Andrew Young's words, because "there has been no confrontation . . . of the kind where they interrupted the network TV programs"[40]—SCLC accelerated plans for "open housing" marches into various parts of greater Chicago, including the white working-class community of Ci-cero, where black families had been violently driven out in the past. Whereas in its early stages the national media paid relatively little attention to the Chicago campaign, when it encountered violent hostility from white racists, both *Time* and *Newsweek* noticed but viewed the campaign as ineffectual, a different stance from their response to the Bull Connor and Jim Clark attacks in Birmingham and Selma. Though the liberal *Newsweek* applauded when the city and SCLC reached a ten-point "open housing agreement," the largely King-friendly maga-zine distanced itself from King's tactic of "provocation" that touched "the white man's most sensitive nerve."[41]

In effect, the national media viewed the grim conditions of ghetto life through an ideologically narrow framework that focused on the quality of inner-city residents' interaction with city government, while King's campaign explained the concentrated inequality of ghetto life in broader economic terms. The same media framing occurred with the Poor People's campaign, which King and the SCLC mustered in late 1967 and early 1968, ambitiously aimed at mobilizing the nation's poor of all races in a campaign of disruption, school boycotts, factory sit-ins, and a mass march on Washington by the unemployed.

The Poor People mobilization reflected King's growing radicalization, his be-lief that the nation's deep racial and class inequality was rooted in its capitalist political economy. Yet King realized that he couldn't continue to have access to political and media institutions if he made these views public. David Garrow's biographical account relates conversations King had with staffers and with the Marxist C. L. R. James. According to the former, King

> asked us to turn off the tape recorder. He talked about what he called democratic socialism, and he said, "I can't say this publicly, and if you say I said it I'm not gonna admit it" . . . and he talked about the fact that he didn't believe that capitalism as it was constructed could meet the needs of poor people, and that what we might need to look at was a kind of socialism, but a democratic form of socialism.[42]

Needless to say, this Martin Luther King is invisible in media culture's public memory.

King's moral sensibility led him eventually to speak out forcefully against the Vietnam War, even if it cost him access to his allies in the Johnson administra-tion. In April 1967, King took to the pulpit of the Riverside Church and delivered a ringing condemnation of the war, observing that he could "never again raise my voice against the violence of the oppressed in the ghettos without having first spoken clearly to the greatest purveyor of violence in the world today—my own government." Decrying the United States for siding with "the wealthy and the secure while we create a hell for the poor," King declared that if there were no change in U.S. policy, "there will be no doubt in my mind . . . that we have no honorable intentions" in Vietnam.[43]

The media response was immediate. At a time when the American public was sharply divided on the war, the *Washington Post* dismissed King's speech as a "reflection of his disappointment at the slow progress of civil rights and the war on poverty," calling some of King's remarks "sheer inventions of unsupported fantasy." The *Post* added another charge: King had "done a grave injury to those who are his natural allies . . . and an even graver injury to himself. Many who have listened to him with respect will never again accord him the same confidence. He has diminished his usefulness to his cause, to his country and to his people. And that is a great tragedy."[44]

In a long editorial titled "Dr. King's Error," the *New York Times* also condemned King for a "disastrous" attempt to link "his personal opposition to the war . . . with the cause of Negro equality," noting that this would "lead not to solutions but to deeper confusion." The *Times* also blasted King for "recklessly comparing American military methods to those of the Nazis."[45] *Life* magazine chimed in by calling King's speech a "demagogic slander that sounded like a script for Radio Hanoi" and noted that King "goes beyond his personal right to dissent when he connects progress in civil rights here with a proposal that amounts to abject surrender in Vietnam." In doing so, "King comes close to betraying the cause for which he has worked so hard so long."[46] These media responses to King echoed their unquestioned support for the war's ideological justification.

Media Outsiders: Militant Rhetoric, Black Power, and the Poor

King's ventures outside the boundaries of legitimate discourse tarnished the favored media image of the civil rights leader whose powerful voice stood in contrast to those variously deemed illegitimate by the media. King's legitimate voice was resurrected by the media in its embrace of the "I Have a Dream" King after his death, but the boundaries that applied to King consistently cast an array of racial activists as illegitimate outsiders. These included the "young hypermilitants" of SNCC, the uncooperative Mississippi Freedom Democratic Party, the stirring street orator Malcolm X, the black power movement as a whole, inner-city blacks who struck out in rage against the hopelessness of their conditions, and, of course, the Black Panther Party.

When the Mississippi Freedom Democratic Party (MFDP) challenged both the segregated Mississippi party regulars and national party leadership at the 1964 national convention, they were surprised to find themselves resisted by a Johnson administration nervous about a divided convention and the potential for losing the southern white vote. They were, after all, the only delegation elected in a primary open to all,[47] and their courageous struggles through the voter registration project and their absolute belief in the rightness of their cause predisposed them to believe they could prevail on the national stage, if not in Mississippi—especially after the powerful testimony of sharecropper and inspiring MFDP leader Fannie Lou Hamer before the credentials committee was carried on national television. Hamer had been the target of brutal violence and jailing during the voter drive. In her powerful cadence, she intoned, "If the Freedom Democratic Party is not seated now, I question America. . . . Is this America? The land of the free and the home of the brave? Where we have to sleep with our telephones off the hook, because our lives be threatened daily?" At the end of her comments, she wept.[48]

Despite President Johnson's hastily called press conference that preempted much of Hamer's speech, the networks knew good television when they saw it and later aired Hamer's full impassioned testimony. However, once the Johnson position became clear, the boundaries of media legitimacy reemerged. The president offered the MFDP a "compromise" that would seat the regular Mississippi delegation if they signed a pledge to support the party's ticket and would seat two administration-designated MFDP members as delegates-at-large with the rest of the MFDP delegates to be seated as "honored guests." Although Johnson enlisted the help of King and other national leaders to persuade the MFDP to accept his offer, the MFDP rejected it as a form of tokenism that was unjust on its face and an affront to its members who had endured so much violence, without federal protection, during the voter drive. As Staughton Lynd later wrote, "What was at stake as it seemed to the SNCC people there, was not so much the question, Should the compromise be accepted? as the question, Are plain people from Mississippi competent to decide?"[49]

During this conflict, the national media showed clear favoritism for the legitimate voices—the national Democratic leadership—and impatience bordering on contempt for the sharecroppers and "radicals" from Mississippi. ABC correspondent Paul Good later recalled of the convention,

> The convention was, in short, a lively, complicated, many-sided story which television, given the glut of air time available, could have laid out objectively before the American people. Instead, exhibiting the egocentric arrogance increasingly evident in a medium—half reportorial and half show biz—and reflecting the subjective identification with the White House establishment, television commentators often behaved before the Mississippi Negroes as proctors charged with keeping order rather than seekers after the roots of disorder.[50]

Dismissing the "moralistic obstinance" of the MFDP, *Newsweek* embraced the position of "black moderates" who were suggesting that "Fannie Lou Hamer, the Freedom Democrat's leading mouthpiece, is showing disturbing demagogic tendencies—attacking middle-class Negroes and whites, American policy in Vietnam, and Martin Luther King."[51] The magazine's dismissal of Hamer would seem to reflect class and perhaps gender bias common to the national media during the 1960s. Mary King reported a confrontation between Hamer and vice-presidential aspirant Hubert Humphrey after the MFDP was told that Humphrey, at one time a strong civil rights advocate, would not be nominated as vice president if the MFDP didn't back off. Hamer "glared" at Humphrey and asked, "Mr. Humphrey, do you mean to tell me that your position is more important than Mississippi's four hundred thousand black lives?" Humphrey later told the MFDP's Ed King, "The President has said he will not let that illiterate woman on the floor of the Democratic convention."[52] Despite everything, the MFDP worked to support the Johnson ticket in Mississippi.

However, the SNCC-led grassroots movement experienced profound disillusionment with national politics and began to shift in the direction of the black power movement that was to emerge in 1966. In their disillusioned isolation, SNCC began to exhibit qualities that showed up later in other movements of the era when their voices were excluded from legitimate discourse. Writing of the "atmosphere of mutual distrust and recriminations," Charles Payne observed, "Time and again, the substance of ideas could not be discussed because of a climate of suspicion and emotional strain, so that the organization was unable to implement any new projects or even effectively maintain old ones. The climate would become progressively more debilitating." Payne cited Mary King's recollection that "until late 1965 it was possible to disagree in SNCC and yet not feel reviled, because the underlying bonds were strong. Personal hostility was now [in 1965] being expressed."[53]

Part of this shift was the growing need on the part of many black SNCC staffers to define their public identity, or, as Mary King put it, to "redefine their self-image" independently of the burdens a racist culture imposed on them.[54] As a SNCC position paper put it, "If we are to proceed toward liberation, we must cut ourselves off from the white people. We must form our own institutions, credit unions, co-ops, political parties, write our own histories."[55] In this sense, they were gravitating toward the assertive black consciousness being expressed by Malcolm X, and clearly journeying outside the boundaries of conventional media understanding.

Malcolm's black nationalism and the black power movement he influenced were frequently labeled as racist because of their denunciations of "the white man" who historically had enslaved and oppressed African Americans. A segment of the news progam *News Beat*, "The Hate That Hate Produced," which aired on WNTA in New York City in 1959, first brought the Nation of Islam's message to public light. While the media at times acknowledged and provided mass publics with glimpses of Malcolm's charismatic personality, the media stance toward Malcolm and the black power movement was to treat both as mirror opposites of the other bad guys of the era's racial struggles: the violent white racists in the South. The national media interpreted black "power" in the conventional manner of power *over*, suggesting an equation between black power advocates and white supremacists, rather than an expression of something more compatible with democratic empowerment: the power *to* that resulted from freeing oneself from the shackles of internalized, as well as external, oppression. As Stokely Carmichael said of the use of "black power" chants, "This isn't anti-white. It's just a way of sayin' that we're not ashamed of bein' black. We need to be proud of bein' black. We need it bad."[56]

As the media began to notice a new national assertiveness among blacks around the time of the Birmingham campaign, they simultaneously began to take note of Malcolm's growing following. A lengthy *New York Times* article on the new "assertive spirit" among Negroes noted in a subheading that "Racial Pride" and "Black Nationalism" were becoming viewed as a "Powerful Force for Change." The article introduced Malcolm with a photo and caption, "Black Muslim Head: Malcolm X, leader of extremist group in New York," and described him as being "of impressive bearing" and "endowed with a shrewd mind." Much of the article analyzed different perspectives on black nationalism, noting that "other Negro leaders are very conscious of the growing popularity of Malcolm X."[57]

However, media coverage of Malcolm almost never explored the philosophical and personal foundation for his rhetoric, but instead was loaded with suggestive language and fraught with the threat of violence Malcolm posed. Malcolm's rhetorical rejection of nonviolence "toward those who are violent with us"—forceful *rhetoric,* but not actual violent behavior—was asserted within the framework of self-defense. In the media's frame, however, violence was only justifiable in defense of the state, the nation, or other authorities that the media deemed legitimate, and any form of racial protest triggered fears of racial violence.

This tendency showed up consistently in the relatively few newsmagazine articles about Malcolm. *Newsweek* published an article at the same time as its Birmingham piece in which it described the "increasingly restless and militant mood" of the "New Negro" as "more aggressive," "ambivalent about whites," and "freighted with dynamite." The article contained a widely dispersed photograph of a determined, finger-pointing Malcolm, with the caption, "You cannot integrate," and went on to worry about the impact of the new mood on King's campaign in Birmingham.[58] *U.S. News* chimed in with a short boxed article entitled "Brother Malcolm: His Theme Now Is Violence" on March 23, 1964.[59] A week later, the conservative magazine published a more nuanced article, titled "Now It's a Negro Drive for Segregation," that not surprisingly gave fairly favorable notice to Malcolm's opposition to integration, his advocacy of "straightening out" the moral and spiritual lives of ghetto residents, and his belief that the only "real solution" is for "our people to go back to Africa."[60] Simultaneously,

Newsweek ran a patronizing piece entitled "Malcolm's Brand X," trying to square the Malcolm X who was "an apostle of bitter black nationalism" with the charismatic leader's "ingratiating" aptitude for the "white man's art of communication." The article ominously went on to detail Malcolm's split from the Nation of Islam and his observation that 1964 "threatens to be a very explosive year on the racial front and . . . I myself intend to be very active in every phase of the American Negro struggle for human rights."[61]

Several months later, in a rare mainstream appearance of Malcolm's own words, the *Saturday Evening Post* ran a pre-publication segment of Malcolm X's *Autobiography* titled "I'm talking to You, White Man." Malcolm's words were framed by the magazine's editorial stance. The magazine's subheading noted that Malcolm, "the explosive Black Muslim rebel who defies both white and Negro leadership," "tells a story that swings from violence and degradation to religion and racism." The magazine's cover featured a close-up of Malcolm's determined face and the caption: "Exclusive: 'More and worse riots will erupt!' Malcolm X: His own story of crime, conversion, and Black Muslims in action."[62] In its accompanying editorial, the magazine made its position clear: "What lends importance to Malcolm's otherwise depressing tale is that he is a leader of the Black Muslims, a sort of Negro Ku Klux Klan. Nobody knows just how large a following he has, but unquestionably the militant hatred he preaches was behind some of the violence of the summer riots in the North."[63] While the magazine noted that "society must share the blame for making Malcolm X the angry and possibly dangerous man that he is," it observed with apparent relief that in a "poll which *The New York Times* took in Harlem—by coincidence just before the [summer 1964] riots—[Martin Luther] King has more than 12 times as many followers as Malcolm X."[64]

Not surprisingly, media accounts of Malcolm's assassination contrasted sharply with accounts of King's death. *Newsweek* titled its story "Death of a Desperado," and asserted that Malcolm's "overwhelming talent was still talk; he always followed his tongue instead of his wasted mind." The magazine titled its review of Malcolm's autobiography "Satan in the Ghetto."[65] *Time* made up for past inattention by including a three-page summation of Malcolm's life in its March 5 issue, leading with two police mug shots from Malcolm's youth in 1944 and characterizing Malcolm as a former "pimp, a cocaine addict and a thief" and more recently as an "unashamed demagogue" whose "gospel was hatred" and whose "creed was violence." The magazine criticized black leaders for sanctifying Malcolm as a "brilliant" leader who had "moderated his views," singling out King for blaming Malcolm's death on a "society sick enough to express dissent with murder."[66] The *New York Times* also weighed in with editorial reflections on "an extraordinary and twisted man" who turned "many true gifts to evil purpose." The newspaper viewed Malcolm's life as "strangely and pitifully wasted."[67]

Generally, the media reduced the black power movement to a similar frame of race hatred and threatening violence. The black power slogan was introduced to the world during the follow-up to the 1966 James Meredith solitary march across Mississippi, when some of the younger SNCC marchers chanted "Black Power" while marching. From that point through the black power convention in Newark in 1967, the national media tended toward three frames for interpreting black power: obscuring its meaning behind the fiery media personality of spokespersons like Stokely Carmichael, returning again and again to the "anti-white, black racist" interpretation, and linking it closely to the threat of violence. *Time* minced no words in its first report on the new black power phenomenon, expressing a common refrain with its title, "The New Racism." *Time*'s article led with reference to the Supreme Court's dictum in *Brown v. Board of Education* that "the old 'separate but equal' doctrine was antithetical to American democracy," and proceeded to announce, "Today, a dozen years later, many militant ideologues are impatient with what they consider the glacial pace of progress in civil rights. They espouse instead a *racist philosophy* that could ultimately perpetuate the very separatism against which Negroes have fought so successfully. Oddly, they are not white men but black, and their slogan is 'Black Power!'"[68]

A *Life* editorial on July 22, 1966, was headlined "'Black Power' Must Be Defined," and then set the stage for its discussion by citing the NAACP's Roy Wilkins's assertion that black power represented "a reverse Mississippi, a reverse Hitler, a reverse Ku Klux Klan. It is the father of hatred and the mother of violence." The piece then moved to Vice President Humphrey's warning that "there is no room in America for racism of any color, and we must reject calls for racism, whether they come from a throat that is white or one that is black." The magazine proceeded to dismiss as naïve and counterproductive the possibility that black power was "not a call to racist violence but a move to separatism," then ended the editorial by concluding that if it simply meant the "marshalling of all available Negro strength to gain legitimate political and economic goals, well and good."[69]

Gender Boundaries

Grounded in the activism of other movements, as well as the awakening national concern for equal rights, the women's liberation movement emerged at a time when the protest spectacle was in full bloom and media frames were well established. Protest movements were widely regarded as outsiders, and the movement activists had to get their message across amidst the "clutter" of media protest. As Patricia Bradley has observed, it was difficult to "get media attention when it was sought in orderly ways."[70]

Compounding the usual difficulties protesters faced in trying to convey their meanings through the media, the women's movement, like the black power movement, had to do more than make instances of oppression visible in the media. They had to raise public consciousness the way their own consciousness had been raised: to understand that offending behaviors were demeaning or oppressive. The movement's drive to change public consciousness drew it naturally to ways the existing consciousness was shaped and perpetuated by media, schools, and the family. Not only was the wider media culture deaf to many of the movement's meanings, but so were many if not most of the women activists' male comrades in the era's movements. The ideological construction of gender in the early to mid-sixties was such that almost all men and most women began with the assumption that much of what the women's movement targeted as oppression was part of the natural order of things—a context also encountered by the gay rights movement that emerged a year or so later.

The more radical feminism of many of the movement's pioneers—veterans of civil rights, antiwar, and New Left struggles—was intensified in good part by the blatant sexism they encountered within these supposedly democratic movements. As the editors of *Dear Sister* put it, movement women's anger derived from a "sense of betrayal typical of divorce" because they had "felt so much a part of the left and had such high expectations of it."[71] As Patricia Bradley has observed, "The specific anger at New Left men came to be represented, by media and by [some] women themselves, as anger at men as a class."[72]

Indeed, the women's movement became a *women's* movement through what Naomi Weisstein has called a "cognitive revolution"[73]—a coming to consciousness about the oppression of women *as* women, irrespective of age, race, or class.[74] This consciousness was the product of two forces: (1) the jarring contradictions between movements committed to egalitarianism, the intrinsic value of personhood, and democratic decision making and the often degrading experiences of women in these movements, and (2) the sharing of personal stories and experiences in consciousness-raising (C-R) groups, "bitch sessions," or "rap sessions." In 1965 SNCC's Casey Hayden and Mary King decried the "caste system" of activist work in the civil rights movement: "Women seem to be placed in the same position of assumed subordination in personal situations, too. It is a caste system, which, at its worst, uses and exploits women."[75] Sharing their private experiences in consciousness-raising groups led women to shed disempowering patterns of self-blame and to see broader patterns of sexism around them.

Thus, in the same way that other protesters defined by media discourse as outsiders sought "free spaces" separate from the mainstream culture, women sought *their* free spaces apart from men in the movement as well as from the wider society. As women challenged the sexism around them, they frequently encountered hostile reactions by men who were variously clueless about their own sexism, threatened by the women's assertiveness, or felt that the push for women's liberation threatened to divide movements for racial justice or an end to the war. In 1967, an anonymous group of "SDS Women" issued a call "To the

Women of the Left" in which they argued, "Women must not make the same mistake the blacks did at first of allowing others (whites in their case, men in ours) to define our issues, methods and goals. Only we can and must define the terms of our struggle. The time has come for us to take the initiative in organizing ourselves for our own liberation."[76] As Ellen Willis put it, women's outsider position was "exactly analogous to the black power position, with male radicals playing the part of white liberals. . . . Substitute man-woman for black-white and that's where I stand. With one important exception: while white liberals and radicals always understood the importance of the black liberation struggle . . . radical men simply do not understand the importance of our struggle."[77]

These experiences and C-R sessions gave rise to radical feminism's critique of the wider culture, what Alice Echols termed the "most vital and imaginative force within the women's liberation movement." As Echols put it, "Radical feminists argued that women constituted a sex-class, that relations between women and men needed to be recast in political terms, and that gender rather than class was the primary contradiction. . . . Radical feminists articulated the earliest and most provocative critiques of the family, marriage, love, normative heterosexuality and rape."[78] It was precisely this critique, as opposed to the more liberal, equal rights-equal access criticisms raised by groups like the National Organization of Women (NOW), that remained outside media culture's boundaries of legitimacy.[79] As Patricia Bradley has observed, "the lessons and culture of the antiwar Left provided the media training ground" for the more radical activists in the movement, producing increasingly dramatic actions confronting the "symbols of systemic female repression," actions often fueled by women's anger at the deaf culture that surrounded them. These occurred, Bradley notes, "after years of polite petitions, conferences, and legal activities failed."[80]

In challenging society at large in the context of late-sixties activism, then, women's groups seized on dramatic public actions as a vehicle for addressing forms of oppression in the wider society and attempting to raise society's consciousness. Their actions ran the gamut of many comparable actions in civil rights and antiwar movements of the time, from efforts to "desegregate" bars that were closed to women (as most were at the time) to sit-ins that challenged the editorial policies of magazines like *Ladies Home Journal* or the banking and investment policies of financial institutions; from confrontational protests like the 1968 action against the Miss America pageant to stickers and stamps proclaiming "This Ad Insults Women" or "Offensive to Women" that could be prominently displayed on offending public material, even to Yippie-like agitprop actions: "Zaps" by the Women's International Terrorist Conspiracy from Hell (WITCH) or quick, theatrical actions that satirically targeted institutions like Chase Manhattan Bank, Revlon, and a bridal industry fair in Madison Square Garden. Some actions attracted media attention; many did not, and sharp disagreements over tactics plagued the movement.[81]

At the same time that feminists deplored the mass media's treatment of women, the media were viewed as a crucial vehicle for accessing the wider public. As Robin Morgan argued, "Leafleting on New York's Lower East side for ten years would not reach the housewife in Escanaba, Mich., but thirty seconds on the six o'clock news would." Therein lay a crucial dilemma faced by outsiders in any of the sixties movements, especially since, in addition to descriptors like "stringy haired" and "braless," the word "*strident* was used on almost any occasion when female behavior did not meet the [conventional] norms," as Patricia Bradley noted.[82]

One example cited in Bradley's work on the movement and the media illustrates the dilemmas the women's movement encountered. A group favoring the legalization of abortion "attempted to have a voice" at a February 13, 1969, New York state hearing on abortion reform held by a committee "composed of fourteen men and one woman, a nun." After failing to "be heard by way of organized channels, the women finally interrupted the hearing with a call for legalization of abortion, not simply reform. However, the committee reacted not to the women's opinions but to their style"—with references to "such rude people" and "the disgraceful conduct of the ladies." Newspaper coverage of the hearings the next day "played up the stridency of the women's objections" in headlines such as "Invade Abortion Hearings" (*Newsday*), "Gals KO Abortion Hearings" and "Gals Squeal for Repeal, Abort State Hearings" (*New York Daily News*), and "Women Break Up Abortion Hearing" (*New York Times*)—all accompanied by photographs and text that "played up confrontation and scolding of committee members." Nevertheless, "press attention provided an impetus" for subsequent passage of the nation's second abortion reform law in New York.[83]

Television anchors typically spun their coverage of young feminists angrily confronting male officialdom in patronizing if not outwardly critical ways. Yet this same coverage could affect young women viewers quite differently, as noted in Susan Douglas's account of a CBS report on U.S. Senate hearings regarding the safety of the birth control pill: "Young women like me, watching this on TV, were yelling, 'Right on!' because it was so thrilling to see women my age taking on these bloated, self-righteous senators who thought girls should be quiet, smile, and serve tea."[84]

As the newsmagazines belatedly came to recognize the new women's liberation phenomenon, their coverage tended to treat the feminist criticism of sexist attitudes and behaviors with open disdain. As Ashley and Olson found in their study of framing techniques found in the *New York Times, Newsweek,* and *Time,* the press "marginalized" the movement through delegitimizing frames (emphasizing movement conflicts, events over goals, women's appearances, the use of belittling quotation marks around words like "liberation," and the like); by comparison, the same media tended to describe later female anti-feminists as "well-organized and attractive."[85] In 1970, *Newsweek* referred to the word "sexist" this way: "Sexist is the women's lib term for male supremacist and an offense to the language we will have to learn to life with."[86]

Eventually, as happened with other movements, there emerged a "legitimate" form of feminism the media understood and sometimes begrudgingly endorsed—namely, a liberal feminism of equal rights and equal opportunities. As recounted by Susan Douglas, newsman Howard K. Smith proclaimed his views in a television commentary:

> "Like the majority of Americans," Smith said, he was "weary of the abrasive type of group protest." While sympathetic to "Indians and Negroes" who had been "genuinely mistreated," Smith confessed to a "modified unsympathy" with women's liberation. He found a "few of their demands," such as equal pay, equal access to "some jobs" and child-care centers "good." He suggested women were already more than equal, since they constituted 53 percent of the population and "they get the most money, inherited from worn-out husbands."[87]

Overall, media treatment of the movement fell within familiar ideological boundaries. On the sympathetic, liberal side, the mass media gradually grew responsive to the clear demonstration of economic inequities and occupational discrimination against women and linked these to anti-discriminatory reforms. At times, liberal responses acknowledged the legitimacy of growing female assertiveness, noting that men might consider making personal accommodations so as not to alienate women with whom they sought relationships. On the unsympathetic, more conservative side, when inequities were acknowledged to be open to question, they were often to be seen as "women's problems" linked to low self-esteem and acquiescence. More commonly, what feminists saw as inequities were viewed as part of the natural order, and the complaining feminists were dismissed as shrill, man-hating malcontents.

In its "Behavior" section in November 1969, *Time* published a three-page assessment of "The New Feminists: Revolt against 'Sexism,'" effectively emptying the movement of significant content by reporting, "To demonstrate their disgust and alienation from sexist society, the angries picket the Miss America contest, burn brassieres [which didn't happen], and dump into 'freedom trashcans' such symbols of female 'oppression' as lingerie, false eyelashes and steno pads."[88] Without providing evidence, the magazine noted that "most middle-aged or older women" were "skeptical if not downright hostile" toward the movement, trotting out the generational frame by observing that "younger women, *part of a rebellious generation,* are fertile ground for the seeds of discontent." In what seems a projection of their own viewpoint, the magazine also noted that "many of the new feminists are surprisingly violent in mood [an oblique reference to training in self-defense], and seem to be trying, in fact, to repel other women rather than attract them." Toward the end of the piece, *Time* acknowledged that the militant women had "drawn attention to some real problems" even as they "aroused a good deal of fury and laughter." The magazine reassured its readers that the movement might not be quite so threatening as it seemed, concluding with the patronizing comment, "With a new sense of self-esteem, which is essentially what the feminists are seeking, even those women who elect to stay at home might be happier, which would of course benefit men as well."[89]

Newsweek published its first feature article on women's liberation on March 23, 1970. One section examined four distinct feminist voices and, presumably for balance and context, another focused on "Other Voices: How Social Scientists See Women's Lib." The four voices were introduced as "pretty, blond Leslye Russel," "tall, elegantly feline Ti-Grace Atkinson," "Roxanne Dunbar . . . one of the first liberationists publicly to advocate masturbation as an alternative to what she sees as the slavery of heterosexuality," and Jo Freeman, "at 24 . . . already both a leading women's lib historian and one of the movement's most effective organizers." The views of social scientists included those of both women and men in the field, and ranged from being guardedly sympathetic ("Many have been sisters in a family where the brother got the better of it—the brother got to go to college, though the girl was brighter. Is she neurotic or justifiably angry?") to scathingly dismissive ("their most conspicuous feature is self-hatred").[90]

On March 30, both *Time* and *Newsweek* covered the sit-in that criticized the editorial policies of *Ladies Home Journal. Newsweek* focused heavily on the protesters' behaviors as they "stormed" the magazine's headquarters and on editor John Mack Carter's response ("one of the most interesting days of my career"). A separate paragraph noted that earlier in the week, forty-six women staffers at *Newsweek* filed an Equal Employment complaint against the magazine charging discrimination in editorial jobs; it also recorded the editor's response.[91] *Time* led with a jab at *Newsweek*'s own "revolt," then described the *Ladies Home Journal* protesters as "more than 100 mod- and trouser-clad feminists" who "marched into" *Journal* headquarters, thereby "scaling new piques" for women's liberation. Noting a male researcher's suggestion—"If you don't like the magazine, don't read it"—*Time* commented that "undaunted, an obstinate group of 30 hunkered down to a day-long vigil" while the editor "demonstrated extraordinary patience." Carter announced that he had agreed to "consider" allowing the women to create a special eight-page "Liberation supplement" for a future issue.[92]

Newsweek followed up with coverage of the special *Journal* "Liberation supplement," patronizingly commenting, "Good politics the supplement may be, but good journalism it is not." The magazine observed that the supplement included the "standard women's lib polemic on job discrimination," the "inevitable group discussion of love and sex," "strangely paranoid first-person accounts" of childbirth experiences, and a "painfully predictable diatribe" on marriage.

The article concluded with *Journal* editor Carter's comment, "'Formerly,' he said with a smile, 'I had little patience with suggestions from non-professionals about the magazine. Now I have none at all.'"[93]

Given the market significance of the female majority, even a conservative newsmagazine like *U.S. News & World Report* took seriously the more liberal or market-linked dimensions of the women's movement: job discrimination, access to careers, and economic inequality. *U.S. News* largely ignored the more radical feminist attacks on sexist attitudes or stereotypes as well as grievances that targeted sexuality, marriage, and child-rearing, but took seriously inequities in job pay. In its first major piece on women's liberation, the magazine reduced women's grievances to economic discrimination and equality, complete with graphs that demonstrated that, in the magazine's concluding words, "It is still 'a man's world,' economically speaking."[94] Similarly, at the same time that *Time* and *Newsweek* gave colorful coverage to the nationwide "Women's Strike for Equality" demonstrations, *U.S. News'* September 7 issue concentrated on "How Women are Doing in Politics." The magazine observed that "politics is still overwhelmingly a man's game" but suggested that this may have had much to do with "women's natural reluctance to push themselves."[95]

In August 1970, *Time* published an article on the movement's campaign against demeaning advertising, which it introduced with reference to the movement's "penchant for oddball causes—from ban-the-bras to communal child rearing," noting that training "their ire" on the "distorted image of women in advertisements" had, however, gained the "militants" "wide support among women." A subsequent article on women's activism in Europe highlighted the "spectacular high jinks" of "Women's Lib, Continental Style" in several countries,[96] and publication of Kate Millett's book *Sexual Politics* brought the author celebrity-like attention and an appearance on *Time's* cover because of the book's successful sales. *Time,* however, dismissed the book as "essentially a polemic suspended awkwardly in academic traction," quoting Millett's dissertation adviser's remark: "Reading the book is like sitting with your testicles in a nutcracker." A lengthy assessment of women's lib also reviewed multiple examples of "angry" women's publications, "idiotic" efforts to change language usage, and raging women who viewed their "bodies as male-occupied territory."[97]

A few months later, *Time* returned to Millett for a second, critical look. Noting that "other critics were dissecting both book and movement," the magazine brought another media boundary into play, noting that "Millett herself contributed to the growing skepticism about the movement by acknowledging at a recent meeting that she is bisexual"—an admission the magazine asserted was "bound to discredit her as a spokeswoman for her cause." The article concluded by making the boundaries of legitimacy explicit: "Chances are that society will heed only the movement's legitimate demands. All the rest—motivated by what Helen Lawrenson calls the 'splenetic frenzy of hatred for men' voiced by 'these sick, silly creatures'—is likely to remain unacceptable to all but the sickest and silliest."[98]

In the early to mid-1970s, the newsmagazines—particularly *Newsweek* and *Time*—revisited the women's movement from time to time to assess tangible progress made by women, schisms in the movement, tensions between white and black women, and eventually the backlash against feminism led by Phyllis Schlafly. Throughout, the magazines retained their disdain for feminist "extremism." In 1971, *Time* published an unusual two-page editorial on "Women's Lib: Beyond Sexual Politics." Warning against "extremism in any movement" and "female chauvinism," the magazine argued for moderate versions of three "extreme" movement "propositions": (1) certain behavioral and occupational expectations had made it difficult for women to become "autonomous beings," (2) "only by learning how society has hobbled her can a woman heal herself," and (3) "most men treat women as sexual objects." Among the items ridiculed by *Time* were women's workshops on "rape in marriage" and women's attacks on the male-perpetrated myth of vaginal orgasm.[99] A 1972 *Time* essay criticized feminists' efforts to use gender-neutral language by labeling it "Sispeak," comparing it to Orwell's Newspeak of *1984*. Clearly not getting the movement's argument about language, the magazine compared the "new lexicographers" to "Humpty Dumpty in *Through the Looking Glass:* a word may mean whatever they want it to mean."[100]

Public consciousness-raising by the women's movement had several salient effects as it encountered the boundaries of mass media discourse. First, it stretched the boundaries so that the media began to take seriously feminism's liberal grievances. One way of measuring this absorption can be found in the relatively few articles on the women's movement published in the pages of *Esquire,* the self-described "Magazine for Men" that affected a hip journalistic style. In a July 1970 piece, "Cutting Loose," feminist Sally Kempton traced the origins of her anger against men and outlined her personal perspective on women's liberation. An essentially sympathetic look at women's liberation, the article suggested that women basically needed to gain better self-esteem.[101] In January 1971, the magazine published an angry screed against the movement, entitled "The Feminine Mistake," in which Helen Lawrenson didn't bother to conceal her disdain toward the women's liberation activists. Accompanied by a full-page artist's sketch of a large braless woman holding up her burning bra and echoing the common mainstream response to the black power movement, Lawrenson blasted the "phony movement" for demanding "not equality, but the absolute subjugation of men, or even their elimination," thereby fulfilling what Kempton had previously declared was the basis of men's inaccurate fear of liberated women—that they would "rule men as men have ruled women."[102]

In July 1973, a special issue of *Esquire* included a celebrity-oriented photo collage of the magazine's "five favorite moments" in women's liberation, a series of quotes (some overtly hostile, some quite supportive) from diverse public figures responding to the question, "When Did You Begin to Take the Women's Movement Seriously?" and Sara Davidson's lengthy essay on movement "Foremothers" and the "paths their ideas and personal lives had taken." Davidson commented that by 1973 "the mood of the original feminists has changed utterly. The anger is gone, and in its place there seems a blend of sadness, softness, compassion, and exhaustion."[103] In one of the responses to *Esquire*'s question about taking the women's movement seriously, radical attorney William Kunstler noted:

> I began to take the women's movement seriously when, through it, I
> began to understand the extent of my own chauvinism. Like racism,
> male chauvinism is endemic in this society and both states of mind are
> perpetuated by a blind refusal to acknowledge the depth and tenacity of
> their existence deep within our psyches. Neither can be eradicated by self-
> deception, rhetoric or even the best of intentions. Only confrontation on
> an individual or mass basis between those most directly affected and their
> oppressors, overt or covert, can transform our myth of sexual and racial
> equality into a reasonable reality.[104]

Kunstler's response suggests a second way the women's movement, including some of its radical arguments, succeeded in raising consciousness among men. Many of the issues women grappled with were manifest in their most intimate relationships with men—lovers, partners, friends, brothers, and fathers. As arenas within which some of the movement's struggles would play out, these relationships offered the potential of a different—and, in a sense, far more democratic—kind of discourse from the one that played out in the mass media. In face-to-face confrontations where some form of personal relationship existed, women were, in effect, their own medium of communication. The relationship provided the opportunity for genuine conversation that could, if both parties were open to learning from the other, produce mutual understanding. Some men in the movement were open enough to examine their own sexism, just as some whites were open to examining their own racism, and thus were able to be supportive. Painful clashes occurred, to be sure, but the new meanings women were expressing presented opportunities for men, too, to evolve and grow beyond their own sexist repression. These interactions helped to spread radical awareness among men as well as women that society needed to be transformed to nurture the full liberation and development of human beings irrespective of gender.

Absorption into the culture, however, meant something quite different. Again, *Esquire* provides an example. In 1975, the magazine published a piece, "The Guilty Sex," depicting "how American men became irrelevant." This was followed a year later by an article proclaiming "The Year of the Lusty Woman" and "It's okay to be a sex object again" and eventually a 1978 satire on the "New Rules of the Mating Game," which profiled eight types of "new men" and their relationships with women. As women found their way into what had largely been a men's magazine, feminism was transformed into new models of male behavior (sexual and otherwise) that male readers could sort through and try on. As the author put it, "Bravo to the men trying to loosen up enough to try some new lines."[105]

Finally, both the rising tide of liberal feminism and the often angry rhetoric and dramatic action of radical feminism became a major target of backlash. In 1973, *Newsweek* carried an editorial by conservative author Midge Decter that decried the ease with which society's institutions, including the media, had been caught up in the "great tide of fashion" that was women's lib. With classically wild overstatement, Decter noted the "record speed" with which women's lib allegedly "came to dominate all the channels of public discussion and exchange." She accused normally "tough-minded" social commentators of "piously . . . chanting a litany of modern women's enslavements and oppressions," thereby elevating herself as a truly tough-minded woman who knew better than to "believe that the women's libbers actually meant what they said in their indictment of men, of civilization in general, and ultimately of nature itself."[106]

In 1975, *U.S. News* revisited the gender inequities it had examined in 1970 and noted the "unprecedented pace" at which the nation was "moving towards equality of the sexes. The magazine observed, however, that there was "growing alarm and resentment" among middle-class women toward "man-hating, family-destructive radical feminism."[107] The backlash would become more strident and more pervasive in the "culture wars" unleashed in the 1980s, aided by references to iconic images left over from "man-hating, family destructive" women's liberation.

Despite a media predisposition to view any form of protest as a form of deviance, the boundaries of media discourse were not impenetrable. Especially as images of the violent repression of nonviolent blacks in the South reached a national audience, and, later, against a backdrop of legitimate civil rights grievances, the women's movement began to gain recognition for equity concerns and media discourse provided a range of debate between legitimate liberal and conservative/backlash meanings of these movements. Via a variety of explicit critiques, pejorative labels, and the failure to take their grievances and arguments seriously, however, the mass media consistently cast those who targeted deeper institutional ills outside the bounds of legitimate discourse. While this discourse helped to spawn the very militancy and violence the media obsessed about and the forces of backlash would feast upon, the sixties trajectory would be profoundly intensified by the war in Vietnam.

5

Vietnam and the Spheres of Media Discourse

Power always thinks it has a great soul and vast views beyond the comprehension of the weak; and that it is doing God's service when it is violating all his laws.
—John Adams, letter to Thomas Jefferson, February 2, 1816

It is the responsibility of intellectuals to speak the truth and expose the lies.
—Noam Chomsky, "The Responsibility of Intellectuals," 1967

In contrast to public memory of the "good" civil rights story, the American war in Vietnam remains a kind of recurring, highly contested, yet seemingly inexplicable nightmare in mass media culture. In 1985, for example, *Time* published a special issue, "Vietnam: Ten Years Later," in which it reviewed "The War that Went Wrong" and "The Lessons It Taught." Ten years later, the magazine ran another special section, "Vietnam: Twenty Years Later, It Still Haunts Us." And in 1988, in a special section looking back at the events of 1968, *Time* characterized the war as a "dark hallucination, the black magic that would come and take the young and bear them off to the other side of the world and destroy them." Thus the war "alienated the young from their elders." The magazine concluded that the war taught Americans two lessons. To an angry New Left, it confirmed that "Amerika" was "not merely mistaken or even bad, but evil." For the rest of America, *Time* asserted, the "nation had made a bad mistake. Americans, who love a winner, detest thinking of themselves as losers, and they saw themselves distinctly as losers after Tet."[1]

Time's accounts are, of course, only a few of the seemingly innumerable retrospectives on Vietnam aired in the mass media culture over the years. In addition to the curious use of the word "hallucination," this brief citation from the magazine's account is noteworthy in several respects. It avoids assigning blame or responsibility for the war, presumably seeking to avoid alienating a significant bloc of potential readers. Its reference to the destructiveness of the war refers to only one kind of victim of that destruction, America's youth; the magazine fails to mention the staggeringly greater destruction wreaked by the United States on the Vietnamese people and countryside. And it contains major distortions that reflected the conventional political discourse of the day. With an accent on the Tet Offensive, the war is said to have had two major divisive effects: dividing the young against the old (the generational theme) and setting New Leftists who saw Amerika as evil against the rest of the nation who viewed the war as a mistake because they weren't used to the United States losing wars. The broad antiwar movement's moral condemnation of the war disappeared in *Time*'s attribution of war opposition to self-centered youth, the familiar "generation gap," and those who simply hated their country, all reinforced by the total absence of references to the destruction in Indochina.

It is, of course, unfair to pin too much on a single passage from one magazine's retrospective—though *Time* only compounds these distortions in the rest of the cited article. However, three points about *Time*'s coverage pertain to mass media culture writ large. One is that the primary consideration about the war is that it was something done to us. There is no denying the enormous pain and trauma suffered by hundreds of thousands of American soldiers, their families and loved ones, and by the vast millions who felt deeply betrayed by their nation's leaders. But it is important to examine what did this "to us." It certainly wasn't a hallucination, nor was it simply war. It was a particular war constructed and sustained by American policy makers in a conscious effort to carry out the nation's postwar foreign policy.

Second, the war did not divide young from old or an angry New Left from a nation ashamed of losing a war. Americans of all ages and from all walks of life learned that the war was a frightening contradiction of much of what they believed about their country. If the war caused a significant divide in the United States, it would seem that the most pervasive divide was one between the people and their government, most directly the political authorities who contributed to the course of American intervention in Vietnam. Americans came to believe that their government had betrayed them and had betrayed the hundreds of thousands of very young men who willingly went to war on the basis of beliefs they had learned in grade school—beliefs deeply etched into their consciousness by the pervasive and idealized public memory of the Second World War, the countless ceremonies of remembrance in which they participated, and the specific ways their government described the crisis in Vietnam.

In 1971, for the first time, most Americans viewed the war as "morally wrong."[2] In 1978, the Chicago Council on Foreign Relations conducted its quadrennial poll regarding U.S. foreign policy and found that 72 percent of the public believed "the Vietnam War was more than a mistake, it was fundamentally wrong and immoral"—a substantial majority sentiment that would stand up over the sixteen years that the Council reported on responses to that question, long after the immediate memory of the war and domestic turmoil had faded.[3]

Third, in contrast to views held by the large majority of the public, the media culture's dominant theme about the war was that it was a mistake of some kind—either the hawkish view that blamed government officials for not letting the troops win[4] or a dovish view that emphasized erroneous governmental readings of Vietnamese culture and history. For whatever reason, the media discourse suggested the United States deviated from its normally benign and successful foreign policy.

In brief, the media culture's remembrance of the war struggles to square public memory of the war with the "mythic reality" with which the war was consistently justified throughout its duration. In exploring the curious "appeal" of war, psychologist Lawrence LeShan has referred to mythic reality as the world of perceptions totally dichotomized between "we" who are good and an "enemy" who is all bad—a compelling reality normally constructed by those in power well in advance of war. Sensory reality, by contrast, is the world as we normally experience it.[5] During the war, successive administrations repeatedly tried to sustain the war's mythic reality by imbuing events with meanings that contradicted the war's sensory realities.

The boundaries of sensory reality are fluid and open to the possibility of change, while mythic reality is, in Erik Erikson's phrase, a realm of "totality," an "orientation to reality" that "includes an absolute boundary of perception and concepts. Nothing inside must be left outside, nothing that must be outside can be tolerated inside."[6] Mythic reality is thereby sustained by a media culture that defends a nation's ideological beliefs against sensory realities that challenge them. As longtime *New York Times* war correspondent Chris Hedges put it, mythic reality requires that "defeats" are viewed as "signposts on the road to ultimate victory." The enemy is demonized "so that our opponent is no longer human." Sustaining mythic reality is so important to states that they commonly seek to silence those domestic voices who question the need for war, those who "give us an alternative language" that recognizes "the humanity of the enemy" or does "not condone violence as a form of communication."[7]

The war's mythic reality evolved from Cold War propaganda proclaiming the United States as "defender of the free world" against a powerful enemy ruthlessly bent on world domination, propaganda often mirrored by that of its Soviet counterpart. As Jacques Ellul has noted, propagandists may believe their propaganda, yet they still manipulate the public to acquiesce in their policies because it is in their interest to do so.[8] Belief in the application of Cold War propaganda to Vietnam was reinforced by a culture infused with glowing public memory of the "Good War," to say nothing of beliefs inculcated early in life about the noble role played by the world's "oldest democracy." Mythic reality is also reinforced by liberal ideology's predisposition to explain events in individualistic rather than systemic or structural terms, thereby effectively reducing a war's objectives to the unquestioned "good intentions" of officials seeking to carry out the consensual benign purpose of American foreign policy. Good intentions, however, don't make a war moral, though in retrospect they help to sustain belief that it was at worst a mistake.

The American war in Vietnam is an archetypal example of the erosion of mythic reality in the political culture writ large, although it took a long time for this to happen. It is also a pivotal case history in how the mass media aided the erosion of mythic reality in one sense while sustaining it in another, eventually helping to restore a mythical story of the war in the nation's public memory. While government officials consistently strove to sustain mythical belief throughout the war, the media role was more complex, spanning the spheres of consensus and legitimate controversy in covering the war and the sphere of deviance in covering much of the antiwar movement.[9] While boundaries of legitimate discourse effectively marginalized challenges to the consensual beliefs about the war and its purpose, media images were one of the vehicles through which the public could see sensory realities of the war that challenged those beliefs. Media images were also the primary vehicle through which the public could see those who viewed the war as fundamentally immoral.

Thus public discourse during the war was a kind of "debate" between three parties: hawks who defended war policies or advocated stronger tactics, doves who criticized policies that were not working as claimed and advocated finding a way to negotiate the American exit, and, essentially, images of protesters in the streets who became increasingly vocal and militant, at times embracing symbols (like NLF flags) that many viewed as anti-American. The argument that the post-1954 war was created by the United States and that the United States was therefore responsible for the deaths of millions of Indochinese civilians in direct contradiction of the Geneva Conventions was effectively excluded within the mass media.

Still, the general public eventually came to view the war as "not a mistake, but fundamentally wrong and immoral," and for this reason, as we shall see, powerful elites have gone to great lengths to "correct" this reading of the war. The popular media culture has managed to maintain the conventional boundaries of interpreting the war, contradicting much of the public's actual memories of the war. People are thereby likely to still carry wounds from the war in their private lives, yet the public memory provides no opportunity for a full public reckoning with the meaning of one of the darker chapters of American history—a truth and reconciliation process that could start to bridge a number of divides that have been perpetuated by the media culture, and one that might generate a clearer public demand for a different kind of American foreign policy. Instead, the public memory sustains a mythic reality about American foreign policy while repeatedly revisiting safely legitimate interpretations of Vietnam.

The Boundaries of Legitimate Discourse

Until around 1962, coverage of American intervention in Vietnam fit neatly into a noncontroversial Cold War consensus. From that point onward, as voices of legitimate dissent expressed doubts about and eventually opposition to the war, war coverage also incorporated the sphere of legitimate controversy. Yet the range of legitimate opinion stayed within what Edward Herman and Noam Chomsky have called the "bounds of controversy," by "taking for granted that the United States intervened in the service of generous ideals, with the goal of defending South Vietnam from aggression and terrorism and in the interest of democracy and self-determination."[10] Daniel Hallin distinguished journalistic behavior in these two spheres as follows:

> In situations where political consensus seems to prevail, journalists tend to act as "responsible" members of the political establishment, upholding the dominant political perspective and passing on more or less at face value the views of authorities assumed to represent the nation as a whole. In situations of political conflict, they become more detached or even adversarial, though they normally will stay well within the bounds of the debate going on within the political "establishment," and will continue to grant a privileged hearing particularly to senior officials of the executive branch.[11]

The mass media repeatedly facilitated the discourse of good intentions by using official language that not only shielded the public from the sensory realities of the war but sustained a kind of insider groupthink that helped shield officials from the sensory realities of policies they adopted.[12] In one illustrative instance in early 1966, General Maxwell Taylor remarked of civilian suffering caused by B-52 bombing raids notorious for their imprecision: "I would doubt if we would find many of the [bombing strikes] hitting exactly where we would like them to . . . but the over-all effect has been very helpful." Similarly, in words that call to mind the "collateral damage" phrase of the 1991 Gulf War, Taylor described the napalming of Vietnamese children as an "unhappy concomitant" of the air war.[13] Or, as Secretary of Defense Robert McNamara infamously put it, the Rolling Thunder bombing campaign in the North raised a troubling public relations problem because of the "distorted" way most people might view it: "The *picture* of the world's greatest superpower killing or seriously injuring 1000 noncombatants a week, while trying to pound a tiny backward nation into submission on an issue whose merits are hotly disputed, is not a pretty one. It could conceivably produce a costly distortion in the American national consciousness and in the world image of the United States — especially if the damage to North Vietnam is complete enough to be 'successful.'"[14]

From outside the boundaries of legitimate discourse, what McNamara described wasn't a "picture," but a sensory reality that defined the war. As Jonathan Schell put it, what was called the "air war" was "actually . . . a one-sided air slaughter, mostly of civilians."[15] Thus to define it as a public relations problem seemed like a kind of madness, a way of perceiving the world that denied if not reversed reality. These kinds of distinctions characterized the difference between the range of discourse within mass media on the one hand, and the morally anguished, angry discourse occurring in the free spaces of underground or independent media, antiwar rallies, and private conversations outside the boundaries of mass media. For some in the antiwar movement, the contrast between their perspective and those contained within legitimate discourse validated their more radical or systemic criticism.

Beginning around 1962, the voices of war critics—soon called "doves" by the mass media—began to emerge, largely expressing skepticism about the unceasingly upbeat reports on the war's progress coming from officials in the Kennedy administration but also raising questions about the counterproductive effects of support for the repressive Ngo Dinh Diem regime the United States had installed in South Vietnam. As the war escalated, casualties mounted and antiwar protests emerged, doves began to argue that escalation policies were a mistake and that the war was too costly in terms of the lives of U.S. soldiers, social disorder, and damage to the economy. Some doves decried the level of violence the United States unleashed in Vietnam, though these comments tended to emphasize the counterproductive impact of the violence rather than seeing it as the defining feature of the war.

News content within the mass media thereby both legitimized dissent and circumscribed its range. Legitimate dissent spread through the halls of Congress and the op-ed pages of the nation's newspapers as a public debate between "hawks" and "doves" became increasingly prominent. Relatively liberal papers like the *New York Times* and *Washington Post* differed in their editorial positions on the war from more conservative papers like the *Chicago Tribune* and *Wall Street Journal*. Liberal columnists vied almost daily with conservative columnists. The "point of view journalism" of the three prominent newsmagazines meant they blended editorializing into their often colorful news accounts.[16] *Newsweek* began to distinguish itself as the most liberal of the three once it was bought by the *Washington Post* in 1961, and was the most responsive to the younger population's tastes as these became more visible in the media culture. *Time,* traditionally loyal to Republicans, maintained a fairly consistent conservative stance, almost acting as a propaganda mouthpiece for the administration. By about 1967, however, reflecting shifts in public and elite opinion, the magazine was coming to view the war as a stalemate and was quite critical of several Nixon administration policies late in the war. *U.S. News* was consistently conservative, representing the harder right wing of public discourse, early on advocating a more rapid intensification of the military assault in Indochina.[17]

Outside the boundaries of mainstream discourse, however, a very different picture of the war was spreading—fed by stories told by returning soldiers or others who traveled to Vietnam, occasional graphic photographs or televisual glimpses in the mainstream media, reports and commentaries in the independent progressive media, and pamphlets and oratory at antiwar rallies. These sources provided important glimpses into the sensory realities of the war: soldiers' stories or field reporters' accounts contrasted the ferocious tenacity of the Viet Cong guerrillas against the South Vietnamese (ARVN) army's apparent unwillingness to fight; news of the South Vietnamese government's repression undercut rhetoric about freedom and democracy; historical information about the Geneva Convention and U.S. obstruction of reunification elections undermined the war's propaganda argument; and exposure of administration lies about the popular support for the South Vietnamese government, the sources of Viet Cong weaponry, and North Vietnamese "aggression" in the Gulf of Tonkin eroded the government's credibility.

These and other stories opened the door to recognition that the original Viet Minh and the later National Liberation Front were guerrilla-based struggles for national self-determination against successive external invaders: the French, the Japanese, and the Americans. They revealed that civilian noncombatants were routinely victimized as U.S. troops sought to find and destroy the forces that were widely supported by and hidden among the civilian population and as massive air power wreaked unfathomable destruction. According to the *Encyclopedia of the Vietnam War*, "From 1962 through 1973, the U.S. dropped nearly 8 million tons of bombs on Vietnam, Laos, and Cambodia. South Vietnam received about half that tonnage, making it the most bombed country in the history of aerial warfare"[18]—more than doubling the total tonnage dropped by the Allies during the entire Second World War. These kinds of perceptions not only produced antiwar criticism, but also generated disbelief in, if not emphatic condemnation of, the government's justification for the war. By contrast, in James Landers's account, the news media "remained generally uncritical towards military operations in Vietnam until autumn 1967"—when Secretary Robert McNamara and the *Wall Street Journal,* among others, were becoming convinced the war was not "winnable." In the aftermath of the Tet Offensive in 1968, the media adopted the same "more critical tone" about the war's progress that was being expressed privately by government policy makers.[19]

The antiwar movement was energized by moral horror at what many increasingly saw as a war of U.S. aggression against a tiny nation that posed no threat to the United States, aggression that unleashed unspeakable levels of violence against a largely impoverished civilian population. In effect, many in the moralistic antiwar movement asked: "Does the United States have the right to intervene in Vietnam?" and answered with a resounding "No!" Within legitimate discourse, even raising such a question was unimaginable. Such a right of intervention was simply assumed.

Viewing the war as illegitimate and unjustifiable was, in effect, a step toward a more radical comprehension of the U.S. role in the world, though many antiwar activists never developed such a comprehension, at least while the war was raging. A radical comprehension of the war saw U.S. military aggression as a concomitant of the United States consciously pursuing an American-dominated global system designed to provide stable and ready access to the economic resources of the underdeveloped world. In effect, a radical argument, like other antiwar arguments, represented a reversal of mainstream ideology—namely, that the economic imperative of seeking a good investment climate in Third World nations contradicted the essence of democracy because it required governments in these nations to pursue policies that inherently frustrated the aspirations of the mass of people, generating the kind of unrest and insurgencies that were then put down by repressive anticommunist regimes.[20] From inside the realm of conventional ideology, market investments are viewed as helping the people of these nations, and communist uprisings were by definition imposed by ruthless outsiders following orders from Moscow. From outside the boundaries of conventional ideology, the uprisings were called "communist" for propaganda reasons, whether or not they were led by or connected to communist parties, whereas insurgencies largely arise because of the repressive conditions and human suffering caused by the regimes and the exploitative policies required to maintain a good climate for international investment. The greatest threat to capitalist hegemony came from the prospect of Third World nations withdrawing from the system, as they would if they were to follow a model of development independent of the U.S.-dominated system, particularly if they were to become part of the pro-Soviet orbit.

Variously expressed, this perspective was, and has remained, consistently inaccessible through the mainstream media, though the war in Vietnam caused many to begin to see this imperial imperative behind U.S. policy making. Inside the boundaries of mainstream discourse, radical arguments were quickly dismissed as pro-Soviet arguments, even though most radical critics were highly critical of both the domestic oppression and imperial ambitions of the Soviet Union.[21] By downplaying or shielding the public from the extensive and brutal sensory realities produced by U.S. policies, the mass media reinforce system-sustaining ideologies.

While causing successive administrations significant political discomfort through its war coverage and airing of dissent and criticism, media coverage of the war from 1962 right down to the present day has consistently upheld the legitimate purpose of U.S. intervention—precisely the point the antiwar movement came to vehemently dispute. Yet media discourse has consistently treated arguments and evidence that the war was illegitimate as themselves illegitimate, if not anti-American. During the war, it did so through the boundaries of its own legitimate discourse on the war and in the ways it covered antiwar protest in the sphere of deviance.

The Spheres of Consensus and Legitimate Controversy

From the earliest U.S. support for French colonial reentry into Indochina after World War II until the erosion of the Diem regime in 1962–63, the mythic reality of American postwar culture provided the context for media coverage. One early study of that coverage in four major newspapers concluded,

> It was in the 1950s, not the 1960s, that this distant and undeclared war became established in the minds of both the public and public officials as a showdown between the forces of Communism and anti-Communism, vital to the "free world." . . . What the press did to help establish these views is important. . . . The press echoed the administration in its definition of the Indochinese situation. In only one instance was the basic assumption of underlying United States policy questioned. The terms of the debate hardened at a very early stage in policymaking, and remained constant throughout. . . . Much of the information gathered by the press . . . was administration-sponsored, directly or indirectly.[22]

Within mass media, support for American policy was simply unquestioned, framed by Cold War perceptions, an American ideology of "modernization,"[23] and broader Western ethnocentrism and racism.[24] This belief system may be chronically costly given that the vast U.S. superiority of military force and high-tech weaponry clouds the vision of decision makers, who fail to perceive the counterproductive political impact of using these weapons, thereby exacerbating the fact that the United States often intervenes on the wrong if not ultimately the losing side of popular political struggles in much of the underdeveloped world.

In Cold War media discourse, communists were by definition the aggressors, thus reducing the fervidly anticolonial, communist-led Viet Minh to the role of "puppet" or "satellite" for the "world Communist conspiracy." The 1945 Vietnamese declaration of independence that quoted the anticolonial U.S. Declaration was thereby framed as a product of the Japanese occupation during World War II.[25] Partition of Vietnam during the 1954 Geneva Convention was seen as a compromise forced upon "the Vietnamese" and "the Vietnamese Government"—meaning the West's client regime in the South—by the belligerent aggressors, the anticolonial, communist-led Viet Minh forces.[26] Sensory realities in Vietnam—from the widespread anticolonial sentiment and popular support for Ho Chi Minh to the tens of thousands of civilian casualties in the South under the U.S.-backed Diem regime—were essentially invisible in mainstream news reporting. The major U.S. role in establishing, arming, training, and supporting the repressive Diem regime in the South was absent except as it was imbued with American "democratic" intentions.

The ideological construction of the noble defense of South Vietnam against aggression from the North relied on the public invisibility of the formative U.S. role in creating the entity called South Vietnam by obstructing internationally sanctioned reunification elections. U.S. obstruction of democracy in Vietnam thereby disappeared into the black hole of media memory. As Marilyn Young wrote in her historical account of the war, "What could not be acknowledged was that Vietnam was one country, that the war in the South was between contending Vietnamese forces, the weaker of which had in large measure been created by the United States itself, and that it was to ensure the triumph of its creation that . . . American combat troops were fighting in Vietnam."[27] Defense against aggression, then, became the linchpin of government propaganda about the war from 1956 onward, repeatedly echoed in media discourse. The notion that the Vietnamese forces were struggling to reunify their country in the face of Western intervention was inadmissible in mainstream discourse, even as it animated some of the more colorful expressions of antiwar protests.

The pattern of legitimate controversy about the war became apparent in the early years of elite dissent as first John Kennedy and then Lyndon Johnson escalated the war as a way to reverse the failure of previous policies. By 1960, repression by the highly unpopular Diem triggered the formation of the National Liberation Front, consisting of a variety of South Vietnamese dissident groups headed by former Viet Minh operatives in the South. President Diem labeled the groups the Viet Cong, a pejorative for Vietnamese communists.[28] The Kennedy years saw a sharp escalation of U.S. military power unleashed against the growing unrest in the South. The Strategic Hamlet program forcibly relocated peasants into barbed-wire camps, leaving the remaining countryside, including their home villages, a "free fire zone" where American pilots ("advisors") and their South Vietnamese clients engaged in massive bombing, defoliation, crop destruction, and napalm attacks, resulting in tens of thousands of civilian casualties.[29]

Perceiving a contradiction between U.S. policy and political opinion in South Vietnam, a few voices of critical dissent began to emerge, ranging from Senate Majority Leader Mike Mansfield and well-placed academics like Hans Morgenthau and John Kenneth Galbraith to outsiders like the radical pacifist A. J. Muste and linguist Noam Chomsky, Trotskyists from the Socialist Workers Party, religious pacifists from the Fellowship of Reconciliation or American Friends Service Committee, activists from Women Strike for Peace, and youth-dominated organizations like SNCC and SDS.

While most news reports during this time emphasized U.S. gains in the effort to save South Vietnam from communist aggression, a few reports cast doubt on the effectiveness of U.S. policy. *New York Times* correspondent Homer Bigart penned a lengthy analysis in July 1962 under the pro-government headline, "Vietnam Victory Remote Despite U.S. Aide to Diem," suggesting that Diem seemed "incapable of winning the loyalty of his people" and raising questions about the "combat effectiveness" of the South Vietnamese military.[30] A few weeks later in *Newsweek,* François Sully reported the "unpleasant truth" about the war: it seemed to be a "losing proposition."[31] Both news accounts were cast in the prevailing frame of U.S. policy: defending South Vietnam against aggression from the North. In fact, Bigart's lengthy piece noted that there seemed valid grounds for U.S. optimism as long as the Viet Cong did not receive substantial outside aid—referring, of course, to the alleged foreign aggressors in the North. As Daniel Hallin has documented, despite clashes between Saigon reporters and their New York editors, news reporting during this period "all took place within the narrow confines of a tight consensus on the nature of world politics and the American role in it; none brought into question the premise that the preservation of an anti-Communist Vietnam was indeed a legitimate goal of the United States."[32]

Glowing administration reports of "turning the corner" in South Vietnam seemed sharply contradicted by front-page photographs of a burgeoning Buddhist revolt against Diem, personified by the images of Buddhist monks' self-immolation on the streets of Saigon. While the searing images were a catalyst to antiwar voices and more open criticism of U.S. policy within independent media like the *Nation* and the *New Republic,* mainstream discourse was couched in terms of "Diem's intransigence" that "troubled the U.S." and reassertion of the "good intentions" argument—that the United States would insist on "prompt action" to remedy Buddhist claims of "discrimination."[33]

In the wake of the Kennedy assassination, after a U.S.-backed coup had toppled the unpopular Diem, Lyndon Johnson and officials of the Kennedy team faced a familiar and recurring dilemma. If a South Vietnamese regime was repressive and unleashed violence against the South Vietnamese countryside, it would only exacerbate popular resistance; on the other hand, if the regime sought a broader base of popularity among the South Vietnamese people, it would have to move toward some kind of rapprochement with the forces of resistance. Since the latter was consistently equated with losing Vietnam to the communists, it was considered unacceptable, if not outright unimaginable.

In fact, successive South Vietnamese governments were showing increasing signs of willingness to move toward some form of neutralization or rapprochement with the guerrillas in the South—a major concern for U.S. policy makers. The way out of the dilemma, the administration decided, was to plan for a sustained escalation of the war in the South and aerial bombardment of North Vietnam. As George Kahin concluded in his detailed study of U.S. intervention, "The conviction that bombing the North would strengthen the morale of the faltering Saigon government and its resolve to continue fighting the Viet Cong was clearly a major factor" underlying the administration's post–Tonkin Gulf air strike and congressional resolution.[34] However, since the attack against the North would take the war into new territory—and, according to mythic reality, another nation—the administration needed to present a persuasive rationale for its escalation. Events in the Gulf of Tonkin off the coast of North Vietnam provided the administration with the pretext for escalating the war. As the administration presented its account, North Vietnamese patrol boats subjected U.S. destroyers that were on "routine patrol in international waters" to a "deliberate and unprovoked attack," in Defense Secretary McNamara's words.[35] The mass media and almost the entire Congress accepted the administration's account in full, thereby leading to passage of the Gulf of Tonkin Resolution that legitimized the planned escalation of the war.

In sensory reality, however, the destroyers had been cruising in North Vietnamese waters as part of OPlan 34A covert operations—U.S.-backed South Vietnamese commando raids against coastal North Vietnam. In addition, two days before the "unprovoked attack," South Vietnamese gunboats carried out heavy raids against two islands in North Vietnamese waters. On August 2, as the *Maddox* approached these same islands, three North Vietnamese PT boats repeatedly sped toward the *Maddox* in V-formation, then rapidly veered off. Viewing themselves under attack, the *Maddox* opened fire and the PT boats responded by firing torpedoes that missed the destroyer. Damaged by the *Maddox*'s guns, the PT boats retreated. A second "attack," later found to be entirely unsubstantiated, was said to have occurred on August 4. Announcing retaliatory raids against North Vietnam's "supporting facilities," President Johnson denounced the North's "open aggression on the high seas," but reassured his audience that the United States sought "no wider war."[36]

New York Times reports of the Tonkin incidents were based exclusively on administration sources. The *Times* editorialized that the attack "is now seen in ominous perspective to have been the beginning of a mad adventure by the North Vietnamese Communists." Confirming the *Times*' myopia about which side was engaging in "mad adventure," the paper also dismissed "Senator [Wayne] Morse's charge that [the Resolution] conveys a 'blanket authority to wage war'"[37]—precisely its actual effect.

The *Times* also printed editorial commentaries from twenty-eight newspapers around the country, unanimously supporting the Johnson administration, expressing indignation at the "unprovoked attack," speculating about "Red Chinese" intentions to "test our resolve," and warning that "if the [Reds] seek a wider war, they can have it."[38]

Provocative actions by the United States and/or the South Vietnamese were virtually invisible in the media throughout the crisis. *Time* detailed the administration's "measured and fitting response" in a three-page, action-filled account, while *Newsweek* devoted seven pages to an article supporting the government titled "Vietnam: 'We Seek No Wider War.'"[39] The hawkish *U.S. News & World Report* framed the attack as a Vietnamese provocation that legitimized full-scale war on the part of the United States and warned ominously that Ho Chi Minh would have to "think long and hard about any action that might lead to his country's being blown apart by U.S. bombings." The *U.S. News* report also displayed a photograph of Communist Chinese troops, asking if China was "looking for a pretext to intervene openly" in Vietnam.[40]

Sentiment in Congress followed suit. The House passed the administration's resolution unanimously, and the Senate passed it with only Senators Wayne Morse of Oregon and Ernest Gruening of Alaska voting against it. Senator J. William Fulbright, who floor-managed the resolution for the administration, later bitterly resented the administration's "lies" that led to his support—lies about the provocation for the August 2 attack, the existence of the August 4 attack, and the absence of any intention of pursuing a "wider war."[41] Quite clearly, the Johnson administration had effectively manipulated perceptions in Congress and the media to view the Tonkin events as unprovoked aggression by the North and the administration's response as "limited and fitting," as President Johnson put it. Not surprisingly, a Harris poll showed Johnson's popularity surging from 42 to 72 percent in the wake of the Tonkin incident, while support for his Vietnam policies rose from 58 to 85 percent.[42]

As the United States took steps toward implementing the plan for sustained bombing of North Vietnam ("Operation Rolling Thunder"), the administration needed to prepare public opinion for bombing that went beyond the "reprisal" air strikes carried out after the Tonkin events—the latter referred to by the *Times'* liberal columnist Tom Wicker as stepped up "U.S. resistance to Vietcong infiltration."[43] A campaign of sustained bombing threatened to draw widespread public criticism—as, indeed, it did. Thus, before Rolling Thunder got under way, the administration released a "White Paper" on February 27, 1965, designed to legitimize the escalated U.S. bombing campaign by placing it in the context of what it termed a "Communist program of conquest" directed against a "sovereign people in a neighboring state" of South Vietnam.[44]

Noting that "it is important for free men to know what has been happening in Vietnam," the White Paper cited evidence of voluminous Soviet-bloc weaponry used by the Viet Cong, arguing that South Vietnam was "fighting for its life against a brutal campaign of terror and armed attack inspired, directed, supplied, and controlled by the Communist regime in Hanoi." It also added ominously that "recently the pace had quickened, and the threat has now become active."[45] The *New York Times* report was headlined "U.S. White Paper Brands Hanoi as an 'Aggressor' and Hints at Air Attacks." Max Frankel's article summarized the White Paper's arguments and reported extensively on its documentation of "more sophisticated" enemy weapons.[46] Despite an earlier *Times* report that the majority of Viet Cong weapons were American-made and "captured in battle from South Vietnamese forces,"[47] the *Times* article—as well as the newsmagazine reports—contained not a word of skepticism about the alleged weaponry.

Outside the bounds of mainstream mass media, however, a different story was being related. Analyzing the government's own evidence in his independently published weekly newsletter, journalist I. F. Stone exposed the government's claims as propaganda. Noting that "none of [the evidence] is discussed frankly in the White Paper," for "to do so would be to bring the war into focus as a rebellion in the South," Stone contended that the rebellion "is largely dependent on popular indigenous support for its manpower, as it is on captured U.S. weapons for its supply."[48] The small-circulation *New Republic* led its story on the White Paper by noting, "The best that can be said about the State Department's White Paper on Vietnam is that it is entirely unconvincing. The worst is that it is contradictory, illogical, and misleading. It has a desperate purpose: to prepare the moral platform for widening the war."[49]

Shortly after Rolling Thunder began, the first units of U.S. Marine combat troops were deployed to South Vietnam, purportedly to defend U.S. air bases used in operations against both the North and South. As with bombing "reprisals," troop deployments were limited in size to minimize the public perception that the administration was undertaking a major escalation. By late spring 1965, the United States had 56,000 soldiers in Vietnam, significantly more than the 39,517 "communist infiltrators" from the North, most of whom were returning to their homes in the South.[50]

Thus 1965 marked the beginning of what the mass media have referred to ever since as the "Vietnam War" against North Vietnam, since everything prior to 1965 is framed as a crisis that the United States was trying to help the South Vietnamese resolve. Nonetheless, as the veteran French journalist Bernard Fall noted at the time, "what changed the character of the Vietnam war was *not* the decision to bomb North Vietnam; *not* the decision to use American ground troops in South Vietnam; but the decision to wage unlimited aerial warfare inside the country [of South Vietnam] at the price of literally pounding the place to bits."[51] The substantial escalation brought antiwar protest to a significant level of visibility within the mass media.

From this time forward, the war continued to escalate as more and more American troops were deployed amidst never-ending government proclamations that these escalations and deployments were the fix needed to ensure the success of the United States' noble endeavor. Yet the public grew increasingly skeptical over time, and the antiwar movement that emerged in 1965 became, itself, part of the news story about Vietnam, albeit in a sphere of deviance distinct and separated from legitimate discourse about the war.

Antiwar Activism: The Sphere of Deviance

The newly escalated war in Vietnam, in particular the bombing of North Vietnam, was the catalyst that ushered in an unprecedented eight-year span of turbulent antiwar activity on the part of the American citizenry, echoed by huge antiwar mobilizations in much of Europe and elsewhere. From the earliest national mobilization in April 1965 through the infamous Christmas bombing of 1972, significant mass mobilizations against the war occurred virtually every spring and fall. In addition, uncountable numbers of local or campus actions occurred in this era: silent vigils, street-corner or campus rallies, pickets, door-to-door canvassing, poetry readings, concerts, religious services, marches, sit-ins, street theater, building takeovers, draft resistance, draft board actions, troop-train obstructions, highway obstructions, war crime trials and Winter Soldier hearings, acts of sabotage, and bombings of targeted buildings. One study of *New York Times*–covered protests counted more than 750 distinct demonstrations involving more than 2,250,000 protesters from 1964 through 1971, with "little slackening off in 1971."[52]

As distinct from the southern civil rights movement, the antiwar movement faced the strategic problem of how to raise public consciousness and mobilize public sympathies against a distant war that was reinforced by long-established beliefs about the U.S. role in the world, especially when many of the war's sensory realities remained clouded by legitimate media discourse. And, of course, public officials and media alike were prone, in their own ways, to denigrate antiwar claims. Finally, while social movements of the 1960s were generally decentralized and highly diverse, the antiwar movement was particularly so. Initially, groups that were predisposed to view the war critically ranged from longstanding religious-based pacifists like the American Friends Service Committee and Fellowship of Reconciliation to dissenting academics to various leftist sects like the Socialist Workers Party.[53] Student-based groups that opposed the war, notably SDS and SNCC, were themselves highly decentralized and largely inclined to focus on issues other than the war. Although the large national mobilizations were organized by variously named coalitions of these and other groups, antiwar actions were frequently generated by locally based, even spontaneous groups targeting local, war-related practices, often off the national media's radar. Seeking tangible connections to the war, activists often confronted or resisted Selective Service practices, and students targeted university recruitment and research activities. Individuals, small groups, and local factions could freely express their own antiwar agendas and were constantly searching for new ways to get their message through so as to expose the war's real costs.

Eventually the war convulsed college campuses and local communities. As Jerome Skolnick wrote in 1969, "the antiwar movement is not a fixed group of people; it is something that has been happening to America." The report went on to note that "demonstrations" were "typically an *outcome* of events uncontrolled by the movement. Moreover, it is usually the response to the demonstration that catapults it . . . into the status of an 'event.'"[54] The media were free to choose what kinds of actions they found newsworthy, and given the media penchant for dramatic storytelling, highly imagistic and conflictual actions came to represent the antiwar movement in the public's eye.

While the media sphere of legitimate controversy grew more agitated over the war, in part because the protests helped to make the war a continuing public issue, the antiwar movements' arguments about the war's purpose and morality remained "unworthy of being heard."[55] Protests were repeatedly denigrated by both political officials and media commentators at the same time that U.S. escalation of the war sharpened moral outrage among antiwar people. There remained no place in mass media's public discourse for the evidence and explanation that formed the core arguments of the antiwar movement. As the war escalated, as the government denigrated them, and as the media belittled their meaning, antiwar alienation and frustration would grow apace.

The most comprehensive study of media coverage of the antiwar movement, Melvin Small's *Covering Dissent,* reviewed accounts of major national protests in the *New York Times,* the *Washington Post,* available major network telecasts, *Time* and *Newsweek,* two Michigan dailies, and two independent, left-leaning weeklies, the *Village Voice* and the *National Guardian.* Of the mainstream mass media, Small noted that "time and time again, those who reported major antiwar demonstrations concentrated on violent and radical—albeit colorful—behavior on the fringes of the [antiwar] activity, undercounted the crowds, and ignored political arguments the protesters' leadership presented. In addition, because of a misapplication of the 'fairness doctrine,' especially on television, journalists bent over backwards to present the views and activities of counterdemonstrators and administration spokespersons in order to balance those of the doves."[56] By comparison, Small discovered that "much to my astonishment" the "treatment of antiwar demonstrations" in the *Village Voice* and the *Guardian* "was often more detailed, accurate, and objective, if more breezy, than that of the seven mainstream sources I previously analyzed."[57]

Media framing of antiwar protest activity began with the first major national protest on April 17, 1965, organized by SDS in Washington, D.C., and attended by 20,000 or more protesters. Among the many speakers at the rally, Senator Ernest Gruening traced the war's history, Yale historian Staughton Lynd explained the parallels between the American Vietnam experience and the French experience in Algeria, I. F. Stone detailed the administration's many policy errors in Vietnam, Robert Moses linked the war to the civil rights struggle, and SDS president Paul Potter moved the crowd with an eloquent radical critique of the war. Potter urged the protesters to "name the system" responsible for the war and oppression in the South and called for a social movement of "people who are willing to change their lives, who are willing to challenge the system, to take the problem of change seriously."[58] Folksingers Joan Baez, Phil Ochs, Judy Collins, and the Freedom Voices provided politically charged music throughout the rally.

Media coverage of the event set the tone for the years that followed, though in this case none of the national newsmagazines covered the protest. According to Small's account, CBS aired a report on the Saturday evening of the protest but focused primarily on the White House picketing rather than the larger rally, highlighted the "beatnik-like" characteristics of protesters, and gave almost as much attention to the tiny group of counter-protesters. Both the *New York Times* and *Washington Post* provided such minimal coverage of the rally that, as Small put it, "it was difficult to determine just what policies, short of opposition to the war," the speakers advocated, despite the fact that their speeches represented "thoughtful and rather sophisticated critiques of administration foreign policy."[59] Both papers undercounted the crowd and overplayed the presence of students and youths in the crowd. The *Times* highlighted the appearances and behavior of four participants, noting that in general "beards and blue jeans mixed hand in hand, and several girls pushed baby carriages."[60]

Todd Gitlin has elaborated on ways the *Times* coverage distorted the protest. First, the dismissive treatment of SDS stood in sharp contrast to a *Times* article written by Fred Powledge a month earlier about "The Student Left—Spurring Reform." Powledge's piece drew on substantial interaction with students on several campuses, contained excerpts from SDS's Port Huron Statement, and, in Gitlin's words, "conveyed respect and a certain distanced sympathy." Nothing of the sort emerged in media accounts of the first major antiwar demonstration in the United States in decades. By comparison, the *Guardian* report headlined its story, somewhat hyperbolically, "The Greatest Peace Demonstration in American History," and printed long excerpts from the speeches of Staughton Lynd and Paul Potter. As Gitlin observed,

The *Times* piece *deprecated* the size and significance of the march (the photo, the reference to "the principal occupant in the White House"); *marginalized* it by identifying it with youthful deviance ("a handful of adults," "a number of their elders," "beards and jeans"); *trivialized* it by failing to cover the call, the picket signs, or the speeches; and *polarized* it to its ostensible right-wing equivalent by choosing a wire-service photo that likened Left to Right. The frame was also *generational*. Meanwhile, the story failed to report politically significant interracialism or internal divisions within the movement.[61]

Noting that the *Guardian* compared the *Times* article to *Times* coverage of the 25,000-person civil rights march in Selma three weeks before, Gitlin commented, "It is fair to conclude, as the *Guardian* did, that opposition to the Vietnam war was as illegitimate for the *Times* as civil rights was legitimate. . . . Strikingly, in important ways, the *Times* was covering demonstrations as the Johnson administration saw the world."[62] He concluded, "It would be *de rigueur* to observe that the *Guardian* coverage was ideological. The *Times'* coverage was no less so."[63]

After the April demonstration, campus "teach-ins" that began at the University of Michigan in March spread to upward of fifty campuses across the country, highlighted by the televised national teach-in on May 15 in Washington, D.C., and a protest-oriented teach-in attended by over twenty thousand people on the Berkeley campus a week later. After reporting on several of the campus teach-ins, the *Times* anticipated later antiwar coverage with its lead on the Berkeley teach-in: "At 12:55 A.M. this morning a bleary-eyed, bearded young man whose gray sweatshirt bore the inscription 'Let's Make Love, Not War,' stretched out on the grass outside the Student Union and went to sleep in the darkness."[64] Many *Times* reports were perfunctory notices. Some focused on threats or protests against the teach-ins; others, like a *New York Times Magazine* article about an Oregon teach-in, conveyed some of the substance of the debates being held.

Over the late spring and summer of 1965, as the administration deployed an additional 50,000 U.S. troops to Vietnam and increased draft calls, it sought to control whatever public relations damage the spring protest and teach-ins might have inflicted. The FBI began infiltrating SDS chapters and prepared a memo linking SDS to communism. The administration recruited supportive students to tour Vietnam and speak in various locales around the country, created a propaganda film, "Why Vietnam?" and mobilized official support for the American Friends of Vietnam.[65] Despite these efforts, early polls from May 1965 to March 1966 revealed that about 25 percent of the public felt that the deployment of U.S. troops in Vietnam was a mistake.[66] Antiwar activities continued to spread during the summer months, occasionally breaking into mass media discourse. In August, Americans got a rare glimpse of the ground war's dark side as a CBS segment documented American marines igniting the thatched roofs of Vietnamese village dwellings.[67]

The mass media took more significant notice of the "International Days of Protest" organized for October 15–16. Rallies and various small-scale actions occurred in eighty cities across the United States, the largest in New York and Berkeley/Oakland, California. Anticipating the fall events, press reports zeroed in on plans for so-called "student demonstrations." An October 4 *New York Times* article mentioned the plans in the context of the Berkeley police chief's references to alleged "student riots" and "revolutionary activity" that had occurred at the University of California campus during the previous year's Free Speech Movement. The chief warned that "individuals dedicated to the promotion of Communist ideology" (a regularly recurring distortion) would seek to direct and benefit from "youthful restlessness."[68] In response to a late October–early November Gallup poll question about communist involvement in antiwar demonstrations, 58 percent felt the communists were involved "a lot" and another 20 percent felt they were "somewhat" involved.[69]

Media coverage of the fall protest continued the patterns that characterized press coverage the previous spring: undercounting the protest size, "balancing" protesters and counter-protesters, ambiguously highlighting whatever violence occurred (though it was initiated by counter-protesters), and framing the stories with dismissive statements from public officials. In Small's account, "more than half the [*Washington*] *Post*'s copy dealt with hecklers, paint-throwing, and scuffles in New York and California that attained 'near-riot proportions,'" while the paper simultaneously counted only 10,000 marchers (instead of 20,000–25,000).[70] Todd Gitlin noted that the *Times*' "roundup story" on October 16 "devoted one-third of forty-two paragraphs to counter-demonstrators or to administration statements," whereas its page-two story on Senator John Stennis's attack on SDS contained no SDS response. He also noted that, like the *Times*, CBS "emphasized *violence, counterdemonstrations,* and *official statements.*"[71]

The newsmagazines also covered the weekend's activities in telling fashion. *Newsweek* eagerly pronounced the movement's obituary, labeling the total national turnout of 100,000 as disappointing to the movement (though providing no evidence of this) and speculating that the antiwar movement may have reached its "saturation point." The magazine also included Senator Thomas Dodd's charge that the protests were "communist-run."[72] *Time* derided the demonstrators as "a ragtag collection of unshaven and unscrubbed—they could be called Vietniks," a disparaging term, like "peaceniks," that the magazine would use to describe antiwar protesters for years to come. The magazine also suggested inaccurately that the weekend's protests brought out more counter-protesters than actual demonstrators.[73] Both *Time* and the *New York Times* simultaneously speculated that the war in Vietnam had reached a positive "turning point" for American policy.

Again, none of the media accounts paid significant attention to the content of rally speeches about the war, though both the *Guardian* and *Village Voice* published lengthy excerpts from one or two of the speeches. For its part, the conservative weekly the *National Review* headlined its article on the International Days of Protest "Day the Vietcong Attacked the United States."[74]

In a dismissive October op-ed titled "The Stupidity of Intelligence," the *Times* chief Washington columnist, James Reston, patronized the antiwar movement in his lead paragraph:

> It is not easy, but let us assume that all the student demonstrators against the war in Vietnam are everything they say they are: sincerely for an honorable peace; troubled by the bombing of the civil population of both North and South Vietnam; genuinely afraid that we may be trapped into a hopeless war with China; and worried about the power of the President and the Pentagon and the pugnacious bawling patriotism of many influential men in the Congress.

Then, apparently feeling he had generously represented the protesters, he continued, "A case can be made for it. In a world of accidents and nuclear weapons and damn fools, even a dreaming pacifist has to be answered." Reflecting the Johnson administration's view, Reston argued that the presumably naïve protesters were

> inadvertently working against all the things they want . . . they are not
> creating peace but postponing it . . . not persuading the President or
> Congress to end the war, but deceiving Ho Chi Minh and General Giap into
> prolonging it. They are not proving the superior wisdom of the university
> community but unfortunately bringing it into serious question.

Reston took pains to distance his establishment perspective from Senator Stennis's rightist demand that the administration "pull up the anti-draft movement 'by the roots and grind it to bits.'" At the same time that the United States was escalating the war, Reston argued that the demonstrators were "protesting not against the nation that is continuing the war, but against their own country that is offering to make peace."[75]

The War and Antiwar Movement Take
Center Stage

By the end of 1965, the number of U.S. ground troops in Vietnam had swollen to 184,000. Draft calls increased dramatically in 1966. Over the next three and a half years, the American fighting force in Vietnam grew to 550,000, while the aerial bombardment of South Vietnam, North Vietnam, Laos, and Cambodia became increasingly savage. In contrast to *Newsweek*'s hopeful prediction that antiwar protest was at a "saturation point," from 1965 to 1970, national antiwar protests grew in size and militancy, and local actions became almost a commonplace on or near the nation's campuses. Protesters' appearances became increasingly bedraggled as trappings of the counterculture spread from 1967 on.

In 1966, a draft resistance movement emerged, and public opinion began to shift away from support for the administration's war.[76] Whereas in March, 25 percent felt the United States had "made a mistake in sending troops to fight in Vietnam," that number grew to 35 percent in September 1966, 41 percent in July 1967, and 46 percent in October 1967.[77] Some media reports were beginning to refer openly to the war as a "stalemate." By late 1967, important elements of the political and economic elite believed the war could not be won without endangering national political and economic stability, and antiwar sentiment had spread throughout much of American society. Whether horrified by the continuing carnage of the war, alienated by government lies and a war that wasn't working, or weary of the growing social unrest—or all of the above—by 1968 a majority of Americans wanted the war to end. By late 1969, an unprecedented antiwar movement among war veterans and active-duty soldiers was growing. Yet the war machine ground on and on and on, to the continuing horror of antiwar activists and much of the public.

Through it all, the media remained fixated on the deviant characteristics of antiwar protesters, with the single exception of the nationwide October 1969 Moratorium.[78] The manifestation of protests—their appearance, their intensity, their militancy, their size—was newsworthy, but never what they said about the war. As with the racial movement, mass media coverage was both drawn to violence yet fundamentally critical of any form of social disorder. It also provided a ready forum for legitimate voices of officialdom to condemn or explain the antiwar activists in mainstreamese. Conservative voices repeatedly denounced the protests as communist, communist-inspired, or communist-organized, without producing a shred of evidence at any point. Sometimes joining in these blanket denunciations, Johnson administration liberals and their supporters like James Reston were quick to denounce the protests as "aiding the enemy" and "extending the war" even as the war administration was "working for peace."

Nineteen sixty-six was notable for legislative hearings held by the Senate Foreign Relations Committee, presided over by Senator J. William Fulbright. As a traditional arena for legitimate debate and dissent, the hearings provided the media dramatic coverage that included among other things gentle critiques of administration policy from General James M. Gavin and longtime diplomat George Kennan—all within a framework of containing communism. With almost 60 percent of the public viewing at least some of the hearings, they "made dissent legitimate for many observers," in Melvin Small's words, much like the Eugene McCarthy presidential campaign did in 1968. The media covered the hearings "fairly, fully, and prominently," according to Small, and "no other antiwar activity, if one can call it that, was treated so well by the press."[79]

By contrast, coverage of the spring mobilizations reverted to the usual formula. Despite the fact that protests were even more peaceful and slightly larger than the fall Days of Protest, and whatever violence occurred was again instigated by counterdemonstrators, the media emphasized violence without attribution and juxtaposed coverage of antiwar deviance with upbeat or sympathetic accounts of the war's progress. The *Times* observed that the parade was "marked by sporadic violence and egg-throwing," and described a "fist-swinging melee" that occurred when a "group of youths carried the orange, gold, and blue flag of the National Liberation Front, the political arm of the Vietcong" past a group of "young men" from the American Legion and the Veterans of Foreign Wars.[80]

Newsweek opened its report with an even more damning juxtaposition: "As US troops score a succession of fresh victories in Vietnam, peace groups in the U.S. doggedly cranked up" demonstrations full of "strident marchers."[81] As Small observed, the protests, for once, "did better in *Time,* which simply ignored the Days of Protest." Overall, "Unless the crowds grew larger or their activities became more unusual, they did not impress. Journalists paid less attention to the antiwar movement during the spring of 1966 than they had during the fall of 1965 when it was more novel."[82]

In late 1966 and early 1967, legitimate sources provided the public with a glimpse of the war that either expressed or corroborated antiwar views. As noted in chapter 4, Martin Luther King Jr.'s condemnation of the war was instantly followed by a chorus of denunciation by the major national media. Something similar occurred when widely esteemed *New York Times* journalist Harrison Salisbury visited Hanoi and filed reports on the civilian deaths and destruction of nonmilitary sites caused by U.S. bombing at the end of 1966. In Daniel Hallin's words, Salisbury's reports "treated the North Vietnamese as though they belonged to the Sphere of Legitimate Controversy, summarizing their views as a Washington reporter might summarize those of American officials"—whereas, typically, the media "painted an almost one-dimensional image of the Vietnamese and Vietcong as cruel, ruthless, and fanatical," clearly assigning them to the "sphere of deviance."[83]

Salisbury's dispatches raised far from trivial concerns, since his report that the United States was bombing the dikes in North Vietnam revealed that the United States was violating international agreements pertaining to war crimes and crimes against humanity.[84] Predictably, the rebuttals were swift and outspoken. Salisbury's *Times* colleague Harrison Baldwin cited "virtually unanimous" military officials "in all the services" proclaiming the effectiveness of U.S. bombing strategy and disputing the North Vietnamese estimates reported by Salisbury as "grossly exaggerated." Baldwin also cited sources who belittled the dike-bombing charge, though later information revealed extensive U.S. bombing of the dikes in North Vietnam.[85] In direct contradiction of the Geneva Conventions, CIA director Richard Helms observed, "The idea that we mustn't bomb the dikes because that will kill a lot of innocent civilians, . . . we mustn't mine harbors because that may kill innocent civilians—this whole idea is one of the reasons I believe history will find that we were unsuccessful in the war. . . . *Wars are not pleasant affairs.*"[86] The *Washington Post*'s story on the Salisbury reports was titled "Hanoi Seen Exploiting Civilian Casualties" and parroted the administration's response. The State Department's *American Opinion Survey* "accurately noted that the majority of the press was more anti-Salisbury than anti-bombing but that the administration had taken a hit for its lack of credibility."[87]

Shortly after the *Times* published Salisbury's dispatches, it published a report that underscored the damaging potential such mass media revelations posed. A group of student body presidents and campus editors from 100 college campuses signed an open letter to President Johnson warning that the United States might "find some of her most loyal and courageous young people choosing to go to jail rather than bear their country's arms." The students commented on their "growing sense—reinforced by Mr. Harrison Salisbury's recent reports from Hanoi—that too often there is a wide disparity between American statements about Vietnam and American actions there."[88]

By 1967, dissent was widespread and gaining a new cast of legitimacy in wider arenas of American life. Yet the war, administration intransigence, and mass media framing of dissent continued unabated. A spring mobilization in New York and San Francisco generated what was at the time the largest antiwar demonstration in American history. More than 200,000 turned out for a rally in Central Park, which included a countercultural "Be-In," an organized draft card burning by about 170 young men, and a parade from the park to a rally at the United Nations that was addressed by Martin Luther King Jr., Stokely Carmichael, and other black leaders. Another 60,000 turned out for the San Francisco rally. However, despite the numbers and the peaceful rally, the *New York Times* again played up the violence ("eggs tossed at parade") and the presence of counterdemonstrators. A front-page photo showing King addressing the UN rally was balanced by one showing a handful of "youths staging a sideline demonstration counter to the antiwar march" and displaying signs reading "Support Our GI's," "End Hanoi Sanctuary," and "Uncle Ho Wants You; We Don't." Considerable attention was given to the draft-card burning, but the *Times* provided a physical description of the draft card burners rather than their explanation of their actions. The only substantive comments about the draft-card burning were disparaging quotes from onlookers ranging from "I think it's terrible" to "I'd be out there, too, but I don't know. I don't think it'll do any good."[89]

Time published a two and a half page article on the "Dilemma of Dissent" in which it described the various marches around the country as a "spring cleaning" of the protester's "passions." The magazine disdainfully noted that "the avowed aim of the 'Spring Mobilization to End the War in Viet Nam' was to demonstrate to President Johnson and the world the depth of feeling in the United States against the conflict. The end result—aside from probably delighting Hanoi's Ho Chi Minh—was to demonstrate that Americans in the springtime like to have fun."[90] The article highlighted the "kooky costumes" and "painted faces of the psychedelic 'potted' participants," the presence of "Vietniks and Peaceniks, Trotskyites and potskyites" and a "contingent of 24 Sioux Indians." Balancing this apparent potpourri of crazies was a description of Vice President Hubert Humphrey, "just back from two weeks in Europe," who "with tears welling in his own eyes" said, "America needs to tell the world of the lives it is saving. We need to be known as a nation of peacemakers not just peace marchers." By comparison, in *Time*'s account, the rally was without substance.[91]

Antiwar frustrations were running high, and the sense that the nation was headed toward cataclysmic disaster was compounded by the disturbing images of the massive riots in Newark and Detroit during the summer. In Tom Wells's account,

Young American men were still being sent off to die. More bombs were falling. The war's violence was so gruesome it was hard to imagine worse, and the policymakers seemed committed to drawing the thing out to the last drop of blood. . . . Frustration over the movement's apparent inability to inhibit the war was "*very* widespread" among activists by the summer of 1967, [Bruce] Dancis remembered. Even the massive Spring Mobilizations had failed to deter officials. It was mind-boggling that the administration could ignore *that* sea of humanity.[92]

Andrew Kopkind began his *New York Review of Books* essay in the summer of 1967: "To be white and a radical in America this summer is to see horror and feel impotence." As Berkeley organizer Frank Bardacke put it, "Despair became a cliché among young white radicals."[93]

Feeling nothing was working to move the war in a less catastrophic direction, many in the movement, including national organizers, began to debate ways of increasing the level of confrontation against the war. At the same time, other factions in the antiwar movement went in less militant directions. Martin Luther King Jr., Dr. Benjamin Spock, and Robert Scheer announced plans for "Vietnam Summer," an antiwar canvassing effort envisioned by Gar Alperovitz. Upward of 3,000 canvassers began going door to door to campaign against the war throughout American cities and towns, largely beneath the media radar. In still another direction, the Vietnam Veterans Against the War was born, along with two groups organized to give a boost to war resistance: Resist, a group of adults organized to support young men who burned their draft cards or refused induction (those who signed their "Call to Resist Illegitimate Authority" were later prosecuted by the federal government), and The Resistance, organized by West Coast antiwar activists to foment public resistance to growing government repression generally and the draft specifically.

In yet another tangent, the counterculture made the social alienation of many young people increasingly visible, especially in the media-hyped "Summer of Love" in Haight-Ashbury. A group that included Abbie Hoffman and Jerry Rubin, later known as Yippies, sought to politicize the alienated young of the counterculture by, among other things, levitating the Pentagon at the mobilization scheduled for October.

In response to spreading antiwar activities, the administration stepped up efforts to mobilize pro-war rallies and marches, and to engage in surveillance, infiltration, intimidation, and provocation of antiwar groups and individuals. Local headquarters for the Los Angeles Vietnam Summer project were fire-bombed, the offices of Chicago-based antiwar groups were burglarized, and the FBI launched an extensive COINTELPRO program in spring 1968 to "expose, disrupt, and otherwise neutralize" New Left, antiwar, and black power groups.[94]

Three antiwar events in October 1967 revealed the movement's turn toward more direct confrontation of "the warmakers": a student protest against Dow Chemical recruiters at the University of Wisconsin, Stop the Draft Week in Berkeley and Oakland, and the national March on the Pentagon. Each produced a marked increase in antiwar militancy, most generally in the aftermath of beatings by police.

The Wisconsin protest sought to block on-campus recruiting for the manufacturers of napalm. University activists conducted a "coercive sit-in" that blocked access to recruiters; when campus authorities called for assistance from city police, the latter swept through the building with billy clubs flailing. Students fled the building and those rallying outside were outraged, taunting the police as they emerged with cries of "Sieg heil!" Police forced their way through with gas and clubs, and some students fired rocks at the police. Calm was eventually restored after a riot-control unit with tear gas and police dogs subdued the weary and bloodied crowd. While some on-site reporters were appalled by the level of police ferocity, mass media accounts essentially termed the protest a "riot." The *New York Times* blandly reported that students boycotted classes after the "riot yesterday when policemen attempted to break up a demonstration over job recruiting." While the article mentioned that the strike was called in response to police brutality, it contained no detail on the previous day's activities, and, as usual, didn't mention the students' grievance: the impact of napalm use in the war.[95]

Stop the Draft Week in the Bay area aimed at blocking the processing of new military recruits at the Oakland induction center. Following a day of sit-ins, arrests, and draft card burnings on both coasts, 3,000 demonstrators were forcefully attacked and driven back by police and a score were hospitalized. The following day, peaceful leafleting of hundreds of tense new recruits proved so ineffectual and demoralizing that organizers planned a new kind of demonstration in which they would employ "greater mobility and aggressiveness" in their efforts to close the induction center in the face of police assaults. In the melee that followed, waves of demonstrators surged back and forth, some wearing hard hats, others throwing tear gas grenades back at the police, still others turning over cars to form street barricades.[96]

Despite opposition from several quarters—notably SDS, which felt that demonstrations had proven futile, and the Socialist Workers Party, which, while radical, was decidedly non-militant, opposing law-breaking activity—the "Mobe," as it became known, forged ahead with plans to raise the stakes to "confront the warmakers" and take the movement "from protest to resistance" at the Pentagon. Plans called for a rally at the Lincoln Memorial followed by an officially sanctioned march to the Pentagon, where civil disobedience involving "stepped-up militance" would occur. Part of Dave Dellinger's thinking for the latter escalation was to indicate to U.S. officials that "there wouldn't be any peace at home if there wasn't peace abroad."[97] A *New York Times* editorial the next day concentrated on the "violent emotions" that were "stirred by the activities of the peace movement" (as opposed to the "violent emotions" stirred by the war) and noted how "epithets such as 'conspiracy,' 'human insects,' and 'agents of death'" were used in Congress to "condemn activities which, it is argued, encourage North Vietnam and lengthen the war."[98] A day later, James Reston penned a column headlined "Everyone Is a Loser: Washington a Sad and Brooding City in Wake of Antiwar Demonstration," noting that "everybody seemed to have lost in the antiwar siege of the Pentagon this weekend."[99] *U.S. News* reported on "Antiwar Protests: A Weapon for Communists" and led with the wild assertion that "Russia is plotting, guiding and helping to finance anti-American and antiwar demonstrations throughout the world—including the U.S."[100]

From 1967 onward, little changed in the media's boundaried coverage of antiwar protests. Reporting on the Pentagon protest emphasized the usual fare of violence, flamboyance, and Viet Cong flags—as did coverage of protest actions through 1972, with the sole exception of the October 1969 Moratorium. However, in its desperation to end the war, the antiwar cause was tending in two different directions. One occurred inside the boundaries of legitimate dissent and focused on antiwar electoral activity—notably the Eugene McCarthy and Robert Kennedy presidential campaigns. The other sought to remain a visible and disruptive reminder that antiwar opposition was not going away but would continue to seize opportunities to delegitimize the war and the warmakers while also confronting any new escalation or atrocity in the war. The two strands came together in Chicago at a crucial turning point of American politics. Media imagery at the Democratic National Convention would be of compelling national importance, as it would also be at the Moratorium, the massive November 1969 mobilization against the war, the 1970 protests against the invasion of Cambodia and the subsequent Kent State and Jackson State student deaths, the 1971 Vietnam Veterans' "Dewey Canyon III" protest, and the May Day protests. Many of the antiwar images provided fodder for an ultimately successful backlash campaign against the 1960s.

6

Visual Drama: The Power of the Image

Vision is a spectator; hearing is a participator.
　—John Dewey, 1927

Photography implies that we know about the world if we accept it as the camera records it. But this is the opposite of understanding, which starts from not accepting the world as it looks.
　—Susan Sontag, 1973

We won, because we made the whole world pay attention to us.
　—Young black man in the aftermath of the 1965 Watts riot

It is difficult to think of the sixties era without conjuring visual images. These may be a wide array of images that at least in public memory have eclipsed their connection to a specific event: long-haired youth, black militants in afros, grieving families, silent peace vigils, helicopters and jungle combat, body bags, inner cities aflame, young people haranguing public speakers, women angrily confronting men, and seas of humanity at protests or outdoor rock concerts. Or they may be specific images engraved in memory by the mass media of the time: well-dressed young African Americans being punched or pulled from their lunch-counter seats, police dogs lunging at a black man in Birmingham, any of several images from the era's assassinations; or a burning Vietnamese Buddhist monk, a Zippo lighter igniting a grass hut, a handgun fired into the head of a captured Viet Cong fighter, a young Vietnamese girl running away from a napalm blast that has burned her clothes off; or it could be a young long-haired youth carefully placing a flower in the barrel of a soldier's gun, the determined face of Malcolm X jabbing with his finger, the exuberant faces of thousands of women marching down Fifth Avenue, or antiwar protesters draped over statues during demonstrations in Chicago or Washington, D.C., or nude swimmers at Woodstock. The list is virtually endless.

These images are not only how many people remember the sixties or learn about them from the media, but they were also an important part of the discourse during the long sixties era. Absent the graphic imagery, the sixties era may well have been significantly different. Images played a crucial role in the evolution of sixties-era movements and in the erosion of their democratic promise. When selected for their dramatic content, images become powerful communicators. Their meaning, however, depends on their viewers' subjectivity, spanning an emotional range from empathic connection to revulsion. Though the mass media provide the words that define the range of legitimate meanings associated with imagery, in a contested culture the images themselves are capable of transcending the media's boundaries through their subjective connection with viewers. In the context of antiwar protest, media images were particularly important in communicating or confirming meanings of the war in Vietnam not contained in legitimate discourse.[1]

With respect to protest movements, media images may also invite the participation of sympathetic audiences, even as news texts disparage the protests. At least two times during the sixties era, media imagery helped to ignite what George Katsiaficas has called an "eros effect," a "massive awakening of the instinctual need for justice and for freedom," in the process producing a contagious protest zeitgeist.[2] The first media images of the student sit-ins helped to incite their rapid spread throughout the South by suggesting that the time to put nonviolent training into practice had arrived. The sit-in images also resonated with students in the North, conveying the sense that, in Rennie Davis's words, "they were us and we were them," that "they were expressing something we were feeling as well."[3] Similarly, in 1968, as Katsiaficas's work documents, images of revolt helped to ignite an era of largely student-based protest extending around much of the world.

On the other hand, these and other protest images could have quite the opposite effect on other media audiences. Not only does the general public tend to look askance at public protests in even the best of times, but the news media's tendency to highlight the more flamboyant or violent kinds of protest activities virtually assures that significant audiences will recoil against what they see — especially, of course, when authoritative officials use these images to cast the protest in the most negative terms possible. Indeed, during and since the sixties, the forces of backlash used a strategy that exploited what I call the audience's "visual thinking." Visual imagery seen by media viewers confirmed the reality that was explained by appeal to commonly held or propagated ideological belief about some form of "outside agitators," to use one common expression of the time.

Thus it was that the many protest images during the sixties era had a polarizing impact on the wider public, typically fed by the ideological rhetoric of officials and media commentators alike. In later years, visual thinking was exploited by linking these same kinds of images with liberal targets that occurred simultaneously, regardless of their actual causal connection. As imagistic media have become more pervasive over time, audiences have become increasingly attention-deficient, making inventive and dramatic imagery even more important as a means of attracting attention and entertaining or seducing audiences, and ushering in what some call "postmodern" culture where images seem to have effaced reality. Visual imagery has largely come to define television news, and through market forces and audience effects it has had a profound impact on the newspaper business and the proliferation of "news" videos on the Internet. While we are still trying to sort out the almost incalculable range of effects produced by our imagistic world, much of the contemporary media discourse reflects the way the forces of backlash have succeeded in converting images from the past into persuasive truths for targeted audiences. Within sectors of today's balkanized society, these have simply become indisputable history.

The Sit-ins: A Dramatic Call to Action

The graphic photographs of the quietly determined students under fire from hostile whites in the early 1960 sit-ins, especially the large photo spreads in *Life* magazine, had a visceral impact on young viewers in the North, drawing them into direct participation in the movement. Robert Moses, who became an inspiring leader in the Mississippi voter registration drive, recalled seeing the photographs while at his home in New York: "The sit-ins, when they broke out, just grabbed me. The pictures of the Southern students. What I became aware of looking at them was *they looked how I felt*. And I responded immediately to that."[4] Cleveland Sellars, who became involved in the Mississippi campaign, remarked, "It gave [us] chills to see people actually hitting away at the system of segregation that existed for so long. And it was young people, a lot like ourselves, and they looked magnificent. They just gave you an overwhelming sense of pride."[5]

These images contrasted sharply with narrow textual reports of the struggle over "squatter's rights," as noted in chapter 4. From his vantage point as a politically conscious senior at Bronx High School of Science, Stokely Carmichael (Kwame Ture) later recalled that on reading about the sit-ins, he thought them "politically inconsequential." However, he continued, "Of course I would completely change my mind the first time I *saw* on TV young Africans calmly sitting at a counter while racist abuse, blows, and the contents of ketchup bottles, full ashtrays, and coffee cups were dumped on their heads. That made a believer of me. Instantly."[6] As Rennie Davis's comment above revealed, white students in the North also felt that the students sitting in were "expressing something we were feeling."[7]

Southern White Violence Gets the Nation's Attention

Following the surge of locally based sit-in activity in 1960, the Congress of Racial Equality (CORE) organized the Freedom Rides with an eye toward using white violence to communicate graphically the South's deviance from national standards. By directly challenging the segregationist practices in southern transportation systems, the integrated Freedom Riders expected to force a conflict between state and federal officials. As CORE's James Farmer put it, "We felt we could count on the racists of the South to create a crisis so that the federal government would be compelled to enforce the law."[8] Escalating violence spurred the newsmagazines to respond with more substantial coverage than they gave the sit-in movement. Three violent attacks in Anniston, Birmingham, and Montgomery, Alabama, provided the newsmagazines with powerful, attention-grabbing drama.

Although their articles were more detached, the magazines' inclusion of photos of the firebombed Greyhound bus and beaten and bloodied riders shocked readers in the North.[9] They not only invited SNCC reinforcements to join and continue the Freedom Rides, but William Sloane Coffin Jr., then the chaplain of Yale, "decided to become a Freedom Rider *after seeing a picture* in his Sunday paper of John Lewis lying on a Montgomery Street, bleeding."[10]

Television, too, dramatized the Freedom Rides once the violent attacks occurred. In David Halberstam's account, the "quantum jump in violence" made the Rides a "national story in the truest sense":

> With television increasingly becoming the critical player in the media as
> the Movement entered the sixties, it was clear that the more *action* a story
> produced, the better. That meant that as far as the media were concerned,
> the Freedom Riders themselves had not been a big story in the beginning,
> when they seemed to be only about riding on buses and eating in terminals.
> The transformation had begun in Anniston, when it had all turned violent.
> . . . The story had changed. It was suddenly producing great footage.[11]

The dramatic media coverage also gave the Kennedy administration a "public relations" crisis, for the violent mobs in Alabama were attracting the attention of the world press. In Richard Lentz's account, the media were able to present a "moral drama uncomplicated by nuances"—one side represented by "mobs running unchecked through the streets, given free rein by Southern lawmen heedless of their duty and their oaths," the other represented by "brave and idealistic young demonstrators, who sought only to assert their rights as Americans."[12] Finally, as Sara Evans has observed, together with the sit-ins, the "freedom rides had an electrifying impact on northern liberal culture. The romance and daring of black youth gave progressives an unassailable cause."[13]

In contrast to the Freedom Rides story, the SCLC/SNCC campaign to desegregate Albany, Georgia, in late 1961–1962 was notable for its relative lack of violence, thereby provoking only minimal media coverage and the absence of a dramatic and clear media message. The failure of the Albany demonstrations to deliver the kind of unequivocal national message that SCLC leaders hoped for was interpreted by the national media as a "final sign that the movement had ended in failure."[14]

Media attention soon shifted to Mississippi and James Meredith's attempt to be the first black person to attend the University of Mississippi. The story's drama was palpable: the solitary figure of Meredith, violent attacks by hostile whites, rioting on the university campus, two deaths and a breakdown in local order, and a federal crisis involving U.S. army troops and a defiant Mississippi governor Ross Barnett. *Time,* in fact, heralded the crisis as "the gravest conflict between federal and state authority since the Civil War," noting prior to the outbreak of violence that it "hovered at the edge of violence and was filled with the potential for tragedy."[15] The episode was a natural for the dramatic, personalized storytelling favored by television news in particular, though the newsmagazines were equally attentive, devoting twenty articles in all to the University of Mississippi events during the fall of 1962. The intense coverage contrasted sharply with the minimal attention given to SNCC's courageous voter registration drive occurring simultaneously among the impoverished populations of the Mississippi Delta.[16]

Birmingham to Selma: Media Images Compel Action

Although media reports were highly critical of the SCLC's "poorly timed" protest in Birmingham in spring 1963, news photographs and television coverage of the ensuing Birmingham events electrified national and world audiences, galvanized the Kennedy administration to action, and sent a surge of bold determination through African American audiences in the rest of the nation — culminating in the spectacular March on Washington in August. As Richard Lentz has described the national news story:

> Birmingham's enduring images were stark and simple. Arrayed on one side were the forces of good — the black men and women marching by the hundreds for the freedom that was their long-denied birthright as Americans; and children, the black children of Birmingham, offering up their bodies, their lives if need be, in a crusade the adults had not won and very likely could not win alone. . . . [On the other were] adversaries representing the antithesis of American principles of equality and freedom. Their encounters in the streets of Birmingham produced powerful images of brutality . . . of white men loosing fierce police dogs and training murderously efficient fire hoses on men, women, and, especially, children, who wanted no more than the rights of any American citizen.[17]

The Birmingham images catapulted the civil rights movement to the center of the national political agenda. The photographs contained sufficient power and emotionality to pierce the normal passivity of media viewers. As Birmingham businessman David Vann later commented of the Birmingham campaign, "It was a masterpiece [in] the use of the media to explain a cause to the general public."[18] The photographs and footage also overwhelmed the more distanced texts of the national news magazines. *Life,* for example, cautioned its readers: "The pictures on these 11 pages are frightening. They are frightening because of the brutal methods being used by white policemen in Birmingham, Ala. against Negro demonstrators. They are frightening because the Negro strategy of 'non-violent direct action' invites that very brutality—and welcomes it as a way to promote the Negroes' cause, which under the law, is right."[19]

As Birmingham chronicler Diane McWhorter recalled, "The dogs and fire hoses dominated the evening news. The scene had been a cameraman's dream," even if one of the national press cameramen, *Life*'s Charles Moore, had been "sickened by what he saw."[20] Eric Sevareid commented on *The CBS Evening News,* "A snarling police dog set upon a human being is recorded in the permanent photoelectric file of every human being's brain."[21] The powerful spread of Moore's photos in *Life* magazine, Bill Hudson's shot of a police dog lunging at the chest of high school sophomore Walter Gadsden spanning three columns at the top of page one of the *New York Times,* lengthy articles dramatized by photographs in *Time* and *Newsweek,* and wire-service photographs carried to the far corners of the world—all brought the message of racial oppression in the South dramatically to life. They spoke a kind of universal language that rippled through the world's media. President Kennedy reportedly said that the photographs made him "sick."[22] He was also concerned about the bad press that the photos were bringing the United States elsewhere in the world.

Finally, the events in the industrial city of Birmingham electrified black audiences throughout urban America, touching off what the *New York Times* termed a "new assertive mood" of black Americans, notably among admirers of the Nation of Islam's rising star, Malcolm X. In the wake of Birmingham and dozens of demonstrations that cropped up in its aftermath, President Kennedy took to the airwaves to introduce his new civil rights bill in what the *Times* called "one of the most emotional speeches yet delivered by a President." Kennedy asserted, "We are confronted primarily with a moral issue . . . as old as the Scriptures and . . . as clear as the American Constitution."[23] While the civil rights bill would have to travel a legislative road strewn with obstacles, it would be signed into law by President Johnson in 1964 as one of the nation's historic landmarks in civil rights history. For three consecutive years following Birmingham, the Gallup poll recorded Americans as citing civil rights as the "most important problem confronting the country."[24]

The Birmingham drama and its aftermath helped to generate a massive public turnout and intense media scrutiny at the August 1963 March on Washington.

Despite publicly aired apprehension about the potential for violence and internal tensions within the movement, the dramatic footage of well over 200,000 marchers filling all visual space around the reflecting pool between the Lincoln Memorial and Washington Monument and the soaring oratory of Martin Luther King Jr. in particular conveyed a powerful sense of national mission revolving around the democratic ideals of freedom, equality, and community. Since the networks preempted regularly scheduled programming to air the march, millions witnessed the ceremonies on television, including King's entire speech. There was little doubt of its powerful impact on those present, or on the millions of Americans who witnessed it through the media. Shortly thereafter, NBC aired a three-hour program on race entitled "American Revolution '63," without commercial interruption. The program included Mississippi's segregationist governor Ross Barnett denouncing the "television revolution" that "publicized and dramatized the race issue far beyond its relative importance"—one of the earliest instances of backlash against the "liberal" national media.[25]

Following passage of the Civil Rights Act and SNCC's voter registration drive that culminated in Freedom Summer, SCLC and SNCC joined forces in Selma, Alabama, in 1965 for a march to Montgomery. Sheriff Jim Clark's reputation, like that of Birmingham's Bull Connor, made Selma a likely place for a brutal government reaction to civil rights protest. After weeks of confrontation, arrests, and violence—including the murder of twenty-two-year-old Jimmie Lee Jackson—the signal event in Selma occurred on March 7, 1965, when over 500 marchers gathered to cross the Edmund Pettis Bridge en route to their fifty-four-mile trek to the state capitol in Montgomery. With news reporters and camera crews in attendance, the marchers were blocked by Sheriff Clark and the Alabama State Highway patrol. The marchers waited while Clark ordered them to disperse. When the marchers quietly refused to yield, the state troopers waded into the marchers pushing, prodding, firing tear gas, and swinging billy clubs as they went, followed by club-swinging police mounted on horseback. In response to the brutal onslaught, the television networks interrupted regular network programming (ABC broke into the film *Judgment at Nuremburg*) to air footage of the violent attack. As Mayor Smitherman of Selma recalled, "When that beating happened at the foot of the bridge, it looked like war. That went all over the country. And the people, the wrath of the nation came down upon us."[26]

The effect of what became known as "Bloody Sunday" was electric. Hundreds of people from all over the United States, including a number of highly visible celebrities, came to help the effort in Selma, chiefly to carry out a follow-up to the banned march. A violent attack on three white Unitarian ministers that resulted in the death of Rev. James Reeb added fuel to the national firestorm over Selma. President Johnson took to the airwaves to announce his voting rights legislation and concluded with words that John Lewis recalled forty-three years later on the night of Barack Obama's election: "It's all of us who must overcome the crippling legacy of bigotry and injustice. And we *shall* overcome."[27] After a federal court ruling upheld the marchers' rights, the march proceeded to Montgomery where the television and press cameras recorded the movement's triumphal return to the site of the 1955 bus boycott.

The Invisible World of Race, Class, and Inner-City Rage

Images of violence by southern white authorities against nonviolent black activists revealed the oppressive realities of Jim Crow with searing impact for much of the nation's viewers. When mostly poor blacks who had long been invisible in the nation's media[28] erupted in violent rage against the oppressive conditions of life in the nation's inner cities, the public response was substantially different.[29] Along with the war, the urban insurrections and police and military responses from 1964 to 1968 produced some of the most viscerally disturbing imagery of the era.

Like much of the historical culture of Jim Crow, the tangible conditions of inner-city life were largely invisible to most white Americans. Blacks had been fleeing the South for the promising opportunities of the industrial North for several decades, and their migration accelerated in the postwar years. Yet conditions in the North fell far short of the promise. In part because of a shifting economy, in part because of racism in labor unions, entry-level jobs were largely unavailable to a population largely disadvantaged by appalling educational deficits in the South. Racist practices by suburban and urban realtors, political gerrymandering, and racially based school assignment policies, along with federal urban renewal and highway policies, all helped to trap the new migrants (as well as a new wave of Latin American immigrants) in huge ghetto tracts isolated from the opportunities of urban life. Poverty was rampant, spawning growing criminal activity and illicit drug trafficking. Residents had to battle against the psychological effects of powerlessness and hopelessness. Perhaps more important, the subjective dimensions of these living conditions—what it felt like to be a black person in the inner city—remained largely beyond the comprehension of most Americans.

It was this world and the rage and despair it generated that began to speak through literary works of the post–World War II era. Ralph Ellison's 1947 novel *Invisible Man* begins,

> I am invisible, understand, simply because people refuse to see me. . . .
> When they approach me they see only my surroundings, themselves, or
> figments of their imagination—indeed, everything and anything except
> me. . . . You wonder whether you aren't simply a phantom in other people's

minds. . . . And let me confess, you feel that way most of the time. You ache with the need to convince yourself that you do exist in the real world, that you're a part of all the sound and anguish, and you strike out with your fists, you curse and you swear to make them recognize you. And, alas, it's seldom successful.[30]

James Baldwin published his essay *The Fire Next Time* in 1963. In his opening "letter" to his nephew, Baldwin spoke of his younger brother:

> But no one's hand can wipe away those tears he sheds invisibly today, which one hears in his laughter and in his speech and in his songs. I know what the world has done to my brother and how narrowly he has survived it. And I know, which is much worse, and this is the crime of which I accuse my country and my countrymen, and for which neither I nor time nor history will ever forgive them, that they have destroyed and are destroying hundreds of thousands of lives and do not know it and do not want to know it.[31]

The book ended with Baldwin's appeal to "relatively conscious whites" and "relatively conscious blacks" to "end the racial nightmare" and "change the history of the world." Baldwin warned that failing to do so would fulfill the biblical prophecy articulated in a slave song, "God gave Noah the rainbow sign, No more water, the fire next time!"[32]

The "next time" came during the mid-1960s, after several years of civil rights struggle in the South. After Birmingham exploded in a short-lived riot in 1963, Cambridge, Maryland, erupted in what *Life* hyperbolically called "racial war" in July. Violence in Jacksonville, Florida, in spring 1964 was reported by *Time* in a piece headlined "Toward a Long, Hot Summer."[33] Starting with Harlem and Rochester, New York, and northeast Philadelphia in 1964, moving to the Watts section of Los Angeles in 1965 and cities like Cleveland and Chicago in 1966 and Newark and Detroit in 1967 — spanning over fifty cities across four years prior to the nationwide outburst of rage following Martin Luther King's assassination in 1968 — the nation's inner cities exploded in rage and frustration.

Along with the hopeful winds of change in the South, presidential rhetoric that boldly embraced the legitimacy of black interests and the brief surge of hope triggered by the War on Poverty and Community Action Program were contradicted daily by jarring reminders that little of life in the inner city was changing — fueling what many academic and social commentators called the "revolution of rising expectations."[34] Classically, the mass media and even some policy analysts adopted what William Ryan called "blaming the victim," seeing the adaptive (if also dysfunctional) behaviors of inner-city residents as the source of their problems.[35] Even rising expectations could be framed as a characteristic flaw of ghetto dwellers; *Newsweek* described them as "rising expectations that can never be satisfied."[36]

The most constant and brutal reminder experienced by young black men in particular was the arbitrary and violent presence of a white police force. Typically the catalyst for the "riots," as they were called, was an act of police brutality that caused something to snap inside these residents. For example, as Newark's Community Action agency (the United Community Corporation, or UCC) was encountering roadblocks in their empowerment, an act of apparent police brutality in 1967 blew up into what was at the time the most massive and destructive of the decade's riots.[37] Prior to the Newark riot, the nation's newsmagazines failed to carry a single article about the Community Action Program in the city, while the *New York Times* ran a total of three articles on the UCC-city conflict from the beginning of 1965 to the aftermath of the 1967 riot. Each of the *Times* articles was framed around the actions and perspectives of elected officials critical of the UCC.[38] Once Newark exploded, however, the national news media gave vivid saturation coverage to the violence and destruction of the 1967 riot, as they did with the 1965 Watts riot and the massive Detroit riot that followed on the heels of Newark.[39]

Throughout this time period, the national media gravitated toward the pictures of violence and destruction, blazing buildings, looting, and clashes with armed police and National Guardsmen, followed by photographs of countless city blocks that looked like they had been carpet-bombed in wartime. If anything consistently generated attention-grabbing visuals in the era's domestic struggles, it was the urban riots. For television viewers, the dramatic violence and the clashes between police and inner-city residents were about all they saw, and the violence was repeated through the summer months for six "long, hot summers" of increasing intensity.

The 1965 Watts riot in Los Angeles was the first of the urban insurrections to take center stage in the mass media, with dramatic, sobering coverage on the nightly news. Both *Newsweek* and *Time* put graphic photographs on their front covers, yet their efforts to make sense of the week's news did little to provide readers with an understanding of the forces that triggered the violence. *Time*'s coverage was more visually dramatic without shedding much light on why the Watts riot occurred. Two full pages of photos showed a policeman "guarding captured looters," inner-city males "stealing shoes from [a] store window," National Guardsmen "patrolling the rubble," a "pillaged furniture store blazing out of control," and black youths "playing with [a] rifled cash register." For several pages, *Time* focused exclusively on the acts of violent "savagery," the cop-hating bravado of young black males, rampaging gangs of "Negroes" overturning or burning cars or throwing Molotov cocktails into stores, and cries of "Here comes Whitey—get him!"[40]

Near the end of the article, *Time* gestured toward explanation, asking, "What caused the disorders?" Noting that "there were as many explanations as there were points of view," the magazine suggested a list of possibilities: the "unusual heat wave," the "Negroes' . . . isolation and poverty in a land of conspicuous plenty," a "lack of communication" between whites and blacks, a lack of "Negro leadership" in Watts, and "the biggest single cause": the Los Angeles Negro's "migration to an alien and fiercely competitive urban world" where his "past miseries and future expectations have been callously exploited." Without explaining who or what might be "exploiting" urban blacks, *Time* quoted at length L.A. police chief William Parker's backlash attack that shifted the blame to civil rights leaders: "You can't keep telling [these people] that the Liberty Bell isn't ringing for them and not expect them to believe it. You cannot tell people to disobey the law and not expect them to have a disrespect for the law. You cannot keep telling them that they are being abused and mistreated without expecting them to react." After which, *Time* concluded, "Riots such as those in Los Angeles have no real object—and therein lies the pity and the danger."[41]

Newsweek's nine-page article also included graphically disturbing photographs, but the magazine seemed to make more of an effort to explain why the riot occurred. Under the heading "The Reasons Why," the magazine briefly reviewed poverty and unemployment statistics and noted that Watts was a "world of seemingly doomed youths, one third [of whom] come from broken homes."[42] Conceding that these conditions were "typical of Negro slums across the United States," the magazine noted that "only a handful have erupted in rebellion."[43] Adding that "sociologists had their own pet theories, too," the magazine chose to highlight "the inherent violence and upside-down values of the slums, the pressure of rising expectations that can never be satisfied . . . [and] the desire for kicks in a boring world."[44]

The 1965 Watts riot received substantial media coverage in part because its scale so greatly eclipsed that of earlier disturbances. Media coverage of the insurrections of 1966 and 1967 followed form, at times seeking new angles for coverage and reflecting public pressures to reduce the inflammatory coverage. A five-page *Newsweek* article on the Chicago insurrection of 1966 focused on "Cops on the Spot," including eight photographs depicting various aspects of inner-city police work, leading with a three-column photograph with the caption, "Through a riddled prowl car windshield in Chicago, a cop's-eye view of a riotous world he never made." The piece concluded with a Minneapolis editor's blame-the-victim observation: "When Southern Negroes move North, they transfer their hatred of the Southern police to the Northern policeman."[45]

With these kinds of reports as their source of information, it was impossible for the public to come to an understanding of the deep chasm between police and inner-city residents, much less the psychological wounds that led to explosions of rage. Nor would they learn anything about the kind of police brutality that would trigger the formative actions of the Black Panther Party for Self Defense. The summer of 1967 provided the longest and most continuous, frightening imagery and television footage of the sixties era.

Not surprisingly, black and white Americans came to quite different conclusions about the causes of urban unrest. According to a 1967 Harris poll published in *Newsweek,* 45 percent of white adults volunteered that "outside agitation" was one of the "two or three main reasons" for the riots, whereas only 10 percent of Negro adults responded that same way.[46] In fact, two weeks before the *Newsweek* poll, in the midst of lengthy coverage of the 1967 Detroit riot, the magazine included a full-page article on H. Rap Brown as the "firebrand" who, officials in Cambridge, Maryland, charged, "lit the fuse" that began rioting there in 1967.[47]

Quite clearly, the riots — and media coverage of the riots — were helping to propel the American public toward the "two societies" the Kerner Commission warned about in 1968.[48] When given a list of "commonly cited causes of rioting," in the 1967 Harris poll, blacks emphasized conditions many of them experienced, while whites focused on characteristics of "Negroes." Sixty-seven percent of blacks versus 34 percent of whites cited "lack of jobs for young Negroes," 68 percent of blacks versus 39 percent of whites cited "lack of decent housing for Negroes," and 49 percent of blacks versus 9 percent of whites cited "police brutality against Negroes." The only "causes" whites cited more frequently than blacks were "desire of Negroes to loot stores" (26 to 9 percent) and "desire of Negroes for violence" (23 to 13 percent).[49]

Finally, the urban insurrections revealed the affective empowerment the media culture encouraged as the sixties era evolved. *Newsweek*'s Watts coverage concluded with a comment from a "Negro Pastor": "Here's the man who doesn't have any identity. But *tonight* he has the Los Angeles Police Department and the Los Angeles Fire Department upset. He has the National Guard called out. Tonight he is somebody."[50] The rioters had forced the city to respond — "winning," as the Watts youth noted earlier, because "we made the whole world pay attention to us."[51] It was, however, a pyrrhic victory. The power embodied in the riots may have forced greater attention from city officials, but it was largely cathartic, symbolic, and short-lived — in contrast to the potentially more enduring power generated by the organizing processes the media ignored — especially since the riots helped to generate a political backlash against the federal poverty program and Great Society liberalism generally.

Radical Feminism: Seen, Not Heard

While the mass media eventually acknowledged the legitimacy of the women's movements' liberal objectives, feminists' efforts to raise public consciousness about the demeaning effects of society's confining gender roles and stereotypes, as well as its violent behavior toward women — in sum, the multitude of ways that young girls and young women learned that their primary social identity revolved around pleasing men — ran into the same dynamic of mass media that black power and antiwar movements encountered. Their arguments were largely dismissed, distorted, or ridiculed in media texts, whereas their dramatic actions, their use of symbolic "agitprop," often gained media attention. The women's movement never became a violent or a particularly militant movement; that, after all, would be embracing the culture's prototypically male behavior trait. Yet women were angry; they refused to be pushed around or to conform to society's stereotypes. As Ellen Willis put it, "At a time when feminism itself was tearing off layers of protective skin and focusing our attention on feelings we'd spent our lives suppressing, it was not surprising that women should resist any further attacks on their defenses."[52]

Given the media culture's pervasive sexism, women often engaged in media-seeking agitprop actions that sought a symbolic confrontation with the institutions that oppressed women. At times, perhaps, because of their anger, at other times because they were either short-sighted in constructing an action or they underestimated the way the media response would distort *their* meanings, the movement engaged in actions that created the images and stories that would be used against them—for decades afterward. As with the other movements' actions, one audience understood the symbolism and in one way or another joined or supported the struggle. Yet the very same actions alienated significant numbers of others and became highly useful to the forces of political backlash. Indeed, movement activists were often divided over the effects of these actions, and as was the case with other outsider groups, these divisions hardened as the sixties era evolved.

Actions varied widely. The liberal National Organization of Women persuaded the *New York Times* to abandon its gender-separated job listings, while the radical feminist group WITCH used guerrilla-like tactics to "hex" Wall Street, leaving their "WITCH" insignia plastered on the walls and the statue of George Washington—the latter described by Robin Morgan as a "ritual against a symbol of patriarchal, slave-holding power."[53] Women's groups organized boycotts of products that were advertised in sexist ways—notably Canada Dry, with its slogan "A Good Soda Is Like a Good Woman: It Won't Quit on You," and National Airlines for its "Fly Me, I'm Cheryl" campaign—and different women's groups placed stickers in prominent public places, ranging from "This ad is offensive to women" to an angry "Fuck Marriage—Not Men."

One early protest that catapulted women's liberation onto the media stage was the demonstration that confronted the 1968 Miss America pageant in Atlantic City only days after the Democratic National Convention in Chicago. The pageant was a particularly blatant symbol of society's pervasive tendency to reduce women to a single dimension of physical beauty (and a single standard for that dimension). Yet, as organizer Robin Morgan noted, the pageant touched on an array of concerns "for us lefty Women's Liberationists. . . . She touched capitalism, militarism, racism, and sexism."[54] Thanks to a *New York Post* preview that inaccurately predicted "Bra Burners and Miss America," the protest was well attended by the media. A "Freedom Trash Can" was placed at the site where women were encouraged to throw away constricting clothing designed to enhance their sex appeal to men—bras, girdles, corsets, high heels, and the like—along with items like a torn-up copy of *Playboy*. The media, however, picked up on the image of feminists as "bra burners"—an epithet that has become common fare among those who have disparaged feminism ever since. As Ruth Rosen has written in her history of the women's movement, bras "seemed to mean a great deal to those journalists who couldn't tell the difference between the sexual revolution and women's liberation. And so the myth spread that women's liberationists burned bras as an act of defiance. A sexy trope, the media used it to sell papers."[55] Women picketed on the Atlantic City boardwalk, sang feminist versions of songs like "Ain't She Sweet," crowned a live sheep Miss America, challenged women passersby, were the target of hostile and sexist comments yelled by men in the crowd, and, inside the convention hall, unfurled a huge banner proclaiming " WOMEN'S LIBERATION" from the balcony during the outgoing Miss America's farewell speech.

Television news provided glimpses of the protest in the course of covering the pageant, but the network that carried the pageant live scrupulously avoided showing the "Women's Liberation" banner. Afterward, while debriefing the action, several participants concluded that the individuals who made signs that read "Up Against the Wall, Miss America" or "Miss America is a Big Falsie" had violated the group's decision to have no "anti-woman" signs. As Carol Hanisch remarked, anticipating schisms that would appear later, the signs "hardly raised any woman's consciousness and really harmed the cause of sisterhood. Miss America and all beautiful women came off as our enemy instead of as our sisters who suffer with us."[56]

Early the next year, WITCH held a protest against a bridal fair held in Madison Square Garden. In addition to hexing the "manipulator-exhibitors," the protesters chanted, "Confront the Whoremakers" (an echo of the antiwar movement's "confront the warmakers" slogan at the 1967 Pentagon march) and sang "Here Comes the Slave, Off to Her Grave." As Robin Morgan later reflected, "We were obviously doing something right—but we were doing it wrong. The Bridal Fair protest was a new low for us in our pattern of alienating all women except young, hip, Leftist ones like ourselves. . . . Our leaflet was mindlessly against marriage without taking the trouble to explain why, or to differentiate between the patriarchal *institution* of marriage and what 'marriage' as a committed bond of love might mean."[57] As Morgan explained, "We were too busy doing actions. . . . We were women who identified politically with the confrontational tactics of the male Left and stylistically with the clownish proto-anarchism of such groups as the Yippies."[58]

Not surprisingly, the largely male press was instantly preoccupied with the visual images presented by the "women's libbers," as they were called. Prone to describing women by their looks, the mass media translated actions aimed at the exploitation of stereotypical female beauty to mean that feminists were ugly and anti-sexual as well as anti-male — and eventually that feminists were invariably lesbians. Indeed, the media were quick to note the exceptions to their own stereotype about women's libbers (see the *Life* cover of Germaine Greer in the photo gallery). A 1971 *Newsweek* story on Gloria Steinem carried the headline "A Liberated Woman Despite Beauty, Chic and Success."[59]

One somewhat successful counterblow against media ridicule was the large NOW-inspired "Women's Strike for Equality" march of August 26, 1970, a couple of weeks after the House of Representatives passed the Equal Rights Amendment. Part of the event's success came from front-page photographs like the one in the *New York Times* that conveyed the boisterous exuberance and apparent unity of a huge crowd that looked relatively mainstream (including some women of color and more than a few men). The *Times* also included three individual marchers' photographs below the start of its article, including an older woman with a sign revealing the words "equal rights," a young mother with a child in a backpack carrier, and a young woman in a stylish hairdo and sunglasses. The visual coverage conveyed an image of American womanhood united, thus compensating for snags in the day's successes: divisions within the movement, disappointing turnout at other locales around the country, other *Times* articles that previewed the march's "central concern" for "free abortion on request," a brief article entitled "Leading Feminist Puts Hairdo before Strike," another headlined "Traditional Groups Prefer to Ignore Women's Lib."[60] Still, ABC News began its coverage with Howard K. Smith reading a Spiro Agnew quotation: "Three things have been difficult to tame. The ocean, fools, and women. We may soon be able to tame the ocean, but fools and women will take a little longer." Smith ended ABC's coverage of the day's rallies by quoting West Virginia senator Jennings Randolph's characterization of the women's movement as "a small band of braless bubbleheads."[61]

One of the earliest *U.S. News* articles on the movement contained a brief look at what it called the "generally good-humored, colorful and orderly — but not massive . . . Women Strike for Equality" marches. Two photos of women carrying flowers and Equal Rights petitions to Congress and "airline stewardesses" picketing for maternity leave outside the White House were captioned "Siege of Capitol Hill" and "Siege of White House," respectively.[62] *Time*'s coverage of "Women on the March" noted how the Fifth Avenue parade provided "not only protest but some of the best sidewalk ogling in years," and commented that the day was a "victory for the less flamboyant elements" of the movement, with "no charred bras and few of the shock tactics of earlier local demonstrations."[63]

In her speech to the 1973 Houston convention of the Women's Political Caucus, Congresswoman Shirley Chisholm maintained that many women viewed feminists as "anti-male, anti-child, and anti-family." Noting that the media tended to focus on "the young girl shaking her fist and screaming obscenities at an abortion rally" rather than giving serious attention to the substantive issues, Chisholm cautioned that movement "excesses" had also contributed to these stereotypes.[64] Products of media preoccupation and the emotion of the time, these stereotypes have become a defining part of the permanent public memory of second-wave feminism.

The War in Vietnam: Seeing through Mythic Reality

Although the mass media contained the debate over the war within the boundaries of conventional ideology about the U.S. role in Southeast Asia, photographic or televisual imagery conveyed some of the war's sensory realities, confirming to some and revealing to others the moral horror of the war and giving the lie to the official propaganda about the war's progress and the government's "good intentions." One striking example of a photograph's impact comes from Bernard Lee's memory of Martin Luther King Jr. flipping through magazines until coming upon a 1967 *Ramparts* magazine article on "The Children of Vietnam":

> When he came to *Ramparts* magazine he stopped. He froze as he looked at the pictures from Vietnam. He saw a picture of a Vietnamese mother holding her dead baby, a baby killed by our military. Then Martin just pushed the plate of food away from him. I looked up and said, "Doesn't it taste any good?" and he answered, "Nothing will ever taste any good for me until I do everything I can to end that war."[65]

One of the earliest images to break through the early, respectful questioning of administration strategies was the front-page photograph of the self-immolation of a Buddhist monk in 1963. While the news media were reporting that military leaders were brimming with confidence about "turning the corner" in Vietnam, longstanding Buddhist resentment toward the repressive Diem regime erupted in demonstrations that were brutally crushed. On June 11, a Buddhist monk named Thich Quang Duc sat in the middle of a Saigon intersection, was doused in gasoline by fellow monks, and lit a match. Press photographs and television footage taken while he was being consumed by fire were carried in news reports all over the world with dramatic effect, despite media texts that minimized the crisis. While independent progressive magazines like the *New Republic* and the *Nation* argued that the United States should sever its ties with Diem and begin discussions with Ho Chi Minh with the aim of supporting Vietnamese nationalism as a buffer against presumed Chinese expansion, mainstream media texts were far more muted. *Time* magazine contended that the Buddhist action was designed to "force" President Diem to "knuckle under to demands for increased religious freedom," noting that "Diem's intransigence troubled the U.S." Readers were reassured that the "U.S. would publicly condemn" Diem's "treatment of the Buddhists unless he took prompt action," and that American "warnings . . . seemed to sink in." The article provided few insights into the Diem regime's repression, nor did it raise any broader questions about U.S. policy.[66]

Subsequent immolations and repression by the Diem government heightened awareness of the tensions within South Vietnam, leading to open letters from several groups of prominent citizens urging the administration to reexamine its Vietnam policy and/or calling for a UN-sponsored international conference on Vietnam. Legitimate dissent was out in the open, and anti–Vietnam War expression began to appear at other public events like the annual Easter march for disarmament in New York.

A second significant imagistic breakthrough occurred in August 1965 when CBS correspondent Morley Safer accompanied a Marine unit in a sweep of the village of Cam Ne. With instructions to "level it" if they received "one round from the village," the Marines "received one burst of automatic fire from an unidentified direction [and] poured in 3.5 rocket fire, 79 grenade launchers, and heavy and light machine-gun fire," then "moved in proceeding first with cigarette lighters then with flame throwers, to burn down an estimated 150 dwellings," according to Safer's account in the next day's *New York Times*.[67] CBS cameras captured the Marines setting fire to thatched roofs with Zippo lighters. At one point, soldiers fired a grenade launcher at "an old man" just as he entered the doorway of what turned out to be a room full of children he had been running back to warn. The village was burned to the ground. In his television report, Safer noted,

> The day's operation burned down 150 houses, wounded three women, killed one baby, wounded one marine, and netted these four prisoners who could not understand questions put to them in English. Four old men who had no idea what an I.D. card was. Today's operation is the frustration of Vietnam in miniature. There is little doubt that American firepower can win a military victory here. But to a Vietnamese peasant whose home is a — means a lifetime of backbreaking labor — it will take more than presidential promises to convince him we are on his side.[68]

The next day's *New York Times* reported the Defense Department official's response: "There is no new policy of toughness towards civilians. Our policy is still to bend over backward even at possible cost of U.S. lives."[69]

Safer's account is notable for three reasons. First, as innumerable later accounts from soldiers, journalists, and international observers confirm, it captured vividly and precisely the contradiction between U.S. firepower used in a counter-guerrilla war and a political struggle that required the United States to "win the hearts and minds" of the Vietnamese peasants, as the "pacification" program put it. The visual drama was profound. Along with Safer's poignant report, it would clearly have a more profound emotional impact on viewers than the Defense official's response read by the news anchor in New York. The clip, in short, was a public relations disaster for the administration, revealing fundamental questions about the futility and immorality of what the United States was doing in Vietnam.[70]

In addition, the news clip's powerful impact made it instantly controversial, the subject of public denunciation by administration officials and an alleged late-night personal call from President Johnson to CBS president Frank Stanton blasting CBS for "shitting" on the American flag. As David Halberstam reported, Johnson also asked how CBS could "employ a Communist like Safer, how could they be so unpatriotic as to put an enemy film like this?"[71] As Bernard Fall wrote, "When the famous newsreel was shot showing Marines burning down houses with lighters, the reaction among officialdom in Saigon was not so much one of distress that the incident had happened as one of furor at the reporters for seeing and reporting it."[72] Although media personnel rallied in defense of Safer's report and praised his "exceptional courage,"[73] the "inflamed reaction to Safer's story," in Chester Pach's words, "revealed the narrow limits of acceptable war reporting on television."[74]

Finally, the image of American troops igniting Vietnamese huts with lighters became so engraved in the minds of the war's defenders that it came to define their charge of "adversarial" war reporting by the media, despite the fact that, as Lawrence Lichty put it in his study of television coverage of the war, "The Cam Ne story is famous for being the exception to the rule."[75] As Daniel Hallin put it, a report like Safer's is "the stuff of which the myths about Vietnam reporting are made—the crusading reporter or 'adversarial journalist' exposing what the government refuses to admit about the war."[76] Few if any war reports had a comparable impact until the My Lai story broke in 1969.

Several of the straightforward photographs from the war—of limbless children, stoic survivors of a violent village sweep, peasants being herded off to strategic hamlets, and the like—provided glimpses of the painful sensory realities of war. These would weigh heavily on those who had come to view the war as abhorrent. They revealed a profound reality of the war not acknowledged within mainstream media—that the war was systematically victimizing the very people the government claimed "we" were in Vietnam to help. As a corollary, this meant that young American soldiers, indoctrinated with propaganda about the help the United States was bringing to the people of Vietnam, were traumatized by killing or witnessing the killing of civilians—or, witnessing the killing or maiming of their fellow soldiers by people who seemed to be civilians. Yet, for others in the wider public, the mass media discourse that reinforced the war's mythic realities cut off connection with the war's primary victims. These were merely war pictures. The enemy Other presumably deserved to be victimized. So thoroughgoing was the dehumanizing system of mythic reality that Noam Chomsky was led to lament, "We have to ask ourselves whether what is needed in the United States is dissent—or denazification. The question is a debatable one."[77]

However intermittent they may have been, the images didn't stop coming, a fact that contributed to the erosion of support for the war and the credibility of official propaganda. A few additional photographs became icons of the war's horror. One was Eddie Adams's photograph and television footage of South Vietnamese policeman Lo An shooting a captured Viet Cong suspect in the head during the Tet Offensive in 1968—a time when attacks by the North Vietnamese army and the Viet Cong brought actual combat out in the open where it could be captured by the media's cameras. Along with other reports and photographs from Tet, the Lo An shooting, like the Morley Safer report, became a central focus for later attacks on an overly "adversarial media."[78]

While the infamous My Lai massacre clearly went beyond the bounds of what most military people recognized as legitimate military combat, it provided a powerful representation of how the war systematically victimized hundreds of thousands of innocent civilians, including children. The power of those images may well have propelled some individuals, acting out their own righteous anger, to denounce returning soldiers as "baby killers"—a theme exploited by later propaganda efforts to depict the antiwar movement as anti-soldier.[79] As with the powerful photograph and television footage of the young girl, her clothes burned off by napalm, running toward American soldiers, these images were vivid representations of the war's horror, linked for war opponents to the fact that the United States instigated the war and was wreaking massive destruction on much of Indochina. Invariably, as they became engraved in public memory, each of the most powerful photographs became a focal point for subsequent government and conservative efforts to attack the media and resurrect the war's mythic reality.

Media and Antiwar Symbolism

The boundaries of legitimate media discourse about the war were, for many Americans, reinforced by the kinds of imagery the media used to "tell the story" of the antiwar movement. In the early days of antiwar protest, the media used protest photographs that juxtaposed antiwar forces with those that were more legitimately "patriotic," thereby marginalizing antiwar sentiment. As the war continued to escalate, protests helped to put the war more forcefully on the public agenda. Antiwar opinion grew in the public at large and among credible elite actors, the latter legitimizing but also mainstreaming dissent. Blocked from conveying their antiwar argument in mass media, antiwar forces sought symbolic ways of communicating this opposition and grew more militant in their protest actions. As Melvin Small observed, media executives (as well as protesters) thereby faced a paradox:

> Those who run the media personally prefer civilized, adult, dissenting activities where rowdies do not use profanity and carry Viet Cong or Cuban flags. But such decorous affairs are not very exciting or newsworthy. Although a large meeting of prominent individuals opposing the war politely might receive favorable attention, after a while, unless such meetings or marches become even larger or new glamorous leaders join them, they will start to appear in shorter stories toward the back of the newspaper or at the end of the newscast.[80]

Even as the general public became increasingly opposed to the war, they also grew more hostile to the antiwar movement they were witnessing in the media, especially after the 1968 Democratic National Convention.[81]

Probably the most modest in appearance of the national protests, the first national demonstration against the war in April 1965 graphically revealed the media's photographic balancing. As Todd Gitlin has documented, the *New York Times* selected a three-column photograph for its front-page article that displayed roughly equal numbers of "students protesting Vietnam policy" and "a counter demonstration" that was "carried on by others" across the street, whereas in actual numbers there were 150 times as many antiwar protesters at the rally as there were counterdemonstrators. The numerous antiwar signs, with professionally printed lettering, were unreadable in the distant photo. Other UPI photographs that were rejected by the *Times* revealed the paper's effort to minimize the protest's significance: "Two showed a mass of antiwar pickets carrying signs bearing readable slogans; one shows a large mass at the antiwar rally at the Washington Monument; and the other two give an accurate sense of the degree to which the antiwar people outnumbered the counterdemonstrators."[82] Similarly, in covering the fall 1965 protests in New York, the *Times* juxtaposed a protester's sign that read "Get Out of Viet-Nam" with a counter-protester's sign that read "Win in Viet Nam."[83]

Along with labeling antiwar resistance and counter-recruitment efforts as "draft-dodging," media visuals sometimes suggested a contradictory relationship between antiwar protest and American G.I.s — despite the prevalence of antiwar banners proclaiming "Support our G.I.s — Bring Them Home." At the time of the spring 1966 protests, the *Times'* front-page report dichotomized the war and antiwar movement with two four-column photographs. The photograph on top showed a long line of Marines wading ashore from their boats near Saigon to "safeguard the Saigon River." The picture underneath showed "opponents of United States action in Vietnam march[ing] down Fifth Avenue."

Mindful of the media potency of symbolic action, as well as the media's deafness to their arguments, some antiwar activists were quickly drawn to visible, if not dramatic symbolism as a means of communicating their outsider perceptions and feelings about the war through their actions. In one controversial action that drew considerable criticism within the movement, some antiwar protesters began to carry Viet Cong flags as early as fall 1965. Antiwar leader David Dellinger considered the flag displays "senseless" and "inflammatory" and recalled that, during a later visit to Hanoi, Vietnamese leaders observed that American protesters should carry American flags rather than Viet Cong flags.[84] Not surprisingly, the media immediately zoomed in on these colorful displays of antiwar alienation. In its editorial on the November 1965 SANE march in Washington, the *Times* neatly distinguished between the "responsible" march leaders seeking what the *Times* considered legitimate ends ("more intensive efforts" to "achieve a negotiated end of the Vietnamese conflict") and "an influx of extremists who insist on parading under the Vietcong flag and otherwise doing their utmost to outrage millions of Americans."[85]

By 1967, generalizing from the flag imagery with their own visual thinking, the media not only equated the antiwar movement writ large with anti-Americanism but interpreted the symbolism to mean the movement equated the Vietnamese enemy with moral purity. *Time* magazine equated moral criticism of an American war—and a few demonstrators carrying Viet Cong flags—as a "double standard that assumed Washington's guilt and Hanoi's innocence."[86] A *New York Times* editorial attacked the spring rallies for depicting "the United States as the epitome of evil and the Vietcong guerrillas and their North Vietnamese allies as the epitome of good," maintaining that "the demonstrators are pursuing a double standard."[87] Apparently within mythic reality, there were only two possible ways of viewing the war: one in which "we" were all good and "they" were all bad, and the other the opposite. The anti-American theme quickly rebounded through the culture via popular bumper stickers that read: "America: Love It or Leave It."

In covering the October 1967 March on the Pentagon, *Time* typecast the protesters as "hard-eyed revolutionaries and skylarking hippies, ersatz motorcycle gangs and all-too-real college professors," and chose to highlight the most inflammatory protest symbols: "red and blue Viet Cong flags mingled with signs affirming that 'Che Guevara Lives' and posters asking 'Where is Oswald When We Need Him?'"[88] In the political aftermath of the Pentagon march, as pollster Louis Harris put it in *Business Week,* the public seemed to say, "If this is what opposition to the war means, then count me out."[89]

Images and particularly television footage of police violence and angry protester defiance played a significant role in the singularly polarizing Democratic National Convention in Chicago in 1968. After a year of traumatic events—Tet, the assassinations of both Martin Luther King Jr. and Robert Kennedy, the student takeover at Columbia, major uprisings in Paris and Prague, as well as increasing government repression in COINTELPRO—the media stage was set for volatile dramatics. Perceptions on each side of the Chicago struggle reflected the media-hyped pronouncements of the other side's darkest intentions,[90] and hundreds of undercover government agents monitored, infiltrated, and provoked demonstrator activities.[91] As Todd Gitlin put it with reference to the Chicago mayor, "the Daley regime took earlier media reports at face value and rioted against what was actually a small, confused, and intimidated radical presence."[92] Outside the highly contentious Democratic convention that nominated Hubert Humphrey and defeated the efforts of antiwar Democrats to adopt an antiwar plank in the party's platform, the "Battle of Chicago," as *Newsweek* later titled its piece, was about violence in the streets.

Encouraged by Mayor Daley's rhetoric and his stonewalling of the protesters' efforts to gain permission for rallies and marches, the police were on the offensive from the outset, driving an early gathering of youths hoping to "crash" for the night out of Lincoln Park with tear gas, mace, and nightsticks. A similar attack the next day forcefully broke up a rock music performance and the Yippie "Festival of Life," and the following day police stripped off their identification badges and, with billy clubs swinging, waded into crowds gathered for an "unbirthday party" for Lyndon Johnson. As police applied force, increasing numbers of the protesting youths responded by taunting police and throwing rocks and anything else they could get their hands on. After journalists and news photographers were attacked with particular vehemence, the media finally zeroed in on the story about police violence.[93] As Dave Dellinger recalled,

> For three days we couldn't believe that the brutal police assaults were getting so little attention in the mass media. But as more and more newsmen (including Dan Rather and Mike Wallace) got assaulted, gradually the whole country began to see or hear what was happening. Public consciousness of just how brutal the police riot was finally spread throughout the country in a way that hadn't happened on many previous occasions when the police assaults had been just as brutal but more limited to the demonstrators.[94]

After being violently attacked by police in Grant Park, angry protesters gathered outside the convention site. Told to disperse by police, some sat down in anticipation of their arrest; others chanted, "The whole world is watching." Then, in Doug Dowd's memory, "All hell broke loose" as police unleashed their fury on the protesters, swinging billy clubs wildly at anyone in their path—a sight Dowd recalled as one he would "never forget."[95] Highlighted by dramatic television footage, the media brought the street violence into American homes. Television coverage played on the visual dramas occurring both in and outside the convention hall, airing earlier footage of the police attack outside the Hilton, while the newsmagazines later provided lengthy, graphic coverage: *Newsweek*'s eighteen-page "Battle of Chicago" and *Time*'s "Survival at the Stockyards" were both filled with colorful photographs of protesters, police, convention delegates, and the usual fare of celebrities.

Much to the shock of many of the protesters who had witnessed staggering police violence, the "whole world" that watched—at least in the United States—ended up siding with the violent police over the protesters whom the media commonly referred to as "hippies" and "yippies." Immediately following the convention, public opinion polls indicated that 56 percent of the public approved of Mayor Daley's handling of the convention disorders, and 71 percent thought the security measures by police were justified.[96] In fact, nearly 40 percent of whites who supported U.S. withdrawal from Vietnam believed Daley's police had used "insufficient force."[97] Clearly, millions of Americans did not like what they were seeing, and more blamed the protesters than the police. Media coverage and growing violence were having a polarizing impact. As Todd Gitlin put it, the media's images "helped render the street-fighting style legitimate *within* the movement as they helped render it anathema to audiences *outside*."[98]

It turned out on later study that identifiable audiences were to have particularly pronounced and polarized readings of police behavior during the convention. African Americans and young people overwhelmingly felt the police used excessive force in Chicago, whereas rural whites, the elderly, and those with less than a high school education were inclined to side with the police.[99] These divisions would prove fruitful to subsequent efforts by candidates Richard Nixon and George Wallace in their appeals to working-class Americans and "law and order." According to Philip Converse and Howard Schuman, in 1968, antiwar protesters were the most negatively rated of a "wide range of political leaders and groups." Of note, "63% of those believing the war was a mistake viewed protesters negatively, and even of the group favoring complete withdrawal from Vietnam, 53% put the protesters on the negative side of the scale."[100]

In sharp contrast to the violence of Chicago, and drawing on wide support from university faculties, religious leaders, and Senate doves, the October 1969 Moratorium on "business as usual" was observed by millions of Americans from all walks of life. About 100,000 gathered on the Boston Common, while an estimated quarter of a million engaged in antiwar activities in New York. Public officials took part in rallies in several major cities. Colleges and universities, secondary schools, courtrooms, town squares, veterans' cemeteries, movie sets, and the steps of the Capitol bore witness to various expressions of antiwar opinion. In Charles De Benedetti's account, "the main force of the Moratorium was the willingness of ordinary and respectable citizens to conduct collective actions that indicated their wish 'to have done with Vietnam' and to restore domestic harmony."[101]

Aided by visuals of everyday Americans peaceably dissenting from the war, the Moratorium produced the only instance in which the antiwar movement gained wide and mostly favorable coverage in the nation's mass media. CBS and NBC aired ninety-minute specials on the Moratorium, while ABC devoted most of its regular newscast to Moratorium events and administration responses. NBC's programming included a sixteen-minute captioned collage uninterrupted by any newscaster commentary, what Melvin Small characterized as "astounding coverage, full of emotional vignettes,"[102] although the next night's account quickly cast the antiwar activity in a more negative light by leading with Hanoi's endorsement of the Moratorium. The day's activities dominated the front page of the *New York Times,* which hailed it with descriptors like the "largest so far" and "unique." Subsequent analysis of the day's impact was more favorable than unfavorable. The *Washington Post* devoted five pages to the "massive" and "peaceful" rallies in various locales. For the first and only time, *Time* ran a generally favorable five-page article highlighting a visual description of protesters who presumably looked like the magazine's readers: "Small-town housewives and Wall Street lawyers, college presidents and politicians, veteran demonstrators and people who have never made the 'V' sign of the peace movement—thousands of Americans who have never thought to grow a beard, don a hippie head-band or burn a draft-card—planned to turn out on M-day to register their dismay and frustration over Viet Nam."[103] *Newsweek,* too, devoted sections of two issues to the day's activities, leading with "Nixon in Trouble," and following with a spectacular portfolio of color photographs from around the country, concluding that there had "never been a phenomenon quite like it."[104] Reflecting the growing split among economic elites, even *Business Week* and the *Economist* gave the Moratorium favorable play.

Fearing the potential public response, and with its credibility with Hanoi undermined by the Moratorium, the Nixon administration temporarily shelved its "Duck Hook" plan to massively escalate attacks against North Vietnam. Instead, President Nixon went public with an appeal to the "great, silent majority" of Americans for their support.

A month later, however, after Vice President Agnew's attacks against the media (see chapter 7), media coverage of the gigantic Moratorium/Mobilization protest in Washington returned to normal, much to the Nixon administration's satisfaction. The television networks "paid scant attention to the largest antiwar demonstration in American history" while it was under way, though they took note of the nonviolent March Against Death.[105] CBS highlighted a spinoff group of militants who raised havoc at the Department of Justice, while NBC noted that the "largest" rally was "almost totally peaceful." NBC anchor David Brinkley predicted, inaccurately, that it was "probably the last mass rally of the antiwar movement." Overall, the media paid no attention to the content of speeches, assuming a stance that seemed to ask why there was a need for demonstrations if the president was withdrawing U.S. troops from Vietnam. As Small reported, the issue was whether the protest would remain peaceful, "as if that had been the main goal of the demonstration."[106]

The massive 1969 actions, combined with a stonewalling Nixon administration and the continuation of the administration's "Vietnamization" program of phased withdrawal of American troops, left antiwar activists with a vexing dilemma: What could they do that could possibly top the fall 1969 protests? In this context, organizing for spring 1970 demonstrations became increasingly difficult. That all changed, however, when President Nixon announced on April 30 that U.S. forces had invaded Cambodia. The president's Orwellian warning about the United States becoming a "pitiful, helpless giant" if it failed to act against both external and internal challenges only added to the rage many Americans felt at this expansion of the war.[107] Spontaneous protests sprung up on campuses around the country, and within a few days a national student strike movement had taken hold. And then on May 4, units of the Ohio National Guard that had been called onto campus to protect buildings at Kent State University unexpectedly opened fire on student demonstrators, killing four students (two of whom were not protesters) and wounding nine others. At that point, the campuses exploded across the country. The student strike spread to hundreds of the nation's colleges and universities, and antiwar activities erupted in almost any imaginable form, from symbolic funerals and flag lowerings to rallies and marches to blockades and sit-ins. In Tom Wells's account, "It was an exhilarating time for most protesters. The antiwar movement was alive as never before. The political possibilities seemed stupendous. A truly general strike against the war was not inconceivable."[108]

The Kent State killings and the shooting deaths of two black students ten days later at Jackson State College in Mississippi clearly jolted the media as well as much of the rest of the United States.[109] The dramatic photograph of the young woman screaming as she crouched beside one of the dead students appeared on newspaper front pages around the country, and *Life* carried its usual dramatic tableau detailing the girl's encounter as well as several huge photos of the national guard kneeling and firing at the protesters. The spectrum of legitimate media opinion ranged from liberal *Newsweek*'s articles titled "My God, They're Killing Us" and "Who Guards the Guard?" to the more conservative *Time* editorial "Violent Protest: A Debased Language" and its lengthy feature report "At War with War" that contained an inflammatory series of photographs: students "burning Nixon in effigy at Tulane," "Berkeley demonstrators throwing tear gas back at police," longhaired young men swimming naked in the Washington reflecting pool, and "animal blood in Washington." *Time*'s Kent State segment focused on "Martyrdom that Shook the Country" and provided both a blow-by-blow account leading up to the shooting, a sympathetic glimpse of the "outnumbered and partially encircled" National Guardsmen, and brief, sympathetic profiles of each of the victims. With almost no attention paid to what the activism was about, the *U.S. News* piece buried the Kent State events within a sub-article that traced a student-generated "Build-up to Tragedy at Kent State" and placed it within a series of alarmist articles about selected events of spring 1970.[110]

The antiwar movement continued to play out for more than two years as U.S. troops remained in Vietnam amidst a deepening sense of frustration and despair. The movement did manage to mobilize one more massive demonstration on April 24, 1971, when another half million assembled in Washington, followed a week later by the street-action turmoil of the May Day effort to "shut down Washington" via "mass civil disobedience." Coming at a time when the majority of Americans for the first time believed that the war was "morally wrong," media responses were somewhat sympathetic to the peaceful April gathering but outspokenly critical of the more volatile May Day street actions.

One reason the media responded more favorably to the April protest was the visually dramatic and emotionally powerful Dewey Canyon III protest organized by the Vietnam Veterans Against the War. As a kind of veterans' "invasion" of Washington, the VVAW contingent of about a thousand veterans and Gold Star mothers marched to Arlington National Cemetery, where they were at first blocked from entry but eventually allowed to hold a silent memorial for the dead in Indochina. In subsequent days, veterans carried out guerrilla theater outside the Capitol, lobbied members of Congress, tried to turn themselves in to the Pentagon for war crimes, camped on the Mall (violating a government ban that was not enforced), and, in a powerfully poignant and emotion-filled ceremony, approached the fenced-off Capitol steps, where they threw away their war medals and denounced the war. Satirically named after Defense Department jargon for the U.S. invasion of Laos, Dewey Canyon III captured the attention of the mass media and placed the Nixon administration in the awkward position of seeming to defy the will of its own soldiers in prosecuting the war. The photographs and television footage of bedraggled veterans, some disabled, denouncing the war and honoring their fallen brothers while throwing their medals over a fence the government had constructed to protect the Capitol from these invaders provided a potent sensory reality of the soldiers' deep alienation from the war in which they had fought. Along with a front-page photograph of one vet throwing his medals over the fence, the New York Times noted that the VVAW protest was "one of the more poignant and eloquent protests" that would have "an impact far greater than its numbers." The paper labeled the protest the "last and most emotional" of the week's demonstrations against the war.[111]

Media acknowledgment of the compelling power of the medals protest contrasted sharply with the way the media all but ignored the Winter Soldier hearings the VVAW had held a few months earlier. Dozens of veterans came forward with painful public testimony about atrocities they had witnessed or committed during the war. Winter Soldier offered no powerful images and only repeated damning condemnations of the war's inherent atrocities. Unlike the visual atrocities of My Lai, or the drama of disabled and alienated vets throwing their medals at the U.S. capitol building, Winter Soldier barely registered in the nation's media.

In the end, media imagery of the many dramatic and colorful events of the sixties era probably had two major kinds of effects. First, during the era, the images provoked powerful responses among the millions who viewed them, responses that on the one hand revealed often-obscured realities or evidence of heroic actions that invited millions of Americans to act, and on the other hand provided millions of other Americans with a profound sense that their ordered world was slipping away. The emotions produced by the images quickly became the object of two significant forces: voices of political backlash that provided a reassuring answer for the fears and resentments aroused among some viewers, and commercial forces that returned again and again to the images and stories they knew would resonate with wide audiences.

7

System Response: Generational Hype and Political Backlash

We're right at the center of everything. . . . Now it's us, we're right in the center reading about ourselves in the newspaper. It's youth. Everything is youth.
—Student speaking to Thomas J. Cottle, quoted in *Time's Children*, 1971

Activists fall into three basic categories: radicals, idealists, and realists. The first step is to isolate and marginalize the radicals. They're the ones who see inherent structural problems that need remedying if indeed a particular change is to occur. To isolate them, try to create the perception in the public mind that people advocating fundamental solutions are terrorists, extremists, fear mongers, outsiders, communists, or whatever. . . . The goal is to sour the idealists on the idea of working with the radicals. Instead get them working with the realists. Realists are people who want reform but don't really want to upset the status quo.
—Consultant speaking to corporate executives,
quoted in Kim Bobo, Steve Max, and Jackie Kendall,
Organizing for Social Change, 2001

In 1964, when hundreds of students from northern campuses joined the Freedom Summer movement in Mississippi, when mostly younger African Americans in some of the nation's northern cities erupted in riotous rage, and when students at Berkeley engaged in what became known as the Free Speech Movement, the mass media woke up to the fact that something beyond the southern struggle to end Jim Crow was happening. Engaging in their own kind of visual association, the mass media zeroed in on the most visible common denominator among these and other activities. Their answer was youth, a new generation of questioning, rebellious baby boomers.

The national news media never let go of the generational frame. While student antiwar protests on college campuses sought to target and remove institutional connections to the war, the media routinely labeled antiwar rallies at other sites as student protests regardless of the mixed ages of participants or the older age of most organizers and speakers. Even feminism was framed as a youth movement—for example, *Time* attributed the women's movement to "younger women, part of a rebellious generation," who were therefore "fertile ground for the seeds of discontent."[1] And, of course, commercial media had been attentive to the baby boom generation and its musical tastes going back into the 1950s when rock and roll and other symptoms of "cultural rebellion" were taking off. That particular commercial fascination would accelerate as signs of a counter-culture emerged in the mid-sixties.

Along with the increasingly expressive images emerging in the media, the generational explanation provided the basis for two kinds of system responses to sixties era social movements. One used the appeal of images, behaviors, and lan-guage of youth to feed the young with a sense of their historical importance as a generation. The other used the threat posed by these same images and behaviors to argue that this generation had fallen under the sway of destructive influences that thereby posed an obvious threat to society. The first of these responses was fundamentally commercial. It offered the young a kind of visual association that empowered them in one way or another. Yet to the degree they succumbed and remained at that level of visual thought, it co-opted their "rebellion."

The second kind of response was, in a variety of forms, ideological backlash. While its proponents may well have found the images and behaviors alarming, they linked them via ideological belief to the political targets they sought to transform. Indeed, one backlash strategy—the federal government's domestic Counterintelligence Program (COINTELPRO)—used government infiltration and provocation to create a more tumultuous spectacle in order to discredit the protest movements.[2] The media images were particularly useful foils for the out-of-power Republicans and conservatives to gain political credibility with the electorate, most notably with two important elements of the Democrat's New Deal coalition: the white South and the Catholic working class. As Piven and Cloward have observed, "Just as people have to be mobilized to support parties and the issues and candidates they put forward, so do they have to be mobilized to desert them."[3] For these audiences, appearance confirmed explanation.

The increasing visibility of behaviors that veered further and further outside the boundaries of conventionality gave the backlash charges increasing validity and urgency, especially among those who felt both alienated by what they saw and left out of the nation's largely liberal discourse of the time. The war greatly compounded both antiwar frenzy and public disenchantment. Thus it was, for example, that in the middle of the turbulence of 1968 a white father of five in North Carolina vented his frustrations in a letter to Senator Sam Ervin, using words that reflect the year's searing images as well as the backlash rhetoric of political leaders:

> I'm sick of crime everywhere. I'm sick of riots. I'm sick of "poor" people demonstrations. . . . I'm sick of the lack of law enforcement. . . . I'm sick of Vietnam. . . . I'm sick of hippies, LSD, drugs, and all the promotion the news media give them. . . . But most of all, I'm sick of constantly being

kicked in the teeth for staying home, minding my own business, working steadily, paying my bills and taxes, raising my children to be decent citizens, managing my financial affairs so I will not become a ward of the City, County, or State, and footing the bill for all the minuses mentioned herein.[4]

Talkin' 'bout Generations: From Students to Youth Culture to Youth Market

Challenges to received authority were inherent in the nature of academic life, at least within the liberal arts curriculum. Furthermore, with young people finding themselves away from parental restrictions among large numbers of their peers, campus life invariably simmers with the exploration of personal and sexual relationships. Well before 1964, small groups of students had been actively challenging various campus practices—so much so that University of California president Clark Kerr was moved to observe that one had to "pretend" that perennial acts of student agitation were "something new."[5] In 1963, a thoughtful *New York Times Magazine* article entitled "College Morals Mirror Our Society" detailed ways the "college generation" was in "open revolt against official codes of campus morality."[6] In spring 1964, *Newsweek* applied the hyperbolic term "revolution" it had used to describe civil rights agitation in 1963 to the "morals revolution" on the nation's campuses.[7] Small groups of students were agitating against what they termed *in loco parentis,* the various ways in which their colleges and universities had assumed the parental role of guiding their moral development (i.e., at least formally constraining their sexual activity).

By fall 1964, however, there was a new energy on several campuses. As Freedom Summer students returned to their campuses determined to address injustices and remove irksome regulations that got in their way, they energized what rapidly became known as the "student movement." Greeted by resistant authorities who saw them as the problem and media that saw them as "the issue," the students drew on the organizing principles and direct action techniques of the civil rights struggle to generate publicity for their efforts to confront wrongs and to reach wider audiences of youth and the general public with their causes.

The Campus Revolt: Free Speech and Beyond

Berkeley's Free Speech Movement became, as Kirkpatrick Sale put it, the "Fort Sumter" of campus unrest from 1964 on, in part because of the movement's colorful trajectory and in part because students at Berkeley and other campuses were expressing their deepening disenchantment with their university and college experiences. In Sale's words, "The basic source of the Berkeley protest was more involved than the desire for political activity or a restructured university, and more difficult to admit and deal with. It was of course ... the desire of young people to say something, to do something about the American society they lived in, the society that made them feel useless, exploited, guilty, paternalized and consumerized, that allowed monstrous ills to be perpetrated."[8] As Berkeley's Mario Savio put it, the university was the place "where people begin seriously to question the conditions of their existence," yet instead it turned out people "with all the sharp edges worn off."[9] This was the postwar "multiversity" proudly proclaimed by Clark Kerr, the institution through which government, the scientific community, and business collaborated in producing a generation of highly functional "managers." As an earlier book by Paul Goodman had put it, students were coming to feel that they were "growing up absurd," in an "apparently closed room."[10]

The catalyst for Berkeley's protests was the university's response to student activists' direct action challenging racial discrimination in San Francisco's hotels. The university banned student groups from leafleting, recruiting, and fundraising at tables that had long been available to passersby at the university's Sather Gate area. Responding with civil disobedience, Berkeley grad Jack Weinberg was arrested for sitting at his table. A spontaneous thirty-two-hour rally and public discussion—what participant Michael Rossman called "an incredible dialogue" of "all different points of view"[11]—ensued as students surrounded the police car that held Weinberg, and a wide coalition of student groups across the political spectrum protested the university's violation of their free speech rights. Speakers removed their shoes and carefully used the car roof as a speaking platform.

The struggle between students and an administration bent on punishing those who flaunted its rules persisted through the academic year. Once a physical confrontation had occurred, media coverage of the Free Speech Movement responded in classic fashion—in Sale's words, with "constant sensationalistic newspaper and television coverage."[12] After the initial arrests, police car forum, and the suspension of student activists, students engaged in a peaceful sit-in in the administration building, a lively time during which students gave speeches about their education and the university crisis, and clusters of students did their homework, played music, and danced in various corridors before police dragged them away. *Time* published the first newsmagazine article on the campus upheaval, full of colorful references to the students' "battle cry" and their "Joan of Arc" (folksinger Joan Baez) as they "stormed" the administration building. After two paragraphs that described the police sweep that cleared the building, *Time* provided a scant two-sentence reference to the ban against recruitment and information tables that had generated the initial protest and asserted that the students "and off-campus agitators" had earlier "battered" and "rocked" the surrounded police car. *Time* referred to the "self-styled Free Speech Movement" as "dominated by civil rights militants, Trotskyite groups, and members of a Communist front" and concluded with Kerr's comment that activists at the demonstration had "been impressed with the tactics of Fidel Castro and Mao Tse-tung."[13]

Shana Alexander's "Feminine Eye" column in *Life* noted that the students were "obsessed by a huge, terrifying IBM-shaped monster they called the mul-tiversity, *misusing* somewhat a term coined by California's distinguished presi-dent, Clark Kerr."[14] At the hostile end of the spectrum, *U.S. News & World Report* published a three-page "exclusive" interview with California's conservative education superintendent, Max Rafferty, entitled "A Cure for Campus Riots." Rafferty concluded that the "Communist groups" who "have always established themselves on State-university campuses" had succeeded in joining with the normally insignificant "exhibitionists" with "beards and pimples" to tap into stu-dents' feelings of "creeping facelessness and loss of identity" on a campus that had "been allowed to get too big."[15]

By the spring semester, the war in Vietnam had become a campus issue pro-ducing a more radical edge to campus activism, and signs of countercultural ac-tivity were becoming visible on and off the Berkeley campus, as well as in San Francisco. Noting the raft of publications about the Berkeley protests, Sale ar-gued, "Somewhere in its depths, the nation knew that Berkeley was more than an enlarged panty raid, was speaking, albeit haltingly, to something profound."[16] In the spring, *Newsweek* framed the unrest in glib generational terms, leading its account with the observation that "the young" had successfully " 'Beatle-ized' the nation" and might be about to "Berkeley-ize it as well." *Newsweek* asked, "Clearly, this generation demands to be heard as well as seen. But just what is it saying?"[17] Drawing on a Harris poll and wide-ranging student comments, the magazine organized its explanation into two major headings: "The Problem: Making the Grade," and "Activism — Protesting Too Much?" While puzzling over the new generational outlook, the magazine's poll findings actually indicated close compatibility between student opinions and those of their parents and older Americans generally. Nonetheless, the writers observed that "indications are that American youth is asking for a truce in the *endless war between genera-tions*."[18] In effect, the magazine brought the notion of intergenerational conflict to students' attention, not the other way around.

With Red Scare and other hyperbolic frames, media coverage was well wide of the mark in understanding the student unrest — as the Berkeley slogan "The issue is not the issue" suggested. *Newsweek*'s spring article, in fact, included a satirical headline from a Carleton College student newspaper: "What's Bugging Them? ADULTS: THE TROUBLED GENERATION." Despite its own contrary evidence, *Newsweek* concluded, "A discontinuity exists not only between parents and chil-dren, but between the malleable youngsters and . . . [those who] run the world." The magazine tweaked the latter discontent to mean "today's undergraduates cannot cope with the achievements of today's advanced scholars."[19]

Countercultural Youth

At the beginning of 1967, *Time* anointed the "Under-25 Generation" its "Man of the Year" on its cover and followed with an article liberally sprinkled with the common generational cues: young celebrities, growing antiwar sentiment, and multiple references to drugs (which *Time* linked to increasing suicide rates "in much of the world"), sexual promiscuity, and rock music. *Time*'s writers offered several explanations for the new generation's behaviors: their material security, competition for high grades, and sympathy for the civil rights cause, and suggested that a "compelling reason for adult *angst* is that the young seem curiously unappreciative of the society that supports them."[20] In mid-decade, it seemed, the media struggled for explanations for what it defined as a generational phenomenon, while the young struggled to articulate what felt wrong about the society they were asked to join. What seems clear is that much of the media's "mainstreamese" made little sense in the eyes of the young.

Around the same time that campus activism was taking off, an alternative "hippie counterculture" was emerging in communities like San Francisco's Haight-Ashbury section and New York's East Village. In contrast to the high spirit and hopefulness of civil rights and early student activism, the counterculture's pioneers were more sharply alienated from the wider society's preoccupation with postponed gratification and material acquisition. Recoiling from what they saw as society's hypocrisy, its manipulation of human beings and the environment, its violence toward those who did not cooperate with the "system's" imperatives and the profound psychic costs borne by those who did, these mostly young people were withdrawing from the prevailing institutions of educational, social, and political life.[21] Their alienation sharpened dramatically and their numbers grew as the war in Vietnam became more visible and omnipresent. They began to wear their alienation in disheveled or "mod" attire, long hair, and hip street lingo and were drawn to live with or near each other. Sometimes seeking media exposure to tell their story to their fellow youths, they found the media's distorted efforts to understand their world both comical and alienating. And so, as communities of the disaffected began to crop up around the country, so did what became an extraordinary culture of alternative or underground media combining radical politics and underground culture with event coverage and personal notices.[22]

The mass media of the time, of course, couldn't leave the counterculture alone. It was far too colorful, bizarre, and newsworthy by virtue of its manifest Otherness and, eventually, its media-influenced popularity among the young. Perhaps more than any other area of the 1960s, the counterculture was subjected to massive sensationalism and screaming alarmism through virtually all mainstream media, both of which helped attract new and ever-younger elements into the counterculture, in the process transforming it.

In addition to youthful sexual mores, the mass media were drawn early on to what eventually became the dominant frame for understanding—and remembering[23]—the counterculture: drugs. The media reported on Timothy Leary and Richard Alpert's experimentation with LSD and subsequent firing from the Harvard faculty in 1963, but in early 1966, after doctors reported on LSD-induced psychiatric breakdowns, the media shifted into panic mode: "Epidemic of Acid Heads" (*Time,* March 11), "Spread and Perils of LSD" (*Life,* March 25), "Dangers of LSD" (*Time,* April 22), "Murder by LSD?" (*Newsweek,* April 25), and, of course, the right-wing's reflexive red-baiting, "Moscow-brewed LSD" (*National Review,* May 17)—ironic given the fact that the CIA had been conducting LSD experiments on unknowing Americans.[24]

After San Francisco's Haight-Ashbury community held their first "Human Be-In" in February 1967—a celebratory "gathering of the tribes," complete with Bay area rock bands, psychedelic attire, dancing, and, yes, drug use—the media took notice. *Newsweek* ran a four-page article on "Dropouts with a Mission," complete with two pages of colorful photographs of various countercultural celebrities (Jerry Garcia and "Pigpen" of the Grateful Dead, Timothy Leary) and variously exotically attired hippies. While the photo spectacle no doubt captured *Newsweek* readers' attention, the article's text observed that most of the participants were caught up in the "gentle anarchy" of the moment, a "love feast, a psychedelic picnic, a hippie happening." Indeed, the magazine was taken in by appearances, embellishing the hype: "External things [like hair and general attire] no longer make the difference." "For the first time men and women are becoming friends again . . . just friends," and "Sex is not a matter of great debate because as far as they are concerned the sexual revolution is accomplished." Gender roles were apparently liberated with "women voluntarily choosing traditional feminine chores" in "new kinds of family systems." Even LSD seemed both ubiquitous and benign: "Virtually every hippie has taken LSD, which means that every one has had a 'vision.'" Only the final paragraph recalled a "low as well as a high side to the hippie phenomenon," mentioning as a kind of afterthought a "sizable fringe of teen-age runaways" and "seriously disturbed people," as well as the "dangers of drug-taking."[25]

In sum, *Newsweek*'s youth-friendly portrait read like a travel brochure of sights and sounds that might appeal to young teenagers seeking freedom from the hassles of authoritarian parents or an "uptight" educational system. *Time* followed with its own somewhat darker guide to the counterculture, a July 1967 cover story on "The Hippies," complete with the obligatory six-page collage of colorful, often provocative pictures and captions. After briefly referring to the hippies' "almost childlike fascination" and their preaching "altruism and mysticism, honesty, joy, and nonviolence," the magazine turned to a lengthy discussion of drugs, reducing "hippiedom" to a "cult whose mystique derives essentially from the influence of hallucinogenic drugs." While the article observed with some accuracy that the counterculture's drug use was "wholly alien to the rationale of Western society," unlike "other accepted stimuli, from nicotine to liquor," the magazine went no further to examine society's "rationale" that drove people to use "accepted stimuli."[26]

Shorter and equally alarmist articles appeared in *U.S. News & World Report.* After a "Spotlight on 'Hippies': A First-Hand Report" provided a brief glimpse into a Washington "pot" party,[27] the magazine published a three-page article in October entitled "Hippies—A Passing Fad?" The latter article highlighted the movement of hippies into "tribal [i.e., communal] living arrangements" and a stereotypical if somewhat valid generational clash between Great Depression parents and their children who "managed to read something sinister" into their parents' lives and were moving "resolutely in the other direction—from riches to rags." The magazine concluded by quoting a California assemblyman's warning that "hippies are potentially the greatest threat facing the nation's traditional social structure," but then speculated hopefully that perhaps the "whole hippie movement may turn out to have been just another fad."[28]

Nineteen sixty-seven was the year of the much ballyhooed "Summer of Love" during which the mass media and the rock music industry endlessly hyped the counterculture. While Scott MacKenzie's popular hit "(Are you Going to) San Francisco?" resounded with lyrics such as "Summertime will be a love-in there," and "All cross the nation . . . there's a whole generation / With a new explanation," the Gray Line Bus Company sponsored "hippie-hop" bus tours that took curious elders through the streets of the Haight and provided them with a "glossary of hippie terms" to help guide the uninitiated. Gray Line proudly advertised the tours as "the only foreign tour within the continental limits of the United States."

Haight chronicler Charles Perry observed that media publicity's "shallow gleanings" produced "in effect an advertisement for the neighborhood, but not the kind that had been hoped for. The press advertised free love, free lunch in the Panhandle, tolerance for the crazy and outcast, and a New Age governed by the power of love and innocence. So it brought in not only visionaries but insecure young people unable to find a place for themselves, dropouts content with the basics of life, outcasts and crazies."[29] And, indeed, young teenagers began to flock to the Haight area during the summer months. The experimentation with drugs and lifestyles carried out by somewhat older, more mature populations spread downward to younger and younger populations, with predictable results. One study of the youthful population of the Haight during the summer of 1967 found that roughly 15 percent made up a religiously obsessive or emotionally disturbed "fringe," 40 percent were "true believers" who were invested in the mystique of the Haight as a model for the world, and about 45 percent were "attracted by the no-hassle lifestyle of the dropout." According to the Haight-Ashbury Research Project's director, Dr. Stephen Pittel, the fringe group tended to come from cold, authoritarian families, the believers came from supportive families with whom they maintained contact, and the dropouts came from families that demanded high achievement but discouraged independence.[30]

Haight residents certainly noticed the destructive impact of the runaway migration. After the summer deluge, community residents held a "Death of Hippie" funeral event, complete with a coffin with the words "Hippie, Son of Media" painted on the side.[31] The countercultural community recognized its own destruction, brought about through the attention of the gawking media. Noting that "the media tend to isolate the weirdest aberrations and consequently to attract to the movement many extroverted poseurs," historian Theodore Roszak criticized "the young" for their "miserably bad job of dealing with the distortive publicity with which the mass media have burdened their embryonic experiments. Too often they fall into the trap of reacting narcissistically or defensively to their own image in the fun-house mirror of the media."[32]

In 1969, when hip promoters advertised a major rock festival outside of Bethel, New York, Woodstock became a countercultural mecca, attracting upward of half a million young people to "three days of peace and music." The promoters expected about 50,000 to attend, paying $18 for festival tickets. They and their facilities were overwhelmed by the massive crowds that streamed onto the festival farmland, producing both a memorable free festival and a potential nightmare in community sustenance (if not crowd control). The fact that the festival took on a celebratory feeling through torrential rains and rousing music could be attributed to both the high spirits of those in attendance and a contagious wave of communal voluntarism that infected not only townspeople and others who came to the festival's assistance, but outsiders like the press and police. The *New York Times* reversed the skeptical tone of its early reporting, noting a police officer's praise for the "courteous, considerate and well-behaved kids" in the paper's wrap-up editorial and observing presciently that "comrades-in-rock, like comrades-in-arms, need great days to remember."[33] *Time* was classically hyperbolic yet prescient in capturing much of the future media's hype, with a lengthy article titled "The Message of History's Biggest Happening."[34]

With the benefit of hindsight, the youthful counterculture of the 1960s and the environmental forces that produced it marked a crucial turning point in American media culture and politics, accelerating the media culture's shift away from the material politics of who gets what, when, and why to a cultural politics grounded in personal expression. The generational preoccupation of the media would prompt a variety of responses: a sense of affective empowerment among the young, an effort by the Yippies to politicize countercultural youth through media theatrics, consumer capitalism's ultimately co-optive adaptation of "hip culture" and endless attention to generational tastes, and, of course, political and cultural backlash.

Generational Backlash: From Pop Psychology to Ideological History

The generational frame was an easy way for the media to encompass the entire range of visible turbulence it was covering in the latter 1960s, especially as political protest and countercultural appearance began to converge. While the media made frequent reference to the "generation gap," attacks on the young began to appear in the media as early as 1965, when, for example, the president of the Los Angeles Chamber of Commerce proclaimed that the "generation of youth that is discontented, restless, and rebellious" was the nation's leading problem.[35]

With "explaining youth" the question, the easiest answer was to scrutinize their parents and speculate about ways the young were encouraged to be self-indulgent by "permissive" parenting—a theory that evolved from a misreading of pediatrician Benjamin Spock's guide *Baby and Child Care,* used by many postwar parents. While it is quite possible that some parents read Spock's emphasis on the individuation of the developing child as permission to indulge their children, the permissive parenting theory also ignored the way postwar consumer culture systematically encouraged both self-indulgence and other-directedness.

In seeking to explain both the counterculture and the rise of student activism, the media gravitated toward several psychological or pop-psychology voices to authenticate their conclusions. Longshoreman Eric Hoffer's 1951 book *The True Believer* had argued that history's great mass movements were populated by "misfits" who longed to transcend their lives of failure by being part of a great historic movement. In the mid-1960s, Hoffer's book became a popular source for explaining the social movements of the time—particularly his argument that youth whose "restless groping for an identity" led them to "join any mass movement and plunge into any form of spectacular action." With a slim 1967 volume titled *The Temper of Our Times,* his own public television show ("Conversations with Eric Hoffer"), and a well-publicized hour-long interview with CBS television's Eric Sevareid, Hoffer provided pungent commentaries on the "New Age." With a nod to their similar class origins, Hoffer praised President Johnson as "one of us," thereby earning him an invitation to the White House and wider publicity for his views.[36]

The year 1968 was a particularly fruitful one for generational backlash. Freudian psychoanalyst Bruno Bettelheim received substantial media attention when he charged at the annual convention of the American Orthopsychiatric Association in Chicago in 1968 that the "civil disobedience, contemptuous attitudes towards the police, and emotional attacks on President Johnson were damaging the mental health of the young." Bettelheim blamed "liberals, the press and teachers who failed to assert their authority" rather than the actual institutions and events targeted by youthful protesters. He further muddied the waters of responsibility: "We send our children off to school to make their way into the system, and then *tell them the system is lousy. We vilify the President as a man who is killing babies* and then ask our children to respect authority." In reality, it was the experiences of the young, encountering either arbitrary acts of authority or rationalizations that perpetuated racism, inequality, and the war in Vietnam that taught some of them that "the system" was "lousy." It was young protesters, not the targeted "liberal" journalists and teachers, who vilified the president for "killing babies" in antiwar chants. Bettelheim's view that "the system" could be changed "in the voting booth" was, in the minds of many protesters, being contradicted by what experience was teaching them in 1968. Cautioning that "we" should "keep adult concerns away from children," Bettelheim echoed a growing sense among political leaders that the mass media spawned "some of these riots." [37]

Later, responding to a 1969 student takeover of a University of Chicago building, Bettelheim simply asserted from afar that "many of these kids are very sick. They need a psychiatrist." [38] In a subsequent *New York Times Magazine* article, entitled "Children Must Learn to Fear," Bettelheim attributed violence "on our campuses and on our streets" to inadequate superego controls that reflected society's (meaning social authorities as opposed to the market's) removal of "both inner and outer controls." Reflecting his own brand of Freudian theory, Bettelheim wrote, "Without sex repression, there is no prolonged span of intellectual learning. And the same goes for fear. Without fear, there is no inner control over instinctual tendencies." [39] Bettelheim's view was subsequently picked up by *New York Times* columnist William V. Shannon, who asserted that the "attack" on the nation's universities and their ideals "comes from youngsters who are ignorant of those ideals, from others who are emotionally disturbed and prone to violence, and from still others who have willfully chosen to be political totalitarians." Shannon concluded that Bettelheim "accurately defined the problem. In the main they are badly brought up children." [40]

One major work that gained leverage in the wider culture because of its "authoritative" application of the generational frame was social theorist Lewis Feuer's *The Conflict of Generations,* a lengthy work published in 1969 that examined a variety of historical student movements. While on the faculty at Berkeley during the Free Speech Movement, Feuer had been, in the words of Reginald Zelnick, "one of the FSM's most rancorous critics." [41] His thesis was that student movements generically combined the "motives of youthful love" with a "destructive pole" of nihilistic self-destruction rooted in the "conflict of generations." Like Bettelheim, Feuer looked to the psychological needs of the young as the causal explanation of activism he found objectionable.

Feuer's selective ideological frame was fairly transparent in his treatment of the "New Student Left." He likened participatory democracy to "Soviet democracy" and "Leninism updated," referring to it as "action by a small, dictatorial elite translated into the language of the 'nonviolent' movement." [42] He characterized the antiwar teach-ins of 1965 as a "demand for special status and privilege" on the part of academics who had the gall to believe that "it was incumbent upon the administration to defend its policies before the academic community." He maintained that the "student movement began to turn rapidly from the civil rights issue to that of Vietnam" in 1965 because civil rights "no longer offered as good an emotional opportunity for conducting a generational struggle," not because of the emergence of the black power movement or the escalation of and growing media attention to the war in Vietnam that year. The antiwar aspect of the "generational struggle" was simply the "emergence of anti-Americanism as a student ideology."[43]

"Expert" commentaries by the likes of Hoffer, Bettelheim, and Feuer lent authority to media frames that zeroed in on characteristics of protesters and youth generally to explain dramatic newsworthy events to older Americans. All three appeared to be commentators who had studied the young. As observers, all three applied their own experiences, professional and otherwise, as frames for understanding the era's events. A few psychologists actually did engage in investigative research into the lives of young Americans. One of the foremost of these was Yale psychologist Kenneth Keniston, who explored the makeup of the "young radicals" of the 1967 Vietnam Summer in some empirical depth. As Keniston himself put it, "Given the failure of liberal theories to anticipate the growing disaffection of the affluent young, it was inevitable that other views would emerge. Most of these views are not worthy of serious consideration: they select some single factor like parental permissiveness, the war in Vietnam, the idealism of youth, faculty instigation, Communist conspiracy, or the Oedipal complex as satisfactory explanations of what is happening."[44] In fact, Keniston's young radicals did not fit the mold. Drawing on in-depth interviews with the Vietnam summer activists, Keniston found that their activism was an outgrowth of their values of tolerance, equality, and fairness that echoed the kinds of values their parents had stressed in raising them.[45]

One problem in explaining actions taken by protesters, of course, is that different individuals engaging in public actions behaved as they did for a wide variety of reasons, and the mass media were reflexively drawn to visual representation of the most bizarre and deviant of these acts. It is undoubtedly the case that some individuals drawn to the counterculture or to militant protest were acting at least partially out of internal drives. Indeed, these individuals may have been responding more than anyone else to the cues and opportunities provided by drama-seeking news media. Many of the backlash commentaries read as if they were based on observations of media events rather than systemic examination like Keniston's, though in some cases individual commentators had been directly impacted by a specific encounter with angry youth. Yet, while riddled with their authors' subjective and ideological perspectives, they provided credentialed support for attacks on sixties movements by those seeking elected office. The latter often used pop psychology as the explanation for behaviors that were becoming increasingly visible to American audiences. Erased from backlash accounts and media reports generally was a more complex explanation that, among other things, took into account ways the mainstream media's framing of legitimate discourse affected the political dynamics of the time. The claims of outsiders, never considered legitimate in the mass media — or by the authors of backlash commentaries — could be legitimately ignored thanks to the kinds of explanations that came from the backlash "authorities."

Other academics, writers, and policy intellectuals joined the backlash in 1968. The *New York Times Magazine* published three commentaries on the late-sixties upheavals, ranging from the left to right ends of legitimate intellectual discourse. All three zeroed in on the more extreme forms of confrontational politics accessible in the mass media. On the left, social democrat Irving Howe used the successful nonviolent politics of the civil rights movement as a framework for denouncing the "black desperadoes" and New Leftists of 1968 for their "politics of desperation." Howe spoke precisely and with some force against the more anti-liberal excesses of these movements. Yet his analysis failed to provide an answer to an antiwar movement that viewed the war as morally horrific and found this view excluded from the legitimate discourse of mass media. He denounced antiwar tactics that "look like civil disobedience" (e.g., recruitment sit-ins), maintaining that "acts of conscience violating the law can be taken seriously only if they are concerned with the most fundamental moral issues." By implication, Howe seemed to say, Vietnam was not such an issue.[46]

A Columbia student whose bloodied face spanned the top of the first page of Howe's article wrote a letter to the *Times* objecting to his being labeled a "student militant," noting that he had joined with hundreds of other students and faculty outside the building Columbia students had occupied as a "witness" against violence, prepared to be arrested. He and the others, however, were "merely clubbed and beaten indiscriminately and without mercy" by the police — a sample of conditions Howe's article did not adequately address.[47]

Somewhere closer to the center, liberal diplomat George Kennan decried the "banners and epithets and obscenities and virtually meaningless slogans" that had replaced the dispassionate discussion of public affairs he associated with the Wilsonian ideal of the academy. Referring to photographs that "may be seen daily," he observed: "On the one side, there is angry militancy, full of hatred and intolerance and often quite prepared to embrace violence as a source of change. On the other side is a gentleness, passivity and quietism — ostensibly a yearning for detachment from the affairs of the world, not the detachment Woodrow Wilson had in mind."[48] While the latter was an "escape into a world which is altogether illusory and subjective," the former was full of an "extraordinary certainty" of the "correctness of its own answers." To be sure, more than a few antiwar protesters did express their views with an unmistakable moral certainty, yet, as was the case with Howe, Kennan was dismissive toward the deep moral horror the Vietnam War engendered in much of the movement, noting that their "conviction that right is on their side" seemed "particularly out of place at just this time." Reflecting the perspective of the insider policy intellectual that he was, Kennan argued that the complexity of Vietnam required "years of disciplined and restrained study, years of the scholar's detachment." He therefore dismissed the moral indignation of the young protesters who, he asserted, "have not studied very much."[49]

While, ironically, Irving Kristol's more conservative response accurately read the movement's feeling that "American life and American society" were "devoid of both moral authority and moral significance," he rejected the "New Politics" that "would give moral direction and moral purpose to American life." Particularly galling for Kristol were "liberal reformers" like Robert Kennedy in 1968, who showed a "keen sensitivity" to the "political mood of young people on the campuses and black militants in the ghettos."[50] Kristol's rejection of the "barren" agenda of reform provided the backdrop for his own conservative responses to issues like poverty and social welfare.

Electoral Backlash: Roots of the Right Turn

As the out-party of American politics in the mid-1960s, the Republicans were in position to draw on the disturbing media spectacle to mobilize an effective and seemingly populist political backlash. Their success is dramatically revealed by the eight-year electoral swing between 1964, when Democrat Lyndon Johnson captured 61.3 percent of the popular vote, and 1972, when Richard Nixon was reelected with 60.9 percent of the popular vote, winning every state in the Electoral College except Massachusetts (and the District of Columbia). From the perspective of party changeover, it is notable that this dramatic shift occurred without the nation experiencing a major economic recession.

Although the largely liberal output of American politics wouldn't completely evaporate until corporate America joined in the backlash and produced Ronald Reagan's startling election in 1980, the New Deal coalition had been fractured by the time Nixon was first elected in 1968. As the Kennedy and Johnson administrations became identified with the civil rights struggle, the previously solid Democratic South began to shift party loyalties, starting with Barry Goldwater's capture of five southern states in 1964. Nixon's explicit "Southern Strategy" was even more successful, sweeping the entire South in 1972.

The forces of backlash were also able to play on the antipathies of many white Americans in the North as well as the South, particularly those working-class Americans who had only recently gained some of the trappings of middle-class life in the postwar years. Aided by politicians' rhetoric and visual association, the socially conservative Catholic working class could find plenty in the media spectacle that seemed demeaning of them.[51] Conservatives repeatedly labeled the poverty program a government "handout" paid for by the hard-earned money of the working class. Unlikely to enjoy the level of material security that upper-middle-class college students had come to assume, working and lower-middle-class whites in the North could also readily respond to appeals that labeled inner-city blacks and student protesters as "ungrateful" recipients of government handouts or affluent privilege.

Furthermore, the highly visible counterculture could be counted on to offend the sensibilities of financially hard-pressed, working-class families who taught their children the importance of respect for authority, respect they believed was crucial for their children to improve their prospects of material security. Militant antiwar youth carrying Viet Cong flags were another eyesore for that class of Americans whose sons disproportionately bore the burden of fighting in Vietnam—even if, for that very reason, working-class Americans were more likely than their upper-middle-class counterparts to oppose the war.[52] Finally, many working-class men, accustomed to asserting their toughness on the job, could be counted on to respond negatively to the more strident manifestations of feminism's challenge to sexist attitudes and behaviors.

In the early going, civil rights, racial unrest, and "law and order" were most directly relevant to the backlash strategy—a strategy that has persisted on the Right through the notorious "Willie Horton" ad during the 1988 George H. W. Bush campaign down to racially coded appeals against Barack Obama's candidacy in 2008 and attacks on his presidency ever since.[53] As with more general attacks against the sixties, the conservative backlash has exploited visual association by playing on the apparent simultaneity of media unrest and a liberal administration, blaming the latter for the former. Ironically, the Right's critique of paternalistic Big Government echoed New Left criticism of the Great Society, although conservatives have never acknowledged this connection. Instead, they have consistently lumped liberal government programs together with New Left and countercultural rebels to explain visible social problems and behaviors. Congressman Newt Gingrich's 1994 attack on the Clinton administration for its allegedly "Great Society, counterculture, McGovernik" policies was one of the more creative uses of what social scientists would call a spurious correlation.[54]

Media evidence of social unrest and increasing violence provided an effective foil for political leaders who appealed to public fears about personal safety and linked actual increases in violent crime to sixties social movements while blaming the liberal welfare state for both. In his acceptance speech at the 1964 Republican National Convention, Goldwater roused the Republican faithful with stormy warnings about the "license of the mob and of the jungle," linking these to Democrats who had allegedly allowed "violence on the streets" to flourish.[55] His warnings seemed validated when, days after the speech, New York police clashed with demonstrators protesting a police shooting and the murders of the three civil rights volunteers in Mississippi, and Harlem and black sections of Brooklyn erupted in rioting and looting—one of the decade's first major inner-city riots.

In his campaign, Goldwater articulated themes that formed the core of conservative attacks for years to come. He attacked liberals for "telling people again and again that the federal government will take care of everything for them," thereby producing the "decline of individual responsibility which is the base cause of the rise in crime and disregard for law and order." Liberals, he maintained, encouraged the "deterioration of the home, the family, and the community, of law and order, of good morals and good manners."[56] In a more pointed reference to the civil rights movement, Goldwater asserted that inner-city lawlessness derived from the doctrine of civil disobedience. Aided by frequent, racially coded references to "states' rights," Goldwater's campaign played well in the white South. Although his bid for the presidency foundered on perceptions of reckless hawkishness in foreign policy, Goldwater's outspoken conservatism won the hearts of young conservatives marginalized by the Johnson landslide and resentful of the media attention to the leftish, "generational" protest spectacle, and who thereby became even more determined to gain control of the public agenda in the coming years.[57]

Ronald Reagan, who stirred the Republican faithful with a ringing speech in support of candidate Goldwater, took on the mantle of law and order in his 1966 campaign for governor of California, exploiting fears aroused by the Watts riot of 1965. Like Goldwater, Reagan denounced "leaders of the Negro community" who "urged civil disobedience," which encouraged "lawlessness" in places like Watts. Reagan contended that these leaders thereby "forfeited their right to leadership" since civil disobedience "had no place in a democracy"[58]—a direct contradiction of the movement view expressed in 1970 by Howard Zinn: "civil disobedience . . . is *not* our problem. . . . Our problem is civil obedience."[59] Aligning nonviolent civil disobedience in the South with the highly visible violence in the inner cities, Reagan created a unified racial Other out of two diametrically opposed actions, in the process tarring both with the same anti-democratic brush. Without saying so explicitly, Reagan's rhetoric fused two wings of white backlash in the South and the North.

With the Free Speech Movement in Californians' rearview mirror, along with emerging signs of the counterculture, Reagan also railed against the "small minority of beatniks, radicals, and filthy speech advocates" who had "brought shame" to the Berkeley campus, turning it into a "rallying point for Communists and a center for sexual misconduct."[60] After the California Senate Subcommittee on Un-American Activities had labeled the Berkeley campus a "haven for communism, homosexuality, and immorality,"[61] Reagan gave a dramatic address in which he spelled out in detail the "sexual misconduct" allegedly occurring at a dance sponsored by a Berkeley antiwar group. According to a staffer in Governor

Pat Brown's campaign, polls showed that "Berkeley" became the "most negative word you could mention" in the state. In Michael Flamm's reading, Reagan offered himself as the voice of popular grievance about the perceived loss of control amidst the rootlessness of modern life.[62]

In October 1966, *Newsweek* carried a lengthy report on "The White Backlash, 1966." The magazine also reported the surprising victory in the Georgia Democratic primary of segregationist gubernatorial candidate Lester Maddox, who in 1964 had chased civil rights protesters from his café with a revolver and ax handle. A subsequent article focused on a riot in San Francisco that led the magazine to ask whether it would seal Governor Pat Brown's fate in his race against Reagan.[63] Aided by a vibrant grassroots campaign in conservative enclaves like Orange County, Reagan stunned national pundits by sweeping into office, aided by large numbers of white working-class Democrats—eventually to be known as "Reagan Democrats"—who abandoned Governor Brown.[64]

While the Johnson administration responded to campaign charges with its own "war on crime," the liberal response, as Flamm pointed out, was ambivalent in its presentation because the administration's commitments to civil rights progress in the South excluded playing the racial card that had been employed by both Goldwater and Reagan. Instead, administration officials like Attorney General Ramsey Clark included southern *white* lawlessness in statements that criticized lawlessness in the inner cities. Johnson lost his clear legislative mandate in 1966 when Republicans gained forty-seven House seats in the midterm elections.

The stunning, widely televised conflagrations in Newark and Detroit during the summer of 1967 ratcheted up the level of fear in white suburbia and provided the Right with dramatic visual references for its claim that the administration's effort to attack the root causes of urban crime through the War on Poverty had thereby failed. The tepid liberal response had a difficult time being heard in the climate of growing violence at home and abroad. Confidence in the administration's liberal policies was declining, especially after the 1968 Kerner Commission published its finding that, despite federal efforts, the nation was moving toward "two societies—one black, one white—separate and unequal," with "white racism" fingered as a principal cause.[65] The left's explanation of why federal policies had been inadequate for addressing the complex institutional causes of poverty and crime remained outside the realm of legitimate media discourse, inaccessible to the wider public.[66]

In the aftermath of the Democratic Party's 1968 Chicago debacle, the Nixon campaign—along with the insurgent third-party effort of George Wallace—successfully exploited public fears. Wallace showed surprising strength with white, working-class, and lower-middle-class voters in the North, while carrying five southern states. A "New Nixon" used lavish television advertising that denounced violent protests, rejected the idea that poverty was a major cause of crime, targeted a Supreme Court that "coddled criminals," and maintained that

"America needed a revival of traditional morality to restore respect for law and decency."[67]

Ever vigilant for new trends or a potentially significant shift in public opinion, the mass media made much of the backlash theme in the immediate aftermath of the Democratic National Convention in 1968. In successive weeks following its coverage of the Chicago convention, *Newsweek*'s cover stories anticipated the two dominant strains of post-sixties response: political backlash and a hyping of sixties images and myths tinged with ironic references to passing youth. The first featured "George Wallace and the Third Party Threat," while the second revolved around a generationally framed inquiry into the reasons for "revolutionary youth" that asked, "Is Dr. Spock to Blame?" on a cover featuring a toddler wearing buttons with slogans like "Up Against the Wall, Mother" and "Don't Trust Anyone Over 7."[68]

By late 1969, the media were highly attentive to the backlash being cultivated by forces on the Right. In October, for example, *Newsweek* devoted much of its issue to "The Troubled American: A Special Report on the White Majority," using language that drew heavily on the rhetoric of backlash campaigns. The article's lead paragraph lumped together familiar late-1960s images with telling language: "All through the skittish 1960s, America has been almost obsessed with its alienated minorities—the incendiary black militant and the welfare mother, the hedonistic hippie and the campus revolutionary. But now . . . suddenly, the focus [in *Newsweek*] is on *the citizen* who outnumbers, outvotes and could, if he chose to, outgun the fringe rebel." Waxing Nixonian, *Newsweek* asked, "How fed up is the little guy, the average white citizen . . . ?" Much of the magazine's report drew on a Gallup poll of "middle-income," white Americans, spreading over twenty-one pages and ending with speculation about the "perils of beards and sandals" and the possibility that the 1970s might be a "GOP decade."[69]

Notwithstanding a late surge by Democratic candidate Hubert Humphrey, Nixon won an extremely narrow popular margin of victory, made more significant by his comfortable electoral margin in the South. The days of a one-party Democratic South were over, and the "Southernization" of American politics, as Flamm put it, had begun in earnest. The law and order issue had taken hold with significant portions of the American electorate. As Flamm argued, "The rise of law and order signaled an end to the brief era of liberal ascendancy."[70] The implications of this shift would soon spread into other areas of reaction to the 1960s.

The Early Cultural Attack: "Liberal Media," the Campuses, and Feminism

Despite the fact that the mass media played up conservative themes and consistently disparaged protest that in their view threatened violence, the Right continued to express grievances they had long nurtured against the national media, going back at least to the days of Senator Joseph McCarthy and the role CBS newsman Edward R. Murrow played in McCarthy's fall. During the sixties, southern segregationists attacked the national media for their fairly sympathetic reporting on the civil rights movement, and the Goldwater campaign combined its southern strategy with attacks against the "Eastern liberal press." As the media spectacle of the 1960s loomed larger, especially on television, critical responses grew. Believing that television coverage of rioting fostered copycat behaviors, government pressure prompted media self-censorship in the coverage of urban disorders.

Public resentment toward the antiwar protests visible in the media was also rising in the latter years of the sixties. In Melvin Small's study of media antiwar coverage, "Chicago in 1968 was probably the turning point. . . . The television coverage of the streets of Chicago during the 1968 Democratic convention brought the audience resentment boiling forth."[71] National media reporters who had been victimized by police violence were at least briefly critical of the police and the Daley administration, which put them on the opposite side of the public opinion majority that was more sympathetic toward the police.[72] As Rick Perlstein observed, "[Richard] Nixon paid attention. The public was on *his* side in his war against the media."[73] With public disenchantment toward the media on the rise, the national media quickly returned to routine coverage, and the newsmagazines in particular turned immediately to highlight the newly discovered "law and order" mood in the nation.

When he gained the White House in 1968, Richard Nixon brought with him grievances he had long nursed against the "East Coast elite." The media were a particularly nettlesome target for Nixon's wrath. In former aide William Safire's recollection, Nixon "had contempt for them, as elitist, antidemocratic, lordly, arrogant lookers-down-their-noses at the elected representatives of the folks, and he did everything he could get away with to destroy them."[74] In addition to old scars like the 1960 Kennedy-Nixon debates and the 1962 California gubernatorial campaign—at the conclusion of which Nixon bitterly informed the press they wouldn't "have Dick Nixon to kick around any more"—the Nixon White House was highly critical of the fact that by 1969 the media were as skeptical of the administration's Vietnam policy as the rest of the country.

The Nixon administration introduced a theme that would later play a significant role in shaping post-sixties discourse about the Vietnam War. Engineering a campaign to blame both media and the antiwar movement for what it saw as the failure of American resolve in Vietnam, the administration portrayed both as out of step with the nation and hostile to the interests of American soldiers.[75] As Jerry Lembcke argued, the administration reframed the debate "from this-war-is-about-U.S.-objectives" to "this-war-is-about-the-men-who-are-fighting-the-war," in an effort to create a schism between the soldiers and the antiwar movement.[76]

After the widely observed and peaceful Moratorium in 1969, the administration went on the offensive with what White House aide Bill Gavin termed an "unrelenting propaganda drive" involving pro-administration "front groups," newspaper ads, letters to the editor, leaflets, and the like.[77] In a widely reported speech, Vice President Agnew characterized the Moratorium as the creation of "an effete corps of impudent snobs who characterize themselves as intellectuals."[78] Deputy director of White House communications Jeb McGruder wrote a memo to Nixon's chief of staff, H. R. Haldeman, noting that Nixon had made twenty-one requests in the prior thirty days for action related to specific "unfair" (read: critical) news coverage and suggesting five strategies for making a "major impact" on news reporting. The strategies, which were acted upon, included an "official monitoring system through the FCC as soon as Dean Burch is officially on board as Chairman," using the anti-trust division and the IRS to investigate various media, showing favorites in sharing information with the media, and using the Republican National Committee for "major letter writing efforts of both a class and a quantity nature."[79]

After President Nixon's "silent majority" speech struck a responsive chord with the wider public on November 3, the president exulted about the speech's effectiveness in marginalizing both the media and antiwar movement: "We've got those liberal bastards on the run now. We've got them on the run and we're going to keep them on the run."[80] Angered by press criticism of Nixon's speech, presidential speechwriter Pat Buchanan subsequently drafted a response that was edited by the president and delivered by Agnew on November 13, two days before the massive antiwar demonstration scheduled for Washington. Agnew attacked the television networks for airing critical commentary by Averill Harriman, who had been President Johnson's chief negotiator at the Paris Peace talks, and called on the American people to "let the networks know that they want their news straight and objective"—meaning, in effect, government policy was precisely as government propaganda described it. In addition, Agnew attacked the "big-city liberal media" as a "tiny and closed fraternity of privileged men, elected by no one," who enjoyed a "monopoly sanctioned and licensed by the Government." Although the majority of Americans wanted the United States out of Vietnam, he continued, "The views of this fraternity do not represent the views of America."[81] On the same day, Dean Burch, former Republican Party chairman and the new head of the Federal Communications Commission, engaged in media intimidation by phoning the three TV networks and asking for transcripts of remarks by their reporters and commentators after Nixon's Vietnam "silent majority" speech.

Agnew's comments set off a firestorm of controversy in the media and the halls of Congress, triggering voluminous editorial commentary in both print and television media. The heads of the three major networks issued immediate statements defending their practice of editorial commentary and denouncing the vice president's intimidation of the media. On November 20, Agnew widened his attack in a speech to the Montgomery (Alabama) Chamber of Commerce, denouncing criticism that he sought to intimidate the media and adding the allegedly slanted news coverage of the *New York Times* and *Washington Post* to his list of culprits—singling out a *Times* editorial that had criticized his condemnation of the Moratorium, the sole occasion in which the *Times* had editorially supported a major antiwar protest. Disparaging the antiwar movement as the "arrogant few who march under the flags and portraits of dictators, who intimidate and harass university professors, who use gutter obscenities to shout down speakers with whom they disagree," Agnew boldly articulated the administration's new line of attack by observing that he would not "remain silent" while the heroes who received posthumous Medals of Honor for service in Vietnam were "vilified" for a "dirty, immoral war." The "time for blind acceptance" of media opinions, he declared, "is past."[82] On November 23, the vice president explained his decision to speak out in an article written for *Life* magazine: "Like the great silent majority, I had had enough."[83]

In April 1972, the Nixon administration filed an antitrust suit against the three major TV networks, and during the 1972 presidential campaign the White House successfully channeled its attacks on antiwar protesters and Democratic candidate George McGovern through the syndicated columns of conservative reporters Rowland Evans and Robert Novak, known among other things for dubbing McGovern as favoring "acid, amnesty, and abortion."[84]

The Nixon administration's campaign to discredit the media and prod it to the right gained support from a little-known writer for *TV Guide* named Edith Efron, who in 1971 wrote a book titled *The News Twisters,* a project underwritten by a grant from the Historical Research Foundation, an organization backed by right-wing money.[85] After reviewing a history of "rightist complaints" about being treated as a "lunatic fringe," Efron developed her own highly subjective methodology for detecting bias in news reporting by totaling words she considered for and against different candidates in the 1968 election—presented, of course, as rigorously objective with the aid of graphs and selected quotations. In one example, a report on Nixon being heckled by antiwar protesters was labeled "anti-Nixon," whereas a report on Humphrey being heckled was classified as "pro-demonstrators"—both therefore counting as examples of "liberal bias."[86] Such "objective" measures led Efron to conclude that the television networks had followed the "elitist-liberal-left line" in all controversies, "actively slanting" their coverage against the administration's war policies, against the "white middle-class majority," and, astonishingly enough, in favor of the Viet Cong and "black militants" as well as Democratic candidate Hubert Humphrey.[87]

Although Efron's methodology was later subjected to damning criticism from a variety of professional and academic sources,[88] the book gained national visibility by making it onto the *New York Times* best-seller list, thanks to efforts by the Nixon administration. Much later, White House "dirty tricks" expert Charles Colson acknowledged that he was ordered by the president to "get it on the best-seller list," which he did by using reelection funds to buy up all available copies from the bookstores the *Times* used to create its list.[89] Aided by highly favorable reviews in William F. Buckley's *National Review* and the neoconservative journal *The Public Interest,* Efron's book went on to be cited again and again as an authoritative study by later critics of the "liberal media." For that reason, former conservative activist David Brock has labeled Efron the "founder of the modern right-wing media criticism industry."[90]

Such right-wing attacks would increase sharply in the aftermath of Watergate and the Vietnam War, as conservatives sought a public scapegoat for both the fall of the Nixon administration and the failure of U.S. policy in Vietnam. By that time, however, a broader reaction to the 1960s was being mobilized by the corporate sector.

Business Backlash

Now we have women marching in the streets! If only things would quiet down!
—Arthur Burns, chairman of the Federal Reserve Board, 1972

On June 28, 1966, the advertising firm Deutsch & Shea ran a major ad in the *New York Times* asking, "Has Business Become a Dirty Word? Ask the Class of 1966." Noting that 88 percent of "today's college graduates" preferred careers "anywhere but business," the ad countered young people's "mistaken belief" that business had "failed to commit itself to the human issues of our time," itemizing ways the corporate sector had contributed to "the public good in the past five years alone."[91] In the end, the ad claimed, the "Class of '66" failed to "get the message," not "because American business has failed to face up to basic social issues," but "because we have failed to communicate to the young in a language that has meaning for them." The problem, from the vantage point of corporate America, was one of communication. Urging business leaders to "tell them . . . on and off the campus . . . that we see the prospects for as brave a world for man as they do," the ad went on to remind its readers that socially responsible business leaders were saying that "'what's good for the nation, and for the world, is good for business.' And they're proving they mean it."

By August 1971, things seemed more serious. Two months before he was appointed to the Supreme Court by President Nixon, Lewis Powell, a corporate attorney and member of the boards of eleven corporations, wrote a confidential memo to Eugene Sydnor Jr., the director of the U.S. Chamber of Commerce, detailing what he claimed was an unprecedented, "broadly-based" attack on the "American economic system." In yet another example of visual association, drawing from a handful of business and right-wing sources, Powell conflated examples of New Left violence with the "most disquieting voices" of criticism coming from the "perfectly respectable elements of society: the college campus, the pulpit, the media, the intellectual and literary journals, the arts and sciences, and from politicians." The "movement against the system" was thereby being led by the "most articulate, the most vocal, and most prolific" members of these communities.[92]

Powell's claims were sweeping, but his evidence was exceptionally thin. For example, in citing the campus as the "single most dynamic source" of attacks on the system, Powell singled out "social science faculties" which "usually" included "members who are unsympathetic to the enterprise system." Yet his evidence consisted of noting that these faculties "ranged from Herbert Marcuse, Marxist faculty member at the University of California at San Diego [the only named faculty member] . . . to the ambivalent liberal critic who finds more to condemn than to commend." The threat posed by these faculty was enhanced by the fact that they were "often personally attractive and magnetic" as well as being "stimulating teachers" who were "prolific writers and lecturers" and who "exert[ed] enormous influence—far out of proportion to their numbers." Powell pieced together this "evidence" with a classic mistaken explanation of the views of disenchanted youth. Asking why "so many young people were disaffected to the point of being revolutionaries," he cited a *Barron's National Business and Financial Weekly* study that "said: 'Because they were taught that way.'" Accurately observing that universities were heavily supported by the business sector, that their boards of trustees were "overwhelmingly composed of men and women who are leaders in the system," and that the mass media were themselves "owned and theoretically controlled by corporations which depend on profits and the enterprise system to survive," Powell went on to bemoan the tendency of the "enterprise system" to tolerate if not participate in "its own destruction." Sounding a theme that was to become pervasive throughout much of media culture in the coming years, Powell characterized the corporate world as victimized by a powerful onslaught against it, noting that "businessmen have not been trained or equipped to conduct guerrilla warfare with those who propagandize against the system, seeking insidiously and constantly to undermine it."[93]

Powell's alarmist tone in describing the "movement against the system" and what he called the system's "appeasement" provided the backdrop to his call to marshal the "ingenuity and resources of American business" against "those who would destroy it." Beyond more effective "public relations" on the part of corporations, he called for a coordinated and well-financed "long-range planning and implementation" effort on the part of the collective business community. That effort, Powell contended, should include universities hiring "highly qualified scholars in the social sciences that do believe in the system," the creation of a Speaker's Bureau from the top echelons of American business, and a staff of scholars who would evaluate social science textbooks used in the colleges and universities.[94] Asserting that "on many campuses freedom of speech has been denied to all who express moderate or conservative viewpoints," Powell noted that the two essential ingredients of the campus campaign were "to have attractive, articulate, and well-informed speakers," and, ominously, "to exert whatever degree of pressure—publicly and privately—may be necessary to assure opportunities to speak."[95]

As for the wider public's opinion, Powell urged a major campaign focusing on the media, including keeping the television networks "under constant surveillance." Complaints "should be made promptly and strongly" to the media and the Federal Communications Commission. Of particular concern, Powell observed, was the "daily 'news analysis'" of national news programming that, he claimed with no supportive evidence, "so often includes the most insidious type of criticism of the enterprise system."[96] As support for his argument, Powell appended to his memo a column from the conservative *Richmond Times-Dispatch* summarizing the findings of the recently popularized Efron book.[97] In the end, Powell argued, it was time for a well-planned, coordinated effort and a "more aggressive attitude" on the part of the business community. "There should be no hesitation to attack the Naders, the Marcuses and others who openly seek destruction of the system," Powell asserted. (Ralph Nader's main claim to fame at that point was publication of *Unsafe at Any Speed*, his documentation of the automobile industry's resistance to safety features in their cars, and the particularly hazardous Chevrolet Corvair.) In addition, Powell argued, the Chamber's "faculty of scholars" should be encouraged to publish articles in popular and intellectual magazines as well as professional journals. Since, as he put it, "one finds almost no attractive, well-written paperbacks or pamphlets 'on our side,'" Powell encouraged a wave of books that would combat "news stands . . . filled with paperbacks and pamphlets advocating everything from revolution to erotic free love."[98]

Powell concluded his section on "A More Aggressive Attitude" with the exhortation: "It is time for American business—which has demonstrated the greatest capacity in all history to produce and influence consumer decisions—to apply their great talents vigorously to the preservation of the system itself."[99] As later events would reveal, Powell's urgent appeal helped to set in motion forces that subsequently transformed the nature of public discourse in the United States for decades to come. His memo became a virtual blueprint for the well-orchestrated attack on the 1960s that followed during the 1970s.

The Rise of Anti-Feminists

These chicks are our natural enemies! The only subject to [sic] feminism that is worth doing is on this new militant phenomenon and the proper Playboy *approach is to devastate it.*
    —Hugh Hefner, internal *Playboy* memo, 1970

If you're on the right track, you can expect some pretty savage criticism.
    —Phyllis Chesler, 1999

In addition to "liberal media," a "traitorous" antiwar movement, and "revolutionary" campuses, the early cultural backlash against the sixties singled out for attack the women's movement and, a bit later, the fledgling gay rights movement. Early magazine articles like Helen Lawrenson's "The Feminine Mistake" in *Esquire* in 1970 had scornfully ridiculed the movement.[100] As noted earlier, when liberal feminism began to gain some credibility in mass media, conservative critics denounced both the movement and the media. In *Newsweek,* for example, Midge Decter, with characteristic exaggeration, claimed that women's liberation had come to "dominate all the channels of public discussion and exchange" with record speed.[101]

A number of small groups used appropriately pithy acronyms to gain media recognition. A New York woman founded the group Men Our Masters (MOM), which subsequently gained attention in the *Christian Science Monitor* and presented a MOM award to Representative Emanuel Celler (D-N.Y.), an important opponent of the proposed Equal Rights Amendment (ERA). Another group named itself Happiness of Womanhood and began a campaign to do battle with "those who dragged the word 'housewife' through the mud." The acronym HOW suggested that they were intended to be a counterpart to the liberal women's group NOW. HOW organized a "Happiness Rally" in Los Angeles that coincided with the national Women's Strike for Equality.[102] Others included Happiness of Motherhood Eternal (HOME), Women Who Want to Be Women (WWWW), American Women Against Ratification of the ERA (AWARE), and Females Opposed to Equality (FOE). Another voice gaining a significant following was Marabel Morgan, author of *Total Woman,* published in 1973. Morgan's answer for women's frustrations was total deference to their husbands: a woman should "listen attentively to her husband," "admire his every trait," and "pander to his every whim."[103]

The most formidable opponent to the women's movement was probably Phyllis Schlafly, a longtime conservative affiliated with Barry Goldwater's 1964 presidential bid.[104] Schlafly founded the Eagle Forum in 1972 and, under its umbrella, Stop ERA!, an organization funded in significant part by the ultraconservative John Birch Society.[105] Drawing on her experience publishing a monthly conservative newsletter, "The Phyllis Schlafly Report," since 1967, Schlafly launched a tightly controlled propaganda campaign utilizing grassroots activism against passage of the ERA. Following Senate approval of the ERA in November 1972, Schlafly distributed her first anti-ERA essay, "What's Wrong with Equal Rights for Women," to her conservative readers. In it, she proclaimed, "One group [of women lobbying for the Equal Rights Amendment] is the women's liberationists. Their motive is totally radical. They hate men, marriage, and children. They look upon their husbands as the exploiters, children as an evil to be avoided (by abortion if necessary), and the family as an institution which keeps women in 'second-class citizenship.'"[106]

Though joined by many other voices on the Right, Schlafly's campaign became the single most prominent voice against the ERA and, through it, the women's movement. Her charges against the ERA ranged wildly—warning that it would require same-sex public restrooms, provide constitutional guarantees of abortion and gay rights, and eliminate preferential veterans' benefits. Readership of her *Report* grew tenfold as the ERA battle intensified, and Schlafly gained mainstream media access as a regular newspaper columnist and television talk show guest. By 1975, *U.S. News* observed that "the counterrevolution" was winning the ERA battle because it was "getting across the idea that the proposed amendment imperiled the American family and would usher in a new age of 'unisex toilet' and 'coed' armed forces."[107]

Although the Equal Rights Amendment was passed by both houses of Congress and ratified by thirty states within a year, it stalled as the backlash grew stronger. One central factor in the growing backlash was the Supreme Court's *Roe v. Wade* abortion decision, handed down in 1973. Long an issue among women's groups, the Court's support for abortion rights became a red flag that triggered a growing backlash from Catholics and the ascendance of the Religious Right. A reluctant Congress passed an extension for the states' ratification of the ERA in 1978, but by 1982 it was clear the tide had turned and the amendment faded from view. Expressing the ascendant backlash view, Moral Majority founder Jerry Falwell proclaimed in 1980, "We must stand against the Equal Rights Amendment, the feminist revolution, and the homosexual revolution."[108]

Media and the "End of the Sixties"

In contrast to the attacks on the "liberal media"—but also because of the direct attacks and the proverbial mass media fear of getting too far out in front of their mass audiences—1968 was the year the nation's newsmagazines, typically the source to which Americans turned to capture the meaning of daily news events, seemed to be anticipating a return to normalcy. *Time*'s special feature on "The Graduate" on June 6 featured a cover photo of a peace-symbol-wearing college graduate with the banner "Can You Trust Anyone under 30?" On September 20, the cover featured a portrait of the vice presidential nominee with a graffiti-like "GOP" scrawled on it and a banner reading, "Agnew, Becoming a Household Word." On October 4 *Time* ran a feature story on "Law and Order" and two weeks later published "The Revolt of the Right" along with caricatures of George Wallace and General Curtis LeMay.

By September 1969, *TV Guide* belatedly announced that the networks were going to retrench in their "coverage of the Left," shifting instead to "exploring middle- and lower-middle-class Americans."[109] The Nixon administration's campaign of harassment and intimidation against "liberal" media was having its desired effect. In late 1969, the newsmagazine covers captured and distanced themselves from the turmoil of the times and began to anticipate an end to a decade rapidly defined by its most turbulent images. *Time*'s issue on the peaceful October Moratorium was labeled "Moratorium: At War with War." On November 14 the cover featured Agnew's attack on the media, headlined "Agnew: Nixon's Other Voice." The following week, "Counterattack on Dissent" was the banner, with the faces of Agnew, Nixon, and Dean Burch on one side, the three major network news anchors on the other, and angry young protesters in the middle. The issue included an article entitled "The Unelected Elite" that profiled the major television news personalities, and another piece on the Mobilization which stated that "once again" Americans had "turned out to march, argue and declaim over Vietnam," but adding what it curiously called "a major difference": this time, the "opponents of dissent also demonstrated in force [though with no reference to numbers], making a counterattack and purposeful counterpoint to the antiwar protesters."[110]

Time's December 12 issue (with a cover highlighting "The Consumer Revolt" and a headshot of Ralph Nader) ran a story on Charles Manson with the sweeping generalization "Hippies and Violence" as a headline, another on the Fred Hampton–Mark Clark murders titled innocuously "Panthers and Police at War," and coverage of the My Lai investigation. There was also a lengthy essay on "The Army and Viet Nam: The Stab-in-the-Back Complex," featuring complaints by General William Westmoreland and other top brass that a "Versailles complex" (i.e., French "abandonment of the Algerian war") might be evident in politicians' reluctance to support a "full mobilization of U.S. manpower" and attacking "ignorant critics" of the war who "simply do not understand Viet Nam or the nature of the fighting there."[111] Lest there be any doubt about what *Time* considered newsworthy, the December 19 issue featured a special section entitled "Into the 70s: From Violence to New Values"; the December 26 cover asked, "Is God Coming Back to Life?"; and the January 5, 1970, cover featured *Time*'s "Man and Woman of the Year: The Middle American."

These influential media seemed more than ready for the sixties to be over. In their coverage, they provided two clear generalizations about the era: it was ending, and its end was caused by social movements moving to extremes, largely self-destructing through violence and mayhem that had alienated the rest of the American public.

Bob Dylan and Pete Seeger at a 1962 rally in Greenville, Mississippi. Folk music was an important early medium for conveying civil rights meanings to a wider public. © Danny Lyon, 1962, Magnum Photos.

One of the inspiring photos of the sit-ins, this from the original Greensboro, North Carolina, Woolworth lunch counter. © Bettman/CORBIS, 1960.

Visual imagery of the firebombed Freedom Ride bus in Anniston, Alabama, provided a stark example of violent southern resistance to civil rights. © Associated Press/str, 1961.

Front-page photograph of Birmingham police dogs attacking civil rights marchers.
© Associated Press/Bill Hudson, 1963.

Birmingham fire hoses turned on peaceful protesters provide shocking evidence of Jim Crow
injustice. © Charles Moore, Black Star.

Alabama state police confront John Lewis and Hosea Williams leading nonviolent civil rights marchers in Selma, Alabama, before pummeling them with billy clubs. © 1965 Spider Martin. All Rights Reserved. Used with permission.

Armed U.S. troops protect firefighters amidst wreckage from the Washington, D.C., riots in the aftermath of Martin Luther King Jr.'s assassination. © Burt Glinn, 1968, Magnum Photos.

Iconic sixties-era image of U.S. Olympic medalists Tommie Smith and John Carlos raising their fists in the black power salute during the 1968 Olympics. AP File Photo, 1968.

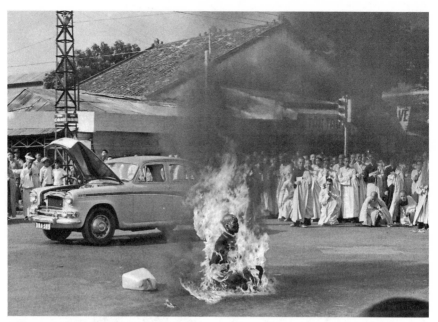

Self-immolation of Buddhist monk Thich Quang Duc provided alarming evidence of the struggle against the U.S.-backed Diem regime in South Vietnam. © Associated Press/Malcolm Browne, 1963.

The war's "sensory realities" glimpsed in this image of a captured Vietnamese woman interrogated by U.S. and South Vietnamese forces. © Keystone/Hulton Archive/Getty Images.

The 'Other War' in Vietnam

LIFE

TO KEEP A VILLAGE FREE

After a fishing trip, a Marine and his young friend return to Hoa Hiep

AUGUST 25 · 1967 · 35¢

An example of the way a magazine cover reinforced mainstream framing of the war: the United States "helping" to keep the Vietnamese "free." © Rentmeester/Time & Life Pictures/ Getty Images.

Another side of the war's "sensory realities" exposed: soldiers in hell appealing for help in getting the wounded out of the jungle. © Associated Press/Art Greenspon.

Eddie Adams's famous photo of South Vietnamese general Lo An shooting an NLF suspect in the head during the Tet Offensive, 1968. © Associated Press/Eddie Adams, 1968.

Famous photo of Vietnamese women and children rounded up and killed in a ditch during the My Lai massacre. The image helped spawn the "baby killer" epithet directed at returning U.S. soldiers. © Associated Press/Life Magazine, Ronald L. Haeberle.

Powerful image of burnt Vietnamese children fleeing napalm attack, one of the war's iconic images. © Associated Press/Nick Ut, 1972.

When compared to *Time*'s cover after the 1975 fall of South Vietnam (next page), the magazine's cover after the My Lai massacre reveals the pattern of "unworthy" (My Lai) victims and "worthy" (South Vietnamese) victims. Reprinted through the courtesy of the editors of *Time Magazine.* © 2010 Time, Inc.

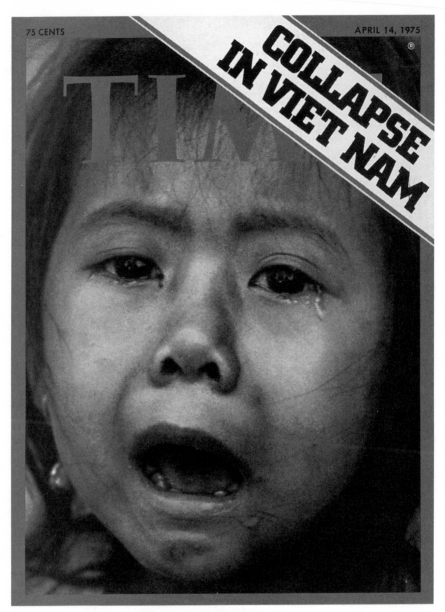

Compared to the My Lai cover on *Time,* this is an example of "worthy" victims featured in the media. Reprinted through the courtesy of the editors of *Time Magazine.* © 2010 Time, Inc.

Chicago as an armed camp epitomized by masked National Guardsmen stopping protesters'
medic. © Raymond Depardon, 1968, Magnum Photos.

With coffins bearing placards with the names of dead soldiers and destroyed Vietnamese villages, a dramatic march against the war winds its way toward a massive rally on the mall in Washington, D.C., in November 1969. © Jack Moebes/CORBIS.

A polarized America is captured by John Filo's photograph of Kent State student Alan Canfora waving the Viet Cong flag and facing down National Guardsmen who were about to open fire on protesting students, killing four. © John Filo. Used with Permission.

Jarring image of U.S. soldiers throwing their medals onto the Capitol Steps as part of the 1971 Vietnam Veterans Against the War protest. © Leonard Freed, 1971, Magnum Photos.

Spirited women fill New York's Fifth Avenue in the 1970 Women's Strike for Equality March. The wording of Bella Abzug's sign gives anti-feminists "evidence" for their claims that the movement is anti-motherhood and anti-family. © Bob Adelman, 1970, Magnum Photos. © Keystone/Hulton Archive/Getty Images.

Life cover reveals typical sexist framing of the time. © Vernon Merritt III/Time & Life Pictures/ Getty Images.

A symbol of what the government feared: a coming together of radical movements. Women's liberation banner at the New Haven protest in support of Black Panthers Bobby Seale and Erica Huggins on trial. © David Fenton/Hulton Archive/Getty Images.

Black Panthers Huey Newton and Bobby Seale in full armed regalia—a potent visual icon of the era. © Associated Press/*San Francisco Examiner*.

Time magazine highlights the shifts occurring as popular culture explores new sixties-relevant themes. Reprinted through the courtesy of the editors of *Time Magazine*. © 2010 Time, Inc.

One example of popular culture's baby boomer fixation: *Time* declares "Boomers Turn 40."
Reprinted through the courtesy of the editors of *Time Magazine*. © 2010 Time, Inc.

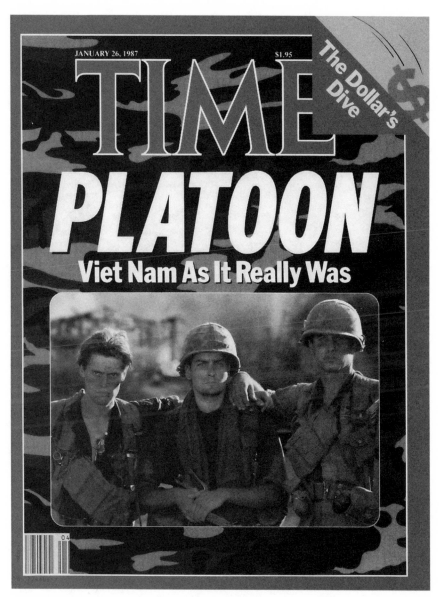

In a classic representation of pop culture, *Time* hails *Platoon*'s depoliticized war as "Viet Nam as it really was." Reprinted through the courtesy of the editors of *Time Magazine*. © 2010 Time, Inc.

The wounds of war: Vietnam vets grieve for lost buddies at Maya Lin's Vietnam Memorial.
© Hiroji Kubota, 1992, Magnum Photos.

TIME

Everybody's Hip
(And That's Not Cool)

1994 *Time* cover captures and satirizes the pervasive culture of "hip." Reprinted through the courtesy of the editors of *Time Magazine.* © 2010 Time, Inc.

In classic style, *Time* frames feminism as anti-male. Reprinted through the courtesy of the editors of *Time Magazine.* © 2010 Time, Inc.

8

Media, Militancy, and Violence: The Making of "Bad Sixties" Icons

Those who make peaceful revolution impossible will make violent revolution inevitable.
    —John F. Kennedy, 1962

Wherever they went, the Americans were the masters, so the [Black] Panthers would do their best to terrorize the master by the only means available to them. Spectacle.
    —Jean Genet, *Prisoner of Love,* 1992

The years from, say, 1964 to 1974 fairly reeked of violence, most of it officially inspired, sanctioned, or encouraged. The Vietnam War, the murders and beatings that were the normal response to the nonviolent tactics of the civil rights movement, the suppression of the Watts uprising and the urban ghetto riots, the murders of the Kennedy brothers and Martin Luther King, the police action at the Democratic National Convention of 1968, the tear gas sprayed by helicopter upon campuses, the murder of students by police and National Guard at Berkeley, Kent State, Jackson State, and Orangeburg provided a seemingly endless succession of shocks, a shattering first-hand experience in the delegitimation of the authority of the state.
    —Sheldon Wolin, "The Destructive Sixties and
    Postmodern Conservatism," 1997

For many activists, the latter half of the sixties provided contradictory dynamics. On the one hand, as noted earlier, by 1967 many in the movement were hitting a psychological wall, feeling despair over the continuing onslaught in Vietnam, the violence in Newark and Detroit, and the sense that demonstrations to date had seemingly registered little if any effect. The momentum of earlier years' reformism had run out and seemed to be reversing. The forces of backlash were becoming more prominent. The prospects for change were dimming. The movement's sense of isolation from the realm of mainstream politics and discourse was growing profound. Chicago police attacks and the murders of Black Panthers Fred Hampton and Mark Clark convinced some that the government was waging war on the movement.

Indeed, the federal government's COINTELPRO operations targeted virtually the whole range of sixties social movements: civil rights groups, SDS, the antiwar movement, the Black Panther Party, the Young Lords, the Yippies, the American Indian Movement, the Socialist Workers Party, and the women's movement. For example, on the one hand, in 1964, COINTELPRO targeted Martin Luther King Jr. and sought to provide more conservative black leaders with damaging information about King that would "convince them of the danger of King to the over-all [*sic*] civil rights movement." On the other, in 1968, COINTELPRO sought to "discredit" what it called "black nationalist groups" in the eyes of the "responsible Negro community," the "white community, both the responsible community and . . . 'liberals,'" and, finally, "Negro radicals."[1] In addition to invasive surveillance and infiltration, the FBI sought to provoke violence and other forms of militant expression as part of its program of preventing "black nationalist groups and leaders from gaining respectability" and preventing a "coalition of militant black nationalist groups" from forming. J. Edgar Hoover's March 4, 1968, memo also specified the need to prevent the "rise of a black 'messiah'" (ominously mentioning King, Stokely Carmichael, and Elijah Muhammad by name, in addition to the already martyred Malcolm X), and to "neutralize" what he called "potential troublemakers . . . before they can exercise their potential for violence."[2] As Robert Goldstein put it in his history of political repression since 1870, "covert, as well as overt, political repression reached massive levels during the Vietnam war era."[3]

Activists were violently attacked, inner-city youths were violently harassed, and a horrifying war ground on and on, irrespective of rising public opposition—thereby producing an increase in militant expression among youthful elements of the black power and antiwar movements and the New Left. As Jack Weinberg observed of Berkeley's Stop the Draft Week in 1967, "We were becoming much more alienated from society and much more willing to be disruptive of that society, and basically we began moving to the view that we wanted to make the cost of pursuing the war abroad the ungovernability of the society at home. . . . The question of moving American society, changing people, really was getting lost."[4] Or, as Weinberg's colleague Suzy Nelson commented, "We began to see ourselves as glue in the keyholes, as obstacles in the way of the system fulfilling its potential for wreaking destruction all over the world. . . . I think we sort of lost the idea that we could be victorious."[5]

In 1969, longtime antiwar organizer Norma Becker observed of the same period that younger activists in the movement had "become *extremely* radicalized, terribly frustrated, enraged, and [they] put their hearts and souls into their political work and experienced the despair of watching the war escalate." Becker noted that "the more successful the demonstrations became in terms of numbers, in terms of [media] coverage—it was like banging their heads against a stone wall."[6] A year later, as David Dellinger put it, antiwar activists struggled to "overcome the feelings of frustration and despair that have gripped people after they discovered that neither a million people in the streets (November 1969) nor several hundred schools and colleges on strike (May 1970) [have] altered Washington's determination" to win the war.[7]

On the other hand, the media were providing a seemingly unending spectacle of young alienated people who, the media insisted, were a new generational force. With its cameras drawn to turbulent protests of one kind or another, the media spectacle suggested the very path to empowerment alluded to by Jack Weinberg: forcing concessions from government through increasing disorder instead of working to change public opinion, especially when opinion against the war was already highly significant. The sharp escalation of militancy, in turn, enabled the powerless and invisible as well as the era's social movements to gain visibility as well as the alarmed attention of government officialdom. Militant action enabled the Black Panther Party, briefly, to check harassment by police patrols. It also enabled the antiwar movement to heighten pressures on the Nixon administration to end the war on terms it did not seek.[8] The latter, in particular, is no mean feat, especially when it is contrasted to the ineffectiveness of a significantly less militant Iraq antiwar movement, even if that movement was initially far larger and more globally pervasive at a much earlier stage.

Yet the long-term price of sixties militancy for movement building and the prospects for a radical democracy have, for at least forty years, been steep. Referring to the war in Vietnam, Richard Flacks observed:

It has helped to build the Left. But people on the Left can't responsibly worry about much else as long as it goes on. And the more they accept the responsibility for trying to end the war, the more militant they become—and the more they sense their own impotence, isolation, and alienation from the larger society. . . . The war helps to build the radical movement, but the necessary obsession to work to end it is, in many ways, incompatible with *achieving* such a movement.[9]

Two groups in particular have remained as the dominant icons of sixties militancy in the media culture: the Black Panther Party (and more broadly, militant black nationalists) and the Weather Underground (and more broadly, militant factions of the New Left and antiwar movement). As is the case with other imagistic icons of the sixties era—most notably stoned hippies and radical feminists—these icons became instant foils for backlash, and they remained as media culture points of reference for those seeking to scapegoat the sixties. Over time, for the most part, they have been so thoroughly discredited in the mass media culture that they are simply presumed to be without any redeeming qualities, or so the forces of backlash have asserted with no formidable voices countering their assertions. The media account suggests there is no need to try to understand the behaviors of these groups in the context of their times.

On the other hand, in the realm of serious scholarship, both the Panthers and Weather Underground have been the focus of significant historical research as well as biographical and autobiographical reflection.[10] Considerable light has been shed on the varying practices of local Panther chapters and on the context of Weather actions. From time to time, efforts to tell the militants' story—particularly in film—make a small dent in the mass media culture, though typically these are subjected to immediate denunciation by the forces of backlash.[11]

Violence and the Macro-Effects of Media Culture

Though the mass media culture of the time did not cause the era's violence, media coverage and portrayal of social movement participants compounded the effects of events and personal experiences that encouraged violence. In the visual media of the 1960s, appearance, rhetoric, and behavior—rather than ideas and argumentation—became the key signifiers of radical criticism, as they had for youthful alienation in the counterculture. Radical discourse was not only historically stigmatized and marginalized in the American mainstream, there was no place for it within mass media discourse. Militancy, on the other hand, invited media attention. Furthermore, the media's generational frame for virtually all late-sixties turbulence conveyed the sense of an empowered generational revolt well beyond young activists' actual, instrumental power—in this sense providing an alluring invitation much the way media coverage of the counterculture invited the increasingly alienated behaviors of young teenagers.

In 1969, the Skolnick Report to the National Commission on the Causes and Prevention of Violence predicted, accurately, that two "lines of development within the peace movement" were "likely to flourish in the years ahead": the "increasing preference for structural analysis as opposed to moral protest" and a growing tendency for violence. Of the former, the Commission noted:

> After a certain number of months and years of begging their elected
> leaders to take mercy on the people of Vietnam and to meet the crisis at
> home, protesters inevitably begin asking themselves whether they have
> been conceiving of the problem truly. Why, protesters ask, has the United
> States become, in Robert Hutchins' words, "the most powerful, the most
> prosperous, and the most dangerous country in the world"? Is it possible
> that our Vietnam involvement is "not a product of eminent personalities or
> historical accidents . . . ?"[12]

In addition to scornfully dismissing antiwar activists for "aiding the enemy" or "undercutting the administration's effort to find peace," government officials and media columnists fanned the flames of antiwar militancy and social polarization. Shortly before the killings at Kent State, for example, Governor James Rhodes of Ohio met with the press and denounced the "vicious form of campus-oriented violence" being "perpetrated by dissident groups and their allies" and vowed, "We are going to *eradicate* the problem. . . . These people just move from one campus to the other and *terrorize* the community. They're worse than the brownshirts and the Communist element and also the night riders and the vigilantes. They're the worst type of people that we harbor in America."[13] To which a "soft-spoken girl" responded in an interview, "If the president thinks I'm a bum and the governor thinks I'm a Nazi, what does it matter how I act?"[14] By 1970, in polarized America, Rhodes's inflammatory remarks found a sympathetic audience in surprising quarters. As reported by James Michener, "a depressing number" of four hundred Kent State students interviewed for his book were "told by their own parents that it might have been a good thing if they had been shot."[15]

At the individual level, the old saw that "violence breeds violence" is not only well grounded but is certainly validated in many cases involving sixties actors. As social workers who deal with family abuse patterns know well, experiencing one's self (or one's community) as a victim of violence leaves people more prone to using or responding with violence themselves.[16] Police violence was the spark that ignited the tinder box of inner-city frustration and despair, and police violence was the catalyst for the Black Panther Party's initial action of tailing police cars and monitoring police activity while carrying visible weapons. Weatherman Bill Ayers recalled of his participation in the 1966 urban riot in Cleveland, "I remember lying facedown on a hard, hot street, gas in my eyes and smoke in my mouth, an M-16 poking into my ribs. It was off the scale, and something came unhinged then."[17] Karl Armstrong, who two years later planted a bomb that blew up the Army Math Research Center at the University of Wisconsin, inadvertently killing a graduate student working inside, had a similar reaction to his experience at the Democratic National Convention in Chicago. Noting that he had urged those around him to sit down and be "peacefully arrested" by the approaching Chicago police, Armstrong continued,

> The police came and started hitting people. I mean they weren't interested
> in arresting anybody, just hitting people and then dragging them off by
> the hair. And I remember [being] seated on the asphalt and trying to get
> up and people tripping over people and my face going into the asphalt. It
> was bedlam. While I had my face in the asphalt, in that split second, I said
> I'm never going to be caught in a position like this again. If they're going to
> make war on us, we're going to make war on them.[18]

Psychologist Kenneth Keniston wrote of the militancy arising in the late 1960s that it was a "symptom of the pathological violence of American life" evident at the time in police repression and the massive American bombing of Vietnam.[19] Just as the American bombing of North Vietnam was meant as a form of communication to leaders in both North and South Vietnam, the state violence that political theorist Sheldon Wolin recalled as pervasive in the sixties era was also meant to communicate something: namely, that protesters' argument against the violence inflicted upon the Vietnamese had no standing in legitimate discourse. Even nonviolent actions taken in opposition to the state's authority were typically delegitimized and labeled as "violence" or "violence-causing."

Finally, exclusion from legitimate media discourse heightened the need to assert one's identity outside that discourse. As Jean-Paul Sartre wrote in his preface to Frantz Fanon's *Wretched of the Earth,* "We only become what we are by the radical and deep-seated refusal of that which others have made of us."[20] As noted below, one can find repeated references to the empowering liberation of "fighting" or violent action among members of Weatherman, particularly in their formative stages prior to their self-inflicted 1970 townhouse explosion.

In effect, the media spectacle of the late 1960s was an invitation to increasing militancy and/or violence on the part of any groups sharply critical of society's mainstream. As the Skolnick report further predicted, "The [antiwar] movement's current mood of disenchantment with existing institutions will both generate new forms of militancy and spread into new segments of the American public."[21] Not only were the Panthers and the militant edges of the New Left notable icons of this kind of expressive politics, but radical feminists, the American Indian Movement, the Young Lords, and the Gay Rights movement burst onto the scene with forceful and riveting expressions of their own radical outsider identities.

These late-sixties activities share three notable common denominators. They were mostly carried out by young people. Their politics were in some sense radical; that is, they targeted for change some fundamental characteristic of the wider society, which placed their argument and analysis clearly outside the bounds of legitimate discourse. And they engaged in some form of expressive militancy. While their relatively youthful membership (some ranging into their thirties) may have contributed to their unrestrained behavior, their youth cannot explain their militancy, since only these relatively few young people, and even relatively few whose politics were radical, took this path of militant expression. What seems crucial is that the political perspectives of all these groups lay outside the boundaries of media discourse. Their perspective was just too "extreme" to be taken seriously within legitimate discourse. In effect, they and others who shared their outsider perspective were not viewed as capable of explaining their own cause; they were simply ignored or summarily dismissed unless they acted out their militancy, their anger. In these circumstances and given the perception that militant action produced palpable effects and captured media attention, it is hardly surprising that some responded with violence, particularly if they had been recipients of violence themselves.

Media One-Dimensionality: The Black Panthers — All Violence, All the Time

Rather than seeing the Panthers as the vanguard of a visible, guerrilla insurgency in the country, they might be better understood as practitioners of an insurgent form of visibility, a literal-minded and deadly serious kind of guerrilla theater, in which militant sloganeering, bodily display, and spectacular actions simultaneously signified their possession and yet real lack of power.

—Nikhil Pal Singh, *Black Is a Country,* 2004

During the 1960s, America's inner cities were violent places, especially for young African American and Latino males whose only readily available gathering places were street corners. As illustrated in books like Claude Brown's *Manchild in a Promised Land,* Malcolm X's *Autobiography,* and Elliot Liebow's *Street-Corner Society,* the street corner was the scene for watching the action, dealing drugs, playing the "dozens," and just "hangin' and jivin'." It was precisely this turf that was persistently targeted by the cities' largely white and often physically brutal police forces. As if to demonstrate their power over the inner city, police would cruise the streets and then, spotting a group of black males on a corner, pull over, throw the young men up against the wall, search them, verbally abuse them, and in some cases beat them.[22]

It was in this environment in the early sixties that the voice of Malcolm X began to reach these young men, urging them to have a sense of pride, to stand up for themselves. Malcolm's voice had the ring of authenticity, coming as it did from a man who had lived and hustled on the city streets before finding in the Nation of Islam a powerful message of empowerment. For Malcolm, the Nation of Islam rejected not only the self-destructive path of drugs but what Malcolm argued was a self-defeating path of nonviolently appeasing the white power structure.

Thus it was in 1966 that two black students at Whitman College in Oakland, Huey P. Newton and Bobby Seale, decided to organize the Black Panther Party for Self-Defense. Over the course of their history, the Panthers' trajectory would bear the imprint of their origins, particularly the volatile and contradictory personality of Newton. This occurred in part because the mass media were from the start preoccupied with the Panthers' most charismatic leaders, their inflammatory rhetoric, their guns and threatening uniform of black berets and leather jackets, their aggressiveness toward police, and their subsequent encounters with violence.

During the Panthers' formative years from 1966 to 1969, violence, criminality, and aggressive language dominated all national newsmagazine articles, with most conveying the clear but inaccurate impression that the Panthers were the aggressors in all their clashes with police.[23] This media attention, in turn, helped attract to the Panthers a volatile and diverse population of young blacks from the streets, including some who, unsurprisingly, had criminal records. In his account of his life as a Panther, Flores A. Forbes recalled, "While I had read about the Panthers that had been killed by the police . . . what I really had on my mind was the black leather jacket and how I would look in one with my black beret cocked to the side with my afro sticking out."[24] Yet the radical content of the Panthers' critique of American institutions and imperial foreign policy was virtually invisible, or at best caricatured by the mass media. The same could be said of the powerfully effective grassroots organizing of chapter leaders like Fred Hampton in Chicago or the range of community service and community-organizing activities adopted by several Panther chapters by 1968. In effect, from the beginning, the Panthers were frozen in a one-dimensional media image of a violent criminal gang spouting leftist revolutionary rhetoric.[25]

Newton and Seale's initial "Ten-Point Platform" called for black self-determination, full employment, trial by juries of their peers, freedom for black "political prisoners," and an end to the urban black community's "robbery by the white man." Point Seven demanded, "We want an immediate end to POLICE BRUTALITY and MURDER of black people."[26] In late fall 1966, in an effort to get the inner-city population—particularly its young—mobilized, the Panthers organized police patrols to monitor the notoriously brutal Oakland police. Reflecting what Newton had been learning in night law school, a group of legally armed Panthers would follow police cars through the city streets. When the police stopped to harass street-corner youths, the Panthers would also stop, get out of their car, ostentatiously load their guns—following the existing legal code—and observe the police, ensuring that the rights of the targeted youths were not violated. As such, the strictly legal armed patrols were a tactic to put a stop to police harassment and a means of emboldening the inner-city black population. They had an unmistakable impact on both. As Flores Forbes put it, "It was a scene that people in the community saw, and it informed black people not just in Oakland, but throughout the country that you had the right, not only to bear arms, but you had a right to defend yourself against a police officer if they attacked you unjustly."[27]

Except for the local Bay area press, the Panthers' initial Oakland action was not noticed by the national media. It was, however, noticed by the police and California political authorities, who immediately began a campaign to change the state laws governing the possession and use of weapons. This led to the Panthers' next action, in effect an escalation of the same tactic with a wider audience. On May 2, 1967, a group of black-clad, fully armed Panthers strode into the California state legislature in Sacramento to protest the new gun legislation. After the Panthers took a wrong turn through the doors to the floor of the assembly and were subsequently arrested, some of the national media took note of this new aggressive group. The *New York Times*, perhaps influenced by the Panthers' appearance, anticipated subsequent media reports in noting at the opening of its account that with "loaded rifles and shotguns in their hands, members of the *antiwhite* Black Panther party marched into the state Capitol today."[28] Yet when asked by white newsmen if the Panthers hated white people, Bobby Seale angrily responded, "We don't hate nobody because of their color; we hate oppression." Indeed, the Panthers' record backed up Seale's words.[29]

From that point on, reflecting their preoccupation with potent visuals, dramatic action, celebrity personalities, and the threat of violence, the mass media defined the Panthers by their appearances and rhetoric as a violent, largely criminal paramilitary group. They systematically failed to hear or consider relevant what William Gamson and Gadi Wolfsfeld would call the Panthers' "alternative language" and "underlying ideas."[30] Typical early coverage came in the aftermath of an April 1968 shootout between police and the Oakland Panthers that resulted in the death of seventeen-year-old Panther Bobby Hutton. While both *Time* and *Newsweek* covered the shootout and included token Panther comments, both magazines' stories were dominated by police testimony and framed in ways that suggested the Panthers were the aggressors. *Time,* for example, opened its story with reference to the "maelstrom of looting and arson" that followed Martin Luther King's recent assassination. Without noting that the Panthers, who were highly critical of pointless "rioting," had spread out through the Oakland community urging young blacks to keep cool—the Skolnick Commission credited them with preventing rioting in Oakland[31]—the magazine went on to observe that "Oakland's police were deeply involved in a bitter private race feud of their own. Ranged against them was a strutting band of hyper-militants, styling themselves the Black Panther Party for Self Defense. The Panthers, armed and angry, are defiantly demanding a facedown." The magazine proceeded to observe suggestively that "routine police procedure provided the invitation to bloodshed" without noting how that "procedure" inflamed tensions in the community. Police accounts of the shootout were "balanced" by a brief reference to Panthers who "shrilled murder, claiming Hutton's hands were raised."[32]

Newsweek gave its readers a short-cut introduction to the Panthers as a "particularly bizarre bunch [of] militant Negro extremists who model themselves after Malcolm X and take their motto from Mao Tse Tung, 'Political power comes through the barrel of a gun.'" After reviewing previous Panther events—the police patrols, Sacramento, and murder charges brought against Newton[33]—*Newsweek* described the shootout, relying exclusively on police accounts.[34] By contrast, in a more personalistic account in the *Saturday Evening Post,* Don Schanche reviewed far more detail about the clash, including trial testimony and his own follow-up investigation, and concluded, "My own examination of the house that was destroyed by police gunfire left me with the distinct feeling that [Eldridge] Cleaver, not the police, had truth on his side."[35] Following the *Newsweek* model, several newsmagazine articles provided equally dramatic and one-sided attention to the subsequent trial of Huey Newton and its aftermath.

By 1968, the Panthers had instituted more substantive community organizing and service programs, like their "breakfast-for-children," an effort to provide hot meals for poor inner-city children that also served as an opportunity to raise community consciousness about inner-city hunger and its link to broader poverty in America and the Third World. The first newsmagazine reference to the breakfast program appeared in *Newsweek* in May 1969 in an article that began with a typical frame focusing on Panther style and symbolism: "They were all of white America's nightmares of the black revenge come chillingly to life—an armed, angry guerrilla cadre uniformed in black berets, black leather, black looks and devoted almost obsessively to guns." Referring to the breakfasts, the article asked if the Panthers had "turned pussycat" and assured its readers that, no, the "vanguard of the black revolution" had "begun experimenting" with a form of "escalation" that was "decidedly unrevolutionary," meaning, presumably, the breakfasts were not violent events.[36] Given the media's total preoccupation with the one-dimensional, violent Panthers, their only plausible interpretation of the breakfast program within this frame was that it represented a desperate public relations effort to cover for their group's violent criminality.

The FBI, however, had a somewhat different view. As the breakfast programs began to spread, the FBI added the Panthers to the government's COINTELPRO efforts. The breakfast for children program was singled out for "eradication," since FBI director J. Edgar Hoover observed that it was the "best and most influential activity going for the BPP and as such, is potentially the greatest threat to efforts by authorities . . . to neutralize the BPP and destroy what it stands for."[37] Part of the FBI's effort involved providing the news media with scare stories about Panther activities. By August 1969, a *Newsweek* article focusing on the Panthers' efforts to form a "United Front against Fascism" with other groups on the left concluded with Hoover's public declaration that the Panthers represented the "greatest threat to the internal security of the country."[38] With the green light from Hoover, state repression of the Panthers moved into high gear.

By December 1969, amidst government pronouncements that the Panthers were a growing threat, legal charges had been brought against two groups of Panthers in New York and New Haven, the first on charges of an alleged bombing "conspiracy," the second (targeting Panther leaders Bobby Seale and Erica Huggins) on charges of murdering young Panther Alex Rackley. Both evolved into sensational trials, in 1970 and 1971, generating substantial media coverage, and both resulted in acquittals of all the principals.

The event that triggered the most significant media controversy about the Panthers was the Chicago police raid on Panther headquarters that resulted in the deaths of Panthers Fred Hampton and Mark Clark. Later investigation revealed that Hampton and Clark had been murdered in their sleep as part of a planned police assault that was assisted by a police infiltrator. Initially described as a "shoot out" between police and heavily armed Panthers, news reports ranged from the *Chicago Tribune*'s account that passed along almost verbatim Chicago district attorney Edward Hanrahan's deceitful press statement about the "vicious Black Panther attack,"[39] to a *Time* report on "Police and Panthers at War," to *Newsweek*'s initial report, "Panthers: Shoot it Out." The latter juxtaposed the Hanrahan account with Panther claims, including Panther attorney Charles Garry's contention that the raid "brought to 28 the number of Panthers killed by police this year."[40] The *New York Times*' first report relied exclusively on police accounts, with the exception of the final sentence: "Bobby Rush, Black Panther deputy minister of defense, charged later that Hampton was 'murdered' while he slept in bed in a 'search and destroy mission' by the Administration."[41]

Almost immediately after the raid, on-site investigations revealed that the police had fired all but a single shot *into* the Panthers' apartment, supporting Rush's charge of murder. In the days and weeks following the killings, a wide variety of voices challenged the Chicago police and called for formal investigation. Between December 6 and December 29 the *New York Times* carried six separate reports, citing charges coming from the American Civil Liberties Union, the NAACP, the United Auto Workers, nine Democratic members of Congress, and a coalition of black community organizations. A feature article on December 14, written by Earl Caldwell, was entitled, "Declining Black Panthers Gather New Support from Repeated Clashes with Police."[42]

The newsmagazines followed suit with *Time*'s December 19 article on "Police and Panthers: Growing Paranoia" and *Newsweek*'s longer feature article on "The Panthers and the Law" on February 23, 1970. Both articles were framed by classic, stereotypical images of threatening Panther bravado. Yet both articles also seemed sobered by the impact of the government's prosecution of the Panthers as well as the actions in Chicago. *Newsweek* questioned how viable the Panthers would be with so much of their leadership in jail or under prosecution, but hastened to add Attorney General John Mitchell's warning that the Panthers continued to be a "menace to national security." Still, *Newsweek*'s opening paragraph focused on the Panthers' performativity with the kind of rhetorical flourish more typically found in the expressive, personalized style of "New Journalism" writers like Norman Mailer and Tom Wolfe:

> They were the Bad Niggers of white America's nightmares come chillingly
> to life—a black-bereted, black-jacketed cadre of street bloods risen up
> in arms against the established order. They were, they announced, the
> Black Panthers, and the name alone suggested menace. They swaggered,
> blustered, quoted Mao, preached revolution, flashed their guns everywhere
> and sometimes used them. They addressed white power in harangues
> that began with F—— and mother-f—. . . . They are guerrilla theater

masterfully done, so masterfully that at a point everybody began to believe them and to be frightened of them. . . . They are Media Age revolutionaries, gifted with words, good at sloganeering (POWER TO THE PEOPLE), irresistibly photogenic, scary on television, masterful at poster art from their first effort.[43]

Disturbed by the government's public proclamations, the Hampton-Clark murders, and the national and local prosecution of Panther leaders, well-connected white liberals began to raise funds for the Panthers' legal defense. Prominent figures like Leonard Bernstein held "meet and greet" gatherings between well-heeled, white New York philanthropists and selected Panthers. On January 15, 1970, an article in the *New York Times* fashion section highlighted humorous anecdotes of Panther-benefactor conversations in Bernstein's "elegant Park Avenue duplex."[44]

In one of the few published articles on media coverage of the Panthers, Michael Staub argued that the surge in media attention that began in 1969 reflected mainstream society's "moral panic" following the Chicago raid and the "specter of wealthy white liberal support for black militancy."[45] Careful analysis of news accounts before and after the Chicago raid suggests that there was more continuity in media coverage than Staub asserted, but that indeed "moral panic" became visible in news articles and commentaries denouncing allegations of a government plot against the Panthers and ridiculing the fund-raising efforts by supportive liberals.[46]

Over the two and a half years from the May 1967 Sacramento action to the Hampton-Clark murders, the national newsmagazines published a total of eleven articles about the Panthers. But in the two years after the December 1969 Chicago police action, the newsmagazines published forty-eight articles focusing on the Panthers. Almost half of these were particularly attentive to the New York and New Haven trials, or related events like pro-Panther protests at Yale University. The magazines highlighted the colorful personalities involved (and, in the New York case, their angry, confrontational courtroom behavior) and provided the appearance of balance by juxtaposing the two sides in adversarial criminal proceedings. However, magazine articles typically revolved around the state's case against the Panthers, often highlighted with dramatic testimony from informers. "Balance" was sometimes provided by brief mention of inflammatory rhetoric (and sometimes behavior) on the part of Panther suspects or their supporters.[47]

A backlash began to appear in the media targeting respectable liberal voices who supported the legal defense of persecuted Panthers or insisted on justice for Hampton and Clark and the liberal media that allegedly hyped patently false claims of government extermination. None of the voices audible in mainstream media defended any Panthers' activities; in fact, many took pains to separate themselves from Panther politics. What seemed to generate the scathing critiques was the image of the Panthers as victims—an image that seemingly lent the Panthers a degree of legitimacy and thereby threatened the one-dimensional depiction of the Panthers as an aggressive criminal element attacking white society.[48]

Two articles define this backlash. One was author Tom Wolfe's "Radical Chic: That Party at Lenny's," a colorful, ironic *New York* magazine account that juxtaposed the earnest inquiries of New York's naïve upper crust against the street language and savvy of the Panthers.[49] Leonard Bernstein's legitimate liberal objective was most clearly stated on the article's final page: "If we deny these Black Panthers their democratic rights because their philosophy is unacceptable to us, then we are denying our own democracy." Yet the article's overall tone of ironic ridicule suggested that its readers were more hip than the gullible Bernsteins and their wealthy guests. *Time* picked up on the Wolfe essay in its own heavily ironic report on "That Party at Lenny's," while the *New York Times'* own version appeared a bit earlier in a Sunday magazine article entitled "Rapping with the Panthers in White Suburbia."[50] Wolfe's "radical chic" made its way into common parlance as a more general reference to a supposedly gullible liberal elite naïvely supporting leftist causes because it was fashionable to do so—a variant on later right-wing efforts to link liberal opponents with sixties radicals (e.g., Barack Obama and Bill Ayers) in order to denigrate liberals.[51]

The other widely publicized backlash article was Edward Jay Epstein's investigative *New Yorker* piece published in 1971, in which the media critic provided what appeared to be authoritative documentation that the mass media had uncritically and grossly overstated the argument that the government was engaged in a genocidal attack on the Panthers.[52] Reviewing quotations from the *New York Times,* the *Washington Post,* the *Christian Science Monitor, Time,* and *Newsweek,* Epstein created a clear impression that the prestigious national media had simply accepted as factual Panther attorney Garry's assertion that Hampton and Clark were the "27th and 28th" Panthers killed by police. Along with other media references to a "lethal undeclared war" and a "growing suspicion that something more than isolated local police action was involved," Epstein's claim that the media accepted the idea that a "virtual open season" had been declared against the Panthers rested on his contention that the media uncritically accepted Garry's exaggerated numbers as fact.[53] His article correctly raised questions about both Garry's initial claims and three individual news reports, yet his uncorroborated reliance on his own investigation into the deaths of nineteen Panthers and his conclusion about the numbers in news reports suffered from several shortcomings.

First, the article's clear implication that the media were unduly sympathetic to the Panthers rested in part on Epstein's charge that two of the nation's leading papers, the *New York Times* and *Washington Post,* reported the exaggerated Garry numbers as factual, without labeling them as "claims" by the Panther attorney.

Yet the three specific instances he cited were cases where the papers had attributed the numbers in earlier articles, and thus the papers had at most exercised questionable judgment in not mentioning the attribution in each instance.[54] Any implication that the media were overly sympathetic to the Panthers, however, was completely misleading. Overall, the mass media were entirely dismissive if not outspokenly critical of the Panthers, failing to take seriously any of their arguments or ideas while simultaneously responding almost viscerally to violent rhetoric and the Panther's style.

The real target of Epstein's criticism, beyond these few cases, turned out to be the fact that claims of "genocide" and "political assassination" had been echoing (though simultaneously contested) through the mass media because they were being voiced by legitimate, moderate black voices like Ralph Abernathy, Julian Bond, and Whitney Young.[55] Targeting narrowly selected instances of undue media "sympathy" for militant leftist expression, while ignoring the broader patterns of media coverage, would later become a trademark in the decades-long attack on liberal media that began in 1969. One effect of this attack, not surprisingly, has been that the media grew correspondingly more tentative in criticizing established power.[56]

Second, in the guise of providing a seemingly objective corrective to overly sympathetic media, Epstein's article was a vehicle for his own interpretive bias. After reviewing all his evidence, Epstein concluded that John Kifner's charge in the offending *New York Times* article—that the Nixon administration had "at least contributed to a climate of opinion among local police . . . that a virtual open season has been declared on the Panthers"—was "historically inaccurate."[57] However, grounds for precisely such a perception were expressed by none other than a Chicago policeman referring to the Hampton-Clark killings. Howard Saffold, a member of the Afro-American Patrolmen's League, observed of FBI director Hoover's proclamations about the Panther threat:

> The police community is sort of a built-in reward and punishment system
> of its own, and you get a lot of rewards when you go after who the boss says
> is the bad guy and you get him. And I think what J. Edgar Hoover was able
> to do was to give police officers the impression that it was ok, it was open
> season. You didn't have to worry about the law. I think what he in effect said
> was, "It's our ballgame, guys. We've got the authority. We have the capacity.
> Let's crush 'em."[58]

As documented later by the Senate Intelligence Committee and others, the Nixon administration and the FBI were indeed involved in a coordinated effort to neutralize the Panthers.[59]

The third way that Epstein's article was significant was that it became, in effect, the final word on the subject for commentators who have since helped to confine public discourse on the Panthers to the one-dimensional depiction of violent criminals—in other words, returning the media frame to its initial dismissive take before the Panthers-as-victims gained brief legitimacy within the mass media. Fifteen years after the first salvo in the media attack, well after the campaign against the "liberal media" and hysterical "Sixties" had borne fruit, the *Washington Post*'s centrist columnist, Richard Cohen, cited the Epstein article and joined in its conclusion that, in Cohen's words, "the public was misled by a press that was unwilling to verify the facts for itself."[60]

Gail Sheehy's 1971 investigation of the New Haven Panther trial, *Panthermania: The Clash of Black against Black in One American City,* was written in the highly subjective style of the era's New Journalism, without documentation.[61] Confessing at the outset that she had "rallied" to the "spellbinding cause" of the Panthers as victims and martyrs, Sheehy asserted (eschewing attribution), "Without verification, Garry's body count passed like gospel throughout the white media." Similarly, the "revulsion" over the murder of Fred Hampton, in her view, "revived the radical Left," since the "police conduct associated with the Hampton murder snowballed into a widespread public belief that the government was out to eradicate the Panthers."[62] Given the content of media discourse, Sheehy's "radical Left" presumably referred to those like the nine House Democrats and the NAACP's Roy Wilkins who defended the Panthers' constitutional rights; similarly, there is no documentation to support her assertion of "widespread public belief" regarding the government's stance toward the Panthers.

Interestingly, Sheehy commented that "[a] year ago I was just as taken up with the Panther cause as anyone else" and proceeded to describe her inclination to "think of all Panthers as martyrs" after the Hampton-Clark killings.[63] The Panther "mania" in the book's title was, in effect, about precisely this uncritical embrace of everything Panther. Sheehy's highly subjective investigation of the Alex Rackley murder in New Haven led her to an equally uncritical embrace of the Right's denunciation of the Panthers and the liberal media that helped "create" them. As she imagined it, "The Panther movement was created by and for the media. The more it was publicized by the liberal white media, the greater the imagined ranks of a black army grew."[64]

Sheehy's writing reveals visual association at work. On the one hand, she responded subjectively to the Hampton-Clark killings and the subsequent claims of government genocide. She was radicalized by the dramatic images and hype commonly found in the media—and little else. In this regard, she may have been like others who were drawn to radicalism by the media images they witnessed—because their subjective response, unlike those of more mainstream audiences, was to feel sympathetic to the outsiders in the media and thereby to simply reverse the official explanation that reduced the Panthers to the one dimension of violent criminality. Discovering that, indeed, some Panthers were violent, misogynistic thugs was sufficient for these observers to make the uncritical subjective switch back to the conventional mainstream view that they all were thugs. One image proved they were "all good," a second image suggested they were "all bad."

In similar manner, several influential commentaries have consisted of "second thoughts" on the part of those who have reflected back on experiences with Panther violence and have written scathing accounts that reinforce the revisionist media line. In a 1967 *New York Times Magazine* article on the Panthers, Sol Stern sought to understand some of the controversial behaviors and styles of the Panthers, while simultaneously distancing himself from their violent rhetoric and fixation with guns. Thirty-six years later, Stern repented for once being a "left-wing crank," noting that, like other "ex-sixties radicals," he "made the unfortunate mistake of thinking that the Black Panthers were a legitimate social protest movement." The reason for his conversion, in addition to the "psychopathic criminals" who surrounded Huey Newton, was the "torrent of articles and books, many written by former sympathizers," that

> voluminously documented the Panther reign of murder and larceny within their own community. So much so that no one but a left-wing crank would still believe in the Panther myth of dedicated young blacks 'serving the people' while heroically defending themselves against unprovoked attacks by the racist police. . . . Except, that is, at the *New York Times,* where the obsession with white guilt and black victimhood apparently trumps every standard of journalistic and historical accuracy.[65]

For Stern, like Sheehy, David Horowitz, and others, there is no middle gray area, no bad *and* good within the Panther world. As one who made his conversion to Reagan conservatism highly visible and one who has led the charge of right-wing polemics against the Panthers, Horowitz was in all likelihood one of those "ex-sixties radicals" Stern referred to.[66] Like Stern and Sheehy, Horowitz has used evidence selectively drawn from the more violent fringes of the late Panther world to cast a wide net and delegitimize everything about the Panthers, extending his repentant condemnation to everything about the 1960s and post-sixties left as a whole. As with other backlash campaigns, these highlighted Panther behaviors are generalized so that they provide a wholly sufficient explanation of who and what the Panthers were. Repeated references to earlier attacks echoing in right-wing accounts have simply confirmed and reconfirmed this "truth." The rest of media discourse has incorporated these images of violent thugs, though the colorful, charismatic personalities of the most visible Panther leaders remain the object of media curiosity and repeated public lectures.

In 1995, Mario Van Peebles sought to correct the massive distortions about the Panthers with his film *Panther.* The film reestablished several authentic realities of the Black Panther Party's history, from their initial use of guns as a tactic to discourage police brutality in the inner city, to the FBI-led efforts to crush the

Panthers, to the Party's breakfast-for-kids program. The film ends with a classic police-Panther shootout. However, in addition to downplaying the role of women in the party, *Panther* ultimately depoliticizes this most political of black power expressions by minimizing exposure to the Panthers' political ideology and defining FBI repression as a conspiracy with organized crime so as to introduce drugs into the ghetto and thereby debilitate inner-city youth. While former Panther chairman Bobby Seale thundered against the film's inaccuracies, the general media response reflected the long-established Panther iconography. *Time* accused the film of "criminal naiveté" and denounced it for suggesting that the Panthers were "idealists and as objects of veneration to today's youth."[67] Right-wing polemicist David Horowitz's Center for the Study of Popular Culture placed an ad in *Variety* calling the film a "two hour lie."[68] In the end, Peebles's effort to correct the prevailing public memory of the Panthers seemed doomed by the very dramatic symbolism used by the historical Panthers—the guns, the black berets and leather garb, the battles with police. Like the Panthers, it too became the subject of media exploitation and backlash attack.

Except for rare media glimpses of serious historical work excavating the history of local chapters or analyzing the Panther phenomenon, these images define mass media discourse on the Panthers. And, to be sure, when a serious consideration of the Panthers shows up in the media, the Right is ready to pounce, dismissing these accounts as if they were the same as the media culture's romanticized treatment of celebrities. Thus, for example, Panther-bashing columnist Kate Coleman described a 2003 conference that she did not attend—"The Black Panther Party in Historical Perspective" at Wheelock College—as having "all the veneer of a scholarly gathering." The bulk of her two scathing articles—"Revisionism: Guess Who's Mything Them Now: The Real Black Panthers Were a Bunch of Thugs" in the *San Francisco Chronicle* and "Black Panthers: Just a Pack of Predators" in the *Los Angeles Times*—revolved around rehashed Huey Newton stories and links between the long-extinct Panthers and the "leap in drive-by shooting deaths in Oakland" in the 1990s.[69]

New Left Militancy and Weatherman

For some in the group that became Weatherman in 1969, as with others in the New Left, police violence at the Democratic National Convention in Chicago was a telling turning point. Bill Ayers recalled the police wading into Lincoln Park and pummeling a friend: "Perhaps this is where the rage got started in the movement, this very night. I'm not sure, but before this, every meeting, every rally, every demonstration was filled with singing, and afterward the singing stopped. When we opened our mouths now, we could only scream. Idealism was there, but in abeyance. The apocalypse approached."[70]

Indeed it did. In the aftermath of Chicago, SDS adopted a Mike Klonsky paper titled "Towards a Revolutionary Youth Movement." In June 1969, at the same time that *New Left Notes* published "You Don't Need a Weatherman to Know Which Way the Wind Blows," SDS came apart at its convention, leaving Weatherman and Revolutionary Youth Movement II (RYM II) issuing a call to "Bring the War Home" in Chicago in fall 1969.

In 1969, desperate young militants began a wave of bombings on and off college campuses. News stories of building takeovers, clashes with police, or bombings became almost daily events.[71] Images conveyed to some a sense of imminent apocalypse. After a rally in Madison, Wisconsin, led by leather-clad black militants, one militant white activist commented, "I distinctly remember one very vivid image, of about twelve or fifteen black guys, all of whom were wearing combat boots and green army jackets, fatigue jackets, and I thought the revolution had arrived."[72]

In her richly reflective memoir of her "life as a Weatherman," Cathy Wilkerson wrote,

> Some of the leaders of Weatherman . . . mistook these youthful expressions of alienation for political consciousness. They confused the seduction of their own images with their ability to nurture a productive organization. . . . Many wanted to be convinced that if a few threw up the barricades, hundreds of thousands would follow.
>
> Throughout its seven years of existence, Weatherman continued to be characterized by this confusion between the power of images to attract attention, and the capability to support the slow construction of the new understanding necessary for a sustainable commitment to change.[73]

RYM II and Weatherman split over strategic differences: Klonsky's RYM II called for "patience, not arrogance" in organizing the white working class, while Weatherman set out on their own ideological path, embracing militant or "revolutionary" action in solidarity with anti-imperial movements in and outside the United States. The 1969 communiqué explained that "the nature of the revolution that we talk about" revolved around the "destruction of US imperialism."[74] Weatherman took the "revolutionary fight" to the streets of Chicago, believing that, in the words of Mark Rudd and Terry Robbins, Weatherman needed to be "a movement that fights, not just talks about fighting," noting that "aggressiveness, seriousness, toughness . . . will attract vast numbers of working-class youth."[75]

Despite efforts by the Panthers' Fred Hampton, antiwar leader Dave Dellinger, and others to talk them out of the action, Weatherman proceeded with the so-called "Days of Rage" in October 1969.[76] Although the event was attended by only a few hundred, the chanting marchers trashed cars and store fronts and clashed violently with well-armed police over the course of several days. Weatherman withdrew, claiming victory on three grounds: that their action would spur other white radicals to commit to their struggle, that they had achieved the coherence of a tight fighting cadre, and that they had inflicted material damage to "imperialist and racist institutions" (including severely wounded policemen), as Weatherman Shin'ya Ono put it. Some of the Weather rationale was based on their reading of the "revolutionary moment": that U.S. imperialism, in Ono's words, had "entered a period of organic crisis, in the Gramscian sense of that term," a crisis of "such intensity, depth, and immediacy as to make the destruction of imperialism and socialist revolution both possible and necessary *in our generation,* that is, in the order of twenty to thirty years, as opposed to fifty or one hundred years."[77]

Not surprisingly, the Days of Rage were widely denounced not only by the mainstream media but by much of the Left. Antiwar leader Dave Dellinger criticized them as did the leftist *Guardian,* and both Robin Morgan and the feminist Bread and Roses collective criticized Weather's machismo and misogynist behavior toward women. Black Panther Fred Hampton denounced the Weather actions as "anarchistic, opportunistic, adventuristic, and Custeristic."[78] Mass media accounts were universally negative and disdainful, referring to the Days of Rage variously as "adolescent adventuring" (*Newsweek*) and a "senseless rampage" (*Time*). To the liberal-Left *Nation*, these were "ill-informed youths shouting irrelevant insults and wielding clubs at available targets."[79] As Jeremy Varon has remarked, "In the Days of Rage, Weatherman revealed itself to the mainstream as monstrous; incapable of being comprehended, the monster had only to be stopped."[80]

Facing prosecution and enraged by the murders of Hampton and Clark, a December 1969 "war council" determined that Weatherman would go underground, disperse into smaller cells in New York, San Francisco, Chicago, and Detroit, and carry out a campaign of clandestine violent struggle against racism and imperialism — in their own words, "Bringing the War Home." Propelled by their "gut checks," early Weather actions were characteristically reckless, which didn't seem to matter until the accidental explosion of a bomb being constructed by members of the New York City cell — a bomb that was at the time meant for a U.S. officers' club dance at Fort Dix, New Jersey.[81] Three Weather people were killed in the blast. The mass media responded with shock and outrage. The *New York Times* editorialized about Weatherman, calling them "Not idealists, Criminals."[82] The FBI stepped up efforts to infiltrate and eliminate Weatherman.

The townhouse explosion also reverberated through the Weather organization. While brashly delivering a communiqué declaring "a state of war" on May 21, a smaller group of chastened Weather members gathered in northern California to reassess their strategies and step back from the path that led toward terrorism.[83] In a communiqué titled "New Morning — Changing Weather," the organization conceded that they had glorified violence, confused martyrdom with commitment, and, acknowledging sexism within the organization, officially changed their name to the Weather Underground. Correcting their "military error" of contemplating actions aimed at killing police or military personnel, the Underground turned toward violent sabotage, or what Dan Berger has termed "armed propaganda," bombing targets carefully selected so as to avoid bloodshed while sending a message. As Berger noted, Weather saw "the greatest error" revealed by the townhouse explosion "to be its own political thinking and attitude, rather than just the bomb's inadvertent detonation or the group's technical inexperience."[84]

The new strategy was designed to use explosives against politically symbolic property while avoiding human casualties by tipping off authorities in advance. Following the killings at Kent State, the Underground went public with its "Declaration of a State of War," announcing Weather plans to blow up a major symbol of American injustice, which turned out to be the Criminal Courts Building in New York City, chosen for its role in the lengthy incarceration of the "Panther 21." Subsequent bombings included the Presidio Army base and military police station in San Francisco, the police statue in Haymarket Square in Chicago (for a second time), and the Harvard War Research Center for International Affairs (the first action by the so-called "Women's Brigade" of the Weather Underground). Later targets reflected responses to provocative acts by the government, among these the U.S. Capitol in response to the expansion of the war into Laos, the California Department of Corrections in response to the murder of George Jackson in prison, and the New York Department of Corrections in response to the police assault against the Attica prison uprising. In effect, Weather Underground actions were meant as symbolic communication to the government (and the wider society) that each new act of oppression or escalation of the war would be met by some violent destruction of related government property. As Dan Berger has noted, the "symbolic resonance of Weather's actions led [Weatherman] Jeff Jones to call the bombings themselves a form of media—not done *for* media attention, but actions that themselves communicated a message." In Berger's analysis, the bombings also "pierced the myth of government invincibility . . . exacting a cost for state or corporate terror."[85]

Along with countercultural expressiveness, racial unrest, and growing antiwar militancy, the case could be made that Weather Underground's strategic use of violence helped to widen the gulf between the movement and the wider public.[86] Violent disruptions visible in the media were inherently unlikely to find many sympathetic readings among general media audiences. Weather's violence—to say nothing of their inflammatory, sometimes crazed rhetoric—came under fire by nonviolent antiwar activists like Daniel Berrigan and Dave Dellinger, and quite clearly it alienated a wider public, including many who were against the war.[87]

Late sixties violence became a useful foil with which the forces of backlash could make their interpretation of events more persuasive, and public opinion seemed persuaded. An October 1970 Harris poll examined the public's view of the "major causes of student unrest" on the nation's campuses. The most cited causes were, in order, "Radical militant student groups" (74 percent), "Irresponsible students who just want to cause trouble" (64 percent), "Radical professors who encourage student revolt" (58 percent), "The continuing war in Vietnam" (54 percent), and "College presidents who are too lenient and permissive" (53 percent). In effect, movement violence meant turning one's back on the possibility of expanding a radical democratic awareness into other sectors of the public. Its two principal audiences were, instead, government officials who would have to incorporate the cost of additional violence into their political calculations and those alienated movement actors, particularly the young, who might rally to the bold militancy of these dramatic actions (and many fewer than expected did so). At the same time, along with other forms of militant confrontation in the antiwar and black power movements, these actions threatened to undermine the authority of a government that seemed unable to maintain order while pursuing a war that was an obvious major cause of disruption.

In their isolation, like other sixties outsiders, Weatherman became increasingly vulnerable to internal dynamics that left democratic interactions far behind, a mixture of self-criticism and strategizing that was infused with a powerful "prove yourself" ethos that took on many meanings: prove your superiority to the afraid-to-fight left intellectuals, prove yourself as a fighter rather than a coward, prove yourself as liberated from monogamous relationships, and so on. Among former members who have testified to brutal, cult-like internal dynamics within Weatherman, Cathy Wilkerson has observed,

> We threw ourselves into the possibility of remaking ourselves as more effective tools for humanity's benefit to the point of sacrificing our own humanity and certainly losing, in the process, our individual voices. . . . During this time . . . we caused no small amount of damage to both ourselves and other organizations, even while tens of thousands felt heartened by our voice of outrage, our sacrifice, and our ability to elude capture.[88]

While I leave to others the task of explaining the bizarre psychodynamics occurring within the self-isolated Weather organization, I would suggest that the media spectacle had something to do with the huge importance the group placed on identity reconstruction and its manifestation in public action. In their own words, Weather's embrace of violence was in part about creating a new identity, shedding their "white skin privilege" in ways they felt fused them with the struggles of militant blacks or the National Liberation Front in Vietnam. As Shin'ya Ono put it, fighting in the streets of Chicago gave meaning to the "abstract phrase 'international solidarity.' . . . We began to *feel* the Vietnamese *in ourselves*."[89] Bernardine Dohrn elaborated on the identity-revealing quality of action by contrasting Weatherman to the conventional public discourse available to Americans:

> We grew up and we didn't learn anything about history, and we didn't understand very much about how you can't always see on the surface. What you see immediately is not necessarily what's at work and what's happening. So, growing up everybody's feeling small and isolated, and made to feel that way their whole lives. We felt that way then. *We were determined to carry out an action that would reveal how passionately we felt and that we were on the other side.*[90]

As Cathy Wilkerson put it years later, "We all needed to belong to something, I reasoned, and once we decided to align ourselves with some particular identity, we looked at the world through that lens."[91]

In conjunction with their own actions and isolation, the media spectacle also seemed to feed an exaggerated sense of affective empowerment among certain Weather members—perhaps blinding them to some of the effects of their actions. In his history of the Weather Underground, Ron Jacobs noted that Weatherman's claim that the Days of Rage was a successful action rested in part on the belief that the "willingness of Weather people to lay their lives on the line would push other white radicals to make a similar commitment," which Jacobs argued was based "naïvely on the belief that media coverage of the Days of Rage had created an image of strength for the watching world, much like the Tet Offensive of the National Liberation Front in 1968."[92]

Instead of interactive exchanges that enabled them to gauge their impact, the bombings were symbolic actions left out there in the public limelight for others to react to however they might. Caught up in the craziness of the time, Weather misread their own impact. Grandiosity and narcissism were plentiful in Weather rhetoric. As Bill Ayers recalled later, "The dreadful and inescapable fact was that it was up to us to rescue everyone. We imagined that the survival of humanity depended on the kids alone."[93] In a 2002 *Washington Post* article recanting his days as a member of Weatherman, Jonathan Lerner noted,

> Our real weapon was youthful swagger, which is cheap and thrilling to use, and magnifies well through the media. . . . We saw ourselves as part of the enormous youth culture and student movements; but as more serious, because we were trying to lead; more committed . . . and braver. So we felt cooler than the rest of our generation . . . felt ourselves to be more heroic and inventive, closer to people like Che Guevara and Simone de Beauvoir than to your average peacenik or hippie.[94]

Weatherman was, of course, not alone in reading the times in this way. Indeed, violence was commonly visible in the media, sixties social movements had evolved into expressive forms of militancy on a variety of fronts, and youthful alienation was at its zenith. Clearly, U.S. imperialism was being challenged by many in the antiwar movement; yet mainstream public discourse failed to take seriously even the possibility that the United States was carrying out an imperial war in Indochina, and there is no evidence that antiwar public opinion in general reflected this view despite majority sentiment that the United States should get out of Vietnam. Furthermore, as critics on the left reminded Weatherman, despite growing antiwar opinion and widespread youthful alienation, there was little evidence to support the argument that the United States was remotely close to a classic revolutionary moment.[95] To suggest that a revolution was possible in "twenty or thirty years" was to place enormous faith in the power that could be mobilized by youthful revolutionaries spurred to action by the demonstration effect of Weatherman's public actions.

Noting that the townhouse explosion was both a symbol of the New Left "going too far" and a catalyst for "pulling back," Jeremy Varon has credited the Weather Underground with coming to recognize limits to the use of violence, in this way distinguishing themselves from the "institutionalized normlessness of killing in the American war in Vietnam."[96] Without wavering from their political commitment to racial and social justice, particularly their support for the Black Panthers and the people of Vietnam, several former Weather men and women have expressed various shades of regret about the path they were once on.[97]

In retrospect, in the absence of sensing the desperate anguish being felt at the time because of the war, it is difficult for most younger people today to see the Weather Underground as anything but a group of crazed renegades madly in love with their self-image as violent revolutionaries—or else, perhaps they romanticize their bravado and style, perhaps even emulating them, as some have done with the Panthers. As is the case with the Panthers, such is the basic characterization available in the media culture today. When Sam Green and Bill Siegel produced *The Weather Underground,* a thought-provoking 2003 film that probed into the meanings of Weather's meteoric trajectory, the mass media responded in a predictable manner. Since the film was nominated for Best Documentary in 2004, it received significant media attention. In response to both the film and media attention, the Right provided the prevailing post-9/11 framework for legitimate conversation about the film—namely that the United States once had its own homegrown "terrorists," the Weather Underground. Despite the fact that Weather's actions were drastically different from those of Al Qaeda or other terrorist organizations, the terrorism frame cropped up frequently, even finding its way into headlines of articles that provided in-depth interviews with the film's key figures. A *Salon* review, for example, focused on Mark Rudd's regrets about the path Weather took; its heading read: "When Terrorism Was Cool."[98]

The most recent repetition of this theme occurred when vice presidential candidate Sarah Palin and others on the Right attacked presidential candidate Obama for his alleged relationship with sixties "terrorist" Bill Ayers. As with the Panthers, the mass media accounts of this volatile past revolved around a contest between an attack on the late sixties and on the most controversial episodes of the era and a provocative glimpse into the media celebrities whose militancy arose mysteriously out of a time of great excess.

Domesticating the Sixties: Capitalism's Cultural Co-optation

The familiar symbols and catchphrases of the young gained currency through films, through radio and television, through albums and rock concerts deftly engineered. . . . By the mid-Seventies, in short, TV had started to resemble what it is today: a good "environment" (as the admakers say) for advertising.
　　—Mark Crispin Miller, "The Hipness unto Death," 1989

"Revolution," once the totemic catchphrase of the counterculture, has become the totemic catchphrase of boomer-as-capitalist.
　　—Thomas Frank, "Why Johnny Can't Dissent," 1997

Sixties social movements challenged much of the postwar capitalist world, yet they all contained within them an expressive, liberatory side that reflected that postwar world's energizing promise of individual freedom. Absent critical self-awareness and sustained political consciousness, the desire for personal self-expression and liberation was susceptible to the co-optive forces of commercialization, especially as capitalism's markets adapted to the emerging new tastes and attitudes of sixties-era youth. By hyping the colorful imagery of the counterculture, for example, the mass media invited young Americans to, as Peter Berg put it, "Act out free."[1] Predictably, Madison Avenue followed suit, pitching products geared to the tastes and language of youth.

Thomas Frank has documented how in the late 1950s and early 1960s, innovative admen began to break from the prevailing pattern of advertising that glorified the trappings of the American dream. The new, satirical advertising was pitched just right to play to youthful disenchantment with the hierarchical, conformist postwar world William H. Whyte wrote about in *The Organization Man*. As Madison Avenue began to respond to the spreading counterculture, Frank noted, "Hip became central to the way American capitalism understood itself and explained itself to the public. . . . Advertising actively compared a new, hip consumerism to an older capitalist ideology and left the latter permanently discredited." The introduction of ironic, hip advertising became, in Frank's words, "The magic cultural formula by which the life of consumerism could be extended indefinitely, running forever on the discontent that it itself had produced. . . .

Hip would become the dynamic principle of the 1960s, a cultural perpetual motion machine transforming disgust with consumerism into fuel for the ever-accelerating consumer society."[2] Frank's work offers important insight into the way capitalism's hegemony was restored via changes in business and advertising culture—a change that reflected, but then converted to market functions, the individualistic and rebellious culture of the young.[3]

As the advertising world was zeroing in on the youth culture, some of the more adventurous television programmers sought to capitalize on the same dynamic of restless youthful alienation. Media critic Mark Crispin Miller has written extensively about the convergence of consumer culture and television, pointing to a dynamic whereby TV producers, attentive to new market tastes, began to seek fresh programming as the novelty of fifties television began to grow stale.[4] Shows ranging from the *Smothers' Brothers Comedy Hour* and *Laugh-In* to *Mod Squad, All in the Family,* and *Mary Tyler Moore* adopted themes that would tap into the attitudes of rebellious youth. As Todd Gitlin has observed, "The blandness of television entertainment in the 1950s . . . was displaced in the 1970s by a style of entertainment that takes account of social conflict and works to domesticate it—to individualize its solutions, if not its causes."[5] Hollywood followed suit with films that either broke through Hollywood conventions and resonated with themes relevant to sixties youth (*Bonnie and Clyde*) or tried to capture the ambiance of the counterculture directly (*Easy Rider* and *Hallucination Generation*).

Commercial media's attention to youth and the social upheavals of the sixties reflected the way in which hegemony is sustained through "negotiations" between public tastes and the institutional imperatives of capitalism. Both youthful rebellion and the monoculture of 1950s capitalism would be affected through these negotiations. In the first place, the attention to and use of youth and rebellion themes by advertisers and the entertainment media alike turned youthful identity formation and rebellion to functional ends responsive to the imperatives of capitalism, most notably shopping and entertainment.

Furthermore, as both Frank and Miller have argued, the commercial appeal to audience desires to be "hip," "with it," or "cool" has over time generated a subversive dynamic that effectively preempts dissent and criticism because the media themselves (ads and television shows in particular) are self-parodying. Frank argues that advertising's play on rebelliousness, individuality, and self-parody—along with the business world's adoption of humane individualism—almost precludes dissent by subverting and channeling the human drive for individual expression: "Today that beautiful countercultural idea, endorsed now by everyone from the surviving Beats to shampoo manufacturers, is more the official doctrine of corporate America than it is a program of resistance. What we understand as 'dissent' does not subvert, does not challenge, does not even question the cultural faiths of Western business."[6]

Miller has argued that "TV coopts that smirking disbelief which so annoyed the business titans of the Thirties" through the use of "preemptive irony." Thus "TV protects its ads from mockery by doing all the mocking."[7] He suggests that TV's entertainment fare embodies the same hegemony-reinforcing dynamic by subverting all authority and individuality. Thus sitcoms routinely flatter their viewers' superiority to the all-too-human "butts of the joke," suggesting "we had better see the joke or else turn into it." However, by laughing at the "butts of the joke," we have joined in the process of self-erasure that leaves us open to the power of consumerism, "TV's sole imperative," as we "try to live up, or down, to the same standard of acceptability that TV's ads and shows define collectively."[8]

Finally, the sixties era clearly manifested a variety of ways in which Americans' social tastes and political attitudes were profoundly fracturing, thereby posing a formidable new challenge to the commercial capitalism's postwar assumptions of a relatively homogenous national market—namely, how to reach a diverse and fragmenting audience through common, corporate media. Market segmentation began to take off in earnest in the sixties, particularly for lifestyle and cultural products, but the diversity of market interests and tastes in turn posed a major challenge to the established system of media oligopoly. Centrifugal market forces helped provoke innovations like cable television and more recently the Internet, media that could more readily tailor programming and information to niche audiences, even to individual tastes. By the 1980s, however, the resulting destabilization of media markets produced significant pressures for neoliberal media policy, namely communications deregulation, which in turn facilitated the vertical integration of media into the giant global conglomerates we have today.[9]

A related phenomena that was accelerated by the counterculture was a burgeoning industry responsive to what some have called the "Human Potential" movement. As Theodore Roszak noted, the counterculture produced a shift whereby "building the good society is not primarily a social, but a psychic task."[10] As such, it opened the door to a whole range of therapeutic, health, and spiritual responses to the same forces the counterculture recoiled against—a mixture of spiritual utopianism, so-called New Age pursuits, and what Carl Boggs has called the "therapeutic revolution: alienation depoliticized."[11] The cumulative effect of these forces is to depoliticize society by drawing the citizenry away from citizenship and reinforcing privatism.

Advertising's Countercultural Pitch

In Thomas Frank's account, ad man Bill Bernbach anticipated the coming counterculture with his groundbreaking "anti-advertising" Volkswagen ads that first emerged in 1959. Pitched in direct counterpoint to the big-finned behemoths of the Big Three U.S. automakers in the late 1950s, Volkswagen ads used humor and a simple layout that spoke directly to viewers' skepticism about consumerist mass society, playing up the car's "ugly" shape, its absence of annual stylish modifications, and its simple practicality with ironic questions like "Could it be that ours aren't the funny looking cars after all?" With consumer skepticism on the rise in the ad-inundated society of the late 1950s, Volkswagen's pitch seemed, by contrast, "honest," yet, as Frank notes, the crucial point of the "new Madison Avenue" was that consumer skepticism was channeled toward greater consumption. To sustain their appeal, Volkswagen's ads soon incorporated self-mockery, suggesting in one 1964 ad that the company didn't engage in dealership gimmicks "maybe because we don't quite understand the system" and, in another, asking about the lack of change in the shape of the VW, "How much longer can we hand you this line?"[12] It seems more than coincidental that the VW "microbus" became a popular counterculture vehicle.

Madison Avenue's co-optation of sixties dissent for profit was deliberate. Although racial minorities and women would soon follow, the rising counterculture of the mid-sixties was probably the first of the newly visible social groups to attract major marketing attention, typically as some variant of a new "generation" (e.g., the "Pepsi Generation"). In early 1967, as the counterculture was approaching peak visibility, an enterprising editor of the advertising magazine *Madison Avenue* published a sixteen-question quiz for older admen who were likely to find the "Now Generation" baffling. As Stuart Ewen reported it, Daniel Moriarty saw the youth culture as "both an antiestablishment challenge and a potential resource to be mined," and Moriarty's references keyed in on the "millions of teeny-boppers, hippies, and Harvard sophs in Fat City with bread in their jeans and a lot of ways to spend it." Throughout Moriarty's pitch, hot political issues like the Vietnam War were "conspicuously absent." It was clear from his quiz that "stylistic elements" and pop-culture references were the crucial codes that needed to be learned if advertisers were to separate the young from their money.[13]

Similarly, a December 1969 issue of *Hear, There & Everywhere,* a magazine for department store promoters, asked, "Can You Rap with the Soul Generation? . . . How many English languages do you speak? Better add soul and rock 'n roll. A hip (not hep) business man should have a nodding acquaintance with such talk." The magazine included its own quiz, to help marketers assess how successful they might be in reaching members of the so-called "Soul Generation."[14] A year later, as the environmental movement was beginning to emerge, the same marketing magazine hit upon "ENVIRONMENT" as the "key word to retail profit, merchandising, promotion," one of the earliest of many appropriations of the language of environmental activism to advance forms of consumption (including "natural" foods, "all natural" ingredients, and "energy-saving"—though electricity-consuming—"green" home appliances).[15] In these cases, the language and icons of alienated youth sectors were taken out of context and reduced to empty (if not contradictory) vehicles for marketing products to potential young consumers. As Ewen observed, the languages and icons of the youth culture, reflecting their alienating encounters with the wider culture, were "reduced to the status of a commodity," their original significance or use value now eclipsed by their exchange value, their "ability to make something marketably 'hip.'" Once their marketability had been exhausted they were, like much of consumer culture, reduced to "cultural waste matter."[16]

The explosion of creative energy in popular music was one of the more potent identifiers of the sixties liberatory spirit, and one that music corporations moved quickly to tap into. One of the better-known ads, for Columbia music, appeared in several underground papers and music magazines in 1968. An eye-catching photograph revealed a half dozen long-haired musicians lounging attentively in what appeared to be a recording studio, with various protest posters featuring contrived slogans like "Grab Hold!" "Music is Love," and "Wake Up!" strewn on the floor. The eye-grabbing heading read, "But the Man can't bust our music." In smaller print, the ad defiantly declared, "The Establishment's against adventure. And the arousing experience that sometimes comes with listening to today's music. So what? Let them slam doors. And keep it out of the concert halls. Nothing can stop great sound makers like Ives, Riley, Stockhausen, Varese or the Moog Synthesizer. They're ear stretching. And sometimes transfixing. And The Man can't stop you from listening. Especially if you're armed with these." Six albums were illustrated in an inset, essentially classical or quasi-classical music pitched to the rebellious minds of youth. Thus a Charles Ives album was touted as "the first shot fired in the Ives Revolution. Ear-shaking portraits of great dissenters." A Terry Riley album was hailed as "the only legal trip you can take. A hypnotic sound experience."[17]

While the ad caused something of a flap at Columbia for identifying the company "too closely" with the counterculture, CBS records continued to advertise in the counterculture's underground papers. Later ads, in Abe Peck's account, featured "an amorous longhaired couple, then a joint-passing circle of hippies, a black, and a headdressed Indian" accompanying the pitch, "'Know who your friends are. And look and see and touch and be together. Then listen'—to Blood, Sweat, and Tears, the Chambers Brothers, and other acts."[18] A later Columbia ad boldly declared, "The Revolutionaries are on Columbia."

As the CBS ads suggest, by 1968 the big record corporations had discovered the money-making potential in the creative dynamism and critical edge of mid-sixties rock music. By the time of the Monterey Pop festival of 1967, rock music had flourished during two years of stunning creative energy in the aftermath of the "British Invasion," heightened by a convergence of folk music's political edge with electronic sound, symbolized by Bob Dylan's "going electric" at the 1965 Newport Folk Festival. At Monterey, the first of the big sixties rock festivals, the tensions between the creative expression of countercultural themes and the commercial imperatives of capitalism began to emerge. Some artists refused to participate in the festival until its profits were donated to educational and musical charities, and the Grateful Dead refused to participate at all unless the festival was free. CBS records executive Clive Davis recalled that Monterey revealed "a very idealistic, very innocent and beautiful philosophy of life," but also a "dramatic change in pop-music group playing that I would bet on."[19] Davis proceeded to sign several of the Monterey acts to lucrative CBS contracts, and a wider commercial talent hunt on the part of several large music producers ensued. The co-optation of the counterculture's music and the related production of wealthy rock celebrities had begun.

Amidst the hype, some believed in the transformative power of rock music. As CBS "house freak" Jim Fouratt put it, "We really believed that the music was coming out of a community, and if that community was expanded because they got our major-label distribution, the message was going to be clear and we were going to take over the world. Capitalism does not work that way. The money cut the artists off from the community."[20] As Robert Santelli has written, "The roots of Monterey Pop . . . and the nonprofit, celebratory theme were soon debauched, distorted, and forgotten. The vision of large profits that arose from the excitement over the commercial viability of the new music and the festival format caused the perversion. Things would never be the same again."[21]

In 1969, *Advertising Age* included a paean to its appropriately named "individual revolution . . . for which young people are the spearhead." Noting lyrics that "feed your mind," the wild names of the new bands, and the endlessly varied fashions of the young, writer Hanley Norins observed, "The Individual Revolution is in full cry. It's not only coming. It's here. So why does anybody resist it at all? Above all, why don't we advertising men lead the revolution and help to make it a viable, positive one?"[22] — meaning, of course, one that would be profitable for the ad companies and their clients.

Finally, a range of advertisements in the latter 1960s played off safe elements of emergent sixties social movements. Middle-class racial minorities began to appear in product advertising, as did professional white women. One of the most blatantly co-optive pitches of this genre was the Virginia Slims cigarette promotion begun in 1968 just as the women's movement was beginning to become visible in the mass media. Patricia Bradley has described the early ads that pioneered a new, dramatic story format that was to become highly popular:

The cigarette campaign, filmed in sepia, featured a series of satiric fictional historical events in the early suffrage movement. In the first commercial an announcer intoned that a "Pamela Benjamin" was caught smoking in a gazebo. "She got a severe scolding and no supper that night." The voice continued, "In 1915, Mrs. Cynthia Robinson was caught smoking in the cellar behind the preserves. Although she was thirty-four, her husband sent her straight to her room. Then, in 1920, women won their rights." The ad concluded in color, with a model, smoking a cigarette against the jingle, "You've come a long way."[23]

Bradley commented, "By all accounts, the campaign succeeded in attracting new female smokers, who may have considered that responding to the campaign was a way of declaring some kind of symbolic allegiance to issues in the women's movement."[24]

In 1969, advertising executive Laurel Cutler captured the commercial potential of women's liberation in a revealing article for readers of *Madison Avenue:* "Many women . . . are throwing out the old forms. They are challenging every institution in our society. At the least, they are questioning all traditional values. . . . Isn't this new woman, this free and loving-every-minute-of-it woman, the heavy user every industry must find and cultivate and multiply?"[25] Pond's hand lotion was one product that responded, appealing to women consumers with the pitch "You need another pious, lily-white, Lady Jane hand lotion like you need a whale-boned girdle," and beginning in 1970 cosmetic companies came out with vaginal deodorants variously pitched as confidence-building and facilitating women's freedom (one brand, a "freedom spray," was advertised next to a political button that read "freedom now").[26] Companies leapt at the chance to erase their former, un-hip pasts. According to Paul Krassner, as the sixties came to an end, "Tampax advertised its tampon as 'Something over 30 you can trust.'"[27]

Entertainment TV Joins the "Revolution"

In their 1997 book *The Revolution Wasn't Televised: Sixties Television and Social Conflict,* Lynn Spigel and Michael Curtin introduced a collection of sixties television studies by noting that hegemony is a "way to understand how the [TV] networks negotiated between the will for social change and the opposing urge for stasis by incorporating revolutionary ideas into the more consensual fictions of television."[28] The studies in their collection, along with several other important works, demonstrate that the entertainment fare of television during and since the 1960s has continually responded to and absorbed dissenting ideas into an arena that is compatible with prevailing ideology, that shrinks the realm of the possible even as it incessantly attends to the new, and, finally, that produces privatized, passive forms of leisure.

After the popularity of initial 1950s sitcoms began to wear thin, one of the more popular television sitcoms of the early 1960s was *The Beverly Hillbillies,* a show lightly satirical of the consumer-driven lifestyle of the 1950s, focusing on a family of Arkansas "hillbillies" who strike it rich by discovering oil on their land

and then migrate to the alluring American Dream state of California. The show's humor revolved around satirizing the nouveau-riche family's botched efforts to live the life of luxury, a theme juxtaposed against the wise traditionalism of the family's patriarch and matriarch. As noted by David Farber, *Beverly Hillbillies* "preached that character was more important than appearance," thereby "contradicting the blandishments of every prime-time commercial sponsor and the entire thrust of the consumer capitalist system." The show exposed the tensions between "discipline and license" and "hard work and hedonism," but "simultaneously defused them with broad humor, turning complex questions about modern society into escapist nostalgia."[29]

As the sixties-era critique sharpened, television responded with shows that played off the currents of disenchantment and dissent among the young. The darkening tone of highly popular Beatles songs, to say nothing of the group's embrace of countercultural lifestyles by around mid-decade, helped launch the television show (and musical career of) *The Monkees*. The quartet who formed the "Prefab Four" had responded to a *Variety* advertisement calling for "4 insane boys, aged 17–21" to play "rock & roll musicians" in a new TV series. More conventionally wholesome-looking than the 1966 Beatles, the Monkees' zany antics brought to mind the Beatles' successful 1964 film *A Hard Day's Night,* itself a humanizing spoof on the band's "Beatlemania" popularity.

After discovering that an initial pilot program alienated older audiences who couldn't get past the long-haired lads, subsequent shows included interviews with individual Monkees designed to show that they were "nice, regular guys after all."[30] The rift between old and young tastes continued to plague the show, particularly in Aniko Bodroghkozy's account, as "cultural signifiers such as long hair, exotic clothing, rock music, and the drop-out lifestyle—all on display in *The Monkees*—increasingly served as indexes of hippiedom." Not surprisingly, press accounts played up the theme of generational conflict, but the show never caught on with countercultural audiences and disappeared after two years. Its main appeal was to a younger "teeny-bopper" crowd, as Bodroghkozy observed, with the band (whose music continued to be heard) nonetheless evoking the "same set of anxieties and moral panics that the burgeoning counterculture evoked among adult observers." "The Monkees may have been the first 'plastic hippies' but plenty would follow," she observed. "Few, however, would work so actively to subvert themselves."[31]

As Bodroghkozy noted, "In the aftermath of 'the Summer of Love' media extravaganza television hippies began popping up all over prime time, especially on law and order programs." While "binaries of 'good kids' and 'bad kids' were continually thrown into question," one social category "not up for grabs" was the "benevolent institution of law and order."[32] In 1968, as the Monkees were leaving TV, *Mod Squad* aired, featuring three troubled youths, all sixties stereotypes: an angry black man with "'Black Power' signifiers: bushy afro, dark shades," a long-haired blond "hippie chick," and an alienated white male.[33] The three had dropped out of "straight society" and gotten in trouble with the law. While on probation, they were organized into the "mod squad" by police captain Adam Greer, their mission, in the words of "The Mod Squad TV Show Unofficial Home Page w/ Pictures and Episode Guide," to "infiltrate the counter-culture and catch the adult crime-lords who preyed on the young kids, but never the kids themselves. While the Mod Squad were 'fuzz,' they certainly weren't 'pigs.' Being from the Flower-Children era, they didn't carry guns; instead, they wore beads and hip clothing and used the slang of the day: 'groovy,' 'keep the faith' and, most notably, 'solid.'"[34] The use of sixties misfits as crime investigators working for the police reversed the archetypal role they played in the news media of the time, yet the co-optive police work sought legitimacy among younger viewers through its focus on organized crime, which by 1968 had indeed begun to prey on the countercultural drug scene in places like Haight-Ashbury. As Bodroghkozy has argued, "In its ideological balancing act, the show could appeal to television's broad audience: the under-thirty viewers could identify with the young protagonists, who were never entirely comfortable with their law-enforcement status, and the older generation could take comfort from the law-and-order format of the show." Yet, she noted, the show generated a conflicted response in the counterculture's underground press — "anger, rage, and disgust, along with a limited amount of grudging support."[35]

Mod Squad carefully negotiated what Stuart Hall has referred to as the "double movement"[36] of resistance and containment at work in popular, market-based media that touched on and made palatable most of the troublesome conflicts of the day: rebellious youth versus the institutions of law and order, race and inner-city black anger, draft resistance and the Vietnam War, even the My Lai massacre. One theme the show avoided challenging was the role of women as the oft-victimized weaker sex — at the time still relatively unchallenged in mainstream circles.[37] As Todd Gitlin has suggested, *Mod Squad*'s contextual appeal ran deeper. Under the firm hand of the paternal police captain, the three youths were "errant sons" (one black, one a daughter) who "had located the father they deserved," and thus the show could appeal to "dismayed parents who wanted to think the best of their errant children while seeing their authority approved in the end."[38] The program, in Bodroghkozy's words, became the "prototype for a wave of 'socially relevant' television programming that would follow it in the years ahead."[39]

Producers of a third popular 1960s show, *The Smothers Brothers Comedy Hour,* veered much closer to the actual political controversies of the day in an attempt to "align themselves with the youth movement," as Bodroghkozy put it,[40] in the process allowing some legitimation of dissent until the show's political commentary became so controversial that CBS dropped it. Unlike *Mod Squad* and other shows of the time, *The Smothers Brothers* succeeded in reaching significant sectors of the era's alienated youth.

Bodroghkozy described a revealing segment that captures the awakening satire of the time and might remind contemporary viewers of *The Daily Show* or *The Colbert Report:* "On Sunday, October 27, 1968, *The Smothers Brothers Comedy Hour* opened with the following teaser: A collage of newspaper headlines about Mexican students rioting appeared on-screen. Cut to Murray Roman, one of the show's writer-comics, dressed as a Mexican police official, proclaiming, 'The reason that the students of Mexico City are rioting this weekend is because of outside agitators.'" After describing similar comments by Soviet officials explaining the Prague uprising, French and Japanese officials doing the same in reference to the May uprising in Paris and Japanese student demonstrations, and finally a New York policeman repeating the same mantra about the Columbia takeover, Bodroghkozy reports, "Suddenly we cut to Tom and Dick Smothers who smiled broadly and, in unison, proclaimed, 'Hi! We're the outside agitators!'"[41]

The show started gently as a variety show that included diverse entertainers and themes. Thus Buffalo Springfield performed their political song "For What It's Worth" with Tom and Dick Smothers spoofing song lines, and Phil Ochs performed his antiwar "Draft Dodger Rag," though Ochs's satirical lyrics might be interpreted by those who didn't know his politics as satirizing draft dodgers. At the same time, the show included plenty of older celebrities performing more conventional fare.[42]

During the show's second and truncated third seasons, however, the Smothers included more explicitly political content and, accordingly, got in trouble with CBS executives. In September 1967, Pete Seeger sang "Waist Deep in Big Muddy," a folk song purportedly about a World War II combat unit ordered to push on across a raging river by their commander. As the waters rise, the unit turns back but witnesses their commander drowning in the deep currents. As a song performed at antiwar rallies in the sixties, "Waist Deep" connoted an anti–Vietnam War theme applicable to the time. The last lines—"Now every time I read the papers / That old feelin' comes on / We're waist deep in the Big Muddy / And the big fool says to push on"—were too much for CBS, which censored it on the grounds that it was insulting to President Johnson. A public uproar ensued over the issue of censorship. Months later—after the beginning of the Tet Offensive that helped lead members of the establishment, including CBS's own Walter Cronkite, to view the war as unwinnable—the song was perhaps somewhat more acceptable, and CBS allowed a second Seeger performance.[43]

Other spoofs on critical dissent followed. The character Goldie O'Keefe became a regular on the show as a comic "hippie chick" who in the persona of an airhead juxtaposed traditional patriarchal constructions with sharp ridicule of conventional assumptions about femininity and an open celebration of mind-altering drugs. Even more volatile material showed up early in the third season. In the wake of the Democratic National Convention in Chicago, Tom and Dick Smothers cleverly used audience responses to their new (rebellious!) mustaches to spoof Democratic Party regulars' tight control of the party convention.[44] CBS cut a later scene that featured Harry Belafonte's critical song "Don't Stop the Carnival," along with relatively tame footage from the convention protests. Ironically, when the Smothers refused to plug in five minutes of substitute programming, CBS sold the time to the Republican Party, which ran an ad for the Nixon-Agnew campaign.[45] Another conflict between the show and network, an appearance by antiwar folksinger Joan Baez, led to censorship not only of the Baez segment but of the whole show. Baez dedicated a song to her husband David Harris, jailed for draft resistance, and openly explained the reasons for her husband's activities. The show was eventually aired later, without Baez's explanation, leaving the reason for Harris's jail term open to speculation about various criminal acts.[46]

Tensions were at a peak between the show's producers and a network worried about public relations and its market. CBS had received an avalanche of mail attacking it for "sympathetic" coverage of antiwar protesters at the Chicago convention, and the network was receiving complaints from affiliates for the show's "sick" humor. Furthermore, the Smothers openly thumbed their noses at the network with spoofs about its censorial hand. Economics became increasingly important as the show's ratings began to fall and some of the show's advertisers complained about the show's content—even though their ads were pitched to the show's youthful audience. In April 1969 tensions between the Smothers and CBS had reached a point where the network terminated the show, producing a raging debate about censorship among mainstream and underground media of the time. In the end, unlike the way that *Mod Squad* provided openings for safe ideological interpretation or the occasionally daring joke on the NBC comedy *Rowan and Martin's Laugh-In, The Smothers Brothers Comedy Hour* identified itself too closely with the dissenting views that had already caused a crisis of authority in many American institutions. As its market appeal narrowed, it became unfit for the commercially driven entertainment medium that is television.

The show that most boldly captured the theme of generational conflict in the 1960s while simultaneously domesticating that conflict was Norman Lear's *All in the Family,* first aired in January 1971 on CBS and enjoying great popularity until 1979. The show, long ranked near the top of *TV Guide*'s list of the "50 Greatest Shows of All Time," has been credited for opening the television floodgates to a wave of more "relevant" comedies, *M*A*S*H, Maude, The Jeffersons,* and the like. Encountering a mixed response when first introduced to CBS executives, *All in the Family* was eventually championed by the same CBS president, Robert D. Wood, who had terminated *The Smothers Brothers,* in good part because he recognized that CBS's more popular entertainment shows—*Gunsmoke, The Beverly Hillbillies, Mayberry R.F.D, The Red Skelton Hour,* and *Hee Haw*—appealed primarily to older viewers in predominantly rural areas, not the rising younger and more urban population. CBS was becoming, in Wood's words, "an aged, or aging, network."[47]

The formula seized upon by Norman Lear revolved around 1960s-era con-flicts played as an ongoing generational clash within the working-class, white-ethnic Bunker family of Queens, New York—mostly revolving around conflicts between Carroll O'Connor's "lovable bigot" Archie Bunker and Archie's son-in-law, Rob Reiner's college-attending, liberal-cause-embracing Michael Stivic. Each of the four persuasive central characters, however, played key roles in the problems that plagued the Bunkers, problems that not only reflected the social and political conflicts of the day but that also broke new ground by encompass-ing more personal issues. Jean Stapleton's Edith Bunker shared Archie's old-fashioned values but played his emotional opposite, while the couple's daugh-ter, Gloria, played by Sally Struthers, balanced her marital commitment with her obvious affection for her parents. Gloria's role also became a vehicle for ex-pressing themes from the evolving women's movement across both generational and gender divides, though never straying too far from conventional norms.[48]

Initially, *All in the Family* stirred widespread controversy because of Archie's overt bigotry, his blustery racism, his sexist put-downs of Edith and Gloria, even his blatant antisemitism. Critical commentary, especially from more liberal sources, targeted the bigotry, arguing that it would legitimize and encourage precisely the kinds of bigoted behaviors liberals had struggled against.[49] Studies of *All in the Family* audiences demonstrated, however, that the show attracted a binary audience. Older, more conservative (and especially white working class) audiences enjoyed Archie's upfront violation of what was later called "political correctness" and his unquestioning embrace of traditional family and religious values. They also laughed at the self-righteous "Meathead" (Archie's nickname for Michael) and the mildly feminist Gloria. On the other hand, younger, "hip" audiences could feel represented by their generational stand-ins while laughing at Archie's invariably illogical argumentation. In reviewing various studies of the show, Aniko Bodroghkozy noted,

> Complicating the differential readings of the show was the fact that even the highly prejudiced viewers who liked and admired Archie tended to admit that Mike usually made more sense. This contradictory and paradoxical reading strategy provides some clues to the ways audiences were negotiating the ideological struggles of the period—viscerally hanging on to familiar, if increasingly residual, structures of feeling, while intellectually accepting the emergent consensus slowly forming from the various social-change challenges to the old order.[50]

Those "familiar structures of feeling" would be important in later efforts to reach these audiences.

However, the tactic of ideological balance within a half-hour comedy about generational conflict helped to domesticate the tense political and social conflicts of the day, not only by bringing them from the realm of public protest into the self-contained world of the sitcom family, but by reducing political conflict to comedic characterization. Indeed, the characters in *All in the Family* are a perfect fit for what Mark Crispin Miller has referred to as television's "erasure of resistant subjectivity." In effect, in Miller's argument post-sixties situation comedy characters become represented by some excessive subjectivity—for Miller, reflecting their "vestigial individuality"—thereby inviting audiences to laugh at these characters, in the process enjoying their own superior enlightenment. Miller, however, argues that the "real point of TV's comedy" in putting down those "hard selves" is to "exalt the nothingness that laughs at them": "Whereas the butt, enabled by his discrete selfhood, pursues desires that TV cannot gratify, we are induced, by the sight of his continual humiliation, to become as porous, cool, and acquiescent as he is solid, tense, and dissident, so that we might want nothing other than what TV sells us. This is what it means to see the joke."[51]

All in the Family was quickly followed by other sitcoms that played on sixties and generational themes. *Mary Tyler Moore*, which actually preceded *All in the Family* by a few months, broke new ground with a single career woman as the popular lead character in a show that played more gently on generational and topical themes. The show's characters, a tight-knit crew at the newsroom of Minneapolis TV station WJM, provided ample opportunity for issues of the day to be explored within a family-like setting.

A year and a half after *All in the Family* first aired, and about two years after Robert Altman's popular film of the same name, *M*A*S*H* debuted on CBS, where it ruled as one of the top ten most popular shows on television for nine of the next eleven years. Both Altman's film and Larry Gelbart's TV show played on public opposition to the Vietnam War through the anti-authority antics of a zany, family-like medical crew forced to deal with the carnage and insanity of the otherwise invisible Korean War. Echoing the kind of ironic humor popularized in Joseph Heller's 1961 best seller *Catch-22*, *M*A*S*H* played off its lovable antiheroes—Hawkeye Pierce, Trapper John McIntyre, and Corporal Klinger, among others—against the show's more conventional "butts"—Major Hoolihan, Colonel Flagg, Major Burns—all of whom earnestly supported the military structure as well as the war. Like *Catch-22*, which was made into a movie in 1970, *M*A*S*H* was just sufficiently removed from the ongoing carnage in Vietnam to be safe enough for TV, yet it tapped into the anti-military and antiwar sentiments of the day. In 1972, *Time* noted, "TV has embarked on a new era of candor. . . . During the season that began last week, programmers will actually be competing with each other to trace the largest number of touchy—and heretofore forbidden—ethnic, sexual, and psychological themes. . . . All the old taboos will be toppling."[52]

In contrast to the relevance themes that emerged on CBS, ABC capitalized on the popular 1973 film *American Graffiti* and its nostalgic look at the loss of innocence in the world of 1950s teenagers—a film that a *Senior Scholastic* review noted was tinged with "a brooding sadness" for "a time that will never come again—a time when life seemed predictable and safe."[53] The result was *Happy Days,* a sitcom introduced in 1974 that revolved around teenage-boy culture placed within the kind of stable family environments that hearkened back to life as it was portrayed in 1950s sitcoms. Not only did *Happy Days*—without any "brooding sadness"—domesticate the James Dean and Marlon Brando rebel characters of the 1950s through the good-citizen character of "the Fonz," it revived nostalgia for a mythical past, nostalgia that would later form a central theme in the presidential candidacy of Ronald Reagan.[54] By then, however, sixties generational themes had themselves succumbed to the nostalgia pitch.

Hollywood Embraces Youth Appeal

As was the case with both advertisers and entertainment TV, the world of popular cinema began to explore themes attuned to the awakening issues of postwar America. As Michael Ryan and Douglas Kellner have argued, "Perhaps the crucial reason for the increase in socially conscious and stylistically innovative films in the later sixties was the liberal and radical social movements of the period . . . and the general loosening of previous strictures against sex and drugs. Radical social and political issues of the sort banished during the Cold War were once again possible topics of popular film."[55]

In 1961, *Raisin in the Sun* critiqued racial intolerance and *West Side Story* did the same while also exposing both the vibrancy and despair of gang life in the inner cities. As Ryan and Kellner put it, *Judgment at Nuremberg* "advocated a liberal indictment of intolerance" that same year.[56] In 1963, *Lilies of the Field* and *To Kill a Mockingbird* both spoke to the possibility of and need for racial cooperation, the latter condemning racism in the old South. The nuclear arms race and Cold War came in for cinematic satire with *Dr. Strangelove* (1964) and *The Russians Are Coming The Russians Are Coming* (1966) and critical perspectives on nuclear ideology with *Failsafe* (1964), *Seven Days in May* (1964), and *The Bedford Incident* (1965).

The film industry was undergoing significant economic and structural changes in the early to mid-sixties. The demise of the old studio system and its replacement by (or absorption into) industrial conglomerates and independent collaborations, and the initiation of a new rating system in 1966, helped to give filmmakers more control over their product and opened up the range of potential filmic subjects. The year 1967 is often seen as the beginning of a new Hollywood era,[57] with films like *The Graduate* exploring youthful alienation from the American Dream, *Guess Who's Coming to Dinner* critiquing the subtle racism of white liberals, *In the Heat of the Night* portraying racism in the South, and

Cool Hand Luke exalting rebelliousness against police authority and southern conservatism.

Set in the Depression era, Arthur Penn's 1967 film *Bonnie and Clyde* can be read as a kind of metaphor for the rebelliousness of the 1960s that was peaking with the events of 1967: Newark and Detroit riots, the Summer of Love, and the confrontational shift in antiwar activism. As with most media accounts, the film played to contradictory responses. Many reviled the film's explicit violence and the bank robbing duo's nonchalant murder of those who stood in their path. The *New York Times* reviewer intoned in response to applauding audiences at the Montreal film festival, "More sober visitors from the United States . . . were wagging their heads in dismay and exasperation that so callous and callow a film should represent their country in these critical times."[58] Others, especially among the young, may have found much to connect with in the film's themes: Bonnie and Clyde's almost playful rebelliousness, their self-absorption and manipulation of the media, even the "Barrows gang" as a kind of surrogate outlaw family. As Jerry Rubin commented, with typical hyperbole, "Bonnie Parker and Clyde Barrow are the leaders of the New Youth."[59] Yet the movie's theme had a dead end. As Faye Dunaway's Bonnie complained in one scene, "When we started out I thought we was going somewhere. This is it. We're just going"—a sentiment that some may have begun to feel by 1967. *Vogue* magazine dismissed *Bonnie and Clyde* in terms that typified mass media accounts of the counterculture of the time as "rebels with no cause beyond the moment's rebellion." As Peter Braunstein suggests, the film was a "perfect example" of what Pagan Kennedy has called "guerilla nostalgia," using the past "as a way of indicting the present."[60]

Two years later, the profitable film *Easy Rider* explicitly exploited the counterculture. In David James's account, "this saga of motorcycle youth, rock and roll, and drugs appropriated" the distinctive styles and motifs of the era's underground films and "cynically inverted the underground's utopianism," making sure that the "counterculture's visions of new forms of community" would "be destroyed by reactionary social elements"—namely the very rednecks who targeted the civil rights movement. Like so many popular films of the time that weaved sixties events into their stories—*The Strawberry Statement* (1970) and *Zabriskie Point* (1970) come to mind[61]—*Easy Rider* failed to communicate "any but the most superficial and alienated sense" of sixties social movements they conveyed.[62] And as Joseph Heath and Andrew Potter have contended, the "death of the rebel protagonist" was becoming a "staple of '60s cinema."[63]

In their analysis of the ideology of Hollywood film, Ryan and Kellner note that these critical late-sixties films provide a counterpoint that romanticizes countercultural themes in effect as ends in themselves, thereby proving compatible with the ways in which consumer capitalism adapted to the counterculture. Thus, they argue, both *The Graduate* and *Bonnie and Clyde* evidence the limitations of the sixties version of alienated white middle class rebellion. The alternatives posed to bourgeois conformity frequently took the form of a search for more personal, self-fulfilling experiences. The self ("doing one's own thing") became a criterion of authenticity, and in many ways this representation cohered perfectly with traditional American individualism. . . . [Similarly,] although the hippie quest [in *Easy Rider*] permits a critique of small-town southern provincialism, it is also essentially aimed toward an idea of freedom that is highly traditional.[64]

As was the case with advertising and television programming, Hollywood's version of the sixties era would subsequently begin to reflect the nation's shift to the Right while simultaneously playing on baby boomer nostalgia. By the mid-1970s capitalism's absorption of countercultural styles and innovations was in full flower. As Jack Whalen and Richard Flacks observed,

most of America was wearing blue jeans. Water beds and granola became staples in middle-class suburbia, and Bob Dylan tunes were programmed on supermarket Muzak. The commodification and absorption of countercultural symbols and styles and practices represented, for many, a kind of relief; instead of waging war on the young, the society and culture were integrating them. But what was remarkable was how little such inclusion changed the central logic of market, bureaucracy, state, and media.[65]

Politicizing Alienated Youth: Yippie! as Advertisement

One response to the alienated counterculture and the media culture of the time were the Yippies, members of the Youth International Party, notable for their dramatic media theatrics as a vehicle for energizing the antiwar movement and politicizing the visibly growing numbers of countercultural youth. As Abbie Hoffman once put it, "Runaways are the backbone of the youth revolution."[66]

Both Abbie Hoffman and Jerry Rubin had been involved in prior political activism in sixties-era social movements. Both developed a media style that effectively commandeered the media's penchant for dramatic action, provocative visuals, and charismatic personalities in order to make their point about the system's decadence. Yet, in playing to the media's imperatives, the Yippies' tactics contained within them both the polarizing effect of expressive militancy and the co-optation vulnerability of the counterculture. In terms of the latter, I would suggest that the media's lure was increasingly one of affective empowerment that, as with advertising, ultimately reinforces narcissistic strains.

Hoffman and Rubin were indisputably gifted in their ability to capture media attention. In Marty Jezer's words, Hoffman's "performance genius was that he made his theater seem spontaneous, but it was always carefully thought out, a conscious act. His critics on the left just thought he was a jester, but he, more than anyone in the country at that time, knew how to use the news medium to get across, in the space of 30 or 40 seconds, a focused political message."[67] Similarly, it was Jerry Rubin's penchant for organizing colorful confrontational politics for Berkeley's Vietnam Day Committee that caused Dave Dellinger to invite him into the planning group for the 1967 Pentagon demonstration. As Rubin put it, "To interest the media I needed to express my politics frivolously. . . . If I had given a sober lecture on the history of Vietnam, the media cameras would have turned off."[68]

Both Hoffman and Rubin had engaged in Yippie-like actions well before they and others formally created the Youth International Party in early 1968. When subpoenaed by the House Un-American Activities Committee (HUAC) in 1966, Rubin appeared in the uniform of an American revolutionary soldier. Though the media were unlikely to capture much of what he said at the hearing, his image made his point: satirizing the committee among young people on college campuses.[69] In 1967, Hoffman, Rubin, Stew Albert, and others entered the gallery of the New York Stock Exchange and floated dollar bills down onto the exchange floor, where clerks and stockbrokers scrambled for the money. Other hi-jinks included setting off soot bombs at New York's Con Edison headquarters, plastering "SEE CANADA NOW" on the façade of the Times Square recruiting booth, and sending marijuana joints in the mail to random people selected from the phone booth.[70] Similarly, in 1968, Hoffman showed up at yet another HUAC hearing in an American flag shirt, which became the instant target of police arrest and media attention. Showing what Stephen Whitfield has termed the "most nimble and inventive mind" of any New Leftists, Hoffman "played all authority as if it was a deranged lumbering bull" and he a "daring matador,"[71] typically with a degree of humor. Hoffman and Rubin joined with a small group of sympathetic spirits in a media-hyped effort to levitate the Pentagon and the October 1967 march.[72] Hoffman later planted a Viet Cong flag atop the Disneyland Matterhorn. And, of course, the Yippies held their much-advertised Festival of Life at the 1968 Democratic National Convention, nominating "Pigasus" as their presidential candidate. Both Rubin and Hoffman played their roles of cultural outlaws to the hilt during the Chicago Seven trial, trying, in Hoffman's words, to make the "outrageous contagious."

With their instinctive feel for visuals and the subjective pulse of their targeted audience, Rubin and Hoffman were, in effect, advertising men for the movement. As Hoffman put it, "We tear through the streets. Kids love it. They understand it on an internal level. We are living TV ads, movies. Yippie!"[73]

While the Yippies doubtless added zest and humor to what was becoming an increasingly bleak political landscape, their approach was limited and carried with it both personal and political costs. The point of the media display was to move alienated youth to join the movement, yet even Hoffman recognized that "inevitably, you *do* alienate people." As media actions became more routinized and media attention waned, the Yippies' political base disappeared. It was, after all, grounded in media, not in political organization. As Todd Gitlin has observed, Jerry Rubin operated as a "freelance broadcaster of symbols, outside any sizable organization," and thus "acquired a *following* instead of a face-to-face political base. His following was organized precisely as a mass media audience: atomized, far-flung, episodic, not alive politically except when mobilized in behalf of centralized symbols of revolt."[74]

At bottom, the continuing glow of media attention seemed to satisfy some inner craving for both Hoffman and Rubin; it made them seem powerful. As Rubin remarked, "Media attention can be comforting. Someone is paying attention, we are having some impact—is the feeling."[75] At times, that affective empowerment of media attention grew out of proportion to reality. In his manicky speech at the 1968 Chicago Festival of Life, Hoffman sarcastically compared his ability to reach American GIs through popular media to the antiwar Left's efforts:

> They're talking about reachin' the troops in Viet Nam so they write in *The Guardian!* That's groovy. I've met a *lot* of soldiers who read *The Guardian,* you know. But *we've* had articles in *Jaguar* magazine, *Cavalier,* you know, *National Enquirer* interviews the Queen of the Yippies, someone nobody ever heard of and she runs a whole riff about the Yippies and Viet Nam or whatever her thing is and the soldiers get it and dig it and smoke a little grass and say yeah I can see where she's at.[76]

He continued, "See Madison Avenue people think like that. That's why a lot [of] SDS's don't like what we're doin'. 'Cause they say we're exploiting; we're using the tools of Madison Ave. But that's because Madison Ave. is effective in what it does."[77]

Through their imaginative actions, both Hoffman and Rubin created themselves as media celebrities—persons known for their well-knownness, to paraphrase Daniel Boorstin.[78] The person eclipsed the cause. By 1969, Dave Dellinger criticized the Yippies for behaving "distressingly like the mirror-image of the culture" they rejected, exhibiting significant "ego-tripping" and "bull-shit" that in the end "got in the way of making a revolution."[79] The Chicago Seven trial was the ultimate media exposure for both Hoffman and Rubin.

When their celebrity status dimmed, both Hoffman and Rubin seemed unable to cope with the lights being turned out in the latter years of the antiwar movement. Reflecting in part his self-described "irrational behavior" at the time of the Chicago Convention, Abbie Hoffman was later diagnosed as manic-depressive.[80] As Jonas Raskin has observed, after the Chicago trial, Hoffman was "stuck in old routines and old poses that felt like a living death."[81] After joining other celebrities on the floor of the 1972 Democratic National Convention—while younger Yippie imitators calling themselves "Zippies" protested with a cake that proclaimed, "Never trust anyone over 30"—Hoffman was floundering. Ignoring his own advice in *Steal This Book,* he was arrested for cocaine use, an event that catapulted him underground, where he took the pseudonym Barry Freed and began working as an environmental organizer—a role he continued after turning himself in and serving brief prison time for the cocaine charge. Struggling with depression, in 1989 Abbie Hoffman ended his life.

Jerry Rubin's response to the end of the sixties was to reinvent himself as a seventies icon by delving into a variety of New Age therapies. Richard Jensen and Allen Lichtenstein wrote that Rubin "worked to maintain and alter his image as a public symbol over a period of thirty years," moving through three iconic stages: a "Radical Period" in the sixties and early seventies, a "Consciousness Period" of the seventies, and a "Capitalist Period" in the eighties when he became a stock analyst on Wall Street.[82] In typical fashion, Rubin announced the second phase with publication of his autobiography, *Growing (Up) at Thirty-Seven,* in which he announced that he was giving up his "one-dimensional, fanatic" past and learning to nurture his "feminine" side, to become a "spiritually high, nonattached human being" capable of being a "true spiritual psychological revolutionary."[83] On July 30, 1980, Rubin announced in a letter published in the *New York Times* that he had taken a position as a stock analyst on Wall Street, noting of his past, "Politics and rebellion distinguished the 60's. The search for self characterized the 70's. Money and financial interest will capture the passion of the 80's."[84] In effect, Jerry Rubin transformed his public persona to fit the media zeitgeist of successive historical eras.

Like the media's version of the 1960s, both Hoffman and Rubin were self-defined in generational terms. Whereas Hoffman remained politically committed but failed to transcend the pull of his celebrated past—perhaps because of his illness—Rubin displayed classic narcissistic tendencies in advertising the self he created in step with the media culture's depiction of aging baby boomers. In effect, Rubin became the prototypical icon for the media's retrospective take on the sixties: self-indulgent wild man turned acquisitive Yuppie. In words that some might direct at his own Weather Underground, Bill Ayers wrote of "cultural anarchists" like Hoffman and Rubin that they were "master disrupters, publicly disputing the suffocating cultural conventions. The downside was the sense of pointlessness, finally, of a kind of self-indulgent theater for its own sake."[85]

10

Reconstructing the Past, Constructing the Future:

Corporate Backlash and the Reagan Revolution

[One] task that had to be undertaken in the post-Vietnam era was to return the domestic population to a proper state of apathy and obedience, to overcome "the crisis of democracy" and the "Vietnam syndrome." These are the technical terms that have been devised to refer, respectively, to the efforts of formerly passive groups to engage in the political process, and to the general unwillingness of the general population to bear the material costs and the moral burden of aggression and massacre.
  —Noam Chomsky, 1979

Who controls the past controls the future. Who controls the present, controls the past.
  —George Orwell, *Nineteen Eighty-Four,* 1949

During the 1970s, the political backlash that began in the 1960s was joined and enormously empowered by a corporate backlash carrying out virtually everything Lewis Powell anticipated in his 1971 memo. As documented in several critical accounts, this was the third time in the twentieth century that capitalist interests pulled together in a concerted propaganda campaign to rescue capitalism from a crisis that threatened it.[1] The first revolved around the role played by the new public relations industry in generating support for American entry into World War I and turning aside the threat of labor militancy after the war. The second arose in response to the Depression and helped to establish the postwar consumer culture while also dampening labor militancy. The third rose in response to forces unleashed during the 1960s era. As Joseph Peschek has observed in his study of American policy-planning organizations: "As the crisis of the 1970s unfolded, elites saw the expansion of liberal democracy as endangering the social order and the economic system they preside over. In differing ways, this contradiction established the terms in which the policy-planners of the center and the right approached the task of rescuing a system in decline."[2]

By most accounts, American capitalism was in crisis in the 1970s. The economy's profitability began to drop precipitously around 1965.[3] Inflation rates were climbing steeply while unemployment rates grew to high levels and productivity rates in the non-farm economy were falling. Furthermore, public support for business, which had gradually grown from 25 percent in 1945 to 75 percent in 1968, fell back precipitously to 1945 levels by 1972.[4] Indeed, the long postwar span of the American economy's unprecedented and widely shared growth was coming to an end.

In addition to declining public support for business, corporate interests were alarmed by the economic challenges posed by the "excesses" of the 1960s: (1) the rise of new and sometimes noisy activist voices—most notably previously marginalized racial minorities, women, and youth—making a range of new demands on both the American polity and the occupational sector; (2) the resulting greater demand for government services and a simultaneous decline in public trust in government; and (3) spurred by the Vietnam War, a rapid decline of public support for defense spending and an interventionist U.S. foreign policy. Indeed, in late 1969, the National Commission on the Causes and Prevention of Violence had recommended reordering national priorities by "reducing military expenditures," and then keeping military spending "level, while general welfare expenditures should continue to increase until essential social goals are achieved."[5]

The result of these challenges, for years thereafter, was a convergence of interests between a corporate sector determined to right the foundering ship of capitalism and right-wing conservatives whose agenda, initially at least, focused on their own electoral ascendancy. In this they were aided by a coalition of organized interests—from the National Rifle Association to the Catholic Church and the new Religious Right—who were galvanized by liberal actions ranging from gun control to abortion. Both the corporate sector and right-wing conservatives sought to take on and reverse what each took to be the evils and excesses of the 1960s.

The combined efforts of corporate interests and right-wing conservatives helped produce the stunning 1980 election of Ronald Reagan along with the defeat of a half dozen significant liberals from the Senate, including several of the outspoken doves of the Vietnam era. As conservative columnist George Will put it in speaking to a *National Review* banquet celebrating Reagan's victory, "It took approximately sixteen years to count the vote in the 1964 election, and Goldwater won."[6] While conservatives exulted, however, the neoliberal free-market regime had taken power. Turning everything over to the market would not only exacerbate conditions that troubled many conservatives as well as progressives, it would leave significant backlash constituencies materially worse off, thereby sustaining their sense of being aggrieved. When material conditions deteriorated sufficiently under conservative Republican administrations, corporate interests—and a wider swath of the public—helped bring Democratic administrations to power. The election of both Bill Clinton and Barack Obama produced new levels of virulence in sixties-linked political backlash, helping once again to divert attention from forces adversely affecting much of the population's material interests. So it goes with the distracting, contradictory media politics under the neoliberal regime.

Capitalism Fights Back

Wealthy conservatives—among them Richard Mellon Scaife, Lynda and Harry Bradley, the Smith Richardson family, and David and Charles Koch—provided the capital that launched the organizational nexus that would begin to transform public discourse in the 1970s. In 1972, the Business Roundtable was established, consisting of 200 CEOs from the largest companies in the United States. With a membership that closely overlapped other significant business groups, including the U.S. chapter of the International Chamber of Commerce, the Roundtable would be described in 1976 as the "most powerful" business lobby in Washington.[7] A year later, boosted by a generous donation from right-wing Colorado beer manufacturer Joseph Coors, the conservative Heritage Foundation was established and would soon play a major role in influencing and trumpeting the policies of the "Reagan revolution." The American Enterprise Institute, founded in 1943 to provide a forum for business interests to influence public policy and public discourse, was refurbished with a multi-million dollar grant from the Howard Pew Freedom Trust. In 1977, the Koch family provided funding that helped establish the free-market Cato Institute.[8]

Another beneficiary of the newly energized conservative largesse was the *Public Interest,* a journal founded in 1965 by a group of scholars and intellectuals initially drawn to the use of social science to improve public policy but increasingly wary of what they viewed as excesses that began to emerge in the mid-1960s. In Lewis Lapham's recollection, co-founder Irving Kristol maintained that "the American system of free enterprise . . . was being attacked by the very people whom it most enriched—i.e., by the pampered children of privilege disturbing the peace of the Ivy League universities . . . and the time had come to put an end to their self-indulgent nonsense."[9] Formerly on the left side of the Cold War anticommunist consensus, the intellectuals involved with journals like the *Public Interest* and *Commentary* became widely known as "neoconservatives." Over time, the former publication moved increasingly to the right because, in Nathan Glazer's view, the journal became "too dependent on what came in over the transom"—submissions that "reflected the increasing energy of conservative think tanks and foundations."[10]

In 1971, the World Economic Forum, consisting of top business, political, and media leaders as well as academic experts, was established and met for the first time at Davos, Switzerland. Through their annual meetings, the WEI prepared the ground for the Uruguay round of the General Agreement on Tariffs and Trade (GATT) negotiations and eventually the establishment of the World Trade

Organization (WTO) — both formative enterprises in the spread of globalizing neoliberalism.

In 1973, at the instigation of David Rockefeller, a group of "highest-level" figures from corporate, financial, and governmental sectors in Europe, North America, and Japan were organized as the Trilateral Commission to explore shared responsibility for maintaining the "wider international system."[11] In 1975, the Trilateral Commission published a study that argued that the "excessive" democratic "surge" of the 1960s had created a "Crisis of Democracy" — meaning that capitalism, its constrained, elite version of electoral democracy, and U.S. global hegemony were all endangered. Written in more judicious language than the typical rhetoric of political backlash, the Trilateralists made dire predictions about democracy's future, asserting the need not only for a "drastic overhaul" of the "policies and institutions" of a troubled "postwar economic system" as well as military security policies, but also the imperative of attending to the institutions of "political democracy."[12] As critic Alan Wolfe put it shortly after the report's publication,

> Social and economic conditions in the United States since 1970 . . . led a number of beneficiaries of U.S. capitalism to question their allegiance to political democracy. . . . *First, the economy itself is in trouble, unable to deliver the prosperity that has always been the main argument in favor of capitalism.* . . . While this was taking place, a second trend made itself felt — *large numbers of people appear to be taking democracy far more seriously than they ever had before.*[13]

The Trilateral report was noteworthy not only because of its prestige as a voice of elite internationalists, but because it viewed the claims made by democracy's citizens during the turbulent sixties era as a threat to "democracy" as it is conceived within the capitalist paradigm. Each of the three regions of global capitalist powers represented on the Trilateral Commission had experienced a surge of political participation, student activism, and public protest during the 1960s. In the report's view, this led to an "overload" of demands on public decision-making systems. Echoing the arguments of Lewis Powell and others, the authors decried the growing presence of "value-oriented intellectuals" (outsiders) who "play to an audience, even if it is a protest type," contrasting these to the more favored "policy intellectuals" (insiders) who "contribute to the process of decision-making."[14]

Writing the section on the United States, political scientist Samuel Huntington's analysis of the problematic "democratic surge" in the United States was particularly revealing. The surge occurred, he observed, not only in most traditional forms of political participation, but in the "marked upswing" of "marches, demonstrations, protest movements, and 'cause' organizations." Huntington took particular note of "previously passive or unorganized groups in the population"—"blacks, Indians, Chicanos, white ethnic groups, students, and women"—who had "embarked on concerted efforts to establish their claims to opportunities, positions, rewards, and privileges which they had not considered themselves entitled to before." The new assertiveness of these groups produced the "reassertion of the primacy of equality as a goal in social, economic, and political life"—a primacy that Huntington would go on to critique.[15]

The main problem with growing public participation was that it produced a "welfare shift"—i.e., "major increases" in government spending for education, social security, public welfare, and public health and hospitals—that threatened the more favored "defense shift" that occurred in the aftermath of World War II—i.e., the postwar build-up in military spending that became a critical component of the U.S. political economy (producing also President Eisenhower's warning against the "unwarranted influence" of the "military-industrial complex" in his farewell address of January 21, 1961). The growth of Great Society programs "seriously disrupted" the "stability" of the postwar defense shift—though Huntington observed this disruption was temporarily reversed by higher military spending during the Vietnam War.[16]

Furthermore, what made these trends particularly problematic was that they enjoyed wide public support. "During the mid-1960s, *at the peak of the democratic surge,* and of the Vietnam war, public opinion on these issues changed drastically," the report noted, singling out the dramatic rise in the percentage of the public that felt the "United States was spending too much on defense."[17] By linking shifts in government spending to shifts in public opinion and the growing public demand of newly activated citizens, the report moved toward its conclusion that the 1960s were a period marked by an "excess of democracy" or a "democratic distemper"—too much public meddling in the system that had worked well for the postwar economy.[18]

The Trilateralist report was a clear expression of the interests of the capitalist system, threatened by the policy, public opinion, and participation shifts in the sixties era and seeking greater public acquiescence to those interests. Alan Wolfe put the opposing case succinctly: "The pessimism of the Trilateral Commission should be the optimism of everyone else. If ruling groups feel they are losing power, it is only because everyone else is gaining it."[19]

Huntington's analysis of tensions between capitalism and democracy reflects the ideological nature of elite responses to the sixties, corresponding closely to the media's sphere of legitimate discourse and at a considerable distance from the experiences of millions of newly activated citizens. In elite reasoning, "increased political participation leads to increased polarization in society."[20] Indeed, polarization was increasing during the 1960s, in part because the inclusion/exclusion dynamic of media attention—visual drama framed within boundaried discourse—helped to produce polarizing expression while the forces of backlash fanned the flames of reaction. Yet more fundamentally, the increasing participation was challenging the status quo, and the beneficiaries of the status quo resisted these challenges. In the case of civil rights, for example, the challenge to the age-old Jim Crow system clearly generated resistance among sectors of the southern white population, thus producing what to Huntington's eye was "polarization." However, absent the activism, the injustices were no less polarizing. They were just quietly endured by oppressed populations largely invisible in the media and thus unseen by much of the public. In effect, then, the elite Trilateral response is similar to that of moderate white clergy in the South who urged Martin Luther King to call off the Birmingham marches—a view King criticized as one "more devoted to 'order' than to justice," that "prefers a negative peace which is the absence of tension to a positive peace which is the presence of justice."[21]

Not surprisingly, the Trilateralist's elite response fingered the protest movements as the problem, instead of the issues that had generated the protests. Huntington similarly argued that the "surge" of "new values" was producing growing mistrust toward government. Though acknowledging that the government's "inability to deal effectively" with the problems of "Vietnam, race relations, Watergate, and stagflation" did "have some impact" on public confidence in government, Huntington dismissed the significance of these factors—even though the impact of the Vietnam War and Watergate on sharply declining public trust has been widely documented.[22] Instead, he returned to a generational theme, highlighting the "new disrespect for authority" and related values of the young as explanations for the decline in trust in government. Conceding that "political leaders, in effect, alienated more and more people" through their actions in the 1960s, he suggested that the "increasing mistrust toward political leaders" came about because activists took "more extreme positions on policy issues."[23]

In the end, the Trilateral analysts echoed the views put forward by generational critics like Bruno Bettelheim and Lewis Feuer and adopted as a dominant frame by conventional mass media reporting. Protesters—meaning the young, women, and minorities—weren't responding to what most viewed as a horrific war, oppressive racism, and pervasive sexism; they were rebelling against authority with their "new values." In short, the report blamed the responses rather than the causes. Where, one wonders, did the "more extreme positions" come from? Typically, they were responses to the policies, actions, and rhetoric of authority, all of which simultaneously spawned increasing mistrust.

The Trilateralists also echoed the backlash responses of both Lewis Powell and the Nixon administration in singling out the mass media and particularly television for contributing to the "new disrespect for authority." In the United States, TV news was seen as both a "'dispatriating' agency" that "portrays the conditions in society as undesirable and as getting worse" and an "excessive check" on presidential power. As with other blame-the-media tropes, the report made it sound as if overly critical media were the problem. In actual practice during the sixties era, the media began to pay attention to some of the dismal conditions that were brought to light by the "previously passive or unorganized groups in the population," in effect making visible what had previously been invisible to the American public. The media "problem" was, in effect, that the media considered the new participation newsworthy. Once this was the case, media imperatives took over and pushed the media toward the visual representation of dramatic social conflict that was interpreted ideologically. As the social tumult worsened, the media paid increasing attention to the argumentation of legitimate doves and other liberal critics within the establishment. These voices, then, became crucial targets for the backlash to the sixties, especially from the conservative end of the political spectrum.

In the Trilateral Commission's view, what was needed was "greater moderation in democracy," which boiled down to two things: a greater role for "expertise, seniority, experience, and special talents in constituting authority," and "more self-restraint on the part of all groups." The latter reflected Huntington's reasoning that echoed the prevailing view of postwar political science: "the effective operation of a democratic political system usually requires some measure of apathy and non-involvement on the part of *some* individuals and groups."[24]

Reversing the "Vietnam Syndrome"

In the aftermath of the horrific Vietnam War experience, members of the American foreign policy establishment, including the class of "policy intellectuals" favored by the Trilateralists, were eager to restore U.S. foreign policy and a damaged U.S. military to their pre-Vietnam stature. The Trilateral Report singled out several ways in which the war's aftermath left the United States less able to maintain its post–World War II role as "the hegemonic power in a system of world order." Samuel Huntington observed that the "manifestations of the democratic distemper" had already "stimulated uncertainty among allies and could well stimulate adventurism among enemies," thereby compounding such "problems" as a weakened executive and public opposition to defense spending. A "turning inward of American attention" was viewed as closely linked to the "downturn in American power and influence in world affairs." In Huntington's conventional framing, the "decline in governability of democracy at home means a decline in the influence of democracy abroad."[25]

The effort to revive the United States' hegemonic stature was, however, more than a problem of international politics. The Vietnam experience had undermined the willingness of the American people to support the kind of military interventionism that was crucial to maintaining hegemony in the postwar world. As Gabriel Kolko argued, "The antiwar constituency barred a return to the pre-

1964 era of social passivity and naiveté, spilling over into all areas of American foreign policy opposition."[26]

As a result, policy elites were eager to root out the deep vein of post-Vietnam public resistance that the Chicago Council on Foreign Relations' quadrennial polls revealed beginning in 1975.[27] If, as the CCFR polls demonstrated, the majority of Americans viewed the United States being in the wrong in Vietnam, if the war was "more than a mistake," they were likely to view new military interventions with instinctive skepticism toward the propaganda used to rouse public support. Skepticism awakened by the Vietnam experience also provided a catalyst for questioning U.S. interventions throughout the postwar era, thus opening up the possibility of discerning an imperial U.S. foreign policy. In contrast to the rhetoric used to justify them, the sensory realities of U.S. interventions reveal the United States protecting a world system geared to the investment opportunities of capital rather than the democratic aspirations of the masses of people in nations where the U.S. intervened—most dramatically in those cases where the masses were directly victimized by the intervention.[28]

In an elite-dominated capitalist system, the intense public skepticism awakened by the Vietnam War was dysfunctional at best and dangerous at worst. As historian Marilyn Young put it, "The fundamental institutions which gave rise to the Vietnam war have hardly changed; what has changed is the *credibility* of the imperialist ideology which justified that war. From the viewpoint of the State, that is the wound that must be healed."[29] With a public that doubted the government's stated intentions, a Congress that was queasy about legitimizing "another Vietnam," and a press corps that had become skeptical of military pronouncements, foreign policy elites had a major problem on their hands any time the United States considered military intervention. Though initially used to describe Vietnam veterans suffering from post-traumatic stress disorder, the phrase "Vietnam syndrome" was soon commandeered by political officials and media commentators alike to describe precisely this resistant attitude toward U.S. military intervention. As the term "syndrome" suggests, elites viewed public resistance as a kind of illness, a dysfunctional deficiency that needed to be healed or corrected. In one instance, neoconservative Norman Podhoretz described it as the public's "sickly inhibitions against the use of military force."[30]

It therefore became crucially important to build public support for the idea that the war in Vietnam was simply a "mistake" made by well-intentioned policy makers who erred in their reading of Vietnam or in the strategies they adopted—thereby reinforcing the boundaries of legitimate discourse that the antiwar movement had repeatedly challenged during the war. Above all, it was important to reassert the benign purpose of American foreign policy, to restore the mythic reality of defending freedom and democracy against the communist hordes—in short, to effect what Noam Chomsky has called the "reconstruction of an imperial ideology."[31]

In the aftermath of the war, as Walter LaFeber has observed, elites began a "remarkable rewriting of the war's history," an effort to rewrite "the record of failed military interventionism in the 1950 to 1975 era in order to build support for interventionism in the 1980s" and to "shift historical guilt from those who instigated and ran the war to those who opposed it."[32] A 1979 study of twenty-eight widely used high school history textbooks noted that they "examined the most bitter conflict in recent American history without calling into question a single fundamental premise surrounding the conflict. The limited margin of debate and dissent was maintained, safe from attacks upon the honor and integrity of our leaders, or upon the nation itself." They concluded that these textbook histories were a form of "old news management."[33]

The first efforts to redefine the past war experience in this manner emerged in the years immediately following the war's end. General William Westmoreland argued in his memoirs and public speeches that the war had been lost because politicians succumbed to a "misguided minority opposition" and followed a "no-win policy."[34] After the war officially ended, the Ford administration encouraged the American people to put the war behind them and move on to deal with pressing economic and domestic issues.

For a number of years, "forgetting" the war also included public neglect of suffering Vietnam veterans, at least until evidence of widespread post-traumatic stress disorder began to seep into public consciousness and veterans themselves battled both the government and corporations like Dow Chemical for relief from multiple aftereffects of the war.[35] The war's legacy for hundreds of thousands of U.S. veterans has, of course, been enormously difficult, producing high rates of suicide, drug addiction, and homelessness as well as illness and birth defects related to exposure to Agent Orange.

As the suffering of American veterans became more visible,[36] the popular line on the war shifted to focus on ways the United States suffered from the war, even as the Right seized upon opportunities to blame the antiwar movement.[37] By 1977, when newsman Ed Bradley asked President Carter if the administration felt the United States had any moral obligation to help rebuild Vietnam, the president waved the question aside with the comment, "Well, the destruction was mutual." The president continued with a restatement of the war's mythic reality: "You know, we went to Vietnam without any desire to capture territory or impose American will on other people. We went there to defend the freedom of the South Vietnamese, and I don't feel that we ought to apologize or to castigate ourselves or to assume the status of culpability."[38] Bradley later recalled that "images of Vietnam," a nation "the United States destroyed," had "flashed across his mind" on hearing Carter's response.[39]

The revisionist campaign continued through the 1970s. In their widely acclaimed 1979 book *The Irony of Vietnam*, Leslie Gelb and Richard Betts argued that the system of Cold War national security policy making "worked," but that the American people eventually grew tired of a war they never really understood.[40] That same year, in *America in Vietnam,* Guenter Lewy sought to minimize the war's brutality in an effort to reestablish its morality and legality, concluding that "the simplistic slogan, 'No More Vietnams' not only may encourage international disorder, but could mean abandoning basic American values."[41] For his part, former President Nixon published a revisionist book with that very slogan as its title. Railing that "rarely have so many people been so wrong about so much," that the Vietnam War was "more misunderstood" than any event in U.S. history, the still-combative Nixon claimed the United States "won the war, but we lost the peace" since "Congress proceeded to snatch defeat from the jaws of victory." For Nixon, "No More Vietnams" meant the United States should ensure that it didn't "lose the peace" to the Soviet Union through similar "Congressional irresponsibility."[42]

Specific international flashpoints required popular reconstruction of the Vietnam War. Two years after the covert U.S.-backed coup overthrew the democratically elected Allende regime in Chile, the first test of congressional reticence to support foreign intervention came in late 1975 when Secretary of State Kissinger urged a reluctant Congress to provide a major increment of open support to rebels in Angola on the grounds that the Soviet Union must not be allowed to believe that the U.S. "will" to meet world "commitments" had waned in the aftermath of Vietnam and Watergate.[43] That same year, while the American media were beginning to trumpet alarms about the genocidal policies of Pol Pot and the Khmer Rouge in Cambodia, a proportionally comparable genocidal bloodbath was being carried out via a U.S.-backed Indonesian invasion of the island nation of East Timor. As Noam Chomsky and others have documented, the East Timor tragedy was long ignored by the U.S. media, eventually being framed in a way that "whitewashed" the role played by the United States[44]—one of the early indicators of post-Vietnam media quiescence.

The year 1979 was a particularly significant turning point in the reconstruction of American interventionism. A fundamentalist Islamic revolution in Iran toppled the U.S.-backed autocracy of the Shah, precipitating the seizure of the U.S. embassy and capture of American hostages, who were then held captive for 444 days, each of which was dramatically noted on nightly TV news. A popular-based leftist revolution toppled the long-entrenched U.S.-backed Somoza dictatorship in Nicaragua and brought the Sandinistas to power, threatening to destabilize U.S. domination of Central America and raising alarms about guerrilla efforts against the U.S.-backed dictatorship in El Salvador. Finally, wary of nationalist sentiment among its own Muslim population, the USSR had established a modern, pro-Soviet regime in neighboring Afghanistan in 1978. With resistance by the Afghan Mujahedeen on the rise, the Soviet army invaded Afghanistan in December 1979. While not publicly known at the time, the United States had previously provided secret aid to the rebels in order to, in Zbigniew Brzezinski's later words, "induce a Soviet military invasion."[45] Subsequent American military assistance to the Mujahedeen was legitimized on the grounds of an alleged Soviet "pincer movement aimed at Iran and the oil regions of the Middle East,"[46] whereas Brzezinski later argued it would "give the Soviets their own Vietnam."[47] As noted by Chalmers Johnson and others, that aid and subsequent American withdrawal from a ravaged Afghanistan once the Soviets left was linked to the "Blowback" of 9/11.[48]

From the perspective of the foreign policy establishment, these events were all warning signs of a hegemon in decline. Compounding the problem, a 1978 Chicago Council on Foreign Relations national poll had found widespread public reluctance to commit U.S. troops to a variety of hypothetical "crisis situations."[49] Although the public would be riled up by dramatic media coverage of the Iran hostage crisis, most remained skeptical that either the Salvadoran or Nicaraguan "crisis situations" posed a threat that justified U.S. military intervention. As U.S. foreign policy grew more aggressive in the later years of the Carter administration and then escalated dramatically under President Reagan, the public remained resistant to any commitment of U.S. troops.

Until the Gulf War in 1990, successive U.S. administrations were reluctant to raise the specter of the Vietnam War by openly deploying massive numbers of U.S. combat troops to international trouble spots. Instead they sought, with mixed success, to avoid inflaming the "Vietnam syndrome" by employing covert action (providing support for the 1973 Chilean coup against Salvador Allende), Vietnam-like counterinsurgency (El Salvador), a U.S.-trained and -equipped proxy army (the Contras in Nicaragua), and quick-strike invasions carried out in the absence of media (tiny Grenada in 1983 and Panama in late 1989). In each case, media publicity about the nature of the U.S. role was sharply curtailed and the range of public discourse narrowly circumscribed, leaving the relevant administrations with a relatively free hand to construct a mythic reality in support of intervention.[50]

Yet public resistance remained a problem, particularly in the case of Central America, so it wasn't until August 1990, when Iraq invaded Kuwait in the crucially oil-rich Middle East, that the George H. W. Bush administration had both a pretext and a convincingly despotic adversary for a massive deployment of U.S. military might. With considerable assistance from mass media that provided an engaging war spectacle largely devoid of evidence of the massive destruction wreaked by U.S. and coalition forces, the war was a brief meteoric success for the Bush administration. Veteran Vietnam War reporter Malcolm Browne compared the press role to that of the Nazi propaganda agency Kompanie: "I've never seen anything that can compare to it, in the degree of surveillance and control the military has over the correspondents."[51] As Reagan media manager Michael Deaver put it, "If you were to hire a public relations firm to do the media relations for an international event, it couldn't be done any better than this is being done."[52] At the war's end, President George H. W. Bush exulted, "By God, we've kicked the Vietnam syndrome once and for all."[53]

Still, the Vietnam ghost has refused to go quietly into the night, as Vietnam memories have been stirred up again and again in the media culture. The war has been a popular stage for Hollywood to explore the drama and tragedy of combat through revisionist frames (see chapter 11), and the news media have returned again and again to conventionally framed renditions of the war each time a candidate for national office has some connection to the war's controversies. Since the 2003 U.S. invasion of Iraq, however, comparisons to the war in Vietnam have been even more telling.

Transition to the Neoliberal Regime

In 1978, William Simon, who had been Nixon's treasury secretary and, as David Brock put it, a "Wall Street venture capitalist who became one of the country's wealthiest individuals by using junk bonds to finance hostile corporate takeovers,"[54] published *A Time for Truth,* a book ghostwritten by Edith Efron. Echoing Lewis Powell and earlier sixties critics, Simon proclaimed, once again, that business was under attack because of its inability to fight back against movements that threatened it. "The target of the 'consumer' movement is *business,* the target of the 'environmentalists' is *business,* and the target of the 'minorities' at least where employment is concerned, is *business.*"[55] Simon laid out a "blue-print" for a conservative, pro-business "counter-intelligentsia" that would shape public discourse in the media and "do battle with spokespeople for the consumer, environmental, civil rights, and feminist movements."[56] In 1980, a new configuration of political and economic interests came together to usher in the neoliberal regime that would dominate American electoral politics for at least the next twenty-eight years.

The influx of corporate funding fueled political campaigns and reforms that ultimately carried out the kind of agenda espoused by the Trilateral Commission report of 1975. They succeeded in turning the economy sharply back in the direction of laissez-faire economics, away from the welfare shift of the Great Society (and New Deal) and toward a revitalized defense shift via a major boost in defense spending. They produced a major deregulation of the economy. They fueled a host of so-called "free trade" agreements that, in the aftermath of the fall of the Soviet Union, have transformed the globe with profound implications for an increasingly fragile ecosphere and a widening gap between haves and have-nots. Finally, they energized a resurgence of an imperial American foreign policy, which under the eventual sway of the George W. Bush administration, boldly proclaimed the United States as the legitimate global hegemon.

In the words of a former Heritage Foundation official, the conservative and corporate foundation effort of the 1970s fueled the "shock troops of the conservative revolution."[57] There are, however, two sides to the "conservative revolution." On the one hand, there is the neoliberal credo of "free market" economics—deregulating the economy, rewarding wealth acquisition, and so on. On the other, conservative voices (of many stripes) have long decried various signs of social deterioration: the erosion of family life, the spread of sexual license at earlier and earlier ages, the loss of a sense of place, the dissolution of valued traditions, among others. Ultimately, the two sides are contradictory. The more things are turned over to the market, the less people can join together and influence the future through the expression of their values and the faster the pace of social erosion.

The convergence between social conservatism and neoliberalism is a kind of historical accident generated by the fact that corporate interests converged with conservatives in believing that the liberalism of the 1960s was to blame for both capitalism's crisis and the turbulence and decadence they saw in the media culture of the time. It has proven highly significant that only one side of the so-called "conservative revolution"—neoliberalism—has been realized, for it has left many of the Right's rhetorical constituencies feeling aggrieved at their displacement by a chaotic world within which they feel powerless and often worse off materially. These constituencies need to be repeatedly reminded that liberalism and those "Sixties" remain their threatening adversaries.

The vehicle that facilitated the convergence of these forces was none other than Ronald Reagan, a movie actor who became the reactionary governor of California, and, as such, a seemingly improbable candidate for president in 1980, especially after his 1976 bid for the Republican nomination fell short. Reagan provided the crucial catalyst for constructing a new, neoliberal future on a reconstructed past.

Ronald Reagan and the Politics of Nostalgia

As a Hollywood actor blessed with an ability to charm people with an affable persona, Reagan's campaign and presidential appearances were carefully managed by media handlers and advisers alike. Reagan was thus particularly successful in tapping into the undercurrent of discontent left over from the 1960s and 1970s with a homespun appeal to mythic recollections of a simpler past when things allegedly worked smoothly. As Daniel Marcus has put it:

> Reagan's effectiveness as a leading symbol of social and cultural nostalgia imbued the conservative political offensive with an overarching sense of a national return to an earlier age, after a period of American decline. By capturing the presidency, the ideologists of nostalgia were able to generate

media accounts of the historical meanings of the 1950s and 1960s and the relevance of those meanings to many aspects of American life—far beyond the cultural fads of the 1970s.[58]

President Reagan's public persona and rhetoric effectively obscured tensions between the agendas of social conservatives and the corporate center. The public policies actually implemented during the Reagan years were largely those desired by the president's corporate backers, not those suggested by the president's nostalgia-laced appeals to social conservatives.[59] Yet by 1979, a number of well-funded right-wing organizations like the Moral Majority, the Committee for the Survival of a Free Congress, and the National Conservative Political Action Committee were mobilized to provide support for the election of Ronald Reagan and the policy agenda of social conservatism. Their lobbying and direct-mail efforts were reinforced by a host of newspapers and publications, as documented in Alan Crawford's 1980 book *Thunder on the Right.*[60]

Given the direct input that organizations like the Heritage Foundation and the American Enterprise Institute had on policy making in the Reagan years, it is hardly surprising that Reagan's policy priorities were right out of the corporate playbook. In this view, the keys to reversing America's alleged decline were to

- roll back "Big Government"—which meant significant cutbacks in government social welfare spending while military expenditures registered their greatest increase since the Vietnam War;
- revive belief in the market economy as the vehicle for achieving widespread prosperity—which meant deregulating environmental, consumer, and worker protections, attacking organized labor for undermining American "competitiveness" and putting "special interests" above the "common good," reducing inflation through a tight monetary policy while simultaneously adopting the novelty of "supply-side economics"—namely, instituting major tax cuts for corporations and society's wealthiest;
- restore public support for defense spending and aggressive foreign policy through saber-rattling, warning against the Soviet "evil empire," and carefully cloaked interventions by the United States and U.S.-trained proxy forces in Central America and the Caribbean.

The outcomes of the Reagan revolution have been well documented.[61] Among other things, the Reagan policies produced the greatest upward redistribution of wealth and income in U.S. history, a pronounced increase in inequality, record-setting federal deficits (which proved politically useful in subsequent efforts to hold down domestic spending), and a new Gilded Age marked by the widely visible consumption of luxuries and the encouragement of get-rich-quick market speculation. In addition, neoliberal policies have had a particularly potent impact on the young, thereby reinforcing the reversal of past student activism.

Cutbacks in public support for higher education were significant, but their impact was greatly compounded by escalating costs of higher education, at least partially driven by the growth of bureaucratic administrative structures as colleges and universities competed to attract a shrinking pool of students. From the 1980s on, students have often graduated with burdensome loans they need to pay off, thereby reinforcing their preoccupation with finding the high-paying jobs the advertising world suggested were both desirable and necessary.

At the same time, the Reagan revolution transformed political discourse in the United States. Much of Reagan's success in leading this transformation stemmed from his ability to appeal to themes of an America in decline—referencing the sixties and seventies—with a remedy drawn from symbolic references to a mythical pre-sixties era. It is more than coincidental that many of the personalities who rose to positions of power during the Reagan years and since were once members of a youthful New Right during the sixties, largely overlooked by media attracted to the more dramatic movements on the left. Among those seemingly influenced by their experiences in the sixties were Dick and Lynne Cheney, Lee Atwater, David Stockman, William Bennett, Dan Quayle, Elliot Abrams, and William Kristol—in addition to pre–baby boomer Newt Gingrich and leftists-turned-rightists like David Horowitz, Peter Collier, and Ronald Radosh.[62]

In general, the Republican campaigns of 1980 focused more on the four years of the Carter administration than on references to the 1960s, although Senator Bill Brock noted in response to Carter's 1980 State of the Union address that the "ideas of the 1960s don't work any more," so the electorate should reject Democrats, the "party of old answers and old ideas."[63] However, as Daniel Marcus has documented, the figure of Ronald Reagan evoked a contrast between the turbulent sixties and a nostalgic vision of the 1950s already popularized on 1970s television.[64] Not only had Reagan railed against many of the sixties disruptions and opposed the era's significant liberal accomplishments like civil rights and voting rights, but during the campaign he aligned himself with the forces of backlash against some of the sixties' most potent symbols: pledging his support for "states rights" while visiting the site of the civil rights workers murdered in 1964, criticizing the Supreme Court's 1962 decision to "expel God from the classroom," and then, in a speech to the Veterans of Foreign Wars, criticizing the inadequate prosecution of the "noble cause" in Vietnam, noting that "to give way to feelings of guilt as if we were doing something shameful" was to dishonor the memory of those who died.[65] Reagan seemed less concerned about honoring the living veterans of the war, for, as D. Michael Shafer has observed, his "first act in office was to freeze hiring in the [Veterans'] Readjustment Counseling Program," and he "soon moved to eliminate all Vietnam veteran outreach programs, including an employment training program for disabled veterans."[66]

In a paid political broadcast on election eve, Reagan elaborated on his vision of the past:

Not so long ago, we emerged from a world war. Turning homeward at last, we built a grand prosperity and hopes, from our own success and plenty, to help others less fortunate. Our peace was a tense and bitter one, but in those days, the center seemed to hold. Then came the hard years—riots, assassinations, domestic strife over the Vietnam war, and in the last four years, drift and disaster in Washington. . . . For the first time in our memory, many Americans are asking, "Does history still have a place for America, for her people, for her great ideals?"[67]

Reagan's very persona—his ready reference to simplified virtues of past and present, his appeal to optimism based on individual and national strengths, even his militant rhetoric toward communism—all hearkened to a mythic, nostalgic past full of the very iconic themes that had for years been passed down through cultural media like film, television, and grade school textbooks. The era Reagan evoked was the world of easy-going paternal authority (Robert Young in *Father Knows Best*), of heroic masculinity closely linked to fabled American conquests (the films of John Wayne, himself a nostalgic icon identified with the conquest of the western frontier and American victory in World War II), of 1950s-era school textbooks that portrayed American history as the "city on the hill" that inspired the rest of the world, of self-contained, contented American families (*Ozzie and Harriet, Leave It to Beaver,* and the contemporary *Happy Days*). Reagan's pitch, in short, was nostalgic for a time that never really existed. As Charles Taylor wrote of Gertrude Himmelfarb's polemic against the sixties, *One Nation, Two Cultures:*

> Implicit in all conservative hand-wringing about the sorry state of our culture, in whatever era that hand-wringing has appeared, is a longing for some lost golden age. But when was this paradisiacal era? If you started with "One Nation, Two Cultures" and worked your way backwards through all the similar tomes that have appeared in the last hundred years, it would be like traveling through an infinity of mirrors, each reflection leading you farther back without ever reaching an endpoint.[68]

Reagan's use of nostalgia-inducing homilies and pithy expressions of American virtues, along with his ready storehouse of illustrative anecdotes real or imagined, made for good television. They were also difficult for critics to refute in the increasingly short span of television news reports, at least without appearing hostile to timeless values that resonated with the public. *Time* magazine greeted Reagan's election by naming him "Man of the Year" for 1980, observing, apparently without irony, that "intellectually, emotionally, Reagan lives in the past. That is where the broad vision comes from; the past is his future." While somewhat skeptical at the time that Americans would embrace this vision, the magazine predictably referenced popular culture in observing that "after several years of *The Deer Hunter* and *All the President's Men,* perhaps *The Ronald Reagan Story* is just what the country ordered."[69]

Reagan repeatedly genuflected toward a benign past that he or his campaign handlers essentially created as the antidote to the darkest images available from the 1960s. Against the "riots, assassinations, and domestic strife" of the sixties era and the recent "drift and disaster," Reagan juxtaposed rugged individualism, hard work, thrift, traditional morality, and stable family life. Yet the era Reagan glowingly evoked was one in which his common rhetorical target, government "handouts," in the form of the G.I. Bill, had in fact played a substantial role in fostering the growing white middle class of the postwar years.[70] Furthermore, Reagan freely reconstructed the past. As Daniel Marcus observed, "In 1960, Reagan described [John F.] Kennedy's program as basically communist; by 1980 he was invoking Kennedy in order to appeal to old-time Democratic voters disillusioned with post-1965 liberalism."[71] Yet, once in office, he inspired young Americans with the opposite of Kennedy's inaugural message by elevating the pursuit of private material gain to the level of a social good. Indeed, Reagan's pro-market rhetoric had the effect of ennobling self-interest and the pursuit of wealth, thus helping to remove the shame associated with a massive increase in benefits to the wealthy while simultaneously cutting back on aid to the poor— producing what the mass media liked to call "compassion fatigue." As political scientist Sheldon Wolin has put it, Reagan's administration engaged in "pseudotraditionalism":

> The appeal to the past and its values was not meant to point the way back to the past. Such a notion is totally incongruous in an administration so completely beholden to corporate interests. . . . Rather it was meant to ease the path toward the future. Pseudotraditionalism mediates between the average citizen and the harsh reality that modernization imposes on even the most highly technologized societies. Pseudotraditionalism helps to mask the costs of adaptation to the intensely competitive political economy being ushered in.[72]

In Marcus's words, "Reagan's policies were meant to assist business in the process of constant modernization, which contributed to the social upheaval his nostalgic image tried to assuage."[73]

Political scientist Michael Rogin observed that Reagan's personality fit this contradiction perfectly; his combination of personality characteristics and professional background was uniquely suited to the times and an increasingly imagistic media culture. Drawing on his cinematic past, Reagan espoused the values of production. But, as a product of the cinematic world, he displayed the narcissistic characteristics of a celebrity. In Rogin's words, "The celebrity displays personality. He pleases others; intimate before mass audiences, he plays at privacy in public. Neither a repressed interior nor an intractable reality exercise claims over the celebrity, for he exists in the eye of the beholder. Since he replaces reality by fantasy, his pleasure and reality principles do not collide."[74]

Rogin's study documented Reagan's elevation of himself as a "hero of American cultural myths" through the use of movie quotes. "Go ahead. Make my day," the president warned Congress while promising to veto a tax increase, echoing Clint Eastwood's dare in *Sudden Impact*. Thus while Reagan's rhetoric helped to blur the boundaries between cinematic fiction and reality, Reagan himself seemed so much a product of his Hollywood background that, Rogin argues, he was unable to make the distinction himself.[75] Indeed, Reagan's saber-rattling anticommunism reflected his war film roles and Hollywood experience. After American hostages in Lebanon were released in 1985, Reagan remarked, "Boy, I saw *Rambo* last night. Now I know what to do the next time this happens."[76] Citing Fredric Jameson's work on the "cultural turn" toward postmodernity, Rogin observed that "Reagan's easy slippage between movies and reality" was a perfect fit for a "political culture increasingly impervious to distinctions between fiction and history."[77]

Presidential comments increasingly carried the day, with little correction from the media—or, for that matter, from Democrats caught up in their own move to the safe center. Reality was becoming increasingly virtual as presidential rhetoric combined with media imagery to transform the meaning of the past. Thus, in a 1982 press conference, Reagan rambled unchallenged through a fantastic reconstruction of the Vietnam War in terms that stood historical reality on its head. North and South Vietnam were depicted "previous to colonization" as "two separate countries," which a benign world was "helping . . . become independent nations" through elections that "Ho Chi Minh refused to participate in." As a result of the latter, the United States sent military advisers "in civilian clothes" to help South Vietnam develop an army to "defend itself," until the advisers "began being blown up where they lived, in walking down the street by people riding by on bicycles and throwing pipe bombs at them," until the attacks got so furious that "John F. Kennedy authorized the sending in of a division of marines."[78]

As Daniel Marcus has argued, "The ability of the Reagan movement to move the country beyond the effects of the Sixties was symbolically illustrated by Reagan's survival of an assassination attempt by John Hinckley shortly after taking office." Aided by his "image of tough-guy strength" and his self-effacing "humorous aplomb," Reagan "evoked the calm, secure presence of the suburban sitcom dad." His popularity surged in the wake of the attempt on his life, helping to build support for his budgetary and tax policies. In Marcus's view, Reagan's survival of the assassination effort was "the most popular act of his first term."[79]

Greatly assisted by adept media handlers, his own on-camera presence, and a fourth estate cowed by well-orchestrated attacks against liberal media, Reagan's presidency ushered in a political discourse saturated with illusory symbolic politics. As Douglas Kellner has put it,

The Reagan team was able to turn politics into images, spectacles, and stories, by producing narrative frames for its policies and figurehead. Drawing on his experience as a master of illusion and narrative, Reagan was able to dramatize political issues as simple conflicts between evil and good. ... The Reagan presidency was thus the United States' most highly realized administration produced for and scripted according to television codes and frames—that is, the first fully simulated presidency—and Ronald Reagan was clearly the most highly developed television president.[80]

However, the transformation of media discourse was not accomplished solely through the efforts of Reagan and his handlers. The infusion of foundation funding from the 1970s onward made possible a series of books, journals, and articles that provided a supportive foundation for the Reagan revolution. Manhattan Institute books included George Gilder's 1980 volume *Wealth and Poverty,* which critiqued the social welfare state and promoted supply-side economic policy that formed the core of Reagan's major economic innovation, the Economic Recovery Tax Act of 1981. The Hoover Institution's Thomas Sowell emerged as an important black voice of dissent from Great Society liberalism, embracing free-market economics in such books as *Race and Economics* (1976, before joining Hoover) and *Markets and Minorities* (1981). With support from the John M. Olin Foundation, Charles Murray's *Losing Ground: American Social Policy, 1950–1980,* published in 1984, patched together highly selective evidence to support sweeping arguments that government social welfare efforts exacerbated the problems of poverty—chiefly by creating dependency on government "handouts." While Murray's claims and findings have been widely contested and critiqued in the social science literature, *Losing Ground* received wide publicity, particularly in the neoconservative journals that were also beneficiaries of general support from conservative foundations.

These were only a few of the more widely publicized of the tidal wave of books and articles providing justification for, and proclaiming, the Reagan revolution. Together, they formed the beginnings of a right-wing echo chamber in which publication of one study was reinforced by laudatory reviews and citations through the newly revitalized conservative media. Ultimately, they helped to transform the debate over government policy, manufacturing the assumption that the Great Society was an abject policy failure. During the Reagan years, only a few lonely books were published refuting the new conservative orthodoxy, despite the fact that, in reality, the percentage of Americans living in poverty had been sharply reduced during the Great Society years of the 1960s, whereas that percentage rose sharply during the 1980s.[81] While the foundation-supported output helped to expedite the Reagan policy agenda, as the 1980s progressed and public policy moved to the right, the focus of a significant portion of these works began to shift onto more cultural targets.

11

The "Sixties" Nostalgia Market and the Culture of Self-Satire

There's a real fight going on . . . over what we can roughly describe as popular memory. . . . Since memory is actually a very important factor in struggle . . . if one controls people's memory, one controls their dynamism. And one also controls their experience, their knowledge of previous struggles.
—Michel Foucault, interview on "Film and Popular Memory," 1975

Multiplicity, choice, reshaping one's self, refining one's sense of identity—these days, these are the values of the marketplace as well as those of the opposition.
—L. A. Kauffman "Small Changes, Radical Politics since the 60s," 1995

As the neoliberal regime solidified under the presidency of Ronald Reagan, several forces were converging that would shape the media culture of the new era. One significant shift was a newly energized consumer culture, enabled by the policies of neoliberalism, driven by the lure of affluent acquisitiveness, and reinforced by sophisticated, hip advertising. The accumulation of wealth was relegitimized by neoliberal ideology at the same time that neoliberal policies redistributed wealth upward. The United States seemed to be launched on a new Gilded Age.

Commercial forces, however, had to contend with a populace that was significantly different from the market democracy of the 1950s. The national audience, the American "imagined community," and the national market of postwar America had been permanently fractured by the diversification of tastes, interests, and identities associated with the "new voices" of the sixties and the breakdown of racial and gender barriers. It would no longer be as straightforward to pitch a television program, a news broadcast, or a product to a wide swath of the public via a single medium, especially in light of the heightened skepticism left over from the sixties. Postmodern, post-Fordist Capitalism was in full sway.[1]

Society's fragmentation provided a powerful incentive for the development of technologies like cable TV, satellite TV, and digital media to enable more effective marketing to niche markets and audiences. The higher-risk media climate added to political pressures to deregulate the media. Deregulation under both Presidents Reagan and Clinton provided the impetus for media mergers and acquisitions, leading to far greater concentration of media ownership (horizontal integration) in the 1980s and 1990s and the conglomerated ownership of diverse forms of media content as well as the means of its distribution (vertical integration) during and since the 1990s. The effects, as recounted by Robert McChesney, probably the most prolific writer on the subject, have been profound. Not only is the "notion that independents will sprout up to challenge the existing giants" a thing of the past, but "the implications of this concentration and conglomeration for media content are largely negative." Writing in 1999, McChesney went on to observe:

> On the one hand, media fare is ever more closely linked to the needs and concerns of a handful of enormous and powerful corporations . . . with clear stakes in the outcome of the most fundamental political issues, and their interests are often distinct from those of the vast majority of humanity. By any known theory of democracy, such a concentration of economic, cultural, and political power into so few hands—and mostly unaccountable hands at that—is absurd and unacceptable. On the other hand, media fare is subjected to an ever-greater commercialization as the dominant firms use their market power to squeeze the greatest possible profit from their product. This is, in fact, the most visible trend in U.S. media today.[2]

The second major shift affecting media culture was the political system's turn to the right, along with its rationalization for "free market" economics, both enabled by the well-funded campaigns that responded to the sixties. This shift, along with the televisually charismatic president, cowed the potentially adversarial media and largely captured the Democratic Party as well as the Republicans. As Douglas Kellner has documented, "At bottom, corporate/conglomerate mergers integrated the major television networks more centrally into the power structure of transnational capitalism during the Reagan years, and television responded by taking a conservative turn that was generally supportive of Reagan's economic policies."[3] In addition to the passage of time, both the unleashing of consumerism and the turn to the right helped to create a market for sixties nostalgia.[4]

Reflecting these forces, the sixties era was pervasively reduced, in rough sequence, to the rebellion of impetuous baby boomers maturing into Reagan-era Yuppies and then to the more divisive boomer "battles" that candidate Obama sought to distance himself from. In this context, the most common way to attract the largest audience possible is to provide music or images that evoke baby boomer nostalgia for an increasingly distant youth while simultaneously casting that rebellious youth in a story frame that fits into the zeitgeist of the 1980s and 1990s and beyond, simultaneously appealing to more conservative audiences' nostalgia for the "innocent" days before the sixties. More narrowly, a range of specific sixties events have been commercially useful in targeting specific audiences. In Orwellian fashion the oppositional meaning of sixties movements were converted into their antithesis: a depoliticized form of participation in the consumer and entertainment culture of capitalism. Within this array of media representations, the democratic meanings of the sixties era have largely disappeared, while, predictably, the relevance of more radical sixties criticism to the contemporary world has never been broached.

"Sixties" Discourses

This media culture has produced a kind of dynamic interplay between the commercial forces of deregulated capitalism and the rhetorical arguments of conservatives. Commercial forces continue to seek out potential narcissists they can empower through the latest fads, the edgiest entertainment, and, of course, the always captivating media icons of the sixties: Black Panthers, the Summer of Love, Woodstock, and the like. The content of this incessant market-driven quest drives conservatives mad, often with good reason. Typically, conservative ideology singles out targets like the "liberal media" and something they like to call "sixties sensibilities" as the major problems facing society. But conservatives' criticism has consistently missed the mark. While conservative political interests clearly benefit from attacks on the forces they blame for "sixties sensibilities" — "Big Government" and "liberal media" — the contradiction between capitalism and conservative values remains obscured by this diversionary discourse.

Two examples illustrate this distracting discourse. One was the bizarre dialogue in 1992 between a sitting vice president, Dan Quayle, and a television character, Murphy Brown, from a CBS sitcom of the same name. Brown, played by Candace Bergen, was the star anchorwoman and investigative reporter of a fictional television newsmagazine, *FYI*. Appealing to hip liberal audiences with Brown's liberal feminism and its satirical jabs at mass media news, the show became the subject of a Quayle campaign speech after the pregnant, unmarried Brown character chose to raise her child as a single mom. Quayle's criticism of Brown for devaluing the role of fathers and promoting single parenthood triggered a public debate on "family values." Playing on an old theme, Quayle broadened his attack to include the "cultural elite" who "mock us in newsrooms, sitcom studios and faculty lounges across America."[5] Later in the 1992–93 season, a *Murphy Brown* episode titled "You Say Potatoe, I Say Potato" (a jab at Quayle's infamous spelling snafu at a grade school) used footage from Quayle's speech in an *FYI* show that examined the diversity of family life in the United States. Within the fictional frame of the show, it appeared that Quayle and the fictional Brown were actually speaking directly to each other. Needless to say, the Quayle-Brown flap was subsequently used to promote future shows.

The second illustration comes from the summer of 1987, twenty years after the infamous "Summer of Love," when the media were full of news, musical, and entertainment references to the summer that the mass media discovered and hyped, eventually destroying the countercultural community of Haight-Ashbury—an anniversary the mass media have revisited without fail every decade. The tidal wave of media references provoked an op-ed piece by *Washington Post* columnist Jonathan Yardley, who opened with the lament, "It would be difficult to think of a more depressing piece of news, but there you have it: The Sixties are back." Yardley proceeded to create a retrospective picture of the past that would have qualified him as a speechwriter for Ronald Reagan. His diatribe began with a reference to a *New York Times* quote that the sixties were a "time of ideological commitment and a sense of purpose," to which Yardley responded:

All of which is baloney. The Sixties had almost nothing to do with genuine ideological commitment or sense of purpose, and neither does the revival. The Sixties were adolescent rebellion masquerading as a political movement, while the current popularity of the decade's symbols and totems seems to be almost entirely a matter of commercial exploitation. . . . The plain truth is that the Sixties were a period of unfettered self-indulgence on the part of the privileged children of America's middle class, and that the decade's legacy is, with the rarest of exceptions, lamentable.[6]

Yardley was certainly right about the commercial exploitation twenty years later, but to continue his attack on the sixties, he needed to construct a peculiar definition of that era: "During the Sixties—which actually began around 1965 and ended about a decade later—little of lasting value was accomplished either politically or culturally." The sixties, in short, was a particular phenomenon rather than a historical era of interrelated events. To make sure his audience didn't get confused by actual history, Yardley went on to assert, "Apologists for the time like to claim, for example, that the civil rights movement was part of the Sixties, when in fact it had begun long before then."[7] In short, "the Sixties" represented the era within which social movements were critical of fundamental American institutions, their actions commanding increasing media attention and evolving in increasingly expressive directions.

Yardley's sixties reflect all the stereotypes commonly aired throughout the backlash era. The "tidal wave of immoderation" was "powered by" adolescents' psychological "needs" to "break away from parental supervision and discipline." Instead of being a time of "idealism" and "commitment," the sixties was "utterly unrelated" to those qualities and a period of "the most intense self-indulgence." Yardley dismissed the antiwar movement as having "far less to do with principled or reasoned resistance than with the avoidance of military service." Its "real legacy," it turned out, was the "yuppies of the Eighties" and the "decline of the university" brought about by the "wholesale capitulation of university faculties and administrations to the demands of the Sixties' 'rebels.'"[8]

If anything, the sixties Yardley described was an accurate description of the young runaways attracted to the counterculture by the media hype of the time. It is also significant that Yardley's diatribe was against the sixties being "back," when in fact there was no evidence that anything from the sixties was back except for media exploitation of sixties "freak" shows. In both cases what seemed to be most irritating to Yardley was not the historical sixties, but the media's commercial pitch appealing to youthful self-indulgence. Yet he never really addressed where this commercial pitch comes from. In the end, commercial media served up imagery and a consumer pitch that provided the Right with another opportunity to flail away at a past consisting of the imagery and stories that the media have preserved for mass consumption. Media "history" thus consists of recycled media stories and imagery from the past. The political discourse about the sixties that the media offer us are akin to watching a self-contained ping-pong match between two uses of those stories and imagery—commercial and ideological. It is, to say the least, a discourse full of irony.

Nostalgia and the Culture of Advertising

The Sixties are more than merely the homeland of hip, they are a commercial template for our times, a historical prototype for the construction of cultural machines that transform alienation and despair into consent. . . . Every few years, it seems, the cycles of the sixties repeat themselves on a smaller scale, with new rebel youth cultures bubbling their way to a happy replenishing of the various cultural industries' depleted arsenal of cool. New generations obsolete the old, new celebrities render old ones ridiculous, and on and on in an ever-ascending spiral of hip upon hip.
   —Thomas Frank, *The Conquest of Cool*, 1997

In Thomas Frank's account, the culture of advertising and the culture of business caught on to the subjective appeal of individuality and personal rebellion during the sixties and, over time, have refined a pitch designed to evade and subvert the individual's "resistant subjectivity"[9] in order to incorporate that individual into the smooth flowing operations of profitable capitalism. In making "hip" the language of both consumption and production, Frank claimed, business resolved what Daniel Bell called capitalism's "cultural contradictions" between self-indulgent consumption and hierarchical, gratification-postponing production—"at least symbolically," in Frank's words.[10] In the end, Frank argued, "what we understand as dissent does not subvert, does not challenge, does not even question the cultural faiths of Western business," because it is "no longer any different from the official culture it's supposed to be subverting."[11]

As Frank's reference to "new rebel youth cultures" suggests, the culture of "hip consumerism" has continued to evolve. As the work of Juliet Schor, Douglas Rushkoff, and others documents, through a marketing "feedback loop," advertisers watch young teens to find out what things are "cool" or "in," and the teens, in turn, watch advertisers to figure out how to behave. This process turns teens into "exhibitionists," thereby reinforcing narcissistic tendencies in society.[12] Or, as Stuart Ewen has put it, teens learn to construct a self "for public consumption."[13]

With respect to the 1960s, this dynamic is embodied in advertisers' exploitation of musical clips or symbols evocative of sixties rebelliousness to sell their products. What was once an icon associated with opposition to the system thereby becomes either a mass-produced commodity itself or the seductive hook to draw one into consumption. As noted previously, such was the sixties-era Volkswagen. After the Reagan years and media hype about baby boomer sellouts (and after the demise of the Volkswagen Beetle), the car manufacturer pitched an entirely new Beetle to baby boom consumers with the line, "If you sold your soul in the 80s, here's your chance to buy it back."

In another example, the classic Alberto Korda photograph of Latin American revolutionary Ernesto "Che" Guevara—like those of Malcolm X or Ho Chi Minh—was a popular icon among sixties youth, eventually finding its way onto T-shirts and other attire after Che was tracked down and killed in Bolivia in 1967. To exhibit a Che poster at the time symbolized opposition to a system that many among the young viewed as violent, oppressive, and imperialistic in carrying out a vicious war. Years later, the same image of Che became fashionably hip, appearing on varieties of chic clothing and leading the conservative *Washington Times* to proclaim gleefully, "Che Guevara: Icon of Capitalism."[14]

Back in the late 1960s, Yippie Abbie Hoffman gained considerable media notoriety when he was arrested for wearing a shirt made from an American flag while attending a 1968 House Un-American Activities Committee hearing. Hoffman appeared again in the flag shirt more than a year later on the *Merv Griffin Show*, during which the portion of the TV screen that showed Hoffman was blackened to prevent viewers from seeing his shirt.[15] In the heat of the times, Hoffman's attire was viewed as inflammatory, even dangerous, provoking denunciatory letters to the editor and retaliatory repression. It was also imitated in a variety of oppositional expressions.

Years later, in the wake of flag-hyping super-patriotism—which Chris Hedges has characterized as a form of narcissism[16]—connected to U.S. wars in the Persian Gulf region, popular clothing manufacturers like Tommy Hilfiger produced wide varieties of clothing displaying U.S. flags. Flag wearers had become transformed from society's oppositional outcasts to stylish patriots. Predictably, the satirically critical magazine *Adbusters* followed with a Hilfiger "subvertisement" featuring several sheep grazing in front of a U.S. flag and the slogan, "Tommy—Follow the Flock,"[17] while flag-waving patriotism was later satirized by mock U.S. flags that featured major corporate logos in place of the white stars. Absent political transformation, the cycle of satirical expression, cooptation, and subsequent satirical expression never ends. Indeed, flag wearing came full circle when high school students near San Francisco were sent home from school for being "disrespectful toward Mexican-American students" when they wore patriotic, flag-adorned T-shirts on Cinco de Mayo. In this case, flag wearing was a kind of protest that reflected precisely the kind of media discourse I am writing about—one in which, after years of backlash, white students apparently feel sufficiently aggrieved by the symbolic attention to Latino immigrants that they need to declare their identity as ("true") Americans. Instead of being drawn into an interactive, educational experience, they are punished by overzealous administrators, thereby generating more backlash against "political correctness."[18] So it goes in the circularity of expressive, symbolic media discourse.

Countercultural attire, or at least some of it, has also been absorbed into the fads and fashions of commercial styles. Self-made tie-dyed T-shirts of the sixties evolved years later into brightly colored, mass-manufactured styles for young people making a cool statement. Practical and inexpensive blue jeans migrated from the farm or factory to middle-class, urban campuses among bohemian students in the fifties and young civil rights volunteers wearing denim overalls and work shirts in the sixties. By the late sixties, jeans became fashionable throughout the youth culture; for women, jeans were part of their shift from "ladylike" attire. In the counterculture, the more ragged the jeans, the better, since they provided an excuse for increasingly playful forms of decoration or self-exposure and also sent a message of down-and-out bohemianism. In the 1970s, one clothing manufacturer after another jumped on the blue-jeans bandwagon. By the Reagan 1980s, blue jeans had become a billion-dollar industry as chic clothing designers like Gloria Vanderbilt and Calvin Klein created their own brands of designer jeans, making their products highly desirable—and expensive. Other counterculture simulations followed: pre-washed and pre-bleached jeans and jeans with pre-torn holes in them.

At times, clothing advertisers have pitched their products with direct appeals to sixties nostalgia. One multi-page 1980s ad invited viewers to "return with us to those thrilling days of yesteryear" above a collage of peace pins. On turning the page, a two-page spread provided a classic montage of popular media images—Jimi Hendrix, Martin Luther King Jr., JFK, Woodstock, the Beatles' Rolls Royce, the 1969 Mets, psychedelic ties—and a text that proclaimed,

> It was a decade unlike any other in the history of this country. Ten years that have affectionately become known as the sixties. A decade of enormous social change, political upheavals, and where the activities of the day ranged from the ridiculous (how many people could squeeze into a Volkswagen) to the sublime (meditating along with your favorite Maharishi).

It was a decade that saw man first walk on the moon. And the New York Mets win their first World Series, a feat many saw as even more improbable.

A decade in which four guys from England came west to the U.S. and changed music forever. And 400,000 people from all across America traveled north, to upstate New York, and a piece of history known simply as Woodstock.[19]

Having emptied the decade of any political content other than mere mention of "political upheavals"—no Vietnam, no civil rights or racial struggles, no student rebellion, no women's movement—the ad avoided potentially divisive references, appealing instead to nostalgia for youth and the excitement and playfulness of the time. The ad made its final pitch to whatever undercurrent of unease might exist in the get-rich eighties.

Finally, it was a decade in which hemlines got shorter, ties got wider, and the official uniform was faded jeans, T-shirts, and a pair of Frye boots. It was a uniform that symbolized a belief on the part of those who wore it (did anybody not?) in things that were simple, honest and enduring. So to the often asked question these days, "Where can you find those values that were so important to us all back in the 60's?" we have our own answer. At any of the stores you see listed below. In men's sizes 7–13 and women's 5–10.[20]

In short, while reinforcing conventional media wisdom that the sixties largely consisted of conforming faddishness ("uniforms" and values held by "us all") and that baby boomers had sold out in the 1980s, the ad suggests that wistful longing for a more ethical life can be satisfied simply by—what else?—purchasing a pair of boots.

Even the war in Vietnam was not immune to commodification. Attenders at a *Miss Saigon* performance in Philadelphia could purchase "Vietnam-war-related coffee mugs, lighters[!], match boxes, t-shirts, and a special boxed set of CD's with pop-up representations of North Vietnamese troops entering Saigon."[21]

As the Virginia Slims cigarette campaign revealed, expressions of women's liberation were another major target of advertisers who belatedly chucked their overtly sexist advertising in an attempt to cash in on shifting tastes and attitudes that began in the sixties. A 1978 Enjoli perfume ad noted, "I can bring home the bacon, fry it up in a pan, and never, never, never let you forget you're a man." In 1988, *Good Housekeeping* launched a "New Traditionalist" woman campaign in a variety of national publications. The ads played up images of former careerist women happily ensconced in their traditional but expensively renovated homes and attending to their model children—noting that they were responding to "deep-rooted values" by serving the needs of their husbands, children, and homes. Using appropriate feminist-speak, the ad proclaimed the New Traditionalist woman as one who "made her own choices" and "started a revolution" while assuring readers that "she's not following a trend. She *is* the trend. . . . In fact, market researchers are calling it the biggest social movement since the 60s." *Good Housekeeping* confirmed the "social movement" a year later in an ad that read, "My mother was convinced the center of the world was 36 Maplewood Drive. . . . I'm beginning to think my mother really knew what she was doing."[22]

Perhaps, however, no phenomenon of the 1960s has been utilized for commercial purposes more pervasively than the era's popular music—rock and folk—as well as the celebrities who performed it. Sixties music, of course, easily evokes sixties memories among baby boomers and allows them to project onto the music their own subjective meanings. Most generically, the music provides an effective vehicle for producers seeking to play on baby boomer's nostalgia for lost youth and vitality irrespective of the political issues of the day. The use of classic sixties songs in television advertising has become so commonplace that few are even likely to notice the irony. Among the early entries, Nike bought the rights to the original Beatles' recording of "Revolution" to advertise its sneakers, while Sunkist used claymation raisins rocking out to Marvin Gaye's rendition of "I Heard It through the Grapevine." Bob Dylan's highly political "The Times They Are a-Changin'" first accompanied an ad for the Big Six accounting firm Coopers & Lybrand, and later was part of the pitch for a major Canadian bank.[23] Among car manufacturers, Mercedes-Benz was sold to the tune of Janis Joplin's song of the same name, while Mercury Cougars were pitched to young drivers with Steppenwolf's "Born to be Wild" (as they were later with "Proud Mary" and the Beatles' "Help"). Over the three years of the Cougar ad campaign, the average age of Cougar drivers fell from forty-four to thirty-five.[24]

The Rolling Stones' "Satisfaction," the Byrds' version of Pete Seeger's "Turn, Turn, Turn," Crosby, Stills, Nash, and Young's "Teach Your Children," the Rolling Stones' "Start Me Up," and John Lennon's "Imagine" are only a few of the many other sixties-era songs and celebrities linked to later commercials. "Imagine" was used by an American Express advertisement that depicted haunting images of hungry children and suggested to its audiences, "Imagine if every time you bought something with your American Express card, or made a purchase through an American Express Financial Advisor, you helped feed someone who was hungry."[25] In a culture so full of irony, political satire, if not dissent, has a more challenging task in seeking to distinguish itself from the cultural clutter.

It's obviously difficult to gauge the full impact of the nostalgic pitch of sixties music, although like much media fare it would seem to shape and thereby restrict the imagination of its audience. Reflecting a variant on visual thinking, one young reporter for the *Newton Kansan* began a 2003 article on the timeless-ness of challenging the status quo:

> Is it possible to be nostalgic for something you've never experienced? I have asked myself this question for years in an attempt to explain what happens to my brain when Jefferson Airplane comes across the radio waves, and what it is that jogs my memory when I hear the opening notes to 'Me and Bobby McGee.' When I listen to music from the '60s and early '70s, I feel like I'm back in time on the Washington Monument [Mall?], joining the Freedom Rides, and hitchhiking in San Francisco, of course with flowers in my hair.[26]

Finally, one of the more famous media-celebrated icons of the 1960s, the 1969 Woodstock Festival, has been recycled again and again by promoters and adver-tisers eager to reap the profits to be gleaned by commercial Woodstock reunion festivals. Like the counterculture generally, Woodstock reflected the apolitical "politics" of youth—a combination of highly tolerant "do your own thing" indi-vidualism and a yearning for community apart from the nation at war. After the festival one Woodstock participant published a poem, "The Hip Fantasy," in the New York underground paper *Rat:*

> We were in one cosmic entity, our unity was our power . . .
> we arrived like refugees seeking our places in the final Armageddon . . .
> I was free, and that's what we're
> all about . . . we saw our revolution, and
> we built it, and we made it baby, and I dug it so much that I'd kill
> to make it happen forever.[27]

The hyperbolic sentiments expressed in those lines suggest Woodstock's market-ing potential, to say nothing of its grip on the mass media's imagination. As *Time* put it, Woodstock was "history's biggest happening."[28]

The twenty-fifth anniversary of the original festival saw perhaps the most ambitious effort to relive the past. "Woodstock '94" was a heavily advertised and commercially backed opportunity for boomers to connect with a bit of his-tory they may have missed and for young fans to hear some of their favorite bands. The news media lavished considerable attention on the festival, playing up the "generations in conflict" theme. The *New York Times,* for example, noted that the younger generation of attenders "had to put up with their own set of stereotypes," which, no surprise, came from boomers (as opposed to commer-cial media culture) who "had pegged them as the generation of Nintendo and MTV, isolated and alienated and passive." In the *Times'* reckoning, the younger generation was "sullen because their elders had all the pre-AIDS fun and took all the good jobs," yet having "seen the movie 'Woodstock,'" they were now "determined to experience it. Afterward, perhaps, they would not feel so all alone."[29]

Equally banal, though more satirically hip, was a Pepsi television ad that appeared in the days leading up to the 1994 festival—the same Pepsi that, back in the day, pitched itself to the youthful "Pepsi Generation." In fact, the ad is a brilliant example of the "hip" advertising that Mark Miller argues "erases resistant subjectivity," since it mocks everything and invites viewers to laugh smugly along with the ad as they "stay young" by sipping Pepsi. Backed by the music of Canned Heat's "Goin' Up the Country" (performed at the original Woodstock and featured in the film), the ad opens with traffic flowing into the festival site and a local's voice bemoaning, "Here come those darn hippies again." The balance of the ad lavished ironic humor on the reunion of aging and once drug-using boomers—one woman says, "Is that you, Pigpen?" and they embrace; Woodstock performer John Sebastian asks Country Joe MacDonald if he remembers when "we did this before," and MacDonald, looking around in obvious befuddlement, replies, "No." A second theme set up for ridicule is that of now-affluent boomer sellouts. One reunion attender is on his cell phone ordering marble appliances for his bathroom, while another looks over the adjacent farmland and bemoans the fact that no one thought of building "condos" on it. A group of pre-teens who gather at a fence overlooking the festivities sees the well-dressed horde in attendance and shakes their heads in amazement, uttering the hope that the overweight dancers won't "go skinny-dipping." Obviously, these youngsters have been exposed to the media-hyped mythical event, since one of them proudly announces to his friends that "this is the anniversary of a historic event," but when a friend asks which one, he declares, "Watergate." Even the ill-informed young (and presumably the media culture that helps to keep them that way) are fair game for satirical ridicule. No one and no principle is invulnerable to the searing irony of the camera lens and advertiser's copy. In the end, viewers are invited to "stay young"—and presumably more hip than anyone in the ad—by enjoying a Pepsi.

The Woodstock icon continues to sustain its hold on the commercial imagination. Subsequent Woodstock revivals occurred in 1999 and 2004. A 2006 music festival in Hertfordshire, England, was pitched as "Hedgestock," a cultural gathering for "hedge fund" holders with all the predictable accoutrements.[30] That same year, a firm called Signatures Network secured licensing rights to the "most recognized and important name in pop culture and social history: WOODSTOCK" and proclaimed, "In keeping with the true spirit of the Sixties and its mantra of Peace, Love, and Harmony, Signatures Network will develop a Woodstock Lifestyle Brand that will embrace the Sixties spirit and energy," including fashion, accessories, and home décor among other commodities—but, obviously, excluding sixties politics.[31] And, of course, in 2009, a round of fortieth anniversary concerts and celebrations received wide media play.

Television's "Sixties"

The culture of the Sixties, then, gave way to our culture of TV: a great change that—literally—made no difference, for it meant that prior differences were now dissolved within TV's new and improved universe. . . . [The] culture of TV . . . represents . . . the fulfillment of an old managerial ideal: to exact universal assent, not through outright force, but by creating an environment that would make dissent impossible. [Emphasis in original]
    —Mark Crispin Miller, "The Hipness unto Death," 1989

Paralleling Thomas Frank's argument about advertising, Mark Crispin Miller has argued that "criticism" has become the "culture of TV," thereby co-opting viewers' "smirking disbelief" through its own "spirit of mockery." Noting that "TV's basic purpose is to keep you watching," Miller argues,

> What the spectacle reveals, then, are not only the commercial forces that demand our continual consumption, but these largely unacknowledged facts of American life: the degradation of experience by technology; the demise of public culture in all its forms; and the warlike relations between men and women, between blacks and whites, and the complicated, hidden animosity between the upper stratum and the spreading underclass—tensions that TV reveals even as it both sentimentalizes and exacerbates them.[32]

Like advertising, television programming has continued to use 1960s themes while simultaneously playing to the conventional tastes of its contemporary audiences. Thus, for example, *The Cosby Show* debuted in 1984 during the Reagan years. Reflecting the show's original intent, the highly successful career couple of Dr. Cliff Huxtable (Bill Cosby) and attorney Clair Huxtable (Phylicia Rashad) and their five children became the vehicle for counteracting mass media's denigrating images of African Americans, at the same time reassuring white America that upper-middle-class African Americans could deal effectively with all the family dilemmas many white Americans faced—with the occasional issue of racism encountered by their children resolved with the help of Cosby's self-deprecating wit. Yet, like any other sitcom, the show reflected its historical epoch: Cliff and Clair would occasionally tell their children stories from the good-old nostalgia-tinged civil rights days, within their sumptuously comfortable home. More subtly, as Mark Crispin Miller has argued,

> Cliff always wins; but this modern Dad subverts his kids . . . by seeming to subvert himself at the same time. His is the executive style, in other words, not of the small businessman as evoked in the fifties, but of the corporate manager, skilled at keeping his subordinates in line while half-concealing his authority through various disarming moves: Cliff rules the roost

through teasing put-downs, clever mockery, and amiable shows of helpless bafflement.[33]

As Miller notes, *The Cosby Show* eased white audiences' worries about the threatening black underclass. By the 1980s, "American whites need such reassurance because they are now further removed than ever, both spatially and psychologically, from the masses of the black poor," and on *The Cosby Show,* "it appears as if blacks in general can have, or do have, what many whites enjoy, and that such material equality need not entail a single break-in. And there are no hard feelings."[34] Despite its ideological compatibility with its day, the very unreality of the Huxtables' existence for most African Americans, in turn, spawned a continuing sequence of black and working-class family sitcoms, each outdoing the previous ones in edging toward "reality."[35]

Nostalgia for the good-old sixties, in turn, spread to other family sitcoms, like *Family Ties,* in which generational conflict themes from the past were turned on their head. This time, the hip, liberal Keaton parents repeatedly clash with their sharp-talking, market-embracing Reaganite son, Alex, played by Michael J. Fox. As was the case with *All in the Family,* the show provided ideological balance in which viewers could laugh at whichever character was the greater butt of the joke in their own ideological frame. The parents' liberal values and nostalgic sixties' reminiscences contrasted with Alex's self-serving pragmatism; yet, as Daniel Marcus has noted, "as impetuous and immature as Alex is, he seemingly has time and determination on his side in his battle against the mild Sixties homilies of his parents. Perhaps that is why Ronald Reagan claimed it as his favorite show on television."[36]

Another clever twist on the controversial late 1960s–early 1970s was *The Wonder Years* (1988–1993), in which the adult narrator revisits scenes from his sixties-era childhood. Episodes revolved around issues of awakening teenage sexuality and romance, friendship and personal values, within a suburban family household—filtered through the narrator's voice of adult maturity. Through these stories, the show accomplished two things: the prevailing image of a time conventionally represented as the "bad sixties" was softened and humanized through the show's preoccupation with more universal themes of growing up, and the narrator's role, in turn, imbued the show with the voice of mature adulthood, able to see foibles of the past yet evoking nostalgia for the promise of innocence that can never return. And, as Jerry Herron has argued, in a show that played freely on sixties-era popular culture and advertising, *The Wonder Years* "invokes history as a problem, and potential source of nostalgic longing, and then proceeds to solve it by translating the past into consumerist information. . . . The adult viewer is invited to consume, as entertainment, his informationally summoned inner childhood."[37]

Like much of the rest of American culture, *The Wonder Years* was itself the target of satire on another show that elevated the oppositional themes of the 1960s to an animated art form, *The Simpsons* (1989–). In fact, as Herron suggests, *The Simpsons* nicely fit the insurgent Fox network's effort to take on established network fare, for Bart Simpson's confrontational politics are "purely oppositional." Along with its animation format, the Simpson's satirical edge allowed Fox to move the show in its second year to Thursday night opposite the hugely popular *Cosby Show,* thus not only accelerating the latter's decline but "humiliating" the very "history on which the presumptive authority" of not only Cosby but any human actor is based. "It's as if these Cosby-like renditions of family values" encountered by members of the Simpson family "were imported into the space of the cartoon in order to be humiliated out of their presumptive, if mawkish, power; in order to be defeated, that is to say, by a more relevant economy of watching."[38]

Reflecting what Herron has called the "rewriting of the nostalgias" necessary to sustain consumer culture, diverse nostalgic themes continue to recur throughout the consumer culture. More recent examples of sixties-linked television shows include *Dharma & Greg* (1997–2002) and *American Dreams* (2002–2005). *Dharma & Greg* revolved around the marriage between Dharma, the free-spirited daughter of hippie parents (one a self-described "revolutionary"), and Greg, the conservative attorney who is the son of uptight, blue-blood parents. Most of the show's dramas rested on the complementarity of the couple's personalities, as well as their often conflictual interaction with the two sets of parents. Yet sixties stereotypes kept emerging, to be dealt with in classic revisionist fashion. Dharma, for example, urges Greg to "find his bliss" in one show, so he quits his lucrative job. Yet Dharma, it turns out, is the one who cannot live without the material comforts she has grown accustomed to, thanks to Greg's money. *American Dreams,* set in the early to mid-1960s, relived sixties events from *American Bandstand* to the 1964 Philadelphia riots to Vietnam within a framework that focused on the struggles of young Americans growing up. Declining audiences killed the show after three seasons.

Hollywood's "Sixties"

Movies are better than real life. If you go to enough movies, movies become real life, and real life becomes a movie.
    —Jules Feiffer, 1969

While film is a medium with its own structures—the capacity for in-depth character or plot development, for example—and great potential for powerful emotive experience, films designed for the popular entertainment market invariably reflect the kinds of imperatives that shape other mass media. The wider the market they seek, the more sensitive they must be to conventional and dominant market tastes. As Michael Ryan and Douglas Kellner have observed, movies "promote ideology by linking the effect of reality to social values and institutions in such a way that they come to seem natural or self-evident attributes of an unchanging world," and their "conventions habituate the audience to accept the basic premises of the social order."[39] Though entertainment films that represent historical events invariably distort history, they are capable of contributing significantly to an era's public memory of the past.

Within the framework of mass commercial imperatives, filmic representations of the sixties era, or events within that era, can be described as liberal (friendly toward sixties movements, critical of war, racism, etc.) or conservative (unfriendly toward the sixties, restoring pride in American soldiers, etc.) or, often, readable in both liberal and conservative ways. It is impossible in this space to do justice to the vast array of popular films that in one way or another touch on the sixties and sixties movements or themes, but a sampling suggests the contributions film has made to public memory of the sixties.

Friendly-to-the-sixties films might place an activist past in a favorable light by depicting a former sixties activist playing a socially constructive or reformist role—such as The Big Fix (1978)—or otherwise adapting to pragmatic life challenges in their respective post-sixties eras. In Running on Empty (1988), Hollywood revisited the world of militant revolutionaries Annie and Arthur Pope, who were forced underground in the aftermath of blowing up a napalm laboratory and (in an echo of the Wisconsin bombing of 1970) accidentally maiming a janitor who happened to be in the building. The film revolves around the couple's relationship with their teenage son, who in the course of developing his musical talent falls in love with his piano teacher's daughter, and thus feels the need to break away from his family's nomadic underground lifestyle to live his own life. Amidst the intergenerational tensions, the parents come to realize they must let their son go, ultimately risking their cover to provide for him. The film ends after Arthur realizes he is becoming the kind of authoritarian father that he once rebelled against—echoing the backlash theme that New Left anger was basically a form of rebellion against authoritarian father figures—and the parents drive away in search of their new identity on the run.

John Sayles's small-market film The Return of the Secaucus Seven (1980) focused on the spontaneous reunion of a group who had been arrested together en route to a sixties antiwar demonstration. While the protagonists share reminiscences, their sexual liaisons create tensions among them. Their still-idealistic politics are nuanced—one member of the group works hard to convince the others that her partner is okay, despite his belief in the political system—and their career paths (ranging from social services to arts to unsure) are authentic reflections of where young sixties activists might find themselves at the end of the seventies.

The impact of mass-market influences in the revisionist 1980s can be seen by comparing *Secaucus* to the substantially more popular film *The Big Chill* (1983), also about a reunion of former sixties activists. While *The Big Chill* can be read as "friendly" to the sixties in its characters' heavy dose of acted-out nostalgia for their youthful past (as well as in its score of classic sixties hits), the film became the consummate vehicle for popular culture's reframing of the sixties to fit the prevailing ideology of the Reagan era. *The Big Chill*'s reunion is one of affluent, middle-aged ex-sixties rebels—Yuppies in the jargon of the day—for the funeral of their friend Alex. While the reunion plays on nostalgia for good times long past among the wide boomer audience, flavored perhaps with a hint of guilt for "selling their soul," as the later Volkswagen ad put it, it casts them as little more than self-absorbed narcissists, thereby affirming the popular characterizations emanating from sixties critics. Throughout, the film tries to maintain a delicate balance between competing visions of the sixties.

Although the actual 1960s are invisible in the film, they are omnipresent in the group's nostalgic memories: "I was at my best," one declares, while another laments that there's "no good music anymore." In contrast to the affluent funeral attenders, Alex, who committed suicide, becomes an invisible stand-in for the invisible past, the "only one of us to stay true to the sixties." One member of the group wonders, "Where did Alex's hope go?" Another's remark suggests that the idealism of the past was self-defeating: "Something about Alex was too good for this world." One of Alex's "favorite songs"—appropriately, the Rolling Stones' "You Can't Always Get What You Want"—is featured prominently in the film's score.

Meanwhile, except for those viewers moved by the film's nostalgic pitch, there is little to recommend the aging boomers to mass audiences. Their 1980s yuppie affluence—from elegant funeral attire to luxury cars—pervades the film from the very beginning. Their reunion weekend consisted of acting out stereotypical sixties tropes—"sex, drugs, and rock & roll"—by consummating long-buried lust for each other, smoking dope, and dancing to popular sixties hits while cleaning up their communal meals. They discuss their investments, the "scum" who are their legal clients, complain that "I no longer know how to handle myself stoned," and end up gathering to watch a videotape they filmed of themselves over the course of their reunion—an ultimate act of narcissistic self-absorption.

Echoing Ronald Reagan extolling the virtue of acquisitive self-interest, the film tries to negotiate the emotions of baby boomers made uncomfortable by their alleged sellout in the 1980s Gilded Age. One man remarks to his friend, "Who'd have thought we'd ever make so much bread, two revolutionaries like us. It's a good thing it's not important to us." These ex-activists attribute their loss of hope to the inevitable aging process, demanding children and stagnant relationships, and the pressures of high-powered careers—not, as might be the case in the real world of sixties activists, to the battering they took from the incessant war in Vietnam, recurring echoes of the Vietnam intervention in Central America, or the political mainstream's sharp turn to the right. *The Big Chill* avoids all these potentially divisive themes. As the one outsider present at the reunion declares, "No one ever said [life] was going to be fun." For those mature enough to acknowledge this wisdom, the film seems to declare, the sixties are, fortunately, long over.

Big Chill themes were so pervasive in 1980s media culture that the news media later referred to baby boomers as the "Big Chill generation."[40] Five years after *The Big Chill,* the film *1969* sentimentalized the late sixties as a series of icons and vignettes—hippie attire, frequent drug use, student demonstrations, the sexual revolution, and music from Canned Heat and Credence Clearwater Revival—and a story that largely reduces conflict over the Vietnam War to a father-son dispute. When two pals hitchhike home from college, they encounter a series of domestic tensions, most notably perhaps the clash between Scott (Kiefer Sutherland) and his stern military father (Bruce Dern), a conflict brought to a head by Scott's older brother, a Marine, being shipped to Vietnam. After spending the summer living out a countercultural fantasy, Scott returns home to find that his brother has been killed. The death becomes a metaphor for social healing, as it brings father and son together. The whole town turns out for a surreal antiwar march in which it appears many do not understand why they're participating. According to reviewer Lynn Darling, the film was "a sanitized, romantic version of the '60s that should play well to dreamy 16-year-olds in tie-dyed T-shirts, but will come as a nasty shock to anyone who happens to have made it through the era itself."[41]

Revisionism seems to have been popular in 1988. Another film, *Mississippi Burning,* told the powerful story of the murders of three Mississippi Freedom Summer volunteers. Yet it did so with a hegemony-reinforcing twist: instead of a movement galvanized by courageous African Americans standing up to the worst racism in America, Hollywood's version sets two FBI investigators as the force for good against stereotypical racist rednecks. Blacks are reduced to roles of passive victims and prayerful spectators, ultimately thankful for the intercession by their white federal saviors. The film reinforced what was rapidly becoming the narrowed, hegemonic story of the civil rights struggle in the mainstream media culture: that racist rednecks in the South oppressed southern blacks, but, when the national government and the American people realized this was the case, they repaired the southern system, thereby affirming the noble American experiment in democracy.[42]

With the media culture full of distortions and clichéd stereotypes from the 1960s, some directors used the film media to try to correct the record in public memory. Spike Lee's *Malcolm X* (1992) sought to tell Malcolm's story in his own words, drawing on the black leader's famous autobiography. Yet, as H. Gray has noted, the mass-market film contained a tension between the "constant quest for legitimacy and the need to quell and displace fears at the same time that it calls them forth."[43] Lee's Malcolm (Denzel Washington) succeeded in humanizing stereotypical images of him as a racist, but it simultaneously helped to feed the commodification of sixties celebrities. "Malcolm-mania" took off in the form of the black leader's image or the simple "X" on sweatshirts, baseball caps, jackets, refrigerator magnets, and the like. Purchasers could symbolically express their alienation from the mainstream culture by wearing Malcolm. A similar dynamic occurred with Mario Van Peebles's *Panther* (1995; see chapter 8). Though the film left audiences with the reminder that blacks in the 1990s were using guns against each other instead of the Man, *Panther* audiences were left with no recourse other than to imitate the Panther performative style, which, indeed, was precisely what a group calling themselves the "New Black Panthers" did, though with a substantially different, black nationalist consciousness.[44]

By 1994, with the Clinton administration in office and the Republicans touting their ultraconservative "Contract with America," *Forrest Gump* became one of the year's blockbuster hits. The poignant tale of the innocent and mentally challenged Gump is set against a montage of images and events that recreate America's story from the post–World War II years up to the present. Tom Hanks's Oscar-winning performance animates Gump's plucky innocence, his encounters with the many sixties-era forces that shattered Americans' innocence, his improbable physical skills, and his embrace of simple but timeless ethical principles — "family values" in the rhetoric of the time — that see him through his many trials. Director Robert Zemeckis selected familiar icons from the 1960s as a way of bringing a sense of realism to the Gump story.

Yet what are the images Forrest encounters? First, the film presents events of the "good sixties," using black-and-white documentary footage: the John F. Kennedy inaugural and the civil rights movement's desegregation campaigns in the South. With the aid of computer-assisted photography, a grainy black-and-white Gump can be seen in the crowd greeting President Kennedy and among those watching Governor George Wallace as he blocks desegregation at the University of Alabama. After an improbable football career at the university, Forrest is encouraged to enlist in the army and heads to Vietnam. From this point on, the filmic recreation of sixties events shifts — as media coverage of sixties movements shifted in mid-decade — into full-color dramatizations of the "bad sixties."

The only glimpse moviegoers have of the Vietnam War is an ambush Forrest's unit encounters while on patrol. With exploding napalm-like flames (used by the enemy) erupting all around them and gunfire blazing out of the jungle, Forrest uses his speed to carry his wounded commander Lieutenant Dan and his best friend Bubba to safety. Lieutenant Dan loses his legs from the blast, however, and Bubba dies in Forrest's arms. The war in Vietnam, in short, is reduced to one in which invisible Vietnamese inflict gruesome damage on young American men. The Vietnamese themselves and their bomb-shattered country are entirely invisible. Going beyond President Carter's revisionist pronouncement that the "destruction was mutual," the war is affirmed as something the Vietnamese did to Americans.

On his return, Forrest finds himself at an antiwar rally, where he bumps into his childhood love, Jenny, now attired in hippie garb. The scenes that follow are right out of a rightist attack on a sixties rogues gallery. Speaking to an antiwar rally, the uniformed Gump's words are conveniently inaudible as the sound system breaks down; the film thus avoids alienating a significant audience segment by declaring a position on the war. Jenny's boyfriend, cast as an SDS leader with no redeeming qualities, shouts clichéd antiwar slogans, calls Forrest a "baby killer," and slugs Jenny in the face, causing Forrest to lose his cool and attack him. Threatening Black Panther lookalikes spew epithets at America's white racism. And, finally, Jenny's role embodies a variety of blame-the-sixties mythologies circulating in popular media. Growing up with an abusive father, Jenny falls in with the folk crowd, begins to smoke dope, performs naked in a folk club, is featured in *Playboy*, gets strung out on hard drugs, and eventually dies of an AIDS-like disease.

Perhaps reflecting the film's corroboration of pervasive media culture assumptions about the past, actor Tom Hanks maintained that the film was "nonpolitical and thus non-judgmental."[45] CNN's *Crossfire* devoted an evening to whether the film was biased in a left- or right-wing direction. In a review titled (what else?) "Generation Gump," the *Economist* termed the film the "ultimate exercise in boomer nostalgia" for a generation "still fixated as ever on the traumas and dramas of the 1960s," as if these were represented in the film.[46]

The Vietnam War has been a potent subject for scores of films that can be read as "liberal" (portraying the war in a critical or dark light) or "conservative" (resurrecting potent mythical realities of the war and American foreign policy) — or, in most cases, a mixture of both. For the most part, however, the non-documentary films are stories of soldiers' lives in and after warfare. Almost without exception (*Born on the 4th of July* might qualify as one), the films depoliticize the war, removing entirely any critical consideration of the United States' responsibility for the war and personalizing the war's dark side (e.g., killing civilians) through characters that either were simply cold-blooded (Sgt. Barnes in *Platoon*) or personally vengeful (Sgt. Meserve in *Casualties of War*).

The initial round of popular late 1970s Vietnam films — *Apocalypse Now, The Deer Hunter,* and *Coming Home* — began to bring controversial aspects of the war into the limelight. *Apocalypse Now* provided a metaphor for the war's madness as well as a setting for soldiers' heroism; *The Deer Hunter* focused on the burden borne by the working-class community that sent its sons to war; and *Coming Home* highlighted the damage borne by both a wounded vet and an unrepentant soldier who felt betrayed by his country. The latter two, of course, framed the war around its damaging effects on Americans.

The Deer Hunter, in particular, introduced revisionist imagery of the war into the story of the horrors experienced by three American soldiers. In the film's war, North Vietnamese troops improbably sweep through a village tossing grenades into villagers' hiding places, an explicit reversal of the common and controversial U.S.-South Vietnamese practice. The Viet Cong, portrayed as a gang of swarthy mobsters, imprison American soldiers in what appear to be tiger cages (almost entirely submerged in water), a reversal of a common practice the South Vietnamese government used for suspected dissenters. The American prisoners are forced to play Russian roulette for their captors' entertainment, providing the film with some of its tensest moments while reversing the imagery of the famous Eddie Adams photograph of the South Vietnamese official assassinating an NLF prisoner with a handgun to his head. In brief, actual war imagery that suggested the Americans and their clients were the bad guys was reversed to convey the opposite message: the Vietnamese adversaries were the bad guys.[47]

The soldiers-victimization theme took different directions in the popular films of the 1980s. Three notable films provided more graphic and accurate glimpses of aspects of the war: *Platoon's* night patrols in the jungle, *Hamburger Hill's* account of an actual though brutally pointless battle to uproot an entrenched enemy, and *Full Metal Jacket's* portrayal of the brutal dehumanization of Marine boot camp. While *Full Metal Jacket* exposes misogynist and racist/imperial dimensions of the war, along with the deterioration of American forces, it is essentially dark, offering no recognition that the war was being resisted at the time its action occurred. *Hamburger Hill* essentially blames antiwar youth and resisters for the soldiers' suffering. *Platoon* offers the war as inexplicable, with central character Chris concluding at the end, "We fought ourselves"—a theme made explicit in Lee Iacocca's commentary that introduced the VHS release. Iacocca called the film a "memorial to all the men and women who fought in a time and in a place *nobody really understood,*" yet "they were called and they went. That in the truest sense is the spirit of America."[48]

Reflecting the spread of right-wing revisionism, a second group of films—*Uncommon Valor* (1983), *Missing in Action* (1984), and *Rambo: First Blood Part II* (1985)—targeted for blame a government that allegedly abandoned American prisoners of war in Vietnam, providing frustrated viewers with fantasies of revenge. All were part of a broader effort to restore the dominant myths and narratives of American warfare—including, importantly, the remasculinization of the American soldier.[49] In critic Harry Haines's words, despite the existence of some accurate representation in the popular Vietnam War films, they crucially "dislocate the source of the veterans' shattered belief system."[50]

In many ways, the Vietnam films merged with wider, more explicitly ideological forces to reinforce postwar myths about Vietnam. As Jerry Lembcke has observed, Nixon administration attacks on the antiwar movement in 1969 sought to create a split between soldiers (many of whom were antiwar) and the movement (many of whom supported the soldiers and wanted them home). The urban legend of "spat-upon" soldiers greatly reinforced this schism. Lembcke's search for documentation of spitting incidents found only a few press reports of pro-war people spitting on *antiwar* veterans, though he noted there was "plenty of grist for mythmaking" in the general climate of division about the war and hostile comments made to returning veterans (noting that "most of the documentable hostility emanated from pro-war groups and individuals," including the Veterans of Foreign Wars and American Legion). On the other hand, films like *Coming Home* "created an American mind-set receptive to suggestions that veterans were actually spat upon."[51]

Though a legend like spat-upon soldiers cannot be disproven, what seems significant about it is, first, that it is an apt metaphor for the way many soldiers felt returning from the hell of Vietnam to a divided America, and, second, that the legend places the blame for hostility toward soldiers on the antiwar movement, which in its organized expressions was supportive of the soldiers. In the war's later years, individuals who acted out their own anger against returning soldiers by calling them "baby killers" were arguably engaged in visual association, unable or unwilling to think past the My Lai photographs that emerged in 1969. Years later, as the United States prepared for the Gulf War, "Support the troops" had become a conscious campaign aimed at "correcting" this mythical past—in the process, once again marginalizing expressions of antiwar opposition.

Similarly, as Bruce Franklin has carefully documented, the right-wing POW-recovery films help to perpetuate the myth that the American enemy continued to hold Americans prisoners of war—a myth, Franklin observes, that began with the Nixon administration's decision to combine POW and MIA categories and use the total number of unaccounted Americans as a rationale for continuing the war against North Vietnam. "Almost entirely absent from public consciousness was the truth," Franklin concluded: "the government of the United States had concocted the POW/MIA issue in the first place, had perpetuated it for decades, and since 1982 had actively collaborated in turning it into a national myth"[52]—one, it might be added, that continued to victimize the families of a few thousand unaccounted-for American soldiers, to say nothing of the vets who continue to focus their anger on this apparent government betrayal.

The real victims of this public discourse are the nation's inability to come to a full reckoning with the moral lessons of the war, and the veterans—already victimized by government propaganda and lies—who are denied a full comprehension of what happened and why it happened, and perhaps an accurate target for their very legitimate anger. As Bruce Franklin put it, "When we recognize and confront all that we—and the peoples of Indochina—have truly lost and that will remain forever missing in Vietnam, Laos, and Cambodia, perhaps we can at least recover some of our lost moral and psychological health."[53] Whereas that suggests the appropriateness of a Truth and Reconciliation process, as Michael

Klein has put it, "Films like *Platoon* or *Rambo II* or *The Deer Hunter* cannot heal the American psyche, cannot reconcile lingering divisions in the American people about U. S. involvement in the war in Vietnam. . . . They do little to enhance our consciousness of history or to clarify our understanding of the political, economic, and ideological factors that sustained the war or that brought the war to an end."[54]

News Media and Public Memory

Time *makes time disappear. Everything is the same. There is no history. . . .*
The essence of Time *is that it destroys the present, the past, and the future.*
  —Murray Bookchin, 1982

Theoretically, national news media reporting could correct the myths and images of a commodified sixties permeating entertainment and consumer media. However, since these media are themselves commercially driven enterprises, it should be no surprise that they, too, have repeatedly replayed the themes of generational rebellion, individual freedom, and inexplicable anarchism at the same time that they have provided a compliant vehicle for the denunciatory attacks of the anti-sixties backlash. Since the 1960s, the news media have repeatedly revisited iconic sixties personalities and events—from the March on Washington to Woodstock—on notable anniversaries, providing postmodern snapshots commonly framed around an aging generation and the hegemonic politics of the time of publication. As one study of the news media's construction of "collective memory" has noted, the "negotiation of collective memories" of key sixties events like the Watts riot of 1965 and the Chicago convention of 1968 was "still on-going in the early and middle 1980s,"[55] and it continues still. As was evident in the 2008 presidential campaign, the media still ask if the sixties are really over.

Mass media debate about the meaning of this past has been dominated by two perspectives: an ascendant Right attacking the alleged failures of Great Society liberalism and the overly indulged excesses of youth versus a tepid liberal response defending selective domestic programs, lamenting a foreign policy misadventure, and hearkening back to a simplified, iconic version of the civil rights struggle in which all of America (outside of a few rednecks) woke up to and corrected the wrong of southern apartheid. As the ascendant Right flooded the media with distorted claims, misinformation, and outright fabrication about past government policy "failures," the antiwar movement, the aftermath of the Vietnam War, and new overseas interventions, the only legitimate alternative lay within the centrist parameters of the market economy.

Dominated by the likes of a few 1960s celebrity-radicals whose politics shifted with the winds of change (notably Jerry Rubin, Eldridge Cleaver, and

David Horowitz), the mass media frame of generational change has obscured the reality that is well documented by a host of sociological studies: most activists from the 1960s have retained their political values and commitments even as they moved through changes commonly associated with aging and family and career responsibilities.[56] Idealized civil rights events and iconic personalities like Rosa Parks and Martin Luther King Jr. are viewed through the rose-colored mists of time, while the specter of Vietnam continues to defy puzzled media imaginations, though not, apparently, the majority of the American people. Protest against subsequent U.S. interventions has invariably drawn comparisons to the typically pejorative imagery of anti–Vietnam War protest. "Bra-burning" feminists, "racist" black militants, and "spitting" or flag-burning antiwar activists are also common tropes.

Throughout the media snapshots, the system-supportive framing of media stories during the sixties has both been sustained and pushed to the right by the longstanding campaign of Rightist propaganda. One of the most common focal points for sixties retrospection has been the highly colorful, once-threatening, but now safely co-opted counterculture. A 1980 *Washington Post* feature article, "How the Sixties Ended [that theme again] with a Federal Grant," focused on the New Buffalo commune in New Mexico. The commune's members experienced various transitions, from early years of hard work, unstructured communal living, and, of course, drugs and the exchange of sexual partners, through lean years when the women abandoned the commune because "the men were so hopeless," to a current cooperative effort at solar-powered dairy farming, the latter funded by a federal Appropriate Technology grant. The article concluded, "Thus ended the '60s. Not with a bang or a whimper but with a federal grant."[57]

A March 1987 *Newsweek* article featured a retrospective on the "Graying of Aquarius," focusing on some quaint remnants from the past—individuals who "cling to the values—and they're still called hippies." While the individuals portrayed were demonstrably trying to live lives committed to simplicity and self-reliance (while also participating in political campaigns around topical issues like abortion rights, apartheid, and nuclear power), *Newsweek* portrayed them as seemingly stuck in a frame from the past, noting that "the smell of incense still wafts down from Earth People's Park," where "on a quiet night you can still hear the White Album being played." Noting that some received welfare while others lived in "plant-laden Victorian houses in Cambridge or Boulder with $500 bikes in the halls and $200 cars in the driveway," the magazine observed that "not all hippies have made a successful adjustment to the 1980s," singling out one couple who lived in a one-room cabin without running water or electricity.

In *Newsweek's* simplistic, discourse-reinforcing generalization, however, all were "hippies, survivors of that once vast band of romantics who imagined that the mighty river of American civilization could somehow be turned from its course by sex, drugs, and rock and roll"—dreams that were, the magazine noted, "launched with industrial-strength hallucinogens." Reflecting on these curious survivors, *Newsweek* concluded its article with a classically vacuous imagistic snapshot: "Someday no one will believe there was a time when young men and women tried to stop a war with music and bring down a president with flowers; or that they could have sex with dozens of strangers and run the risk of nothing more serious than body lice." Seemingly unwilling to alienate potential readers by traveling too close or too far from the hippie phenomenon, the magazine boldly concluded, "It is time to move on, but not yet time to forget."[58] Twenty years later, a LexisNexis search of major publications and TV and radio broadcasts uncovered 991 articles on the ever-magnetic "Summer of Love." In the 2008 presidential campaign, a John McCain ad played McCain's record as a former POW against the same "Summer of Love" imagery.

Mass media accounts of retrospective sixties conferences or notable class reunions often reduced the gatherings to nostalgia-evoking events among aging boomers, often in sharp contrast with the experiences of reunion participants themselves. Yet, as Mark Rudd wrote of the reunion of Columbia's class of 1968 (noteworthy for the spring 1968 seizure of campus buildings), "What we were feeling was the opposite of nostalgia. . . . We introduced ourselves to each other and found that all the people present had gone on, in a dazzling variety of ways, to create lives that more than fulfilled the promise of what we started in those buildings."[59]

In 1988, both *Time* and *Newsweek* seized upon the pivotal year of 1968 to reflect back on the turbulent past. *Newsweek* titled its cover article, "Will We Ever Get Over the 60s?" One article on "Decade Shock" spun off the controversy over vice presidential candidate Dan Quayle's war avoidance in the National Guard and the withdrawal of Supreme Court nominee Douglas Ginsburg after he admitted to smoking pot and asked, "Will the baby-boom generation ever come to grips with the '60s?" A longer personal essay by *Newsweek* writer Tom Mathews incorporated a number of insightful personal reflections in an overview of "the Sixties complex" that gave ample play to iconic themes of assassinations, good civil rights, drugs, draft avoidance, the campus "revolution," and sex.[60]

Time headlined its cover story "1968: Like a Knife Blade, the Year Severed Past from Future." The writing in *Time*'s nine-page feature article calls to mind the imagistic "things-happened" presentation of the Frye boots ad, as well as Murray Bookchin's remark about *Time* making time disappear. *Time* chose 1811 as a metaphor for 1968, a year in which, the magazine reported, natural upheavals occurred inexplicably only to subside as things returned to normal. The big stories of 1968 were represented by iconic imagery: Eddie Adams's photograph of the South Vietnamese police chief shooting the NLF suspect in the head, a beleaguered President Johnson at his desk, a Columbia student audaciously smoking President Grayson Kirk's cigar during the students' building occupation, angry youths at the Chicago convention fronted by a young man giving the police the finger, the assassinated King and Kennedy, the black power salute of U.S. Olympians Tommie Smith and John Carlos, Soviet tanks facing down Czech protesters, a rally of flag-waving French students, the seduction scene from *The Graduate*, a triumphant Richard Nixon waving from the Miami convention platform, a starving child in Biafra, and, finally, the "earth-rise" photo taken from Apollo 8 behind the moon.[61]

A collage of sixties imagery can evoke wide-ranging meanings in the memories of readers of a certain age. Yet by themselves they explain nothing, in effect cutting off younger readers from any understanding of the sixties. In this vacuum, *Time* injected a text that framed events in the safely conventional terms popularized by right-wing and centrist revisionism: "Militarily, Tet was a defeat for the Communists. But once again in Viet Nam and in the American mind, *illusion triumphed over reality.* America, and much of the rest of the world, regarded Tet as shocking proof that the war was a disaster for the U.S., unwinnable"—an opinion, as opposed to illusion, about the war's reality that has continued to be shared by millions of Americans, including policy makers and military strategists. *Time* simply asserted that Tet was for the communists "an enormous victory. It turned American opinion decisively against the war," thereby ignoring ample evidence that Tet was less a conversion than a confirmation of antiwar opinion, already at 47 percent in late 1967 and continuing to rise in the months after Tet. Daniel Hallin argues that Tet was "less a turning point than a crossover point, a moment when trends that had been in motion for some time reached balance and began to tip the other way," and the crucial "tipping" occurred among elite policy makers and their audiences.[62] In retrospect, *Time* concluded, "Viet Nam taught America something about its fallibility," a lesson, the magazine suggested, the nation may have "overlearned."[63]

The rest of *Time*'s retrospective repeated a smattering of events and perspectives befitting *Time*'s postmodern pastiche and conventional framing. King's assassination was mentioned in conjunction with Black Panthers taking up guns and "shooting it out with police in Oakland"—when, in fact, after King's death, the Panthers were in the streets urging inner-city youth to remain calm. Student uprisings at Columbia, in Paris, and elsewhere erupted out of nowhere, their origins invisible, though "psychologically coordinated" in the "nervous system of a global generation," in the magazine's glib phrasing—no suggestion of the conditions or even the media images that played a role in the spreading revolt. In the end, the account of Apollo 8 reassured readers that America was returning to normal by the end of the tumultuous year.

Like the war in Vietnam, the urban insurrections of the sixties were revisited when an anniversary or current event made them salient. Yet these relatively rare occasions were largely an opportunity to reframe the discussion of "inner-city problems" to fit the dominant ideology of the time—a dialogue between the ascendant Right's interpretation and a contemporary recollection of Great

Society approaches. The massive riot that occurred in Los Angeles in 1992 in the wake of a jury's acquittal of the policemen accused of the widely observed (via a personal videotape) beating of a black man named Rodney King provided a unique opportunity to revisit the urban upheavals and discourse of the sixties. Like its earlier predecessors, the '92 riot that swept through South Central Los Angeles provided vivid footage of violence, looting, and destruction that shocked a public largely ignorant of the conditions of inner-city life.

The obvious visual similarity to past insurrections, however, prompted media retrospectives on the failures of American urban policy, asking why the riot occurred after more than twenty-five years of public policies allegedly designed to deal with the urban concentrations of poverty. Mainstream media explanations revolved around a debate between the Reagan-Bush approaches to urban poverty and those of the Johnson administration's Great Society.[64] Bush administration officials attributed the riot to the failures of Great Society liberalism and the "dependency" fostered by government "handouts." Liberal defenders of the Johnson policies fingered the years of Republican "benign neglect" of racial minorities, particularly the inner-city poor. Each offered its own meaning for "empowering" the poor, liberals through programs to provide job training for the unemployed, to counter drug dependency, and to improve deteriorating schools; conservatives by cutting off the dependency on government programs and instead encouraging job creation through "enterprise zones."

Entirely missing in this debate was any reference to the form of participatory empowerment that was once embedded in the early Community Action Program of the 1960s, to say nothing of the way the rising hopes for empowerment fostered by the program encountered both institutional resistance and police brutality, thereby igniting violent rioting and political backlash—a history that could have shed light on the problems still faced by residents of Los Angeles and other urban centers. A LexisNexis search covering the four months following the '92 riot revealed only a single column—an editorial in the *St. Petersburg Times*—that mentioned CAP in the course of discussing the Los Angeles riot. The column, "Placing Blame for the L.A. Riots Is Not So Simple," noted that "such *misbegotten measures* as the Community Action Program" were what "fell aside, after the innovations of the 1960s." The author noted that CAP's idea of "maximum feasible participation" was "appealing in principle" but "led to angry clashes between Community Action officials and local elected officials"—which was apparently sufficient to dismiss efforts at collective self-empowerment on the part of the poor as "misbegotten."[65] Gone from public memory was the possibility of giving thoughtful consideration to a more radically democratic alternative to liberal and conservative public policies that had obviously failed to resolve the tensions and hopelessness of inner-city life. Political discourse was correspondingly diminished.

Baby Boomers Forever

As the years have passed, the media culture's collective memory of the 1960s has been reduced to a single dominant frame: a media-indulged generation has been repeatedly translated into a persistently self-indulgent generation continually facing "new challenges" associated with the life cycle. Indeed, the most common way the sixties have been commodified in the mass media culture is through their being equated with—in effect, owned by—the populous baby boom generation. This commodification has several effects.

First, it distances the sixties from the millions of Americans born too late to have any real personal memory of the sixties era. If baby boomers own the sixties, only they can really understand the meaning of all those images, songs, celebrity faces, and the like. Cut off from those meanings, younger audiences become "outsiders" to these media "Sixties," similar to the way that conservative youth in the 1960s were "outsiders" to the youths who dominated media images of the time.

Second, the commercially driven, generational fixation continues. Baby boomers continue to be defined en masse as an exploitable market as these once-rebellious youngsters encounter the pressures of families and careers, struggles with health and financial issues related to aging, their allegedly damaging impact on Social Security funds, and, more recently, the "new" challenge of retirement and entering old age in "new" ways. In 2001, *USA Today* reported that baby boomers were "redefining" aging, declaring as fact, "Baby-boomers, who once turned in their antiwar signs for Lexuses and 3,500-square-foot homes, are leaving behind 'me generation' attitudes. Instead they're searching for balance, lasting relationships, and spiritual values, sociologists say." A quote from one such specialist is, perhaps, more revealing than intended: "Boomers 'will have more effect on the *image* of aging than any generation in history,' says David Wolfe, author and consumer-behavior specialist in Reston, Va."[66] Similarly, in an article subtitled "A Generation Begins to Redefine 'Golden Years' and Retirement Housing on Its Own Terms," a partner in the Yankelovich consulting firm gushed, "Boomers are busting out all over. Boomers are not redefining aging. They are redefining youth."[67]

A third effect of this media bombardment is that the baby boomer market continues to be indulged, or affectively empowered, by the media. A May 19, 1986, *Time* cover read, "Baby Boomers Turn 40," and, inside, the magazine proclaimed, "The Baby Boomers were the Spock generation, the Now generation, the Me generation." In classic marketspeak, the magazine went on to observe, "Nor were they exactly shy about all the attention. Through high times and hard times, no other group of Americans has ever been quite so noisily self-conscious."[68] Nineteen years later, a November 28, 2005, issue of *Newsweek* featured a lengthy cover article, "Ready or Not: Boomers Turn 60," complete with a colorful collage of famous baby boomer faces. In addition to all the standard newsmagazine departments, the magazine's online site contained a feature area called "Boomer Files." As is the case with advertising, the generational stories in the newsmagazines have generally been nostalgic, playing on appeals to happier, younger days.[69] Furthermore, the media commonly refer to baby boomers being in power, and thus—in classic visual think—generationally responsible for all kinds of contemporary social woes. As a *Time* article on "Generation X" put it in 1990: "The boomer group is so huge that it tends to define every era it passes through, *forcing society* to accommodate its moods and dimensions."[70] According to the market dialectic, boomers were empowered.

And yet, the bombardment is such that outsiders are made to feel disempowered by their exclusion from it (thus the right-wing attacks against the Clinton White House complained about the "baby boom generation" being in charge).[71] It is hardly surprising that many younger Americans correspondingly resent the media boomer fixation. In 1995, *USA Today* published a lengthy article about "The GenX Philosophy"—a classic media effort to "understand" a new generation of youth. The article led with the assertion that "Generation X has had enough of baby boom politics," which meant, the article went on to explain, in a wildly creative construction that echoed right-wing attacks: "As disillusioned twentysomethings see it, Democrats have buried them under $5 trillion of debt to support social programs that failed"—not only a grossly inaccurate generalization but highly ironic in light of the budgetary surplus achieved during the Clinton years. One young woman was quoted claiming, "In the Sixties, [youth] asked the same government that had been oppressing them to solve all of their problems. This monstrous bureaucracy that we have today is their legacy; it's their Frankenstein."[72] A 2006 article in *Adweek,* "Having Bored You about the '60s, They'll Now Bore You about the 60s," led with: "Sick of hearing about baby boomers? Be patient, they'll die off soon enough."[73] In its pitch to younger generations, the *Adweek* article is a kind of commercial variant on Andrew Sullivan's political complaint about the "debilitating, self-perpetuating family quarrel of the Baby Boom generation that has long engulfed all of us."[74]

Discourse that reflects on the 1960s through the generational frame is ultimately self-referential and narcissistic, and therefore politically impotent and irrelevant. Add in the clash between conservative attacks on sixties sensibilities and the media's continuing spiral into edgier, more in-your-face come-ons, and it becomes possible to see this public discourse as the ultimate victory of a self-satirical consumer culture incessantly distracting and co-opting impulses that might rise up against it. At least for now, it represents the victory of consumer capitalism.

12

Cultural Politics and Warlike Discourse

Frustrated that their political power has not translated into cultural hegemony, conservatives are methodically attacking cultural institutions— particularly the universities and the arts—ostensibly for being subverted by radicals, but actually for their persistent liberalism, especially that mushy pluralistic habit of allowing cultural dissidents on the premises.
   —Ellen Willis, *No More Nice Girls,* 1992

Three decades down the road from the sixties, the nation's political discourse may be driven by conservatives, but they, although by many measures triumphant, seem aggrieved because politics seems peripheral to, and largely impotent against, the cultural forces and institutions permeated with what conservatives consider the sixties sensibilities.
   —George Will, foreword, *Reassessing the Sixties,* 1997

By the end of the Reagan-Bush years, the Right had solidified its place in American politics and neoliberalism had come to define the parameters of political debate. Despite the political dominance of conservative and corporate agendas, as George Will suggested, conservatives continued to be provoked by the degree to which the nation's discourse seemed dominated by a liberal and narcissistic public culture. Two aspects of that culture, often linked in political attacks, have been particularly galling to the Right. One is the perception that much of commercial media—and, more broadly, public space—is saturated with evidence of incivility, immorality, indecency, irresponsibility, and/or self-indulgence. However subjectively these may be defined, there is ample evidence that these are valid and legitimate concerns, and not only for conservatives.

The other factor driving the Right's animus is that they have seen in all these phenomena echoes of the hated sixties. In fact, the Right invariably engages in some kind of spurious associational thinking to link virtually all social grievances, real or imagined, back to the sixties. One variant on this thinking simply borrows the mass media's generational frame to assert that the "sixties generation" is now (by virtue of age?) "in power" in whatever institutions the Right is targeting. Another variant is to generalize from anecdotal cases to assert that "sixties radicals" now dominate the nation's cultural institutions—unleashing, among other things, a scourge of "totalitarian political correctness," a curricular takeover by multiculturalism, and virtual administrative control by anti-male "gender feminists" on the nation's campuses. As Harvey Silverglate, an attorney who founded the Foundation for Individual Rights in Education (FIRE), asserted, "You had a generation that was talking about free speech all the time. And then when they got into positions of power, their first response was to restrict it."[1] Similarly, an incessant drumbeat of charges of "liberal media bias" coming from lavishly supported right-wing attacks has established the formidable public myth that the mass media are "liberal" when—with the telling exception of Fox News—they have been persistently and professionally centrist and neoliberal, always safely within the boundaries of legitimate discourse.[2]

Space does not allow a full analysis of these voluminous attacks, but they damage democratic discourse in three ways: they are often wildly exaggerated if not egregiously inaccurate; they feed a sense of victimization and polarization within the body politic; and they supplant a potentially open discussion of the nation's political, economic, and social policies with a distracting symbolic discourse.

First, the exaggerations suggest an agenda that seeks a return to the monoculture of the 1950s, a culture that simply assumed that its norms applied to all humans. In touting their objectivity, they reject the relevance of diverse subjectivity, in the process failing to give adequate consideration to their own subjectivity. A variant of these assumptions is the conservative argument that the post-sixties integration of women and racial minorities into mainstream political and occupational worlds and the rise of global neoliberalism after the fall of the Soviet bloc have ushered in a world that is post-feminist, post-Marxist—and even, in the aftermath of the Obama election, post-racial. Echoing the "end of ideology" argument of the late 1950s, they argue that we have arrived at the "end of history," as Francis Fukuyama put it.[3] The fundamental debates and divisions of yesterday are no longer relevant. Thus anyone still targeting racism or sexism must have a supremacist agenda of some kind, or any president suggesting the need for even modest social welfare programs must be a closet socialist.

Second, these cultural attacks emulate yet have vastly exceeded the very victim-speak rhetoric they complain about, in the process poisoning public discourse with their "warlike" charges. By capitalizing on feelings of victimization among people who are in various ways disempowered in today's political and economic world, they create a warlike mythic reality for their followers who become predisposed to ignore any argumentation from the "enemy." The attacks have succeeded in extending the enclave mentality that occurred within late-sixties social movements excluded from legitimate discourse to much of the media culture, making it increasingly difficult to have a democratic discourse in which different groups converse with each other to discover common ground and mutual interests. Through their emphasis on visual drama and dumbing down of political discourse, the mass media greatly assist this enclave tendency.

There certainly have been excesses of personal attack, "political correctness," "speech codes," and the like by the targeted groups on the nation's campuses and elsewhere in the culture, and, indeed, these do go all the way back into the sixties era. However, these targeted excesses, while at times transgressing the boundaries of civility or even common sense, have usually reflected justified anger at being delegitimized if not excluded from the mainstream culture, whereas attacks against "political correctness" and its ilk have been generated for the most part by those who are privileged in today's economic, political, and occupational hierarchies (even if their anger may be a valid response to excess or personal attack). Historical patterns of injustice and exclusion against women, African Americans, Latinos, Native Americans, and non-heterosexual Americans persist, even if media appearances and post-sixties gains among the middle classes make it seem otherwise. We have a long way to go before we achieve a democratic culture. The trick, as Cornel West put it, is to "preserve the possibility of universal connection."[4]

Finally, the heavily symbolic discourse of American politics that derives from the media culture and the history of these attacks diverts attention away from legitimate criticism of the nation's *material politics*—primarily its economy and the economy's consequences for environmental despoliation and ecological erosion, inequality, and the nation's wars. Indeed, these attacks attempt to strengthen the culture of capitalism at the expense of democracy. It is no accident that, during the 2008 election, public disenchantment with the long wars in Iraq and Afghanistan and the sharply deteriorating economy gave material politics greater salience than the usual politics of distraction.

The Attack on the University

In the 1980s, it seemed, at last, that the Sixties were over. They were not. It was a malignant decade that, after a fifteen year remission, returned in the 1980s to metastasize more devastatingly throughout our culture than it had in the Sixties, not with tumult but quietly, in the moral and political assumptions of those who now control and guide our major cultural institutions. The Sixties radicals are still with us, but now they do not paralyze the universities; they run the universities.
—Robert Bork, *Slouching towards Gomorrah*, 1996

The Right's attack on the university grew out of early alarms about the state of the nation's campuses during and after the late 1960s. Lewis Powell was not alone in expressing his concerns about the regard American students had for business. In 1971, Pepsico CEO Donald Kendall warned of the nation's "economic illiteracy" among the younger generation.[5] In 1975, James J. Kilpatrick wrote an article entitled "Why Students Are Hostile to Free Enterprise," in which he employed spurious association to make the highly misleading claim that a Gallup poll commissioned by Oklahoma Christian College demonstrated that the "typical college student . . . moves sharply to the left during his four years in higher education."[6] Kilpatrick also referenced a 1973 speech in which former Deputy Secretary of Defense David Packard urged the Committee for the Corporate Support of American Universities to be more selective in avoiding support for those "whose faculties regard free enterprise with contempt."[7] Similar concerns were raised about elementary and secondary education. An American Enterprise Institute report advocated a shift in priorities from promoting "educational equity" to promoting "economic growth for the nation" and preserving a "common culture by teaching students the basic values upon which American capitalism is based."[8]

Foundation funding supported the establishment of a variety of institutions that have attempted to reshape American colleges and universities. As Ellen Messer-Davidow has put it, "the Right has manufactured the attack on liberalized higher education by means of a right-wing apparatus dedicated to making radical cultural change."[9] The Madison Center for Educational Affairs generated early attacks on progressive elements on university campuses, largely through its sponsorship of conservative student newspapers on sixty-six campuses.[10] The Intercollegiate Studies Institute also provides support for conservative faculty, students, and programming and for what it calls "independent college journalism" on college campuses. It also provides $1,000 in prize money for "Campus Outrage" essays revealing alleged "excesses of politically correct students, faculty, or administrators in higher education."[11] The neoconservative Committee for the Free World founded the Coalition for Campus Democracy in 1982, an organization that by 1987 evolved into the National Association of Scholars, the key academic group leading the attack on "political correctness" and yet another entity seeking stories from alleged conservative victims of "left-academics."[12] Paul Weyrich, a co-founder of the Heritage Foundation in 1973 and the Moral Majority in 1979 and president of the Free Congress Foundation, joined with fellow conservatives to launch what they called "cultural conservatism" in the mid-1980s, aiming to "conserve traditional Western culture" against alleged threats in many quarters, including a greatly embellished specter of multiculturalism that sought to broaden the range of artistic and literary works in college curricula.[13]

In addition to the campaign to transform college campuses, the Right's cultural attack zeroed in on institutions like the National Endowment for the Humanities (NEH), the National Endowment for the Arts (NEA), and the Public Broadcasting System (PBS). During the Reagan years, William Bennett was appointed head of the NEH and subsequently issued a report entitled "To Reclaim a Legacy," which grew out of dissatisfaction with the inadequacy with which students were being educated about "the culture and civilization of which they are members" and linked an alleged "drift toward curricular disintegration" to a "collective loss of nerve and faith on the part of both faculty and academic administrators during the late 1960s and early 1970s."[14] After Bennett was appointed secretary of education in the Reagan administration, Lynne Cheney replaced him at NEH and produced a number of reports calling for the transformation of university humanities curricula while consistently nominating conservatives to the NEH National council. As Representative Chester Atkins (D-Mass.) noted, under Cheney there was "a slow process at the NEH of granting the far right ideological veto power," which violated the NEH's "history of being isolated from political considerations."[15]

One early book that drew on support from the conservative John M. Olin Foundation was Allan Bloom's 1987 best seller *The Closing of the American Mind,* a broadly philosophical lament about the state of higher education and the "impoverished souls of today's students." Bloom placed his critique in the context of the great political philosophers of the Western tradition that were his academic specialization. From this vantage, Bloom railed against youth culture and its "value" relativism, young peoples' "addiction" to rock music, and their trivialization of eros via sexual licentiousness.

While much of *The Closing of the American Mind* poses a critique of transformations that were occurring in American culture, particularly those manifest in the behavior of the young, it is clear that Bloom's animus is directed at the 1960s, particularly at the changes he witnessed in the universities from the mid-sixties on. In his own words, the "wandering and wayward energies" of students "finally found a political outlet" by this point in the decade, and the universities responded by granting them "every concession other than education." Bloom's animus was most intense in his denunciation of what he saw as faculty capitulation to the demands of Cornell's black students who, in their frustration, had taken over a university building in 1969, arming themselves with guns for their own "self-defense." As a Cornell faculty member, Bloom's outrage was understandable—as, for that matter, was the anger of the black students. Nonetheless, he moved from the case he witnessed to a sweeping dismissal of essentially all forces that challenged the detached academic world he loved. As he put it, "So far as universities are concerned, I know of nothing positive coming from that period [the sixties]; it was an unmitigated disaster for them," whereas "the fact is the fifties were one of the great periods of the American university."[16] The rest of the sixties social movements—notably the antiwar movement and feminism—fared equally badly in Bloom's account. In Bloom's view, "appeasement failed and soon the whole experiment in excellence was washed away, leaving not a trace."[17]

Bloom saw the causes of the youth culture and the push for academic relevance in the young themselves rather than the societal forces that were increasingly penetrating the sheltered world of higher education. Except for brief mention of early civil rights activity, little outside the youth culture merited any serious consideration in Bloom's analysis of the 1960s. The war in Vietnam rated a single brief mention, unrelated to student protests.[18] In a chapter entitled "The Self," Bloom hinted rather strongly that narcissism was relevant to his critique, yet he failed to ask what forces might be producing that narcissism.

While raising valid points about American culture, *The Closing of the American Mind* ended up as a one-sided and seemingly embittered critique of the sixties. It echoed the general conservative complaint against mass culture while failing to notice the degree to which mass culture is largely the product of corporate institutions of mass consumption that manipulate popular tastes and needs. As a best seller, it helped to feed the reconstruction of the past occurring in media culture generally in the 1980s and 1990s.

Bloom's book was followed by a steady stream of foundation-supported polemics on the alleged liberal or left takeover of higher education: Charles Sykes's *Profscam* (1988) and *The Hollow Man* (1990), Page Smith's *Killing the Spirit* (1990), Roger Kimball's *Tenured Radicals* (1990), Dinesh D'Souza's *Illiberal Education* (1991).[19] Kimball and D'Souza's books kicked off the campaign against "political correctness" (discussed below). Foreshadowing Robert Bork's *Slouching towards Gomorrah* (1996), Kimball opined:

> Who could have guessed that administrators would one day be falling over themselves in their rush to replace the "white Western" curriculum of traditional humanistic studies with a smorgasbord of courses designed to appeal to various ethnic and racial sensitivities? Who could have predicted that the ideals of objectivity and the disinterested pursuit of knowledge would not only be abandoned but pilloried as products of a repressive bourgeois society? No, the radical ethos of the Sixties has been all too successful, achieving indirectly in the classroom, faculty meeting, and by administrative decree what they were unable to accomplish on the barricades.[20]

By the early 1990s, Ellen Messer-Davidow described the vast network of attack in traditional economic production terms:

> The articulated systems — think tanks, training institutes, foundations, grass roots organizations, and legal centers — are the manufacturing apparatus. The articles, opinion pieces, letters, and news stories, as well as a range of actions, are the individual products. The conservative journals and books, the think-tank seminars, and the grassroots lobbying efforts, together with the mainstream media, are the distribution system. . . . [all designed] to leverage changes in national and local institutions, which in turn can be used to (re)constitute individuals as subjects and agents of a conservative society.[21]

In Messer-Davidow's words, this apparatus has targeted the universities in order to "gain control of this important means of socio-cultural production and reproduction" through a two-pronged effort to "attack progressive trends and strengthen the conservative presence in higher education."[22]

The National Committee for Responsive Philanthropy, which has issued several reports documenting the ideological campaigns of conservative foundations, noted that their "first and primary purpose has been to build and strengthen an intellectual edifice to support conservative social and public policy views." Their "second purpose" has been to

> develop an organizational network of faculty, students, alumni and trustees to oppose and reverse progressive curricula and policy trends on the nation's campuses. This network has launched a highly sophisticated attack on "liberal" higher education, first by developing and popularizing the idea that a dominant and intolerant left has eroded academic standards and the space for free intellectual inquiry and then by using this critique to press for change in American higher education, particularly with respect to university admissions practices, curricular trends, faculty hiring and funding.[23]

Like anyone else, conservatives obviously have every right to invest their funds in efforts that reflect their political views. Yet two characteristics of this campaign are particularly disturbing in terms of their impact on democratic discourse. The first is that in their exaggerated and distorted claims, in addition to what are at times vicious attacks on their opponents, they engage in precisely what they accuse their opponents of doing, greatly compounding the polarization, if not poisoning, of public discourse in the United States. "Victimspeak" now seems like a dominant form of discourse. The campaign against "tenured radicals" and multiculturalism in colleges and universities is couched as an attempt to restore the integrity of academic standards of neutrality and rigor, to say nothing of the virtues of "Western civilization." Yet in its alleged effort to "rid the campus of politics," in Harvey Mansfield's words,[24] it is blatantly political, if not anti-democratic.

The other disturbing characteristic of this campaign is its convergence with corporate interests' response to the sixties era. Not only has the convergence enabled a tidal wave of institutions and publications that have transformed media discourse and effectively remarginalized the Left, but this campaign has accelerated the erosion of not only the civic culture, but culture in general—in ways that undermine their own conservative concerns. The narcissistic, it's-all-about-me culture driven by consumer capitalism, about which conservative critics like Allan Bloom legitimately complain, has resulted not from liberal politics but from abandoning the project of political community altogether and turning everything over to the market—the foundational value of neoliberalism that conservatives have consistently embraced.

"Political Correctness"

Influenced by popular books like Bloom's *Closing of the American Mind,* mass media attention to "political correctness" took off in the years following the Reagan presidency, an indication of the Right's growing frustration with the persistence of the sixties "cultural revolution" after the Reagan administration had seemingly promised conservatives so much. While the "PC" term had roots in the correct "party line" arguments of various Marxist sects, it had been used self-satirically within the New Left and the women's and environmental movements even as fragments of these movements began to practice forms of "correctness" themselves. Public awareness of "political correctness" on the nation's college campuses can probably be traced to an October 1990 *New York Times* article Richard Bernstein wrote about a Western Humanities Conference in Berkeley, California. While the conference explored questions of multiculturalism and "correctness" through wide-ranging debate, Bernstein's article, "Political Correctness and Cultural Studies," was heavily skewed toward the attacks on PC, noting how the term suggested "Stalinist orthodoxy." After briefly mentioning one Stanford student's explanation of the thinking behind multiculturalism, Bernstein spent the rest of the article highlighting the claims of Roger Kimball, Allan Bloom, Bard president Leon Botstein (who criticized both sides of the campus debate), a critic of a new University of Texas writing course, and a Berkeley grad student who attacked the "fundamentalism" of "politically correct discourse."[25]

Bernstein's attack was followed two months later by a *Newsweek* cover story on PC, "Taking Offense," that wondered if the various forms of "political correctness" might not be "the new McCarthyism." While acknowledging that "hundreds of experiments" were occurring on different campuses, the article quickly transformed diverse efforts to confront prejudice among students into a "creed," a "totalitarian philosophy" requiring all students to "affirm" the presence of homosexuals and other minorities and "study their literature and culture alongside that of Plato, Shakespeare, and Locke." Echoing another much-ballyhooed myth cited by PC critics, the article explained that PC was "the program of a generation of campus radicals who grew up in the '60s and are now achieving positions of academic influence." Among the exaggerated claims left unchallenged in the *Newsweek* article was one Berkeley professor's assertion that "an overwhelming proportion of our courses are taught by professors who really hate the system."[26]

The number of major-media citations on "political correctness," as recorded by LexisNexis, increased dramatically in those years, beginning with a mere 10 in 1989 and rising to 44 in 1990, 901 in 1991, 1,599 in 1992, 2,326 in 1993, and 3,316 in 1994. The term remains a staple of public discourse: in 2007 the same LexisNexis sources recorded 4,188 citations. *Newsweek* alone had 51 articles in 1990–1991 dealing with political correctness issues on campuses. As John Wilson found, the flood of mass media articles in late 1990 and early 1991 were almost uniformly critical of the Left and accepted the conservatives' attacks without questioning their accuracy or their motives. By using a few anecdotes from a few elite universities, the conservative attacks created a PC epidemic in the eyes of the media, and in herd-like fashion journalists raced to condemn the "politically correct" mob they had "discovered" in American universities.[27] As Barbara Epstein has observed, the Right's framing of the debate in terms of campus "radicals" is "intellectually sloppy. It labels people as radicals who do not deserve to be so described," and it "masks the political agenda of the neoconservatives" which, she argued, was "not so much to undermine the already feeble left, but to pull the liberal-conservative middle—which actually dominates the world of universities, foundations, and publishing houses—toward the right."[28]

Whatever excesses have been uncovered, they are commonly repeated in exaggerated ways through the Right's highly publicized campaign. One might, for example, contrast the extensive publicity given to Roger Kimball's arguments—not only in his book's promotion and sales through the Harper & Row publishing giant, but in the repetition of his charges in the mass media (46 media citations in two years on LexisNexis) and what some have called the right-wing media "echo-chamber"[29]—to the relative inattention given to Patricia Aufderheide's slim volume *Beyond PC: Towards a Politics of Understanding,* published by a small independent publisher (a single brief media mention in two years). While Kimball's book was an unfettered polemic, Aufderheide's edited book contained a range of views in the PC debate (including polemics by the National Association of Scholars and Dinesh D'Souza), a number of specific pieces correcting distortions about their campuses, and, as the title suggests, several pieces that without rancor sought a healthier democratic dialogue on the nation's campuses.[30]

One of the PC critics included in the volume, eminent historian C. Vann Woodward, observed that university campuses that were once "centers of civil rights activists" have become "places where instances of bigotry are frequent." Woodward suggested that affirmative action efforts to promote racial harmony had increased the "perception and complaint of racial hostility."[31] Yet it seems far more likely that offensive incidents have occurred because young people feel greater permission to make racial, sexist, or homophobic statements in the context of widely visible, Rightist statements castigating the motives of women or racial and sexual minorities. Woodward also critiqued the "resegregation" of campuses that provided separate housing and curricula populated by minorities, arguing that they exacerbated racial disharmony. Yet, like many critiques that focused on the most proximate cause, Woodward's argument overlooked the fact that both the migration of minority students to supportive enclaves and the oft-attacked "balkanized" curriculum of women's or gender studies, African American studies, Latino studies, and gay and lesbian studies have been responses to ways their worlds have been resisted or suppressed in both curricular and cultural mainstreams. Furthermore, as Joan Wallach Scott observed in the same volume, "A pluralism or multiculturalism failing to recognize that difference is a relationship—*and* that it is a structured relationship that cannot be undone simply by individual fiat or by denial of asymmetries of power—encourages separatism. Indeed, it provides the conceptual basis for it in an essentialism that denies the historical basis for difference."[32]

Both PC excesses and the overwrought counterattack have done significant damage to the climate on the nation's campuses. As Barbara Epstein has observed, they have generated what she calls "self-intimidation in the name of sensitivity to racism, sexism, and homophobia, which tends to close down discussion and make communication more difficult."[33] Overzealous enforcement of "speech codes" and punitive responses to racially insensitive remarks are particularly inappropriate for institutions that are supposed to be about educating young people. On the other hand, various kinds of required exposure to diversity training (ridiculed as "manipulative" or "totalitarian" by the Right) designed to awaken understanding among groups would seem to be not only appropriate but a necessary feature of educational institutions in the twenty-first century. And approaches modeled after "restorative justice" practices that bring perpetrator and victim into face-to-face exchange could enhance mutual understanding (i.e., educate) where offensive speech has occurred. The more effective programs of this kind aim at precisely the "possibility of universal connection," as Cornel West put it.

The other major cost of the anti-PC attacks is that, while eroding the civic culture, they also move the discussion away from examining the forces that strengthen capitalism's damaging hold on higher education. In Bill Readings's analysis, the contemporary university is becoming "a transnational bureaucratic corporation" shaped by the political and economic forces that have prevailed within the neoliberal regime.[34] Among these forces are significant cutbacks in public support for higher education initiated by the Reagan administration and sustained by its successors (at least until the Obama administration); dependency on external research funding that reflects increasingly utilitarian or corporate objectives; the swelling of a vast layer of middle-management administrators devoted to the tasks of fund-raising and public relations or charged with addressing "problem areas" like campus safety, student life, and potentially litigious parents or faculty; students increasingly worried about their economic futures in the volatile world of globalization and increasingly devoted to finding high-paying jobs in order to pay off burdensome college debts; the increasing emphasis on the use of "performance indicators" applied to teaching and other areas of faculty activity; and publication of national college rankings in publications like *McLean's* and *U.S. News & World Report,* based upon (what else?) quantitative performance indicators.

Not only are many of these trends counter-educational, but, as Readings observed, they position anyone who would challenge them as resisting "public accountability," which really means "the logic of contemporary capitalism, which requires 'clear measures to establish university performance.'" The administrative university has been designed in ways to "make the exclusive rule of business management not seem discontinuous with the prior role of the University."[35]

These trends, of course, begin in the earliest years of schooling, with outcomes-based education and No Child Left Behind—to say nothing of what sociologist Stanley Aronowitz points out is a curriculum "oriented to patriotism, obedience, and above all, to the prevailing morality—the 'work ethic,' 'family values,' and citizenship—which equates virtue with responsibility to . . . the nation-state."[36] From top to bottom, American education has become highly corporatized.

From Anti-Feminism to Post-Feminism

Whenever I hear certain men sonorously announcing that the Women's Movement is dead . . . I know of course that they mean we seem less sensational: "Where are all those bra-burners?"
    —Robin Morgan, *Going Too Far*, 1978

Feminism has figured prominently in the campaign against the sixties as well as the anti-PC attacks on college campuses. Even as liberal or "equity" feminism has gained legitimacy in the mainstream culture, befitting the performance-measure norms of capitalism, one of the more virulent forms of cultural sixties-bashing has been the attack on feminism and the women's liberation movement. Feminism has had a somewhat distinctive trajectory because of the way commercial culture has absorbed it into the consumer mainstream.

One study of news media portrayal of the Women's Movement over the span of time from 1969 to 2004 found that the media "exercised considerable discretion in determining which [women's movement] issues it cover[ed]," for example overrepresenting activities related to the abortion issue while under-representing activities related to family issues the organizations addressed. The authors drew two important conclusions from their study: movement organizations, they noted, "are less able to win coverage of the agenda they want to present and more likely to be governed by what the media want to cover," and "the public's sense that the movement is out of touch may have as much to do with what the news media choose to cover as it does with the priorities of the women's movement itself."[37]

From the beginning, the anti-feminism backlash focused on the images and caricatures drawn from past mass media accounts. Defending the vision of feminism they document in the pages of *Dear Sisters: Dispatches from the Women's Liberation Movement,* Rosalyn Baxandall and Linda Gordon observed, "The media—and not only conservative sources—often portray the women's movement through unrepresentative anecdotes and outright falsehoods," thus helping to foster "widespread myths about women's liberation." Among the myths they cite were the movement's alleged rejection of motherhood, the view that children were "only a burden," that participants "hated being women and rejected everything feminine, from bras and long hair to shaved legs and high heels," that participants "were man-haters who tried to belittle and compete with men, often rejecting them entirely and becoming lesbians," "humorless and prudish, quick to take offense," and "whined about life's difficulties and exaggerated the discrimination against women."[38] Conservative columnist Cal Thomas broadened the attack: "Feminist disdain for the family and the sexual revolution have given millions of women the chance to realize their full potential—of abandonment and poverty, that is—and has 'liberated' countless children from the affection and care of their parents."[39]

As noted earlier, much of the imagery and rhetoric that represent "feminism" resulted from a media dynamic that largely excluded the movement's meanings, instead applying conventional interpretation to symbolic or agitprop gestures. Thus the "anti-men," "anti-motherhood," "anti-sex," and "anti-family" backlash charges echoed through the media culture throughout the seventies, eighties, and nineties. In that context, women's strategies—like those of other movements—were, at times, ill conceived. Furthermore, as Baxandall and Gordon acknowledged, media stereotypes, "like most myths," contain a kernel of truth. Thus feminists "did reject confining clothing," did want "help raising children, from husbands and organized day care, as more and more women joined the workforce," "were angry at men who beat them, harassed them, belittled them, and kept them in inferior and dead-end jobs"—and, "in order to be heard . . . sometimes shouted and oversimplified." But, they added,

> Some of these myths contain not a grain of truth. Feminists never rejected motherhood; rather, they sought to improve its conditions. Not only were most feminists romantically involved with men, but all had sons, brothers, fathers, male friends, or coworkers whom they loved. Far from being losers, feminists were typically the most achieving and self-confident of women. . . . Anything but prudes, feminists dedicated themselves to liberating women's sexuality. They were doers, not complainers. They identified discrimination for the purpose of trying to change it.[40]

Beneath the more virulent attacks on "identity politics," one suspects a strain of "threatened-identity politics" on the part of those who embrace rigid gender meanings threatened by the feminist critique. In this manner, the attack against feminism reflects and feeds on an often manufactured sense of victimization even as it denounces feminism as an expression of victimhood. Feminism does indeed challenge the unacknowledged subjectivity of its harshest critics.

Significant foundation support has enabled the publication of books and articles by conservative women like Carol Iannone and Christine Hoff Sommers.[41] Sommers's book, *Who Stole Feminism? How Women Have Betrayed Women,* was published by Simon & Schuster in 1994 to wide acclaim. Presenting herself as an "equity feminist," Sommers framed her book around an attack on "gender feminists" who had "alienated and silenced women and men alike" through a campaign of alleged factual misrepresentation, control over university appointments and curriculum, and domination of fund-raising. Her own book read as a continuing narrative of anecdotal stories tied together with Sommers's sweeping assertions about the "gender war" being waged with great success by the militant feminists. Among her exaggerations: "It is now virtually impossible to be appointed to high administrative office in any university system without having passed muster with the gender feminists."[42] As reviewer Laura Flanders put it, Sommers's book relied "heavily on a handful of oft-repeated, antifeminist anecdotes — or folktales." Flanders also observed that Sommers berated feminists for "victimhood" but simultaneously complained that "to criticize feminist ideology is now hazardous in the extreme."[43] Reviews of Sommers's book in the conservative press simply accepted her assertions as truth: the *Wall Street Journal* ("Ms. Sommers simply lines up her facts and shoots one bulls eye after another") and the *National Review* ("Why Feminism's Vital Statistics Are Always Wrong"). Mainstream media played up the theme of Sommers as a feminist betrayed by her cause (*Time:* "A Feminist on the Outs"; the *Boston Globe:* "Rebel in the Sisterhood") or played along with her stereotyped portrayal of "gender feminists."[44]

While consumer capitalism has exploited images of the successfully "liberated" career woman, along with the more traditional dualism of cheerful housewife and seductive "sexpot," cultural conservatives have never let up in their assault, blaming feminism for everything from rising divorce rates to the decline of Western culture. Through his well-funded talk radio show, Rush Limbaugh introduced the term "Feminazi" into popular usage. In *Slouching towards Gomorrah,* Bork elaborated on familiar Rightist themes: "Radical feminism is the most destructive and fanatical movement to come down to us from the Sixties. This is a revolutionary, not a reformist, movement, and it is meeting with considerable success. Totalitarian in spirit, it is deeply antagonistic to traditional Western culture and proposes the complete restructuring of society, morality, and human nature. Radical feminism is today's female counterpart of Sixties radicalism."[45]

Like many attacks, Bork's statement contains a kernel of truth — radical feminism and sixties radicalism do challenge "traditional Western culture," for example — but Bork's argument distorts the meaning of that challenge. Furthermore, Bork contended, the reformist agenda of "equity feminism" had been realized by the time he wrote his book. "There are no artificial barriers left to women's achievement," he asserted, though three years later a Gallup poll of women over the age of eighteen found that only 4 percent believed that "women are treated as well as men."[46] All other aspects of feminism — a feminist epistemology, the critique of masculinist institutions, the effort to free both women and men from repressive patterns of development, to name a few—were either beyond Bork's comprehension or were lumped together as "radical feminism" and dismissed as "totalitarian": "Many people suppose that feminism today is a continuation of the reform movement of the past. . . . That is not the case; the extremists [for Bork, a "ranting Bella Abzug" or an "icy Gloria Steinem"] *are* the movement."[47]

Bork focused on one of the most common attack stereotypes about feminism: "Perhaps the most vicious aspect of radical feminism is that it *necessarily* criticizes and demeans women who choose to work primarily as mothers and homemakers. They are made to feel guilty and told that their lives are essentially worthless."[48] He repeated the familiar litany of charges: radical feminism "attacks not only men but the institution of the family, it is hostile to traditional religion, it demands quotas in every field for women, and it engages in serious misrepresentation of facts. Worst of all, it inflicts great damage on persons and essential institutions in a reckless attempt to remake human beings and create a world that can never exist."[49]

The Rightist attack on feminism largely succeeded in stigmatizing both the women's liberation movement and the term "feminism." A variety of public opinion polls, dating back into the 1980s, found that women are aware of their mistreatment and support policies that would improve the conditions they encounter. Yet relatively few consider themselves to be "feminists."[50] Naomi Wolf has observed that the number of women willing to identify themselves with the word "feminist" slipped steadily throughout the 1980s even as support for women's rights steadily rose[51]—a trend that brings to mind the way the public grew increasingly opposed to the war in Vietnam and increasingly hostile to the antiwar movement at the same time. Both suggest the difficulties movements face in communicating outside-the-boundary ideas through the mass media. Part of Wolf's effort is aimed at helping feminists and non-feminists alike get beyond the poisoned media discourse.

Wolf's list of explanations for younger women's disengagement from "feminism" includes many plausible reasons, ranging from the media's "dyke-baiting" and caricatures of feminism to young women's job vulnerability and the obscure language of academic discourse. One she called the "hangover habits of the revolutionary left of the 1960s," later alluded to as grounded in "the Marxist-Leninist male left of the 1960s." Other manifestations of what Wolf called "victim feminism" include "contempt for the mainstream media, for women in business, and for female individualism."[52] What Wolf seems to be criticizing here is feminism's radicalism. She is correct in suggesting ways in which this radicalism does not readily resonate with the masses of younger women (at least via mass media), but her response seems framed by her own liberalism. Within her frame, Wolf offers an individualistic (liberal) "power feminism" as the preferred alternative to "victim feminism."

The "power feminism" phrase is useful because it suggests liberal feminism's vulnerability to the mass media's affective empowerment, and thus the need to go beyond the boundaries of liberalism. In 1998, a *Time* cover asked "Is Feminism Dead?" and featured black-and-white head shots of Susan B. Anthony, Betty Friedan, and Gloria Steinem, and then, in color, Ally McBeal, the title character of the TV show that takes place in a hip law firm with a highly sexualized office environment and unisex toilets. The main article was titled "Feminism: It's All about Me!" and featured the self-preoccupied Ally McBeal because, according to *Time,* she was "the most popular female character on television."

In addition to chiding "Clinton-loving feminists" who overlooked the "faults of a man who had been their best provider," much of the article reviewed the exploits of variously sexually "liberated" and narcissistic younger women. Camille Paglia, known for her attacks on feminists, was credited with helping "catapult feminism beyond an ideology of victimhood" by her argument that "female sexuality is humanity's greatest force." Yet, by the end of the article, without ever exploring how female "power" got co-opted back into sexuality-equals-popularity, *Time* concluded by asking, "But is Ally McBeal really progress? Maybe if she lost her job and wound up a single mom, we could begin a movement again."[53]

Whereas post-feminism reduces forms of feminist radicalism to "victim feminism," its own equation of empowerment with media popularity, business success, and "female individualism" suggests that radical feminism — or at least feminist radicalism — remains highly salient in the contemporary world despite the attacks and postmortems. When post-feminists write about "radical feminism," however, they single out the most extreme cases of feminist expression — often highly controversial within feminism. Thus Katie Roiphe critiqued the anti-pornography "Puritanism" of radical feminist Catherine MacKinnon. Or, in reference to Take Back the Night marches on college campuses, she saw victim feminism in the "image that emerges from feminist *preoccupations with rape and sexual harassment.*"[54]

The boundaries of post-feminism and the catalytic images that trigger it can also be seen in Rene Denfeld's book explaining why "so many women my age refuse to join the women's movement." She introduced her thesis by citing a 1992 *Los Angeles Times* article, "I'm Not a Feminist But . . . ," that asserted, "To many, the term *feminist* still evokes images of hairy-legged, humorless extremists who view men as the enemy. In an effort to combat those stereotypes, many feminist leaders have taken aim — at conservatives, at the media, at political leaders, at almost everyone but themselves. By lashing out, they have managed to underscore the militant image that alienated so many Middle American women in the first place."[55] Despite what appears to be a balanced take on feminism, Denfeld's book largely echoed the derogatory characterizations of feminism that permeate media culture. She zeroed in on the more extreme expressions as if they defined feminism, while simultaneously making clear her own preferences for feminism as a "cultural movement" (e.g., a *Glamour* article titled "Your Ob-Gyn Checkup: Read This before You Go"). While observing that feminism has "climbed out on a limb of academic theory that is all but inaccessible to the un-initiated"—a charge arguably true of postmodern theorizing—she generalized that "feminism . . . has become bogged down in an extremist moral and spiritual crusade that has little to do with women's lives."[56] In the end, Denfeld claims, women "choose not to call themselves feminist or participate in women's organi-zations because of feminist attacks on the male sex and the movement's dictates about the sexuality of its members." She goes on to assert that "the truth is that man hating and anti-heterosexuality are firmly entrenched and loudly espoused in today's movement."[57]

Feminism's alleged anti-sexuality is a pervasive distortion in the conserva-tive and post-feminist critiques. No doubt both women and men can evolve to a deeper understanding and more liberated expression of human sexuality, but the consumer culture that post-feminists appear to embrace offers the same old repressive desublimation that Herbert Marcuse wrote about in 1964.[58] Ariel Levy has targeted one example of desublimation in her book about the young women of "raunch culture" who believe they are so "liberated," or even "feminist" that they freely expose their bodies or perform acts of public sexuality. As Levy ob-serves, however, theirs is really a form of narcissistic self-exhibition aimed at consumption by others, with the particular aim of pleasing men.[59] The con-sumer culture offers endless ways women can "liberate" themselves, including, of course, cosmetic or "aesthetic" surgery—now a commonplace.

Even as innumerable articulations of feminist radicalism continue to explore ground left ignored by post-feminism, significant numbers of younger women are embracing what they call "third wave" feminism.[60] As the editors of *Third Wave Agenda* put it, the "third wave goal . . . comes directly out of learning from [the] histories" of earlier feminisms and focuses on "the development of modes of thinking that can come to terms with the multiple, constantly shifting bases of oppression . . . and the creation of a coalition politics based on these under-standings—understandings that acknowledge the existence of oppression, even though it is not fashionable to say so."[61]

Race and Class Revisited

The cultural and Reagan revolutions took place within a single generation, and have proved to be complementary, not contradictory events. . . . The facts are these: The Sixties happened, Reagan happened, and for the foreseeable future they will together define our political horizon.
    —Mark Lilla "A Tale of Two Reactions," 1998

The growth of a black (and Latino) middle class and its increasing visibility in the media culture have produced the groundwork for the myth of a post-racial

America—a myth that seemed validated by the media celebration of Barack Obama's election. Yet, as Thomas Sugrue has documented in his comprehensive study, "white Americans and black Americans diverge sharply in their perceptions of disparities between blacks and whites as well as the socioeconomic progress blacks have or have not made, and the facts bear out the perceptions of black Americans."[62] And as graphically documented in a short 1992 ABC *Prime Time* segment entitled "True Colors," most black Americans regularly encounter discriminatory treatment—sometimes subtle, often not at all subtle—because of the color of their skin, no matter how professional they may look. Racism persists, often in ways that suggest many white Americans still associate black skin with the sociological patterns correlated with the inner-city black underclass—another example of visual association.

What has remained largely unchanged since the Community Action Program was circumscribed in 1965–66 are the conditions that inner-city minorities encounter daily, conditions that continue to breed hopelessness, crime, and gang violence. The policies of the neoliberal regime have done nothing to improve the conditions of the inner-city underclass; indeed, the main outcome, via the "drug war" and "three strikes" policies, has been to incarcerate unprecedented numbers of black males in particular for increasingly long sentences.

So, how then does the Right explain the continuing hopelessness, violence, and drug abuse manifest in this population? The old answer used to be that liberal Great Society government programs produced a cycle of "dependency" that crippled the potential for initiative in the inner-city poor. Yet the pattern persisted after successive administrations from Nixon to the elder Bush had largely decimated the old "war on poverty" and, after the Clinton administration, joined the Republicans' "Contract with America" to "end welfare as we know it." The 1992 Los Angeles riots were a reminder that the inner cities remained potentially explosive.

One noteworthy book that evolved with support from the vaults of right-wing foundations provided an imaginative, new (if broadly familiar) answer. In 1993, reflecting on the "dizzying contrasts of wealth and poverty" that were "deeply ingrained in the basic texture of today's American cities," Manhattan Institute scholar and *Fortune* magazine board of editors member Myron Magnet asked, "What's gone wrong?" Ignoring the impact of neoliberalism and consumer capitalism, he argued that the nightmare of urban poverty was the "result of making a democratic cultural revolution that ended—tragically—by making a travesty of the democratic values it had set out to uphold."[63] This "cultural revolution" was the creation of a "liberal-left-of-center elite" of "opinion-makers, policymakers and mythmakers" who "radically remade American culture, turning it inside out and upside down to accomplish a cultural revolution whose most mangled victims turned out to be the Have-Nots."[64] Magnet essentially reduced sixties-era social movements to clichéd stereotypes from the media-hyped second wave of the counterculture: "kicking free of mechanical rationality and opening your-self to altered states of consciousness" and a "fling with 'protest,' drugs, sexual experimentation, and dropping out."

What is distinctive is that Magnet argued that these qualities "explained" the erosive "underclass culture" of the early nineties, essentially because of behavioral similarities between the two worlds, with one happening before the other. Substituting visual similarity for actual empirical evidence that demonstrated that A caused B, the book drew on the common conservative trope for explaining the social ills of the 1980s and 1990s. Sexual experimentation in the sixties "explained" the surge in unwed teen mothers in the latter 1980s, countercultural drug use "explained" the epidemic of far more dangerous and addictive drugs among the urban poor twenty years later, and countercultural dropping out "explained" the high rate of school dropouts in the inner city. One might recall the way sex and drugs in the sixties "explained" AIDS in *Forrest Gump* a year later.

In the realm of statistical methodology, these are spurious correlations. Because two variables are related or appear similar, one imputes a causal relationship between them when, in fact, both might be explained by some third factor. Magnet did caution that "the Sixties were a quarter century ago and more, and belaboring them now might seem like flogging a dead horse," but he went on to argue that "intergenerational social pathologies such as homelessness and underclass culture don't spring up overnight from trivial causes. They are the mature harvest of seeds sown by the Haves and rooted years ago." For evidence, Magnet pointed to visual appearances, suggesting that his readers should walk through the "encampments of the homeless in America's western cities" where "crowds of young men, mostly white, in their twenties, dressed like refugees from the Summer of Love." They are homeless, Magnet claimed, not because of severe Reagan administration cutbacks in the public housing budget, nor because of an economic downturn, but "because they are enslaved by the specious liberation whose troops have worn that uniform for the past quarter century."[65]

Magnet achieves a kind of feel-good, "populist" conservatism—seeming to be on the side of the poor while simultaneously diverting attention from the forces that are most responsible for the social ills that flourish among the most desperate poor—by observing that most middle-class dropouts in the 1960s had a "margin of safety because of their class," while contemporary "working class kids . . . run a bigger risk." Magnet's book was later cited by President George W. Bush as his "second favorite" book, next to the Bible.[66]

In contrast to Magnet's facile account, social-class inequality remains profound in the United States, a stain on the nation's claim of democracy. Neoliberalism's reliance on the market economy cannot ameliorate poverty because it relies on institutions that require inequality to function effectively. Neoliberalism means making the poor suffer more than they would under liberalism so they will have greater incentive to work; it also means relying on greater profitability (wealth in the hands of the rich) to provide a greater number of demeaning jobs for the poor. On the other hand, while government supports by themselves can improve the material lives of the poor, they can disempower the poor in the process. The only way out of this systemic dilemma, as I argue in the next chapter, is to consider a more radically democratic option.

But what of race, the great American dilemma? Probably the single most promising aspect of Barack Obama's campaign was his address on race in Philadelphia, in which he tried to open some windows of potential understanding between the "two sides" of the nation's racially divided perceptions. Yet beyond the evocative symbolism of election night 2008, there is little evidence of public discourse in which cultural and experiential differences are shared in a mutually enlightening way—at least in the media.[67] What has occurred instead, however, is yet another round of Rightist-generated ad hominem attacks against Obama, some thinly veiled challenges to his American citizenship, others blatant attacks calling him a "socialist" or likening him to Stalin and Hitler. The vitriol is reminiscent of the Right's attacks on Bill Clinton as somehow the manifestation of everything wrong in the 1960s—nicely encapsulated in Newt Gingrich's critique of the Clinton administration's alleged "Great Society, counter-culture, McGovernick" tendencies.

"Liberal Media" Sell American Wars

For too long our culture has said, "If it feels good, do it." Now America is embracing a new ethic and a new creed: "Let's roll."
    —George W. Bush, State of the Union Address, January 29, 2002

I admit it—the liberal media were never that powerful, and the whole thing was often used as an excuse by conservatives for conservative failures.
    —William Kristol, *New Yorker,* May 22, 1995

The other major cultural institution targeted by the Right's sixties backlash has been the mass media, also presumably controlled by baby boomer professionals with "liberal biases." It also seems clear from media behavior during controversial foreign interventions from Central America to the Iraq war that the post-Vietnam attacks on the media produced far greater media passivity toward government propaganda—quite the opposite outcome from what one might expect from the Vietnam experience. And the deregulated, hyper-commercialized media have become increasingly vulnerable to sophisticated efforts to manipulate the visual staging of events while simultaneously less able to explore and explain events in any meaningful depth.

Like the attack on "tenured radicals," the "liberal media" campaign was a variant on the generational theme—namely, that a new class of urban professionals, thoroughly sympathetic to movements of the 1960s, brought its ideological predispositions into the world of journalism, thus providing boundless publicity for environmental, feminist, consumer, and peace movements that posed challenges to the world of business.[68] These arguments were supported by the early-to-mid-1980s publication of survey findings funded by, among others, the John M. Olin and Sarah Scaife Foundations. The Lichter-Rothman-Lichter studies found that the "orientations and preconceptions" of national journalist elites were "politically liberal and alienated from traditional norms and institutions." Furthermore, the authors theorized, "psychological factors" helped to "explain some features of contemporary journalistic behavior, ranging from a focus on scoops to an adversarial stance towards politicians."[69] As interpreted for public consumption by President Reagan's science adviser, George A. Keyworth, "much of the press seems to be drawn from a relatively narrow fringe element on the far left of our society . . . and . . . is trying to tear down America."[70]

The Lichter-Rothman-Lichter studies have been subjected to sharp criticism for their sloppy methodology and the infusion of ideology into their interpretation of their data, notably by the distinguished sociologist Herbert Gans. Furthermore, Gans observed, "their presentation of a mass of data on the personal backgrounds and alleged political opinions and values of journalists" was totally lacking in "evidence that these are relevant to how journalists report the news."[71] Indeed, the Right's case has been constructed on opinion poll data about the alleged values and party preferences of select national journalists, without being able to provide systematic evidence that actual news reporting is liberally biased. Much of the public rhetoric about media bias has been dominated by anecdotal narrative and "eye of the beholder" polemic.[72] In fact, the focus on journalist characteristics diverges sharply from the prevailing social science studies that have demonstrated that actual news reporting is largely shaped by journalistic routines, organizational imperatives, dependency on established sources, and the like.[73] Yet, as Gans has observed, "even journalists from the 'elite media' themselves have cited the work of Rothman and the Lichters uncritically," and "thus, slowly but surely the notion seemingly held by the three researchers that journalists are dangerously liberal is seeping into the conventional wisdom as scientific conclusion."[74]

Public attacks on "liberal media" have tended to focus on instances in which a favored conservative leader or policy is subjected to reporting that contains criticism—as if this were somehow not an appropriate role for mass media in a democratic society. Media coverage of the Vietnam War has been a persistent and effective theme in this campaign from the Nixon-Agnew era onward, so that again popular discourse has been dominated by the metaphor of an overly adversarial media as an "excessive check," as the Trilateralists put it, on the commander-in-chief. Despite previously mentioned documentation that the mass media consistently reinforced the government's framing of the Vietnam

War and only grew more critical as their well-placed sources grew more critical, the myth of media responsibility for the United States' loss in Vietnam has persisted. No one made the argument more vehemently than Robert Elegant did in his 1981 essay "How to Lose a War: The Press and Viet Nam." In Elegant's words,

> The American press, naturally dominant in an "American war," somehow felt obliged to be less objective than partisan, to take sides, for it was inspired by the *engagé* "investigative" reporting that burgeoned in the United States in these impassioned years. The press was instinctively "agin the government"—and, at least reflexively, for Saigon's enemies. . . . For the first time in history, the outcome of the war was determined not on the battlefield but on the printed page and, above all, on the television screen.[75]

Like the alleged journalists' biases, claims of media responsibility for loss of the Vietnam War echoed through the right-wing attack machine.

Throughout the post–Vietnam War years, from the 1983 invasion of Grenada and the 1989 invasion of Panama to the carefully orchestrated Gulf War of 1991, the "War on Terror" launched after 9/11, and the invasion of Iraq in 2003, subsequent administrations have responded to the "television war" in Vietnam by establishing new controls on the flow of information as well as media access to damaging photo opportunities. Indeed, the highly favorable and controlled media coverage of the Gulf War noted earlier, alive as it was with references to the "Vietnam syndrome," can be seen as testimony to the effectiveness of the attack on media for "losing Vietnam."[76] Those few reporters who managed to reveal rare damaging footage of civilian Iraqis killed by the U.S. bombardment, most notably CNN reporter Peter Arnett, were singled out for a tidal wave of attack by the Right. Senator Alan Simpson denounced Arnett as an Iraqi "sympathizer," just as he (Arnett) was a "communist sympathizer" (i.e., questioned the glowing optimism of military officials) during the war in Vietnam.[77]

In addition, of course, television's presentation of the two Iraq wars has embodied all the attributes of consumer-driven, entertainment TV. Though they had complained about lack of access during the Gulf War, the mass media succumbed once again to systematic government distortion and deception in the lead-up to the 2003 invasion of Iraq.[78] Moreover, media complaints led to a creative Pentagon innovation during the war that seemingly met both government and commercial media needs. By embedding reporters with fighting units in Iraq, the media not only got access to both soldiers and (approved) combat operations, but the sense of drama built into news reports escalated significantly. As NPR's Tom Gjelten observed, "We were offered an irresistible opportunity: free transportation to the front line of the war, dramatic pictures, dramatic sounds, great quotes. Who can pass that up?"[79] The government, in turn, got reporters who became close to the soldiers they depended upon for their safety. The public got media reporting that failed to challenge the administration's framing of the war or report critically on the war's politics.

These are the very mass media the Right has accused of having a liberal bias. The Right's campaign has had enormous influence in shaping discourse in the mass media not only because of the resources amassed behind it and its effective exploitation of media technologies, but because of what some have called the "Fox effect," as other networks seek to avoid potential attacks by Fox News. Aided by avid promotions via a network of right-wing talk-radio shows and cable TV programming on the Fox News network, the flow of Rightist polemics against liberal media has been sustained for well over a decade, at times topping best-seller lists.[80] As David Brock, a former insider from the Right's campaign, put it,

> Once upon a time, right-wing strategists, operatives, and financiers believed they could never win political hegemony in the United States unless they won domination of the country's political discourse. Towards this end, a deliberate, well-financed, and expressly acknowledged communications and deregulatory plan was pursued by the right wing for more than thirty years—to subvert and subsume journalism and reshape the national consciousness through the media, with the intention of skewing American politics sharply to the right. The plan has succeeded spectacularly.[81]

Documentation of the degree to which the Right's claims about media bias are aired and accepted within the mass media, as well as refutation of those claims, has been a regular feature of the publication *Extra!,* published by Fairness and Accuracy in Reporting (FAIR), as well as books like Eric Alterman's *What Liberal Media?*[82]

More broadly, one can argue that the right-wing enclave is a subset of a much larger mass media "echo chamber"—or a convergent and increasingly "hyper-commercialized" media world achieved through the astonishing concentration of media ownership produced by the neoliberal policies of the Reagan-Bush and Clinton-Gore administrations. Indeed, the Fox conglomerate owned by conservative media magnate Rupert Murdoch encompasses both the overtly right-wing Fox News and probably the edgiest, most hip-satirical entertainment network (Fox TV). Given the "left-right" screaming match aired on the recently defunct *Counterpoint,* or the combative polemics of Bill O'Reilly and Sean Hannity versus Keith Olbermann, or young audiences' reliance on comic satire by Jon Stewart and Stephen Colbert as "news sources," or, for that matter, war-as-entertainment television—and one can reasonably argue that the "liberal media" problem is really a market-driven, neoliberal media problem.

13

Media Culture and the Future of Democracy

*I believe . . . that unless we continually explore . . . the network of complex
relationships which bind us together, we [will] continue being the victims
of various inadequate conceptions of ourselves, both as individuals and as
citizens of a nation of diverse people.*
—Ralph Ellison, *Invisible Man*, 1947

*The point is, we are all part of the problem and the solution—rhetoric to the
contrary.*
—Robin Morgan, *Going Too Far*, 1978

Democracy is coming to the U. S. A.
—Leonard Cohen, 1992

For the last twenty-five years, students taking my college course on the social
movements and legacies of the 1960s have consistently found the movement
histories powerfully inspiring. Almost to a person, they find considerable connection with the values and sense of empowerment alive in that world. For most
of these years, however, these same students have concluded with a sense of
resignation that they see few places in their own culture where they can make a
significant difference. They have sensed a world that is in trouble, yet they don't
see the vivid signifiers that, in the earlier era, indicated what needed fixing: the
explicit racism of the Old South, the tightly constricted world of sexist gender
roles, or the daily horror of the war in Vietnam. In addition to their own sense
of powerlessness, many of them are, of course, saddled with long-term college
debt that keeps them focused on maximizing their personal marketability after
graduation.

These students are among the relatively few young people who have some
genuine understanding of this turbulent past beyond the media snapshots that
revolve around an older generation's rebellious youth. More often than not, students entering my class say that images of hippies, "sex, drugs, and rock and
roll," war and violence, and a larger-than-life figurehead like Martin Luther King
Jr. are what come to mind when they think of the sixties. More than a few have
commented that what they had previously learned about the sixties or the war
in Vietnam came from seeing *Forrest Gump*. One student commented, "Vietnam
is something you learn about in school on a very surface level. Communism is

bad. Communism spread in Vietnam. America tried to stop it. There was a draft. It was in a jungle."[1]

By now, the media's "Sixties" has been playing so long, it has become a turnoff to many young people. Even the sixties backlash itself seems part of an anachronistic "family quarrel of the baby-boomer generation," as Andrew Sullivan put it.[2] For the most part, young people want to stop feeling like they're being compared to young people in the sixties by a media culture that remains obsessed with generations, and thus they become vulnerable to consumer pitches that flatter them for being more hip than their apparently banal and hopelessly nostalgic elders.

In spring 2008, I noticed a change. Not only were significant numbers of students demonstrably engaged in following, and in some cases participating in, the presidential campaign of Barack Obama, but students in my class seemed to sense that the sixties history had some relevance to the world they were experiencing, and an unprecedented number of students had enrolled in another class I taught on political and community organizing. Symbolically, at least, the Obama candidacy had galvanized them. For the first time in a long time, politics mattered, or so it seemed. The distracting, depoliticizing "politics" that had so long dominated the media spectacle seemed, finally, to have been trumped by real, material politics. Two increasingly unpopular wars were continuing to erode the world's perceptions of their country, and the nation's economy seemed to be in freefall. And one young, charismatic candidate generated new energy with his hopeful campaign for "change." The fact that he was African American confirmed that, at least in that respect, his election would be a historic change.

While Obama's opponent, John McCain, appeared to be a man who had acted with some integrity in his political career, he hearkened back to those baby boomer "family quarrels" that had grown so tiresome. More pointedly, McCain's vice presidential candidate represented yet another effort to sway the electorate through distracting symbolism. Stylishly attractive, Sarah Palin seemed tailor-made for the glitzy world of TV celebrity-hood. Indeed, her folksy speech and media-highlighted personal life were well suited to appeal to those publics long alienated by remnants of the sixties: as a hunter she personified gun owners long "threatened" by gun-control liberals, and as a Christian mother whose daughter was having a child out of wedlock, she symbolized the values of a long-aggrieved anti-abortion population.

This time, however, it didn't take, and the Obama administration was launched, aided by the highest voter turnout since 1968 and a significant margin of victory among the young.[3] Over the first year and a half after the election, however, two familiar strains stood out. Framed within an activist-liberal approach to governing, the Obama administration's major policy initiatives have reflected the perennial constraints and priorities of capitalism's interests—personified by those appointed to the crucially influential positions of economic and foreign policy making. On the other hand, the forces of backlash once again pulled out all the stops in orchestrating public fears and resentments about liberal government—now, ironically enough, called "socialism"—aided at times by thinly veiled racial attacks. Legitimate resentment against a massive taxpayer bailout of the nation's financial institutions was turned via Tea Party mobilizations against health care reform that might actually benefit many of the participants—thereby helping to keep a fundamental reform like single-payer health insurance off the table. These were reminders of how little has changed, except, perhaps, for the level of discourse toxicity.

What lessons, then, might I offer my students from my study of 1960s-era social movements and their interaction with the American media culture and political economy? As I sometimes do in teaching, I start by reciting the popular paraphrase of Antonio Gramsci, urging both "pessimism of the intellect" and "optimism of the will."[4] There is much in the experience of sixties-era social movements that reflects and justifies optimism of the will. People are capable of rising up and challenging conditions that oppress and demoralize them, and these uprisings are capable of having powerful and lasting effects on both the participants and the wider society.

At the same time, it is necessary to understand all the forces that can deflect, distort, and defeat these popular uprisings, and the experiences of sixties social movements recounted in these pages offer important insights. Ultimately, I argue, pessimism of the intellect requires a hard look at the systemic forces that undermine democracy today. At the same time, I also argue that these very conditions suggest reasons for optimism of the will.

The Contemporary Media Culture

This [media] concentration accentuates the core tendencies of a profit-driven,
advertising-supported media system: hypercommercialism and denigration of
journalism and public service. It is a poison pill for democracy.
　　—Robert McChesney, *Rich Media, Poor Democracy,* 1999

The average American's politicalness is trained and developed by the received
culture of television, image and sound replacing words. People don't even
understand what "democratic society" means.
　　—Edward T. Chambers, *Roots for Radicals,* 2006

Today's commercial mass media continue to function as the ideological "boundary-maintaining mechanism" for society's common discourse.[5] Events are framed and interpreted in ways that reinforce the dominant ideological beliefs of a capitalist political economy, even as that economy threatens the globe's future. Within the United States in particular, these boundaries reinforce prevailing myths about the U.S. role in the world, even as media fragments continue to generate skepticism about those myths. As it did in the 1960s, this means that *there is no full public debate* of how public and private institutions work to the detriment of millions of Americans, to say nothing of billions of people around the globe. At bottom, mass media culture needs to incorporate as legitimate all serious argumentation, particularly that of the heretofore excluded left.

Instead, we are largely entertained and distracted by a narrowed debate between two sides that assume that capitalism is here to stay, that it is conducive to democracy, and that with the help of a benign United States this worthy system is being exported for the benefit of people the world over. This fundamental characteristic of our corporate media fails the prerequisite for media in a vital democracy: it enables a wide variety of destructive, if not ghastly, practices to be carried out in the name of the people without their accurately informed consent, and it steers discussion of remedies away from institutional transformation that a fully informed public might favor.

In a variety of ways, then, the media culture that we have inherited from the sixties era has effectively depoliticized the polity, meaning our role as citizens has shrunk while our lives as workers, consumers, and entertainment audiences have greatly expanded. Today's mass media culture is, if anything, more image-driven than it was becoming in the sixties era, and far more saturated with the imperatives of consumerism and entertainment than forty years ago. Politics becomes something consumed. As community organizer Ed Chambers has put it, "You cannot be bombarded with consumerism, debt, and constant worry about your job and security and have any energy left for the common good."[6] Given the importance of emotional connection for commercial entertainment media, the spectacle has become saturated with dramatic conflict, shrill attack and counterattack, colorful personalities, personal scandals, and vivid imagery, while simultaneously being largely emptied of political content and serious explanatory analysis. As a result, as Carl Boggs has put it, politics has "sunk to new levels of personalized and trivialized blather."[7]

As I have argued in these pages, the media culture evolved in this direction because, responding to commercial and ideological imperatives, it excluded a desperately needed full range of argumentation during the sixties era while paying increasing attention to extreme behaviors on the part of those it left out. It subsequently became a vehicle for angry distortions and denunciations that initially played on audiences' feelings of being victimized by what they saw, and it eventually succeeded in bringing us the world we currently inhabit. We are invited to watch, cheer or jeer, and perhaps occasionally take part with our own behavioral outburst. In short, the media spectacle has encouraged the spread of enclave mentalities and a warlike political discourse in much of our culture. What Lawrence Grossberg said of the conservative backlash in the eighties and nineties can be applied generally to the media culture and most of the public: the "real paradox" of the backlash and media culture is that "by repoliticizing and re-ideologizing all of the social relations and cultural practices of everyday life," they have "effectively depoliticized a significant part of the population."[8]

Ironically, perhaps, national elections, arguably the showcase of American democracy, have themselves become permeated by the manipulative and depoliticizing qualities of mass media. Referring to the electoral spectacle as "postmodern democracy," political theorist Sheldon Wolin has observed that the once "rowdy populist carnival" of presidential politics "was sleekly engineered" in the late twentieth century into a "tightly orchestrated production for anointing 'the leader of the free world,' and equating democracy with 'free elections'" even though "a near-majority of Americans" do not vote and "elections are expensive and not free." In a manner similar to consumer culture, the "lavish spectacle of elections flattered" the "sovereign people," even while "the sheer scale and display of money-power [reminded] them of their powerlessness." Likening elections to a "political Superbowl," Wolin went on,

> The thinly veiled contempt for the voter in the lavish display was one of many indications that elections were steadily coming to resemble totalitarian plebiscites, except that in the United States some political ads (i.e., party propaganda) deliberately aimed to discourage citizens from voting, that is from supporting those who governed. Perhaps in postmodernity indifference and apathy, demobilization rather than mobilization of mass excitement, are the necessary conditions of a new form of totality.[9]

The Internet

Although mass media culture continues to be dominated by the same combination of boundaried discourse and commercially driven imagery, the Internet has generated significant shifts from the media culture of the sixties era. It has also become a medium of choice for millions of younger Americans. As an open-ended medium, the Internet provides its users with access to information and interpretation from outside the boundaries of mass media discourse. Indeed, its boundaries are limited only by the human imagination. It also provides an enormously important vehicle for interactive communication that can spread awareness and conversation, and it is a highly significant tool for networking and organizing. Each of these characteristics of Internet technology provides greater potential for democracy. Yet the future impact of the Internet remains unclear, in large part because uses of the technology will reflect evolving social, political, and economic forces.

Three questions about public access to the Internet's potentially unlimited range of information and interpretation are crucial: whether that access will remain socioeconomically skewed, whether "net neutrality" (see below) will be compromised so that most users will be drawn to the Internet predominantly for consumer and entertainment functions, and, finally and most crucially, whether and how much the Internet's unbounded opportunities can widen the boundaries of the common political discourse.

The Internet itself remains vulnerable to the same forces of commercialization and ideological control that currently dominate the mass media, suggesting a future in which these forces, as they did with radio and television, once again distort a medium initially hailed as a boon to American democracy. Lawrence Lessig has provided a telling interpretation of the way that the "environment designed to enable the new is being transformed to protect the old." Positing "two futures in front of us," Lessig suggests that the "one we are taking" looks like this: "Take the Net, mix it with the fanciest TV, add a simple way to buy things, and that's pretty much it. It is a future much like the present." As he put it, "The promise of many-to-many communication that defines the early Internet will be replaced by a reality of many, many ways to buy things and many, many ways to select among what is offered."[10]

Increasing interaction between the mass media and the Internet has provided opportunities for openings in normal media discourse, but the mass market influences on television and the press may well end up shaping the Internet more than the Internet's open discourse shapes those media.[11] It is also an open question whether Internet-stressed newspapers can maintain their already meager levels of investigative reporting.

Finally, in the contemporary media culture, the open-ended, individualized nature of the existing Internet may well accelerate the erosion of the commons into enclaves of like-minded cyber-communities—what Cass Sunstein has called "The Daily Me"[12]—thus accelerating the media culture's centrifugal tendencies.[13] With the corporate mass media remaining the gatekeepers of the discursive commons, the expanded Internet domain will provide endless opportunities for a rich, radical, and often contentious discourse (as it currently does), but, like the alternative or underground press of the sixties era, this discourse will remain marginalized outside the boundaries of society's commons.

Media Reform

If we are serious about democracy, we will need to reform the media system structurally.
    —Robert McChesney, *Rich Media, Poor Democracy,* 1999

The prevalence of this media culture suggests that one important arena for moving society toward more democratic politics is media reform, specifically the effort to rein in the commercialization of mass media, to render the media less accountable to capitalism and more structurally accountable to the people. Indeed, organizing to make capitalism's media more democratic may offer an opportunity for what André Gorz has called "non-reformist reform" that promises to enhance the possibility of broader systemic reform, to say nothing of building a more democratic world.[14]

Such an effort is, in fact, being mobilized on several fronts. Within the United States, a number of progressive groups have emerged that are engaged in important early efforts to counter the many flaws of corporate media. One of these in particular, Free Press, was launched in 2002 by media critics Robert McChesney, John Nichols, and Josh Silver.[15] With growing impetus coming from increasingly well-attended national conferences, Free Press has helped to build a strong network among independent and alternative media while simultaneously addressing the need to reform the "broken system" of corporate media. Among the key themes the organization addresses are "media ownership," "public media," "the future of the Internet," "civil rights and media justice," and "quality journalism," along with the ongoing effort to build the media reform movement.

In recent years, Free Press has joined with a wide spectrum of others, including highly visible conservative groups, to generate public and eventually congressional opposition to corporate efforts to gain Federal Communications Commission (FCC) approval for increased conglomeration of media ownership—one example of an organizing effort that has succeeded in reaching across the political spectacle's traditional ideological spectrum. Another campaign Free Press has supported with some success has been the effort to preserve Internet "neutrality" or "Net Freedom" by preventing the large telephone and cable corporations that provide virtually all public Internet access from "blocking, speeding up or slowing down Web content based on its source, ownership or destination."[16] As with the anti-conglomeration effort, Save The Internet is a coalition of scores of groups spanning the political spectrum, from Free Press, the Feminist Majority, and the "I Hate Bush" blog site to the Christian Coalition of America and the National Rifle Association.[17]

In this sense, organizing to transform the media not only improves the likelihood of effective democracy building, but is itself an arena within which one can glimpse the potential for building a democratic dialectic among broad sectors of the public. While the interchange across the range of these groups has thus far been limited, the media reform movement encompasses those who are typically characterized as mortal adversaries in the attack culture of mass media. They have begun to recognize some of their common interests in halting the increased concentration of corporate power over media. Not surprisingly, while the media reform movement has generated significant interest and discussion among the independent and progressive media, the national news media have largely overlooked their efforts—except for a brief flap caused when Bill O'Reilly of Fox News attacked the "lunatics" at the 2008 national conference.[18]

Toward a Democratic Dialectic

Can't Beat Capitalism? Carve out little alternative communities of principle within it. Can't credibly challenge the state? Set your sights lower and focus on remaking your daily life. Can't build long-term strategies? Opt for dramatic gestures instead.
—L. A. Kauffman, "Small Change: Radical Politics since the 1960s," 1995

While far from perfectly expressed during the sixties era, the vision of a more vital and inclusive democratic culture provides a starting point for addressing the challenges of the current time. As I argued early in the book, in the process of confronting social and political targets, sixties social movements began to explore a democratic dialectic of collective empowerment significantly different from the social dynamics in the postwar market democracy. Society's dominant institutions, including the media, effectively converted that dialectic back into forms that are compatible with market democracy, leaving the vision and experiences of democratic mobilization outside. Indeed, as L. A. Kauffman's quote suggests, mass media culture and its highly conflictual spectacle devalues politics as a field of activity in which humans join with others to shape their collective future. And as Sheldon Wolin has observed of the social program rollbacks induced by the neoliberal regime, they "don't simply reverse previous social gains; they also teach political futility to the Many."[19] Market democracy thereby offers compensatory or "affective" empowerment, for, as Grossberg contended, "Affective empowerment is increasingly important in a world in which pessimism has become common sense, in which people increasingly feel incapable of making a difference."[20]

As a key form of affective empowerment, the consumer imperative has left virtually no public and private space untouched; it shapes the American landscape, the public's leisure activities, and the polity itself. As Juliet Schor wrote in 2006, "The United States is the most consumer-oriented society in the world. People work longer hours than in any other industrialized country. Savings rates are lower. Consumer credit has exploded, and roughly a million and a half households declare bankruptcy every year. There are more than 46,000 shopping centers in the country, a nearly two-thirds increase since 1986."[21] Consumer credit imploded, of course, in the crash of 2008, yet, as George W. Bush argued in the aftermath of the 9/11 attacks, a core requirement for economic recovery has been for Americans to "go shopping." Revived and liberated by neoliberalism and sustained by advertising that flatters consumers' sense of individual significance, advertising has, as Schor added, "proliferated far beyond the television screen to virtually every social institution and type of public space, from museums to zoos, to college campuses and elementary school classrooms, restaurant bathrooms and menus, at the airport, even in the sky."[22] As a form of manipulative propaganda with an implicit ideology about individuals and society,[23] advertising has become what Jacques Ellul called "total propaganda"—or, in Neil Postman's terms, the "background radiation of the social and intellectual universe."[24]

A variation on affective empowerment that emerged from the shrinking political horizon of the late-sixties era was a vast range of therapeutic and spiritual practices under the umbrella of a "Human Potential" movement that has reinforced psychology's individualistic answers to fundamental human and social needs. As critics like Christopher Lasch and Carl Boggs have observed, the therapeutic culture tends to focus on the self in a way that "detaches individuals from their social context."[25] As a consequence, Philip Cushman argued, "if we psychologize and medicalize every human action by ridding it of any significant political cause, we condemn ourselves to denying the effects of the macro structures of our society."[26] Russell Jacoby has taken this reasoning one step further: "The more the development of late capitalism renders obsolete or at least suspect the real possibilities of self, self-fulfillment, and actualization, the more they are emphasized as if they could spring to life through an act of will alone."[27] At the same time, as psychotherapist Nancy McWilliams has observed, contemporary psychotherapy is being "reshaped by descriptive psychiatric diagnosis, pressures from powerful corporate interests," and is therefore "threatened with becoming the servant of the surrounding culture" despite psychotherapists' "core values and beliefs that differ significantly from many values and beliefs that pervade contemporary commercially oriented Western cultures."[28]

Psychology has, of course, been helpful to countless individuals, and psychological awareness provides important insights into the dehumanizing qualities of institutional life and prevailing social dynamics. Karen Stenner's analysis of the "authoritarian dynamic," for example, seems particularly relevant to the way the backlash against the sixties and the "politics of distraction" have aroused and played off public fears.[29] As psychologist Sandra Bloom remarked in the aftermath of the 1991 Gulf War, "All the detritus that we would rather deny—sexism, racism, narcissistic rage, hatred, fear, and loathing—rises to the surface when our national defense is threatened, just like they rise to the surface in the individual who is threatened. The opportunity is therefore presented for a conscious recognition and resolution of the underlying dark forces that secretly motivate so much of human behavior."[30] Observing how psychotherapy had become "disconnected from any wider social meaning, narcissistically preoccupied with helping the individual to adjust," Bloom noted, "The suffering of my individual patients became embedded in a historical and political context out of which could be derived a meaning and purpose both for their pain and for the transformation of this pain into social action and social reconstruction."[31] Finally, psychological insight is also crucially important for a workable understanding of a democratic dialectic, of interaction that reaches across the divides of media culture, whether through community organizing or conflict resolution.

Building Community

Radical democracy is ordinary people participating in active community institutions where they discuss politics and ideas as they work for a better neighborhood, city, state, nation, and beyond.
—Rinku Sen, *Stir It Up: Lessons in Community Organizing and Advocacy,* 2003

One important dimension of generating a radically democratic alternative is the practice known as community organizing. Popularized during the sixties era by longtime organizer Saul Alinsky, community organizing has evolved through a variety of training institutes and organizations in the years since. In addition to the still-operating Industrial Areas Foundation (IAF) that Alinsky founded in 1940, contemporary organizations include, among others, The Association of Community Organizations for Reform Now (the recently maligned ACORN), the Citizen Action network and the Midwest Academy (of Community Organizing), and the church-based People's Institute for Community Organizing (PICO).[32] Most forms of community organizing emphasize helping communities of people come together to articulate their concerns and priorities, recognize their common interests, gain a sense of themselves as members of a mutually supportive community, and act in ways that enhance their political voice within the wider political culture. While organizers play a crucial facilitative role, they typically take a back seat to the wishes of the community and the community-building process. Community organizing also recognizes that democracy involves more than debate and deliberation.[33] It attends to and incorporates the important emotional and psychological dimensions of community, place, and interpersonal engagement in the organizing process, in addition to enhancing participants' political efficacy.[34] As Noam Chomsky has put it, organizing "means that you discover that you're not alone."[35]

While necessary, however, community organizing by itself is far from sufficient for building a democratic future. Grassroots community organizations tend to remain local in their focus, often becoming absorbed into the local political culture and by their nature leaving the institutions of globalizing capitalism and elite-dominated national politics essentially untouched. As the social movements of the sixties era encountered increasing resistance, local organizing evolved into a wide range of neighborhood or community-protection resistance actions in what Harry Boyte called the "backyard revolution."[36] Over time these efforts were conventionally lumped together under the usually pejorative banner NIMBY (Not In My Back Yard), reflecting what Sidney Plotkin has called "enclave localism," a turning "inward and defensive in a world dominated by powerful interests."[37] In effect, for all its promise for democratic community building, localism reflects other individualized responses to capitalism and elite domination. As Manuel Castells has argued, "When people find themselves unable to control the world, they simply shrink the world to the size of their community."[38]

Thus the construction of a radically democratic future cannot remain local, just as the "blessed unrest" that Paul Hawken has described as non-ideological cannot remain inattentive to systemic forces. As Hawken himself put it, the growing number of citizen organizations need to "shift our awareness to the possibility that we will have fundamentally changed the way human beings govern and organize themselves on earth."[39] Or, as David Harvey has written, Not in My Back Yard needs to become translated into a universal principle of environmental justice: "Not in Anybody's Back Yard." In his words, this requires

> confronting the underlying processes (and their associated power structures, social relations, institutional configurations, discourses, and belief systems) that simultaneously generate environmental and social injustices. . . . The fundamental problem in today's world is that of unrelenting capital accumulation and the extraordinary asymmetries of money and political power that are embedded in the process. Alternative modes of production, consumption, and distribution as well as alternative modes of environmental transformation have to be explored.[40]

After fifty years of community organizing, Ed Chambers observed, "It is clear that an analysis of who's got power and why . . . is necessary if we are to relieve the stresses and heal the wounds."[41] To some degree, of course, such awareness flows naturally from the educative function of democratic participation. However, it would seem that an increasingly important function of organizers is to attend explicitly to a community's consciousness of their connections to systemic forces as well as to other efforts like their own. In some form, communities need "master teachers" in the sense that Martin Luther King Jr. and Malcolm X were master teachers who helped their communities understand the forces arrayed against them and inspired them to action. As I suggest above, truly democratic media would also play a significant role in enhancing local awareness of wider connections.

Networking, participation in regional or global conferencing, and coalition building are also crucially important, and events like the Seattle WTO protests of 1999 and the World Social Forum have provided glimpses of international organizing at work.[42] Traditionally, political parties have been the way of organizing broader constituencies, one reason the rightward migration of both the Democratic and Republican Parties over the past few decades has produced several unsuccessful efforts to generate third parties—unsuccessful in large part because the electoral system is structurally and politically stacked against them. Social movements are the other prevailing model for broader-than-local organizing. Thus organizer Rinku Sen urged community organizing to "move into practices that support the emergence of new social movements with the potential to win large-scale progressive change."[43] A number of left-progressive writers have argued that a unified movement could emerge when existing social movements "recognize that they themselves are essentially different facets of one still larger movement all of whose parts must relate positively to one another if the whole and any of the parts will succeed."[44] As John Sanbonmatsu put it in *The Postmodern Prince*, what is needed is an "*organic coalescence* of the various diverse movements for human and non-human liberation into a single universal project to cultivate the basis of a new social order."[45]

Transcending the Media Divide

The democratic dialectic reflects both personal and collective dimensions of empowerment, for democratic empowerment occurs in the context of community and builds a democratic civic culture that, in turn, nurtures individual development and collective empowerment. Democratic theorist John Dewey suggested two dimensions to democratic empowerment: democracy is grounded on conversation and interaction among individuals or between an individual and his or her community, and this democratic interaction involves a mutually educative interaction between self and other, one that expands into wider circles of exchange with new groups of others experienced as equals. These interactions enable one to learn about both oneself and others, in the process gaining a sense of mutuality and common interest.[46]

Reflective democratic thinkers have variously characterized the democratic conversation that needs to occur in our contemporary world. Cultural critic Lawrence Grossberg has written of the need to create "structures of affective commonality *that do not deny differences,* based on principles of justice, fairness, equality, and democracy in economic, political, and cultural terms."[47] On the grounds that "only shared hopes are stable," philosopher Judith Green has offered a "deeply democratic" model that includes "all stakeholders in devising mutually satisfactory solutions to shared problems."[48]

As some of the more powerful moments in sixties social movements suggest, efforts to construct an alternative democratic future can, and indeed must, convey a vision of the democratic future they seek, a vision that can unite the diverse fragments of local, national, and international politics. One compelling way that vision can be communicated to others is through a transparent process that respects people's common humanity. Another way of putting this is that democracy building requires a universalistic discourse grounded in its process, a discovering of commonality through respect for, even celebration of, diversity, rather than a discourse that is assumed to be universal by those elites who work to promulgate it as a governing ideology.

Thanks in good part to the legacy of the sixties and post-sixties eras, our world seems a long way from this kind of universal discourse. In the postmodern world of consumer-driven media culture and Internet enclaves, innumerable manifestations of community, ethnic, religious, racial, gender, and sexual identity have become increasingly important to people, yet the pursuit of what Lawrence Grossberg calls the "construction of social individuality" in enclaves of similar others has not only fragmented the progressive Left, it fragments society and has enabled the polarization of Left and Right. As food and environmental activist Frances Moore Lappé put it, "Unable to satisfy our yearning for connection through common endeavor, we try the next best thing—to feel included because of our outer identities."[49] Like the privatized world of therapy, these communities of identity reflect important aspects of human empowerment. If, however, they remain only expressions of who each of us is in the public spectacle, they are a political dead end, at least with respect to the globe's future. In Grossberg's words, "identity politics . . . loses any common sense of power and oppression."[50]

I don't mean this in a plaintive "can't we all just get along" sense. It involves hard work over a long haul, or what Howard Zinn has called "the long, slow struggle, not *for* equality (that phrase suggests completion), but *toward* equality."[51] In addition to the interchanges between blacks and whites in the "beloved community" of SNCC, two areas where sixties movements made significant headway in getting others to understand their perspectives—albeit not without difficult and sometimes painful argument—were in conversations young people had with their parents about the war in Vietnam and the conversations women had with their male partners. Clearly, the bonds people create in their relationships were and are important to their communicative efforts.

In addition, much of the work that has gone on over the past few decades in the worlds of psychology, conflict resolution, and mediation can and should be fruitfully linked to these political efforts. Organizing efforts can (and do) benefit from insights that help humans move beyond the traditional adversarial and often victimized stances that the contemporary culture fosters. Organizations like the National Coalition Building Institute and the Social Justice Training Institute have well-established training workshops that help to break down the dominant racial, gender, sexual, and religious divisions by starting from common human experiences of marginalization and stigmatization. Truth and reconciliation efforts in some of the world's most troubled and divided societies have helped longtime adversaries, or oppressors and oppressed, move past their ancient injuries into civil discourse—most notably, perhaps, in South Africa. It is also a hopeful sign in the early twenty-first century that, in contrast to their namesakes, the "New SDS" developed procedures that help to ensure mutually respectful dialogue while safeguarding the participation of gender, racial, class, and sexual subgroups in organizational decision making. These kinds of communicative practices can facilitate awareness of the commonalities shared across existing community divisions. Indeed, the largely unaddressed wounds left from the war in Vietnam, if not more generally from the 60s era, suggest that a Truth and Reconciliation process might be conducive to the restoration of democracy in the United States.

Ironically, another factor that may contribute to this process is what might be called polarization fatigue, resulting from thirty to forty years of a political spectacle that has revolved around attack and counterattack. Candidate Barack Obama's Philadelphia speech on race, made in response to the media flap about Rev. Jeremiah Wright's scathing rhetoric, seemed to tap into a wellspring of public desire to hear a different kind of discourse from its political leaders. As news commentator David Gergen noted at the time, the Illinois senator was "one of the rare figures" in public life "who speaks to us as adults."[52] Indeed, John Sanbonmatsu argues, "Critics fail to perceive what is most extraordinary about contemporary praxis, which is not difference but a felt need for unity"—a need he links to eros, the "life principle."[53]

Such a democratic discourse differs profoundly from society's identity polarization within conventional politics. In the latter realm, the only imaginable alternative to the alleged ideological "poles" of liberal Democrats and conservative Republicans is some "third way" combining fiscal conservatism and social liberalism (or, theoretically, their opposites). This imagined alternative might even be capitalism's preferred option. Yet this top-down solution contrasts sharply with a democratic conversation among diverse populations. It thereby perpetuates the depoliticized public's sense of powerlessness while completely failing to grapple with the structural forces producing the world's most profound problems.

Not only that, but the democratic civic culture is battered from two sides: on one, the "liberating" possibilities of the "anything goes" market, on the other, authoritarian conservative responses that seek to curb society's "sixties sensibilities." For democracy, these are corrosive, lose-lose options. Not only that, but as examples like the Soviet bloc and potentially Iran and China suggest, authoritarianism cannot permanently check the seductions of the marketplace. Yet, for a number of reasons, the anything goes market is not a sustainable option either.

Approaching the Crossroads: Capitalism or Democracy?

U.S. global power, as presently conceived by the overwhelming majority of the U.S. establishment, is unsustainable.
    —Anatol Lieven, *America Right or Wrong*, 2004

Our world, it would appear, will either undergo revolutionary changes so far reaching in character that humanity will totally transform its social relations and its very conception of life, or it will suffer an apocalypse that may well end humanity's tenure on the planet.
    —Murray Bookchin, *The Ecology of Freedom*, 2005

Along with the diversion of the entertainment spectacle, the boundaries of mass media discourse help to obscure the fact that the post–World War II archetype is, so to speak, running out of gas. With the ideological support of mass media culture, the American political economy has sought to project the United States as global hegemon and as the arbiter of the only legitimate model for world development. Facing a significant challenge during the sixties era, the American archetype recovered dramatically, effectively marginalized still-active dissent, and, since the fall of the discredited Soviet system, has become the model for global emulation.

While the latter news is typically welcomed with open arms by conventional pundits, fundamental contradictions within this archetype remain enormously problematic. Perhaps most concretely, the American pursuit of global hegemony, facilitated by the permanent war economy, not only generates increasing global hostility and resistance,[54] but also distorts the American political economy in ways that generate the potential for mass resistance within the United States.

Furthermore, the very political economy that has spread throughout the world under the neoliberal regime and is now advertised the world over is rapidly running up against its own, and the earth's, limitations. A world in which billions of people live near the edge of survival while thousands live in staggering, ostentatious wealth widely visible in the global media is a world rife with tensions that inevitably produce violent uprisings and violent repression. The proliferation of wars, fueled by these global tensions and by competition among the world's profit-seeking arms producers, has produced millions of impoverished refugees while accelerating immigration tensions. Within the United States alone, the past thirty-five years of neoliberal economic growth has produced a massive concentration of wealth in a tiny segment of the population, while the nation's median income has remained level and the real income of the lower 90 percent of the population has declined.[55]

Much of the aforementioned tension revolves around the disparities between the so-called "developed" and "underdeveloped" worlds that the postwar archetype of world capitalism has ensured. This tension has intensified with widening inequality under globalizing capitalism. While these conditions continue to raise obvious moral and pragmatic challenges for the American archetype, an increasing number of social and scientific critics have taken this critique one step further to argue that the archetype itself is unsustainable.

Immanuel Wallerstein, author of an important critique of the contemporary capitalist "world historic system," argued in 1996 that this world historic system has entered a period of "terminal crisis" and is "unlikely to exist in fifty years," largely because of four fundamental shifts that accelerated in the post–Cold War world: (1) the deruralization of much of the globe (undercutting capitalism's ability to exploit human and natural resources in sparsely populated rural areas); (2) the ecological crisis that threatens to end what capitalism's economists call the "externalization of costs"; (3) the democratization of world demand that has accompanied but remains in contradiction with the spread of market economics (specifically, the spreading demand for not only the products of capitalism but also the fundamentals of the welfare state: decent wages, housing, and health care, along with educational opportunities for one's children); and (4) the decline under globalization of the very state power that is not only the source of potential amelioration of market excesses but a crucial source of stability and growth for those economies. Wallerstein further noted that Third World "wars of national liberation" ultimately failed [or some would argue, were not allowed] to provide their peoples with a "fully liberatory" alternative to world historic capitalism. Not surprisingly, he argues that satisfaction of the fundamental demands of democratization, for everyone, requires a "radically different system of distribution of the world's resources than we have today."[56]

Exacerbated by pervasive inequality, ecology poses the newest and most fundamental challenge to the prevailing world system. Beginning with the environmentalism that grew out of the later years of the sixties era, ecological thinking not only contradicts one of the crucial ideological foundations of the postwar system—"what's good for business is good for everyone"—but, as Wallerstein noted, it has challenged the market system's externalization of costs. All living beings on the planet bear the costs that do not figure in corporations' cost calculations, because those private calculations are central to capitalism.

However, the environmental problems that were being addressed in the 1970s have broadened from health-threatening pollution and the destruction of natural resources to more systemic and tangible threats to the planet's ability to sustain life. Fossil fuels that have driven the engine of growth-oriented capitalism since the invention of the steam engine are finite, and the imminent arrival of "peak oil" is likely to wreak major disruptions in the economy and lifestyle of the American archetype as the financial and ecological costs of finding and extracting these fuels soar. Even more important, the massive reliance on these fuels throughout the industrial age has reached a point where in aggregate they threaten the ecosphere. The greenhouse effect that is creating unprecedented global warming is accelerated by the combination of global fossil fuel combustion and the destruction of the world's forests to facilitate development and industrialized agriculture. Notwithstanding political propaganda attacks and a few voices of scientific skepticism, the scientific community has grown increasingly alarmed about the fundamental transformations generated by global climate change and has with increasing confidence attributed the magnitude of the change to human causes.[57] Furthermore, the widespread use of pesticides, particularly in industrial agriculture, has compounded the problems of industrial pollution, and thus humanity grapples with the spread of chronic and degenerative diseases linked, at least to some degree, to damage to the human immune system.[58] In addition to dramatic increases in the rate of species extinction, there are also ample signs of the "tragedy of the commons" at work, perhaps most dramatically for the world's fisheries.[59]

From Bill McKibben's warning that capitalism's growth imperative—the "endless More"—is "morphing into a dangerous fantasy,"[60] to Joel Kovel's argument that capital is "incapable of mending the ecological crisis it provokes" and thus "we face a choice between 'the end of capitalism' and 'the end of the world,'"[61] a growing number of analysts argue that the world is approaching a crucial crossroad between a path toward extinction and an alternative future.[62] The spreading pursuit of the American economic archetype in enormous nations like India and China only brings home the point about the globe's viability more forcefully.

Within the world capitalist system, answers to problems of health-threatening pollution or the destruction of natural resources have been shaped according to capitalism's mal-distribution of income and wealth. Thus those with capital have been able to avoid most of the more immediate environmental threats, whereas those without, in their desperation for capital investment, have traded short-term material gains for long-term environmental costs (or at least those in political authority have done so). The ecological consciousness of the commons, however, challenges these inequities by drawing on a radically different set of perceptions and priorities from those at work in the capitalist world historic system. Ecology focuses on the preservation of the whole through respect for the interrelatedness of the parts; capitalism is grounded on the interests of separate individual parts. Without attention to the inequitable environmental burden or the issue of "environmental justice," the radical impact of ecological destruction is diverted into class-based and capitalism-sustaining environmentalism—environment versus jobs.

The key, I argue, is whether the ecological challenge produces system-transforming change, or whether it is simply absorbed into the dominant system. Important ecological thinkers like Amory and Hunter Lovins and Paul Hawken have advocated a future they call "natural capitalism,"[63] suggesting various means by which a market economy can adapt to and advance ecological imperatives. As I suggest below, my own orientation toward a vital, meaningful, and inclusive democracy suggests that "natural capitalism" is, by itself, an insufficient level of change. Yet I acknowledge that these remain open questions that can and should be resolved democratically through a conversation among the citizenry (as opposed to an elite-dominated polity responsive to the imperatives of capital). The existence of private ownership and market exchange seem widely valued aspects of human experience, yet, elevated to dominant principles by capitalism, these imperatives produce the massive accumulation of wealth in the hands of a few, the impoverishment of many, and the resulting elite-dominated polity. The real question may be whether or not organizing for a democratic future can produce sufficient public engagement and consciousness to keep both private ownership and the market within appropriate boundaries and scale. Or, to use terms I have used in this book, whether the market dialectic can be progressively surmounted by a democratic dialectic. That is, can markets be made to serve democracy instead of dominating and distorting democracy as they currently do? Much depends on how we collectively proceed.

At the same time, the treacherous state of the world produced by globalizing capitalism and neoliberal politics provides an opportunity to bridge long-entrenched class divides. Ecological crises provide openings for understanding humans' shared fate, and since mutuality lies at the center of ecological thinking it can provide a window for empathy, for seeing the globe's enormous inequities in a new light. Increasing attention to the importance of life-supporting wages, sanitary drinking water, decent housing, real educational opportunities, and adequate health services for all—*and* to the health of the ecological commons—contains the built-in possibility of a radical popular movement that spans a far broader spectrum of identities and political interests.

Calls for "real democracy" are commonly dismissed as hopelessly utopian by defenders of competitive individualism and status quo institutional arrangements. Yet the question needs to be asked: Is it utopian (i.e., unrealistic) to believe that humans are capable of democratic conversation that builds toward a wider democratic future, or is it utopian to believe that the global system can continue to forge ahead on its current destructive path because its flaws will be effectively eclipsed by some as yet unforeseen technological "fix"? Outside the boundaries of mass media discourse one finds a host of commentaries suggesting the latter is, as Bill McKibben put it, a "fantasy." As Paul Hawken has observed, "Creating genetically modified organisms to address hunger, building pebble bed nuclear reactors to address global warming, or waging opportunistic wars to establish democracies are all forms of downstream thinking that predicated today's dilemmas because none of them address the source of the problem.[64]

Lessons from the Sixties Experience

To be hopeful in bad times is not just foolishly romantic. It is based on the fact that human history is a history not only of cruelty, but also of compassion, sacrifice, courage, kindness. What we choose to emphasize in this complex history will determine our lives.
 —Howard Zinn, *You Can't Be Neutral on a Moving Train*, 1994

What is lost in the media culture's "Sixties" is the powerful experience of people taking history into their own hands, as well as the story of how and why that popular uprising turned into the distortion popularized in media lore. If these had been the stories told to people over the past thirty to forty years, innumerable groups could have sensed their connection to this history, could have learned from it, and might thereby have a greater sense of hope linked to their own potential empowerment. Like their forebears, people would sense their potential to make history in their own time.

This book's focus on what happened in and to the sixties has led me to conclusions that emphasize democracy building, with implications for the Left's efforts to raise consciousness among the wider public. I believe that people on the Left need to converse and build political common cause with those who have significantly different political outlooks. And I believe that community building that can produce acts of defiance remains a crucial avenue for wresting concessions from the powerful. Nonetheless, I am well aware that direct action protest will necessarily remain an important tool in a democracy movement's tool box.

Two specific aspects of the sixties era require careful attention for future democracy building to have a chance to work. One has to do with the issue of the militancy of political expression. The sixties experience, as well as others since the sixties era ended, clearly suggests that the more militant a collective action is, the more likely it is to generate a negative response from a wider swath of the public (to say nothing of government repression), especially as the visible manifestations of the militant action are explained in the conventional terms used by political elites who have easy access to mass media. Over time, more and more Americans came to view the war in Vietnam as immoral, yet more and more Americans also expressed a kind of protest fatigue, if not outright hostility toward antiwar protesters. On the one hand, militant action proved functional in building pressure to end the war; on the other, it helped to generate more vehement hostility toward protest. One could argue that by generating increased public hostility, militancy helped to build public pressure on the Nixon administration to make the militancy-generating problem—i.e., the war—go away. However, in the aggregate, these media-conveyed images became the basis for dominant mainstream texts about the sixties and useful foils in the political backlash that drove American politics to the right.

Mass mobilizations, militant and otherwise, remain politically significant. They generate awareness of the existence of dissent that can be an important catalyst for wider audiences to be more attentive to contested issues; they can provide participants with important sources of outside-the-boundaries interpretation as well as affective empowerment. They can even disrupt what Leslie Sklair calls global capitalism's "smooth running (accumulation of private profits) locally," thereby potentially generating "ways of globalizing these disruptions."[65] However, such disruptions need to be entered into strategically, with full awareness of the kind of coverage mass media typically provide, and therefore of their negative as well as positive effects on different audiences. Tensions between central organizing and local autonomy remain inherently problematic. Indeed, the global justice movement—or, as the mass media like to call it, the "anti-globalization" movement—that followed on the Seattle protests of 1999 encountered dynamics similar to those at work in the sixties, even though the movement had embraced democratic and diversity-respecting techniques like consensus decision making and affinity groups. In her insightful discussion of these strains, Stephanie Ross's observation might sound familiar to former sixties activists:

> The refusal to make decisions that have some binding force on the whole community or to have forms of legitimate leadership thus results in vanguardism by default. This is most readily seen when it is combined with a commitment to diversity of tactics. Not only do some groups emerge as a self-selected avant garde, they do so by deploying tactics which are not only defined as the "radical" [i.e., "militant"] leading edge but which, by their very nature, make the practice of other tactics next to impossible. . . . There is in fact a narrowing of the definition of what constitutes radicalism or even resistance, in implicit moral judgment which privileges risk-taking, regardless of whether the majority believes such risks are worthwhile, effective, or justified.[66]

Thoughtful awareness of past social movements' experiences with mass media is also crucial. Along with the tactical guidelines published by community organizers, writers like Charlotte Ryan have outlined strategies that can help protest movements optimize their impact with mass media, including cultivation of relations with relevant journalists through interaction that helps the journalists at least understand the "outside" perspectives of many protesters, laborious though that process might be.[67] However, given the tendency of most social movements toward decentralization and a healthy degree of spontaneity, the possibility of counterproductive media exposure is ever present, particularly given the predispositions of many media professionals and the structural and ideological imperatives of commercial mass media.

The second problematic issue arising from the sixties-era trajectory is the more general tendency toward expressive politics as politics, particularly the many ways that capitalism's market dialectic has developed to provide "affective empowerment" that deflects real political change. The identity politics of individual expression will remain an important and appealing path, as will a wide variety of therapeutic practices. Yet one of the clear lessons of the sixties era and its aftermath is that expressiveness by itself —or what Rinku Sen has called "identity-without-the-politics"[68]—has diminishing utility, especially as polarization fatigue grows among the public. The crucial distinction would seem to be between emotional empowerment linked to activity that enhances self- and other-awareness, therefore to democratic growth, as opposed to emotional empowerment achieved through the media and consumer spectacle's manipulation.

Making these distinctions requires both political and psychological awareness, or, perhaps, both cognitive and emotional intelligence. Since empathy is a foundation for both a universal discourse and the "spiral of empowerment," a convergence between psychology and politics is, arguably, much needed.

Frances Moore Lappé has argued that our current condition necessitates a shift from the competitive individualism that underpins society's prevailing institutions. Lappé accurately observes that the market economy and liberal politics are grounded on the assumption that humans are essentially competitive and self-interested, on the narrow but self-fulfilling principle that "there isn't enough of anything, neither enough 'goods'—whether jobs or jungles—nor enough 'goodness,' because human beings are, well, pretty bad." These assumptions, in turn, lead us to "mistrust deliberative problem solving, distrust even democratic government, and grasp for an infallible law—the market!—driven by the only thing we can really count on, human selfishness." These beliefs legitimize institutional arrangements that generate a "spiral of powerlessness" within a "thin democracy." In addition, they produce the global ills described earlier, or, as Lappé put it, "wealth concentrates and suffering increases, confirming the dreary premises that set the spiral in motion in the first place."[69]

By contrast, Lappé draws on evidence from the burgeoning field of human brain research that demonstrates an inherent human inclination toward empathy, as well as the need for collaboration and meaning. Herein lies the "possibility of universal connection" Cornel West referred to.[70] As democratic activists like Martin Luther King Jr. have long recognized, humans have a capacity for good or ill, and a key question for society is: which characteristics do the prevailing social arrangements nurture and reward? As Lappé has argued, our thin democracy is "misaligned with human nature" because it "fails to tap the best in us and fails to protect us from the worst." Instead, she argues for a "living democracy" grounded in the fundamental human need to "connect with others, for basic fairness, and for efficacy, as well as the need to feel that our lives matter, which for many people means contributing to something grander than their own survival." These values are as applicable to the economic sphere as the political sphere. Trusting these human traits and humans' ability to learn the skills of deliberative problem solving would lead, Lappé contends, to a "spiral of empowerment" that contrasts sharply with the current spiral of powerlessness. At bottom, thin democracy generates a cycle of fear, while living democracy reinforces a cycle of hope.[71]

John Sanbonmatsu is not alone in contending that this kind of vision, this connection with others, is at root spiritual: "The ultimate spiritual or 'religious' objective of the postmodern prince is to defend this *eros,* the life principle, from every social deformation rooted in *thanatos,* the death-drive. (For what are existing social movements but differing, partial manifestations of *eros*, the *will to life?*)"[72] Indeed, as Herbert Marcuse wrote in 1966, "Today the fight for life, the fight for Eros, is the *political* fight."[73] If that was true in 1966, it is certainly more true today.

In the end, the effort to build a democratic alternative to an increasingly ominous corporate future is, like many moments experienced during the long sixties era, one that can be powerfully self-sustaining. In addition to enabling people to see the forces that impinge on and repress their full humanity, it awakens in people the awareness of possibility—the possibility that things can be done differently, the possibility that people of very different backgrounds and orientations can come together and discover their common humanity. The latter discovery is one of democracy's most powerful rewards, the sense of breaking through preconceptions about differentness to come to an understanding of the other that brings with it a rich, emotional connection.

Notes

Preface

1. Andrew Sullivan, "Goodbye to All That," *Atlantic Monthly,* December 2007, 42.

Chapter 1. The Past as Prologue: Distorted History—
Declining Democracy

1. NBC News, November 4, 2008, www.lexisnexis.com.

2. Ibid.

3. Ibid.

4. See, for example, Matt Bai, "2010's Debates Still Trapped in the 1960s," *New York Times,* May 25, 2010, A17.

5. Tim Reid, "Obama Tries to Revive Campaign with Late Push in Opening State," *Times* (London), September 15, 2007, 53.

6. Discussed in chapter 10 below. See Michel Crozier, Samuel P. Huntington, and Joji Watanuki, *The Crisis of Democracy: Report on the Governability of Democracies to the Trilateral Commission* (New York: New York University Press, 1975), 113.

7. The term neoliberal refers to the extreme, contemporary form of classical liberalism and its embrace of "free" markets. I use the word "regime" in the sense of "relatively durable political regimes" grounded in dominant political coalitions over a span of American presidencies. See Stephen Skowronek, "The Changing Political Structures of Presidential Leadership," in *Debating Democracy: A Reader in American Politics,* 4th ed., ed. Bruce Miroff, Raymond Seidelman, and Todd Swanstrom (Boston: Houghton Mifflin, 2003), 285–296.

8. Tom Hayden, *The Long Sixties: From 1960 to Barack Obama* (Boulder, Colo.: Paradigm, 2009).

9. Ronald Reagan, quoted in Daniel Marcus, *Happy Days and Wonder Years: The Fifties and the Sixties in Contemporary Cultural Politics* (New Brunswick, N.J.: Rutgers University Press, 2004), 61.

10. Sidney Blumenthal, "Reaganism and the Neokitsch Aesthetic," in Sidney Blumenthal and Thomas Byrne Edsall, *The Reagan Legacy* (New York: Pantheon, 1988), 275.

11. Thomas Frank, *The Conquest of Cool: Business Culture, Counterculture, and the Rise of Hip Consumerism* (Chicago: University of Chicago Press, 1997).

12. Lawrence Grossberg, "Rockin' in Conservative Times," in *Dancing in Spite of Myself* (Durham, N.C.: Duke University Press, 1997), 257. See also note 17 in chapter 13 below.

13. Both the market and democratic dialectics represent a form of interaction or interchange between people and the wider community or culture. What I term the market dialectic is referred to by Richard Fox and Jackson Lears as a "dialectic" between the emotional needs of consumers and advertising's manipulation of the empty self with the "culture of consumption." It purports to be democratic because it "gives the consumer what s/he wants," yet it is, as I explain in this and the next chapter, fundamentally undemocratic. See Richard Wightman Fox and T. Jackson Lears, *The Culture of Consumption: Critical Essays in American History, 1880–1980* (New York: Pantheon, 1983).

14. This was a history that saw the sixties as starting hopefully, then spinning out of control, leading to terminal decline. Early retrospective accounts by former SDS activists contributed to this frame: James Miller's *"Democracy Is in the Streets": From Port Huron to the Siege of Chicago,* Todd Gitlin's *The Sixties: Years of Hope, Days of Rage,* and Tom Hayden's *Reunion: A Memoir.* Critics argued the declensionist view neglected movements like feminism that extended well beyond the "end" of the sixties. See Alice Echols, "We Gotta Get Out of This Place: Notes to-

ward a Remapping of the Sixties," in Echols, *Shaky Ground: The Sixties and Its Aftershocks* (New York: Columbia University Press, 2001), 61–74, originally published in *Socialist Review* 22, no. 2 (1992); and Wini Breines, "Whose New Left?" *Journal of American History* 75, no. 22 (September 1988): 528–545.

15. One symptom of the distortions in media discourse is that moderate Democrats like Bill Clinton are reflexively referred to by the Right as "Leftists." Actual left arguments lie outside the boundaries of mass media discourse, as I explain below.

16. Notably Maurice Isserman and Michael Kazin, *America Divided: The Civil War of the 1960s* (New York: Oxford University Press, 2000). Related research on the origins of the "New Right" in the 1960s was also important during these years: see Paul Lyon, *New Left, New Right, and the Legacy of the Sixties* (Philadelphia: Temple University Press, 1996); John A. Andrew III, *The Other Side of the Sixties: Young Americans for Freedom and the Rise of Conservative Politics* (New Brunswick, N.J.: Rutgers University Press, 1997); and Rebecca E. Klatch, *A Generation Divided: The New Left, the New Right, and the 1960s* (Berkeley: University of California Press, 1999).

17. Andrew Sullivan, "Goodbye to All That," *Atlantic Monthly,* December 2007, 42. Ironically, Sullivan's title is identical to one used by feminist Robin Morgan in a 1970 essay denouncing the sexism in the white New Left. Rick Perlstein, author of the *Nixonland: The Rise of a President and the Fracturing of America,* rebutted Sullivan's argument in "Getting Past the '60s? It's Not Going to Happen," *Washington Post,* February 3, 2008, B01ff.

18. I don't mean to suggest that these politics are solely symbolic, just that they have diverted a great deal of energy away from the material effects of neoliberalism while also promising more than they can deliver.

19. C. B. Macpherson, "Democratic Theory: Ontology and Technology," in *Philosophy and Technology: Readings in the Philosophical Problems of Technology,* ed. Carl Mitcham and Robert Mackey (New York: Free Press, 1983), 162.

20. Robert D. Putnam, *Bowling Alone: The Collapse and Revival of American Community* (New York: Simon & Schuster, 2000), 18.

21. See Richard Flacks, *Making History: The American Left and the American Mind* (New York: Columbia University Press, 1988).

22. Attributed to Paul Rockwell, the statement provided a framework of interpretation for the Columbia student takeover in 1968. "The Columbia Statement," in *The University Crisis Reader: The Liberal University under Attack*, vol. 1, ed. Immanuel Wallerstein and Paul Starr (New York: Vintage, 1971), 24.

23. See Howard Zinn, *A People's History of the United States: From 1492 to the Present,* rev. ed. (New York: HarperPerennial, 2005).

24. See Antonio Gramsci, *Prison Notebooks,* ed. and trans. Quintin Hoare and Geoffrey Nowell Smith (New York: International Publishers, 1971).

25. See W. Lance Bennett's *News: The Politics of Illusion,* 7th ed. (New York: Longman, 2006).

26. Daniel Hallin, *The "Uncensored War": The Media and Vietnam* (Berkeley: University of California Press, 1989), 116.

27. Ibid., 116–117, emphasis added.

28. As Hallin notes, the "boundary-maintaining mechanism" phrase comes from Talcott Parsons, *The Social System* (New York: Free Press, 1951). See Hallin, *"Uncensored War,"* 117.

29. Edward Herman and Noam Chomsky, *Manufacturing Consent: The Political Economy of Mass Media,* 2nd ed. (New York: Pantheon, 2002), lx. See also Douglas Kellner, *Television and the Crisis of Democracy* (Boulder, Colo.: Westview Press, 1990); and Michael Parenti, *Inventing Reality: The Politics of New Media,* 2nd ed. (New York: St. Martin's Press, 1993).

30. Todd Gitlin, *The Whole World Is Watching: Mass Media in the Making and Unmaking of the New Left* (Berkeley: University of California Press, 1980), 271, emphasis in original.

31. Gadi Wolfsfeld and William A. Gamson, "Movements and Media as Interacting Systems," *Annals of the American Academy of Political and Social Science* 528 (July 1993): 119.

32. See Hallin, *"Uncensored War,"* 116–117.

33. Albert O. Hirschman, *Exit, Voice and Loyalty: Responses to Decline in Firms, Organizations, and States* (Cambridge, Mass.: Harvard University Press, 1970).

34. I am indebted to Todd Gitlin's analysis of the way media imagery invited certain actions and behaviors among members of SDS. See Gitlin, *The Whole World Is Watching*.

35. Jonathan Yardley, "The Sixties Revival: Echoes from an Empty Decade," *Washington Post*, July 24, 1987, C2. I discuss Yardley's column further in chapter 11.

36. John Sanbonmatsu, *The Postmodern Prince: Critical Theory, Left Strategy, and the Making of a New Political Subject* (New York: Monthly Review Press, 2004), 35.

37. Jerry Rubin, *Do It! Scenarios of the Revolution* (New York: Ballantine, 1970), 106, quoted in Melvin Small, *Covering Dissent: The Media and the Antiwar Movement* (New Brunswick, N.J.: Rutgers University Press, 1994), 18–19.

38. As told to Bayard Rustin, quoted in Milton Viorst, *Fire in the Streets: America in the 1960s* (New York: Simon & Schuster, 1979), 341.

39. Sara M. Evans and Harry C. Boyte, *Free Spaces: The Sources of Democratic Change in America* (Chicago: University of Chicago Press, 1992), 17.

40. For a rich account of the underground press of the era, see Abe Peck, *Uncovering the Sixties: The Life and Times of the Underground Press* (New York: Pantheon, 1985).

41. John Dewey, *Democracy and Education* (1916; reprint, New York: Free Press, 1966), 87.

42. Paul Hawken, *Blessed Unrest: How the Largest Movement in the World Came into Being and Why No One Saw It Coming* (New York: Viking, 2007), 4.

43. See Toni Morrison, *Paradise* (New York: Knopf, 1998), 212; and Richard Flacks, *Making History*, 8.

44. See, for example, David Neiwert, *The Eliminationists: How Hate Talk Radicalized the American Right* (Sausalito, Calif.: PoliPoint Press, 2009). Citing the widespread "frustration, disillusionment, the justified anger and the absence of any coherent response," Noam Chomsky has likened the current moment to Weimar Germany. See Chris Hedges, "Noam Chomsky Has 'Never Seen Anything Like This,'" *Truthdig*, April 19, 2010, www.truthdig.com/report/item/noam_chomsky_has_never_seen_anything_like_this_20100419. Others dispute the potential for fascism. See the discussion in Matthew Rothschild, "Chomsky's Nightmare: Is Fascism Coming to America?" *The Progressive*, June 14, 2010, 14–21.

45. Discussed in chapter 13. See Frances Moore Lappé, *Getting a Grip: Clarity, Creativity and Courage in a World Gone Mad* (Cambridge, Mass.: Small Planet Media, 2007).

Chapter 2. Roots of the Sixties: Contradictions between Capitalism and Democracy in Postwar America

1. Quoted in Stuart Hall, "Citizens & Citizenship," in *New Times: The Changing Face of Politics in the 1990s*, ed. Stuart Hall and Martin Jacques (London: Lawrence & Wishart, 1989), 174.

2. Hannah Arendt, *The Human Condition* (Garden City, N.Y.: Doubleday Anchor, 1959), 51.

3. C. B. Macpherson, *Democratic Theory: Essays in Retrieval* (London: Clarendon, 1973), 57.

4. From Mill's *Considerations on Representative Government,* in John Stuart Mill, *Utilitarianism, Liberty, and Representative Government* (London: J. M. Dent & Sons, 1910), 217.

5. Or as Jean-Jacques Rousseau argued more than two centuries ago, democracy reflects humans' "natural" impulse for commiseration (*pitié*)—the "natural repugnance to see any sensitive being perish or suffer." Jean-Jacques Rousseau, *The First and Second Discourses,* trans. and ed. R. D. Masters and J. R. Masters, 3rd ed. (New York: St. Martin's Press, 1964), 95. Cited in David E. Ingersoll, Richard K. Matthews, and Andrew Davison, *The Philosophical Roots of Modern Ideology: Liberalism, Communism, Fascism, Islamism* (Upper Saddle River, N.J.: Prentice-Hall, 2001), 88.

6. E. E. Schattschneider, *Party Government* (New York: Holt, Rinehart & Winston, 1942), 11–16, and *Two Hundred Million Americans in Search of a Government* (New York: Holt, Rinehart & Winston, 1969), 5. Both are quoted in David Adamany's introduction to E. E. Schattschneider, *The Semisovereign People: A Realist's View of Democracy in America* (New York: Harcourt, Brace, 1975), xii–xiii.

7. See, for example, Marco Iacoboni, *Mirroring People: The New Science of How We Connect with Others* (New York: Farrar, Straus & Giroux, 2008); and Daniel Goleman, *Social Intelligence: The New Science of Human Relationships* (New York: Bantam, 2006).

8. See her "spiral of powerlessness" and "spiral of empowerment," discussed in chapter 13 below. Frances Moore Lappé, *Getting a Grip: Clarity, Creativity and Courage in a World Gone Mad* (Cambridge, Mass.: Small Planet Media, 2007).

9. John Dewey, *Freedom and Culture* (New York: G. P. Putnam, 1939), 162, quoted in Sheldon S. Wolin, *Politics and Vision,* expanded ed. (Princeton, N.J.: Princeton University Press, 2004), 516.

10. Immanuel Wallerstein put it this way in reference to neoliberal globalization: "The market can no more transform the economic prospects of the poorer 75% of the world's population than taking vitamins can cure leukemia." Immanuel Wallerstein, *The End of the World as We Know It: Social Science for the Twenty-First Century* (Minneapolis: University of Minnesota Press, 1999), 29.

11. As expressed in James Madison's famous essay, "Federalist #10," written to urge ratification of the Constitution. James Madison, Alexander Hamilton, and John Jay, *The Federalist Papers,* ed. Isaac Kramnick (New York: Viking, 1987).

12. Sheldon Wolin, "Elitism and the Rage against Postmodernity," in *The Presence of the Past* (Baltimore: Johns Hopkins University Press, 1989), 48.

13. For rich historical detail on this era, see Paul Starr, *The Creation of the Media: Political Origins of Modern Communications* (New York: Basic Books, 2004); Douglas Kellner, *Television and the Crisis of Democracy* (Boulder, Colo.: Westview Press, 1990); Michael Schudson, *Discovering the News: A Social History of American Newspapers* (New York: Basic Books, 1978); and Erik Barnouw, *A History of Broadcasting in the United States: Volume I, A Tower of Babel* (New York: Oxford University Press, 1966).

14. W. Lance Bennett, *News: The Politics of Illusion,* 8th ed. (New York: Pearson Longman, 2009), 189, 194–210.

15. Michael Schudson, *The Sociology of News* (New York: Norton, 2003), 66.

16. Neil Postman, *Amusing Ourselves to Death: Public Discourse in the Age of Show Business* (New York: Viking Penguin, 1985), esp. chapter 5.

17. Garth Jowett and Victoria O'Donnell, *Propaganda and Persuasion* (Newbury Park, Calif.: Sage Publications, 1986), 7.

18. Jacques Ellul, *Propaganda: The Formation of Men's Attitudes,* trans. Konrad Kellen and Jean Lerner (New York: Vintage, 1965), 27.

19. Quoted in Noam Chomsky, *Turning the Tide: U.S. Intervention in Central America and the Struggle for Peace* (Boston: South End Press, 1985), 235.

20. Walter Lippmann, *Essays in the Public Philosophy* (Boston: Little, Brown, 1955), 39–40.

21. As Lippmann put it, the "democratic fallacy" was its preoccupation with the "origin of government" (the people) rather than with the "processes and results." See Walter Lippmann, *Public Opinion* (1921; reprint, New York: Free Press, 1997), 196. Noam Chomsky quotes Lippmann's phrasing in *Hegemony or Survival: America's Quest for Global Dominance* (New York: Metropolitan Books, 2003), 6. For a more detailed analysis of the thinking of Lippmann, Bernays, and others, see Stuart Ewen, *PR! A Social History of Spin* (New York: Basic Books, 1996).

22. See Harold Lasswell, "Propaganda," *Encyclopedia of the Social Sciences* (1933), 12:521–528.

23. Alex Carey, *Taking the Risk out of Democracy: Corporate Propaganda versus Freedom and Liberty* (Urbana: University of Illinois Press, 1995), 18. A broader and more general picture of the "creation of the corporate soul" is documented in Roland Marchand, *Creating the Corporate Soul: The Rise of Public Relations and Corporate Imagery in American Big Business* (Berkeley: University of California Press, 1998).

24. Adam Smith, *The Wealth of Nations* (1776; reprint, Chicago: University of Chicago Press, 1976), 477.

25. See Edmund L. Andrews, "Greenspan Concedes Flaws in Deregulatory Approach," *New York Times,* October 24, 2008, 1.

26. Garrett Hardin, "The Tragedy of the Commons," *Science* 162 (December 1968), 1243–1248. This dynamic has been applied more generally to capitalism in the writing of social ecologist Murray Bookchin. See, for example, Murray Bookchin, *The Ecology of Freedom* (Palo Alto, Calif.: Cheshire, 1982).

27. An ideological belief expressed most openly in the apocryphal 1953 remark of Charles Wilson, "What's good for General Motors is good for the country, and what's good for the country is good for General Motors," but clearly present in the rationale for the federal government "bailout" of 2008. See Harold B. Hinton, "Approval Is Likely," *New York Times*, January 23, 1953, 1ff.

28. See Thomas C. Schelling, *Micromotives and Macrobehavior* (New York: Norton, 1978).

29. Wallerstein, *The End of the World as We Know It,* 32.

30. See the classic account by Harry Magdoff, *The Age of Imperialism: The Economics of U.S. Foreign Policy* (1969; reprint, New York: Monthly Review Press, 2000). See also Immanuel Wallerstein, "The Rise and Future Demise of the World Capitalist System: Concepts for Comparative Analysis," *Comparative Studies in Society and History* 16, no. 4 (September 1974): 387–415; and David Harvey, *The New Imperialism* (New York: Oxford University Press, 2005).

31. Alexis de Tocqueville, *Democracy in America* (1840; reprint, Indianapolis: Hackett Publishing Company, 2000), book 2, chapter 5.

32. In effect, an American counterpart to the nineteenth-century European "public sphere" described by Jürgen Habermas in *The Structural Transformation of the Public Sphere: An Inquiry into a Category of Bourgeois Society,* trans. Thomas Burger and Frederick Lawrence (Cambridge, Mass.: MIT Press, 1989). For a contemporary democratic theorist's advocacy of such a sphere, see Benjamin Barber, *Strong Democracy: Participatory Politics for a New Age* (Berkeley: University of California Press, 1984).

33. See, for example, the documentation in Alex Carey, *Taking the Risk out of Democracy: Corporate Propaganda versus Freedom and Liberty* (Urbana: University of Illinois Press, 1997).

34. Elizabeth A. Fones-Wolf, *Selling Free Enterprise: The Business Assault on Labor and Liberalism, 1945–1960* (Urbana: University of Illinois Press, 1994), 15.

35. *Fortune* editor Daniel Bell itemized the "prodigious" apparatus of the campaign: "1,600 business periodicals, 577 commercial and financial digests, 2,500 advertising agencies, 500 public relations counselors, 4,000 corporate public relations departments and more than 6,500 'house organs'" with a "combined circulation of more than 70 million." In Bell's words, the "staggering" output of this campaign amounted to "the most intensive 'sales' campaign in the history of industry." Bell's study, "Industrial Conflict and Public Opinion," was included in A. Kornhauser, R. Dubin, and A. Ross, eds., *Industrial Conflict* (New York: McGraw-Hill, 1954), 240–256, quoted in Carey, *Taking the Risk out of Democracy,* 30.

36. V. O. Key, *Politics, Parties, and Pressure Groups* (New York: Crowell, 1958), 106–107, cited in Carey, *Taking the Risk out of Democracy,* 79.

37. Fones-Wolf, *Selling Free Enterprise,* 1.

38. Carey, *Taking the Risk out of Democracy,* 27.

39. A key stepping stone toward this end was the 1946 midterm election in which the Re-

publicans won control of both houses of Congress. Among the new members of Congress were Joseph McCarthy and Richard Nixon (who had accused his "lip service American" opponent of consistently voting the "pro-Moscow line" and fronting for "un-American elements"). Quoted in William H. Chafe, *The Unfinished Journey* (New York: Oxford University Press, 2006), 98.

40. The article, written by Edward Shils, was published in *Encounter.* See Godfrey Hodgson, *America in Our Time: From World War II to Nixon, What Happened and Why* (New York: Vintage, 1976), 74. The phrase "end of ideology" was popularized by the publication of Daniel Bell's book, entitled *The End of Ideology and the Exhaustion of Political Ideas in the Fifties* (Glencoe, Ill.: Free Press, 1960), and its subsequent embrace by President John F. Kennedy.

41. On this and other contradictions, see Stephanie Coontz, *The Way We Never Were: American Families and the Nostalgia Trip* (New York: Basic Books, 1992).

42. Chafe, *The Unfinished Journey,* 111.

43. Ibid., 112.

44. See Michel Crozier, Samuel P. Huntington, and Joji Watanuki, *The Crisis of Democracy: Report on the Governability of Democracies to the Trilateral Commission* (New York: New York University Press, 1975); and the discussion in chapter 10 below.

45. Quoted in Daniel Hellinger and Dennis R. Judd, *The Democratic Façade,* 2nd ed. (Belmont, Calif.: Wadsworth, 1994), 258, emphasis added.

46. See Gabriel Kolko, *Confronting the Third World: United States Foreign Policy, 1945–1980* (New York: Pantheon, 1988), 48.

47. George Kennan, "Review of Current Trends, U.S. Foreign Policy" (Report by the Policy Planning Staff, U.S. State Department, PPS/23), in *Papers Relating to the Foreign Policy of the United States,* vol. 1, 1948, 524, quoted in Hellinger and Judd, *Democratic Façade,* 253.

48. See Stuart Ewen, *Captains of Consciousness: Advertising and the Social Roots of the Consumer Culture* (1976; reprint, New York: Basic Books, 2001). See also John Kenneth Galbraith, *The New Industrial State,* 4th ed. (Boston: Houghton Mifflin, 1985).

49. Philip Kotler, professor of marketing at the Kellogg School of Management, Northwestern University, quoted in *Financial Times,* May 29, 2003, 9.

50. Stuart Ewen argues that the consistent objective of industrialists was the social control or "pacification" of the workforce. Ewen, *Captains of Consciousness,* 27.

51. I draw on Lynn Spigel's figures that utilized information contained in Cobbett S. Steinberg, *TV Facts* (New York: Facts on File, 1980). Lynn Spigel, *Make Room for TV: Television and the Family Ideal in Postwar America* (Chicago: University of Chicago Press, 1992), 1.

52. See Bennett, *News: The Politics of Illusion,* 32–72.

53. Neil Postman has argued cogently for the way photography combined with the world of incoherence, irrelevance, and impotence introduced by news by teletype to produce, with television, news that is essentially meaningful only as entertainment. See Neil Postman, *Amusing Ourselves to Death: Public Discourse in the Age of Show Business* (New York: Penguin, 1986).

54. Susan Sontag, *On Photography* (New York: Farrar, Straus & Giroux, 1977), 5, 10.

55. See Joseph Schumpeter, *Capitalism, Socialism, and Democracy,* 3rd ed. (London: Allen & Unwin, 1950).

56. Bernard Berelson, Paul F. Lazarsfeld, and William N. McPhee, *Voting: A Study of Opinion Formation in a Presidential Campaign* (Chicago: University of Chicago Press, 1954), 314–315.

57. Benedict Anderson's historical study of nationalism notes the importance of the "mass ceremony" of daily newspaper reading as one of the early forms of imagining one's nation. See Anderson, *Imagined Communities: Reflections on the Origin and Spread of Nationalism,* 2nd ed. (London: Verso, 2006), 32–35.

58. See Robert McChesney, *Rich Media, Poor Democracy: Communication Politics in Dubious Times* (New York: New Press, 1999).

59. David Halberstam, *The Fifties* (New York: Ballantine, 1994), 506.

60. Quoted in Lynn Spigel and Michael Curtin, *The Revolution Wasn't Televised: Sixties Television and Social Conflict* (New York: Routledge, 1997), 3.

61. Quoted in Coontz, *The Way We Never Were,* 171.

62. Cohen's study documents many such themes of postwar consumerist culture. See Lizabeth Cohen, *A Consumer's Republic: The Politics of Mass Consumption in Postwar America* (New York: Random, 2003), 113. See also Wendy Kozol, *Life's America: Family and Nation in Postwar Photojournalism* (Philadelphia: Temple University Press, 1994).

63. Sven Birkets, *The Gutenberg Elegies* (Boston: Faber & Faber, 1994), 214–215, quoted in Robert D. Putnam, *Bowling Alone* (New York: Simon & Schuster, 2000), 245–246.

64. Marty Jezer, *The Dark Ages* (Boston: South End Press, 1982), 110.

65. Philip Cushman, *Constructing the Self: Constructing America: A Cultural History of Psychotherapy* (Cambridge, Mass.: Perseus Publishing, 1995), 78–79.

66. John Berger, *Ways of Seeing* (New York: Penguin, 1977), 142, 132.

67. Poppy Cannon, quoted by David Halberstam, *The Fifties,* 496.

68. Berger, *Ways of Seeing,* 132.

69. Ibid., 133.

70. David Riesman, with Nathan Glazer and Reuel Denney, *The Lonely Crowd: A Study of the Changing American Character,* abridged and rev. ed. (New Haven, Conn.: Yale University Press, 2001), 20–21.

71. Philip Cushman, *Constructing the Self,* 80.

72. As John Berger has put it, "Publicity [advertising] is, in essence, nostalgic. It has to sell the past to the future. It cannot itself supply the standards of its own claims. And so all its references to quality are bound to be retrospective and traditional." Berger, *Ways of Seeing,* 139–140.

73. Thus, according to Cushman, throughout the consumerist era since World War II, the field of psychology has increasingly focused on "narcissism, schizophrenia, and borderline personality disorders" as prominent forms of mental illness. Cushman, *Constructing the Self,* 80.

74. Berger, *Ways of Seeing,* 134.

75. Ibid., 148–149.

76. Chris Hedges, *War Is a Force That Gives Us Meaning* (New York: Anchor Books, 2002), 10.

77. Cited in James B. Twitchell, *Adcult USA: The Triumph of Advertising in American Culture* (New York: Columbia University Press, 1996), 93.

78. See, for example, Arlie Russell Hochschild, *The Commercialization of Intimate Life: Notes from Home and Work* (Berkeley: University of California Press, 2003).

79. Twitchell, *Adcult USA,* 110.

80. C. B. Macpherson, *The Life and Times of Liberal Democracy* (Oxford: Oxford University Press, 1977), 5.

81. In addition to David Riesman's *Lonely Crowd* mentioned earlier, these included William Whyte, *The Organization Man* (New York: Simon & Schuster, 1956); C. Wright Mills, *The Power Elite* (New York: Oxford University Press, 1957); Paul Goodman, *Growing Up Absurd* (New York: Random House, 1960); and Vance Packard, *The Hidden Persuaders* (New York: David McKay, 1957). Other postwar intellectual currents, like existentialism, were becoming widely consumed, particularly by many younger readers.

82. Malvina Reynolds, "Little Boxes" (1962), *Ear to the Ground* (Smithsonian Folkways Records, 2000).

83. See William Hamilton Harris, *The Harder We Run: Black Workers since the Civil War* (New York: Oxford University Press, 1982), chaps. 6 and 7.

84. See Lewis Mumford, *The City in History* (New York: Harcourt, Brace & World, 1961); Jane

Jacobs, *The Death and Life of Great American Cities* (New York: Random House, 1961); and Percival Goodman and Paul Goodman, *Communitas: Means of Livelihood and Ways of Life,* 2nd ed. (New York: Vintage, 1960).

85. As Putnam put it, "The two decades following 1945 witnessed one of the most vital periods of community involvement in American history." Putnam, *Bowling Alone,* 54–55.

86. Abraham H. Maslow, "A Theory of Human Motivation," *Psychological Review* 50, no. 4 (1943): 370–396.

87. Paul Goodman, "Poverty of the Great Society," in *The Great Society Reader: The Failure of American Liberalism,* ed. Marvin E. Gettelman and David Mermelstein (New York: Random House, 1967), 518n26.

88. Herbert Marcuse, *One-Dimensional Man: Studies in the Ideology of Advanced Industrial Society* (Boston: Beacon Press, 1964), 3, 10.

Chapter 3. An Awakening Democratic Dialectic: From Action to Empowerment in the 1960s

1. See Edward P. Morgan, *The Sixties Experience: Hard Lessons about Modern America* (Philadelphia: Temple University Press, 1991).

2. See Hazel Erskine, "The Polls: Demonstrations and Race Riots," *Public Opinion Quarterly* 31, no. 4 (Winter 1967–68): 655–677.

3. See Frances Fox Piven and Richard A. Cloward, *Poor People's Movements: Why They Succeed, How They Fail* (New York: Vintage, 1979), 4–5.

4. Barbara Deming, "Nonviolence and Radical Social Change," in *Revolution and Equilibrium* (New York: Penguin, 1971), 223.

5. Michael Lipsky, "Protest as a Political Resource," *American Political Science Review* 62 (December 1968), 1144–1158.

6. Noam Chomsky, *For Reasons of State* (1973; reprint, New York: New Press, 2003), 290.

7. In the language of social movement research, the media response helps to define the "ideological understandings" and "cultural symbols" of the "master protest frame" that reaches wider audiences.

8. William Gamson, "Social Movements and Cultural Change," in *From Contention to Democracy,* ed. Marco G. Guigni, Doug McAdam, and Charles Tilly (Lanham, Md.: Rowman & Littlefield, 1998), 59.

9. Murray Bookchin, *The Ecology of Freedom* (Palo Alto, Calif.: Cheshire, 1982), 339.

10. Much of the "Port Huron Statement" was written by Tom Hayden, one of the early, articulate voices for grassroots meanings of democracy.

11. Students for a Democratic Society, *Port Huron Statement* (Chicago: n.p., 1966), 6, 8, emphasis added.

12. Ibid., 5.

13. Ibid., 7, emphasis in original.

14. Ibid., 8.

15. Martin Luther King Jr., "I See the Promised Land," in *A Testament of Hope: The Essential Writings and Speeches of Martin Luther King, Jr.,* ed. James M. Washington (New York: HarperCollins, 1991), 286.

16. Quoted in Juan Williams, *Eyes on the Prize: America's Civil Rights Years, 1954–1965* (New York: Penguin, 1987), 244. The book is the "companion volume" to the PBS television series of the same name.

17. Charles M. Payne, *I've Got the Light of Freedom: The Organizing Tradition and the Mississippi Freedom Struggle* (Berkeley: University of California Press, 1995), 101.

18. Francesca Polletta, *Freedom Is an Endless Meeting: Democracy in American Social Movements* (Chicago: University of Chicago Press, 2002), 24.

19. Quoted in Tom Wells, *The War Within: America's Battle over Vietnam* (Berkeley: University of California Press, 1995), 15.

20. Michael Rossman, "The Wedding within the War," in *"Takin' It to the Streets": A Sixties Reader,* ed. Alexander Bloom and Wini Breines, 2nd ed. (New York: Oxford University Press, 2003), 84, emphasis in original.

21. "SDS Call for a March on Washington," in Bloom and Breines, *Takin' It to the Streets,* 183.

22. Paul Potter, "Speech to the April 17, 1965 March on Washington," in *The Sixties Papers: Documents of a Rebellious Decade,* ed. Judith Clavir Albert and Stewart Edward Albert (New York: Praeger, 1984), 218–219.

23. Quoted from a Vietnam Day Committee news release in Charles DeBenedetti, *An American Ordeal: The Antiwar Movement of the Vietnam Era* (Syracuse: Syracuse University Press, 1990), 127.

24. Saul Alinsky, *Rules for Radicals: A Practical Primer for Realistic Radicals* (1973; reprint, New York: Vintage, 1989), xxvi, 11.

25. Paul Goodman, "People or Personnel," in *Participatory Democracy,* ed. Terrence E. Cook and Patrick M. Morgan (San Francisco: Canfield Press, 1971), 52–53. In contrast to the consumer culture, Goodman meant that communities of people, rather than isolated individual consumers, would decide matters for themselves.

26. Rosalyn Fraad Baxandall, "Catching the Fire," in *The Feminist Memoir Project: Voices from Women's Liberation,* ed. Rachel Blau DuPlessis and Ann Snitow (New York: Three Rivers Press, 1998), 213.

27. As Doug McAdam has argued, the civil rights struggle's "ideological understandings" and "cultural symbols" were "appropriated" by subsequent "insurgent groups," while a "student left master frame" was adopted by the global eruption of student-based protest in 1968. Doug McAdam, "Culture and Social Movements," in *New Social Movements: From Ideology to Identity,* ed. Enrique Larana, Hank Johnston, and Joseph R. Gusfield (Philadelphia: Temple University Press, 1994), 42.

28. Ibid., 39.

29. As Piven and Cloward have put it, the system loses legitimacy in people's perceptions when they view rulers and institutional arrangements as "unjust and wrong," and people shift toward action when they shed their "fatalistic" outlook or their sense of themselves as "helpless." A correlate of seeing the system as illegitimate is viewing one's self as having "rights." See Piven and Cloward, *Poor People's Movements,* 4.

30. Nathan Teske, *Political Activists in America: The Identity Construction Model of Political Participation* (Cambridge: Cambridge University Press, 1997), 55.

31. Thus, for example, psychotherapist Alice Miller writes of parents who learned the "art of not experiencing feelings" in their own upbringing being unable to respond to their children as the persons they really are. See Alice Miller, *The Drama of the Gifted Child: The Search for the True Self,* rev. ed. (New York: Basic Books, 1997), 6–10.

32. Ralph H. Turner, "Ideology and Utopia after Socialism," in Larana et al., *New Social Movements,* 79–100.

33. Quoted in Dick Cluster, ed., *They Should Have Served That Cup of Coffee* (Boston: South End Press, 1979), 25.

34. Carol McClurg Mueller, "Building Social Movement Theory," in *Frontiers in Social Movement Theory,* ed. Aldon D. Morris and Carol McClurg Mueller (New Haven, Conn.: Yale University Press, 1992), 292.

35. For an in-depth account of the variety of institutional forces generating civil rights activism, see Aldon Morris, *Origins of the Civil Rights Movement* (New York: Free Press, 1984).

36. Quoted in Williams, *Eyes on the Prize,* 66, emphasis added.

37. Drawn from David Halberstam's interview with Diane Nash. David Halberstam, *The Children* (New York: Fawcett, 1999), 5.

38. Doug McAdam, *Freedom Summer* (New York: Oxford University Press, 1988), 127.

39. See Paul Good, *The Trouble I've Seen: White Journalist/Black Movement* (Washington, D.C.: Howard University Press, 1975).

40. Quoted in Wells, *The War Within*, 36–37.

41. C. Douglas Lummis, *Radical Democracy* (Ithaca, N.Y.: Cornell University Press, 1996), 35–36.

42. Quoted in the television documentary *Eyes on the Prize*, "Ain't Scared of Your Jails, 1960–61" (DVD; Alexandria, Va.: PBS Video, 2006). See also Halberstam, *The Children*, 139.

43. Nathan Teske, *Political Activists*, 55–56.

44. Halberstam, *The Children*, 62. As John Lewis recalled, pointing to the photograph of himself as a student coming out of jail, "I had never had that much dignity before. . . . It was exhilarating—it was something I had earned, the sense of the independence that comes to a free person" (140).

45. Bernice Johnson Reagon, interviewed in Williams, *Eyes on the Prize*, 177.

46. Halberstam, *The Children*, 8–9.

47. Quoted in *Freedom on My Mind*, dir. Connie Field and Marilyn Mulford (VHS; San Francisco: California Newsreel, 1994).

48. Cohn-Bendit is quoted in Wini Breines, *Community and Organization in the New Left: 1962–1968* (South Hadley, Mass.: J. F. Bergin, 1982), 30.

49. This is what Ross et al. have called a "fundamental attribution error." See J. Michael Ross, Reeve D. Vanneman, and Thomas F. Pettigrew, "Patterns of Support for George Wallace: Implications for Racial Change," *Journal of Social Issues* 36, no. 2 (1976): 69–91. Doug McAdam, *Political Process and the Development of Black Insurgency, 1930–1970* (Chicago: University of Chicago Press, 1982), 50.

50. Halberstam, *The Children*, 75.

51. Jo Freeman, *The Politics of Women's Liberation* (New York: David McKay, 1975), 118.

52. Baxandall, "Catching the Fire," 210; Ann Popkin, "The Personal Is Political: The Women's Liberation Movement," in Cluster, *They Should Have Served That Cup of Coffee*, 187.

53. Betty Friedan, *The Feminine Mystique* (New York: Dell, 1964).

54. Quoted in Williams, *Eyes on the Prize*, 76.

55. From an interview in ibid., 177.

56. Quoted in Howell Raines, *My Soul Is Rested* (New York: Penguin, 1983), 151.

57. Webb was twelve at the time of the march. Sheyann Webb and Rachel West Nelson, as told to Frank Sikora, *Selma, Lord, Selma: Girlhood Memories of the Civil-Rights Days* (Tuscaloosa: University of Alabama Press, 1980), quoted in Bloom and Breines, *Takin' It to the Streets*, 56.

58. Susan Brownmiller, *In Our Time: Memoir of a Revolution* (New York: Dial Press, 1999), 68. The name was an ironic play on the State Department "truth squads" that traveled to college campuses in 1965 preaching the Johnson administration line on the Vietnam War.

59. Halberstam, *The Children*, 61.

60. Kathleen Cleaver, "Women, Power, and Revolution," in *New Political Science* 21, no. 2 (1999): 231–232.

61. Howard Zinn, *You Can't Stay Neutral on a Moving Train: A Personal History of Our Times* (Boston: Beacon Press, 1994), 122.

62. Ann Oakley, "Feminism, Motherhood, and Medicine," in *What Is Feminism?* ed. Juliet Mitchell and Ann Oakley (New York: Pantheon, 1986), 140.

63. Quoted in Wells, *The War Within*, 36.

64. Williams, *Eyes on the Prize*, 88.

65. Quoted in *Berkeley in the 60s*, Kitchell Films in association with P.O.V. Theatrical Films (VHS; San Francisco: California Newsreel, 1990).

66. Baxandall, "Catching the Fire," 210.

67. Quoted in *America's War on Poverty: City of Promise* (VHS; Alexandria, Va.: PBS Video, 1995).

68. See Thomas J. Sugrue, *Sweet Land of Liberty: The Forgotten Struggle for Civil Rights in the North* (New York: Random House, 2008), 373.

69. Quoted in *America's War on Poverty: City of Promise*.

70. Ibid.

71. David Stoloff, "The Short Unhappy History of Community Action Programs," in *The Great Society Reader: The Failure of American Liberalism*, ed. Marvin Gettelman and David Mermelstein (New York: Random House, 1967), 231–239.

72. Both Bernstein and Malafronte's quotations come from *America's War on Poverty*.

73. Ibid. Importantly, community organizing was also unable to produce job openings in the established order.

74. The outbursts of mass violence known as riots throughout the mass media were often called "insurrections" or "rebellions" by those who perceived their political, if unorganized, character.

75. It should be noted that the Newark CAP experience not only helped lay the groundwork for the "riot" that exploded as expectations were dashed, but that in the riot's aftermath the UCC successfully pressured the city to reduce the scale of its urban renewal (and poverty removal) program and led to the election of Newark's first black mayor, Kenneth A. Gibson, in 1970. For a grassroots account of the Newark experience, see Tom Hayden, *Rebellion in Newark: Official Violence and Ghetto Response* (New York: Random House, 1967).

76. As Charles Payne wrote of civil rights organizing in the South, "The frames used to cover the civil rights movement were multiple and shifting, but they were always such as to obscure the organizing process." Payne, *I've Got the Light*, 392.

77. Ibid., 368. King's quote is taken from her *Freedom Song: A Personal Story of the 1960s Civil Rights Movement* (New York: William Morrow, 1987), 484.

78. Both recollections are contained in Amy Kesselman, with Heather Booth, Vivian Rothstein, and Naomi Weisstein, "Our Gang of Four: Friendship and Women's Liberation," in DuPlessis and Snitow, *Feminist Memoir Project*, 50–51.

79. Cathy Wilkerson, *Flying Too Close to the Sun: My Life and Times as a Weatherman* (New York: Seven Stories Press, 2007), 262, 275.

80. Sixties historians and sixties activists seem to have widely varying ways of dividing the sixties era. I suspect one factor influencing these divisions, including perhaps my own, is one's age as the sixties evolved.

81. In the Till case, the North's black newspapers and magazines like *Jet* were particularly crucial in bringing the Till murder and aftermath to the attention of northern black populations.

82. See Barbie Zelizer, *Covering the Body: The Kennedy Assassination, the Media, and the Shaping of Collective Identity* (Chicago: University of Chicago Press, 1992).

83. See Clayborne Carson, *In Struggle: SNCC and the Black Awakening of the 1960s* (Cambridge, Mass.: Harvard University Press, 1981); and Emily Stoper, *The Student Nonviolent Coordinating Committee: The Growth of Radicalism in a Civil Rights Organization* (Brooklyn: Carlson Publishing, 1989).

84. Marshall Ganz, quoted in *Freedom on My Mind*.

85. Robert Moses, quoted in ibid.

86. Quoted in Stoper, *The Student Nonviolent Coordinating Committee*, 235.

87. See chapter 5, note 5.

88. Stoper, *The Student Nonviolent Coordinating Committee*, 296.

89. Quoted in Bloom and Breines, *Takin' It to the Streets*, 225.

90. See chapter 1, note 27.

91. Milton Viorst, *Fire in the Streets: America in the 1960s* (New York: Simon & Schuster, 1979), 176.

92. Milton Mankoff and Richard Flacks, "The Changing Social Base of the American Student Movement," *Annals of the American Academy of Political and Social Science* 395 (May 1971): 65.

93. See Rick Perlstein, *Nixonland: The Rise of a President and the Fracturing of America* (New York: Scribner, 2008).

Chapter 4. Race, Class, and Gender: The Boundaries of Legitimate Media Discourse

1. Charles M. Payne, *I've Got the Light of Freedom: The Organizing Tradition and the Mississippi Freedom Struggle* (Berkeley: University of California Press, 1995), 392.

2. *Report of the National Advisory Commission on Civil Disorders* (New York: Bantam, 1968), 383.

3. Taylor Branch, *Pillar of Fire: America in the King Years, 1963–65* (New York: Simon & Schuster, 1998), 49. As Melvin Small wrote of media coverage of antiwar protests, "The media generally do not look favorably upon movements that oppose official policy" but "tend to support those who operate within the system and denigrate oppositional activities of ordinary citizens." Melvin Small, *Covering Dissent: The Media and the Anti-Vietnam War Movement* (New Brunswick, N.J.: Rutgers University Press, 1994), 13.

4. Ralph David Abernathy, *And the Walls Came Tumbling Down* (New York: Harper & Row, 1989), 272–273.

5. Todd Gitlin, *The Whole World Is Watching: Mass Media in the Making and Unmaking of the New Left* (Berkeley: University of California Press, 1980), 53.

6. Herman and Chomsky have used these terms in documenting the American mass media's dichotomous treatment of the (worthy) victims of U.S. adversaries and the (unworthy) victims of U.S. or client-state activities. See Edward Herman and Noam Chomsky, *Manufacturing Consent: The Political Economy of the Mass Media,* 2nd ed. (New York: Pantheon, 2002), esp. chapter 2.

7. "Squatter's Rights," *Newsweek,* February 22, 1960, 27–28.

8. King observed that the sit-ins were easing southern blacks' frustration with the "deliberate speed" and "token integration" of court litigation and stressed the principle of dignified and disciplined nonviolence. "Full-Scale Assault," *Newsweek,* February 29, 1960, 24–25.

9. "Terror?" *Newsweek,* March 7, 1960, 30.

10. "Turmoil in Dixie: Tennessee to Alabama," *Newsweek,* March 7, 1960, 30.

11. In its account, *Time* labeled the white toughs "familiar flotsam: the duck-tailed, side-burned swaggerers, the rednecked hatemongers, the Ku Klux Klan" in the narrowly titled article "Complicated Hospitality," *Time,* February 22, 1960, 20.

12. "Sitdown Erupts into Racial Riot," *New York Times,* February 24, 1960, 28; and "Chattanooga Quells Racial Clash," *New York Times,* February 25, 1960, 1.

13. "A Pattern for Peace?" *Newsweek,* March 21, 1960, 50–51, emphasis added.

14. "Next for the South?" *Newsweek,* March 28, 1960, 25.

15. Mary King, *Freedom Song: A Personal Story of the 1960s Civil Rights Movement* (New York: William Morrow, 1987), 213–214.

16. Ibid., 223.

17. Ibid., 222.

18. Ibid., 244.

19. Ibid., 231.

20. Claude Sitton, "Negro Vote Drive in Mississippi Is Set Back as Violence Erupts," *New York Times,* October 24, 1961, 28.

21. "Prospectus for the Summer," undated mimeographed copy of a SNCC working paper, cited by Fred Powledge, *Free at Last? The Civil Rights Movement and the People Who Made It* (New York: HarperCollins, 1991), 562.

22. James Atwater, "If We Can Just Crack Mississippi. . . . ," *Saturday Evening Post,* July 25, 1964, 16, quoted in Clayborne Carson, *In Struggle: SNCC and the Black Awakening of the 1960s* (Cambridge, Mass.: Harvard University Press, 1981), 112.

23. Moses added, "The Press were a critical part of the struggle in Mississippi, and they knew it. Their telling the story . . . [and] the media circus that followed was going to have the biggest impact." *Freedom on My Mind,* dir. Connie Field and Marilyn Mulford (VHS; San Francisco: California Newsreel, 1994).

24. "South Girds for Crisis," *New York Times,* June 4, 1964, 6.

25. Excerpted from Staughton Lynd, *Living inside Our Hope: A Steadfast Radical's Thoughts on Rebuilding the Movement* (Ithaca, N.Y.: Cornell University Press, 1997), 29.

26. See Robert McFadden, "First Murder Charge in '64 Civil Rights Killings of 3," *New York Times,* January 7, 1965, 1ff.

27. Powledge, *Free At Last?* 569–570. As Clayborne Carson has observed, the federal government failed to change its policy regarding protection of civil rights workers and instead focused its full "resources solely on the Philadelphia incident." Carson, *In Struggle,* 115.

28. "Limpid Shadows of Violence," *Life,* July 3, 1964, 32–34.

29. "Mississippi—'Everybody's Scared,'" *Newsweek,* July 6, 1964, 15–18. A week later, *Newsweek* ran one story on "Conversations on U.S. 45" in Mississippi, exploring the resentful feelings of white Mississippians, and a second story by Louis Harris, reporting on "The 'Backlash' Issue," *Newsweek,* July 13, 1964, 21–25.

30. As one volunteer put it, "We were all watching the CBS TV show—about 100 of us. . . . Walter Cronkite told how the whole country was watching Mississippi. . . . A Negro by my side spoke. . . . 'You know what we're all doing. . . . We're moving the world.'" Doug McAdam, *Freedom Summer* (New York: Oxford University Press, 1988), 71.

31. Powledge, *Free At Last?* 570.

32. Quoted in Payne, *I've Got the Light of Freedom,* 284.

33. Lynd, *Living inside Our Hope,* 34–35.

34. Ibid., 35.

35. "Waving the Red Flag," *Newsweek,* April 12, 1965, 30–31.

36. Richard Lentz, *Symbols: The News Magazines and Martin Luther King, Jr.* (Baton Rouge: Louisiana State University Press, 1990), 78, 80.

37. "Poorly Timed Protest," *Time,* April 19, 1963, 30–31. See Lentz, *Symbols,* 78–97.

38. "The Aim: Registration," *Time,* January 29, 1965, 21. See Lentz, *Symbols,* 145–146.

39. Lentz, *Symbols,* 340, 150–156.

40. Quoted in David Garrow, *Bearing the Cross: Martin Luther King, Jr. and the Southern Christian Leadership Conference* (New York: Vintage, 1988), 498.

41. "White Consensus: 'They're Trying to Go Too Fast,'" *Newsweek,* August 22, 1966, 24.

42. Garrow, *Bearing the Cross,* 591–592. James's reflections are included on 716–717n19.

43. Ibid., 552–553.

44. "A Tragedy," *Washington Post,* April 6, 1967, A20.

45. "Dr. King's Error," *New York Times,* April 7, 1967, 34.

46. *Life,* April 21, 1967, 4, quoted in Garrow, *Bearing the Cross,* 554.

47. The regular Mississippi Democratic Party and its primary were virtually closed to black participation.

48. Hamer's remarks are recorded in Juan Williams, *Eyes on the Prize: America's Civil Rights Years, 1954–1965* (New York: Penguin, 1988), 241–242.

49. Quoted from Staughton Lynd, "Coalition Politics or Nonviolent Revolution?" *Liberation*, June–July 1965, 19, in Todd Gitlin, *The Sixties: Years of Hope, Days of Rage* (New York: Bantam, 1987), 162.

50. Good, *The Trouble I've Seen: White Journalist/Black Movement* (Washington, D.C.: Howard University Press, 1975), 206.

51. "Waving the Red Flag," *Newsweek*, April 12, 1965, 28. The magazine's "moralistic obstinance" reference to MFDP emerged in a February 7, 1966, article entitled, "Panther on the Prowl" (20–21), focusing largely on the SNCC voter registration effort in Lowndes County, Alabama.

52. King, *Freedom Song*, 347.

53. Payne, *I've Got the Light of Freedom*, 368.

54. King, *Freedom Song*, 497–498.

55. Student Nonviolent Coordinating Committee, "The Basis of Black Power," in *Takin' It to the Streets: A Sixties Reader*, 2nd ed., ed. Alexander Bloom and Wini Breines (New York: Oxford University Press, 2003), 118.

56. From a June 25–26 edition of *Southern Courier*, written by David R. Underhill, in Stokely Carmichael [Kwame Ture], with Ekwueme Michael Thelwell, *Ready for Revolution: The Life and Struggles of Stokely Carmichael (Kwame Ture)* (New York: Scribner, 2005), 510.

57. *New York Times*, April 23, 1963, 20.

58. "'I Like the Word Black,'" *Newsweek*, May 6, 1963, 27–28.

59. "Brother Malcolm: His Theme Now Is Violence," *U.S. News & World Report*, March 23, 1964, 19.

60. "Now It's a Negro Drive for Segregation," *U.S. News & World Report*, March 30, 1964, 38–39.

61. "Malcolm's Brand X," *Newsweek*, March 23, 1964, 32.

62. Malcolm X, "I'm Talking to You, White Man," *Saturday Evening Post*, September 12, 1964, 30–35ff.

63. "The Lesson of Malcolm X," *Saturday Evening Post*, September 12, 1964, 84.

64. Ibid.

65. "Death of a Desperado," *Newsweek*, March 8, 1965, 24–25; "Satan in the Ghetto," *Newsweek*, November 15, 1965, 130–131.

66. "Death and Transfiguration," *Time*, March 5, 1965, 23–25.

67. "Malcolm X," *New York Times*, February 22, 1965, 20.

68. "The New Racism," *Time*, July 1, 1966, 11–13, emphasis added. Interestingly, back in April 1965, *Time* observed that Carmichael "has no more use for black racism than white." "Inside Snick," April 30, 1965, 74.

69. "'Black Power' Must Be Defined," *Life*, July 22, 1966, 4.

70. Patricia Bradley, *Mass Media and the Shaping of American Feminism, 1963–1975* (Jackson: University Press of Mississippi, 2003), 57.

71. *Dear Sisters: Dispatches from the Women's Liberation Movement*, ed. Rosalyn Baxandall and Linda Gordon (New York: Basic Books, 2000), 52.

72. Bradley, *Mass Media and the Shaping of American Feminism*, 56.

73. Naomi Weisstein, "Naomi Weisstein Speaks," a section of Ann Kesselman et al., "Our Gang of Four: Friendship and Women's Liberation," in *The Feminist Memoir Project: Voices from Women's Liberation*, ed. Rachel Blau DuPlessis and Ann Snitow (New York: Three Rivers Press, 1998), 34.

74. It is important to note, however, that tensions between the largely white upper-middle-

class women's liberation movement and both working-class women and women of color cropped up frequently over the movement's trajectory.

75. Casey Hayden and Mary King, "Sex and Caste: A Kind of Memo," in Baxandall and Gordon, *Dear Sisters,* 21–22. Later on, New Left activists Marge Piercy and Robin Morgan angrily denounced their male counterparts. Marge Piercy, "The Grand Coolie Damn," in *Sisterhood Is Powerful: An Anthology of Writings from the Women's Liberation Movement,* ed. Robin Morgan (New York: Vintage, 1970), 421–438; and Robin Morgan, "Goodbye to All That," originally published in the New York underground paper *The Rat* when it was taken over by women, in Baxandall and Gordon, *Dear Sisters,* 53–57.

76. SDS Women, "To the Women of the Left," in Baxandall and Gordon, *Dear Sisters,* 28.

77. Ellen Willis, "Letter to the Left," ibid., 51.

78. Echols added that radical feminists "fought for safe, effective, accessible contraception; the repeal of all abortion laws; the creation of high-quality, community-controlled child-care centers; and an end to the media's objectification of women. They also developed consciousness-raising—the movement's most effective organizing tool." Alice Echols, *Daring to Be Bad: Radical Feminism in America, 1967–1975* (Minneapolis: University of Minnesota Press, 1989), 3–4.

79. Although NOW repeatedly raised issues about sexist stereotyping, restrictive gender socialization, and the like, the group tended to do so in less confrontational ways. See Bradley, *Mass Media and the Shaping of American Feminism,* 212.

80. Ibid., 48, 57.

81. One study of newspapers in Britain and Los Angeles found that the major circulation newspapers provided readers with "sparse" coverage and "little information" about the women's liberation movement in its early stages (from July 1968 through June 1969). Monica B. Morris, "Newspapers and the New Feminists: Black Out as Social Control?" *Journalism Quarterly* 50 (Spring 1973): 37–42.

82. Bradley, *Mass Media and the Shaping of American Feminism,* 74.

83. Ibid., 57–58.

84. Susan J. Douglas, *Where the Girls Are: Growing Up Female with the Mass Media* (New York: Three Rivers Press, 1994), 172. Douglas's account contains numerous examples of condescending dismissal by CBS and ABC anchormen and commentators.

85. Laura Ashley and Beth Olson, "Constructing Reality: Print Media's Framing of the Women's Movement, 1966 to 1986," *Journalism and Mass Communication Quarterly* 75, no. 2 (Summer 1998): 263–277.

86. "Women's Lib: The War on 'Sexism,'" *Newsweek,* March 23, 1970, 74.

87. Douglas, *Where the Girls Are,* 179.

88. See the discussion of the Miss America protest in chapter 6.

89. "The New Feminists: Revolt against 'Sexism,'" *Time,* November 21, 1969, 53–56, emphasis added.

90. "Women's Lib: The War on 'Sexism,'" *Newsweek,* March 23, 1970, 71–77.

91. "Woman Power," *Newsweek,* March 30, 1970, 61.

92. "Woman-Power," *Time,* March 30, 1970, 50.

93. "Liberating the Journal," *Newsweek,* August 3, 1970, 44.

94. "Rebelling Women—The Reason," *U.S. News & World Report,* April 13, 1970, 35–37.

95. "How Women Are Doing in Politics," *U.S. News & World Report,* September 7, 1970, 24–27.

96. "Women's Lib, Continental Style," *Time,* August 17, 1970, 23–25.

97. "Who's Come a Long Way Baby?" *Time,* August 31, 1970, www.time.com/magazine/article/0,9171,876783,00.html.

98. "Women's Lib: A Second Look," *Time*, December 14, 1970, 50.

99. "Women's Lib: Beyond Sexual Politics," *Time*, July 26, 1971, 36–37.

100. "Sispeak: A Misguided Attempt to Change Herstory," *Time*, October 23, 1972, 79.

101. Sally Kempton, "Cutting Loose: A Private View of the Women's Uprising," *Esquire*, July, 1970, 53–57.

102. Helen Lawrenson, "The Feminine Mistake," *Esquire*, January 1971, 83ff.

103. Sara Davidson, "Foremothers," *Esquire*, July 1973, 71ff.

104. "When Did You Begin to Take the Women's Movement Seriously," *Esquire*, July 1973, 102.

105. Judy Jarvis, "New Rules in the Mating Game," *Esquire*, July 4, 1978, 42. See also Stephen Koch, "The Guilty Sex: How American Men Became Irrelevant," *Esquire*, July 1975, 53–57; and Judy Klemesrud, "The Year of the Lusty Woman," *Esquire*, December 19, 1976, 33–37.

106. Midge Decter, "The Paradox of Women's Liberation," *Newsweek*, January 22, 1973.

107. "The American Woman: On the Move—But Where?" *U.S. News & World Report*, December 8, 1975, 54–74.

Chapter 5. Vietnam and the Spheres of Media Discourse

1. Lance Morrow et al., "1968: Like a Knife Blade, the Year Severed Past from Future," *Time*, January 11, 1988, 12–23. The war characterizations are on 20, the two lessons on 21.

2. Tom Wells, *The War Within: America's Battle over Vietnam* (Berkeley: University of California Press, 1994), 491.

3. The percentage of Americans feeling the Vietnam War was "more than a mistake, it was fundamentally wrong and immoral," was again 72 percent in 1982, 68 percent in 1986, 71 percent in 1990, and 59 percent in 1994, twenty-one years after the war's end and following the Gulf War and President George H. W. Bush's pronouncement that "by God, we've kicked the Vietnam Syndrome once and for all." See "American Public Opinion and U.S. Foreign Policy, 1975" (1979, 1983, 1987, 1995, and 1999), the Chicago Council on Foreign Relations.

4. Or as Ronald Reagan put it in his remarks at the Vietnam Memorial on November 11, 1988, "Perhaps at this late date we can all agree that we've learned one lesson: that young Americans must never again be sent to fight and die unless we are prepared to let them win." Ronald Reagan Presidential Library, www.reagan.utexas.edu/archives/speeches/1988/111188b.htm.

5. Lawrence LeShan, *The Psychology of War* (New York: Helio, 1992), 31ff.

6. Erik Erikson, "Wholeness and Totality," in *War,* ed. L. Bransom and G. W. Goethals (New York: Basic Books, 1964), 122. Cited in LeShan, *Psychology of War,* 149n41.

7. And of course enemy states do the same. Chris Hedges, *War Is a Force That Gives Us Meaning* (New York: Anchor, 2002), 15, 21.

8. Jacques Ellul, *Propaganda: The Formation of Men's Attitudes* (New York: Vintage, 1973), 60.

9. Media studies have predominantly focused on the years from 1965 onward. From 1965 to 1973, an average of about 51 million people watched one of the three major networks' evening news programming on any given night, 38 million read one of the three major newsmagazines, nine million listeners were reached by radio news programming, and 80,000 people outside of metropolitan New York read the *New York Times*. While *Times'* readers were concentrated in the more educated, higher income sectors of the population, the newsmagazines were also an important source of information for society's elites. In addition, the two wire services, AP and UPI, provided war news to the nation's 1,750 newspapers. James Landers, *The Weekly War: Newsmagazines and Vietnam* (Columbia: University of Missouri Press, 2004), 2.

10. Edward Herman and Noam Chomsky, *Manufacturing Consent: The Political Economy of Mass Media,* 2nd ed. (New York: Pantheon, 2002), 169.

11. Daniel Hallin, *The "Uncensored War": The Media and Vietnam* (Berkeley: University of California Press, 1986), 10.

12. See Graham Allison's account, *Essence of Decision: Explaining the Cuban Missile Crisis* (New York: HarperCollins, 1971).

13. Quoted in Wells, *The War Within,* 68.

14. Quoted in ibid., 155–156, emphasis added. As Noam Chomsky later observed in reviewing McNamara's 1995 book on Vietnam, *In Retrospect,* "the 'tiny backward nation' is North Vietnam, which certainly suffered, though it was the *South Vietnamese* who bore the brunt of the assault that McNamara directed," emphasis in original. Noam Chomsky, "Memories," *Z Magazine,* July–August 1998, 3.

15. Jonathan Schell, "Remembering Robert McNamara," *Nation,* August 3/10, 2009, 24. Schell's essays about the destruction of Vietnamese villages were later published in *The Real War* (Cambridge, Mass.: De Capo Press, 2000).

16. As James Landers observed, newsmagazine articles often worked editorial stances into their reports through "stance words," adjectives or adverbs and verbs that conveyed judgment or tone. By discarding "all pretense of objectivity," their "commentary came to be stated as fact," with each newsmagazine pitching its ideological slant to its "like-minded" readers. Their weekly as opposed to daily deadlines also allowed them greater leeway in synthesizing the week's events and interpreting their significance. Landers, *Weekly War,* 10, 11, 4.

17. Thus *U.S. News* criticized early Johnson administration restrictions on bombing areas of North Vietnam that policy makers felt might hazard intervention in the war by China. Ibid.

18. Earl H. Tilford Jr., "Air Power, Role in War," *The Encyclopedia of the Vietnam War,* ed. Spencer Tucker (New York: Oxford University Press, 1998), 7.

19. See Landers, *The Weekly War,* 4.

20. On the latter point, see the explanation provided in Daniel Hellinger and Dennis R. Judd, *The Democratic Façade,* 2nd ed. (Belmont, Calif.: Wadsworth, 1994), esp. 296–304.

21. The radical argument applies as readily to post–Cold War U.S. foreign policy, of course. In fact, the continuation in U.S. defense spending and U.S. military bases after the Cold War ended was one reason a Cold War analyst like Chalmers Johnson came to view U.S. policy as imperial in nature. See Chalmers Johnson, *Nemesis: The Last Days of the American Republic* (New York: Holt, 2008).

22. Susan Welch, "The Press and Indochina," in *Communication in Inter-national Politics,* ed. Richard L. Merritt (Urbana: University of Illinois Press, 1972), 207–231, quoted in James Aronson, "The Media and the Message," in *The Pentagon Papers: The Defense Department History of United States Decisionmaking on Vietnam,* Gravel ed., vol. 5 (Boston: Beacon Press, 1972), 43. Welch studied coverage in the *New York Times, Washington Post, San Francisco Chronicle,* and *Chicago Tribune.*

23. For an influential example of the latter, see Kennedy advisor Walt W. Rostow's "non-Communist Manifesto" in *The Stages of Economic Growth: A Non-Communist Manifesto* (Cambridge: Cambridge University Press, 1960).

24. See the perceptive critique of an American "technowar" grounded in assumptions of the Western scientific tradition by James William Gibson, *The Perfect War: The War We Couldn't Lose and How We Did* (New York: Vintage, 1988).

25. See "Province Is Sliced from Indo-China," *New York Times,* May 12, 1945.

26. See "Partition in Vietnam," *New York Times,* May 19, 1954, 30, and "Red Propaganda Fight," *New York Times,* July 24, 1954, 3. In fact, partition at the 17th parallel was the West's choice, effectively forced upon the Viet Minh, who maintained that the cease-fire line should have been drawn farther south of the 17th parallel since much of the countryside in the southern part of Vietnam was loyal to them.

27. Marilyn Young, *The Vietnam Wars, 1945–1990* (New York: Harper Perennial, 1991), 179.

28. "Viet Cong" became the mass media's label of choice for the National Liberation Front, while American troops routinely referred to them as "VC" when not using racist terms such as "gooks" and "slopes."

29. Longtime Indochina observer Bernard Fall calculated an estimate of 160,000 civilians killed in South Vietnam prior to U.S. escalation in 1965. Bernard Fall, "Viet-Cong: The Unseen Enemy in Viet-Nam," in *The Vietnam Reader: Articles and Documents on American Foreign Policy and the Viet-Nam Crisis*, ed. Marcus Raskin and Bernard B. Fall (New York: Vintage, 1965), 261.

30. Homer Bigart, "Vietnam Victory Remote Despite U.S. Aid to Diem," *New York Times,* July 25, 1962, 1ff.

31. François Sully, "Vietnam: The Unpleasant Truth," *Newsweek,* August 20, 1962, 40.

32. Hallin, *The "Uncensored War,"* 48.

33. The first two terms were part of *Time*'s coverage; the latter was part of *U.S. News & World Report*'s coverage of "a religious struggle in Vietnam." "Trial by Fire," *Time,* June 21, 1963, 32; "When a Monk Became a Human Torch," *U.S. News & World Report,* June 24, 1963, 8.

34. George McT. Kahin, *Intervention: How America Became Involved in Vietnam* (New York: Knopf, 1986), 217; more generally, see Kahin's detailed account of U.S. deliberations and interactions with the successive governments of General Duong Van Minh and General Nguyen Khanh, 182–235.

35. As told to the House Foreign Affairs Committee, quoted in Young, *The Vietnam Wars,* 120.

36. Cited in Denise M. Bostdorff, *The Presidency and the Rhetoric of Foreign Crisis* (Columbia: University of South Carolina Press, 1994), 70.

37. "The President Acts," *New York Times,* August 5, 1964, 32; and "Congress and Vietnam," *New York Times,* August 8, 1964, 18.

38. "Editorial Reactions to Asian Conflict," *New York Times,* August 7, 1964, 8.

39. "Foreign Relations: A Measured and Fitting Response," *Time,* August 14, 1964, 11–13, and "Vietnam: 'We Seek No Wider War,'" *Newsweek,* August 17, 1964, 17–27.

40. "Bigger War for U.S. in Asia?" *U.S. News & World Report,* August 17, 1964, 21ff.

41. See Young, *The Vietnam Wars,* 121.

42. Louis Harris, *The Anguish of Change* (New York: Norton, 1973), 56. Both figures are cited in Wells, *The War Within,* 11.

43. Tom Wicker, "Peril for Washington," *New York Times,* February 11, 1965, 12.

44. *Aggression from the North: The Record of North Vietnam's Campaign to Conquer South Vietnam* (U.S. Department of State Publication 7839), in Marvin E. Gettleman et al., *Vietnam and America: A Documented History* (New York: Grove Press, 1985), 254.

45. "Text of U.S. White Paper on North Vietnam's Growing Role in War in the South," *New York Times,* February 28, 1965, 30ff.

46. The "most conclusive proof" of this was a sunken ship later revealed to be a CIA plant. See Kahin, *Intervention,* 290. Max Frankel, "Policy Is Altered," *New York Times,* February 27, 1965, 1ff.

47. Charles Mohr, "Questions on Air Strike," *New York Times,* February 8, 1965, 14ff.

48. I. F. Stone, "A Reply to the White Paper," March 8, 1965, in *In a Time of Torment* (New York: Random House, 1967), 212–218.

49. "The White Paper," *New Republic*, March 13, 1965, 5–6.

50. Young, *Vietnam Wars,* 142.

51. Bernard Fall, "Vietnam Blitz: A Report on the Impersonal War," *New Republic,* October

9, 1965, reprinted in Milton J. Bates et al., *Reporting Vietnam: American Journalism, 1959–1975* (New York: Library of America, 2000), 110, emphasis in original.

52. William R. Berkowitz, "The Impact of Anti-Vietnam Demonstrations upon National Public Opinion and Military Indicators," *Social Science Research* 2 (1973): 3.

53. For a thorough account of the early antiwar organizations and their evolution, see Charles DeBenedetti, with Charles Chatfield, *An American Ordeal: The Antiwar Movement of the Vietnam Era* (Syracuse: Syracuse University Press, 1990), chaps. 1–3.

54. Jerome H. Skolnick, *The Politics of Protest* (New York: Ballantine, 1969), 33, emphasis in original.

55. See chapter 1, note 27.

56. In the account that follows, I supplement Small's findings and those of Todd Gitlin and others with my own reading of news accounts and editorials in the *New York Times, Time, Newsweek,* and *U.S. News & World Report.* Melvin Small, *Covering Dissent: The Media and the Anti-Vietnam War Movement* (New Brunswick, N.J.: Rutgers University Press, 1994), 2.

57. Ibid., 5.

58. Potter's speech is excerpted in Alexander Bloom and Wini Breines, eds., *Takin' It to the Streets": A Sixties Reader,* 2nd ed. (New York: Oxford University Press, 2003), 174–178.

59. Small, *Covering Dissent,* 38.

60. "15,000 White House Pickets Denounce Vietnam War," *New York Times,* April 18, 1965, 1ff. A secondary article about counterdemonstrators who sat down to block a bus bringing marchers from Cornell University and Syracuse to Washington was ambiguously headlined "Cornell Marchers in Melee." *New York Times,* April 18, 1965, 3.

61. Todd Gitlin, *The Whole World Is Watching: Mass Media in the Making and Unmaking of the New Left* (Berkeley: University of California Press, 1980), 58–59, emphasis in original. See Gitlin's analysis of the *Times* photograph in the next chapter.

62. Ibid., 59–60.

63. Ibid., 53.

64. "33-Hour Teach-In Attracts 10,000," *New York Times,* May 23, 1965, 26.

65. The AFV was established in the 1950s to mobilize support for U.S. policy in Vietnam. It remained active throughout the war, joined by other government-sponsored "citizen" groups. As the war escalated, the White House tried to keep its connection to the AFV carefully hidden so the AFV's credibility would not suffer. Cited in Wells, *The War Within,* 34.

66. John E. Mueller, *War, Presidents and Public Opinion* (New York: John Wiley, 1973), 54–55.

67. See discussion in the next chapter.

68. Seymour Topping, "Vietnamese Refugees Fleeing to Cambodia," "More Student Demonstrations over Vietnam Policy Planned," *New York Times,* October 4, 1965, SU2_2. As Todd Gitlin has observed, the absence of quotes around "student riots" suggested that this was the *Times'* "objective description" of the 1964 Berkeley Free Speech Movement (about which the term "riot" would be a highly subjective distortion). Gitlin, *The Whole World Is Watching,* 80.

69. Gallup poll, November 19, 1965, Survey 719-K, Question 19c.

70. Small, *Covering Dissent,* 50.

71. Gitlin, *The Whole World Is Watching,* 94, emphasis in original.

72. "Battle of Vietnam Day," *Newsweek,* October 25, 1965, 98.

73. *Time,* October 22, 1965, 25, quoted in Small, *Covering Dissent,* 53–54.

74. T. J. Wheeler, "Day the Vietcong Attacked the United States," *National Review,* December 14, 1965, 1157–1159.

75. James Reston, "Washington: The Stupidity of Intelligence," *New York Times,* October 17, 1965, E10.

76. For further discussion of the resistance, see chapter 6.

77. Mueller, *War, Presidents and Public Opinion,* 54–55. Mueller attributes the rise in opposition to the war to the rise in American fatalities. However, as E. M. Schreiber points out, it is impossible statistically to separate out the rising U.S. deaths from the duration of public exposure to the war itself, much less the growing turmoil at home. See E. M. Schreiber, "Anti-War Demonstrations and American Public Opinion on the War in Vietnam," *British Journal of Sociology* 27, no. 2 (June 1976): 225–236.

78. Very significantly, the October Moratorium occurred when substantial elite opinion (and a majority of Americans) was critical of the war and the event was noteworthy for peaceful participation of Americans from all walks of life, thereby contrasting sharply with the previous year's image of violence at the Chicago national convention.

79. Small, *Covering Dissent,* 61–62.

80. "Thousands on Fifth Ave. March in Vietnam Protest," *New York Times,* March 27, 1965, 1ff.

81. Small, *Covering Dissent,* 63.

82. Ibid.

83. Hallin, *"Uncensored War,"* 147–148.

84. Namely, the rulings of the Nuremburg trial, which convicted German officials, and the Geneva Conventions of 1949, to which the United States was a signatory.

85. Harrison Baldwin, "Bombing of the North," *New York Times,* December 30, 1966, 1. The *Pentagon Papers* revealed internal discussions among policy makers about bombing the dikes in order to cause mass starvation. See the discussion in Noam Chomsky, *For Reasons of State,* rev. ed. (New York: New Press, 2003), 69–70, 225–226.

86. Quoted in Wells, *The War Within,* 157–158, emphasis in original.

87. Small, *Covering Dissent,* 66–67.

88. "Student Leaders Warn President of Doubts on War," *New York Times,* December 30, 1966, 1.

89. "100,000 Rally at U.N. against Vietnam War," *New York Times,* April 16, 1967, 1ff.

90. "The Dilemma of Dissent," *Time,* April 21, 1967, 20.

91. Even the presence of Martin Luther King Jr. as one of the speakers was framed entirely by references to three nonparticipating black leaders and their criticism of King's antiwar position. Ibid., 20–22.

92. Wells, *The War Within,* 158, emphasis in original. Wells draws on his interview with Bruce Dancis, a president of SDS at Cornell in 1967.

93. Both Kopkind and Bardacke's comments are quoted in Todd Gitlin, *The Sixties: Years of Hope, Days of Rage* (New York: Simon & Schuster, 1987), 246.

94. See DeBenedetti, *American Ordeal,* 186–187, 225.

95. "Boycott at Madison," *New York Times,* October 20, 1967, 1.

96. For further discussion of Stop the Draft Week militancy, see chapter 8.

97. Quoted in Wells, *The War Within,* 176.

98. "The Vietnam Dissent," *New York Times,* October 22, 1967, 208.

99. James Reston, "Everyone Is a Loser," *New York Times,* October 23, 1967, 1.

100. "Antiwar Protests: A Weapon for Communists," *U.S. News & World Report,* November 13, 1967, 12–14.

Chapter 6. Visual Drama: The Power of the Image

1. Thus Susan Sontag compared imagery from the Korean and Vietnam Wars, noting that "there was, ideologically, no space" for images of "the cruelty of unlimited American firepower" in Korea, whereas journalist used photographs of Vietnamese suffering because they "felt

backed in their efforts to obtain those photographs." Susan Sontag, *On Photography* (New York: Picador, 1977), 18.

2. George Katsiaficas, *The Imagination of the New Left: A Global Analysis of 1968* (Boston: South End Press, 1987), 10. CBS News' Eric Sevareid had a jaundiced and patronizing view of the contagious spread of movements (in this case, the women's movement), reflecting mass media's more distanced mainstream perspective: "Many movements grow by simple contagion, thousands discovering they are in pain, though they hadn't noticed it until they were told." Quoted in Susan J. Douglas, *Where the Girls Are: Growing Up Female with the Mass Media* (New York: Three Rivers Press, 1995), 164.

3. Quoted in Milton Viorst, *Fire in the Streets: America in the 1960s* (New York: Simon & Schuster, 1979), 176.

4. *Freedom on My Mind*, dir. Connie Field and Marilyn Mulford (VHS; San Francisco: California Newsreel, 1994).

5. Ibid.

6. Stokely Carmichael with Ekwueme Michael Thelwell, *Ready for Revolution: The Life and Struggles of Stokely Carmichael (Kwame Ture)* (New York: Scribner, 2003), 139, emphasis added.

7. See note 3 above.

8. Quoted in Juan Williams, *Eyes on the Prize: America's Civil Rights Years, 1954–1965* (New York: Penguin, 1988), 147.

9. "Trouble in Alabama," *Time,* May 26, 1961, 16; "Days of Violence in the South," *Newsweek,* May 29, 1961, 21–22; "Aftermath of Freedom Rides?" *U.S. News & World Report,* June 12, 1961, 4.

10. Coffin and six colleagues joined the rides from Montgomery to Jackson, Mississippi. Diane McWhorter, *Carry Me Home: Birmingham, Alabama: The Climactic Battle of the Civil Rights Revolution* (New York: Touchstone, 2001), 239, emphasis added.

11. David Halberstam, *The Children* (New York: Fawcett, 1998), 314, emphasis in original.

12. Richard Lentz, *Symbols, the News Magazines, and Martin Luther King* (Baton Rouge: Louisiana State University Press, 1990), 51–52.

13. Sara Evans, *Personal Politics: The Roots of Women's Liberation in the Civil Rights Movement and the New Left* (New York: Vintage, 1980), 60.

14. David Garrow, *Bearing the Cross: Martin Luther King, Jr., and the Southern Christian Leadership Conference* (New York: Vintage, 1988), 216.

15. "The Edge of Violence," *Time,* October 5, 1962, 15.

16. See chapter 4.

17. Lentz, *Symbols,* 75–76.

18. Quoted in Williams, *Eyes on the Prize,* 191.

19. "Provocation, Reprisal Widen the Bitter Gulf," *Life,* May 17, 1963, 32ff.

20. McWhorter, *Carry Me Home,* 373.

21. Quoted in ibid., 22.

22. Taylor Branch, *Pillar of Fire: America in the King Years, 1963–65* (New York: Touchstone, 1998), 87.

23. *New York Times,* June 12, 1963, 20, quoted in Branch, *Pillar of Fire,* 107–108.

24. Doug McAdam, *Political Process and the Development of Black Insurgency 1930–1970* (Chicago: University of Chicago Press, 1982), 197–198.

25. "The American Revolution of '63," Frank McGhee, NBC, September 2, 1963.

26. Quoted in Williams, *Eyes on the Prize,* 273.

27. Ibid., 278.

28. As the Kerner Commission put it, the media "have not communicated to the majority of

their audience—which is white—a sense of the degradation, misery, and hopelessness of living in the ghetto. . . . The news media have, we believe, contributed to the black-white schism in this country." *Report of the National Advisory Commission on Civil Disorders* (New York: Bantam, 1968), 383.

29. One study of public responses to racial demonstrations and riots found the public generally unsympathetic or hostile to specific protests (Selma was the exception) and overwhelmingly negative in their reactions to Watts, Harlem, Rochester, and Jersey City riots in 1964 and 1965. Hazel Erskine, "The Polls: Demonstrations and Race Riots," *Public Opinion Quarterly* 31, no. 4 (Winter 1967–68): 655–677.

30. Ralph Ellison, *Invisible Man* (1947; New York: Signet, 1952), 7–8.

31. James Baldwin, *The Fire Next Time* (New York: Dell, 1962), 15.

32. Ibid., 21, 141.

33. "Thirty Miles Divide Folly and Reason," *Life,* July 26, 1963, 18–25; and "Toward a Long, Hot Summer," *Time,* April 3, 1964, 28–29.

34. The "urban riots" of the 1960s were a heavily studied phenomenon, the focal point of at least two presidential commissions, several book-length accounts, and a myriad of academic journal articles. The best known of these was probably the Kerner Commission report. See note 28 above.

35. See William Ryan, *Blaming the Victim* (New York: Pantheon, 1971). In a study of media attention given to the so-called Moynihan Report (based on Daniel Patrick Moynihan's chief authorial role in generating the Department of Labor report, *The Negro Family: The Case for National Action* [Washington, D.C.: U.S. Government Printing Office, 1965]) that critiqued flaws in the "Negro Family Structure," Carl Ginsburg observed, "None of the stories or editorials repudiated the 'Negro Family Structure' as the source of black impoverishment. Nor did they propel inquiry into the social and economic factors that exclude blacks from sharing equally in America's wealth. Rather, the news reports fell neatly into the Moynihan pattern, limiting themselves to a *description* of the conditions of black poverty." Carl Ginsburg, "Race and Media: The Enduring Life of the Moynihan Report," Monograph Series 3 (New York: Institute for Media Analysis, 1989), 16, emphasis in original.

36. "After the Blood Bath," *Newsweek,* August 30, 1965, 19.

37. See Tom Hayden, *Rebellion in Newark: Official Violence and Ghetto Response* (New York: Random House, 1967).

38. "$1.5 Million Poverty Plans Are Submitted by Newark," *New York Times,* July 1, 1965, 22; "Newark Aides Seek Antipoverty Role," *New York Times,* November 1, 1965, 1; and "Newark Stirred over Poverty Aid," *New York Times,* December 12, 1965, 81.

39. The Watts riots revealed a similar contrast between pre- and post-riot coverage. Without either a single black editor or reporter, the *Los Angeles Times* carried only two major stories on the black community in the twenty years prior to 1965, then exploded with coverage of the riot. See David Farber, *The Age of Great Dreams: America in the 1960s* (New York: Hill & Wang, 1994), 114.

40. "Trigger of Hate," *Time,* August 20, 1965, 12–19.

41. Ibid., 19.

42. "After the Blood Bath," *Newsweek,* August 30, 1965, 16.

43. Ibid., 17.

44. Ibid., 19.

45. "Summer '66: Cops on the Spot," *Newsweek,* June 27, 1966, 22–26.

46. "After the Riots: A Survey: How the Flare-ups Affected U.S. Racial Attitudes," *Newsweek,* August 21, 1967, 19.

47. "The Firebrand," *Newsweek,* August 7, 1967, 28. Back in 1965, *U.S. News* had blamed Martin Luther King Jr. and other "Negro agitators" for the racial unrest in the North. "When

Negroes Tried to Shock a Friendly City," *U.S. News & World Report,* September 13, 1965, 46–48.

48. See note 28 above.

49. "After the Riots," *Newsweek,* August 21, 1967, 19.

50. "After the Blood Bath," *Newsweek,* August 30, 1965, 19, emphasis in original.

51. From an exchange with Bayard Rustin, detailed in Viorst, *Fire in the Streets,* 341.

52. Ellen Willis, "Radical Feminism and Feminist Radicalism," in *No More Nice Girls: Countercultural Essays* (Middletown, Conn.: Wesleyan University Press, 1992), 135.

53. Robin Morgan, "WITCH Hexes Wall Street," in *Going Too Far: The Personal Chronicle of a Feminist* (New York: Vintage, 1978), 75.

54. Quoted in Brownmiller, *In Our Time: Memoir of a Revolution* (New York: Dial Press, 2000), 36.

55. Ruth Rosen, *The World Split Open: How the Modern Women's Movement Changed America* (New York: Viking, 2000), 160–161. See also the *Esquire* illustration discussed in chapter 4 (in Helen Lawrenson's article, "The Feminine Mistake," *Esquire,* January 1971, 83ff.); and Patricia Bradley, *Mass Media and the Shaping of American Feminism, 1963–1975* (Jackson: University Press of Mississippi, 2003), 148.

56. Carol Hanisch, "Excerpt from a Critique of the Miss America Protest," in *Dear Sisters: Dispatches from the Women's Liberation Movement,* ed. Rosalyn Baxandall and Linda Gordon (New York: Basic Books, 2000), 186.

57. Morgan, "Three Articles on WITCH," in *Going Too Far,* 74, emphasis in original.

58. Ibid., 72.

59. See Bradley, *Mass Media and the Shaping of American Feminism,* 94.

60. Linda Charlton, "Women March down Fifth in Equality Drive," *New York Times,* August 27, 1970, 1; Linda Charlton, "Women Seeking Equality March on 5th Ave. Today," *New York Times,* August 26, 1970, 44; "Leading Feminist Puts Hairdo before Strike," *New York Times,* August 27, 1970, 30; and Lacey Fosburgh, "Traditional Groups Prefer to Ignore Women's Lib," *New York Times,* August 27, 1970, 44.

61. Susan J. Douglas, *Where the Girls Are: Growing up Female with the Mass Media* (New York: Three Rivers Press, 1995), 163.

62. "How Women Are Doing in Politics," *U.S. News & World Report,* September 7, 1970, 24–27.

63. *Time,* September 7, 1970, 12–13.

64. See Bradley, *Mass Media and the Shaping of American Feminism,* 97.

65. Cited in Garrow, *Bearing the Cross,* 543.

66. "Trial by Fire," *Time,* June 21, 1963, 32.

67. "Burning of Village Described," *New York Times,* August 4, 1965, 2.

68. CBS News broadcast, August 5, 1965, quoted in Hallin, *"Uncensored War,"* 132.

69. "Burning of Village Described," *New York Times,* August 4, 1965, 2.

70. As an example of the latter effect, the magazine *Saturday Review* raised over $10,000 from its readers to help rebuild the village of Cam Ne.

71. Halberstam's account also detailed the intense deliberations within CBS when they received the film clip and had to decide whether or not to run it. As Fred Friendly, head of CBS News, anchor Walter Cronkite, and producer Ernie Leiser watched the clip, in Halberstam's account, they "knew they had to go with it. It was not so much that they wanted to as that *they simply could not fail to use it.*" David Halberstam, *The Powers That Be* (New York: Knopf, 1979), 489–490, emphasis in original.

72. Bernard Fall, "Vietnam Blitz: A Report on the Impersonal War," *New Republic,* October 9, 1965; from Milton Bates et al., *Reporting Vietnam: American Journalism, 1959–1975* (New York: Library of America, 2000), 113.

73. See George Gent, "C.B.S. President Backs War News," *New York Times*, January 29, 1966, 55, and Douglas Robinson, "Press Club Gives Awards for 1965," *New York Times*, April 23, 1966, 32.

74. Chester Pach, "And That's the Way It Was," *The Sixties: From Memory to History*, ed. David Farber (Chapel Hill: University of North Carolina Press, 1994), 104.

75. Quoted in Edward Herman and Noam Chomsky, *Manufacturing Consent: The Political Economy of Mass Media,* 2nd ed. (New York: Pantheon, 2002), 201.

76. Hallin, *"Uncensored War,"* 132. See, notably, Robert Elegant's 1981 essay, "How to Lose a War," discussed in chapter 12. As Hallin noted (234n43), Elegant insinuated that "Safer staged the incident in a training village," a claim contradicted by the military's own account.

77. After reviewing the distancing words of established policy intellectuals and an account of a 1968 Chicago Museum of Science and Industry exhibit at which visitors of all ages were invited to fire helicopter machine guns at Vietnamese huts, Chomsky commented, "These and a thousand other examples testify to moral degeneracy on such a scale that talk about the 'normal channels' of political action and protest becomes meaningless or hypocritical." Noam Chomsky, *American Power and the New Mandarins: Historical and Political Essays* (New York: Vintage, 1969), 16.

78. See, notably, Peter Braestrup, *Big Story: How the American Press and Television Reported and Interpreted the Crisis of Tet in 1968 in Vietnam and Washington*, 2 vols. (Boulder, Colo.: Westview Press, 1977).

79. See chapter 10, note 37.

80. Melvin Small, *Covering Dissent: The Media and the Anti-Vietnam War Movement* (New Brunswick, N.J.: Rutgers University Press, 1994), 14.

81. See Tom Wells, *The War Within: America's Battle over Vietnam* (Berkeley: University of California Press, 1994), 283–284, 299, 511.

82. Todd Gitlin, *The Whole World Is Watching: Mass Media in the Making and Unmaking of the New Left* (Berkeley: University of California Press, 1980), 47.

83. "Pressures," *New York Times*, October 24, 1965, E1ff.

84. David Dellinger, *From Yale to Jail: The Life Story of a Moral Dissenter* (New York: Pantheon, 1993), 206.

85. The *Times* also sniffed, "It is tragic that the actions of exhibitionists—many of them openly pro-Peking—now threaten to upset the useful purpose the demonstration might have served in promoting a valid [i.e., legitimate] debate." "March on Washington," *New York Times*, November 27, 1965, 30.

86. "The People: The Dilemma of Dissent," *Time*, April 21, 1967, 22.

87. The *Times* framed its interpretation of the day's activities with dismissive references to "Communist-organized" "ban-the-bomb" protests that "failed on moral grounds" and pacifists' demonstrations "against the use of military force under any circumstances" that "have no relation to political reality." "The Peace Protest," *New York Times*, April 16, 1967, 30.

88. "Protest: The Banners of Dissent," *Time*, October 27, 1967, 23.

89. Quoted in Charles DeBenedetti, with Charles Chatfield, *American Ordeal: The Antiwar Movement of the Vietnam Era* (Syracuse: Syracuse University Press, 1990), 203, from "Sizing up the Public on the War," *Business Week*, February 24, 1968, 37.

90. As was their style, the Yippies (Youth International Party) were particularly dramatic with wild rhetorical predictions of events that would occur during the convention. On Yippie "threats" and the way humorless officials and media interpreted these, see Todd Gitlin, *The Sixties:Years of Hope, Days of Rage* (New York: Bantam, 1987), 322.

91. According to David Farber, there were about a thousand federal agents in Chicago, and by midweek, "military intelligence estimated that one in six demonstrators was an undercover government agent." David Farber, *Chicago '68* (Chicago: University of Chicago Press, 1988), 170.

92. Gitlin, *The Whole World Is Watching*, 169. Indeed, Chicago's police "rioted," in the words of the later Walker Commission investigative report. See The National Commission on the Causes and Prevention of Violence, *Rights in Conflict* [the Walker Report] (New York: Grosset & Dunlap, 1968).

93. In Farber's account, forty-three reporters, photographers, and cameramen were beaten by the police during the convention. CBS carried twenty-eight hours of convention coverage, thirty-two minutes of which focused on the demonstrators, while NBC carried sixty-five minutes on the demonstrators out of thirty-five hours on the convention. Farber cites the Walker Report (*Rights in Conflict*) and Bill Matney, "The Shattering Effects of Television News," *Columbia Journalism Review*, August 1969, 3–4. Farber, *Chicago '68*, 290n148.

94. Dellinger, *From Yale to Jail*, 536.

95. Inside the convention, the Democratic Party was dissolving in bitter dispute before the public's eyes, as Senator Abraham Ribicoff of Connecticut denounced the "Gestapo tactics" of the Chicago police in the streets outside the hall.

96. DeBenedetti, with Chatfield, *American Ordeal*, 229.

97. Wells, *The War Within*, 283.

98. Gitlin, *The Whole World Is Watching*, 196.

99. See John P. Robinson, "Balance Theory and Vietnam-Related Attitudes," in *Political Attitudes and Public Opinion,* ed. Dan D. Nimmo and Charles M. Bonjean (New York: McKay, 1972), 347–353. While working-class Americans were more likely to be critical of the war in Vietnam than their upper-middle-class counterparts—their sons, after all, carried most of the war's burden borne by Americans—they were also more likely to be alienated by the antiwar movement they witnessed in the Chicago debacle.

100. Philip E. Converse and Howard Schuman, "'Silent Majorities' and the Vietnam War," *Scientific American* 222, no. 6 (June 1970): 24. I address the issue of militancy and its effects in chapter 8 below.

101. DeBenedetti, with Chatfield, *An American Ordeal*, 256–257. The quoted phrases were drawn from "The Unsilent Opposition," *New Republic*, November 15, 1969, 9.

102. Small, *Covering Dissent*, 98.

103. "Strike against the War," *Time*, October 17, 1969, 17. A week later, however, *Time* assessed "M-Day's Message to Nixon" more critically, leading with the negative observation that "their numbers were not overwhelming. Probably not more than 1,000,000 Americans took an active part in last week's Moratorium Day." "M-Day's Message to Nixon," *Time*, October 24, 1969, 16ff.

104. "The Meaning of the Moratorium," *Newsweek*, October 27, 1969, 30ff.

105. Small, *Covering Dissent*, 120. The March Against Death was a particularly moving event in which marchers carrying the names of dead American soldiers or destroyed Vietnamese villages marched to the cadence of a funeral drumbeat past the White House gate, where they called out the soldier's name and placed the placard in a coffin.

106. Ibid.

107. Nixon denied that the U.S. action was an "invasion," claiming instead that it was a temporary "incursion" by U.S. troops to find and destroy the "headquarters for the entire Communist military operation in South Vietnam," the so-called COSVN that, in fact, didn't exist. See Marilyn Young, *The Vietnam Wars, 1945–1990* (New York: Harper Perennial, 1991), 247–248.

108. Wells, *The War Within*, 429.

109. Although it needs to be noted that the media's double standard toward black as opposed to white deaths continued to prevail as the Jackson State killings received far less media attention.

110. "Build-up to Tragedy at Kent State," *U.S. News & World Report*, May 25, 1970, 19.

111. "Veterans Discard Medals in War Protest at Capitol," *New York Times*, April 24, 1971, 1ff., and "Demonstration in Washington," *New York Times*, April 26, 1971, 34.

Chapter 7. System Response: Generational Hype and Political Backlash

1. "The New Feminists: Revolt against 'Sexism,'" *Time,* November 21, 1969, 53.

2. See Ward Churchill and Jim Vander Wall, *The Cointelpro Papers: Documents from the FBI's Secret Wars against Domestic Dissent* (Boston: South End Press, 1990), and Robert Justin Goldstein, *Political Repression in Modern America: From 1870 to the Present* (Cambridge, Mass.: Schenkman, 1978).

3. Frances Fox Piven and Richard A. Cloward, "Movements and Dissensus Politics," in *Cultural Politics and Social Movements,* ed. Marcy Darnovsky, Barbara Epstein, and Richard Flacks (Philadelphia: Temple University Press, 1995), 237.

4. From a letter written by Curt Furr to Senator Sam J. Ervin, June 18, 1968, cited in Michael W. Flamm, *Law and Order: Street Crime, Civil Unrest, and the Crisis of Liberalism in the 1960s* (New York: Columbia University Press, 2005), 1.

5. *Berkeley in the 60s* (VHS; New York: First Run Features, 1990).

6. Grace and Fred M. Hechinger, "College Morals Mirror Our Society, *New York Times Magazine,* April 14, 1963, 208ff.

7. "The Morals Revolution on Campus," *Newsweek,* April 6, 1964, 52ff.

8. Kirkpatrick Sale, *SDS* (New York: Vintage, 1974), 165.

9. Mario Savio, "An End to History," in *"Takin' It to the Streets,"* 2nd ed., ed. Alexander Bloom and Wini Breines (New York: Oxford University Press, 2003), 91–92.

10. Paul Goodman, *Growing Up Absurd: Problems of Youth in the Organized Society* (New York: Vintage, 1960).

11. Michael Rossman, "The Wedding within the War," excerpted in Bloom and Breines, *Takin' It to the Streets*, 84.

12. Sale, *SDS,* 166.

13. "To Prison with Love," *Time,* December 11, 1964, 60.

14. Shana Alexander, "You Don't Shoot Mice with Elephant Guns," *Life,* January 15, 1965, 27, emphasis added.

15. "A Cure for Campus Riots," *U.S. News & World Report,* May 17, 1965, 70–72.

16. Sale, *SDS,* 166.

17. "Campus '65: The College Generation Looks at Itself and the World around It," *Newsweek,* March 22, 1965, 43ff.

18. Ibid., 45, emphasis added.

19. Ibid., 43, 46, 47.

20. "Man of the Year: The Inheritor," *Time,* January 6, 1967, www.time.com/time/magazine/article/0,9171,843150,00.html.

21. See Doug Rossinow, "'The Revolution Is about Our Lives': The New Left's Counterculture," in *Imagine Nation: The American Counterculture of the 1960s and 70s,* ed. Peter Braunstein and Michael William Doyle (New York: Routledge, 2002), 100. See also Edward P. Morgan, *The Sixties Experience: Hard Lessons about Modern America* (Philadelphia: Temple University Press, 1991), chapter 5.

22. See Abe Peck, *Uncovering the Sixties: The Life and Times of the Underground Press* (New York: Pantheon, 1985).

23. Thus, for example, a 2007 History Channel feature on "The Hippies" (Lou Reda Productions, 1997) gave significant play to the discovery of LSD as the single-most prominent causal factor explaining the counterculture.

24. See Martin A. Lee and Bruce Shlain, *Acid Dreams: The Complete Social History of LSD: The CIA, the Sixties, and Beyond* (New York: Grove Press, 1994).

25. "Dropouts with a Mission," *Newsweek,* February 6, 1967, 92–95.

26. "The Hippies," *Time*, July 7, 1967, 18–22ff.

27. "Spotlight on 'Hippies': A First-Hand Report," *U.S. News & World Report*, May 8, 1967, 61–63.

28. *U.S. News & World Report*, "Hippies—A Passing Fad?" October 23, 1967, 42–44.

29. Perry estimated that at least 75,000 lived in the psychedelic community by fall 1967. Perry, *The Haight Ashbury: A History* (New York: Vintage, 1985), 271.

30. Pittel's research is detailed in ibid., 293.

31. Peter Coyote, *Sleeping Where I Fall* (Washington, D.C.: Counterpoint, 1988), 135.

32. Theodore Roszak, *Making of a Counter Culture* (New York: Anchor, 1969), 36–37.

33. Michael T. Kaufman, "Generation Gap Bridged as Monticello Residents Aid Courteous Festival Patrons," *New York Times*, August 18, 1969, 25.

34. "The Message of History's Biggest Happening," *Time*, August 29, 1969.

35. Quoted in Tom Wells, *The War Within: America's Battle over Vietnam* (Berkeley: University of California Press, 1994), 365.

36. References from *The Temper of Our Times* are drawn from an essay review by Jack Newfield, "Idealists without Illusions," *New York Times*, February 26, 1967, BR2. See also Jack Gould, "TV Review," *New York Times*, September 20, 1967, 95; and Roy Reed, "Johnson Pleased by a Philosopher," *New York Times*, October 8, 1967, 29.

37. John Leo, "Mental Ills Linked to Disrespect," *New York Times*, March 22, 1968, 49, emphasis added.

38. Donald Janson, "Chicago U. Ready for Sit-in Siege," *New York Times*, February 1, 1969.

39. Bruno Bettelheim, "Children Must Learn to Fear," *New York Times Magazine*, April 13, 1969, 125ff.

40. William V. Shannon, "One Man's View of the Unquiet Campus," *New York Times*, April 28, 1969, 40.

41. Reginald E. Zelnik, "On the Side of the Angels: The Berkeley Faculty and the FSM," in *The Free Speech Movement: Reflections on Berkeley in the 1960s*, ed. Robert Cohen and Reginald E. Zelnick (Berkeley: University of California Press, 2002), 268.

42. Lewis Feuer, *The Conflict of Generations: The Character and Significance of Student Movements* (New York: Basic Books, 1969), 410.

43. Furthermore, a Jew himself, Feuer also cited reports about the participation of Jewish students in various New Left actions—a theme picked up by later sixties-bashers—to suggest that the "generational conflict was the deepest psychological problem of the Jewish students." Ibid., 414, 419–431.

44. Kenneth Keniston, *Youth and Dissent: The Rise of a New Opposition* (New York: Harcourt, Brace, Jovanovich, 1971), 375.

45. Kenneth Keniston, *Young Radicals: Notes on Committed Youth* (New York: Harcourt, Brace, & World, 1968).

46. Irving Howe, "The New 'Confrontation Politics' Is a Dangerous Game," *New York Times Magazine*, October 20, 1968, 27ff.

47. John F. Khanlian, "Casualty," *New York Times*, November 3, 1968, 364.

48. George Kennan, "Rebels without a Program," *New York Times Magazine*, January 21, 1968, 23.

49. Ibid.

50. Irving Kristol, "The Old Politics, the New Politics, The *New*, New Politics," *New York Times Magazine*, November 24, 1968, 49ff.

51. See Thomas J. Sugrue and John D. Skrentny, "The White Ethnic Strategy," in *Rightward Bound: Making America Conservative in the 1970s*, ed. Bruce J. Schulman and Julian E. Zelizer (Cambridge, Mass.: Harvard University Press, 2008), 171–192.

52. See Harlan Hahn, "Correlates of Public Sentiments about War: Local Referenda on the Vietnam Issue," *American Political Science Review* 64, no. 4 (December 1970): 64, and John P. Robinson and Solomon G. Jacobson, "American Public Opinion about Vietnam," *Peace Research Society (International) Papers* 10 (1968): 75.

53. See Michael W. Flamm, *Law and Order: Street Crime, Civil Unrest and the Crisis of Liberalism in the 1960s* (New York: Columbia University Press, 2005), 183–184.

54. See Philip Gailey, "A New Political Order," *St. Petersburg Times*, November 13, 1994, 1ff.

55. Flamm, *Law and Order*, 31. As I argue below, this recurring and widely accepted conservative argument has never confronted the degree to which the market economy has been most systematically responsible for the erosion of social order.

56. Ibid., 42.

57. See Mary C. Brennan, *Turning Right in the Sixties: The Conservative Capture of the GOP* (Chapel Hill: University of North Carolina Press, 2007).

58. Flamm, *Law and Order*, 71. The quoted phrases are all Reagan's except for Flamm's wording that Reagan maintained civil disobedience had "no place in a democracy."

59. Howard Zinn, "The Problem Is Civil Obedience," in *Voices of a People's History of the United States*, ed. Howard Zinn and Anthony Arnove (New York: Seven Stories Press, 2004), 484.

60. Ronald Reagan, "The Morality Gap at Berkeley," speech presented in San Francisco, May 12, 1966, from Ronald Reagan, *The Creative Society* (New York: Devin-Adair, 1968), quoted in Daniel Marcus, *Happy Days and Wonder Years: The Fifties and Sixties in Contemporary Cultural Politics* (New Brunswick, N.J.: Rutgers University Press, 2004), 71.

61. Flamm, *Law and Order*, 72.

62. All references are from ibid., 69–73. The Brown staffer quote (in Flamm) was by Frederick G. Dutton, interviewed by Amelia R. Fry, August 15, 1978, in *Democratic Campaigns and Controversies, 1954–1966,* Bancroft Library, Berkeley.

63. "Politics: The White Backlash, 1966," *Newsweek*, October 10, 1966, 27–29.

64. Kurt Schuparra, *Triumph of the Right: The Rise of the California Conservative Movement, 1945–1966* (New York: M. E. Sharpe, 1998), 138. Cited in Flamm, *Law and Order*, 213.

65. *Report of the National Advisory Commission on Civil Disorders* (New York: Bantam, 1968), 1–2.

66. See, for example, Richard A. Cloward and Frances Fox Piven, eds., *The Politics of Turmoil: Essays on Poverty, Race and the Urban Crisis* (1965; New York: Pantheon, 1974). See also earlier discussion of the Community Action Program.

67. The wording is Flamm's, not Nixon's. Flamm, *Law and Order*, 174.

68. *Newsweek*'s "George Wallace and the Third Party Threat" issue was published on September 16, 1968, and the "Is Dr. Spock to Blame?" issue on September 23.

69. The magazine also quoted Eric Hoffer, the "bare-knuckled philosopher": "You better watch out. The common man is standing up and someday he's going to elect a policeman President of the United States." "The Troubled American: A Special Report on the White Majority," *Newsweek*, October 6, 1969, 22–43.

70. Flamm, *Law and Order*, 179.

71. Melvin Small, *To Kill a Messenger: Television News and the Real World* (New York: Hastings House, 1970), xi.

72. See the related discussion and notes 96–100 in chapter 6.

73. Rick Perlstein, *Nixonland: The Rise of a President and the Fracturing of America* (New York: Scribner, 2008), 337, emphasis in original.

74. Safire, of course, went on to become a member of that allegedly liberal "East Coast elite" as a columnist for the *New York Times*. William Safire, *Before the Fall: An Insider's View of the Pre-Watergate White House* (New York: Doubleday, 1975), 364–365. Cited in David Brock, *The*

Republican Noise Machine: Right-Wing Media and How It Corrupts Democracy (New York: Crown, 1964), 23.

75. For an account of Nixon's campaign against the media and demonstrators, see Goldstein, *Political Repression in Modern America*, 494–500.

76. Jerry Lembcke, *The Spitting Image: Myth, Memory, and the Legacy of Vietnam* (New York: New York University Press, 1998), 51.

77. Tom Wells, *The War Within: America's Battle over Vietnam* (Berkeley: University of California Press, 1994), 379–380.

78. Marjorie Hunter, "Agnew Says 'Effete Snobs' Incited War Moratorium," *New York Times*, October 20, 1969, 1.

79. Memorandum of October 17, 1969, included in William E. Porter, *Assault on the Media: The Nixon Years* (Ann Arbor: University of Michigan Press, 1976), 244–246.

80. Quoted, along with other colorful Nixonian epithets, by Tom Wells in *The War Within*, 386–387.

81. E. W. Kenworth, "Agnew Says TV Networks Are Distorting the News," *New York Times*, November 14, 1969, 1.

82. "Transcript of Address by Agnew Extending Criticism of News Coverage to the Press," *New York Times*, November 21, 1969, 22.

83. William Borders, "Agnew Explains: 'I'd Had Enough,'" *New York Times*, November 24, 1969, 31.

84. See Brock, *The Republican Noise Machine*, 116–117.

85. According to Brock's account, the foundation was established by a bequest from Alfred Kohlberg, a "close associate" of Senator Joseph McCarthy and "head" of the anticommunist China Lobby. See ibid., 19.

86. Though significant amounts of her own data contradicted her assertions, some claims—as in the bar graphs that showed that 69 percent of all words referring to black militants were favorable, as opposed to only 31 percent unfavorable—were staggeringly subjective. Edith Efron, *The News Twisters* (Los Angeles: Nash Publishing, 1971), 40–41, 354–355.

87. Ibid., 18, emphasis added.

88. In the *Washington Post,* longtime news analyst Ben Bagdikian labeled the book "dishonest, inaccurate" and a "demonstration on how to doctor evidence." The *St. Louis Post-Dispatch* contended that "the book is no genuine study of TV news performance, but a 1972 campaign document designed to twist network coverage to the right." These and other examples are noted in Brock, *The Republican Noise Machine*, 20–21.

89. "Remembrances," *Newsweek*, May 2, 1994, 24, cited in ibid., 19.

90. Brock, *The Republican Noise Machine*, 18.

91. The Deutsch & Shea ad originally appeared in the *New York Times* on June 28, 1966. It is duplicated in Mitchell Goodman, *The Movement towards a New America* (Philadelphia: Pilgrim Press, 1970), 703.

92. Lewis F. Powell, "Confidential Memorandum: Attack on the American Free Enterprise System," August 23, 1971, published as "The Powell Memo," April 3, 2004, at www.reclaim democracy.org/corporate_accountability/powell_memo_lewis.html, 2.

93. Ibid., 5, 6, 4.

94. Ibid., 7.

95. Ibid., emphasis added.

96. Ibid., 8.

97. Brock, *The Republican Noise Machine*, 40. This circularity of argument on the Right later became known as the right-wing "echo chamber." See, for example, Sheldon Rampton and John Stauber, *Banana Republicans: How the Right Wing Is Turning America into a One-Party State* (London: Robinson Publishing, 2004).

98. Powell, "Confidential Memorandum," 6, 9, 11 .

99. Ibid, 11.

100. See chapter 4, note 102.

101. Midge Decter, "The Paradox of Women's Liberation," *Newsweek*, January 22, 1973, 7.

102. See Patricia Bradley, *Mass Media and the Shaping of Feminism, 1963–1975* (Jackson: University Press of Mississippi, 2003), 256.

103. Quoted in Ruth Rosen, *The World Split Open: How the Modern Women's Movement Changed America* (New York: Viking, 2000), 318.

104. Schlafly wrote and distributed *A Choice Not an Echo*, a popular campaign book that spelled out the conservative argument in the 1964 race. She was also a delegate to the Republican National Convention on three different occasions.

105. See Janet K. Boles, *The Politics of the Equal Rights Amendment: Conflict and the Decision Process* (New York: Longman, 1979), cited in Bradley, *Mass Media and the Shaping of Feminism*, 259.

106. Quoted in Bradley, *Mass Media and the Shaping of Feminism*, 262. The second "type of women" referred to professional women interested in equal pay for equal work.

107. "The American Woman on the Move, but Where?" *U.S. News & World Report,* December 8, 1975, 55, cited in ibid.

108. Jerry Falwell, *Listen, America!* (Garden City, N.Y.: Doubleday, 1980), 17.

109. Todd Gitlin, *The Whole World Is Watching: Mass Media in the Making and Unmaking of the New Left* (Berkeley: University of California Press, 1980), 279. Indeed, by 1971, one survey of press coverage noted a "subtle tendency" of the press to engage in "self-censorship" by pulling back from controversial issues. Fred Powledge, *The Engineering of Restraint* (Washington, D.C.: Public Affairs Press, 1971), 7, cited in Goldstein, *Political Repression in Modern America*, 496.

110. "Parades for Peace and Patriotism" (23–24 and 26–27) was, along with "The Uneducated Elite" (20–22), part of an issue focus on "The Nation: Politics of Polarization," *Time,* November 21, 1969.

111. "The Army and Viet Nam: The Stab-in-the-Back Complex," *Time*, December 12, 1969, www.time.com/time/printout/0,88816,840467,00.html, 2.

Chapter 8. Media, Militancy, and Violence: The Making of "Bad Sixties" Icons

1. Quoted in FBI memos dated December 1, 1964, and March 4, 1968, in Ward Churchill and Jim Vander Wall, *The COINTELPRO Papers: Documents from the FBI's Secret Wars against Dissent in the United States* (Boston: South End Press, 1990), 98, 110–111.

2. March 4, 1968, memo from J. Edgar Hoover to the Albany field office, quoted in ibid., 110–111.

3. Robert Justin Goldstein, *Political Repression in Modern America: From 1870 to the Present* (Cambridge, Mass.: Schenkman Publishing, 1978), 530. For a range of moving personal accounts of government repression, see Bud Schultz and Ruth Schultz, *It Did Happen Here: Recollections of Political Repression in America* (Berkeley: University of California Press, 1989).

4. Jack Weinberg, quoted in Mark Kitchell, *Berkeley in the 60s* (VHS; New York: First Run Features, 1990).

5. Ibid.

6. While many older activists felt the 1969 Mobilization had been highly successful, in part because of the massive turnout, to their astonishment younger activists ridiculed the protest as ineffective. Wells, *The War Within: America's Battle over Vietnam* (Berkeley: University of California Press, 1994), 398.

7. Quoted in ibid., 463.

8. See, for example, Noam Chomsky's discussion of the "limits of civil disobedience" and his refutation of Andrew Greeley's argument that mass antiwar protests prolonged the war by alienating significant swaths of the public. Chomsky, *For Reasons of State* (1970; reprint, New York: New Press, 2003), 285–297.

9. Richard Flacks, "Whatever Happened to the New Left," quoted in Wini Breines, *Community and Organization in the New Left, 1962–1968: The Great Refusal,* 2nd ed. (New Brunswick, N.J.: Rutgers University Press, 1989), 120.

10. In addition to richly reflective autobiographies, edited works, and local studies, several works have explored in depth the issues of militancy and violence in and against the Panthers and Weatherman. See in particular Jeremy Varon, *Bringing the War Home: The Weather Underground, the Red Army Faction, and Revolutionary Violence in the Sixties and Seventies* (Berkeley: University of California Press, 2004); Dan Berger, *Outlaws of America: The Weather Underground and the Politics of Solidarity* (Oakland: AK Press, 2006); and Curtis J. Austin, *Up against the Wall: Violence in the Making and Unmaking of the Black Panther Party* (Fayetteville: University of Arkansas Press, 2006). Jane Rhodes's *Framing the Black Panthers: The Spectacular Rise of a Black Panther Power Icon* (New York: New Press, 2007) provides important documentation of Panther history in the context of media and critical commentary from the party's emergence through the 1970s.

11. See the discussion of Mario Van Peebles's 1995 film *Panther* and Sam Green and Bill Siegel's 2004 film *The Weather Underground* later in this chapter.

12. Jerome H. Skolnick, *Politics of Protest: A Task Force Report Submitted to the National Commission on the Causes and Prevention of Violence* (New York: Ballantine, 1969), 76–77.

13. Quoted in Rick Perlstein, *Nixonland: The Rise of a President and the Fracturing of America* (New York: Scribner, 2008), 486, emphasis in the original.

14. Ibid.

15. James Michener, *Kent State: What Happened and Why?* (New York: Random House, 1971), 408. Michener reports many of the graphic comments on 406–415.

16. Although, according to one text, social science findings have been mixed on the cycle of violence theory. See Harvey Wallace, *Family Violence: Legal, Social, and Medical Perspectives*, 5th ed. (New York: Allyn & Bacon, 2007).

17. Bill Ayers, *Fugitive Days: A Memoir* (Boston: Beacon Press, 2001), 79.

18. Karl Armstrong, in *Vietnam: The War at Home*, dir. Glenn Silber and Alexander Brown (VHS; MPI Video, 1986).

19. Kenneth Keniston, "The Agony of the Counterculture," in Harrison Salisbury, ed., *The Eloquence of Protest: Voices of the 70s* (Boston: Houghton Mifflin, 1972), 221, cited in Varon, *Bringing the War Home,* 168.

20. Jean-Paul Sartre, preface to Frantz Fanon, *The Wretched of the Earth,* trans. Constance Farrington (New York: Grove Press, 1963), 17, quoted in Varon, *Bringing the War Home,* 88.

21. Skolnick, *Politics of Protest,* 78.

22. See *Report of the National Advisory Commission on Civil Disorders* (New York: Bantam, 1968), 302–305.

23. See Edward P. Morgan, "Media Culture and the Public Memory of the Black Panther Party," in *In Search of the Black Panther Party: New Perspectives on a Revolutionary Movement,* ed. Jama Lazerow and Yohuru Williams (Durham, N.C.: Duke University Press, 2006), 324–373.

24. Flores A. Forbes, *Will You Die with Me? My Life and the Black Panther Party* (New York: Atria Books, 2006), 22.

25. As Curtis Austin put it, the Black Panther Party "took the great leap forward and for the first time presented the American government with the long-feared threat of a minority uprising. Posing that threat cost it its life." Austin, *Up against the Wall*, 335.

26. "What We Want/What We Believe," reprinted in *The Black Panthers Speak*, ed. Philip S. Foner (Philadelphia: J. S. Lippincott, 1970), 3.

27. Flores Forbes, interviewed by Amy Goodman on "Democracy Now," November 22, 2006, www.democracynow/org/article.pl?sid=06/11/22/156254.

28. "Armed Negroes Protest Gun Bill," *New York Times*, May 7, 1967, 23, emphasis added.

29. Quoted in *Eyes on the Prize II*, "Power! 1967–68" (VHS; Alexandria, Va.: PBS Videos, 1989).

30. William A. Gamson and Gadi Wolfsfeld, "Movements and Media as Interacting Systems," *Annals of the American Academy of Political and Social Sciences* 528 (July 1993): 119.

31. Cited in Charles E. Jones and Judson L. Jeffries, "'Don't Believe the Hype': Debunking the Panther Mythology," in *The Black Panther Party Reconsidered*, ed. Charles E. Jones (Baltimore: Black Classic Press, 1998), 40.

32. "Shoot-Out on 28th Street," *Time*, April 19, 1968, 17–18.

33. Newton was charged with killing an Oakland policeman. He was eventually convicted of voluntary manslaughter, though the conviction was later reversed because of a judge's error. Newton was ultimately freed after two subsequent inconsequential trials and three years in prison.

34. "Panther Hunt," *Newsweek*, April 22, 1968, 38B.

35. Contained in Don Schanche, *The Panther Paradox: The Liberal's Dilemma* (New York: David McKay, 1970), 224.

36. "Guns and Butter," *Newsweek*, May 5, 1969, 40.

37. See Ward Churchill, "'To Disrupt, Discredit and Destroy': The FBI's Secret War against the Black Panther Party," in *Liberation, Imagination, and the Black Panther Party*, ed. George Katsiaficas and Kathleen Cleaver (New York: Routledge, 2001), 87. The FBI Airtel from the director to twenty-seven field offices, May 15, 1969, is quoted in Tracye Matthews, "'No One Ever Asks, What a Man's Place in the Revolution Is': Gender and the Politics of the Black Panther Party, 1966–1971," in Jones, *Black Panther Party Reconsidered*, 292, drawing from Huey P. Newton, "War against the Panthers: A Study of Repression in America" (Ph.D. diss., University of California, 1980), 109.

38. "Radicals: Gathering of the Clans," *Newsweek*, August 4, 1969, 32.

39. The *New York Times*, which quoted these words from Hanrahan, also contained the testimony of police sergeant Daniel Groth, claiming that "there must have been six or seven of them firing. The firing must have gone on for 10 or 12 minutes." John Kifner, "Inquiry into Slaying of 2 Panthers Urged in Chicago," *New York Times*, December 6, 1969, 29.

40. "The Panthers: Shoot It Out," *Newsweek*, December 15, 1969, 37.

41. "Police in Chicago Slay 2 Panthers," *New York Times*, December 5, 1969, 1.

42. *New York Times*, December 14, 1969, 64.

43. "The Panthers and the Law," *Newsweek*, February 13, 1970, 26.

44. Charlotte Curtis, "Black Panther Philosophy Is Debated at the Bernsteins," *New York Times*, January 15, 1970, 48.

45. Michael Staub, "Black Panthers, New Journalism, and the Rewriting of the Sixties," *Representations* 57 (Winter 1997): 53–72.

46. See Morgan, "Media Culture and Public Memory," in Lazerow and Williams, *In Search of the Black Panther Party*, 324–373.

47. See ibid.

48. One of the earliest such attacks was published in the conservative *National Review* on December 30, 1969. Titled "The Persecution and Assassination of the Black Panther Party as Directed by Guess Who," it attacked the respectable voices—the Illinois NAACP, the United

Auto Workers civil rights council, and Roy Wilkins—that had been raised in criticism of the Hampton-Clark murders. *National Review*, December 30, 1969, 1306–1307.

49. Tom Wolfe, "Radical Chic: That Party at Lenny's," *New York*, June 8, 1970, 26–56. Wolfe's article was later expanded into his book *Radical Chic and Mau-Mauing the Flak-Catchers* (New York: Farrar, Strauss & Giroux, 1970).

50. "That Party at Lenny's," *Time*, June 13, 1970, 81–83. Gerald Emanuel Stearn, "Rapping with the Panthers in White Suburbia," *New York Times Magazine*, March 8, 1970, 15ff. William F. Buckley Jr. also weighed in with a dismissive essay, "Have a Panther to Lunch," *National Review*, February 10, 1970, 168.

51. The *New York Times* later revived the "radical chic" epithet in a prominently featured article that largely ridiculed the fund-raising efforts for the defense of convicted ex-Panther Mumia Abu Jamal, titled "The Case that Brought Back Radical Chic," *New York Times,* August 13, 1995, C1. The *Times* article was the catalyst for Michael Staub's analysis and his contention that "mobilized memories of the sixties" were being used "for the purpose of ridiculing and neutralizing political activism in the nineties." See Staub, "Black Panthers, New Journalism," 53.

52. Edward Jay Epstein, "The Panthers and the Police: A Pattern of Genocide?" *New Yorker,* February 13, 1971, 45–76.

53. See ibid., 45–47.

54. For more detail, see my discussion of Epstein's article in Morgan, "Media Culture and the Public Memory of the Black Panther Party," in Lazerow and Williams, *In Search of the Black Panther Party*, 349–352.

55. The controversy over numbers of dead Panthers proceeded to rage publicly through a variety of media, extending even to *Senior Scholastic*'s "teacher's edition"—hardly evidence that Garry's claims blanketed the media, as Epstein's article initially implied though much later in the article qualified. See Morgan, "Media Culture."

56. In this case, in fact, the *Washington Post* issued an apology for its nonreferenced use of the Garry figure, an apology *Time* magazine—the main competitor with the *Post*-owned *Newsweek*—was quick to jump on. "Mea Culpa," *Time*, March 8, 1971, 45.

57. Epstein, "The Panthers and the Police," 76.

58. *Eyes on the Prize II:* "A Nation of Law? 1968–71" (VHS).

59. Although Epstein would not have known this at the time of his article, it may have had a significant bearing on the discrepancies between Panther perceptions and Epstein's report. For example, while Epstein concluded that ten Panthers died at the hands of police, at least four of the remaining nine Panther deaths were attributed to the black militant group US, targeted by COINTELPRO efforts to seed animosities between them and the Panthers. Given J. Edgar Hoover's hostile rhetoric and their own well-grounded suspicions about police informants, the Panthers could validly perceive these deaths as part of a concerted effort to eliminate them.

60. Richard Cohen, "An Epidemic of Inaccuracy," *Washington Post*, May 22, 1988, W11. The initial salvo in the media attack was spearheaded by the Right in a 1973 article, "The 'Black Genocide' Myth," *National Review*, February 16, 1973.

61. Writing of the New Journalism accounts by Tom Wolfe and Sheehy, Michael Staub observed that "Wolfe, like Sheehy, utilized the narrative freedom of New Journalism in order to move subtly and cleverly from perspective to perspective—none of them completely his own nor identifiably anyone else's." Staub, "Black Panthers, New Journalism," 66.

62. Gail Sheehy, *Panthermania; The Clash of Black against Black in One American City* (New York: Harper & Row, 1971), x.

63. Ibid., ix.

64. Ibid., 8.

65. The *Times*' crime, in Stern's eyes, was a Holland Carter review of an exhibit of Panther photographs, in which he, according to Stern, lectured on the "justice of black violence."

"Soundings: 'Ah, Those Black Panthers! Beautiful!'" *City Journal* 13, no. 3 (Summer 2003): 12–13.

66. See, for example, Peter Collier and David Horowitz, *Destructive Generation: Second Thoughts about the '60s* (New York: Summit, 1989). For more on this campaign, see chapter 12.

67. Richard Corliss, "Power to the Peephole," *Time,* May 15, 1995, 73.

68. Michael Eric Dyson, "The Panthers, Still Untamed, Roar Back," *New York Times,* April 30, 1995.

69. See my discussion in "Media Culture and the Public Memory of the Black Panther Party," in Lazerow and Yohuru, *In Search of the Black Panther Party,* 358.

70. Ayers, *Fugitive Days,* 131. See also Susan Stern quote in Varon, *Bringing the War Home,* 94–95.

71. In 1970, the Scranton Commission reported that there had been 8,200 "bombings, attempted bombings, and bomb threats" attributable to "campus disturbances and student unrest." Report of the President's Commission on Student Unrest (Washington, D.C.: U.S. Government Printing Office, 1970), 38.

72. Comments by Ken Mate in the aftermath of post–Kent State protests, quoted in *Vietnam: The War at Home* (VHS).

73. Cathy Wilkerson, *Flying Close to the Sun: My Life and Times as a Weatherman* (New York: Seven Stories Press, 2007), 284.

74. "You Don't Need a Weatherman to Know Which Way the Wind Blows," initially disseminated in 1969, reprinted in *Sing a Battle Song: The Revolutionary Poetry, Statements, and Communiqués of the Weather Underground, 1970–1974,* ed. Bernardine Dohrn, Bill Ayers, and Jeff Jones (New York: Seven Stories Press, 2006), 67–68.

75. "Bring the War Home," *New Left Notes,* July 23, 1969, quoted in ibid. As Cathy Wilkerson recalled, Weatherman was "trying to reach white youth on the basis of their most reactionary macho instincts, intellectuals playing at working-class toughs." Quoted in Harold Jacobs, ed., *Weatherman* (San Francisco: Ramparts Press, 1970), 43.

76. David Dellinger, *From Yale to Jail: The Life Story of a Moral Dissenter* (New York: Pantheon, 1993), 387–388.

77. Shin'ya Ono, "A Weatherman: You Do Need a Weatherman to Know Which Way the Wind Blows," reprinted in Jacobs, *Weatherman,* 228, emphasis added.

78. Quoted in Varon, *Bringing the War Home,* 81.

79. "Wild in the Streets," *Newsweek,* October 20, 1969, 42; "Poor Climate for Weathermen," *Time,* October 17, 1969, 24; "Custeristic," *Nation,* October 27, 1969, 428.

80. Varon, *Bringing the War Home,* 84.

81. In Mark Rudd's account, the Fort Dix action was being advocated by a small group in the New York cell, led by Terry Robbins (one of the three who died in the townhouse explosion), and it was sharply denounced by Bernardine Dohrn, speaking for the West Coast contingent. See Mark Rudd, *Underground: My Life with SDS and the Weathermen* (New York: William Morrow, 2009), 213.

82. *New York Times,* March 13, 1970, 38.

83. At least in the sense that terrorism involves the intentional taking of human life, as opposed to sabotage that involves destruction of politically targeted property.

84. Berger, *Outlaws of America,* 130.

85. Ibid., 151.

86. It is at least well documented that the wider public was becoming increasingly hostile to antiwar demonstrations they saw as militant, destructive, and, ironically, "hippie-like." See, for example, E. M. Schreiber's finding that "suggests that Vietnam war protesters were unpopular not because they were expressing opposition to the war in Vietnam, but simply because of the behavior in which they were engaged; they were dissenters, deviants and were evaluated ac-

cordingly." E. M. Schreiber, "Anti-War Demonstrations and American Public Opinion on the War in Vietnam," *British Journal of Sociology* 27, no. 2 (June 1976): 230.

87. See, for example, the essays in Jacobs, *Weatherman*. At the same time, it is probably fair to say that some of the symbolic bombings were greeted by quiet cheers from many in the movement.

88. Wilkerson, *Flying Close to the Sun*, 263–264.

89. Ono, "You Do Need a Weatherman," 241, emphasis added.

90. *Underground*, dir. Emile DeAntonio, with Mary Wexsler and members of the Weather Underground Organization (VHS; New York: First Run Features, 1976), emphasis added.

91. Wilkerson, *Flying Close to the Sun*, 259.

92. R. Jacobs, *The Way the Wind Blew: A History of the Weather Underground* (London: Verso, 1997), 66.

93. Or, as Ayers added, with presumable irony, "Sex was, of course, our own personal invention, our own generational discovery." Ayers, *Fugitive Days*, 141, 142–143.

94. Jonathan Lerner, "I Was a Terrorist," *Washington Post*, February 24, 2002, W24ff.

95. For a counterargument that the United States was in a state of near-revolutionary turmoil at the end of the 1960s, see George Katsiaficas, *The Imagination of the New Left: A Global Analysis of 1968* (Boston: South End Press, 1987).

96. See Varon, *Bringing the War Home*, 188, 194.

97. See in particular Wilkerson, *Flying Close to the Sun;* and Rudd, *Underground*. For reflections on the morality of violence, see Naomi Jaffe's comments published on the *Upstate Films* website after release of the film *The Weather Underground*, www.upstatefilms.org/weather/jaffe.html (accessed May 24, 2010); and the discussion in Varon, *Bringing the War Home*, 187–195.

98. Andrew O'Hehir, "When Terrorism Was Cool," *Salon*, June 7, 2003, www.salon.com/entertainment/feature/2003/06/07/weatherman.

Chapter 9. Domesticating the Sixties: Capitalism's Cultural Co-optation

1. Peter Berg, in *It Was Twenty Years Ago Today*, dir. John Sheppard (VHS; London: Granada Television, 1987).

2. Thomas Frank, *The Conquest of Cool: Business Culture, Counterculture, and the Rise of Hip Consumerism* (Chicago: University of Chicago Press, 1997), 26, 54, 68. See also Daniel Bell, *The Cultural Contradictions of Capitalism* (1978; reprint, New York: Basic Books, 1996); and Jackson Lears, *Fables of Abundance: A Cultural History of Advertising in America* (New York: Basic Books, 1994).

3. See also Juliet B. Schor's discussion of the "Marketing of Cool" in her *Born to Buy: The Commercialized Child and the New Consumer Culture* (New York: Scribner, 2004); and Douglas Rushkoff's essay, "The Pursuit of Cool," *Sportswear International*, North American ed., no. 150 (June 2001): 4–6, www.rushkoff.com/essay/sportswearinternational.htm.

4. See Mark Crispin Miller, "The Hipness unto Death," in Miller, *Boxed In: The Culture of TV*, 3rd ed. (Evanston, Ill.: Northwestern University Press, 1989), 3–27.

5. Writing of the hegemonic process, Gitlin observed that hegemony is an "unequal collaboration, in which the large-scale processes of concentrated production set limits to, and manage, the cultural expressions of dominated (and dominating) groups." Todd Gitlin, "Television's Screens: Hegemony in Transition," in *American Media and Mass Culture: Left Perspectives*, ed. Donald Lazere (Berkeley: University of California Press, 1987), 241–242.

6. Thomas Frank, "Why Johnny Can't Dissent," in *Commodify Your Dissent: Salvos from the Baffler*, ed. Thomas Frank and Matt Weiland (New York: Norton, 1997), 44.

7. Miller, "Hipness unto Death," 14.

8. Mark Crispin Miller, "Big Brother Is You, Watching," in Miller, *Boxed In,* 309–331.

9. See Robert W. McChesney, *Rich Media, Poor Democracy: Communication Politics in Dubious Times* (New York: New Press, 1999), especially 15–29.

10. Theodore Roszak, *The Making of a Counter Culture* (New York: Anchor, 1969), 49.

11. See Carl Boggs, *The End of Politics: Corporate Power and the Decline of the Public Sphere* (New York: Guilford, 2000), 177–185.

12. As Frank observes, of course, the Volkswagen was transformed by advertising from its original niche as the "everyman" car favored by the Nazis to the widely popular and hip "anti-car." Frank, *Conquest of Cool,* 55, 60–67.

13. Among the quiz questions cited by Ewen were: "1) To 'blow your mind' *a.* refers to sniffing glue, *b.* refers to a sudden lapse of memory at exam time, *c.* means to be overwhelmed by an idea or an event." And "7) Buffy Sainte-Marie and Phil Ochs are *a.* leading singer-composers, *b.* student leaders at Berkeley, *c.* inventors of skin jewelry." Stuart Ewen, *All Consuming Images: The Politics of Style in Contemporary Culture* (New York: Basic Books, 1988), 249.

14. Marketers were asked to select the correct meaning of terms like "Heavy" ("meaningful" or "villain"), "Rap" ("knock opponent" or "a conversation"), "Bummer" ("sponger" or "negative experience, bad job experience") and "Ego-Trip" ("soulful" or "self-centered"). Ibid., 250.

15. Ibid., 251.

16. Ibid.

17. The Columbia ad is reproduced in Abe Peck, *Uncovering the Sixties: The Life and Times of the Underground Press* (New York: Pantheon, 1985), 164.

18. Ibid., 170.

19. Quoted in ibid., 170.

20. Quoted in ibid. By contrast, as the radical *Guardian*'s cultural critic Irwin Silber put it, "Our goal is not to get our message out on 10 million Columbia records, but to take over Columbia records and make it part of a people's socialist system based on human need and human expression." Ibid., 169.

21. Robert Santelli, *Aquarius Rising: The Rock Festival Years* (New York: Delta, 1980), 59. For a discussion of the transformation of popular music and its link to the counterculture, see Edward P. Morgan, *The Sixties Experience: Hard Lessons about Modern America* (Philadelphia: Temple University Press, 1991), 187–196.

22. Quoted in Frank, *Conquest of Cool,* 108.

23. Patricia Bradley, *Mass Media and the Shaping of American Feminism 1963–1975* (Jackson: University Press of Mississippi, 2003), 211.

24. Ibid.

25. Laurel Cutler, "She's Doing Her Own Thing," *Madison Avenue,* May 1969, 29, quoted in Thomas Frank, *Conquest of Cool,* 153.

26. Quoted in Frank, 153–155.

27. Paul Krassner, "On the 40th Anniversary of Woodstock," *Huffington Post,* August 14, 2009.

28. Lynn Spigel and Michael Curtin, eds., *The Revolution Wasn't Televised: Sixties Television and Social Conflict* (New York: Routledge, 1997), 9.

29. David Farber, *The Age of Great Dreams: America in the 1960s* (New York: Hill & Wang, 1994), 54–55.

30. Aniko Bodroghkozy, *Groove Tube: Sixties Television and Youth Rebellion* (Durham, N.C.: Duke University Press, 2001), 67–68.

31. Ibid., 68, 60, 75.

32. Ibid., 81.

33. Ibid., 195, 165.

34. The site also claims that "the show worked because of its clothes, its language, its attitudes and, of course, its timing. The show's topics, such as student unrest and anti-war statements could only have worked in the late 60s." See Graeme Smith, "The Mod Squad in Color," www.chezgrae.com/modsquad (accessed May 31, 2010).

35. See Bodroghkozy, *Groove Tube,* 169ff.

36. Stuart Hall, "Notes on Deconstructing the Popular," in *People's History and Social Theory,* ed. Raphael Samuel (London: Routledge & Kegan Paul, 1981), 228. Cited in Bodroghkozy, *Groove Tube,* 168.

37. See Bodroghkozy's analysis of specific shows' themes in *Groove Tube,* 172–197.

38. Todd Gitlin, *Inside Prime Time* (New York: Pantheon, 1985), 139.

39. Bodroghkozy, *Groove Tube,* 164.

40. Ibid., 123.

41. Ibid.

42. Ibid., 128.

43. Ibid., 129–134.

44. Ibid., 140–142.

45. Ibid., 145.

46. Discussed in ibid., 144–147.

47. Gitlin, *Inside Prime Time,* 206. Gitlin's seminal work provides important insight into the programming concerns of television's executives.

48. See the episode summaries in Richard Adler, ed., *All in the Family: A Critical Appraisal* (New York: Praeger, 1979), 272–318.

49. See Laura Z. Hobson, "As I listened to Archie Say 'Hebe' . . . ," *New York Times,* September 12, 1971, D1. See also Adler, *All in the Family,* xxiv–xxviii.

50. Bodroghkozy, *Groove Tube,* 230.

51. Mark Crispin Miller, "Big Brother Is You, Watching," 326–327.

52. "The Team behind Archie Bunker & Co.," *Time,* September 25, 1972, 48.

53. "Films," *Senior Scholastic,* October 4, 1973, 24, quoted in Daniel Marcus, *Happy Days and Wonder Years: The Fifties and Sixties in Contemporary Cultural Politics* (New Brunswick, N.J.: Rutgers University Press, 2004), 22.

54. Marcus, *Happy Days and Wonder Years,* 28.

55. Michael Ryan and Douglas Kellner, *Cinema Politica: The Politics and Ideology of Contemporary Hollywood Film* (Bloomington: Indiana University Press, 1988), 6.

56. Ibid., 3.

57. See ibid., 6.

58. Bosley Crowther, "Shoot-em-up Film Opens World Fete," *New York Times,* August 7, 1967, 32.

59. Jerry Rubin, *Do It! Scenarios of the Revolution* (New York: Ballantine Books, 1970), 122.

60. All quotes—Bonnie's complaint, *Vogue's* characterization, and Kennedy's term—are drawn from Peter Braunstein, "Forever Young: Insurgent Youth and the Sixties Culture of Rejuvenation," in *Imagine Nation: The American Counterculture of the 1960s and '70s,* ed. Peter Braunstein and Michael William Doyle (New York: Routledge, 2002), 261–262. See also Pagan Kennedy, *Platforms: A Microwaved Cultural Chronicle of the 1970s* (New York: St. Martin's Press, 1994), 9.

61. Aniko Bodroghkozy's examination of these and other late-sixties films (e.g., *Woodstock, Getting Straight,* and *The Activist*) and their reception in sixties underground papers led her to conclude that "Hollywood's attempt to commodify and package youth rebellion did not occur without a struggle by the intended audience for these offerings." Aniko Bodroghkozy, "Reel

Revolutionaries: An Examination of Hollywood's Cycle of 1960s Youth Rebellion Films," *Cinema Journal* 41, no. 3 (Spring 2003): 55.

62. David E. James, "'The Movies Are a Revolution'—Film and the Counterculture," in Braunstein and Doyle, *Imagine Nation,* 299.

63. Joseph Heath and Andrew Potter, *Nation of Rebels* (New York: HarperBusiness, 2004), 63.

64. Ryan and Kellner, *Cinema Politica,* 21, 23.

65. Jack Whalen and Richard Flacks, *Beyond the Barricades: The Sixties Generation Grows Up* (Philadelphia: Temple University Press, 1989), 270.

66. Quoted from Hoffman's *Revolution for the Hell of It* in Todd Gitlin, *The Sixties: Years of Hope, Days of Rage* (New York: Simon & Schuster, 1987), 236. Originally conceived in December 1967 by a group including Abbie Hoffman, Jerry Rubin, Paul Krassner, Stew Albert, Ed Sanders, Anita Hoffman, Robin Morgan, Phil Ochs, and others, the Yippies grew out of early media-savvy actions of Hoffman and Rubin in particular.

67. Comments on sixties-1@lists.village.virginia.edu, October 2, 2000.

68. Jerry Rubin, *Growing (Up) at Thirty-Seven* (New York: M. Evans, 1976), 98–99, quoted in Richard J. Jensen and Allen Lichtenstein, "From Yippie to Yuppie: Jerry Rubin as Rhetorical Icon," *Southern Communication Journal* 60, no. 4 (1995): 340.

69. See Todd Gitlin, *The Whole World Is Watching: Mass Media in the Making and Unmaking of the New Left* (Berkeley: University of California Press, 1980), 171.

70. See Gitlin, *The Sixties,* 233.

71. Hoffman's words, from his book *Square Dancing in the Ice Age* (Boston: South End Press, 1982), are quoted in Stephen J. Whitfield, "The Stunt Man: Abbie Hoffman (1936–1989)," in *Sights on the Sixties,* ed. Barbara L. Tischler (New Brunswick, N.J.: Rutgers University Press, 1992), 104, 108.

72. One of the chief organizers of the Pentagon march, Dave Dellinger remarked, "I remember being thrilled and excited that this whole new element of humor and creativity and youthful zest was coming into things. . . . I felt [the levitation] showed the breadth and diversity and vitality of the opposition. But especially it was a lively, imaginative thing that just appealed to me." Quoted in Tom Wells, *The War Within: America's Battle over Vietnam* (Berkeley: University of California Press, 1994), 180.

73. Quoted from Hoffman's *Revolution for the Hell of It* in Gitlin, *The Sixties,* 236. Gitlin also observed that both Hoffman and Rubin "received job offers from three advertising agencies" after Chicago.

74. Gitlin, *The Whole World Is Watching,* 172–173, emphasis in original.

75. Quoted from Rubin, *Do It!* 106, in Melvin Small, *Covering Dissent: The Media and the Antiwar Movement* (New Brunswick, N.J.: Rutgers University Press, 1994), 19. See also James E. Miller, *Democracy Is in the Streets: From Port Huron to the Siege of Chicago* (New York: Simon & Schuster, 1987), 243–244.

76. Abbie Hoffman, "Media Freaking: Talking to the Yippies," in Mitchell Goodman, *The Movement toward a New America* (Philadelphia: Pilgrim Press, 1970), 361.

77. Ibid., 362.

78. Daniel Boorstin, "From Hero to Celebrity: The Human Pseudo Event," in *Inter/Media: Interpersonal Communication in a Media World,* ed. G. Gumpert and R. Cathcart (New York: Oxford University Press, 1979), 25.

79. Quoted from Dellinger's *Liberation* article in Jonas Raskin, *For the Hell of It: The Life and Times of Abbie Hoffman* (Berkeley: University of California Press, 1996), 188.

80. Ibid., 164.

81. Ibid., 191.

82. As Jensen and Lichtenstein argued, "Rubin was able to present the self-definition he

wanted to the public as well as attract the media's attention. . . . [He] refused to be frozen in one image but changed when necessary in order to remain a symbol of currently popular attitudes and beliefs." Jensen and Lichtenstein, "From Yippie to Yuppie," 333–334.

83. Quoted in ibid., 339.

84. Jerry Rubin, "Guess Who's Coming to Wall Street?" *New York Times,* July 30, 1980, 21.

85. Bill Ayers, *Fugitive Days: A Memoir* (Boston: Beacon Press, 2001), 204.

Chapter 10. Reconstructing the Past, Constructing the Future:
Corporate Backlash and the Reagan Revolution

1. See in particular Alex Carey's examination of corporate interests in the United States and Australia, *Taking the Risk out of Democracy: Corporate Propaganda versus Freedom and Liberty*, ed. Andrew Lohrey (Urbana: University of Illinois Press, 1997); David Miller and William Dinan's account of corporate propaganda in the United States and the United Kingdom, *A Century of Spin: How Public Relations Became the Cutting Edge of Corporate Power* (London: Pluto Press, 2008); and Elizabeth Fones-Wolf's study of the post–World War II United States, *Selling Free Enterprise: The Business Assault on Labor and Liberalism* (Urbana: University of Illinois Press, 1994).

2. Joseph Peschek, *Policy-Planning Organizations: Elite Agendas and America's Rightward Turn* (Philadelphia: Temple University Press, 1987), 241.

3. See Edward N. Wolff, *Poverty and Income Distribution*, 2nd ed. (Hoboken, N.J.: Wiley-Blackwell, 2009). See also the discussion in Juliet B. Schor, *Plenitude: The New Economics of True Wealth* (New York: Penguin, 2001), 13–14.

4. The percentages represent those surveyed who responded affirmatively to the question "Does business achieve a good balance between profits and service to the public?" From Daniel Yankelovich, *The Changing Business Environment* (Washington, D.C.: National Association of Manufacturers, 1972), quoted in Carey, *Taking the Risk Out of Democracy*, 145.

5. "Violence Panel Bids U.S. Combat Causes of Unrest," *New York Times,* December 13, 1969, 1.

6. Dinesh D'Souza, *Ronald Reagan: How an Ordinary Man Became an Extraordinary Leader* (New York: Free Press, 1997), 73, quoted in Daniel Marcus, *Happy Days and Wonder Years: The Fifties and Sixties in Contemporary Cultural Politics* (New Brunswick, N.J.: Rutgers University Press, 2004), 75.

7. G. William Domhoff, *The Powers That Be* (New York: Vintage, 1979), 79, cited in Miller and Dinan, *A Century of Spin*, 74.

8. Lewis H. Lapham, "Tentacles of Rage: The Republican Propaganda Mill, A Brief History," *Harper's Magazine*, September 2004, 34–35. Miller and Dinan depict both the initial Heritage funding and the boost in AEI resources as responses to the Lewis Powell memo.

9. Lapham, "Tentacles of Rage," 36.

10. Ibid., 4.

11. From Trilateral Commission, "About the Organization," www.trilateral.org/about.htm (accessed May 26, 2010).

12. Michel Crozier, Samuel Huntington, and Joji Watanuki, *The Crisis of Democracy: Report on the Governability of Democracies to the Trilateral Commission* (New York: New York University Press, 1975), 1–2.

13. Alan Wolfe, "Capitalism Shows Its Face: Giving Up on Democracy," *Trilateralism: The Trilateral Commission and Elite Planning for World Management,* ed. Holly Sklar (Boston: South End Press, 1980), 296, emphasis in original. Wolfe's article originally appeared in the *Nation*, November 29, 1975.

14. Crozier, Huntington, and Watanuki, *Crisis of Democracy*, 4–5.

15. Huntington also singled out the growing number of strikes by unionized public employees as a target of concern. Ibid., 61–62, 104.

16. Despite the high level of defense spending, the Trilateralists singled out the welfare shift as the principal cause of a rising federal deficit that, in turn, contributed to "the inflation that plagued the United States, along with most other industrial countries, in the early 1970s." Ibid., 72–73.

17. Crozier, Huntington, and Watanuki, *Crisis of Democracy*, 71, emphasis added.

18. Ibid., 113, 106.

19. Wolfe, "Capitalism Shows its Face," 306.

20. Crozier, Huntington, and Watanuki, *Crisis of Democracy*, 84.

21. Martin Luther King Jr., "Letter from Birmingham City Jail," in James M. Washington, ed., *A Testament of Hope: The Essential Writings and Speeches of Martin Luther King, Jr.* (New York: HarperCollins, 1991), 295.

22. Crozier, Huntington, and Watanuki, *Crisis of Democracy*, 107–108. See, for example, "How Americans View Government: Deconstructing Distrust," Survey Report, Pew Research Center for the People and the Press, March 10, 1998.

23. Crozier, Huntington, and Watanuki, *Crisis of Democracy*, 78.

24. Ibid., 113–114, emphasis added.

25. Ibid., 105–106, emphasis added.

26. Gabriel Kolko, *Anatomy of a War: Vietnam, the United States, and the Modern Historical Experience* (New York: Pantheon, 1985), 174.

27. See chapter 5, note 3.

28. See chapter 5, notes 20 and 21.

29. Marilyn Young, "Revisionists Revised: The Case of Vietnam," *Newsletter of the Society of Historians of American Foreign Relations* (Summer 1979): 1–10, quoted in Harry W. Haines, "'They Were Called and Went': The Political Rehabilitation of the Vietnam Veteran," in *From Hanoi to Hollywood: The Vietnam War in American Film*, ed. Linda Dittmar and Gene Michaud (New Brunswick, N.J.: Rutgers University Press, 1990), 85.

30. Podhoretz used the term in critiquing the Carter administration while praising the 1983 American invasion of Grenada, which, he argued, "points the way back to recovery and health." Norman Podhoretz, "Proper Uses of Power," *New York Times*, October 30, 1983, E19.

31. Noam Chomsky, "Toward a New Cold War," in *Toward a New Cold War: Essays on the Current Crisis and How We Got There* (New York: Pantheon, 1982), 190.

32. Walter LaFeber, "The Last War, the Next War, and the New Revisionists," *Democracy* 1, no. 1 (January 1981): 93.

33. William L. Griffen and John Marciano, *Teaching the Vietnam War: A Critical Examination of School Texts and an Interpretive Comparative History Using the Pentagon Papers and Other Documents* (Montclair, N.J.: Allenheld, Osmun & Company, 1979), 171, xix.

34. Quoted in ibid., 95.

35. See Wilbur J. Scott, *Vietnam Veterans since the War: The Politics of PTSD, Agent Orange, and the National Memorial* (Norman: University of Oklahoma Press, 2004).

36. Thanks to the publication of a book like Gloria Emerson's *Winners and Losers: Battle, Retreats, Gains, Losses and Ruins from a Long War* (New York: Random House, 1976).

37. See Jerry Lembcke, *The Spitting Image: Myth, Memory, and the Legacy of Vietnam* (New York: New York University Press, 1998); and the discussion of Vietnam war films in chapter 11 below.

38. "Transcript of President's News Conference," *New York Times*, March 25, 1977, 10.

39. Jacqueline Trescott, "CBS' Ed Bradley: The Anchorman-Reporter as Symbol," *Washington Post,* April 1, 1977, B1ff.

40. Ibid.; Leslie H. Gelb, with Richard K. Betts, *The Irony of Vietnam: The System Worked* (Washington, D.C.: Brookings Institution, 1979).

41. Guenter Lewy, *America in Vietnam* (New York: Oxford University Press, 1979), quoted in LaFeber, "The Last War, the Next War," 94.

42. Richard Nixon, *No More Vietnams* (New York: Arbor House, 1985), 9–10, 165.

43. Prior to this point, aid for the Angolan rebels had been covert, as had the U.S.-engineered coup against Salvador Allende of Chile in 1973. Leslie H. Gelb, "Angola and the Schism in Washington," *New York Times*, December 20, 1975, 9; and David Binder, "Kissinger Reports U.S. Is Weighing Open Angolan Aid," *New York Times*, January 30, 1976, 61.

44. See Edward S. Herman and Noam Chomsky, *Manufacturing Consent: The Political Economy of Mass Media,* 2nd ed. (New York: Pantheon, 2002), introduction.

45. "Interview with Zbigniew Brzezinski," *Le Nouvel Observateur*, January 15–21, 1998, 76.

46. Robert Newman, in *Washington Review of Strategic and International Studies*, July 1978, 117, quoted in William Blum, *Killing Hope: U.S. Military and C.I.A. Interventions since World War II,* updated ed. (Monroe, Me.: Common Courage Press, 2004), 341.

47. Brzezinski utters the "Vietnam" phrase in *Behind the Terror: Understanding the Enemy,* Discovery Channel, 2001. Indeed, as he revealed in a 1998 interview, President Carter signed a secret authorization for U.S. intervention in support of opposition to the pro-Soviet Afghan government, intervention that Brzezinski assured the president would "induce a Soviet military intervention." *Nouvel Observateur*, January 15–21, 1998, 76.

48. See Chalmers Johnson, *Blowback: The Costs and Consequences of American Empire,* 2nd ed. (New York: Holt, 2004).

49. John E. Rielly, ed., *American Public Opinion and U.S. Foreign Policy, 1979* (Chicago: Chicago Council on Foreign Relations, 1979).

50. See, for example, Noam Chomsky, *Necessary Illusions: Thought Control in Democratic Societies* (Boston: South End Press, 1989); Walter LaFeber, *Inevitable Revolutions: The United States in Central America,* 2nd ed. (New York: Norton, 1993); Thomas W. Walker et al., *Reagan vs. the Sandinistas: The Undeclared War on Nicaragua* (Boulder, Colo.: Westview Press, 1987).

51. Quoted from *Village Voice,* February 5, 1991, in Douglas Kellner, *The Persian Gulf TV War* (Boulder, Colo.: Westview Press, 1992), 1.

52. Quoted from *The Fund for Free Expression,* February 27, 1991, in ibid.

53. From Bush speech to state legislators visiting the White House. "Quote of the Day," *New York Times,* March 2, 1991, 2.

54. David Brock, *The Republican Noise Machine* (New York: Crown, 2004), 41.

55. Quoted in ibid., emphasis in original.

56. Ibid., 42.

57. Quoted in ibid., 48.

58. Marcus, *Happy Days*, 37.

59. See Thomas Ferguson, *Golden Rule: The Investment Theory of Party Competition and the Logic of Money-Driven Political Systems* (Chicago: University of Chicago Press, 1995), chapter 5.

60. Alan Crawford, *Thunder on the Right: The 'New Right' and the Politics of Resentment* (New York: Pantheon, 1980).

61. See, for example, Alan Gartner, Colin Greer, and Frank Riessman, eds., *What Reagan Is Doing to Us* (New York: Harper, 1982); John L. Palmer and Isabel V. Sawhill, *The Reagan Record: An Assessment of America's Changing Domestic Priorities* (Cambridge, Mass.: Ballinger, 1984); George E. Peterson and Carol W. Lewis, eds., *Reagan and the Cities* (Washington, D.C.: Urban Institute Press, 1986).

62. See Paul Lyons, *New Left, New Right and the Legacy of the Sixties* (Philadelphia: Temple University Press, 1996); John A. Andrew III, *The Other Side of the Sixties: Young Americans for*

Freedom and the Rise of Conservative Politics (New Brunswick, N.J.: Rutgers University Press, 1997); and Rebecca Klatch, *A Generation Divided: The New Left, the New Right, and the 1960s* (Berkeley: University of California Press, 1999).

63. "The State of the Union: A Republican View," *NBC Nightly News*, January 27, 1980.

64. See Marcus, *Happy Days*.

65. Howell Raines, "Reagan Calls Arms Race Essential to Avoid 'Surrender' or 'Defeat,'" *New York Times*, August 19, 1980, 1, quoted in ibid., 38.

66. D. Michael Shafer, "The Vietnam Combat Experience: The Human Legacy," in *The Legacy: The Vietnam War and the American Imagination*, ed. D. Michael Shafer (Boston: Beacon Press, 1990), 97.

67. Quoted in ibid., 61.

68. Charles Taylor, "Himmelfarb vs. the '60s: There's No Room for Real Life in Gertie's America," www.salon.com/books/feature/2000/02/09/gertie, February 9, 2000.

69. Roger Rosenblatt, with Laurence I. Barrett, "Man of the Year: Out of the Past, Fresh Choices for the Future: Invoking Old Values, Ronald Reagan Must Make Them Work for the '80s," *Time,* January 5, 1981, 10–23. See the discussion by Marcus, *Happy Days*, 60–62.

70. See the extensive discussion and documentation in Stephanie Coontz, *The Way We Never Were: American Families and the Nostalgia Trap* (New York: Basic Books, 1992).

71. Marcus, *Happy Days*, 72.

72. Sheldon S. Wolin, *The Presence of the Past: Essays on the State and the Constitution* (Baltimore: Johns Hopkins University Press, 1989), 23.

73. Marcus, *Happy Days*, 72.

74. As an actor, Rogin noted, Reagan "learned to see himself from the outside in as others see him, not from the inside out." Michael Rogin, *Ronald Reagan, the Movie* (Berkeley: University of California Press, 1987), 6, 9.

75. For several telling examples, see ibid., 8.

76. Ibid., 9.

77. Ibid. The reference is to Fredric Jameson, "Postmodernism, or the Cultural Logic of Late Capitalism," *New Left Review* 146 (July 1984): 58–69.

78. From the *Public Papers of the President of the United States: Ronald Reagan, 1982,* vol. 1, 184–185, cited in Marvin E. Gettleman, Jane Franklin, Marilyn Young, and H. Bruce Franklin, eds., *Vietnam and America: A Documented History* (New York: Grove Press, 1985), xiii.

79. Marcus, *Happy Days*, 73.

80. Douglas Kellner, *Television and the Crisis of Democracy* (Boulder, Colo.: Westview Press, 1990), 141–142.

81. Poverty rates are, of course, a function not only of government programs but also the state of the economy. They also underrepresent the percentage of Americans living lives of intense fiscal distress. Nonetheless, the official poverty rate fell steadily from 19.5 percent in 1963 to 11.1 percent in 1973 and remained quite stable through the 1970s. It rose again significantly in the 1980s, beginning to decline in the latter 1990s only to begin rising again in the early years of the twenty-first century.

Chapter 11. The "Sixties" Nostalgia Market and the Culture of Self-Satire

1. See L. A. Kauffman, "Small Changes: Radical Politics since the 1960s," in *Cultural Politics and Social Movements*, ed. Marcy Darnovsky, Barbara Epstein, and Richard Flacks (Philadelphia: Temple University Press, 1995), 154–160.

2. McChesney, *Rich Media, Poor Democracy: Communication Politics in Dubious Times* (New York: New Press, 2000), 26, 29–30.

3. Douglas Kellner, *Television and the Crisis of Democracy* (Boulder, Colo.: Westview Press, 1990), 140.

4. Arguably, nostalgia for the hopeful earlier sixties was beginning to set in by 1968 when Mary Hopkin's 1968 hit, "Those Were the Days," gained wide popularity.

5. Quoted in Mark Crispin Miller, "The Jewish Media: The Lie That Won't Die," *Extra!* September–October 1996, 19.

6. Jonathan Yardley, "The Sixties Revival: Echoes from an Empty Decade," *Washington Post,* July 24, 1987, C2.

7. Ibid.

8. Ibid.

9. The term is Mark Crispin Miller's from "Big Brother Is You, Watching," in Miller, *Boxed In: The Culture of TV*, 3rd ed. (Evanston, Ill.: Northwestern University Press, 1989).

10. A reference to Daniel Bell, *The Cultural Contradictions of Capitalism* (New York: Basic Books, 1976). See Thomas Frank, *The Conquest of Cool: Business Culture, Counterculture, and the Rise of Hip Consumerism* (Chicago: University of Chicago Press, 1997), 232.

11. Thomas Frank, "Why Johnny Can't Dissent," in *Commodify Your Dissent: Salvos from the Baffler,* ed. Thomas Frank and Matt Weiland (New York: Norton, 1997), 44.

12. On the "marketing of cool" and the "anti-adult bias" of marketing to children, see Juliet B. Schor, *Born to Buy: The Commercialized Child* (New York: Scribner, 2004), esp. 47–55. See also Douglas Rushkoff, "The Pursuit of Cool," *Sportswear International*, North American ed., no. 150 (June 2001): 4–6.

13. In Bill Moyers, *The Public Mind: Consuming Images* (VHS; Princeton, N.J.: Films for the Humanities & Sciences, 1994).

14. Eduardo Kaplan, "Che Guevara: Icon of Capitalism," *Washington Times,* September 25, 2004.

15. Daniel Simon, ed., *The Best of Abbie Hoffman* (Cambridge, Mass.: De Capo Press, 1993), 185.

16. See note 76 in chapter 2.

17. *Adbusters* 20 (Winter 1998): 1.

18. Readers can view the news story and the backlash comments at www.wbtv.com/Global/story.asp?S=12441226, May 6, 2010.

19. The ad text is examined in Stuart Ewen, *All Consuming Images: The Politics of Style in Contemporary Culture* (New York: Basic Books, 1998), 253–255.

20. Ibid.

21. E-mail correspondence from John Baky, who oversees a large collection of material reflecting the commodification of the war in Vietnam—at LaSalle University in Philadelphia.

22. Susan Faludi, *Backlash: The Undeclared War against American Women* (New York: Crown, 1991), 93.

23. See "Bob Dylan Proves the Times Are Changin' Again," *Billboard,* January 22, 1994, 47.

24. "Just in Case You Hadn't Heard—The '60s Are Over," *Time,* January 31, 1994, 23.

25. Reported in *Adbusters* (Spring 1997): 17.

26. Amanda Balzer, "Challenging Status Quo Not Just a '60s' Thing," *Newton Kansan,* October 18, 2003, www.thekansan.com/stories/101802/vie_1018020029.shtml.

27. From *Rat,* August 27, 1969. Quoted in Peck, *Uncovering the Sixties: The Life and Times of the Underground Press* (New York: Pantheon, 1985), 179.

28. See note 34 in chapter 7.

29. Jon Pareles, "Just Who's Woodstock Was It?" *New York Times,* August 28, 1994, 2:1ff.

30. Heather Timmons, "I Saw A Deadhead Sticker on a Bentley," *New York Times,* June 9, 2006, 7.

31. "Woodstock, A Music, Fashion, and Lifestyle Brand Celebrates Peace, Music and the En-

during Spirit of the Sixties," *Yahoo Financial News*, June 12, 2006, www.newscom.com/cgi-bin/prnh/20060612/LAM040-b.

32. Mark Crispin Miller, "The Hipness unto Death," in *Boxed In,* 19.

33. Mark Crispin Miller, "Cosby Knows Best," in *Boxed In,* 72.

34. Ibid., 74–75.

35. For a brilliant deconstruction of television's effort at serious analysis of race in America, see Miller's essay, "Black and White," in *Boxed In*, 137–149.

36. Sidney Blumenthal, "Reaganism and the Neokitsch Aesthetic," in *The Reagan Legacy*, ed. Sidney Blumenthal and Thomas Byrne Edsall (New York: Pantheon, 1988), 275, cited in Daniel Marcus, *Happy Days and Wonder Years: The Fifties and the Sixties in Contemporary Cultural Politics* (New Brunswick, N.J.: Rutgers University Press, 2004), 106.

37. Jerry Herron, "Homer Simpson's Eyes and the Culture of Late Nostalgia," *Representations* 43 (Summer 1993): 14.

38. Ibid., 17–18.

39. Michael Ryan and Douglas Kellner, *Camera Politica: The Politics and Ideology of Contemporary Hollywood* (Bloomington: Indiana University Press, 1988), 1.

40. Among countless media uses of this phrase, a 1994 *Boston Globe* article referenced the "Big Chill Generation's" alleged surprise at finding themselves subject to, what else, age discrimination—the "biggest chill yet for the Big Chill Generation." Don Aucoin, "First, the Big Chill, Then over the Hill," *Boston Globe,* January 20, 1994, 21.

41. Lynn Darling, "TWO STARS 1969," *Newsday,* November 18, 1988.

42. For more on the media culture's characterization of the civil rights movement, see Edward Morgan, "The Good, the Bad, and the Forgotten: Media Culture and Public Memory of the Civil Rights Movement," and Jennifer Fuller, "Debating the Present through the Past: Representations of the Civil Rights Movement in the 1960s," both in *The Civil Rights Movement in American Memory*, ed. Renee C. Romano and Leigh Raiford (Athens: University of Georgia Press, 2006), 137–166, 167–196.

43. H. Gray, "Television, Black Americans and the American Dream," *Critical Studies in Mass Communication* 6 (1986): 378.

44. Bobby Seale joined in the voices denouncing the New Black Panthers for being "like a COINTELPRO operation," providing Fox News with a foil for promotion of conservative views. See the Kam Williams interview, "Chicago 10 Interview with Bobby Seale," under the auspices of the African American Literature Book Club, reviews.aalbc.com/bobby_seale.htm (accessed May 27, 2010).

45. Richard Corliss et al., "The World According to Gump," *Time,* August 1, 1994, www.time.com/time/magazine/article/0,9171,981196,00.html.

46. "Generation Gump," *Economist,* July 30, 1994, 28.

47. For more on these themes, see H. Bruce Franklin, *Vietnam and Other American Fantasies* (Amherst: University of Massachusetts Press, 2000), and *M.I.A. or Mythmaking in America* (Brooklyn: Lawrence Hill Press, 1992).

48. Quoted in Judy Lee Kinney, "Gardens of Stone, *Platoon* and *Hamburger Hill, Ritual and Remembrance,*" in *Inventing Vietnam: the War in Film and Television,* ed. Michael Anderegg (Philadelphia: Temple University Press, 1991), 154, emphasis added.

49. See Susan Jeffords, *The Remasculinization: Gender and the Vietnam War* (Bloomington: Indiana University Press, 1989); and James William Gibson, *Warrior Dreams: Violence and Manhood in Post-Viet America* (New York: Hill & Wang, 1994).

50. Harry Haines, "'They Were Called and They Went': The Political Rehabilitation of the Vietnam Veteran," in *From Hanoi to Hollywood: The Vietnam War in American Film*, ed. Linda Dittmar and Gene Michaud (New Brunswick, N.J.: Rutgers University Press, 1990), 93.

51. Lembcke marshals a host of evidence that suggests strongly that antiwar people spitting on returning soldiers is a constructed event, not a real one. Jerry Lembcke, *The Spitting Image: Myth, Memory, and the Legacy of Vietnam* (New York: New York University Press, 1998), 76, 78, and 9.

52. For further documentation and elaboration see Franklin, *M.I.A. or Mythmaking in America,* esp. chapter 2.

53. Ibid., 175.

54. Michael Klein, "Historical Memory, Film, and the Vietnam War," in Dittmar and Michaud, *From Hanoi to Hollywood,* 38.

55. Jill A. Edy, *Troubled Pasts: News and the Collective Memory of Social Unrest* (Philadelphia: Temple University Press, 2006), 18.

56. See, for example, Doug McAdam, *Freedom Summer* (New York: Oxford University Press, 1988); Jack Whalen and Richard Flacks, *Beyond the Barricades: The Sixties Generation Grows Up* (Philadelphia: Temple University Press, 1989); and the findings and studies cited by Gerald Marwell, Michael T. Aiken, and N. J. Demerath III, "The Persistence of Political Attitudes among 1960s Civil Rights Activists," *Public Opinion Quarterly* 51, no. 3 (Autumn 1987): 359–375.

57. Robert Kaiser, "How the Sixties Ended with a Federal Grant," *Washington Post,* May 18, 1980.

58. "The Graying of Aquarius," *Newsweek,* March 30, 1987, 56–58.

59. Mark Rudd, *Underground: My Life with SDS and the Weathermen* (New York: William Morrow, 2009), 316.

60. Tom Morganthau, Mark Miller, and Marcus Mabry, "Decade Shock: Quayle Controversy Sparks Re-examination of a Complex Time," and Tom Mathews, "Sixties Complex," *Newsweek,* September 5, 1988, 14–18, 18–21.

61. Lance Morrow et al., "1968: Like a Knife Blade, the Year Severed Past from Future," *Time,* January 11, 1988, 12–23.

62. See Daniel Hallin, *The "Uncensored War": The Media and Vietnam* (Berkeley: University of California Press, 1986), 168ff. *Time*'s account, on the other hand, reflected the argument of Peter Braestrup's Freedom House–sponsored study, *Big Story: How the American Press and Television Reported and Interpreted the Crisis of Tet in 1968* (Boulder, Colo.: Westview Press, 1976), and ignored the considerable evidence refuting Braestrup's thesis in print at the time. See, for example, Herbert Schandler, *The Unmaking of a President* (Princeton, N.J.: Princeton University Press, 1977); and Gabriel Kolko, *Anatomy of a War* (New York: Pantheon, 1985).

63. Morrow et al., "1968: Like a Knife Blade, the Year Severed Past from Future," 21. See also chapter 1, note 1.

64. See the detailed research of Benjamin I. Page, *Who Deliberates? Mass Media in Modern Democracy,* chapter 3, "Assigning Blame for the Los Angeles Riots" (Chicago: University of Chicago Press, 1996), 43–76.

65. Edwin M. Yoder Jr., "Placing Blame for the L.A. Riots Is Not So Simple," *St. Petersburg Times,* May 9, 1992, emphasis added.

66. Amy Baldwin, "Boomers Ponder Career Options, Retirement," *USA Today,* July 2, 2001, www.usatoday.com/careers/news2001–0702-boomers.htm, emphasis added.

67. Marilyn Gardner, "Boomers Refuse to Fade into the Sunset," *Christian Science Monitor,* May 16, 2001.

68. "Growing Pains at 40," *Time,* May 19, 1986, www.time.com/time/printout/0,8816,961 401,00.html#.

69. See Carolyn Kitch, "Generational Identity and Memory in American Newsmagazines," *Journalism: Theory, Practice, and Criticism* 4, no. 2 (2003): 185–202.

70. "Living: Proceeding with Caution," *Time,* July 16, 1990, 57, emphasis added.

71. Thus, for example, a 1997 issue of *American Enterprise,* published by the market-

embracing American Enterprise Institute, was devoted to the theme "The Sixties Return." While the issue's contents featured the expected sixties-bashing fare, the cover featured an artist's rendition of a bearded Clinton holding the remains of a marijuana joint and sporting "Hell No We Won't Go" and "Free Huey Newton" buttons on his sweatshirt.

72. Deirdre R. Schwiesow, "The GenX Philosophy: Sixties Legacy: 'This Monstrous Bureaucracy,'" *USA Today*, July 26, 1995, A1.

73. Mark Dolliver, "Having Bored You about the '60s, They'll Bore You about the 60s," *Adweek.com,* July 17, 2006.

74. See chapter 1, note 17.

Chapter 12. Cultural Politics and Warlike Discourse

1. Quoted in Eli Lehrer, "Another Result of Racial Politics on Campus: UnFree Speech," *American Enterprise Online,* April/May 2003.

2. Two of the most comprehensively documented sources for this argument have been Eric Alterman, *What Liberal Media? The Truth about Bias and the News* (New York: Basic Books, 2003); and the many publications of Fairness and Accuracy in Media (FAIR), notably their "Challenging the 'Liberal Media' Claim," *Extra!* July/August 1998, 4–9. More on this below.

3. Francis Fukuyama, *The End of History and the Last Man* (New York: Free Press, 1992).

4. Cornel West, "Diverse New World," *Democratic Left,* July/August 1991, quoted in Patricia Aufderheide, *Beyond PC: Towards a Politics of Understanding* (St. Paul, Minn.: Graywolf Press, 1992), 233.

5. Donald M. Kendall, "The Generation Gap: Economic Illiteracy," remarks delivered before the National Food Brokers Association annual conference, New York, December 5, 1970," *Vital Speeches of the Day* 37 (1971): 245–246.

6. The results demonstrated that older students were more to the left than younger ones, but as with other conservative claims, they demonstrated nothing about the effects of college life. The poll could just as plausibly be read as demonstrating that the Rightist backlash was beginning to bear fruit with younger, more conservative students. James J. Kilpatrick, "Why Students Are Hostile to Free Enterprise," *Nation's Business* 73 (July 1975): 11–12.

7. The words are Kilpatrick's. Ibid.

8. Quoted in Ellen Messer-Davidow, "Manufacturing the Attack on Liberalized Higher Education," *Social Text* 36 (Autumn 1993): 44.

9. Ibid., 43. Without anything remotely like the media attention given to the charges generated by the Right, the research of Messer-Davidow and the National Committee for Responsive Philanthropy (below) has provided detailed documentation of these activities.

10. Ibid., 47.

11. See "Collegiate Network, Campus Outrage Awards, Intercollegiate Studies Institute," www.isi.org/cn/members/polly.aspx and www.isi.org/college_guide/index.aspx (accessed May 27, 2010).

12. The Coalition for Campus Democracy (later the National Association of Scholars) was founded by the neoconservative Committee for the Free World, which included among its members Irving Kristol, Midge Decter, Elliott Abrams, and the John M. Olin Foundation's William Simon. See Messer-Davidow, "Who (Ac)Counts and How," *Journal of the Midwest Modern Language Association* 27, no. 1 (Spring 1994): 29.

13. See ibid., 45–47. Other groups using similar campus-monitoring techniques include Accuracy in Academia and Daniel Pipes's Campus Watch: Monitoring Middle East Studies on Campuses.

14. William J. Bennett, "To Reclaim a Legacy: A Report on the Humanities in Higher Education, National Endowment for the Humanities, ERIC document ED247880, November 1984,"

2, 32, 27. The report drew on deliberations of the Study Group on the State of Learning in the Humanities in Higher Education at NEH.

15. Quoted from John Milne, "Ideology Fuels NEH Funding, Critics Charge," *San Francisco Examiner*, August 1992, B7, in John K. Wilson, *The Myth of Political Correctness: The Conservative Attack on Higher Education* (Durham, N.C.: Duke University Press, 1995), 61. See also Messer-Davidow, "Manufacturing the Attack," note 5, 71.

16. Allan Bloom, *The Closing of the American Mind: How Higher Education Has Failed Democracy and Impoverished the Souls of Today's Students* (New York: Simon & Schuster, 1987), 322.

17. Ibid., 50.

18. Robert Bork's later attack on the sixties took Bloom's avoidance of Vietnam one step further. After attacking the Johnson administration for "fighting a half-hearted war" and accusing student radicals of being anti-American in his first chapter, Bork asserts, "I have discussed Vietnam only to show that the war does not explain the Sixties" and proceeds to leave out further discussion of the war for virtually the entire book. Robert H. Bork, *Slouching towards Gomorrah: Modern Liberalism and American Decline* (New York: Regan Books, 1996): 20–21.

19. One of the more prolific sixties-bashers, David Horowitz, qualifies as an extreme case with his distorted and at times venomous attacks on the sixties and allegedly totalitarian universities, while parading his own revisionist embrace of right-wing doctrine. Gaining cachet with the Right when he denounced his radical past and embraced Ronald Reagan's candidacy, Horowitz's publishing blitz began in 1989 with two books: *Second Thoughts: Former Radicals Look Back at the Sixties,* coedited with Peter Collier, and, coauthored with Collier, *Destructive Generation: Second Thoughts about the Sixties*. His more recent diatribes have recited wild charges against *The Professors: The 101 Most Dangerous Academics in America* (2007), *Indoctrination U: The Left's War against Academic Freedom* (2009), and *One-Party Classroom: How Radical Professors at America's Top Colleges Indoctrinate Students and Undermine Our Democracy* (2009).

20. Roger Kimball, *Tenured Radicals: How Politics Has Corrupted Our Higher Education,* rev. ed. (Chicago: Ivan R. Dee, 1998), 7.

21. Messer-Davidow, "Manufacturing the Attack," 68.

22. The latter, according to Messer-Davidow, includes "supporting conservative colleges and universities, while increasing conservative faculty and programs at other colleges and universities." Messer-Davidow, "Who (Ac)Counts and How," 30.

23. Sally Covington, *Moving a Public Policy Agenda: The Strategic Philanthropy of Conservative Foundations* (Washington, D.C.: National Committee for Responsive Philanthropy, 1997, 2004), 7.

24. Quoted in Messer-Davidow, "Manufacturing the Attack," 67.

25. Richard Bernstein, "The Rising Hegemony of the Politically Correct," *New York Times*, October 28, 1990, 4:1.

26. Jerry Adler et al., "Taking Offense," *Newsweek*, December 24, 1990, 48ff.

27. Wilson, *The Myth of Political Correctness*, 13. Wilson documents some of the "breakthrough for the conservatives" that followed Bloom's popular book on 12–15ff.

28. Barbara Epstein, "'Political Correctness' and Collective Powerlessness," in *Cultural Politics and Social Movements*, ed. Marcy Darnovsky, Barbara Epstein, and Richard Flacks (Philadelphia: Temple University Press, 1995), 8.

29. The progressive media-watch group Fairness and Accuracy in Reporting (among others) has used the term to refer to tendencies among right-wing media to repeat earlier right-wing attacks as authoritative documentation, or more broadly tendencies in mass media to echo uncritically various governmental foreign policy pronouncements.

30. See Aufderheide, *Beyond PC.*

31. C. Vann Woodward, "Freedom and the Universities," in ibid., 40.

32. Joan Wallach Scott, "Campus Communities beyond Consensus," in ibid., 217.

33. Ibid., 8.

34. Bill Readings, *The University in Ruins* (Cambridge, Mass.: Harvard University Press, 1996), 3.

35. Ibid., 26, 31. The "clear measures to establish university performance" quote is drawn from Readings's reference to *Maclean's* 106, no. 46 (November 15, 1993): 48.

36. Stanley Aronowitz, *The Knowledge Factory: Dismantling the Corporate University and Creating True Higher Learning* (Boston: Beacon, 2000), 3–4.

37. Maryann Barakso and Brian F. Schaffner, "Winning Coverage: News Media Portrayals of the Women's Movement, 1969–2004," *Press/Politics* 11, no. 4 (October 2006): 22, 33, 41.

38. Rosalyn Baxandall and Linda Gordon, eds., *Dear Sisters: Dispatches from the Women's Liberation Movement* (New York: Perseus, 2000), 2.

39. Cal Thomas, "The Sixties Are Dead; Long Live the Nineties," *Imprimis,* Hillsdale College, January 1995, www.hillsdale.edu/news/imprimis/archive/issue.asp?year=1995&month=01.

40. Baxandall and Gordon, *Dear Sisters,* 2–3.

41. On Iannone's articles, see Messer-Davidow, "Manufacturing the Attack," 72n14. On Sommers's support, see Wilson, *The Myth of Political Correctness*, 26.

42. Christina Hoff Sommers, *Who Stole Feminism? How Women Have Betrayed Women* (New York: Simon & Schuster, 1994), 273.

43. Sommers's quotes are from Laura Flanders's review, "The 'Stolen Feminism' Hoax: Anti-Feminist Attack Based on Error-Filled Anecdotes," *Extra!*, September/October, 1994, www.fair.org/index.php?page=1246.

44. Ibid.

45. Bork, *Slouching towards Gomorrah,* 193.

46. Ibid., 194. Garry Wills, "Feminism Has Been Defeated in Name Only," *Chicago Sun-Times*, February 27, 1999, 12.

47. Bork, *Slouching towards Gomorrah*, 195.

48. Ibid., 223, emphasis added. Reflecting the right-wing echo chamber, Bork documents his claims by citing the critical generalizations about feminism made by a number of foundation-supported conservative women: Carol Iannone, Christine Hoff Sommers, Midge Decter, Maggie Gallagher, and others. His argument also echoed the one put forward by anti-ERA forces in the late seventies and early eighties: that feminists' agenda belittled and would harm women who were mothers and homemakers.

49. Ibid., 197.

50. The polls are commonly cited by the more conservative "equity feminists." Thus Rene Denfeld cites a 1989 *Time*/CNN poll that found a majority of women believed feminism had advanced women's rights, but only 33 percent considered themselves to be feminists, and, tellingly, 76 percent paid little or no attention to the women's movement. Rene Denfeld, *The New Victorians: A Young Woman's Challenge to the Old Feminist Order* (New York: TimeWarner, 1995), 2. Christine Hoff Sommers cites a 1992 *Time*/CNN poll which revealed that 57 percent of the women respondents felt there was a "need for a strong women's movement," yet 63 percent did not "consider themselves feminists." See Sommers, *Who Stole Feminism*, 18.

51. Naomi Wolf, *Fire with Fire: The New Female Power and How to Use It* (New York: Fawcett Columbine, 1994), 59.

52. Ibid., 66, 68.

53. Gina Bellafante, "Feminism: It's All about Me!" *Time,* June 29, 1998, 48–54.

54. Quoted from Katie Roiphe, *The Morning After: Sex, Fear, and Feminism* (Boston: Back Bay

Books, 1994), in Sarah Gamble, ed., *The Routledge Companion to Feminism and Postfeminism* (New York: Routledge, 2001), 46, emphasis added.

55. Nina J. Easton, "I'm Not a Feminist, But . . . ," quoted in Denfeld, *The New Victorians*, 6.

56. Ibid., 5, 2.

57. Ibid., 26.

58. Herbert Marcuse, *One Dimensional Man: Studies in the Ideology of Advanced Industrial Society* (Boston: Beacon Press, 1964).

59. See Ariel Levy, *Female Chauvinist Pigs: Women and the Rise of Raunch Culture* (New York: Free Press, 2005).

60. See Barbara Findlen, ed., *Listen Up: Voices from the Next Feminist Generation* (Seattle: Seal Press, 1995); Rebecca Walker, ed., *To Be Real: Telling the Truth and Changing the Face of Feminism* (New York: Doubleday, 1995); and Leslie Heywood and Jennifer Drake, *Third Wave Agenda: Being Feminist, Doing Feminism* (Minneapolis: University of Minnesota Press, 1997). See also the more popularly pitched book by Jessica Valenti, *Full Frontal Feminism: A Young Woman's Guide to Why Feminism Matters* (Berkeley, Calif.: Seal Press, 2007).

61. Heywood and Drake, *Third Wave Agenda*, 3.

62. Thomas J. Sugrue, *Sweet Land of Liberty: The Forgotten Struggle for Civil Rights in the North* (New York: Random House, 2008), 533–540.

63. Myron Magnet, *The Dream and the Nightmare: The Sixties Legacy to the Underclass* (New York: William Morrow, 1993), 22.

64. Ibid., 16.

65. Ibid., 35–36.

66. David Brock, *The Republican Noise Machine: Right-Wing Media and How It Corrupts Democracy* (New York: Crown, 2004), 8.

67. Mark Crispin Miller's perceptive analysis of a 1981 NBC program, *"American—Black and White,"* an inquiry into the nature of racism in America, suggests the mass media are an unlikely venue for this discourse. In Miller's analysis, the program managed to belittle "blacks in the very act of taking their side, while dismissing whites entirely." Mark Crispin Miller, "Black and White," in Miller, *Boxed In: The Culture of TV,* 3rd ed. (Evanston, Ill.: Northwestern University Press, 1989), 138.

68. A brief scan of *Vital Speeches of the Day* contents in the early 1990s provides a glimpse into the concerns of businesses being addressed by opinion leaders: "Managing Bad News in America; It's Getting Tougher and It's Getting Worse," or "Image Building: Why Is It So Difficult?"

69. The group's publications were grounded on surveys of various social and political values and psychological profiles of national media journalists as well as top and middle-level management from Fortune 500 corporations (and students at the prestigious Columbia Journalism Graduate School of Journalism). See S. Robert Lichter, Stanley Rothman, and Linda S. Lichter, *The Media Elite: America's New Powerbrokers* (Bethesda, Md.: Adler & Adler, 1986), xii, 294.

70. Quoted in Herbert J. Gans, "Are U.S. Journalists Dangerously Liberal?" *Columbia Journalism Review* (November/December 1985): 29.

71. Ibid., 32.

72. For the distinction between the popular debate and systematic analysis, see Douglas Kellner, *TV and the Crisis of Democracy* (Boulder, Colo.: Westview Press, 1990), 2–6.

73. See, for example, Edward Jay Epstein, *News from Nowhere: Television and the News* (New York: Vintage, 1974); Gaye Tuchman, *Making News: A Study in the Construction of Reality* (New York: Free Press, 1978); Michael Schudson, *Discovering the News: A Social History of American Newspapers* (New York: Basic Books, 1978); Herbert J. Gans, *Deciding What's News: A Study of CBS Evening News, NBC Nightly News, Newsweek, and Time* (New York: Pantheon, 1979); David L.

Paletz and Robert M. Entman, *Media Power Politics* (New York: Free Press, 1981); and W. Lance Bennett, *News: The Politics of Illusion,* 8th ed. (New York: Pearson/Longman 1983, 2009).

74. Gans, "Are U.S. Journalists Dangerously Liberal?" 30.

75. Robert Elegant, "How to Lose a War: The Press and Viet Nam," *Encounter* 57, no. 2 (August 1981): 73.

76. This is a strategy one Republican Party official likened to coaches who "work the refs" by incessant complaining. Quoted in Eric Alterman, *What Liberal Media? The Truth about Bias and the News* (New York: Basic Books, 2003), 2.

77. Douglas Kellner, *The Persian Gulf TV War* (Boulder, Colo.: Westview Press, 1992), 293–294. The Simpson quote was drawn from James Ridgeway, ed., *The March to War* (New York: Four Walls Eight Windows, 1991), 37.

78. Also widely documented, perhaps most powerfully in videos such as Bill Moyers and Kathleen Hughes, *Buying the War* (DVD; Princeton, N.J.: Films for the Humanities and Sciences, 2007); and Norman Solomon, Loretta Alper, and Jeremy Earp, *War Made Easy: How Presidents and Pundits Keep Spinning Us to Death* (DVD; Northampton, Mass.: Media Education Foundation, 2007).

79. Quoted in Robert Jensen, "Embedded Reporters Viewpoint Misses Point of War," *Znet,* June 2003, www.zmag.org/zspace/commentaries/1621.

80. A small sampling of titles, some of which have not made inroads into mainstream culture—presumably proving their authors' complaints—includes the following: Laura Ingraham, *Shut Up & Sing: How Elites from Hollywood, Politics, and the UN Are Subverting America* (Washington, D.C.: Regnery, 2006); Bernard Goldberg, *Bias: A CBS Insider Exposes How the Media Distort the News* (New York: Regnery, 2002); Ann Coulter, *Slander: Liberal Lies about the American Right* (New York: Crown, 2002); Brent Baker, ed., *How to Identify, Expose, and Correct Liberal Media Bias* (Alexandria, Va.: Media Research Center, 1994); Brian C. Anderson, *South Park Conservatives: The Revolt against Liberal Media Bias* (Washington, D.C. : Regnery, 2005); and Mike Gallagher, *Surrounded by Idiots: Fighting Liberal Lunacy in America* (New York: William Morrow, 2005).

81. Brock, *The Republican Noise Machine,* 11.

82. See note 2 above.

Chapter 13. Media Culture and the Future of Democracy

1. Margaret Allen, "Vietnam: Trying to Make a Real Connection," unpublished paper, May 2010.

2. See chapter 1, note 17.

3. See Alec MacGillis and Jon Cohen, "A Vote Decided by Big Turnout and Big Discontent with GOP," *Washington Post,* November 5, 2008, A27.

4. The exact quote, according to *The Columbia World of Quotations* (1996), was "I'm a pessimist because of intelligence, but an optimist because of will." www.bartleby.com/66/84/25784.html.

5. See chapter 1, note 28.

6. Edward T. Chambers, *Roots For Radicals: Organizing for Power, Action, and Justice* (New York: Continuum, 2006), 128.

7. Carl Boggs, *The End of Politics: Corporate Power and the Decline of the Public Sphere* (New York: Guilford Press, 2000), 2.

8. Lawrence Grossberg, *Dancing in Spite of Myself: Essays on Popular Culture* (Durham, N.C.: Duke University Press, 1997), 258.

9. Sheldon S. Wolin, *Politics and Vision: Continuity and Innovation in Western Political Thought,* expanded ed. (Princeton, N.J.: Princeton University Press, 2004), 554.

10. Lawrence Lessig, *The Future of Ideas: The Fate of the Commons in a Connected World* (New York: Random House, 2001), 6–7. Lessig's book picks up on themes developed in Andrew

Shapiro's earlier and more optimistic book, *The Control Revolution: How the Internet Is Putting Individuals in Charge and Changing the World We Know* (New York: PublicAffairs, 1999).

11. Some of these issues are explored in Henry Jenkins, *Convergence Culture: Where Old and New Media Collide* (New York: New York University Press, 2006).

12. Cass Sunstein, *Republic.com* (Princeton, N.J.: Princeton University Press, 2001).

13. One recent study suggests that "ideological segregation" of the Internet has not yet achieved levels Sunstein warned about, instead that most Internet news consumption is concentrated in a small number of relatively centrist sites (Yahoo! News, AOL News, msnbc.com, and cnn.com account for more than 50 percent of all visits), with only a very small proportion of users reading "ideological extreme" sites. While reassuring, perhaps, from a balkanization perspective, the findings suggest most Internet users are exposed to the same kinds of views they would find in the commercial mass media. See Matthew Gentzkow and Jesse M. Shapiro, "Ideological Segregation Online and Offline," Working Paper 15916 (Cambridge, Mass.: National Bureau of Economic Research, April 2010), 4, 18.

14. See André Gorz, *Strategy for Labor: A Radical Proposal* (Boston: Beacon Press, 1964), 7–8.

15. See www.freepress.org. Another, mentioned above, is Fairness and Accuracy in Reporting (FAIR), which provides monthly online documentation of biases in media reporting (www.fair.org).

16. See www.savetheinternet.com/frequently-asked-questions (accessed May 29, 2010).

17. Robert McChesney, *The Problem of the Media: U.S. Communication Politics in the 21st Century* (New York: Monthly Review Press, 2004), 278–283.

18. A LexisNexis search yielded only three newspaper articles about the conference, in Minneapolis–St. Paul and Seattle newspapers. The only television notice the conference received besides O'Reilly's dismissive attack was a Keith Olbermann response on MSNBC that showed a confrontation between conference speaker Bill Moyers and a Fox reporter.

19. Sheldon Wolin, *Democracy Incorporated: Managed Democracy and the Specter of Inverted Totalitarianism* (Princeton: Princeton University Press, 2008), 65.

20. Lawrence Grossberg, *We Gotta Get Out of This Place: Popular Conservatism and Postmodern Culture* (New York: Routledge, 1992), 86.

21. Juliet B. Schor, *Born to Buy: The Commercialized Child and the New Consumer Culture* (New York: Scribner, 2004), 9.

22. Ibid.

23. See Richard Ohmann, "Doublespeak and Ideology in Ads: A Kit for Teachers," in *American Media and Mass Culture: Left Perspectives*, ed. Donald Lazere (Berkeley: University of California Press, 1987), 106–115.

24. See Jacques Ellul, *Propaganda: The Formation of Men's Attitudes* (New York: Vintage, 1965); and Neil Postman, *Amusing Ourselves to Death: Public Discourse in the Age of Show Business* (New York: Penguin, 1985), 79.

25. Boggs, *End of Politics*, 178. See also Christopher Lasch, *The Culture of Narcissism* (New York: Norton, 1991).

26. Philip Cushman, *Constructing the Self, Constructing America: A Cultural History of Psychotherapy* (Cambridge, Mass.: Perseus, 1995), 337.

27. Russell Jacoby, *Social Amnesia* (Boston: Beacon Press, 1975), 64, quoted in Boggs, *End of Politics*, 179.

28. Nancy McWilliams, "Preserving our Humanity as Therapists," *Psychotherapy: Theory, Research, Practice, Training* 42, no. 2 (2005): 139.

29. Karen Stenner, *The Authoritarian Dynamic* (New York: Cambridge University Press, 2005).

30. Sandra L. Bloom, "The Clinical Uses of Psychohistory," *Journal of Psychohistory* 20, no. 3 (Winter 1993): 265–266.

31. Ibid., 261.

32. During the sixties era, among the groups reflecting Alinsky's influence were the SDS ERAP project, César Chavez's United Farm Workers (UFW), and the National Welfare Rights Organization (NWRO).

33. In addition to the significant literature advocating deliberative democracy, see also John Dryzek, *Deliberative Democracy and Beyond: Liberals, Critics, Contestation* (New York: Oxford University Press, 2000); and James Fishkin and Peter Laslett, eds., *Debating Deliberative Democracy* (Malden, Mass.: Blackwell, 2003).

34. See also Frances Moore Lappé's ten "arts of democracy" in her *Getting a Grip: Clarity, Creativity, and Courage in a World Gone Mad* (Cambridge, Mass.: Small Planet Media, 2007), 88.

35. Noam Chomsky, *Media Control: The Spectacular Achievements of Propaganda* (1991; New York: Seven Stories Press, 1997), 35.

36. See Harry Boyte, *The Backyard Revolution: Understanding the New Citizen Movement* (Philadelphia: Temple University Press, 1980).

37. Sidney Plotkin, "Community and Alienation: Enclave Consciousness and Urban Movements," in *Breaking Chains*, ed. Michael Peter Smith (New Brunswick, N.J.: Transaction Publishers, 1991), 14–15, quoted in Boggs, *The End of Politics*, 189.

38. Cited in Paul Gilroy, "Cultural Studies and Ethnic Absolutism," in *Cultural Studies*, ed. Lawrence Grossberg, Cary Nelson, and Paula Treichler (New York: Routledge, 1992), 232.

39. Paul Hawken, *Blessed Unrest: How the Largest Movement in the World Came into Being and Why No One Saw It Coming* (New York: Viking, 2007), 26.

40. David Harvey, "What's Green and Makes the Environment Go Round?" in *The Cultures of Globalization*, ed. Fredric Jameson and Masao Miyoshi (Durham, N.C.: Duke University Press, 1998), 352.

41. Edward T. Chambers, *Roots for Radicals: Organizing for Power, Action, and Justice* (New York: Continuum, 2006), 132.

42. For more, see Jeremy Brecher, Tim Costello, and Brendan Smith, *Globalization from Below: The Power of Solidarity* (Boston: South End Press, 2000); and Donatella della Porta, Massimiliano Andretta, Lorenzo Mosca, and Herbert Reiter, *Globalization from Below: Transnational Activists and Protest Networks* (Minneapolis: University of Minnesota Press, 2006).

43. Rinku Sen, *Stir It Up: Lessons in Community Organizing and Advocacy* (San Francisco: Jossey-Bass, 2003), xliii.

44. Michael Albert, Leslie Cagan, Noam Chomsky, Robin Hamel, Mel King, Lydia Sargent, and Holly Sklar, *Liberating Theory* (Boston: South End Press, 1986), 144, quoted in John Sanbonmatsu, *The Postmodern Prince: Critical Theory, Left Strategy, and the Making of a New Political Prince* (New York: Monthly Review Press, 2004), 160.

45. Sanbonmatsu, *The Postmodern Prince,* 185, emphasis in original.

46. See John Dewey, *The Public and Its Problem* (Chicago: Gateway Books, 1946), and "The Democratic Conception in Education," in his *Democracy and Education* (New York: Macmillan, 1944), 81–99.

47. Lawrence Grossberg, "Rockin' in Conservative Times," in *Dancing in Spite of Myself: Essays on Popular Culture* (Durham, N.C.: Duke University Press, 1997), 269.

48. Judith M. Green, *Deep Democracy: Community, Diversity, and Transformation* (Lanham, Md.: Rowman & Littlefield, 1999), 216. Other theorists who have reflected thoughtfully about these interactions include Ernesto Laclau and Chantal Mouffe, Iris Marion Young, C. Douglas Lummis, Amy Gutmann, and Benjamin Barber.

49. Lappé, *Getting a Grip,* 110.

50. Grossberg, *We Gotta Get Out of This Place,* 377. George Katsiaficas has provided a useful angle on this concern in his essay "The Latent Universal within Identity Politics," *New Political Science* 38/39 (Winter/Spring 1997): 79–88.

51. Howard Zinn, *You Can't Be Neutral on a Moving Train: A Personal History of Our Times* (Boston: Beacon Press, 1994), 33.

52. Anderson Cooper, "Senator Barack Obama Confronts Race Issue," *360 Degrees*, CNN, March 18, 2008.

53. Sanbonmatsu, *The Postmodern Prince*, 19, 223.

54. See Chalmers Johnson, *Blowback: The Costs and Consequences of American Empire* (New York: Henry Holt, 2004).

55. On a host of measures, repeatedly documented, income and wealth have gravitated upward in the decades marked by neoliberal policies. For example, the top 1 percent of households' share of all pretax income was 8.9 percent in 1976 and 23.9 percent in 2005, the greatest concentration of income since 1928. Between 1979 and 2005, the top 5 percent of American families enjoyed an 81 percent increase in income, compared to a 1 percent decline for the lowest quintile of families. In 1962, the wealth of the richest 1 percent of households was 125 times that of the typical household, whereas it was 190 times the typical household wealth in 2004. Wage inequality and tax cut benefits have been similarly skewed over these years. See Chris Hartman, "By the Numbers," Inequality.org, www.demos.org/inequality/numbers.cfm (accessed May 29, 2010). See also "The New Inequality: A Special Issue," *Nation*, June 30, 2008.

56. Immanuel Wallerstein, *The End of the World as We Know It: Social Science for the Twenty-First Century* (Minneapolis: University of Minnesota Press, 1999), 18, and cf. 1–4 and 19–33.

57. U.N. Intergovernmental Panel on Climate Change, "Climate Change 2007: Synthesis Report" (Valencia, Spain: IPCC, 2007), 29.

58. See Fritjof Capra, *The Turning Point: Science, Society and the Rising Culture* (New York: Bantam, 1984), 24.

59. Obviously I only touch on a few of the macro signs of decline here. Others have spelled out the erosion of the global ecosphere in far greater, and more sobering, detail. See, for example, Bill McKibben, *The End of Nature* (New York: Random House, 2006).

60. Bill McKibben, *Deep Economy: The Wealth of Communities and the Durable Future* (New York: Henry Holt, 2007), 4, 34–42.

61. Kovel's argument reflects his analysis of capitalism as a "whole way of being" that incorporates a "gendered bifurcation of nature," not simply as a "set of economic institutions." See Joel Kovel, *The Enemy of Nature: The End of Capitalism or the End of the World* (London: Zed Books, 2007), 4–7. See also John Bellamy Foster, *Ecology against Capitalism* (New York: Monthly Review Press, 2002).

62. In addition to the above, see John Bellamy Foster, *The Vulnerable Planet: A Short Economic History of the Environment* (New York: Monthly Review Press, 1999).

63. Paul Hawken, Amory Lovins, and L. Hunter Lovins, *Natural Capitalism: Creating the Next Industrial Revolution* (Boston: Back Bay Books, 2000).

64. Hawken, *Blessed Unrest*, 20.

65. Leslie Sklair, "Social Movements and Global Capitalism," in Jameson and Miyoshi, *The Cultures of Globalization*, 305.

66. Stephanie Ross, "Is This What Democracy Looks Like? The Politics of the Anti-Globalization Movement in North America," in *Socialist Register 2003: Fighting Identities: Race, Religion, and Ethno-Nationalism* (Halifax, N.S.: Fernwood Publications, 2002), 281–304.

67. See Charlotte Ryan, *Prime Time Activism: Media Strategies for Grassroots Organizing* (Boston: South End Press, 1991).

68. Sen, *Stir It Up*, lxii.

69. Lappé, *Getting a Grip*, 6–7.

70. See chapter 12, note 4.

71. See Lappé, *Getting a Grip*, 25–39, as well as the "spiral of empowerment" illustration inside the back cover.

72. John Sanbonmatsu, *The Postmodern Prince,* 223, emphasis in original.

73. Marcuse's words are the final sentence in "Political Preface," in his *Eros and Civilization* (Boston, Beacon Press, 1966), xxv (also quoted as the final words in Sanbonmatsu, *The Postmodern Prince,* 223), emphasis in original.

Index

Fisk University, 50, 52, 53

Flacks, Richard, 1, 62, 199, 236, 332n21, 333n43, 375n56

Flamm, Michael, 160, 161, 356n4, 358n53, 358n58, 358n62, 358n64, 358n67

Flanders, Laura, 299

folk music, 59, 171, 225, 230, 267, 277. *See also* *specific artists*

Fones-Wolf, Elizabeth, 27, 335n37, 369n1

Forbes, Flores A., 204, 362n27

Forrest Gump (Robert Zemeckis), 5, 276–277, 304, 309

Fortune, 303, 335n35

Foucault, Michel, 259

Fouratt, Jim, 226

Fox Network
  entertainment TV, 272, 308
  news, 288, 308, 315, 374n44, 381n18 (*see also* O'Reilly, Bill)

Frank, Thomas, 5, 221, 222, 224, 263, 365n6, 366n22, 366n25–26, 373n10–11

Frankel, Max, 103

Franklin, Bruce, 279, 374n47

Freedom Rides of 1961, 41, 53, 119–120, 172 (photo), 267, 351n9

Freedom Summer, 50, 59, 61, 70–72, 123
  media and, 70–72, 343n30
  and student movement, 144, 146, 275

Freeman, Jo, 52, 86

Free Press, 315

free spaces, 16, 17, 56, 58, 82, 96

Free Speech Movement, 45, 54, 60, 108, 144, 146–147
  backlash against, 154, 159, 349n68

Friedan, Betty, 52, 196 (photo), 301

Frye boots ad, 266, 282

Fukuyama, Francis, 288

Fulbright, J. William, 103, 111

Full Metal Jacket, 278

Gallup poll, 42, 108, 122, 161, 289, 299

Gamson, William, 12, 15, 43, 205

Gans, Herbert, 306, 379n70, 379n73

Ganz, Marshall, 59

Garman, Betty, 60

Garrow, David, 75, 343n40, 343n46, 351n14, 353n65

Garry, Charles, 207, 363n56

GATT (General Agreement on Tariffs and Trade), 242

Gavin, Bill, 163

gay and lesbian rights movement, 9, 44, 47, 82, 168, 169, 202

Gelb, Leslie H., 248, 371n43

gender
  construction of, 82
  repression and, 83, 89
  roles, 15, 33, 128, 150, 309

generation
  rebellious generation, 6, 15, 85, 144, 280

generational backlash, 153–157

generational explanation for the 1960s, 5, 85, 145, 159, 281. *See also* mass media: generational frame

generational hype, 61, 148, 152, 218, 285–286

generational labels, 1, 222, 224, 268, 274, 277, 285, 286, 374n40. *See also* baby boom generation

"generation gap," 15, 92, 153

Genet, Jean, 197

Geneva Convention, 1954, 97, 99, 112

Geneva Conventions, 94, 350n84

Gergen, David, 322

G.I. Bill, 28, 256

Gilded Age (1980s), 253, 259, 274

Gingrich, Newt, 158, 254, 305

Ginsburg, Carl, 352n35

G.I. rebellion, 42, 110–111. *See also* Dewey Canyon III protest

Gitlin, Todd, 12, 238, 344n49, 350n93, 354n90, 368n66, 368n70, 368n73
  and entertainment television, 222, 229, 365n5, 367n47
  and media reporting on 60s protests, 65, 107, 109, 136, 138, 139, 333n34, 349n56, 349n68

Gjelten, Tom, 307

Glazer, Nathan, 242, 337n70

globalizing capitalism, 18, 288, 318, 323, 326, 327
  confronting, 327–328
  effects of, 8, 18, 322–325
  non-sustainability of, 322–325

global warming, 18, 324, 326

Goldberg, Jackie, 54

Goldwater, Barry, 157, 168, 241
  and Sixties backlash, 3, 158–160, 162

Good, Paul, 77, 340n39

Goodman, Andrew, 71

Poor People's campaign, 74–75
Popkin, Ann, 52
Port Huron Statement, 44, 107, 331n14, 338n10
post-feminism, 302–303
Postman, Neil, 24, 31, 317, 336n53
post-traumatic stress disorder (PTSD), 247, 248
postwar (WWII), 26, 35, 124, 246
  consumer culture of, 337n73
  contradictions in, 36–39
  development archetype, 29, 322–323, 324, 325
Potter, Andrew, 235
Potter, Paul, 45, 106, 107
Powell, Lewis, 165, 243, 245, 251, 289
  memo to Chamber of Commerce, 165–167, 240, 369n8
Powledge, Fred, 71, 72, 107, 343n21, 360n109
Prague uprising of 1968, 138, 230
propaganda, 20, 24, 32, 168, 216
  anticommunist, 27, 93, 98, 109, 111
  and antiwar movement, 109, 111, 135
  and attacks on Sixties, 5, 8
  business, 28, 240, 335n23, 369n1
  commercial advertising as, 316–317
  and global climate change, 324
  media and, 96, 135, 305, 347n26
  Nazi, 250
  political advertising as, 313
  Right-wing, 281
  and Vietnam veterans, 279
  and war in Vietnam, 97, 100, 104, 108, 132, 134, 163
  Weather Underground, 247
protest (in general)
  conditions producing, 41
  defiance, 42, 43, 327
  and public opinion, 41
  See also direct action protest
protest militancy, 13, 14, 17, 28, 61, 100, 115, 156, 200, 214, 219, 220
  audiences for, 217, 236
  backlash and, 155, 200
  and Black Panther Party, 199, 208, 361n10
  and bombings, 15, 105, 214, 216, 218, 273, 364n71, 365n87
  effects of, 327–328
  escalation of war in Vietnam and, 61, 198, 199, 201–202
  exclusion from media discourse and, 57, 90

  media encouragement of, 17, 111, 155, 199, 200, 202
  police repression and, 201–202
  price of, 199, 216
  and public opinion, 217
  vs. radical ideas, 17, 200
"pseudotraditionalism," 256
psychology
  compatibility with capitalism, 317, 337n73
  pop, 153–156
  relevance to democracy, 321, 328
The Public Interest, 165, 242
public opinion
  and antiwar movement, 108, 364n86 (*see also* antiwar movement: public hostility towards; protest militancy: and public opinion)
  and Chicago Convention of 1968, 139, 355n96–99
  and civil rights movement, 42, 122, 352n29
  and feminism, 378n50
  an urban riots, 128, 352n29
  See also Gallup poll; Harris poll; war in Vietnam: and public opinion
public relations, 24, 108, 120, 165, 166, 206, 231, 296
  postwar, 335n35
  and war, 28, 95, 134, 240, 250 (*see also* propaganda)
Putnam, Robert, 9, 337n63, 338n85

Quayle, Dan, 254, 261, 375n60

Rackley, Alex, 206, 211
radical analysis/radicalism, 15, 57, 96, 114, 149, 202, 366n20
  and Black Panther Party, 204
  as distinguished from militancy, 17, 42, 115
  exclusion from mass media discourse, 17, 200
  in the media, as militancy, 200, 211, 217, 328
  relevance of, today, 211, 301, 325, 326, 347n21
  and war in Vietnam, 97–98, 106, 148, 199
"radical chic," 209, 363n49, 363n51
radical hope, 37, 40, 47, 54, 56
Rafferty, Max, 148
Rambo: First Blood, Part II, 256, 278, 280
Ramparts magazine, 132